NALA Manual For
Legal Assistants

The West Legal Studies Series

Your options keep growing with West Legal Studies

Each year our list continues to offer you more options for every area of the law to meet your course or on-the-job reference requirements. We now have over 140 titles from which to choose in the following areas:

Administrative Law	Family Law
Alternative Dispute Resolution	Federal Taxation
Bankruptcy	Intellectual Property
Business Organizations/Corporations	Introduction to Law
Civil Litigation and Procedure	Introduction to Paralegalism
CLA Exam Preparation	Law Office Management
Client Accounting	Law Office Procedures
Computer in the Law Office	Legal Research, Writing, and Analysis
Constitutional Law	Legal Terminology
Contract Law	Paralegal Employment
Criminal Law and Procedure	Real Estate Law
Document Preparation	Reference Materials
Environmental Law	Torts and Personal Injury Law
Ethics	Will, Trusts, and Estate Administration

You will find unparalleled, practical support

Each book is augmented by instructor and student supplements to ensure the best learning experience possible. We also offer custom publishing and other benefits such as West's Student Achievement Award. In addition, our sales representatives are ready to provide you with dependable service.

We want to hear from you

Our best contributions for improving the quality of our books and instructional materials is feedback from the people who use them. If you have a question, concern, or observation about any of our materials, or you have a product proposal or manuscript, we want to hear from you. Please contact your local representative or write us at the following address:

West Legal Studies, 3 Columbia Circle, P.O. Box 15015, Albany, NY 12212-5015

For additional information point your browser at
www.westlegalstudies.com

West Legal Studies
an imprint of Delmar Publishers

an International Thomson Publishing company

NALA Manual For Legal Assistants

Third Edition

Prepared By

The National Association of
Legal Assistants, Inc.

DELMAR

THOMSON LEARNING

Africa • Australia • Canada • Denmark • Japan • Mexico • New Zealand • Philippines
Puerto Rico • Singapore • Spain • United Kingdom • United States

NOTICE TO THE READER

Cover Design: Susan Mathews, Stillwater Studio

Cover Photo: PhotoDisk, Inc.

Delmar Staff

Publisher: Susan Simpfenderfer
Acquisitions Editor: Joan Gill
Developmental Editor: Rhonda Dearborn
Editorial Assistant: Margaret J. Aumic

Production Manager: Wendy A. Troeger
Production Editor: Laurie A. Boyce
Marketing Manager: Katherine M. S. Hans

Printed in the United States of America
6 7 8 9 10 XXX 05 04 03 02

For more information, contact Delmar, 3 Columbia Circle, PO Box 15015, Albany, NY 12212-0515; or find us on the World Wide Web at http://www.delmar.com

International Division List

Asia
Thomson Learning
60 Albert Street, #15-01
Albert Complex
Singapore 189969
Tel: 65 336 6411
Fax: 65 336 7411

Japan:
Thomson Learning
Palaceside Building 5F
1-1-1 Hitotsubashi, Chiyoda-ku
Tokyo 100 0003 Japan
Tel: 813 5218 6544
Fax: 813 5218 6551

Australia/New Zealand:
Nelson/Thomson Learning
102 Dodds Street
South Melbourne, Victoria 3205
Australia
Tel: 61 39 685 4111
Fax: 61 39 685 4199

UK/Europe/Middle East
Thomson Learning
Berkshire House
168-173 High Holborn
London
WC1V 7AA United Kingdom
Tel: 44 171 497 1422
Fax: 44 171 497 1426

Latin America:
Thomson Learning
Seneca, 53
Colonia Polanco
11560 Mexico D.F. Mexico
Tel: 525-281-2906
Fax: 525-281-2656

Canada:
Nelson/Thomson Learning
1120 Birchmount Road
Scarborough, Ontario
Canada M1K 5G4
Tel: 416-752-9100
Fax: 416-752-8102

Spain:
Thomson Learning
Calle Magallanes, 25
28015-MADRID
ESPANA
Tel: 34 91 446 33 50
Fax: 34 91 445 62 18

Library of Congress Cataloging-in-Publication Data
National Association of Legal Assistants.
    NALA manual for legal assistants / prepared by the National
Association of Legal Assistants, Inc. — 3rd ed.
        p. cm.
    Rev. ed. of: Manual for legal assistants, 2nd ed. c1992.
    Includes bibliographical references and index.
    ISBN 0-7668-0393-7 (hc. : alk. paper)
    1. 650 Legal assistants—United States—Handbooks, manuals, etc.
I. Manual for legal assistants. II. Title.
KF320.L4N34   1998   98-23892
340'.023'73—dc21   CIP

Table of Contents

Introduction   1

1   Introduction to the American Legal System   9

2 Legal Research   28

---

3   Ethics   80

7   Investigation

182

8   Pretrial Litigation Skills   207

9   The Legal Assistant and Document Discovery Cases   273

10   Assisting at Trial   314

Glossary: Legal Terminology   329

Appendix   367

Index   400

Acknowledgments

This Third Edition of the NALA Manual for Legal Assistants has been a project of the NALA Continuing Education Council, Brenda A. Mientka, CLAS, Chairperson. The committee chairs for this revision project were Michael K. Gaige, CLA, of Bangor, Maine and V. Sheri Towne, CLAS, of Charleston, South Carolina.

Special appreciation and acknowledgement is extended to Virginia Koerselman, Esquire for reviewing the manuscript of this Third Edition.

The National Association of Legal Assistants, Inc., gratefully acknowledges the contributions of the following committee members to the successful completion of this Third Edition:

Ann Atkinson, CLA
Omaha, Nebraska

Patricia Armstrong, CLAS
Wichita, Kansas

Tita Brewster, CLAS
Redwood City, California

Linda Burns, CLAS
Greenville, South Carolina

Lana Clark, CLA
Solvang, California

Sharon Cohron, CLAS,
  CFLA
Bradenton, Florida

Jane Daffron, CLAS
Richmond, Virginia

Lynn Dean, CLA
Tampa, Florida

Karen Dunn, CLAS
Vail, Colorado

Felicia Garant, CLA
Portland, Maine

Jonathan Kafka
Redwood City, California

Donna Karkos
Topsham, Maine

Kay Kasic, CLA
Napa, California

Vicki Kunz, CLAS
Bismarck, North Dakota

Cynthia McClelland, CLAS
Hilton Head Island
South Carolina

Deb Monke, CLAS
Bloomington, Illinois

Jimmie Murvin, CLAS
Baton Rouge, Louisiana

Shiloh Napier, CLA
Albuquerque, New Mexico

James Orlando, CLA
Jacksonville, Florida

Joey Phelps-Lasater, CLAS
Charlevoix, Michigan

Sharon Lynn Pope, J.D.
Hartford College for
  Women

Pamela Robtoy
St. Louis, Missouri

Karen Sanders-West, CLAS
Wichita, Kansas

Jane Terhune, CLAS
Tulsa, Oklahoma

Vicki Voisin, CLAS
Charlevoix, Michigan

Joan W. Warden, CLA
Charleston, South Carolina

The National Association of Legal Assistants, Inc., gratefully renews its recognition and appreciation to the following contributors to the Second Edition of this manual:

Patricia L. Armstrong,
  CLAS
Wichita, Kansas

Pamela J. Bailey, CLAS
Pittsburgh, Pennsylvania

Lee T. Deuto, CLAS
Jacksonville,
  North Carolina

Karen M. Dunn, CLAS
Vail, Colorado

Amy J. Hill, CLAS
Raleigh, North Carolina

Karen B. Judd, CLA
Champaign, Illinois

Kay Kasic, CLA
Napa, California

Virginia Koerselman, Esq.
Omaha, Nebraska

Connie Kretchmer, CLA
Omaha, Nebraska

Anthony L. Matens
Bloomington, Illinois

Sharon L. Pope, J.D.
Hartford, Connecticut

Karen Sanders-West, CLA
Wichita, Kansas

The National Association of Legal Assistants also renews its recognition and appreciation to the following contributors to the First Edition of this Manual:

Linda R. Babineaux
Lafayette, Louisiana

Nina Baker
Colorado Springs,
   Colorado

Ellen H. Batt, CLA
Huntsville, Alabama

Gert Benz
Morristown, New Jersey

Mary Watts Baylor
Sherman Oaks, California

Susan Bierschbach
El Paso, Texas

Julia Brouhard
Galveston, Texas

Jery Bryce, CLA
Lubbock, Texas

Mary Ellen Buehring,
   CLA
Maitland, Florida

Emma Valborg Carlson,
   PLS
Humboldt, Iowa

Gabriella Carozzino, CLA
San Francisco, California

Una Clark, CLA
La Mesa, California

Shirley M. Collins
Cupertino, California

Janis C. Davidson, CLA
Birmingham, Alabama

David P. Della Penta
White Plains, New York

Kay Eismann
Mt. Vernon, Oregon

Penny L. Fuestel
West Allis, Wisconsin

Twyla Gab, CLA
Brookings, South Dakota

Pat T. Gibson
Paris, Illinois

B. Jayne Greene
Vinita, Oklahoma

Haru K. Hains, CLA
Manasquan, New Jersey

Kathleen J. Hill, CLA
Tallahassee, Florida

Sally Hingley
Key Largo, Florida

Barbara Hutchisson
New Orleans, Louisiana

Jo D. Johnson
Kalispell, Montana

Dorthea Jorde, CLA
Minot, North Dakota

Glynjo Keefer
Long Beach, California

Bruce A. Kesselman
New Brunswick,
   New Jersey

Linda J. Kiernan
Buffalo, New York

Geri Land
Tucson, Arizona

Carol McGill
Boulder, Colorado

Violet McNew, CLA
Boulder, Colorado

Eunice Miller
Waco, Texas

Kayla B. Muse
Tacoma, Washington

William R. Park
San Francisco, California

Doris Paxton
Tucson, Arizona

Mary Ann Pickrell
Sunnyvale, California

Margaret Richards, CLA
Topeka, Kansas

Randi Rochow, CLA
Los Altos, California

Madelyn Russell
Davenport, Iowa

Eloise Schneider
Babylon, New York

Mildred Sheffy
Tulia, Texas

James M. Shriver, Jr.
Schertz, Texas

Dorothy Swicord
Irving, Texas

Florence M. Telling, CLA
Bloomfield Hills, Michigan

Jane H. Terhune, CLA
Tulsa, Oklahoma

Ardeth Thomas
Greenfield, Wisconsin

Joanne Toporski
Brookfield, Wisconsin

Rosemary Westbrook
St. Petersburg, Florida

Cathy Zander, CLA
Meridian, Idaho

Lawyers and educators have expressed interest in this book since it was first conceived. A number of them undertook substantial review and critique of the text for certain chapters and this book is the better for their effort and interest. This group includes the following:

Robert F. Gardner, Esq.
Martin, Gibson & Gardner
Sedalia, Missouri

Barry F. Keller, Esq.
Keller and Avadenka
Bloomfield Hills, Michigan

Virginia Korselman, Esq.
Omaha, Nebraska

Richard L. Meiss, Esq.
Pacific Gas and Electric Co.
San Francisco, California

Lois M. Plowman
Professor, Cerritos College
Norwalk, California

Michael Ropers, Esq.
Ropers, Majeski, Kohn &
  Bentley
San Jose, California

Marty Schiff
St. Louis, Missouri

Foreword

The National Association of Legal Assistants, Inc. (NALA) presents this manual as an educational contribution to the legal assistant profession. It was originally developed:

To serve as a quick reference guide for working legal assistants; and

for use by schools as a teaching aid to expose legal assistant students to the practical skills and techniques required for entry into the profession; and

to assist legal assistants in preparing to take the voluntary NALA Certified Legal Assistant Examination.

This revised manual was completed by many dedicated members who unselfishly gave their time and energy for this very worthwhile project. None of that dedication has gone unnoticed and it is here that NALA gratefully acknowledges the exemplary and concentrated efforts of those professionals.

This manual is a collection of techniques and procedures which can be used by legal assistants nationwide. It is compatible with the Federal Rules of Civil Procedure. However, the purpose of the manual is not to teach federal law or procedures as there are many excellent treatises available on that subject. Further, this book is not intended to offer specific guidance on any state law or procedure since the fifty jurisdictions differ too widely to capsulize all the laws adequately within one volume.

The techniques described are examples of past successful solutions to actual assignments accomplished by working legal assistants. These should be considered as starting points from which changes, adaptations, and modifications can be made by other legal assistants in similar situations.

This manual will serve its purpose if it:

Helps legal assistants achieve a comfortable perspective of themselves; and

inspires them to dedicate themselves to high standards of professional performance and strong ethical and moral commitment to the client and attorney; and

generates enthusiasm and a willing sense of loyalty between legal assistants and their employers.

Dedication

This Third Edition of the National Association of Legal Assistants Manual for Legal Assistants is dedicated to the memory of

Janis Davidson, CLA
NALA President 1979–1980
and
Andrew J. Kasic, Esq.
and
Gerald M. Shea, Esq.

As a tribute to their dedication and support of NALA and of the legal assistant profession.

Introduction

What is a legal assistant? What does one do? What does a job as a legal assistant entail? How much responsibility can or should one assume?

If you are a legal assistant and have not encountered these questions, you are lucky! You may only need this manual for reference or guidance in a particular area of the law. For those who have questions, for students, and for those entering the profession, the National Association of Legal Assistants (NALA) offers this practical aid for the legal assistant.

As the number of legal assistants continues to increase, there is a corresponding need for a workable reference on "what to do" and "how to do it." Realizing that those best qualified to present this information are legal assistants themselves, the National Association of Legal Assistants called upon its members to share their knowledge and expertise. This manual is a culmination of that effort. It is designed to further your understanding of this profession, as well as its duties, responsibilities, and limitations.

What Is the National Association of Legal Assistants?

The National Association of Legal Assistants (NALA) is a professional association for legal assistants which was incorporated in 1975. By the 1990s, NALA had grown to represent over eighteen thousand legal assistants through its individual members, affiliated state and local associations, and certified legal assistants.

Headquartered in Tulsa, Oklahoma, NALA is managed by a professional staff under the direction of a board of directors consisting of members from across the nation.

NALA's goals and programs have been defined to:

- increase the professional standing of legal assistants throughout the nation
- provide uniformity in the identification of legal assistants
- establish national standards of professional competence for legal assistants
- provide uniformity among the states in the utilization of legal assistants

NALA is associated most often with the administration of the Certified Legal Assistant (CLA) and Certified Legal Assistant Specialist (CLAS) certifying programs, the profession's national credentialing mechanism designed to support the legal assistant profession. Other services and programs for member and nonmember legal assistants include:

- **Publications.** Since the late 1970s, NALA has published educational materials for legal assistants such as this Third Edition of the NALA *Manual for Legal Assistants*. In addition, the association also publishes, through West Publishing Company, NALA's *CLA Review Manual*, the NALA *CLA Study Guide and Mock Examination*, and review texts for NALA CLA Specialty Examinations.
- **Periodicals.** *Facts & Findings*, NALA's quarterly magazine, is the professional journal for legal assistants, offering in-depth educational articles and treatises to keep legal assistants informed of current developments in specialized practice areas.
- **Workshops and Seminars.** NALA's annual convention, held in July, offers specialized workshops for both beginning and advanced legal assistants. The association also sponsors four-day courses for preparation for the CLA and CLA specialty examinations.

■ **Occupational Research.** In 1986, NALA initiated its biannual survey of legal assistants to begin extensive research of the legal assistant profession. The questionnaires used for this survey are very detailed in their request for information on the respondents' educational backgrounds and experiences, descriptions of employers, definitions of duties and responsibilities, billing rates, compensation, and benefits. Through this biannual survey, NALA developed a significant study of the profession. In addition to providing a description of this career field every two years, NALA is storing and summarizing a tremendous amount of data showing the growth and development of this field. Much of the information in this introductory chapter is based on these research efforts and the work and contributions of NALA members and committees.

What Is a Legal Assistant?

In 1984, the National Association of Legal Assistants adopted the following definition of a legal assistant:

> Legal assistants, also known as paralegals, are a distinguishable group of persons who assist attorneys in the delivery of legal services. Through formal education, training, and experience, legal assistants have knowledge and expertise regarding the legal system and substantive and procedural law which qualify them to perform work of a legal nature under the supervision of an attorney.

Two years later, the American Bar Association (ABA) defined legal assistants as:

> Persons who, although not members of the legal profession, are qualified through education, training or work experience, who are employed or retained by a lawyer, law office, governmental agency, or other entity in a capacity or function which involves the performance, under the direction and supervision of an attorney, of specifically delegated substantive legal work, which work, for the most part, requires a sufficient knowledge of legal concepts such that, absent the legal assistant, the attorney would perform the task.

These definitions share many similarities. Both state that legal assistants work under the supervision of a lawyer, that legal assistants are qualified through education, training, or work experience, and that legal assistants do substantive legal work. The ABA further states that the work of legal assistants is of such a nature that "absent the legal assistant, the attorney would perform the task."

In 1997, the ABA House of Delegates approved a streamlined definition of a legal assistant:

> A legal assistant or paralegal is a person, qualified by education, training, or work experience who is employed or retained by a lawyer, law office, corporation, governmental agency, or other entity, who performs specifically delegated substantive legal work for which a lawyer is responsible.

This definition maintains the similarities of those discussed previously by keeping the requirement that legal assistants work under the supervision of a lawyer, that delegated work be substantive in nature, and that legal assistants are qualified through education, training, or work experience.

These similarities are the ingredients that separate this profession from other occupations and other professions in the legal field. They are the concepts that make the legal assistant profession unique. There are numerous positions and responsibilities for nonlawyers within the legal profession. However, the membership and services of the National Association of Legal Assistants, including this publication, are designed for those persons whose positions and duties meet the NALA and ABA definitions of a legal assistant.

Legal assistants who free-lance are included in these definitions. Rather than being full-time employees of a law firm, free-lance legal assistants work for law firms on a contract basis, either through their own businesses or through other contractors. These individuals work on the same professional basis and under the same supervisory provisions as legal assistants who work for only one law firm. In recent years, the numbers of free-lance legal assistants and independent contractor businesses have increased. However, the only differences between these legal assistants and those working on a full-time basis for a single employer are the terms of their employment and delivery of services. Free-lance legal assistants are subject to the same, if not more, ethical proscriptions and responsibilities as all legal assistants. The chapter on ethics in this manual will explain the variety of considerations and concepts of law that apply to all legal assistants. Additionally, the Appendix to this manual contains an article authored by NALA which tracks the progress of the legal assistant profession through case law, statute, and regulation.

Who Do Legal Assistants Work For?

The vast majority of legal assistants are found in private law firms, although legal assistants are also employed in banks, insurance companies, corporations, government offices, or are self-employed (freelance). They may work under the direction of just one attorney or several, have a private office or no office, have secretarial assistance or no support, travel frequently or never travel.

NALA's surveys have established that legal assistants generally work in private law firms (75 percent of those surveyed in 1995) on a full-time basis (93 percent) and have a private office (67 percent). Most legal assistants either have a secretary or share a secretary with one or more attorneys (40 percent) or with one or more legal assistants (10 percent), and most (75 percent) travel in connection with their work. Most legal assistants (47 percent) receive direction from one or more attorneys. However, the number of those receiving direction from an office administrator is growing. The legal assistant's work environment depends in large part on the employer, the geographic region, and how the legal assistant's skills are utilized.

One of the questions facing the profession and management studies is that of identifying the relationship between the size of a law firm, as defined by the number of lawyers, and the number of legal assistants. A comparison of annual survey data gathered over the years provides little information for making a definitive statement about this relationship beyond the obvious that larger firms tend to have more legal assistants than smaller firms. Interesting in the trends that are developing is that the numbers of legal assistants employed in firms of like size are increasing across the board.

Professional Standards: Education and Experience

With the recent overwhelming increase in educational programs designed for legal assistant training, a growing number of legal assistants have some sort of formal education beyond high school. The largest growth area has been in two-year associate degree programs with legal assistant training. However, more and more colleges and universities are offering bachelor's degree programs in legal assistant studies and some are offering masters degree programs, although the associate degree remains the largest category of education. Also, the number of employers requiring that entry-level employees have a bachelor's degree is increasing. The growth of educational programs for legal assistants, coincides with predictions for a phenomenal growth of the legal assistant profession.

In addition to the training offered through formal education programs, many law firms and other employers provide in-house training for their legal assistants. In-house training refers to education of the employee by the attorney with regard to legal assistant duties. In addition to review and analysis of assignments, the legal assistant should receive a reasonable amount of instruction directly related to his or her duties and obligations. This preparation of legal assistants is important because most codes of ethical and professional responsibility adopted by bar associations require that attorneys must be assured of the professional competence of their employees.

As a hiring criterion for entry-level employees, many employers require prior legal experience, a minimum level of education, and/or successful completion of the Certified Legal Assistant (CLA) certifying examination. The NALA *Model Standards and Guidelines for the Utilization of Legal Assistants* suggests to the profession the following as the minimum qualifications for a legal assistant:

1. Successful completion of the Certified Legal Assistant (CLA) certifying examination of the National Association of Legal Assistants, Inc.;
2. Graduation from an ABA approved program of study for legal assistants;
3. Graduation from a course of study for legal assistants which is institutionally accredited but not ABA approved and requires not less than the equivalent of sixty semester hours of classroom study;
4. Graduation from a course of study for legal assistants other than those set forth in (2) and (3) above, plus not less than six months' in-house training as a legal assistant;
5. A baccalaureate degree in any field, plus not less than six months' in-house training as a legal assistant;
6. A minimum of three years of law-related experience under the supervision of an attorney, including at least six months of in-house training as a legal assistant, or
7. Two years of in-house training as a legal assistant.

These minimum qualifications recognize law-related work and formal educational backgrounds, both of which should provide the legal assistant with a broad exposure to, and knowledge of, the legal profession. This background is necessary to assure the public and the legal profession that the one being identified as a legal assistant is qualified.

What Does a Legal Assistant Do?

A legal assistant is allowed to perform any task that is properly delegated and supervised by an attorney, so long as the attorney is ultimately responsible to the client and assumes complete responsibility for the work product. The chapter on ethics in this manual will explain in greater detail what a legal assistant cannot do, as well as the variety of considerations and concepts of law that are involved in working as a legal assistant.

Generally, and except as otherwise provided by statute, court rule or decision, administrative rule or regulation, or the attorney's *Code of Professional Responsibility,* a legal assistant may perform any function delegated by an attorney including, but not limited to, the following:

1. Conduct client interviews and maintain general contact with the client;
2. Locate and interview witnesses;
3. Conduct investigations and statistical and documentary research;
4. Conduct legal research;
5. Draft correspondence, pleadings, and other legal documents;
6. Summarize depositions, interrogatories, and testimony;
7. Attend execution of wills, real estate closings, depositions, court or administrative hearings, or trials with the attorney; and
8. Author and sign letters, provided the legal assistant status is clearly indicated and the correspondence does not contain independent legal opinions or direct legal advice.

The tasks of legal assistants vary but usually fall within those functions listed above. Empirical studies show a definite trend toward a concentration of legal assistant time in specialized areas of practice due to the tendency of lawyers to move toward specialized practice. However, NALA surveys continue to show very strong data which suggests the continuing trend that legal assistants generally are assigned a wide range of tasks and responsibilities in varied areas of practice. For instance, 54 percent of the respondents to NALA's most recent survey worked in two to four specialty areas. These are not competing ideas or contradictory statements. It is difficult, if not impossible, to segregate the areas of practice of law or to compartmentalize these specialties so neatly that there is no overlap.

How assignments are given to legal assistants will also vary. Some employers have defined levels of legal assistants; others have no structure. Assignments most commonly come from individual attorneys or through specific departments. Some legal assistants participate in meetings with clients, do legal research, and attend court hearings, while others do not.

Remember, there will be diversity in each and every position filled by a legal assistant. This diversity will depend in large part on the particular requirements for the position, the needs of the attorney and the firm, as well as the background and experience of the legal assistant.

Utilization and Billing

The standards, responsibilities, and utilization of legal assistants received significant endorsement in June, 1989, when the U.S. Supreme Court announced its decision in *Missouri v. Jenkins,* 491 U.S. 274, 109 S.Ct. 2463 (1989). The Eighth Circuit Court of Appeals placed several issues before the Supreme Court regarding the general subject of attorney fee awards under 42 U.S.C. Section 1988. The issue related to the utilization of legal assistants was whether or not, in attorney fee awards, legal assistant time may be reimbursed at market rates, rather than at actual cost. While the question before the Court already assumed that the time was reimbursable under the Code, the question of how the time may be reimbursed required the Court to examine the utilization of legal assistants.

Ultimately, the Court agreed with the decision of the Eighth Circuit Court which had allowed the compensation of legal assistant time at market rates (*see* Appendix). There are many matters of great significance to the profession in the Court's decision. First is the Court's acknowledgment of the general practice of billing legal assistant time at market rates and that these rates are significantly lower than the hourly market rates for attorney time. Second, the Court allowed the time of legal assistants to be considered in the same manner as all professional fees and separate from costs or expenses associated with a case. Finally, the Court encouraged the use of lower cost legal assistants wherever possible as a practice that ensures the cost-effective delivery of legal services and reduces the spiraling cost of litigation.

The Court cautioned, however, that "purely clerical or secretarial tasks should not be billed at a paralegal rate, regardless of who performs them." Herein lies the significance of the Court's decision on the utilization of legal assistants. While strongly encouraging the use of legal assistants through its comment and decision, the Court cautioned just as adamantly that when billing for legal assistant time (or time for any other professional), firms should not bill for any tasks that are clerical or secretarial in nature. The assumption is that the costs for these tasks are already included as overhead expenses in the hourly rates of professionals such as attorneys and legal assistants.

The Court's decision in *Missouri v. Jenkins* has been relied on by other courts in reviewing the propriety of attorney fees awards and compensation within those awards for legal assistant time.[1]

The following list of factors should be helpful in defining billing practices for legal assistants:

1. The firm customarily bills clients at an hourly rate for legal assistant time.
2. The legal assistant has the necessary qualifications through education, training, professional certification, or work experience to function in that capacity under the direction and supervision of an attorney.
3. The legal assistant time and the services performed are clearly identified and documented in the fee request.
4. The tasks performed by the legal assistant are not clerical or ministerial in nature.
5. The tasks performed by the legal assistant involve substantive legal work specifically delegated by and conducted under the direct supervision of an attorney.
6. The tasks performed by the legal assistant are cost effective in the delivery of legal services in that, absent the use of a legal assistant in the litigation, the attorney would have performed the tasks at a higher hourly rate.
7. There is no duplication of efforts by the use of a legal assistant, as the only necessary time for the attorney is in review and supervision of the legal assistant's work to merge it into the attorney's final work product.
8. The training and expertise of the legal assistant are such that they support the requested hourly services performed.
9. In specialized or complex litigation where a higher hourly rate may be sought, emphasis should be placed on the legal assistant's experience, expertise, and type and quality of work.
10. Affidavits, other documentation, or evidence are presented on the prevailing hourly rate in the relevant market area for legal assistant services.[2]

---

[1] For a discussion of the reliance of the courts on *Missouri v Jenkins* see *The Ripple Effect of Missouri v Jenkins Begins: Special Report of NALA President Karen B. Judd, CLA*, Facts & Findings (January, 1990).

[2] See Judd, Karen B., *Legal Assistant Time in Attorney Fee Awards: A Separate and Distinct Compensation*, VIII Facts & Findings (June, 1988).

Compensation

A legal assistant's compensation will likely depend on a number of factors: the type of employer, such as a private law firm or corporation, and its size; the geographic region of employment; the number of years of legal assistant experience; level of education; and other professional achievements, such as the CLA or the CLAS designations.

Depending on these variables, legal assistant salaries range from $20,000 to over $40,000 annually. In its 1995 survey, the National Association of Legal Assistants found an increase of about 7 percent in the average compensation of legal assistants. This average nationwide increase cannot be attributed solely to the two-year time span between the distribution of questionnaires. Increasingly, lawyers have come to recognize the high cost of replacing an experienced legal assistant. Because educational institutions are generally better equipped than law firms to train legal assistants, more positions than ever before are being filled by legal assistants with higher levels of education. The number of Certified Legal Assistants has increased dramatically within the past few years and the NALA surveys reflect a significant increase in the compensation of those with the CLA and CLAS designations (5 percent higher for the CLA as opposed to the non-CLA; 15 percent for the CLAS as opposed to the non-CLA).

The majority of legal assistants are salaried, frequently work in excess of their employers' normal working hours, and are not paid overtime. Fringe benefits can include vacation, medical or other insurance, parking, professional dues, and retirement plans.

Professional Certification and Activities

Legal assistants work under the supervision of attorneys and attorneys shoulder the ultimate responsibility for the work product of legal assistants. However, these facts do not relieve a legal assistant of his or her individual obligation to exhibit ethical conduct and responsibility to the legal assistant profession itself. For example, legal assistants must remain current on such subjects as ethical guidelines, opinions, and case law that affect their professional status, continue their legal education, and demonstrate their competence and their commitment to professional standards. It is through their local, state, and national professional associations that they may address these goals and responsibilities.

The National Association of Legal Assistants offers a national voluntary certification program for legal assistants. This peer-established certification program provides a means for legal assistants to demonstrate their knowledge and expertise in this profession and their commitment to professional development. The Certified Legal Assistant (CLA) designation is generally recognized within the legal community as one means of identifying competent legal assistants. This certification and the use of the CLA designation are available to any legal assistant who meets certain eligibility requirements and successfully completes a two-day examination covering the range of skills and knowledge required of legal assistants. All Certified Legal Assistants must meet certain continuing education requirements in order to maintain the CLA designation which must be renewed every five years.

Legal assistants who achieve the CLA designation may continue their professional accreditation through NALA's specialty certification program. As of 1997, Certified Legal Assistant Specialist (CLAS) designations were available in the areas of bankruptcy, civil litigation, probate and estate planning, criminal law and procedure, real estate law, corporations/business law, and intellectual property. The CLAS designation is earned through successful completion of a comprehensive examination in a topical area mentioned above. Continuing education credit is also awarded for successful completion of a specialty examination.

Recognition of the Certified Legal Assistant program is nationwide. An example of the high regard in which it is held by attorneys in general is the discussion of the program which appears in the 1993 publication *Leveraging with Legal Assistants*, published by the ABA Section of Law Practice Management. On the subject of recruiting legal assistants:

> The legal assistant who can use the CLA designation has a number of advantages, not the least of which is that a hiring lawyer can assume for the CLA appellation that he or she is dealing with an experienced legal assistant who has performed to a high standard. It would be safe to assume that a CLA can immediately bring experience and capability to the practice.

The CLA program has been in existence over twenty years. As of March, 1998, there were 9,211 Certified Legal Assistants in the United States, 749 of whom have achieved a CLA Specialty designation. Three states (Florida, Louisiana, and California) have adopted the CLA as the standard for legal assistants within their own state specialty certification programs. The only other state to offer state-wide certification is Texas, with the CLA being one of the means of qualifying for that examination.

Numerous bar associations offer guidelines for legal assistants, as well as associate membership for legal assistants. Half of the bar associations and bar association sections offering this membership include the CLA credential among the alternate eligibility requirements for membership. The South Dakota Supreme Court has recognized the CLA as a means of identifying competent legal assistants and other courts have awarded higher fees to legal assistants with the CLA designation. In 1995, Mississippi Bar Ethics Committee Opinion 223 (1/19/95) described the CLA as a reputable program and allowed the use of the CLA and CLAS credentials on law firm letterhead listings.

The legal community has also been supportive of the credential economically. Legal assistants with the CLA receive higher salaries nationwide and their work is billed at higher rates. The 1995 NALA Utilization and Compensation Survey showed a significant positive relationship between the CLA credential and legal assistant salaries and compensation. Further, the credential is more highly related to salary and compensation than the level of legal assistant educational training. The Certified Legal Assistant program exists for the legal assistant profession. It is a valuable tool for use by legal assistants in the development of their career path and direction.

Summary

The word *assist* is the basis for the title *legal assistant*. This one word is the key reason for the emergence of, and the ever-growing need and demand for, qualified legal assistants. Legal assistants *assist* attorneys in the delivery of legal services by performing whatever tasks the attorneys delegate. This frees attorneys to do that which only they can do. This *assisting* can be in a direct one-to-one relationship with an attorney, as part of an attorney-legal assistant-legal secretary team, or with a number of attorneys. It is in this spirit of assisting that we must approach the legal assistant profession. This, above all others, is the criterion upon which we will build and expand this exciting, promising, and vital career.

1 Introduction to the American Legal System

The American legal system reflects complexity and diversity in its structure and procedure. In the United States, two sovereigns exercise jurisdiction: the United States (the federal government) exercises authority according to the powers granted by the U.S. Constitution; the state exercises authority through the state and federal constitutions.

In each case, the power exercised is a grant from the people, an expression of the people's choice as to how they will be governed and the limitations upon that governance.

1.00 Law in American Society

An essential element in understanding the law begins with definition. How is law defined? What is law? *The American College Dictionary* defines law as ". . . the principles and regulations emanating from a government and applicable to a people, whether in the form of legislation or of custom and policies recognized and enforced by judicial decision." *Black's Law Dictionary*® also offers a general definition: ". . . law, in its generic sense, is a body of rules of action or conduct prescribed by controlling authority, and having binding legal force. . . ." Common to these definitions are (1) rules of conduct, (2) made by a controlling body, usually a government, and (3) which are enforceable.

How has this controlling force, that is, the government, earned the right or power to make and enforce rules for a people? The answer can be found in the history and theory of legal principles, a brief overview of which follows.

1.001 History, Theory, Philosophy

Legal traditions develop from history, theory, and philosophy. Our American legal system is most often thought to be taken only from English systems. However, in the development of Anglo-American law, four basic schools of thought are commonly identified.

1.0011 Natural Law. In ancient times, the great philosophers from Athens and the great Roman jurists, believed humankind could discover, by reason, the perfect rules of human conduct that were separate from enacted laws. These "natural laws" are not peculiar to any one people, rather they conform to the inherent nature of all people. In other words, they are unchanging rules of conduct discovered only by the rational intelligence of humankind.

Our Founding Fathers, especially Thomas Jefferson and Alexander Hamilton, adopted a revised "natural law" school of thought. They were particularly influenced by John Locke (1632–1704), an English philosopher who wrote on the individual's rights and government's obligations. A good example of Thomas Jefferson's work can be found in the Declaration of Independence:

> When in the course of human events, it becomes necessary for one people to dissolve the political bonds which have connected them with another, and to assume, among the powers of the earth, the separate and equal station to which the laws of nature and of nature's God entitle them, a decent respect to the opinions of mankind requires that they should declare the causes which impel them to separate.
>
> We hold these truths to be self-evident, that all men are created equal; that they are endowed by their Creator with certain unalienable rights; that among these are life, liberty, and the pursuit of happiness.

Our Founding Fathers declared revolution against the king of England based on the thinking that new rules must be established that were consistent with natural rights.

1.0012 Positive Law/Divine Law. Early positivism developed in Europe, reflecting Judeo-Christian traditions and the canon law of the early Holy Roman Empire. Fundamentally, believers held all law is of divine origin and handed down by the sovereign. The positivist focused on four basic principles: (1) law consists of rules, (2) law is different from morals, (3) the sovereign establishes the rules, and (4) legal rules carry sanctions. Although this school of thought was influential, our constitutional principle of separation of church and state was already strongly embedded in American law.

1.0013 Sociological Jurisprudence. This school of thought is concerned with the effects of law and its justifications. When a law is enacted, the proponents of sociological jurisprudence analyze the effects and reasons for the law by applying methods of the social sciences. The adequacy of a legal system is judged by weighing its effect on society against individual interest, special group interest, and the good of the general public.

1.0014 Legal Realism. This school, which best describes our American legal philosophy, has its roots in natural law and sociological jurisprudence. The great jurist Oliver Wendell Holmes (1841–1935) was a pioneer of the realist school. Fundamentally, realists examine what the law is and not what the law ought to be. They use social science to analyze how the law functions and to look for underlying policy.

1.01   Sources of American Law

Federal and state laws come from many different sources. When most of us think of the law, we are generally referring to the statutes or ordinances that are enacted by a legislative body. To understand the American legal system and its sources of law, however, we will have to look further.

The American government is divided into three branches: executive, legislative, and judicial. Each of these branches has several levels: federal, state, and local. Thus, the United States executive branch is headed by the president, the state executive branch by a governor, and the local executive branch by a mayor or similar officer. The same pattern can be found in the legislative branch of government. The United States legislative body is the Congress; the state legislative body is the legislature; and the local legislative body is generally called a city or town council. The judicial branch of government also has three basic levels: the United States (federal) courts, consisting of the U.S. Supreme Court and the lower federal courts of appeals and district courts; state courts reflect this system as well by having a court of last resort, usually referred to as the supreme court, and/or their appellate court, and a trial court. Administrative agencies are sometimes referred to as the "fourth" branch of government because the regulations that they promulgate have the effect of law. Administrative regulations are created at the federal, state, and local levels. (*See* Exhibit 1-1, Sources of American Law.)

1.011 Common Law

The individual states of the United States can trace the development of their legal principles, and to some degree their judicial systems, to medieval England. Common law principles have evolved through judicial decision making. The judge applies principles of law through the analysis of prior court decisions. This is known as *stare decisis,* that is, following the reasoning and decisions of earlier courts when presented with a similar fact situation unless a clear, convincing reason exists to depart from the established precedent. Judicial adherence to the

EXHIBIT 1-1   Sources of American Law

| | **Four Sources of Law** | | | |
	Statutory (Legislatures)	*Administrative Agencies*	*Common Law (Courts)*	*Constitutions*
Federal Level	Congress (Statutes)	Federal Agencies (Regulations)	Federal Courts (Cases or opinions)	U.S. Constitution
State Level	State Legislatures (Statutes)	State Agencies (Regulations)	State Courts (Cases or opinions)	State Constitution
Local Level	City Council (Ordinances)	City Agencies (Regulations)	Local Courts (Cases or opinions)	Charter

principle of *stare decisis* creates consistency in the law. When a similar fact situation arises, the parties and their attorneys can, with some degree of certainty, predict and explain what the law has been and how the courts are likely to decide the dispute. Clearly, there are exceptions because the law does change. This system, however, offers stability and consistency in how legal principles are applied. Because the rules do not change rapidly, attorneys are able to explain to clients what the general law is and how courts have viewed their specific fact situation.

1.012 Statutory Law

Laws that have been enacted by a legislative body are known as statutes or ordinances. Statutes are enacted by either the United States Congress or a state legislative body. The term *ordinance* is generally used when a city or town council passes a local law. The federal legal system is exclusively statutory in nature. There is no federal common law source. However, federal statutes, when challenged, are interpreted by judges. The state legal system, however, is a combination of statutory law and common law principles.

1.013 Administrative Law

Administrative law is similar to statutory law (legislation). It is now well established and judicially accepted that Congress and the state legislatures may delegate some of their constitutional lawmaking authority to administrative agencies. In fact, without these agencies, government could not effectively function. Agencies of the federal government, such as the Social Security Administration, promulgate rules and regulations that have the effect and force of law.

Administrative agencies have the power to exercise quasi-judicial, quasi-legislative, and quasi-executive authority. Their authority is limited by the power granted. Congress can grant to the Social Security Administration, through legislation, the power to hear and decide violations of Social Security regulations. This grant is not unlimited because Congress, under the United States Constitution, is restricted to what it can delegate. In this way, agencies carry out many functions that are simply not possible for Congress to do alone. Because the separation of powers through the three branches of government is fundamental, this "fourth branch" can only function through the authority granted by one of the original branches, specifically, the legislative branch or the executive branch.

1.014 Constitutional Law

The last major source of law is the constitution. There are basically three levels of constitutions: federal, state, and local. The federal Constitution is the supreme law of the land. All other sources of law—legislative, administrative, and common law—are subject to the principles of the U.S.

Constitution. The Constitution embodies general principles regarding the powers granted to the federal government, the powers reserved to the states, and the rights held by citizens, especially in the Bill of Rights, which are the first ten amendments to the Constitution. Because the principles are general, they require frequent interpretation by the judiciary.

In addition to the U.S. Constitution, state and local governments have constitutions. A state's constitution is the supreme law of that particular state; however, it is subordinate to the U.S. Constitution. Local governments may also adopt constitutions, generally referred to as charters, and these are subordinate to federal and state constitutions.

1.02 The American Legal System

Systems provide structure for processing the various sources of law. There is a judicial system and process, a legislative system and process, and an administrative system and process.

The American legal system is founded in common law principles that the colonists brought with them from England. However, Louisiana also follows a civil law system based upon the Napoleonic Code that its settlers brought from France thereby giving it a dual system. The difference between the common law system and Louisiana's civil law system is not so much a difference between what is right and what is wrong as it is a difference in procedure, though each system does have some substantive laws that are unique to it.

Common law does not operate in isolation within our legal system. Each governmental unit (federal, state, and local) has adopted a document that defines and limits its powers in relation to its citizens. At the federal and state levels, this document is called a constitution. A local government, such as a city, may adopt a charter for this purpose.

The U.S. Constitution reflects the method of government adopted by the founders through the governmental branches (legislative, executive, and judicial) created by it, and the specific powers that each branch is authorized to exercise. The legislative branch is authorized to make laws; the executive branch, to enforce laws; and the judicial branch, to interpret laws. This is known as the separation of powers among the three governmental branches. The federal Constitution and most state constitutions include a Bill of Rights that specifically defines those individual rights that no governmental branch can take away, such as the right to a jury trial, and freedon of speech.

The federal Constitution gives Congress the authority to legislate in specific areas, such as interstate commerce and federal taxation. The U.S. Supreme Court is the only court specifically created by the Constitution, although Congress is given authority to add such other, inferior courts as it deems necessary. Since most state constitutions follow a format similar to that in the U.S. Constitution, many parallels can be drawn between the two systems of government. Yet, federal and state governments exist independently of each other. Their authority or jurisdiction is distinct. For further discussion, see Chapter 2, Legal Research.

1.021 Court Systems

At both the federal and state levels, court systems have been established for judicial resolution of legal disputes. Each court system is generally organized in four levels: specialty courts, trial courts, intermediate appellate courts, and supreme courts. Some decisions and appeals, heard and adjudged in state courts, may be appealed further to the U.S. Supreme Court if a federally protected right is involved and if the Court consents (grants *certiorari*) to hear the case. (*See* Exhibit 1-2, United States Judicial System.)

EXHIBIT 1-2   United States Judicial System

FEDERAL JUDICIAL SYSTEM

U.S. Supreme Court
(9 Justices)

U.S. Court of Appeals
(Federal Circuit)

U.S. Courts of Appeals
(12 Circuits)

U.S. District Courts

Certain Administrative
Agencies

Federal Specialty
Courts

Other Federal Courts
of Limited Jurisdiction

STATE JUDICIAL SYSTEM

State Supreme Court

Intermediate Appellate Courts

REMOVAL

Circuit Court
(Superior Court, etc.)

Specialty Courts
(Family & Probate, etc.)

Other Courts of
Limited Jurisdiction

1.022 Federal Court System

The federal judiciary is established in Article III of the U.S. Constitution. However only the Supreme Court is specifically mentioned: ". . . The judicial Power of the United States, shall be vested in one supreme Court, and in such inferior Courts as the Congress may from time to time ordain and establish. . . ." Thus, the federal court system is in large part determined by Congress. In addition, Congress may establish courts under Article I, Section 8 of the Constitution, which states that ". . . Congress shall have the power . . . to constitute Tribunals inferior to the Supreme Court. . . ." Congress has established, for example, the U.S. Tax Court under this section of the Constitution. The difference between the two articles is that under Article III, Section 1, judges hold office for life and compensation can not be reduced during their term. However Article I, Section 8 makes no statement regarding the length of office or the compensation, thus Congress may establish specialty courts, such as tax or bankruptcy, without appointing judges for life or guaranteeing a level of compensation. Congress cannot establish all courts under Article I, however, because Article III, Section 2 describes certain judicial powers granted to the Supreme Court and inferior courts.

The federal court system is composed of four types of courts: (1) the district court, a trial court; (2) the court of appeals, an intermediate appellate court; (3) The Supreme Court, the final appellate court; and (4) specialized courts such as the U.S. Court of Claims and the U.S. Tax Court. This basic four-tier federal system is generally repeated at the state level.

1.0221 District Courts.

1.0221 District Courts.   The federal court system covers the United States, Puerto Rico, the Virgin Islands, and Guam. The federal trial courts serving these areas are the U.S. District Courts, which are geographically located to serve each of the fifty states and Puerto Rico with one or more courtrooms in each state. These courts have federal jurisdiction over civil and criminal matters. U.S. District Courts that have both federal and local jurisdiction serve the District of Columbia, the Virgin Islands, and Guam.

Courts are organized with judges and courtrooms assigned to departments within the court. The more population and litigation, the more courtrooms and judges. Trials may be held, depending on the issues, before a judge, a jury, or specially selected and qualified masters whose powers and limitations are defined by the district court making the appointment.

The district courts are established geographically, with a minimum of one per state (none crosses state lines); currently, there are more than ninety district courts. Larger states, such as Texas, California, and New York, have several district courts within them. District courts are trial-level courts of original jurisdiction. The district court evaluates testimony, hears witnesses, and makes findings of fact and law; most types of trials brought within the federal court system originate here. District courts are general jurisdiction courts in that they hear most types of cases, unlike specialty courts, such as the U.S. Tax Court or U.S. Court of Claims, which hear only single-subject cases. Judges are appointed for life by the president, subject to confirmation by the U.S. Senate.

Certain circumstances allow the removal of some cases or issues from state courts into federal courts, such as diversity of citizenship (parties are domiciled in different states) where the amount in controversy exceeds a minimum amount. When no federal question exists, but where there is diversity of citizenship, the amount in controversy exceeds the minimum proscribed in Title 28, U.S.C. 1332, and the federal court accepts the right of removal as one properly exercised and procedurally correct, the U.S. District Court will apply the law of the appropriate state, whether it is common law, civil code, or the statutes of the state.

1.0222 Courts of Appeals.

1.0222 Courts of Appeals.   The U.S. Courts of Appeals (also referred to as circuit courts) were established as intermediate appellate courts to help relieve the workload of the Supreme Court. The United States has thirteen circuits: eleven represent geographic areas, the District of Columbia is a circuit, and the thirteenth is known as The Federal Circuit. The Federal or Thirteenth Circuit Court of Appeals handles appeals from the U.S. Court of Claims, U.S. Court of International Trade, and other specialized federal courts. There may be more than one division within a single circuit. Three judges are designated from all the judges in the division to sit in each case in each division. Appeals are not heard before juries but before the judges of the division. At least two judges are always present, but the judges may sit en banc (all three judges present). When two of the three judges assigned to a particular case agree on an outcome, the decision is binding.

Courts of appeals hear cases where the appellant (the party appealing) argues that the evidence did not support the trial court's finding or that the trial court erred in the application of the law. The appellate court reviews the record only; no new evidence is admitted, and no witnesses are heard. This court will hear the arguments of the parties' attorneys, review the record of the trial proceedings, and read written briefs submitted by both parties. The court will make its decision based on this information. Most appeals end here. The next appeal would be to the Supreme Court, which exercises discretion in accepting cases. About 4,500 cases are appealed to the Supreme Court annually; the number actually heard averages less than 300.

1.0223 The Supreme Court.   The U.S. Supreme Court is the ultimate interpreter of the United States Constitution. This is the court of last resort, although in most cases, litigants do not have a right to have their appeal heard by the highest court. There are two basic ways appeals reach the Supreme Court: (1) through a *writ of certiorari* (an order to the lower court to send the Supreme Court the record of the case for review) which may or may not be granted by the high court; or (2) through an appeal of right, which exists in certain cases, such as where a state or federal court of appeals has held a state statute violates the U.S. Constitution.

The Supreme Court has nine justices; one chief justice and eight associate justices. Justices are nominated by the President and confirmed by the Senate. These are lifetime appointments. It has original jurisdiction in cases affecting ambassadors, other public ministers, and consuls and in those cases where one of the fifty states is a party. Original jurisdiction is exercised in very few cases. It has appellate jurisdiction in all other cases. The Supreme Court itself is subject to some regulation by Congress. Article III, Chapter 21 of the U.S. Constitution establishes the powers and limitations of the federal judiciary. Sections 1251–1257, Title 2A, Chapter 81 of the U.S. Code confer appellate jurisdiction on the Supreme Court.

1.0224 Specialized Courts.   Federal specialized courts have jurisdictions limited to a specialized subject area, and are considered *inferior courts*. Examples of such courts include the Court of International Trade, the U.S. Claims Court, and the U.S. Tax Court. These courts function as a trial court. Appeals from these first tier courts are made directly to the U.S. Court of Appeal for the Federal Circuit, established by Congress as part of the Federal Courts Improvement Act of 1982.

The U.S. Claims Court renders judgments on the validity of certain types of claims against the United States. Also separate from the U.S. District Court, the U.S. Tax Court renders judgments in federal taxation matters.

A separate U.S. Customs Court deals exclusively with matters of imported merchandise and the activities of customs collectors. The U.S. Court of Customs and Patent Appeals hears appeals and reviews decisions of the Customs Court, the Patent Office, and the Tariff Commission.

1.0225 Administrative Agencies.   The administrative agencies of the federal government carry out the directions of the president as a part of the executive branch. Each is established and authorized by a specific legislative act (enabling act) passed by Congress. Within the boundaries of its particular enabling act, each administrative agency adopts rules and regulations to carry out its purpose. In addition, it is empowered to hold hearings and to render binding decisions in quasi-judicial proceedings that resemble trials. Hearing officers in contested matters may be administrative law judges, referees, hearing examiners, commissioners, or other persons authorized by the agency. Hearing officers are not generally required to be attorneys. Although their work is not controlled or directed by the courts, all appeals from their decisions proceed directly to the U.S. Courts of Appeals. Examples of administrative agencies are the Federal Communications Commission, the Federal Trade Commission, the National Labor Relations Board, the Federal Aviation Administration, the Occupational Safety and Health Administration, and the Equal Employment Opportunity Commission.

1.023 State Court Systems

Although state court systems are not uniform, they share some typical elements. They have trial and appellate level courts, specialized courts, and courts with general and limited jurisdiction. Examples of trial courts with limited jurisdiction would be magistrates courts, small claims courts, and municipal courts that enforce local ordinances. Examples of specialized courts would be family or domestic relations courts and probate courts. The state will also have a trial court with general jurisdiction to hear civil and criminal cases.

Most states have an intermediate appellate court where the losing party has a right of appeal. The appeals court of last resort in most states is the state's supreme court. If the state has an intermediate appellate court, its supreme court may use discretion in accepting cases.

State courts handle an immense volume of litigation, both civil and criminal. Largely because of the defendant's constitutional right to a speedy trial, most courts give priority to criminal cases. This causes some problems in scheduling and rescheduling civil cases, both for procedural matters leading to trial as well as for the trials themselves. It is not unusual to have civil trial dates cancelled or postponed on the court's calendar because of a sudden influx of criminal cases. Attorneys and legal assistants recognize that the litigation process has inherent elements of uncertainty that require an attorney to be ready for trial on schedule, in full knowledge that the trial may not begin on schedule. This uncertainty is the basis for at least a portion of the pressures experienced by the litigation team as trial dates draw near. From state to state, trial court systems may differ (particularly in titles) but usually fit the general outline shown in Exhibit 1-2.

State Supreme Courts have minimal, if any, original jurisdiction. The bulk of their workload derives from their appellate jurisdiction over civil and criminal cases that are appealed from state superior courts and state administrative agencies. From five to nine judges, depending on the state, provide appellate review based upon the record made at the trial court level and intermediate appellate court level, if any. No jury exists at this level, and no new evidence is received. In some states, citizens have an absolute right of review by the state supreme court. In others, supreme court review is discretionary with the court itself.

Superior courts (sometimes called district, circuit, common pleas, or sessions courts) are usually established in each county, parish, or similar region and have sufficient judges and courtrooms to handle the population or litigation within that particular county. Occasionally, judges are "borrowed" from other counties to handle heavy litigation loads. Superior courts generally handle the trial of all felonies, as well as civil litigation over a minimum dollar amount, such as five thousand dollars. In many states, this court is one of general jurisdiction, which means that there is no minimum or maximum dollar amount for the civil suits that it handles. These courts may also handle appeals from inferior courts as a separate and distinct responsibility.

The County court or municipal court is a lower-level court that hears criminal misdemeanor cases and civil cases having a maximum dollar value. Sometimes this court has a separate small claims court, which is limited to very small dollar amounts (five hundred dollars or less, for instance), does not provide for trial by jury, and does not allow parties to be represented by attorneys.

1.024 Jurisdiction

The complexity of law and its administration, together with the multilevel regulation of modern life, often make it hard to identify the best *forum,* that is the location or type of court, in which to present the client's case. Even after all the forums have been identified that have authority to hear a particular matter, difficult decisions often remain. A state may have laws that parallel those of the federal government in certain areas, such as antitrust statutes, securities regulation, equal employment opportunity, and utility regulation. If so, the lawyer must decide whether to lodge the client's claim in the state or federal court or at the administrative level.

A decision on whether to file a civil action in a state superior court or in a county court may depend on the dollar value of damages and the length of time necessary to bring the case to trial. While trials usually can be completed more quickly in a county court, a successful plaintiff may still need to register the judgment with the superior court before it will be given full faith and credit by other courts in other jurisdictions. This is a critical factor when it appears likely that judicial enforcement will be required to collect the judgment.

Further decisions must be made if the potential defendant (or defendants) is domiciled outside the geographical jurisdiction of the forum court. In that case, facts must be established that will give the forum court personal jurisdiction over the defendant. Most states have long-arm statutes that authorize jurisdiction over persons who commit torts within the forum state (such as causing an automobile accident) or who do other things to establish minimum contacts with the forum state.

Even if all of the parties live in the same state, it may still be necessary to decide which court has proper venue to hear the case. Venue relates to the place where the case should be tried, assuming that there is more than one division or department of a court that has jurisdiction. When venue becomes an issue, it is usually resolved by balancing convenience to the plaintiff, convenience to the defendant, where the events occurred, and where the witnesses and other evidence are most readily available.

1.025 Legislative Systems

The power to make law originates with the federal and state legislative bodies. (*See* Exhibit 1-3, How a Bill Becomes a Law.) The "supreme law of the land" is the Constitution; all other laws are subordinate. The Constitution states in Article I, Section 1, "All legislative Powers herein granted shall be vested in a Congress of the United States, which shall consist of a Senate and House of Representatives." The Constitution grants broad powers to Congress, but those powers not specifically granted to Congress are reserved to the states or to the people through the Tenth Amendment, which says that "the powers not delegated to the United States by the Constitution, nor prohibited by it to the States, are reserved to the States respectively, or to the people." This is referred to as the Reservation Clause.

State constitutions similarly grant the power to legislate to a state body, often referred to as the legislature. This legislative body acts within the power granted by the state constitution or by the power reserved through the Tenth Amendment. Collectively, these powers are the police power of the state because they allow the state to enact laws to promote public health, safety, and welfare. Police power is very broad and permits states, for example, to set standards for

EXHIBIT 1-3   How a Bill Becomes Law

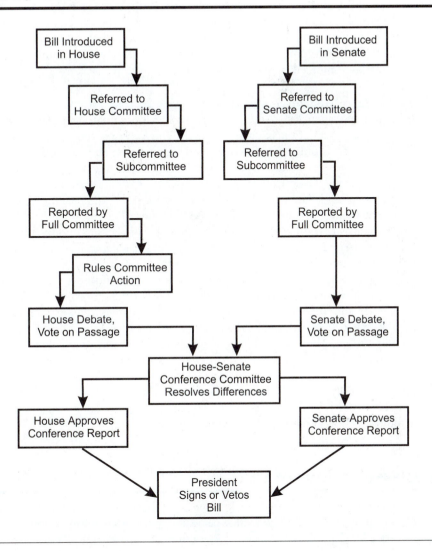

licensing professionals, requirements for operating vehicles, minimum age for marriage, and generally to control any areas unique to the state.

State and federal legislative bodies have many potentially conflicting areas of power. However, the Supremacy Clause of the Constitution (Article VI, Section 2) makes clear that the Constitution is the ultimate law: "This constitution, and the laws of the United States which shall be made in pursuance thereof; and all treaties made, or which shall be made, under the authority of the United States, shall be supreme law of the land; and the Judges in every State shall be bound thereby, anything in the constitution or laws of any State to the contrary notwithstanding."

Another article that tries to clarify the relationship between state and federal power is Article IV, Sections 1 and 2. Section 1 states, "Full faith and credit shall be given in each State to the public acts, records, and judicial proceedings of every other state. And the Congress may by general laws prescribe the manner in which such acts, records and proceedings shall be proved, and the effect thereof." This is called the Full Faith and Credit Clause. Section 2 is referred to as the Privileges and Immunities Clause, and it states, "The citizens of each State shall be entitled to all privileges and immunities of citizens in the several States." Both of these sections of Article IV have been interpreted, through case law, by the U.S. Supreme Court. Laws enacted by Congress are enforced by the judicial and administrative systems.

1.026 Administrative Systems

Administrative agencies are established by a specific act of the legislative branch, but are usually considered an arm of the executive branch. The U.S. Constitution does not specifically provide for the agencies. Some examples of federal agencies are: Federal Deposit Insurance Corporation, the Federal Reserve Board, Environmental Protection Agency, Securities and Exchange Commission, Federal Trade Commission, Farm Credit Administration, Consumer Protection Safety Commission, and National Labor Relations Board. The administrative agencies, which may fall under the control of any one of the three branches of government or classified as independent (*see* Exhibit 1-4, The United States Government), are often authorized by the act creating them to engage in quasi-legislative, quasi-executive, or quasi-judicial activities. In their quasi-executive status, they manage a particular area of interest of law; in their quasi-legislative role, they promulgate rules and regulations that have the force and effect of law; in their quasi-judicial status, they conduct hearings and render and order the enforcement of decisions.

Under the theory of exhaustion of administrative remedies, a person must seek an administrative agency remedy to a problem, if a remedy is available, before seeking relief through a court system. The Administrative Procedures Act (APA) originally adopted in 1946, controls the majority of the administrative processes through the establishment of procedures which must be followed by an agency in its rulemaking and quasi-judicial functions. It is these procedures which generally control whether or not an individual is deemed to have exhausted administrative remedies. Many states have adopted Administrative Procedures Acts which mirror the federal act and function at the state level in the same manner.

1.03 Classifications of Law

It is not a simple task to break down our large accumulated body of laws into simple classifications to study. In general, we speak of our laws in terms of whether they are substantive or procedural, public or private, civil or criminal. As shown in Exhibit 1-5, a law often belongs to more than one classification.

1.031 Substantive and Procedural Law

Substantive law includes laws that regulate, define, and establish legal rights and obligations. Examples of substantive law are contracts, torts, criminal law, corporations, real property, administrative, trusts and wills, and constitutional law.

Procedural law establishes the methods of enforcing the substantive laws. Examples of procedural law are federal and state rules of evidence, rules of civil procedure, and rules of criminal procedure.

Basically, the difference between substantive and procedural law is that the former describes what our rights and obligations are and the latter describes how we apply and enforce the substantive rights.

EXHIBIT 1-4   The United States Government

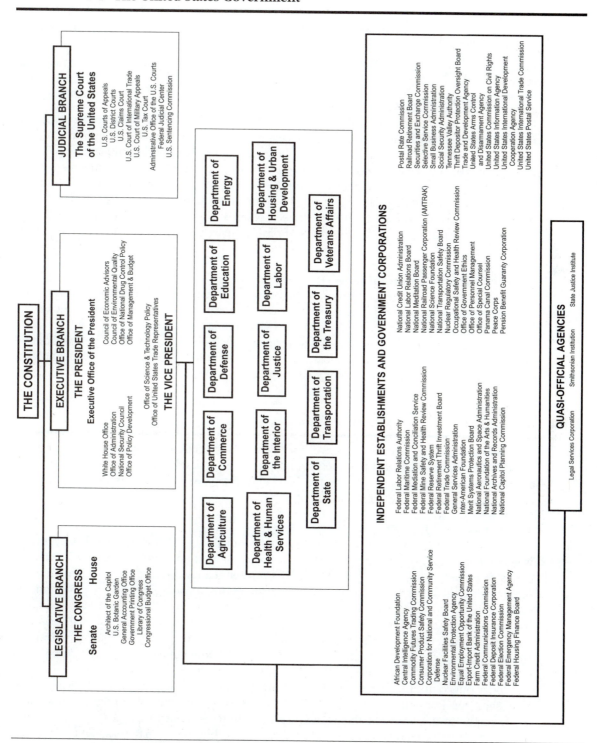

EXHIBIT 1-5   Classifications of Law

Civil Law				Criminal Law	
Public Law		Private Law		Public Law	
Substantive	Procedural	Substantive	Procedural	Substantive	Procedural

1.032 Public and Private Law

Public law is best described as the relationship between persons and their government. For example, constitutional law, in part, describes the relationship between the government and the people. Administrative law is another example, as is criminal law. Constitutional law provides the right to vote, a voice in the government; administrative law describes what entitlement might be available through an agency, such as Social Security benefits; and criminal law defines crime against society, even though the crime may be committed against an individual person.

Private law deals with relationships between people. A breach of contract, a tort, wills and trusts, and corporation law are all examples of private law because they affect person-to-person relationships.

1.033 Civil and Criminal Law

Civil law embodies the whole area of law that exists between persons or between citizens and their government. Some civil law is public and some is private. A suit by the government against a citizen is public even though it may involve a civil wrong.

In contrast, criminal law involves a wrong against the public as a whole. A person accused of a crime has violated society's standard of conduct. Although the crime may also involve a civil wrong, such as assault and battery, criminal law is public law.

1.04 Remedies

Remedies are the legal means to recover for a wrong. In a civil litigation, courts and/or juries must decide the type of relief that the prevailing party is entitled to receive. The type of relief awarded is dependant on the what the party requested as well what is permitted by the applicable substantive laws of the forum.

1.041 Law and Equity

Historically, remedies were divided into legal and equitable. Courts were also divided in this way, so that a court of law could award a legal remedy and an equity court could award an equitable remedy. The courts were limited; if you wanted a legal remedy, that is land, money, or something of value, only a court of law could provide this; if you wanted an equitable remedy, such as an order for a person to perform an obligation under a contract, you had to go to a court of equity. As mentioned earlier in this chapter, the common law principle of *stare decisis* controls in courts of law, while courts of equity apply what are known as "equitable maxims." Some examples of equitable maxims are: "He who seeks equity must do equity." "Equity must follow the law." "He who comes into equity must come with clean hands."

Today our courts are merged, and these distinctions are not as important. The judicial system can issue a legal or equitable remedy. However, the adage "no remedy, no right" still applies. For example, in the area of contract law, if the party feels money damages are inadequate, *rescission* (an order modifying or canceling the parties' obligations) may be sought.

1.05 Alternative Dispute Resolution

No examination of the history of the American legal system would be complete without a glimpse into the future. In what direction is the legal system evolving? Discussions earlier in this chapter focused on the various sources of American Law and its history, theory and philosophy. The name "alternative" implies something new and different, apart from the mainstream. To the contrary, Alternative Dispute Resolution (ADR) is far from new. Some historians view adjudication or litigation as the alternative method. The high rate of negotiated settlements prior to trial would seem to support this theory.

1.051 Historical Perspective

Some form of negotiation and mediation has been employed for centuries. It is as ancient as human civilization itself, and is not limited to western tradition. In early China and Japan religion and philosophy placed a strong emphasis on consensus, persuasion, and harmony. We recall King Solomon's famed wisdom in the child custody battle. In the early days of Christianity, Paul told the congregation at Corinth not to take their disputes to court but to appoint their own people to settle their disputes. In Anglo-Saxon England a wide array of dispute resolution processes were employed, predating English common law. Some of these methods were remarkably akin to our modern day arbitration, mediation, conciliation, and negotiation.

Valerie Sanchez indicates that these processes were available to litigants on a "dispute processing continuum." Sanchez states that in Anglo-Saxon England, judges and arbitrators "often encouraged parties to reach settlement agreements . . . *after* the decision makers had reached a winner-take-all judgment on the merits of the claim *and* announced it to the parties, *but before* those judgments were procedurally 'finalized' in keeping with Anglo-Saxon legal procedure."[1] Thus the decision makers became third party facilitators—commonly known today as mediators.

The major difference between adjudication and ADR is reflected in the Anglo-Saxon methods which gave disputants access to other options, rather than accepting the judgment of the third party decision makers. Negotiation was adjunct to the adjudication process. Then, as now, ADR permitted parties to forge their own resolutions. The control of the outcome was shifted to the parties themselves. Along with control came power—the key to ADR.

1.052 The Multidoor Courthouse Experiment

Though widely credited with coining this metaphor, Professor Sandor did not actually call for a "multidoored courthouse" but a "Dispute Resolution Center." In a paper delivered at the *National Conference on the Causes of Popular Dissatisfaction with the Administration of Justice* (1976), known as the "Pound Conference,"[2] Professor Sandor envisioned a flexible system where a litigant could be channeled through a diverse array of processes—mediation, arbitration, fact-finding, and/or court processes.

As the practice of ADR has evolved, so have the various processes available to disputants. Arbitration (both binding and nonbinding) and mediation are the most prevalent today. Both methods are explained herein, with a greater emphasis on mediation processes. Also available

---

[1] Valerie A. Sanchez, *Towards a History of ADR: The Dispute Processing Continuum in Anglo-Saxon England and Today*, 11 OHIO ST. J. ON DISP. RESOL. __ (1996).

[2] From the 1906 Roscoe Pound speech, *The Causes of Popular Dissatisfaction with the Administration of Justice*, delivered August 29, 1906 in St. Paul, Minnesota, to the ABA's annual meeting. This served as a landmark in the history of procedural reform.

in some jurisdictions are the minitrial, summary jury trial, and moderated settlement conference. A brief description of these processes is included.

1.053 Arbitration

Black's defines arbitration as the "reference of a dispute to an impartial (third) person chosen by the parties to the dispute who agree in advance to abide by the arbitrator's award issued after a hearing at which both parties have an opportunity to be heard."[3] Arbitration may be binding or nonbinding depending on prior agreement of the parties. The arbitration hearing is similar to a trial proceeding but is less formal and doesn't follow strict rules of evidence. Arbitration is often employed in disputes involving labor relations, commercial contracts and intellectual property matters. Parties may enter into arbitration by informal agreement, contractual agreement, or by order of a court. Statutory authority for The Federal Arbitration Act is found at 9 U.S.C. Section 1, et seq., and for the Uniform Arbitration Act at 7 U.L.A. Business & Financial Laws. A majority of states have adopted the Uniform Arbitration Act in some form. The Uniform Arbitration Act serves to validate arbitration agreements by allowing for the filing of motions to enforce, confirm, modify, or vacate arbitration agreements and awards.

The American Arbitration Association, a private, non-profit organization, serves to assist parties by promulgating rules and regulations, providing lists of qualified arbitrators and assisting with logistical matters. Qualification requirements for arbitrators vary by region. Some jurisdictions require a law degree, others do not. The primary requirement is that the arbitrator be impartial.

Disputes in arbitration are best decided by skilled arbitrators who are knowledgeable in that particular field. Arbitrators have virtually total control over the proceedings, including subpoena power. The major advantage of arbitration, like most forms of ADR, is its cost effectiveness. Its major disadvantage is that it places the decision making capability in the hands of a third party.

1.054 Mediation

Mediation is a process wherein an impartial third party assists the parties in a direct negotiation of their dispute. Parties voluntarily work out their own agreement in an informal, private setting. Mediation may be employed outside the court system or as a result of a court order. Many jurisdictions are enacting court ordered mediation in certain substantive areas, most notably domestic law. Other cases that lend themselves especially well to mediation are those where the parties have an ongoing relationship, such as business partners, neighbors, students, etc.

The mediator assists the parties in focusing on their interests, not their positions. Positional bargaining is dangerous as parties have the tendency to become entrenched. The mediator must guide the parties to identify, analyze and separate the issues, and then to rephrase the issues within the context of resolution. To accomplish these goals, the mediator strives to help parties develop their BATNA (best alternative to a negotiated agreement).[4] Mediators help parties to explore options that will satisfy some of the goals of each party, creating an end result that is a win-win situation for all, not the winner-take-all result of the court system.

What makes a good mediator? Credential requirements vary by jurisdiction, particularly for court ordered mediation. First, as with arbitration, the mediator must be impartial. He/she must

---

[3] *Black's Law Dictionary*®, 6th ed., West Publishing Company, St. Paul, MN 1979.

[4] Roger Fisher and William Ury, *Getting to Yes; Negotiating Agreement Without Giving In*, Bruce Patton, Editor, 2nd ed. (New York: Penguin Books USA, 1991).

not only be a good listener, but must guide the parties into listening to each other. The mediator must show parties that they must seek to understand the other before they themselves can be understood. Other valued qualities include the mediator's ability to maintain confidentiality, to be unbiased, open, courteous, tolerant, reliable, attentive, observant, encouraging, etc.

The procedures in arranging a mediation conference consist of educating the parties to the process (including attorneys who may be unfamiliar with mediation), negotiating dates and fee schedules (mediator fees are split among the parties), arranging for the facility where the mediation will occur, and arranging for execution of agreements to mediate.

As the mediation conference begins, as a plenary session, the mediator makes opening remarks which acclimate those present to the process and the expected roles of all participants. These remarks establish the tone of the conference and stimulate interest in the process. The mediator must lay out ground rules so all know what steps the mediator will follow as he/she controls the process. Next the parties, and/or their attorneys, will be asked to make opening statements. Thereafter, the mediator summarizes the key points of each presentation, separating personalities from the problem. This summary is crucial as it lets the parties know they have been heard, sorts out the issues and reframes the problem as a search to satisfy interests.

The mediator may caucus with the parties, a private, confidential meeting with the mediator and each of the parties and their counsel. The caucus permits parties to share concerns, hidden agendas, and perceptions with the mediator in a confidential forum. The mediator may also employ a technique called settle-try analysis, asking questions designed to get parties thinking about probable results of delegating the problem solving to a judge or strangers on a jury. Brainstorming and other option generating techniques may also be employed, both in caucus and plenary session.

When and if agreements are made, the mediator continues to manage the process by having counsel prepare a settlement memorandum to be executed by all parties. The mediator must bring closure to the conflict by memorializing the agreement and, if necessary, reporting the results to the court.

1.055 Other ADR Forms: Minitrial, Summary Jury Trial, and Moderated Settlement Conference

A minitrial (MT) or summary jury trial (SJT) usually takes place after parties have completed substantial discovery. The SJT usually takes place on the eve of trial. Traditional legal assistants (those working in law offices) are often as involved in MT and SJT preparation as for a traditional court trial. The juries of the two differ: SJTs take place before real juries of impartial strangers; MTs before corporate representatives of the parties. Usually the MT is voluntary, generated by motions of the parties. The court may order SJT if the matter has already proceeded to pretrial conference. The SJT often is the final alternative before an actual trial. Judge Thomas D. Lambros, of the U.S. District for the Northern District of Ohio, is generally credited for creating the SJT form of ADR in 1980.[5]

The moderated settlement conference (MSC) is a hybrid form of ADR, combining the minitrial, summary jury trial, and mediation. The three attorneys, who issue a nonbinding opinion.

---

[5] Judge Thomas D. Lambros, *The Summary Jury Trial and other Alternative Methods of Dispute Resolution*, in *A Report to the Judicial Conference of the United States Committee on the Operation of the Jury System*, 103 F.R.D. 461, 463 (Jan. 1984).

Judy Quan, in her *Legal Assistant's Guide to Alternative Dispute Resolution*[6] provides an excellent study of these ADR options. Ms. Quan also gives a view of the growing use of mediation in the bankruptcy courts and explores the role ADR will play in NAFTA (The North American Free Trade Agreement).

1.056 ADR Fears and Misconceptions

Parties to lawsuits often ask, "Why should we bother trying this [ADR]? If we show our hand and it doesn't work out, the other side will have more ammunition to use against us." Within the context of the court system, Federal Rule of Evidence 408 protects all parties. In effect, parties have nothing to lose by trying ADR. A basic tenet of the process is parties are not prejudiced by any efforts to settle. The process often opens lines of communication. All forms of ADR can help to shorten the time necessary to resolve a dispute, even if the matter is not fully settled.

1.057 Role of the Legal Assistant

What is the role of the legal assistant in ADR? Roles may vary depending on jurisdiction and practice. Some jurisdictions permit nonlawyers to serve as arbitrators, mediators and/or other third party facilitators, particularly in the area of construction and business disputes. Experts in these fields, such as architects, real estate professionals, medical and dental technologists, accountants, engineers, etc. are found serving as such facilitators. In some jurisdictions, legal assistants are serving as mediators and service providers; in others, as ADR Coordinators assisting service providers. The key for the legal assistant interested in ADR, as with any other legal specialty, is knowledge and continuing education. Potential for utilizing ADR in informal settings, such as community groups, abound and are not limited to licensed attorneys.

There are many questions about who should train and regulate ADR providers. Some state bar associations are drafting rules and guidelines which exclude nonlawyers from court approved rosters of mediators and ADR service providers. Education of the general public, legal practitioners, and legislators is an ongoing requirement if ADR is to expand into the mainstream of the legal profession and society. One thing is clear—the multidoor courthouse idea envisioned by Professor Sandor has become a reality.

Bibliography

The United States Government Manual. Government Printing Office, 1996–1997.

Federal Civil Judicial Procedure and Rules, as amended to January 6, 1997. St. Paul: West Group, 1997.

Koerselman, Virginia, *CLA Review Manual.* West Publishing Company, 1993.

Scaletta, Phillip J. Jr. and Cameron, George D., III, *Foundations of Business Law.* Business Publications, Inc., 1986.

Schantz, William T. and Jackson, Janice E., *The American Legal Environment.* West Publishing Company, 2nd ed. 1984.

Black's Law Dictionary, 6th ed. West Publishing Company, St. Paul, MN, 1990.

---

[6] Judy Quan, *Legal Assistant's Guide to Alternative Dispute Resolution,* Clark Boardman Callaghan/Estrin Paralegal Practice Series. Deerfield, IL, Clark Boardman Callaghan, 1994, 1995.

Dillon, Fonda M., *From Litigation to ADR,* in *Facts & Findings, The Journal for Legal Assistants.* Vol. XXIII, Issue 2, August, 1996.

Duvall, Suzanne Mann and Scheske, Jack J., *No Mediator is an Island. Relationship Based Management of Legal Assistants and Other Staff in Mediation and Alternative Dispute Resolution Practices. Dispute Resolution Across the Continents,* 22nd Annual International Conference [Society of Professionals in Dispute Resolution], Dallas, TX, October 27–29, 1994.

Fisher, Roger and Ury, William, *Getting to Yes; Negotiating Agreement Without Giving In,* edited by Bruce Patton, 2nd ed. New York: Penguin Books USA, 1991.

Goodheart, Harry G. III and Harness, Cotton C. III, *Circuit Court Civil Mediator Training Program.* Hilton Head Island, SC, December 1–5, 1994.

Lambros, Thomas D., *The Summary Jury Trial and other Alternative Methods of Dispute Resolution,* in *A Report to the Judicial Conference of the United States Committee on the Operation of the Jury System.* 103 F.R.D. 461, 463 (Jan. 1984).

Quan, Judy, *Legal Assistant's Guide to Alternative Dispute Resolution.* Clark Boardman Callaghan/Estrin Paralegal Practice Series. Deerfield, IL, Clark Boardman Callaghan, 1994, 1995.

Sanchez, Valerie A., *Towards a History of ADR: The Dispute Processing Continuum in Anglo-Saxon England and Today,* 11 OHIO ST. J. ON DISP. RESOL. __ (1996).

Sandor, Frank E. A., *Varieties of Dispute Processing,* 70 F.R.D. 111, 131 (1976).

2 Legal Research

2.00 Introduction

This chapter is merely an introduction and is not intended to be a complete course in legal research. It will provide the inexperienced legal assistant with a working background of the mechanics of research but will not satisfy the highly sophisticated needs of an attorney or a fully trained and experienced legal assistant. Most inexperienced legal assistants will receive very limited and specific research assignments in the beginning. The parameters of the research will be clearly defined, some research sources suggested, cases cited, and past research efforts of others will often be made available for guidance in form, style, and preferred format. These will help in determining starting points or checkpoints during the research and reporting tasks. Research assignments will increase in difficulty and complexity as the legal assistant demonstrates skill and craftsmanship and gains the attorney's trust and confidence.

Legal assistants should not be discouraged if their first efforts do not result in immediate success and praise from the attorney for brilliance. In all likelihood, the initial assignment will take much more time than anticipated with the odds against achieving perfect results. Those efforts will not be wasted, however, as they contribute to a practical foundation in research, providing opportunities to try different methods and to identify those most effective. As familiarity with research material and resources increases, the time required to find the law and analyze case decisions will decrease. As individual research techniques become more refined, even less time will be needed to research a given fact situation. Experience, practice, and constructive criticism by others will help the legal assistant develop expertise in stating facts and analyses in professional, concise legal writing.

The law library seems overwhelming and complex at first glance, but as the legal assistant gains familiarity and confidence it will become a friend. While most lawyers maintain a library sufficiently complete to meet the needs of their practice, other libraries are highly specialized and sophisticated with multiple copies of source material and several varieties of sources on the same topics. Looking at the different topic titles and sets of books to determine exactly what sources of information are available in the library, understanding how the library is arranged, and locating the specialized sections is time well spent. It will aid research planning and improve confidence. Where other law libraries are available to the public (such as law school, county, district, state, or federal libraries), write or visit them; meet the librarians; and take note of the procedures that allow access to use, or borrowing of material. Competence in using the library is the key to success in legal research. Use of library resources via the Internet can exponentially increase your information sources with text libraries as well as through card catalogue searches. Library resources at universities as well as government agencies are regularly updated, maintained and available for public access on a limited "on-line" basis as well. Additionally, many law schools have the full text of their law review articles on-line.

CD-ROM technology has reduced the size of many library sources to a compact disk with keyword searching ability. Although the updates are not as frequent as the weekly supplements, and certainly not as frequent as the hourly updates of available on-line subscription services such as WESTLAW® or LEXIS-NEXIS®, CD-ROM technology provides even the smallest firm with the ability to store rooms of books in a CD carrying case.

If the legal assistant is diligent, confidence will be acquired in the ability to research. Legal research is a very rewarding experience, and an exciting challenge; however, it requires full understanding of the research objective by the legal assistant which can be accomplished only when the employing attorney identifies each of the legal principles and issues underlying each assignment.

2.01 Principles of Legal Research

Legal research is an integral part of the practice of law, and its impact on a case can be critical. It is essential that all research be accurate and include the most current data available. The authority controlling the status of the law can change very quickly as decisions come down from higher courts; therefore, the importance of fully updated research cannot be overemphasized.

A working rapport must be established between the attorney and the legal assistant. Mutual respect and trust are essential. The attorney must thoroughly discuss the issue or subject of the research with the legal assistant, including the legal principles, the legal issues involved, the scope of the research, the fact situation, and the time deadline. These must be completely understood by the legal assistant before proceeding. Always remember that the research must be thorough and precise with up-to-the-minute accuracy, or it will have to be redone completely by the attorney. Leave no stone unturned, no case or statute (and the updated pocket parts) unread, and no conflict unresolved without being clearly pointed out. If confusion sets in, seek help.

2.011 Case Law and Statutory Law

The legal assistant must become comfortable with the dual origins of law and legal principles that may influence the client's case. There is "case law" and "statutory law" to consider in most situations. The courts, both federal and state, must apply statutory law where applicable, even in the face of contradictory case law. The only exception to this hierarchy is when a court determines that the statute in question is inconsistent with the state's constitution or the U.S. Constitution. When applying case law, the courts are obligated to follow the appropriate precedents established by prior decisions unless the present circumstances can be distinguished in some way. This method of adhering to the same legal principles in similar cases is the doctrine of *stare decisis* ("let the decision stand"). The product of this doctrine is the ability of the public to examine existing legal standards and predict with some degree of accuracy the likely outcome in a current situation. With respect to goals in legal research, this translates to the following equation: (1) search for applicable statutory law, then (2) search for case law (especially if there is some basis upon which the statutory law is likely to be declared unconstitutional).

2.0111 Case Law. Case law is based in part on legal principles developed from the written opinions by judges in past cases. Case law is part of the tradition of common law dating as far back as medieval England. The exception to this is case law developed in the state of Louisiana, which has its legal origins in France, resulting in case law based upon French legal principles of civil law. However, while the legal terminology may be different, there are many striking similarities in English and French legal principles.

In essence, the written opinions of judges in past cases have established legal principles which are to be followed in future similar cases. These principles, or rules of law, are known as precedent. Most judicial opinions that are reported (published) are those of appellate courts, which establish standards for entire jurisdictions, such as the federal court system or the courts of a particular state. As a result, these are the precedents that can be cited as authority in subsequent cases.

When researching case law, it should be kept in mind that the law of a particular jurisdiction is usually controlling; the law of other jurisdictions may be used to influence and persuade the court, but the court has no obligation to follow it. For example, when performing research for a case that is pending in a particular state, the statutory law and appellate decisions of that state are controlling. However, the law of other states or federal courts may be cited as persuasive authority.

It is important to understand that appeals may be made on nearly any area of the law involved with the trial, such as the basic legal questions involved; the procedural rules, including but not limited to jurisdiction and discovery procedures; introduction of witnesses or evidence; instructions to the jury on the law to apply; and standards. Only the issues tried, appealed, and ruled upon at the appellate level may be properly cited as authority from the appellate decision. All the rest is dictum: interesting in showing how the appellate court reached its decision but not binding. *Dicta* may be helpful in determining how the court might rule on a given matter in the future, even persuasive in arguing that another court should so rule, but it is not law.

2.0112 Statutory Law. Statutory law is different from case law in that statutes are the stated intention of a legislative body to create a standard of permitted or proscribed conduct. The U.S. Constitution, the Bill of Rights, and the subsequent amendments to the Constitution are controlling as the primary written expression of the rights of individuals, and state and federal laws must be consistent with them and encourage the observance of similar desirable objectives. Each state also has its own constitution upon which its statutes are based, and these must be consistent with the U.S. Constitution as well. Counties, as subordinate governmental units of the state, are granted certain powers by the state to legislate rules of conduct within the county by ordinances and codes. Cities and towns are organized under the permission of the state and are granted certain powers to create rules necessary for the execution of their public responsibilities. Each of these entities follow the same basic process of creating a law, whether titled as such or called a "rule," "regulation," "ordinance," or "code."

2.0113 Codes. Codes are collections of statutory or regulatory law by jurisdiction and sometimes by subjects of law within a jurisdiction. A similar term used by some states is *revised statutes*. These collections are updated frequently to include new statutory law and to reflect amendment or repeal of existing statutory law. These codes are organized to facilitate the research process. Typically, all of the laws on a particular area of legislation, such as motor vehicles, are placed under a single heading. This is sometimes known as a title or chapter. The titles are arranged in alphabetical order and then assigned consecutive numbers as well. For example, "agriculture" would be one of the first numbered titles since it begins with "A." The main headings are also arranged in alphabetical order. Within each heading, all of the laws on the particular subject are individually numbered. Thus, new laws can be added to the subject simply by adding new numbers. In addition, each code is accompanied by an extensive subject index that assists the reader in locating the needed information. For example, if one wanted to locate the law that indicated a driver's duty when road conditions are dangerous, one would look in the subject index for such topics as motor vehicles, automobiles, and traffic. Below each main topic are more specific references to the individual laws on the subject. When the correct heading and subheading are located in the index, a two-part number will be found. This generally corresponds to the number assigned to the main heading and the number assigned to the particular law.

Included with the actual text of the statute in the code may be a reference to the initial publication of the statute in the session laws. This enables the reader to locate historical information about the passage of the statute. Many codes are also *annotated*, which simply means that a brief description and reference to any judicial opinions that have interpreted the statute follow the text of the statute. These can be helpful in determining how the statute has been applied in specific past situations and consequently how it is likely to be applied in a present situation.

2.0114 Legislative Intent. Each statute exists for the purpose intended by the entity that passed it. Where the language of a particular statute cannot be clearly understood, or, as is more often the case, opponents claim different meanings for the same words, the researcher may have to look back into the recorded minutes of hearings, committee discussions, and legislative rhetoric to define the original purpose. Many times this is an onerous task, which involves tracking the statute back to its origins as a bill, through committee and public hearings, even to the personal files of the original author of the proposed legislation. In some cases, a federal statute is so important that the U.S. Government Printing Office will publish all the written materials pertaining to it in one or more volumes. The historical data, debates, and comments can be a great aid to the researcher. The legislative intent, more often described as "legislative history" on the federal level, may also be published in looseleaf services available to its subscribers or on the Internet (e.g., the U.S. Environmental Protection Agency makes such information concerning environmental legislation available to the public over the Internet). Some states provide staff members to handle requests for legislative history, or intent. Administrative agencies also have archives of historical information concerning rules they establish from the date of their proposal until publication. It may be necessary when contending with administrative agency rules and regulations to research first the rule, then the agency's own enabling legislation to ensure the agency is not exceeding its own authority as shown by the legislative intent in the statutory law that created the agency.

2.02   Five Steps of Research

While efficiency and productivity in legal research can only be the product of extended practice, some basic steps can help the researcher locate valid authority more quickly and easily. After years of performing legal research, many practitioners still follow these basic steps as a normal course of action. The five basic steps are:

1. analyzing the facts and identifying the problem and subject of research;
2. recognizing the issues or points of law involved;
3. finding the law and expanding the research to access all necessary information, including adverse authority:
4. updating the search; and
5. reporting the research.

2.021   Step One: Analyzing the Facts

Know the factual situation completely and know the client's objective. There may be occasions when the legal assistant will be able to discover an alternative way of obtaining the client's purpose when direct methods, as the client may have proposed, cannot be used. For example, if a man wants an advertising sign erected on his building and city ordinances prohibit certain kinds of signs, there may be an alternative way to accomplish the desired advertising to his satisfaction.

Legal research will be easier if the facts and desired end result are clearly understood. Analyzing the facts and identifying the problem and/or subject are musts. Every legal problem arises from a factual situation; the facts determine whether there is a legitimate cause of action or a valid defense. The facts are the basis of the document to be prepared, such as a will, a bill of sale, a lease agreement, or a complaint.

a. The first essential element in the factual analysis is to identify the parties involved. Determine whether they have any special standing under the law, such as a tenant, a landowner, or a particular class of people (such as all the purchasers of Product X) or whether they are immune from suit.

b. Next, determine the subject matter, such as real or personal property, bodily injury and damages, issues of governmental regulation, or contract execution.

c. Then determine the basis of the action or issue, such as negligence, breach of contract, or strict liability.

d. Now determine what types of relief are available, such as temporary restraining order, specific performance of the contract, or compensatory money damages.

e. Determine the defenses to the claim. Consider the facts and evaluate whether the claim has merit and whether any extenuating circumstances, facts, or law might legally exonerate the opponent, such as self-defense, comparative or contributory negligence of the plaintiff, or impossibility of performance of the contract.

2.022   Step Two: Identifying the Law

When defining the law problems and areas, try to determine:

a. what court or agency has primary jurisdiction;

b. if there are statutes, codes or administrative agency rules or regulations involved; and

c. whether it is a substantive or procedural law problem.

2.023   Step Three: Finding the Law

Finding the law and expanding the search to include all necessary information is the next step and the point at which the true research begins. Again, there are many approaches open to the legal assistant. One of the most useful actions at this point is identifying all related terms, synonyms (same or similar meaning), and antonyms (opposite meaning) for the subject of research. Legal research is aided tremendously by the existence of subject indexes for most authorities. However, one must know what terminology the author used when preparing the index. By first identifying a number of possibilities, the speed of research can be increased while at the same time decreasing the level of frustration at not being able to locate the proper authority.

    If the research problem is in an area of law unfamiliar to the legal assistant, the first step would usually be to read some secondary authority that contains a general commentary and explanation of the subject. (*See* Section 2.04, Sources of the Law in Research.) This allows the legal assistant to become familiar with the general nature and past history of and approaches to the problem and to decide which path the research must follow. The secondary authority generally cites cases and sometimes statutes. These can often provide a starting point for the research. Identifying the leading case on an issue provides a key to many other cases that follow, distinguish, or depart from the leading case holding. At the very least, these sources contain basic principles and relevant terminology and can provide a general familiarity with the subject matter. Because the majority of legal research resources can be accessed through various types of subject indexes, this basic knowledge can greatly assist the researcher when searching for commentary, case law, or statutory law.

    Following examination of secondary sources, it is often necessary to go to the codes and reported judicial opinions of the jurisdiction whose law is being applied in the case under research. While more attention is given to this in the subsequent discussion, it is briefly noted here that codes are accompanied by extensive subject indexes that allow easy access to the particular statute sought. Similarly, all published judicial decisions are briefly described and arranged by subject in what is known as a *Digest*. A digest also has a subject index (called a "descriptive word index") that allows the researcher to locate the specific subject area of research. A key element in both statutory and case law research is knowledge of the relevant terminology. What one might consider the appropriate subject heading for a topic might vary significantly from the actual heading used in the legal resources. Familiarity with the subject, as well as such aids as a legal thesaurus, can take much of the frustration out of this aspect of legal research.

2.024 Step Four: Updating the Search

Updating the search accomplishes two very important objectives. First, it confirms that the legal authority is still accepted as valid by the legislature and the judiciary. Second, it allows the researcher to learn of any subsequent statutes or judicial opinions on the subject that may not yet have been incorporated into the code or published. The most commonly accepted method of updating is through a process referred to as "Shepardizing." This describes the use of *Shepard's Citations* to locate all references to or approval, amendment, or repeal of published statutory or case law. (*See* Section 2.06, Use of *Shepard's Citations* or "Shepardizing".) In addition to examining the subsequent treatment of the case or statute in *Shepard's Citations*, one should also read the actual text of the case or statute to determine if there are any distinguishing characteristics that may affect its applicability to the case at hand. With respect to statutes, it is important to note the date upon which the statute became effective to ensure that it was in effect on the relevant dates in the case being researched.

The completeness of the updating is of paramount importance, since the research must reflect the law as it is currently interpreted. The review of advance sheets, pocket parts, and supplements of codes or statutes is essential. The legal assistant who cites a case as authority for a positive position and later is proved to be in error because a more recent decision reversed the cited authority may find overnight that the attorney's confidence has been lost, along with any further assignments in this interesting and highly important work area.

Caveat: Most cases involve the law as it was on the date of the occurrence; for example, changes in the vehicle code or other law are seldom retroactive. Therefore, be certain to research the applicable law individually from the current date back to the origin of the cause of action. There can be some shocking exceptions. For example, in *Li v. Yellow Cab Co.*, 13 Cal.3d 804, 119 Cal.Rptr. 858, 532 P.2d 1226 (1975), a case establishing in California the system of comparative negligence to assign responsibility and liability for damage in direct proportion to the degree of negligence of each of the parties, the California Supreme Court concluded that the rule of contributory negligence (which had prevailed for years in California law) was overturned and that a rule of limited retroactivity should prevail. The court held that in view of the many pending cases involving matters similar in issue to that in *Li* at the trial and appellate levels, *Li* would apply to all cases in which the trial had not begun before the date the decision became final but would not apply to any case in which trial had begun before that date. It also provided that if any judgment were reversed on appeal for other reasons, the opinion would be applicable to any retrial. Another example is California Code of Civil Procedure Section 1048, *Severance and Consolidation of Causes*, which was completely reworded in 1971 to be operative July 1, 1972. The new act applied to actions commenced on or after July 1, 1972, but not to actions pending on July 1, 1972, and provided that any action to which the act did not apply would be governed by the law as it would exist had the act not been enacted.

Admittedly, these are exceptions, but this type of limited retroactivity or limited applicability of operative dates must be considered in any research.

2.025 Step Five: Reporting the Research and Commenting on the Adversary's Position

Everything done must be reported concisely to the attorney, including the positive research and, if the work effort goal is to rebut the position of another, the research and review of every case cited in support of the adversary's position. Do not accept at face value the adversary's cited positions or authorities as either factually or legally correct statements of the positions taken by the courts in the cited cases. Citing cases out of context, from headnotes, or only from synopsis is a common, though dangerous, activity. Similarly, citing dictum from a case as though it were a tried and considered issue is a technique the legal assistant can avoid only by reading the case in its entirety.

Reviewing the adversary's cited cases provides several benefits, one being an appreciation of the adversary's legal reasoning and/or legal foundation. Many times the legal assistant may find the adversary cited a case that does not help the adversary's position nearly so persuasively as it does the client's; also, other cases favorable to the client's position may be found in Shepardizing the cases developed in the adversary's citations. These finds occur when the legal assistant reads the full case text, not just the headnotes, to be certain the context of the citation is applicable, the interpretation is correctly reported, and it is current law and not a case that has been overturned by subsequent decisions. If the cases cited in the initial document are not valid authority or have been incorrectly interpreted, the report of research must point out these facts as well as the reasoning and cases supporting the legal assistant's own conclusions.

While a report on all the research is essential, carefully think about and consider each bit of information accumulated and decide whether to include or exclude it. This is critical to the clarity of the end result and conclusion. Research requires an intelligent and active mind and the ability to analyze information and to concentrate all efforts single-minded and fixedly on the goal. Practice in legal writing requires familiarity with legal writing styles. Go to the library and read some decisions at random. Learn to analyze the case content. The first few cases may not make any sense, but familiarity with the legal writing style and careful rereadings will create skill in analysis, perception, and measuring the written cases against a given issue. It also will increase the legal assistant's ability to detect relevance or analogy between the reported cases and the factual situation in the instant problem.

The office file of past legal research reports can offer pointers on style and form for the legal assistant to follow. Briefs filed in appellate proceedings can clearly show the organized manner of expression that may be helpful or desired by the office (*see* Section 2.031, Retention of Legal Research). Adapting to the style preferred in the office simplifies the lawyer's review of the finished effort since the form of the report is familiar and he or she can concentrate on the substance of the report or memorandum.

Finally, while most research will entail only a review of authority and will not be incorporated in any formal pleading, the purpose is to provide the lawyer with case law, statutory law, and statements sufficient to enable him or her to measure the law against the facts, thereby reaching a final determination and stating a positive position. Even drafting pleadings requires research, as do law and motion matters, particularly the points and authorities for such documents. In any event, the written product should be clear and to the point, and the writing quality should be above reproach. An evaluation of the factors should be presented in an appropriate, logical and effective manner, and the legal assistant must be confident of the position recommended. Strong decisions in opposition to the proposed point of view must be brought to the attention of the attorney, as well as any distinctions between those cases and the instant problem. If at any time during the research procedure, the legal assistant becomes unsure of a point, it must be discussed fully and freely with the attorney to resolve the doubt, redirect the effort, or get back on the right track. If the attorney won't help, the legal assistant is working in the wrong office.

2.03   Basic Research Procedures and Practices

Certain basic beneficial procedures should be instituted at the start of a career in research to avoid duplication of effort; they also will be invaluable later as starting points.

2.031   Retention of Legal Research

This sounds self-explanatory, but it is not necessarily a simple matter. Some offices maintain complete legal memoranda files whether in hard copy or in their computer system, and all research in the office is categorized, indexed, and filed in a control file. If the office has such a research file system, the legal assistant must become familiar both with the file and the indexing system. Clearly, it is important to take advantage of the past research contained within the file. In large firms, this is often one of the functions of the law librarian. Some firms with such files also have procedures to continuously update the material, or selected categories of material, depending on the specialties of the office. If the employer does not maintain such a file, take the initiative and start one. In any event, the legal assistant must adapt to or devise a suitable system and maintain his or her own research for use in the future, taking care to update the cites in any past memorandum or report before again citing that material as authority. Each update is posted to the research file as well. If the legal assistant is working in a specialized field, such as malpractice, it is helpful to read the West advance sheets on that topic as they come into the office.

The legal assistant can establish the protocol for the research file system through an attorney review process, to maintain the integrity of the law stored. If a new associate prepares a draft brief, not yet reviewed, it should not be immediately downloaded or printed for storage into a research file system. The firm will need to support the law used and maintain whatever is placed in that file through updates and supervision. In a large firm, with a large number of practice areas, this can be a full-time job for a legal assistant or librarian. A justification in maintenance time by the use of coded topics familiar to all firm members (such as the West Key System) can facilitate maintenance and also increase the use by attorneys and legal assistants.

Through the use of Internet software and capabilities offered through some on-line services, WESTLAW and LEXIS-NEXIS, articles and news releases can be automatically downloaded to the legal assistant's computer for review as they become available. This may be the first notice of a new decision to override or modify the existing standard relied upon in a firm's brief, released to the public over the UPI and AP wires that day. Further research is so current that it may not be available without a telephone call (e.g., a decision reached that day with no published case law at that time) and a copy request from the deciding court or agency. The legal assistant appears psychic with up-to-the-minute information for the attorneys.

2.032   Compilation of a Personal Case Book

As the legal assistant researches problems and as new decisions are handed down, he or she should file or record the citations in a case book by topic. An alternative to the case book is to create and maintain an electronic document with the same general format. Also, when researching a problem which is common from both "for and against" sides, that is, filing a claim with a public entity, as opposed to relief from the requirement of filing a claim, or filing a late claim, note the case as applicable to both sides. This book, or electronic document as the case may be, normally is not a detailed description of the case but, rather, a loose-leaf system with general categories, such as malpractice, fraud, or strict liability, which contains the cite or code sections along with the particular point of law to which it applies together with a few lines setting forth the theory as shown in the example below:

PRODUCTS LIABILITY

** Lessor of Personal Property . . .
Doctrine of strict liability in tort applicable.
Fakhoury v. Magner, 25 Cal.App.3d 58, 101 Cal.Rptr. 473 (1972) lessor of furnished apartment liable for injuries when couch partially collapsed.
Price v. Shell Oil Co., 2 Cal.3d 245, 85 Cal.Rptr. 178, 466 P.2d 722 (1970) lessor of truck and ladder to plaintiff's employer liable when ladder collapsed.

2.033 Devise a Workable System to Avoid Duplication in Research

When legal assistants begin their initial efforts to research, many find themselves returning to the same case several times. This is wasted effort and should be avoided. This seems to happen most frequently in the updating process, where the legal assistant is reading many cases and Shepardizing. (*See* Section 2.06, Use of *Shepard's Citations* or "Shepardizing".) Many methods can be utilized, such as keeping lists of citations or titles as cases are read. Find a method and use it faithfully.

2.034 Save Time and Steps

One essential tool for beginning research is a legal dictionary or combination dictionary/thesaurus (*see* Section 2.0511). Dictionaries provide meanings, origins, spellings, and pronunciations. A legal thesaurus can provide synonyms to aid the legal assistant in locating information during research and in writing in a more concise and professional manner. Another useful tool for beginning a research project are "Words and Phrases" dictionaries. These references provide case citations to the subtle meanings which have developed through case law where courts have defined and construed the particular meaning of certain words and phrases.

Up-to-date word processing software is available which includes legal terminology as part of the software package containing both a dictionary and a thesaurus. Legal dictionary and thesaurus materials, as well as "words and phrases" publications are also available electronically on CD-ROM and through on-line services.

2.035 Be Familiar with the Hierarchy of the Courts and the Reporting Systems

Each of the fifty states has established its own court system and rules for those courts, including appellate procedures (*see* Chapter 1, Section 1.023, State Court Systems). A good place to start when researching the structure and procedures of a court system in another state is the *Martindale-Hubbell Law Digest*. These volumes contain summaries of statutory law from all states (as well as U.S. Territories), and are also available electronically through on-line services such as LEXIS-NEXIS. For example, if you looked in the volume which contained a summary of California statutory law, you would be able to determine that California has five courts; small claims court, municipal court, superior court (all of which comprise the trial level courts), the courts of appeal, and the supreme court (the appellate-level courts). Each court has established procedural rules that must be followed. The appellate procedures provide for appeal to the next higher court, for example, from superior court to court of appeal. The legal assistant must be familiar with the state's court system, which decisions are published, the reporting systems of the courts' official reports, and the corresponding commercial (unofficial) reporters and the decisions they cover. The decisions of the trial-level courts are seldom published; the decisions of the appellate-level courts usually are. For instance, the official reports of the California Courts of Appeal are contained in the *California Appellate Reports* (in several series), while *California Reports* contains the official decisions of the California Supreme Court. The *Pacific Reporter*® (part of the national reporter system, *see* Section 2.0543) contains the *unofficial* reports of the California Supreme Court, as well as reports of other western states, but does not contain reports for the California Courts of Appeal. The separate *California Reporter* (still of the national reporter system) contains the *unofficial* reports of both appellate-level courts. Therefore, most California legal assistants, in researching California law, rely on the *California Reporter* rather than the *Pacific Reporter*.

In addition to the more traditional sources discussed above, a search of the Internet will locate official websites for states providing court decisions on-line to the public. For instance, Florida Supreme Court decisions are available to the public via the Internet as are decisions of the South Carolina Supreme Court. *Florida Law Weekly* publishes and maintains past issues and lists recent decisions; however, *Florida Administrative Law Weekly* is not yet available on the Internet. On-line resources are still evolving and do not constitute a comprehensive or complete resource, but neither does the library "down-the-hall" in most law offices. Supplement resources with other material, and determine an effective and efficient method to utilize the strengths of both.

The federal court system has a hierarchy of trial and appellate courts (*see* Chapter 1, Section 1.021, State Court Systems) with separate and distinct reporter systems, official and unofficial, which are similar to those of the states discussed above.

2.04 Sources of the Law in Research

Generally, the law is contained in two types of authority—primary and secondary. Law books and finding aids are categorized in the same manner—primary and secondary.

2.041 Primary Authority

Primary authority is that which is valid authority as to the exact status of the law on any given point, in any state or area, and at any given time. The most persuasive primary authority that can be cited is that of the official report of the highest court, state or federal, (above the trial court-level) that has rendered a decision on the point of law being researched. This may be cited as the controlling law. Examples of this type of authority are the U.S. Supreme Court decisions or the supreme court decisions of the state in which the issue is located; then the Constitution (state or federal); codified laws; Statutes at Large or session laws; administrative rules, regulations, orders, and decisions; and court rules and court decisions in the state where the issue is located. Similar authority from other jurisdictions may be persuasive authority on matters not previously decided in the state but is not mandatory authority.

2.042 Secondary Authority

Secondary authority is any compilation of opinions and/or comments by various authors setting forth their interpretation of the law. This kind of authority is most helpful as an aid in research but does not have the force and effect of law. Examples of this type of authority are annotated case reports, annotated codes and statutes, "restatements" of various laws, encyclopedias, loose-leaf services, index books, dictionaries, digests, form books, treatises, and periodical literature.

Secondary authority is a basic tool. It provides insight into the disputed issue and, many times, quickly directs the researcher to the primary authority being sought. There are occasions when secondary authority can be cited and effectively used to sway or persuade the court to accept a given position as the correct one, but it should be clearly referenced to the attorney as a secondary authority—distinctly different from case law or statutory law or any administrative agency rule. In so-called test cases (a case where the particular legal issue has not been tried and appealed in the state before), where there is no substantive or case law, it may be the only authority available.

2.05 Search Methods—Finding the Law

It is impossible to include in this chapter a detailed discussion of each and every search aid available to the serious researcher. This will review the types of materials available and give a brief discussion of the general categories. Entire books are devoted to this topic (see the Bibliography of this chapter). In addition, the National Association of Legal Assistants has a comprehensive cassette course entitled "Legal Research for the Legal Assistants, Guide to the Use of the Law Library." It covers the subject, case, statutory, and administrative approaches to the law and contains four professionally recorded cassette tapes to supplement approximately a hundred pages of written material.

Regardless of whether you are researching using printed books or electronic media, the same general search methods, techniques, and reasoning apply.

2.051 The Subject or Text Approach

The subject or text approach to the law requires the use of general information sources (secondary authority). In the absence of a specific case or a definite starting place, this is probably the logical starting point. Some of the sources are:

2.0511 Dictionaries. There are various kinds of dictionaries, including single-volume and multivolume glossaries. The single-volume type is represented by *Black's Law Dictionary*, *Ballentine's Law Dictionary*, and, of course, *Webster's Dictionary*. The definitions in the law dictionaries are usually derived from court opinions and are quoted verbatim with citations to the cases. The best known of the multivolume dictionaries is probably *Words and Phrases* by West Publishing Company. This set covers, as nearly as possible, every word and phrase defined by the federal and state courts in opinions rendered since 1658, and the words and phrases are listed in alphabetical order. A smaller version of *Words and Phrases* is produced for some states, for example, *Florida Words and Phrases*. These sets are kept up-to-date by annual pocket parts and revisions. Other standard law dictionaries may be in the firm's library. Dictionaries are secondary authority, and often cited as persuasive authority. They are often good tools for finding references to primary authority. As previously noted, may of these resources, if not all, are available in electronic format via CD-ROM, WESTLAW, LEXIS, and the Internet.

2.0512 Textbooks, Treatises, and Law Reviews. As the primary authorities became more voluminous, lawyers, students, and others began to follow the development of the law in certain fields. As attorneys became more knowledgeable, they began to write treatises and textbooks relating to certain areas of the law. The bibliography at the end of this chapter provides an idea of some of the texts and references available on legal research. Textbooks are available on nearly every area of the law, including discovery procedures, evidence and punitive damages. Periodically, judges, attorneys, and law school professors jointly agree that the law in a particular area needs clarification, modernization, or adjustment to the demands of our changing, complex society. Study groups are formed, such as the American Law Institute, and produce definitive restatements of a law for the area under study, such as the *Restatement of the Law of Torts* or the *Restatement of the Law of Contracts*. This type of authority is secondary and is not the law itself, but it is a strong and persuasive presentation of the way the law should be. Such studies have, in the past, become the law by a court agreeing and overturning the existing law or by being codified and the code being enacted by the various jurisdictions. The *Uniform Commercial Code* is the result of such a restatement and codification procedure. The restatements are widely respected as quotable authority, though secondary, because of the distinguished and highly respected authors who participate in their preparation and because of the sound logic and legal reasoning they represent. Such authority has value to the attorney particularly if directly on point in the instant case, whether in direct conflict with past case law or not.

Law schools publish law reviews, such as the *Cornell Law Review*, the *Harvard Law Review*, and the *Hastings Law Review*. Law reviews contain articles written by professors, lawyers, and students usually including detailed analysis of a particular problem, area of law, or particular case, with copious commentary and voluminous footnote references to primary and secondary authorities on the topic. These materials are secondary authority in that they contain one person's discussion, opinion, viewpoint, and conclusions after examination of the footnoted sources; the theories expressed, therefore, are not universally accepted, so the cases cited in support of their opinions should be read.

2.0513 Newspapers. Newspapers often contain articles concerning lawsuits of local or national interest, as well as reports on matters being considered by state and federal courts of appeal. Access to newspapers across the United States and even around the world has become increasingly inexpensive and available through such on-line sources as the Internet, WESTLAW and LEXIS. There also are newspapers that deal only with legal matters. Examples of such publications on the national level are *Corporate Legal Times*, the *National Law Journal* (which publishes a special Internet edition called *LJExtra!*), and *The American Lawyer*. This kind of exclusive legal newspaper also exists on a local level in many metropolitan areas and are represented by such publications as *The Recorder*, the *Los Angeles Daily Journal*, and the *Kansas Lawyer*. These are secondary, though valuable, sources of current information.

2.0514 Legal Encyclopedias. Many researchers find legal encyclopedias are the best secondary source of information and an excellent place to start research. Encyclopedias give an overall view of the given legal topic and, when properly used, provide an enormous amount of background information, sometimes set out the necessary elements or meaning for any given term, and get the legal assistant off on the right foot in finding the law. Because they contain numerous case citations, the legal assistant who studies them will have a general feeling for the point being researched as well as a place to start the case research to determine the present state of the law. Normally, encyclopedias are multivolume publications, arranged alphabetically and indexed. They are updated continually with cumulative pocket parts or replacement volumes. Here again, do not cite cases from encyclopedias without reading the cases.

Two general legal encyclopedias are available: *Corpus Juris Secundum* and *American Jurisprudence* (both of which are also available in electronic media). *Corpus Juris Secundum*, generally known as *C.J.S.,* purports to cite all American cases. Footnotes in these volumes are extensive. Since this is a West publication, it carries references to the West topic and key numbers, which allows easy transition from one to another of the West publications. As a bound volume created from past cases, extensively edited and proofed, the information is very informative but may be out of date. Every item of interest in the basic volumes must be checked by reference to the cumulative annual pocket parts and by seeking out updated case citators to find any cases on the same matter that may have been decided since the publication of the pocket part. An example of pages in a *C.J.S.* volume and its updating pocket part are shown in Exhibits 2-1 and 2-2. These exhibits clearly show the number of cases concerning issues of contributory negligence and avoidance of injury that occurred between the publication of the 1972 bound volume and the 1996 Annual Cumulative Supplement on the one topic of "———— What Constitutes Ordinary or Reasonable Care."

Three search methods can be applied to *C.J.S.* through the (1) descriptive word index, the fact method of search; (2) the topic analysis method, through its topical outlines; and (3) the words and phrases method or words sprinkled throughout. A separate "Words and Phrases Defined" listing in alphabetical order is located at the back of each volume. *American Jurisprudence 2d (Am.Jur.2d)* reports selected cases. It also contains a general index system. If the researcher is familiar with the area of law, he or she may proceed directly to the volume that contains that topic. If the researcher has difficulty using this method, the volume itself has a volume index (to be used in the same manner as the general index volumes). In the front of every volume of *Am.Jur.2d* are tables of statutes and parallel references. These tables indicate where the statutes cited in the volume are located and the references covered by articles formerly in the first edition of this work. Cross references are cited to: *American Law Reports (ALR)*; *U.S. Supreme Court Reports, Lawyer's Edition*; *U.S. Code Service*; *Am.Jur.Legal Forms*; *Pleading and Practice Forms*; and *Proof of Facts and Trials.*

Out of the national legal encyclopedias have evolved state legal encyclopedias, examples of which are *California Jurisprudence, Texas Jurisprudence, Florida Jurisprudence*, and practice sets, such as *Indiana Law and Practice* and *Florida Law and Practice.*

The value of encyclopedias becomes obvious through examination and use since they give extensive coverage of the law in broad treatment covered by known cases within specific jurisdictions and footnoted to those cases.

2.0515 Indexes, Words and Phrases. Almost every publication contains an index. Some indexes also contain a section entitled "Words and Phrases" containing significant words and phrases used within that publication, in alphabetical order. These are useful in leading the reader quickly to the proper section of the publication.

There also are special indexes for legal periodical literature and periodicals, as well as law review citations. Among these are Jones-Chipman's *Index to Legal Periodical Literature* (covering the period from 1803 until it ceased publication in 1937); *Index to Legal Periodicals* (covering the period from 1926 to date), and *Shepard's Law Review Citations.* These sources can be found in larger libraries, such as law school, county, state, or federal law libraries, as well as in electronic versions.

EXHIBIT 2-1   Sample C.J.S. Page

65A C. J. S.   NEGLIGENCE   §§ 118(1)–118(2)

Where there is an exercise of ordinary care, there is no contributory negligence.[15] Extraordinary care is not required,[16] nor is the ultmost possible caution.[17]

The exercise of ordinary care is the duty imposed, not the possession of knowledge or skill.[18] In order that one may be guilty of contributory negligence, it is not essential that the conduct for which he is responsible shall amount to recklessness,[19] gross negligence,[20] or willful or wanton conduct.[21] Negligence which will bar a plaintiff's recovery is disregard for his own safety, and not necessarily such as threatens to invade any of defendant's legal rights.[21.5]

Rule with respect to use of one's own property. While it has been held that one who fails to take precautions which he might have taken to protect his property from injury resulting from the negligence of another, the danger from which he was fully aware, is guilty of contributory negligence,[22] it has generally been held that the rule which requires one to exercise ordinary care to protect himself from the results of the negligence of others is subject to the exception that, since a person is entitled to use his own premises for any lawful purpose, his failure to protect them from the negligence of another will not be contributory negligence,[23] this being based on the proposition that the rights of one man in the use of his property cannot be limited by the wrongs of another.[23.5] While a person on his own premises is required to exercise less care to protect himself from injury than would otherwise be the case,[24] a man has no right to invite peril, or run into danger, even on his own property.[25]

§ 118(2). ——— What Constitutes Ordinary or Reasonable Care

Ordinary or reasonable care is such care as an ordinarily prudent person, or a reasonably prudent person, would exercise under the same or similar circumstances to avoid injury.

Library References

Negligence ⊂=65, 68.

In determining an issue of contributory negligence, ordinary or reasonable care is such care as an ordinarily prudent person, or a reasonably prudent person, would exercise under the same or similar circumstances to avoid injury.[26] The standard by

---

ley Ice & Fuel Co., Civ.App., 313 S. W.2d 104.

15. Ark.—Corpus Juris cited in Southwestern Gas & Electric Co. v. Murdock, 37 S.W.2d 100, 101, 183 Ark. 565.

Mass.—Rich v. Finley, 89 N.E.2d 213, 325 Mass. 99.

Mich.—Muth v. W. P. Lahey's Inc., 61 N.W.2d 619, 338 Mich. 513—Reedy v. Goodin, 281 N.W. 377, 285 Mich. 614.

R.I.—Peycke v. United Electric Rys. Co., 142 A. 232, 49 R.I. 257.

45 C.J. p 945 note 60.

16. Iowa.—Markle v. Chicago, R. I. & P. Ry. Co., 257 N.W. 771, 219 Iowa 301.

45 C.J. p 945 note 61.

17. Iowa.—Markle v. Chicago R. I. & P. Ry. Co., 257 N.W. 771, 219 Iowa 301.

Mo.—Tribout v. Kroger Grocery & Baking Co., App., 191 S.W.2d 261.

45 C.J. p 945 note 62.

18. Mo.—Schneider v. St. Joseph R., etc., Co., 238 S.W. 468.

19. Pa.—Lloyd v. Noakes, 96 Pa. Super. 164.

44 C.J. p 945 note 64.

Degrees of contributory negligence are not recognized.

Cal.—Lolli v. Market St. Ry. Co., 110 P.2d 436, 43 C.A.2d 166.

N.J.—McGarvey v. Atlantic City & S. R. Co., 8 A.2d 385, 123 N.J Law 281.

20. Okl.—Von Keller v. Ream, 220 P. 330, 93 Okl. 179.

21. Iowa.—Wells v. Chamberlain, 168 N.W. 238, 185 Iowa 264.

Tex.—Texas, etc., R. Co. v. Mitchell, Civ.App., 45 S.W. 945.

21.5 U.S.—Nesbit v. Everette, C.A. Fla., 243 F.2d 59.

22. La.—Mason v. Carter Packet Co., 116 So. 378, 165 La. 904—Factor's, etc., Ins. Co. v. Werlein, 8 So. 435, 42 La.Ann. 1046, 11 L.R.A. 361.

Wyo.—Town of Douglas v. Lore, 375 P.2d 399.

23. U.S.—Leroy Fibre Co. v. Chicago, M. & St. P. R. Co., Minn., 34 S.Ct. 415, 232 U.S. 340, 58 L.Ed. 631.

Ariz.—City of Tucson v. Koerber, 313 P.2d 411, 82 Ariz. 347.

Cal.—Humboldt County v. Shelly, 220 C.A.2d 194, 33 Cal.Rptr. 758—Goodwin v. Braden, 285 P.2d 330, 134 C. A.2d 34—**Corpus Juris Secundum quoted in** Atlas Assur. Co. v. State, 229 P.2d 13, 18, 102 C.A.2d 789—**Corpus Juris cited in** Kleinclaus v. Marin Realty Co., 211 P.2d 582, 584, 94 C.A.2d 733.

Idaho.—Coulsen v. Aberdeen-Springfield Canal Co., 277 P. 542, 47 Idaho 619.

Ky.—**Corpus Juris Secundum quoted in** Leavel v. Kentucky Utilities Co., 275 S.W.2d 792, 794—**Corpus Juris cited in** Dalzell v. McClintock, 171 S. W.2d 467, 469, 294 Ky. 319.

N.Y.—**Corpus Juris cited in** Monacelli v. State, 55 N.Y.S.2d 129, 130, 269 App.Div. 247.

Tenn.—**Corpus Juris quoted in** Nashville, C. & St. L. Ry. v. Nants, 65 S.W.2d 189, 191, 167 Tenn. 1.

Wyo.—**Corpus Juris quoted in** J. J. Mayou Mfg. Co. v. Consumers Oil & Refining Co., 146 P.2d 738, 747, 60 Wyo. 75, 151 A.L.R. 1243.

45 C.J. p 945 note 69.

Placing straw near buildings, resulting in their destruction by reason of prairie fire communicated to straw, was not negligence, preventing recovery.

N.D.—George v. Odenthal, 225 N.W. 323, 58 N.D. 209.

23.5 U.S.—Leroy Fibre Co. v. Chicago, M. & St. P. R. Co., Minn., 34 S.Ct. 415, 232 U.S. 340, 58 L.Ed. 631.

Cal.—Humboldt County v. Shelly, 220 C.A.2d 194, 33 Cal.Rptr. 758—Atlas Assur. Co. v. State, 229 P.2d 13, 102 C.A.2d 789—Kleinclaus v. Marin Realty Co., 211 P.2d 582, 94 C.A.2d 733.

24. Ala.—Hemmings v. Planters Supply Co., 65 So.2d 538, 37 Ala.App. 171.

Tex.—Jordan v. City of Lubbock, Civ. App., 88 S.W.2d 560, error dismissed.

25. Tenn.—**Corpus Juris quoted in** Nashville, C. & St. L. Ry. v. Nants, 65 S.W.2d 189, 191, 167 Tenn. 1.

45 C.J. p 956 note 70.

26. U.S.—**Corpus Juris Secundum quoted in** City of Richmond v. Atlantic Co., C.A.Va., 273 F.2d 902, 915—De Eugenio v. Allis-Chalmers Mfg. Co., C.A.N.J., 210 F.2d 409—Caraglio v. Frontier Power Co., C. A.N.M., 192 F.2d 175—Southern S.

EXHIBIT 2-2   Sample C.J.S. Pocket Part Page

65A CJS 3

7. **Kan.**—Kirby v. Golden, 527 P.2d 962, 215 Kan. 583.

8. **Iowa**—C.J.S. cited in Marean v. Petersen, 144 N.W.2d 906, 913, 259 Iowa 557.

page 30

9.10. **U.S.**—Decker v. Fox River Tractor Co., D.C.Wis., 324 F.Supp. 1089.

§ 118(1).   Care Required to Avoid Injury

9.15. **Mich.**—Bumstead v. Bucht, 143 N.W.2d 789, 4 Mich.App. 4.

9.30. **Distinction based on reasonableness**
U.S.—Messick v. General Motors Corp., C.A.Tex., 460 F.2d 485.

9.40. **Objective and subjective tests**
(2) Other statements.
Fla.—Henry v. Britt, App., 220 So.2d 917.
10. **Cal.**—Barth v. B. F. Goodrich Tire Co., 71 Cal. Rptr. 306, 265 C.A.2d 228.
Ind.—Hunsberger v. Wyman, 216 N.E.2d 345, 247 Ind. 369.
     Kilmer v. Galbreth, 218 N.E.2d 361, 139 Ind. App. 252—Tyler v. Nolen, 248 N.E.2d 186, 144 Ind.App. 665.
Ky.—Keown v. Keown, 394 S.W.2d 915—Goetz v. Green River Rural Elec. Co-op Corp., 398 S.W.2d 712—Jones v. Winn-Dixie of Louisville, Inc., 458 S.W.2d 767.
La.—Chauvin v. U.S. Fidelity & Guaranty Co., App., 223 So.2d 441, application den. 226 So.2d 921, 254 La. 790—Berglund v. F. W. Woolworth Co., App., 236 So.2d 266.
Mo.—Wells v. Wachtelborn, App., 410 S.W.2d 558.
N.C.—Wallsee v. Carolina Water Co., 144 S.E.2d 21, 265 N.C. 291—Gibbs v. Carolina Power & Light Co., 150 S.E.2d 207, 268 N.C. 186.
Ohio—Mobberly v. Sears, Roebuck & Co., 211 N.E.2d 839, 4 Ohio App.2d 126.
Wis.—Willenbring v. Borkenhagen, 139 N.W.2d 53, 29 Wis.2d 464.

Golfer
(2) Must foresee danger from driven golf balls.
Wash.—Wood v. Postelthwaite, 496 P.2d 988, 6 Wash. App. 885, affd. 510 P.2d 1109, 82 Wash.2d 387.

Customer
Fla.—Pensacola Restaurant Supply Co. v. Davison, App., 266 So.2d 682.

page 31

11. **Ga.**—McGinty v. Laird, 155 S.E.2d 685, 115 Ga. App. 704—Townsend v. Central Parking, Inc., 164 S.E.2d 287, 118 Ga.App. 538.
Ill.—Pedrick v. Peoria & E.R. Co., 211 N.E.2d 134, 63 Ill.App.2d 117, affd. 229 N.E.2d 504, 37 Ill.2d 494.
Ind.—Kilmer v. Galbreth, 218 N.E.2d 361, 139 Ind. App. 252—McAllister v. Butler, 220 N.E.2d 540, 139 Ind.App. 613.
Iowa—Cavanaugh v. Jepson, 167 N.W.2d 616.
Ky.—Goetz v. Green River Rural Elec. Co-op. Corp., 398 S.W.2d 712—Bennett v. Southern Bell Tel. & Tel. Co., 407 S.W.2d 403.
La.—Vetters v. Papania, App., 218 So.2d 639.
Md.—Hooper v. Mougin, 284 A.2d 236, 263 Md. 630.
Minn.—Cormican v. Parsons, 163 N.W.2d 41, 282 Minn. 94.
N.Y.—Masciarelli v. Powell, 291 N.Y.S.2d 967, 30 A.D.2d 342, affd. 246 N.E.2d 359, 23 N.Y.2d 929, 298 N.Y.S.2d 510.
N.D.—Wolff v. Light, 169 N.W.2d 93.
Pa.—Kurtzer v. Corgan, 57 Luz.L.Reg. 83.
Tenn.—Dawson v. Sears, Roebuck & Co., 394 S.W.2d 877, 217 Tenn. 72.
Tex.—Sneed v. Fort Worth Transit Co., Civ.App., 427 S.W.2d 920.

Degree and amount of care
(2) Other matters.

Cal.—Gyerman v. U.S. Lines Co., 102 Cal.Rptr. 795, 498 P.2d 1043, 7 C.3d 488.
Pa.—Borsa v. Great Atlantic & Pac. Tea Co., 215 A.2d 289, 207 Pa.Super. 63.

Knowledge of danger
(1) **Okl.**—Henryetta Const. Co. v. Harris, 408 P.2d 522, 28 A.L.R.3d 876.

Heedlessly running into danger
R.I.—Molleur v. City Dairy, Inc., 290 A.2d 214, 110 R.I. 58.

Use of alcoholic liquor as factor
Ill.—Shore v. Turman, 210 N.E.2d 232, 63 Ill.App.2d 315.

page 32

13. **U.S.**—Greyhound Lines, Inc. v. Miller, C.A.Mo., 402 F.2d 134.
Ky.—Burd v. King's Food, Inc., 441 S.W.2d 125.
Mont.—Suhr v. Sears Roebuck & Co., 450 P.2d 87, 152 Mont. 344, 36 A.L.R.3d 602.
Nev.—Otterbeck v. Lamb, 456 P.2d 855, 85 Nev. 456.

Exercise of right or privilege
Mich.—Pollack v. Oak Office Bldg., 151 N.W.2d 353, 7 Mich.App. 173.
14. **Minn.**—Coenen v. Buckman Bldg. Corp., 153 N.W.2d 329, 278 Minn. 193, 28 A.L.R.3d 592.

page 33

15. **Ga.**—Seagraves v. ABCO Mfg. Co., 164 S.E.2d 242, 118 Ga.App. 414, app. after remand 173 S.E.2d 416, 121 Ga.App. 224.
Pa.—Quinn v. Funk Bldg. Corp., 263 A.2d 458, 437 Pa. 268.
16. **Ga.**—Hieber v. Watt, 165 S.E.2d 899, 119 Ga. App. 5.
23. **Tex.**—Salazar v. Bond Finance Co., Civ.App., 410 S.W.2d 839, err. ref. no rev. err.
23.5. **Kan.**—C.J.S. cited in Mid Century Ins. Co. v. Latimer, 508 P.2d 935, 937, 211 Kan. 810.

§ 118(2).   ——— What Constitutes Ordinary or Reasonable Care

26. **U.S.**—Emery v. Northern Pac. R. Co., C.A.N.D., 370 F.2d 1009, app. after remand 407 F.2d 109.
Colo.—Roberts v. Fisher, 455 P.2d 871, 169 Colo. 288.
Fla.—Milby v. Pace Pontiac, Inc., App., 176 So.2d 554, cert. dism. 185 So.2d 467.
Ind.—Kilmer v. Galbreth, 218 N.E.2d 361, 139 Ind. App. 252.
Ky.—Gullett v. McCormick, 421 S.W.2d 352, app. after remand 460 S.W.2d 813—Dale v. E. R. Knapp & Sons, Inc., 433 S.W.2d 880—Creech v. Heaven Hill Distilleries, Inc., 497 S.W.2d 934.
La.—Langlois v. Allied Chemical Corp., 249 So.2d 133, 258 La. 1067.
     Ransom v. Acosta Cleaners, Inc., App., 219 So.2d 224—Roberts v. Tidex, Inc., App., 251 So.2d 509, writ den. 253 So.2d 224, 259 La. 905.
Md.—Honolulu Limited v. Cain, 224 A.2d 433, 244 Md. 590.
Minn.—Cormican v. Parsons, 163 N.W.2d 41, 282 Minn. 94.

page 34

27. **U.S.**—Schultz & Lindsay Const. Co. v. Erickson, C.A.N.D., 352 F.2d 425—Dalldorf v. Higgerson-Buchanan, Inc., C.A.Va., 402 F.2d 419—Mroz v. Dravo Corp., C.A.Pa., 429 F.2d 1156.
Ariz.—Bryant v. Thunderbird Academy, 439 P.2d 818, 103 Ariz. 247, 38 A.L.R.3d 901.
Ark.—Hudgins v. Maze, 437 S.W.2d 467, 246 Ark. 21.
Conn.—Callender v. Lakewood Realty, Cir.A.D., 237 A.2d 106, 4 Conn.Cir. 556.
Del.—Dammer v. Metropolitan Merchandise Mart, Inc., 217 A.2d 688, 9 Storey 247.
Ga.—Seagraves v. ABCO Mfg. Co., 164 S.E.2d 242, 118 Ga.App. 414, app. after remand 173 S.E.2d 416, 121 Ga.App. 224.

NEGLIGENCE   § 118(2)
Page 37

Ill.—Sweeney v. Matthews, 236 N.E.2d 439, 94 Ill. App.2d 6, affd. 264 N.E.2d 170, 46 Ill.2d 64.
Ind.—Memorial Hospital of South Bend, Inc. v. Scott, 300 N.E.2d 50, 261 Ind. 27.
     Jenkins v. City of Fort Wayne, 210 N.E.2d 390, 139 Ind.App. 1, reh. den. 212 N.E.2d 916, 139 Ind.App. 1.
Iowa—Cronk v. Iowa Power & Light Co., 138 N.W.2d 843, 258 Iowa 603.
Ky.—Post v. American Cleaning Equipment Corp., 437 S.W.2d 516—O'Connor & Raque Co. v. Bill, 474 S.W.2d 344.
La.—Guillory v. Allstate Ins. Co., App., 185 So.2d 905, writ ref. 187 So.2d 451, 249 La. 488.
Me.—Roy v. Merrill, 267 A.2d 386.
Md.—Craig v. Greenbelt Consumer Services, Inc., 222 A.2d 836, 244 Md. 95.
Mich.—Koehler v. Detroit Edison Co., 165 N.W.2d 598, 14 Mich.App. 367, affd. in part, revd. in part on oth. grds. 174 N.W.2d 827, 383 Mich. 224.
Miss.—General Tire & Rubber Co. v. Darnell, 221 So.2d 104.
Neb.—Mendoza v. Aguilera, 165 N.W.2d 360, 184 Neb. 94.
N.M.—Lujan v. Reed, 434 P.2d 378, 78 N.M. 556.
     Stewart v. Barnes, App., 451 P.2d 1006, 80 N.M. 102—Wood v. Southwestern Public Service Co., App., 452 P.2d 692, 80 N.M. 164—Perez v. Miller, App., 453 P.2d 383, 80 N.M. 214—Brown v. Hall, App., 458 P.2d 808, 80 N.M. 556, cert. den. 458 P.2d 859, 80 N.M. 607.
N.C.—Holland v. Malpass, 147 S.E.2d 234, 266 N.C. 750.
Ohio—Motorists Mut. Ins. Co. v. Walker, 265 N.E.2d 836, 26 Ohio Misc. 169.
Okl.—Jack Healey Linen Service Co. v. Travis, 434 P.2d 924.
Wash.—Rosendahl v. Lesourd Methodist Church, 412 P.2d 109, 68 Wash.2d 180.
     Papac v. Mayr Bros. Logging Co., 459 P.2d 57, 1 Wash.App. 33—Johnson v. Mobile Crane Co., 463 P.2d 250, 1 Wash.App. 642.

Methods of work
(2) Standards imposed by normal job function.
U.S.—Powell v. E. W. Bliss Co., D.C.Mich., 346 F.Supp. 819.

Crucial question
Wash.—Hoffman v. Gamache, 465 P.2d 203, 1 Wash. App. 883.

Licensee or invitee
Minn.—Peterson v. Balach, 199 N.W.2d 639, 294 Minn. 161.

page 35

29.5. **Or.**—Koch v. Southern Pac. Co., 513 P.2d 770, 266 Or. 335, app. after remand 547 P.2d 589, 274 Or. 499.
30. **U.S.**—Brooks v. Eastern Air Lines, Inc., D.C.Ga., 253 F.Supp. 119.
Miss.—Bozeman v. Tucker, 203 So.2d 795.

page 36

38. **Ill.**—Morehead v. Mayron, 279 N.E.2d 473, 3 Ill.App.3d 425.
La.—Calvert Fire Ins. Co. v. Barlow, App., 215 So.2d 392—Butler v. City of Bogalusa, App., 258 So.2d 599, writ den. 260 So.2d 323, 261 La. 544.
Md.—Stein v. Overlook Joint Venture, 227 A.2d 226, 246 Md. 75.
Mo.—Moore v. Eden, 405 S.W.2d 910. Stoeppelman v. Hays-Fendler Const. Co., App., 437 S.W.2d 143.

page 37

39. **U.S.**—Harner v. Somerset Steel Erection Co., D.C.W.Va., 284 F.Supp. 553.
Ky.—Goetz v. Green River Rural Elec. Co-op. Corp., 398 S.W.2d 712.
Mich.—Pollack v. Oak Office Bldg., 151 N.W.2d 353, 7 Mich.App. 173.
N.C.—Wallsee v. Carolina Water Co., 144 S.E.2d 21, 265 N.C. 291.

Some states, in addition to the indexes in the volumes of the state codes and statutes, have other indexes that may prove more adaptable to the individual researcher's thinking. For example, the state library (usually in the capital city) may publish a special directory listing the types of legislative documents within the library and providing procedural guidance on searching the library for the volumes and on the types of information within them, their availability for loan, the methods of arranging to check out the books, and the names and phone numbers of persons in the library who can assist the researcher. Additionally, there are commercial sources for more detailed indexes that can be helpful. For instance, the Recorder Printing and Publishing Company of San Francisco, California, published *Larmac, Consolidated Index to the Constitution of Laws of California*, a very comprehensive index with an effective subject cross-index. Other states have similar publications. Indexes sometimes are difficult to use for finding the specific area of interest. An alternative then is to use the table of contents, which will lead to the general area of interest, and persistence and review of the general material will suggest or lead to the specific subject of interest, if it is contained in the legal publication. Municipal codes, including many city and county ordinances, are currently located at http://www.muni-code.com, including the ordinance index and the text of the code. Without such a site, the legal assistant must travel to the locale or call, write and send money for copies before identifying the necessary sections desired for research. This website permits a preliminary review of the local code's index and format.

2.0516 Digests. Legal digests are arranged much like legal encyclopedias, except that they do not contain a summary of the law or a particular point. Legal digests are really indexes to the law. The *American Digest System* constitutes the most comprehensive index to American decisions that is available. The system is based on a topic and key number classification scheme that divides the entire body of law into seven major headings, thirty-two subheadings, and over four hundred digest topics. There are over 75,000 subtopics, each representing decisions accumulated under the topic-key number system.

The topic name and the key number, together, serve as a research reference for points of law abstracted from reported judicial decisions. The digest paragraphs are short summaries of the decisions arranged to help locate the decision and its holding(s). Digests also have indexes and tables of cases, as well as "Words and Phrases" compendia, which refer the reader to judicial definitions of words and phrases in court opinions.

An example of the indexes found in digests is Exhibit 2-3. This exhibit clearly reflects the helpful organization and explicit outline of the matters covered or excluded, suggests sources for near-synonymous topics and outlines, and provides topic and key number references to the material covered. Anyone interested in "proximate cause of injury" quickly finds the same topic and key number within the text as shown in Exhibit 2-3.

2.0517 Other Sources. Some other methods that some researchers find expeditious will be mentioned because they can be effective for persons with particular research needs. Every method is only a tool to accomplish a task, and each should be designed to fit the individual and the special task when possible.

One such method takes advantage of a resource that many states have and some do not: an approved state book for forms, pleading and practice, and/or points and authorities. There are many form books commercially published for pleadings and for preparation of legal documents for the client. When one is asked to draft a motion for summary judgment, for example, the state form book of pleading and practice details the specific items that must be

EXHIBIT 2-3   Sample Page from Federal Practice Digest

NEGLIGENCE

SUBJECTS INCLUDED

Failure to use due care, either in respect of acts or of omissions, in performance or observance of a duty not founded on contract, which failure is the proximate cause of unintended injury to the person to whom such duty is owing

Nature and extent of liability for such injuries in general

Nature and effect of negligence or other fault on the part of the person injured contributing to his injury

Comparison of negligence of the parties

Imputation to the person injured of others' negligence

Civil remedies for such injuries

Criminal responsibility for such negligence in general, and prosecution and punishment thereof as a public offense

SUBJECTS EXCLUDED AND COVERED BY OTHER TOPICS

Death, actions for damages for, see DEATH

Manslaughter by negligence, see AUTOMOBILES, HOMICIDE

Particular kinds of property, negligence in care and use of, see MINES AND MINERALS, WATERS AND WATER COURSES, ANIMALS, SHIPPING, COLLISION, and other specific topics

Particular kinds of works, public improvements, etc., negligence in construction and use of, see RAILROADS, BRIDGES, HIGHWAYS, MUNICIPAL CORPORATIONS, and other specific topics

Particular personal relations, occupations, employments, contracts, etc., negligence in respect of duties incident to, see ATTORNEY AND CLIENT, EMPLOYERS' LIABILITY, PHYSICIANS AND SURGEONS, CARRIERS, LANDLORD AND TENANT, BAILMENT and other specific topics

For detailed references to other topics, see Descriptive-Word Index

---

Analysis

I. ACTS OR OMISSIONS CONSTITUTING NEGLIGENCE, ☞1–55.
    A. PERSONAL CONDUCT IN GENERAL, 1–15.
    B. DANGEROUS SUBSTANCES, MACHINERY, AND OTHER INSTRUMENTALITIES, ☞16–27.
    C. CONDITION AND USE OF LAND, BUILDINGS, AND OTHER STRUCTURES, ☞28–55.

II. PROXIMATE CAUSE OF INJURY, ☞56–64.

III. CONTRIBUTORY NEGLIGENCE, ☞65–101.
    (A) PERSONS INJURED IN GENERAL, ☞65–83.11.
    (B) CHILDREN AND OTHERS UNDER DISABILITY, ☞84–88.
    (C) IMPUTED NEGLIGENCE, ☞89–96.
    (D) COMPARATIVE NEGLIGENCE, ☞97–101.

included for a meritorious motion to be acceptable based on the law of that state. It often cites the code section, rule of court, and so on that makes such a requirement. A state-approved points and authorities book can provide the form and language of any issue and cite the actual case giving rise to the acceptable authority. Naturally, the cases must be read to ensure that they are on point and do support the proposed motion.

Another method that can be effective is best demonstrated by an example:

> A legal assistant has the assignment to review a complaint to determine whether an action for strict liability against the client has been properly stated and to draft interrogatories sufficient to reveal the existence of facts known by the adversary that support the cause of action.

Some researchers are very successful in immediately finding the essential elements to prove strict liability by consulting their state book of approved jury instructions. These books are collections of standardized jury instructions, also known as jury "charges," which are approved by the court as to form and language for presentation to a jury by the judge before the jury is sequestered to consider and decide a case. The theory of framing jury instructions has led to creating succinct expressions of each essential element that must be proved for a cause of action to be supported by a jury verdict. Since the pleadings are generally phrased in very broad terms, the jury instructions are a guide to framing interrogatories which develop the exact facts that support or attack the allegations in a set of pleadings, as well as the facts relied upon which hold the party in as a proper party-defendant or (as often is the case in strict liability) as a cross-defendant.

2.052 The West Topic and Key Number System

The West Publishing Company topic and key number system of classification was developed as a comprehensive indexing system to be used by researchers to locate points of law or legal principles. This system is a hallmark of the West Publishing Company encyclopedias, digests, unofficial reporters (such as the national reporter system volumes), and annotated codes, and was made available for licensing to other publishing companies in 1996. Some of the major topic headings are shown in Exhibit 2-4, and Exhibit 2-3 shows the relationship between the topic and the key number subtopics. A quick perusal of the topic and key number chart reveals there are many topics within each division and each topic is further subdivided according to the legal principles or the points of law that fall within its scope. Finer breakdowns within the individual subtopics naturally result, and each subdivision topic is given a *key number*. Every case reported using the West system is first provided with *headnotes*. Each headnote summarizes a salient point of law decided in the case. Then, the headnotes of every published decision are further reviewed for specific case elements and each headnote then provided with a topic and key number reference. For example, headnotes 1 and 2 might be on "Evidence" and headnote 3 might be on "Appeal and Error." Theoretically, this in results in a system where all cases with the same elements are assigned the same topic and key number and will involve fact situations or points of law that have some similarity. The topic and key numbers from all the cases are consolidated into digests which West publishes. Digests are finding tools and a researcher must check the appropriate digest for a given jurisdiction. As an example, for an action in Montana, the appropriate digest would be the *Montana Digest*. These digests are kept up-to-date with cumulative annual *pocket parts* and supplemental pamphlets, in the same manner as the national reporter volumes are kept current using pamphlets and advance sheets with indexes. The most

EXHIBIT 2-4   Example of Digest Topics

DIGEST TOPICS

See, also, Outline of the Law by Seven Main Divisions of Law, Page VII

The topic numbers shown below may be used in WESTLAW searches for cases within the topic and within specified key numbers.

1	Abandoned and Lost Property	37	Assault and Battery	76	Chattel Mortgages
2	Abatement and Revival	38	Assignments	76A	Chemical Dependents
		40	Assistance, Writ of	76H	Children Out-of-Wedlock
3	Abduction	41	Associations		
4	Abortion and Birth Control	42	Assumpsit, Action of	77	Citizens
		43	Asylums	78	Civil Rights
5	Absentees	44	Attachment	79	Clerks of Courts
6	Abstracts of Title	45	Attorney and Client	80	Clubs
7	Accession	46	Attorney General	81	Colleges and Universities
8	Accord and Satisfaction	47	Auctions and Auctioneers		
		48	Audita Querela	82	Collision
9	Account	48A	Automobiles	83	Commerce
10	Account, Action on	48B	Aviation	83H	Commodity Futures Trading Regulation
11	Account Stated	49	Bail		
11A	Accountants	50	Bailment	84	Common Lands
12	Acknowledgment	51	Bankruptcy	85	Common Law
13	Action	52	Banks and Banking	86	Common Scold
14	Action on the Case	54	Beneficial Associations	88	Compounding Offenses
15	Adjoining Landowners	55	Bigamy	89	Compromise and Settlement
15A	Administrative Law and Procedure	56	Bills and Notes		
		57	Blasphemy	89A	Condominium
16	Admiralty	58	Bonds	90	Confusion of Goods
17	Adoption	59	Boundaries	91	Conspiracy
18	Adulteration	60	Bounties	92	Constitutional Law
19	Adultery	61	Breach of Marriage Promise	92B	Consumer Credit
20	Adverse Possession			92H	Consumer Protection
21	Affidavits	62	Breach of the Peace	93	Contempt
22	Affray	63	Bribery	95	Contracts
23	Agriculture	64	Bridges	96	Contribution
24	Aliens	65	Brokers	97	Conversion
25	Alteration of Instruments	66	Building and Loan Associations	98	Convicts
				99	Copyrights and Intellectual Property
26	Ambassadors and Consuls	67	Burglary	100	Coroners
		68	Canals	101	Corporations
27	Amicus Curiae	69	Cancellation of Instruments	102	Costs
28	Animals			103	Counterfeiting
29	Annuities	70	Carriers	104	Counties
30	Appeal and Error	71	Cemeteries	105	Court Commissioners
31	Appearance	72	Census	106	Courts
33	Arbitration	73	Certiorari	107	Covenant, Action of
34	Armed Services	74	Champerty and Maintenance	108	Covenants
35	Arrest			108A	Credit Reporting Agencies
36	Arson	75	Charities		

XIII

1–1

comprehensive digest published by West is the *American Digest*, which indexes and classifies all American case law, state and federal. These digests are called *Decennials*. Starting with the *Ninth Decennial Digest*, West began publishing the series in two parts, Part I covering the first five-year period and Part II covering the second five-year period to make up a full *Decennial Digest*. Prior to the *Ninth Decennial,* the digests were published once every ten years.

Other digests published individually cover the decisions of different courts, such as *The Supreme Court Digest* and the *Federal Practice Digest 4th*. The ultimate value of the West topic and key number system is that once a researcher locates a particular topic and key number, he or she has the "key" to reported American cases that have litigated a particular point or principle of law. If a state digest is checked and there are no cases under the topic and key number assigned to a particular point, then the researcher knows there is a strong possibility that the particular point has not been decided or litigated in that state. The search is then extended to the cases of other states and courts. *Caveat:* Careful consideration must be made when selecting the topic word under which a search for the key number is made since our vocabulary is filled with near synonymous words. The absence of a topic and key number should not be accepted without exhausting the reasonable synonyms, which is another way of saying the human element of decision exercised by West employees in deciding how a subject should be indexed may not always match how the researcher would index a subject. Certain invaluable methods for finding the correct topic and key number are outlined in the sections below.

2.0521 Descriptive Word Method. The descriptive word method becomes the most effective tool when the researcher does not have the name of a case on point or has not yet determined the topic that deals with the issue of interest. Every case decided is based on a fact situation, and the aim is to find other cases based on the same, or similar, fact situation that will provide the authority with which to argue the client's case.

In classifying and indexing cases, editors use words consistently when describing the facts of a case. These words are arranged alphabetically in volumes called "Descriptive Word Indexes" which will, in turn, direct the researcher to the topic and key number relating to cases with similar facts or legal issues. To use this search method, the researcher must analyze the fact situation and list the key words and phrases describing the essential elements. The researcher may have difficulty analyzing problems and choosing descriptive words at first, but the skill will develop with practice. Most descriptive words naturally group themselves around the five elements common to every case, namely:

a. Parties
b. Places and things
c. Acts or omissions that provide a basis for the action or issue
d. Defenses that might apply to an action or issue
e. The ultimate relief sought

The problem for most researchers at the start is to select words that are the same as a significant descriptive word to which a key number has been assigned. The pamphlet *West's Law Finder, a Legal Research Manual* contains an excellent example of the process. (*See* Exhibits 2-5 and 2-6.) *West Federal Practice Digest* (Exhibit 2-3) uses a similar method of topic analysis. Additionally, at the beginning of each digest topic is a note specifying the scope of the topic and a complete breakdown of all subtopics, which are arranged numerically. Each subtopic bears what is called a key number. These numbers are often preceded by a drawing of a small

EXHIBIT 2-5   Copy of Page 19, *West's Law Finder, a Legal Research Manual*

mind that most descriptive words naturally group themselves around the five elements common to every case, namely:

1. **PARTIES**
   Aliens, Children Out-of-Wedlock, Landlords, Physicians, Sheriffs

2. **PLACES AND THINGS**
   Playground, Theater, Office Building, Roller Coaster, Puck, Automobile, Engagement Ring

3. **BASIS OF ACTION OR ISSUE**
   Negligence, Breach of Contract, Slander, Restraint of Trade, Title to Property, Admission of Evidence

4. **DEFENSE**
   Act of God, Assumption of Risk, Contributory Negligence, Usury

5. **RELIEF SOUGHT**
   Damages, Injunction, Eviction, Rescission, Divorce

At a professional wrestling match the referee was thrown from the ring in such a way that he struck and injured plaintiff who was a front row spectator. Does plaintiff have a cause of action? The following analysis shows how the descriptive words for this problem should be selected.

1. **PARTIES**—Spectator, Patron, Arena Owner, Wrestler, Referee, Promoter

2. **PLACES AND THINGS**—Wrestling Match, Amusement Place, Theater. Show

3. **BASIS OF ACTION OR ISSUE**—Negligence, Personal Injury to Spectator, Liability

4. **DEFENSE**—Assumption of Risk

5. **RELIEF SOUGHT**—Damages

The following are actual excerpts from the Descriptive-Word Index of the 6th Decennial Digest showing how several of the above words refer to Theaters 6 which is the Topic and Key Number that carries the wrestling injury cases in all Key Number Digests.

Descriptive-Word Index

ASSUMPTION OF RISKS—Cont'd
Automobiles—
   Burden of proof in action for injuries from operation or use of highways. **Autos 242(8)**
   Evidence of assumption of risk by occupant. **Autos 244(56)**
   Guest passenger, host's failure to look. **Autos 224(1)**
Hockey spectator. **Theaters 6**
Hunting party members. **Weap 18(1)**
Motorboat race, voluntary entry. **Collision 15**
Operation of doctrine. **Neglig 105**
Passengers. **Carr 323**
Patron of amusement device. **Theaters 6**

Swimming pool patron. **Theaters 6**
Tenant. **Land & Ten 168(1)**
Tenant's injuries, evidence. **Land & Ten 169(6)**
Tractor operator voluntarily assisting truck driver. **Autos 202**
Willful and wanton conduct of defendant. **Neglig 100**
Workmen's compensation—
   Abrogation or modification of defense. **Work Comp 772, 2110**
   Failure of employee to elect to come under act. **Work Comp 2114**
Wrestling match spectator injured by referee thrown from ring. **Theaters 6**

ASSUMPTION OF SKILL
Master as chargeable with knowledge

EXHIBIT 2-6 Copy of Page 21, *West's Law Finder, a Legal Research Manual*

Nebraska Digest

⚷6(5) THEATERS & SHOWS

10 Neb D—222

THEATERS AND SHOWS.

Library references

Corpus Juris Secundum reference →

C.J.S. Theaters and Shows § 1 et seq.

⚷2. **Statutory and municipal regulations.**

Neb. An act prohibiting "all public exhibitions of Hypnotism, Mesmerism, Animal Magnetism, or so-called Psychical Forces, for gain", does not prohibit spiritualistic seances, unless they are public and open and for gain, the words "psychical forces" applying to a seance conducted by a spiritualistic medium, but his act as such not violating statute unless it is public and open and for gain. Comp.St. 1929, § 28–1111.—Dill v. Hamilton, 291 N.W. 62, 137 Neb. 723.

The act prohibiting "all public exhibitions of Hypnotism, Mesmerism, Animal Magnetism, or so-called Psychical Forces, for gain", is a valid exercise of police power, since police power to prohibit public exhibitions for money-making purposes or for gain extends to harmful, immoral or indecent performances, though conducted in the name of religion, and violators of such prohibitions are subject to statutory penalties therefor. Comp.St.1929, § 28–1111.—Dill v. Hamilton, 291 N.W. 62, 137 Neb. 723.

A guaranty of $15 to remunerate a medium for conducting spiritualistic seance as religious ceremony in the worship of God and creation of the fund by voluntary contributions of communicants of Spiritualistic Church do not constitute "gain" within statute forbidding public seances for gain. Comp.St.1929, § 28–1111.—Dill v. Hamilton, 291 N.W. 62, 137 Neb. 723.

Internal Key Number breakdown →

⚷6. Liabilities for injuries to persons attending.

(1). In general.

(2). Duty affected by charging for admission, insuring safety or assuming special legal status.

(3). Licensees or invitees.

(4). —— Particular invitees.

(5). Persons liable or entitled to sue.

(6). Limitation of liability.

(7). Particular duties toward participants.

(8). —— Amusement devices.

(9). —— Swimming or bathing.

(10). Particular duties toward spectators.

(11). —— Athletic events.

(12). —— Floor and ground.

(13). —— Lighting, and ushering in darkness.

(14). —— Protection against crowds, assaults and acts of others and ushering in general.

(15). —— Seats and structural defects.

(16). —— Stairs, steps and ramps.

(17). Contributory negligence and assumption of risk.

Point of law in illustrative example →

(18). —— Athletic events.

(19). —— Participants.

(20). Actions in general.

⚷6(5). **Persons liable or entitled to sue.**

Neb. In personal injury action by spectator at wrestling match, instruction that if jury found that while two wrestlers were on ground outside ring they continued to wrestle and when referee attempted to separate them, one of the wrestlers shoved the referee into the spectator and injured spectator, there was no liability against anyone except wrestler who did the pushing, because such pushing was outside that wrestler's scope of employment, was erroneous, since such wrestler was not, as a matter of law, outside the scope of his employment.—Klause v. Nebraska State Bd. of Agriculture, 35 N.W.2d 104, 150 Neb. 466.

Action for injuries sustained by spectator at wrestling match when referee was thrown or knocked from ring and came in contact with spectator was properly dismissed as to one who procured one of the wrestlers, where such wrestler was in nowise in such person's employ or under his control.—Id.

⚷6(10). **Particular duties toward spectators.**

Neb. One who operates a place of public amusement or entertainment is held to a stricter accountability for injuries to patrons than owners of private premises generally; and he is not insurer of safety of patrons but owes to them only what under the particular circumstances, amounts to ordinary and reasonable care.—Fimple v. Archer Ballroom Co., 35 N.W.2d 680, 150 Neb. 681.

⚷6(14). —— **Protection against crowds, assaults and acts of others, and ushering in general.**

Neb. Ordinance rendering it unlawful for operators of public dance halls to permit persons therein while under influence of liquor or engaging in boisterous conduct is for benefit of individual patrons of dances as well as public at large and could properly be made basis of civil action for damages where dance hall patron was injured by bottle thrown by second patron who was intoxicated.—Fimple v. Archer Ballroom Co., 35 N.W.2d 680, 150 Neb. 681.

⚷6(17). **Contributory negligence and assumption of risk.**

Neb. Patron who attended large dance at public dance hall did not assume risk of injury from bottle thrown by second patron who was intoxicated.—Fimple v. Archer Ballroom Co., 35 N.W.2d 680, 150 Neb. 681.

⚷6(18). —— **Athletic events.**

Neb. A spectator at hockey game assumes risk of, and owes duty to protect himself against, such dangers incident to playing of game as are known to him or should be obvious and apparent to reasonable and prudent person in exercise of due care under circumstances.—Tite v. Omaha Coliseum Corporation, 12 N.W.2d 90, 144 Neb. 22.

Neb. A spectator at a wrestling match is required to exercise due care in protecting himself against known dangers or such as should be known and appreciated by a reasonable person in exercise of due care.—Klause v. Nebraska State Bd. of Agriculture, 35 N.W.2d 104, 150 Neb. 466.

Spectator at wrestling match who was injured when referee was thrown or knocked from ring and came in contact with spectator, was not contributorily negligent, so as to preclude recovery for his injuries, because he sat in front row.—Id.

Spectator at wrestling match who was injured when referee was thrown or knocked from ring and came in contact with spectator, did not assume risk of injury because he sat in front row.—Id.

A spectator at a wrestling event assumes risk only of such dangers as are incident to such events, of which he had knowledge or key. This is simply a reminder that the number and title that follow are part of the organized group of topics and subtopics, as seen in Exhibits 2-3 and 2-6.

Beginning at page 21 of *West's Law Finder* (Exhibit 2-6), the researcher is shown how the descriptive word method works:

a. "Parties" equals spectator and a synonym patron, or arena owner, or wrestler, or referee, or promoter, all words that might have been the issue parties in past litigation. Other synonyms could be generated if a search for each proved negative. As it is, patron immediately leads to the topic "Theatre" and the key number 6.

b. "Places" equals wrestling match, amusement place, theatre, and show, and could include auditorium, arena, or others. "Theatre," however is the title of a topic on point.

c. "Basis of Action" produces "Personal Injury" (to a spectator).

d. "Defense" finds an easy entry under "Assumption of Risk."

e. "Relief Sought" produces references to several sources of information.

2.0522 Topic Method. The topic method involves locating the topic under which the point of law has been previously classified. Before relying on this method, be very familiar with the key number classification system. Researchers, particularly those just beginning, very often arrive at the wrong topic. Study and analyze the key number system law chart (Exhibit 2-4); almost invariably it will lead the researcher to the correct topic. If problems still exist, refer to the alphabetic list of digest topics that appears in the front of each digest volume and the *C.J.S.* indexes. In using the descriptive word indexes, the researcher may have difficulty locating the precise key number needed, but they will always lead the researcher to the proper topic, and sometimes, to additional topics for consideration. Every digest has a topic analysis that begins with a "scope-note." Review of the scope-note will often quickly reveal whether the selected topic matches the case factual situation. Select an example based on page 1 of the current key chart to replace this example: For instance, presume a client is involved in an automobile accident where her car was pushed into another because a third vehicle rammed the side of the client's car. This will require a search to determine whether the client is liable for damage to the vehicle she hit. Review of the key number system law chart (Exhibit 2-4) suggests the transaction fits best in the category of "Collision."

2.0523 Table of Cases Method. The table of cases search method is useless unless, or until, the researcher has the name of at least one case that deals with the particular point of law of concern. The name of a case allows the researcher to go immediately to the table of cases in the appropriate state key number digest, reporter key number digest, or the *American Digest* and find from that case what topics and key numbers were used. Once the proper topic and key number are located, all other American cases dealing with the same general point become available for review, analysis, and report.

2.053 The Statutory Approach to Law

Once an initial review of the secondary source material has been completed on a particular issue, the legal assistant has a general understanding of the problem and in all probability has discovered some case on point and found references to one or more statutes or codes. When researching a problem involving a statute, a good rule of thumb is to first read the statute (including all updates) and relevant annotations that may be listed after the statute. As mentioned previously, an annotation is a brief description of a judicial opinion.

Locating a statute is a relatively simple procedure. Statutory laws can be divided into three subdivisions:

a. Federal—U.S. Constitution, congressional legislation, treaties, executive orders, administrative rules and orders, and court rules;
b. State—state constitutions, session laws, uniform laws, administrative rules and orders, and court rules; and
c. Local—municipal charters, county and municipal ordinances and court rules.

When statutes are initially published, they are arranged in chronological order according to the date of passage. However, the statutes passed in a particular legislative session are ultimately incorporated into statutes that were in existence prior to that legislative session, thus creating an ever-growing and changing collection of laws. Because these change so frequently, they are arranged topically. Consequently, if one is familiar with the appropriate terminology relating to a particular subject of law, one can locate all current laws on a specific topic through the use of a subject index to the statutes. Various names for these collections of statutes are used by the different states and jurisdictions. Very often the terms code, annotated statutes, compiled laws, or revised statutes appear in the title of the publication. There are a large number of codes in this country, and each may be composed of one, five, or even several hundred volumes, as in the case of the *United States Code Annotated*. Additionally, some states subdivide their state codes into smaller codes, such as a code of civil procedure, a code of criminal procedure, an insurance code, and so on. A researcher who is encountering a code for the first time should try to become familiar with the organization of the state code, including any smaller codes, and become comfortable with the form and style of the text. At the beginning of the code will be noted the order in which the topics are arranged as titles, parts, or chapters, as well as the system of numbering of the sections and subsections.

The difference between chronologic (such as statutes at large and session laws) and the topical arrangements of codes is of primary importance to the researcher for speed of location, clarity of reading, and ease of updating.

2.0531 Federal Reports.   Federal question research is technical and advanced, and although it will not be discussed in detail, it is important for legal assistants to be aware of common sources of federal statutory and case law.

The U.S. Constitution was signed in 1787 and became operative in 1789. It was the origin of federal law and, as amended, still stands as the supreme law of the land. Most Americans are affected continuously by its provisions, and the discussion of cases and terminology arising directly from the rights guaranteed to individuals by the Constitution (for example, freedom of speech, freedom of the press, and due process) regularly appear in the media. The Constitution is the highest authority available, and the U.S. Supreme Court is the final arbiter in disputes over its provisions. All other federal and state statutes must conform to the guarantees of this document or they will fail. West's *U.S. Code Annotated (U.S.C.A.®)* has several volumes devoted exclusively to the Constitution and the cases that have arisen from disputes over its provisions.

A key to statutory research is that statutes can be found several places: in session laws, in an unannotated code, and in an annotated code. As bills are enacted by Congress they enter the *U.S. Statutes at Large*, the session laws of the U.S. Congress, and may, if permanent, general, and public in nature, be included in the *U.S. Code*. Official copies of the *U.S. Code* can be obtained through the U.S. Government Printing Office. Each such provision as it becomes law can be found in the *Congressional Record* and may be located through the Congressional Information Service/Index. Unofficial reports include the *U.S.C.A., the U.S. Code Service (U.S.C.S.)*, and the *U.S. Code Congressional and Administrative News (USCAAN)*. USCAAN publishes new federal laws as they are enacted and includes some legislative history. Remember when checking annotations to check both the *U.S.C.A.* and the *U.S.C.S.* because different editors make different decisions about what materials to include in annotations. Additionally, there are numerous publishers of *loose-leaf services*. These services monitor and publish new laws along with updated material for subscribers in particular fields of law, such as trade regulation, taxation, antitrust, environmental law, labor, and occupational safety and health law in a loose-leaf format for insertion into binders. Firms that have a substantial specialty practice will generally subscribe to such a service at both the federal and state levels.

Each publisher supplies the legal community with a particular style and format they believe is helpful, easy to use, and clear to its readers. The *U.S.C.A.* supplies the researcher with a variety of routes to the significant material of the statutes and cases which refer to them. Each volume of the *U.S.C.A.* contains all or a portion of the U.S. Constitution or the *U.S. Code* as well as a title page describing the extent of material covered in the volume which is supplemented by detailed tables of contents and indexes.

The *U.S.C.A.* also contains a special index of the popular name of each law enacted by Congress, references to the date of its passage, any amendments, the chapter and statute reference to the statutes at large, its public law designation (if any), the titles and sections under the *U.S. Code*, and any alternative names under which it is listed. (*See* Exhibit 2-7.)

Because not all statutes at large are codified and published in the *U.S. Code*, it is essential to be able to move between the *U.S. Code* and the *U.S. Statutes at Large*. The *U.S.C.A.* provides indexes which meet this need by providing: (1) the year and the session of Congress in which the law was passed; (2) the statute volume in which it is recorded; (3) the date of passage of the statute; and (4) its public law number, along with the sections and pages all cross-referenced to the *U.S.C.A.*, as shown in Exhibit 2-8.

Administrative agencies of the United States must publish their rules and regulations (these terms are used synonymously in administrative law vernacular) in the *Federal Register*. The codification of the various rules of these agencies is found in the *Code of Federal Regulations (C.F.R.),* the official record for such law. The topics in the *C.F.R.* correspond to those found in the *U.S. Code*. Because of the volume of agency rules promulgated, one-quarter of the *C.F.R.* is updated every three months. Therefore, although the *C.F.R.* is well indexed and revised annually, at any given time some volumes will be three months old, some six months old, and some nine months old. The date on the cover of the particular *C.F.R.* volume will tell the researcher when that particular title was last updated, and include a cumulative history of changes from 1964 forward. Anything older is found in a special volume, *C.F.R. Sections Affected 1949–1963*, published by the U.S. Government Printing Office in 1966. The *C.F.R.* contains indexes which aid the researcher in finding the *U.S. Code*, the *U.S. Statutes at Large*, the proclamation, the executive order, or the reorganization plans relied upon by a particular rule or regulation for authority. The *United States Code Service Index and Finding Aids to the Code of Federal Regulations* is another useful tool for moving between the *U.S. Code* and the *Code of Federal Regulations*.

To assist a researcher in delving into the governmental regulatory and administrative agency maze, the U.S. Government Printing Office annually publishes the *United States Government Manual*. This manual describes all executive branch and regulatory agencies and cites the

EXHIBIT 2-7   Sample Entry, *U.S.C.A.* Popular Name Table

AAA Farm Relief and Inflation Act (Wagner-Lewis $500,000,000 Emergency Relief Act)   Page 1

*32090 UNITED STATES CODE ANNOTATED

POPULAR NAME TABLE FOR ACTS OF CONGRESS

Through Pub.L. 105-41

Name of act, alternate/descriptive name (if any), and enacting credit:

AAA Farm Relief and Inflation Act (Wagner-Lewis $500,000,000 Emergency Relief Act) (May 12, 1933, ch. 25, 48 Stat. 31)

Section of ch. 25	USCA Classification
1	7 USCA§ 601
2	7 USCA § 602
3	7 USCA § 603
4	7 USCA § 604
7	7 USCA § 607
8	7 USCA § 608
8a	7 USCA § 608a
8b	7 USCA § 608b
8c	7 USCA § 608c
8d	7 USCA § 608d
8e	7 USCA § 608e-1

9	7 USCA § 609
10	7 USCA § 610
11	7 USCA § 611
12	7 USCA § 612
13	7 USCA § 613
14	7 USCA § 614
15	7 USCA § 615
16	7 USCA § 616
*32091 17	7 USCA § 617
18	7 USCA § 618
19	7 USCA § 619
20	7 USCA § 620
21	7 USCA § 623
22	7 USCA § 624

<This list contains only sections enacted by this Public Law. To retrieve all sections affected by this law, see May 12, 1933, ch. 25 in USCA-TABLES database.>

7 USCA§§ 601 to 604, 607, 608, 608a to 608d, 608e-1, 609 to 620, 623, 624

Additional subject matter contained in Revised Title:

See 31 USCA §§ 5301, 5304

EXHIBIT 2-8 Sample Page, Index of *U.S. Code* Cross-reference to *Statutes at Large*

1990				STATUTES AT LARGE		
	1990—101st Cong.—104 Stat.				USCA	
May P.L.	Sec.		Page	Tlt.	Sec.	Status
4 101–280	5(d)		159	18	207	
	5(e)		159	18	208	
	5(f)		159	18	216	
	6(a)(1)		160	26	1043	
	6(a)(2), (3)		160	26	1043	nts
	6(b)		160	31	1344	nt
	6(c)		160	18	208	nt
	6(d)(1)		160	5	3393	
	6(d)(2)		160	5	7701	
	6(d)(3)		160	22	3945	
	6(d)(4)		161	10	1601	
	7(a)		161	5 App. 7	501	
	7(b)		161	5 App. 7	502	
	7(b)(1)		161	2	441i	
	7(b)(2)		161	2	31–1	
	7(c)		161	5 App. 7	503	
	8		162	2	31–2	
	9		162	5 App. 6	105	nt
	10(a)		162	31	3730	
	10(b)		162	10	2397a	
	10(c)		162	10	2397a	nt
	11		163	5 App. 6	101	nt
101–281	1(a)		164	49 App.	1475	
	1(b)		164	49 App.	1475	nt
	2		164	49 App.	2210	
9 101–286	1		171	16	551	nt
	101 to 106		174	16	551b	nt
	201		174	16	551b	nt
	202		174	16	551b	
	203		175	16	551c	
	204(a)		175	16	558c	
	204(b)		175	16	18i	
	204(c)		175	43	1737	
17 101–292	1		185	16	460aaa	
	2		185	16	460aaa–1	
	3		185	16	460aaa–2	
	4		187	16	460aaa–3	
	5		188	16	460aaa–4	
	6		188	16	460aaa–5	
	7		188	16	460aaa–6	
	8		189	16	460aaa–7	
	9		190	16	460aaa–8	
101–293	1, 2		192	13	23	nt
101–296	1 to 4		197 to 199	31	5111	nt
22 101–298	1		201	18	175	nt
	2		201	18	175	nt
	3(a)		201, 202	18	prec. 175, 175 to 178	
	3(b)		203	18	2516	
	3(c)		203	18	prec. 1	
24 101–301	1(a)(2)		206	25	450m–1	
	1(a)(3)		206	25	608	
	1(b)		206	25	608	
	2(a)(1) to (3)		206	25	450b	
	2(a)(4)		206	25	450c	
	2(a)(5)		206	25	450e–1	
	2(a)(6)		206	25	450i	
	2(a)(7)		207	25	450j	
	2(a)(8), (9)		207	25	450j–1	
	2(a)(10)		207	25	450m	
	2(b)		207	25	450m–1	
	2(c)		207	5	3371	
	3(a)		207	25	478–1	
	3(b)		207	25	473	
	3(c)		207	25	477	
	4		207	25	713f	nt
	5(a)		207	25	2019	
	5(b)		207	25	2508	

644

statutes under which they function, their subordinate units, and other organizational data, as well as the types of information each agency can provide. It is an excellent general reference and informational tool.

Many of the loose-leaf services, mentioned in passing above, follow the publications of these agencies and supply their subscribers with the most recent changes in timely fashion. Additionally, electronic versions of the government publications and official reports mentioned above, as well as some of the loose-leaf services, such as *BNA*, are available on the Internet and in CD-ROM versions.

2.0532 *Federal Court Rules.* Federal courts establish rules of procedure to guarantee a uniform system of presentation of cases. These rules are subject to controversy and interpretation, and the courts are sometimes requested to decide the meaning of a rule. Court resolutions of questions about the proper interpretation of rules from 1940 to the present will be found in a series of volumes called the *Federal Rules Decisions*®. The *Federal Rules Service* is a similar publication which reports on decisions interpreting and construing federal rules. Both are excellent tools for researching questions concerning the federal rules of civil procedure. Of course, the U.S. Government Printing Office publishes *Rules of Civil Procedure for U.S. District Courts* and all other federal rules. This official publication, like all other official publications, provides only the text of the material without reference to cases. The unofficial publications by the commercial firms, such as the *Federal Civil Rules Handbook*, provide explanations of the meaning and intent of the rules in the form of footnoted cases.

2.0533 *State Reports.* Each state has a similar range of statutory authority controlling or directing the lives of its citizens. The same basic procedures for proposing legislation, introducing bills, and enacting them into law is followed whether the state legislature meets annually or every other year. The executive branch of the state government (the governor and the regulatory and administrative agencies) generates executive orders and rules and regulations in a manner similar to the federal system. In many cases, however, there are areas of overlapping responsibilities between the state and federal jurisdictions that must be considered by the researcher. Some of these areas are education, health and welfare, housing, occupational health and safety, and utility regulation. Great care must be exercised to determine the exact problem and whether it is responsive to state statute, federal statute, or both. The basic sources of state statutory law are:

a. State Constitution. The constitution of each state is the ultimate source of the laws for that state. Here, again, check to be certain some article or section has not been amended or repealed. The state's highest court, the supreme court in most states, is the final authority on the interpretation of the state's constitutional provisions, though some of those rulings may be appealed for decision by the U.S. Supreme Court where a conflict between rights under the state and the U.S. Constitution are alleged.

b. State Codes and Statutes. These are the laws of the state, passed by the legislature and signed by the governor (or passed over his or her veto). Once the governor signs the legislation, the statute is published as a session law and consolidated chronologically with the current legislative session's accumulation. If the particular bill provided for the acceptance of a code in its codified form, it will be found both in the chronologic and the code version of the law. The researcher will find parallels between the research aids for the federal system and the research aids for the state statutory law. Each state has a printing office that supplies official copies of the statutes and codes. Similarly, there are commercial publishers that produce the unofficial publications. In California, for example, there are two publications that cover the state's codes: *West's Annotated California Codes*, and *Deering's California Codes*. California's codes are divided topically much like the *U.S. Code* and the *U.S.C.A.* The arrangement of the content is similar to the *U.S.C.A.* in that it provides quick reference in the code to the statutes for each section, the historical notes, library references, and the derivation of any section, as well as the West Topic and Key Number references for research in other West sources. Clearly, care must be taken to ensure the latest amendments are included. Each volume is updated annually with pocket parts containing amendments to the sections in the volume, as well as additional annotations. (Annotations are compilations of cases and historical matter dealing with various aspects of a code or statute, with short summaries of decisions and case citations. They contain cases ruling both for and against.) Always check the volume to determine its date of publication and for a pocket part. If there is a pocket part, check to see if there have been any changes. If there is no pocket part, it may be the most recent replacement volume. However, if there are several years between the publication date in the front of the volume and the time of the research, take the extra step of checking for a missing pocket part. CD-ROM versions of the state statutes, with and without annotations are also available. This provides better searching capabilities, but is not updated as frequently (annually) unless the law firm is with a service which provides updates of the CD-ROM as laws are modified, repealed, etc., even in special sessions of the legislature. The librarian in the office or in the nearest major law library can be of assistance. The volumes also contain legislative history, cross-references, and collateral references. Each book of codes and statutes reflects the effective dates of the statutes and the date the statutes were passed in a given year.

State regulatory and administrative agencies are empowered by the legislature that created them to propose and publish (after public comment or hearing) rules and regulations necessary for the discharge of their responsibilities. Often they also are empowered to enforce their own regulations, subject to appeal, of course. Many times these state agencies parallel federal ones and must work in concert with them on matters of mutual concern but within their specified areas of jurisdiction. *Caveat:* Research in statutes alone is ineffectual unless the cases (cited in the annotated code volumes) are studied to determine how the courts construed and interpreted the rules. It is obvious that finding cases analogous to the researcher's problem is helpful, whether the decisions support or refute the client's desired position. The attorney, armed with the past decisions, can adapt the theory, choice of jurisdictions, and strategy or at least advise the client of the most effective and economic course of action.

2.054 Case Approach to the Law

Case research is clearly the backbone of all legal endeavors in the United States. Even in cases of "first impression," where the court never before has heard or decided the disputed issue, the decision is influenced by the principles and reasoning of the courts in past similar cases and decisions. Sometimes, a dissent (the individual opinion of a judge disagreeing with the majority decision) becomes the choice of later judges who recognize that changes in social structure or mores call for a change in the law. These landmark cases do not come about without persuasion based on logic and the views presented in past decisions, by study groups (such as the American Law Institute), and in law review articles, among other sources. Reading and distinguishing the cases is essential. Reporting the results of the research in easily recognizable form contributes to the value of the research by aiding the reader's understanding and appreciation of the views researcher/writer.

2.0541 Case Citation. The uniform procedure for citing cases is:

a. by the parties surnames (full names of business entities should be included);
b. the volume number of the reporter containing the case;
c. the abbreviated name of the reporter;
d. the page number where the case begins;
e. the parallel citation (if the case is published in two separate law reports);
f. the date; and, if necessary,
g. the court that rendered the decision.

The latter is required if the reporters (official and parallel) in which the case is published contain decisions of more than one court. It is essential to know which of the courts rendered the decision because the authority of one court may be more persuasive than another or even mandatory. The Harvard Law Review Association publishes *A Uniform System of Citation*, (also known as *"The Blue Book"*) which illustrates the proper way to cite cases, statutes, and other legal authorities. The researcher is cautioned to follow these rules rather than to follow the form used in an authority. It is not uncommon for incomplete citations to appear within a published authority.

"Parallel authority," mentioned above, refers to the fact that some cases are printed in more than one publication. When this occurs, one will be designated as the official reporter and the other as the unofficial reporter. As a general rule, the state-authorized publication is the official or parallel cite and the commercially published copy of the decision is the unofficial cite. When the same decision is published in more than one location, the citations are referred to as parallel cites. *A Uniform System of Citation* includes a table of the federal and state governments and indicates the appropriate method of citing to the official (and unofficial, if any) publication. It should be noted that many states no longer publish their own cases and instead adopt the commercial publication as the official citation. In these states, the case is published in one location, so there is only one citation reference to a report. Parallel cites are not generally used in the statutory citation of laws that have been incorporated into a code.

Citations should omit the first names or initials of natural persons who are plaintiffs or defendants (except in administrative cases), but the entire name of fictitious entities, such as companies or corporations, should be used. For example, cite *Smythe v. Jones*, NOT *John Smythe v. Earl Jones*; BUT *J. M. Smythe Co. v. Smith and Sons Inc.*, NOT *Smythe v. Smith et al.*

With the advent of the availability of court decisions, statutes and regulations on the Internet, published directly by the courts and other electronic services, a system of "neutral citation" not dependant on the national or official reporter volume and page number has also become acceptable. These citation forms are set forth in the latest edition of *A Uniform System of Citation*. An example of citing to other electronic publications which appear on the Internet appeared in the U.S. Supreme Court opinion *Denver Area Education Telecommunications Consortium, Inc., v. FCC, et al*, 116 S.Ct. 2374, 64 LW 4706 (June 1996), at footnote 4. The form of the citation was: Author (when known), Title, Date last modified (or visited), URL (which is the Internet address), and looked like this: "[4]See, *e.g.*, Lynch, Speedier Access: Cable and Phone Companies Compete, at http://www.usatoday.com/life/bonus/cb006.htm (June 17, 1996) (describing cable modem technology); Gateway 2000 ships first Destination big screen TV-PCS, at http://www.gw2k.com/corpinfo/press/1996/destin.htm (April 29, 1996) (describing computer with both cable TV and Internet reception capability)." The most widely referred to source for citing to the Internet is Janice Walker's "MLA Style Citations of Electronic Sources." http://www.cas.usf.edu/english/walker/mla.html (October 13, 1996), and Harnack and Kleppinger's "Beyond the MLA Hand-

book: Documenting Electronic Sources on the Internet." June 10, 1996. <http://www.falcon.
eku.edu/honors/beyond-mla> (October 13, 1996).

2.0542 Federal Reports.   Certain federal cases are reported both officially and unofficially.
U.S. Supreme Court cases are reported officially in *U.S. Reports. Caveat:* Volumes one through
ninety must be cited with the name of the official court reporter who compiled the volume and
the volume number, for example, *Marbury v. Madison*, 5 U.S. (1 Cranch) 137. There were a
number of different reporters over the years who imposed their own numbers on the volumes
they compiled. Citing their name and volume obviates any confusion. The unofficial reporters
include the *Supreme Court Reporter* (a portion of the national reporter system), which began at
Volume 106 of the *U.S. Reports*, and the *Lawyer's Edition of the U.S. Supreme Court Reports.* Some
researchers like *Supreme Court Reporter* since it incorporates the topic and key number system
in the annotation, while others prefer the *Lawyer's Edition* series because they include a summary
of the arguments of counsel on both sides of the question.

The U.S. Supreme Court publishes its decisions immediately on ruling on an issue as a "slip"
decision; slip opinions from the Court are available electronically on the day of the ruling or by
mail subscriptions. Subscribers to the mail service receive their copy about two weeks after the
decision is announced. There are unofficial loose-leaf services that fill the same function but
even more quickly than the mail subscription to the official report. Subscribers to both the
Supreme Court Reporter and the *Lawyer's Edition* also receive advance sheets containing the
decisions as they will appear in the forthcoming bound volumes. Slip opinions are also available
on WESTLAW and on LEXIS. The U.S. Supreme Court and many state Supreme Courts, also
publish the text of recent decisions on the Internet.

U.S. Courts of Appeals decisions are originally published in nominative reports (reports
carrying the name and volume number of the reporter who compiled them) for each federal
court, both district courts and circuit courts of appeals, creating a confusing and voluminous
problem. West Publishing Company accumulated the most important federal decisions, both of
district and courts of appeal cases, and published them in a thirty-volume set called *Federal
Cases*, dated up to 1880. U.S. District Courts and Courts of Appeals stopped publishing volumes
of decisions, and now publish some (but not all) of their decisions as slip opinions. West
accumulated the slip opinions and published them in bound volumes as the *Federal Reports*
until 1932. In that year, West began the *Federal Supplement*, which accumulated the selected
district court and customs court decisions, leaving the *Federal Reporter* to cover only the decisions
of the courts of appeals, court of patent appeals, and the court of claims.

In 1940, West began publishing the *Federal Rules Decisions®* series, which covers decisions
of all the federal courts on procedural law matters as well as articles or speeches on the topic.

Another source for federal case reporting is the *American Law Reports—Federal*, which
includes specially selected and annotated federal court decisions. Citation to any of the above
"unofficial" reporters is usually acceptable under local district or appellate court rules, a matter
easily checked by examination of the court rules in the jurisdiction of the researcher's interest.

The *Supreme Court Reporter*, the *Federal Reporter*, and the *Federal Supplement*, are part of
the national reporter system and use the West topic and key number system.

2.0543 The State Court Reports.   Most states have official reports. In California, for example,
there are two official reports: *California Reports*, containing reports of cases decided by the
California Supreme Court since March 1850, and *California Appellate Reports*, containing reports

of cases determined in the state's district courts of appeal since May 1905. Not all state decisions are published in the official reports, because the supreme court can mark some decisions "Not to be Published in Official Reports."

California decisions too recent to be bound are reported in paperback volumes called "advance sheets," that contain both supreme court and appeal decisions, appropriately paginated as they will be in their respective future bound volumes.

Many states do not have a satisfactory method of reporting recent decisions, and the delay in publication of the decisions is a distinct disadvantage to the lawyer and the researcher. As a result, about one-fifth of the states have discontinued production of an official state reports system in favor of a commercial series, which is more efficient to use, current, and indexed. In such states, the series is designated as the official reporter of the state; for example, the *Southern Reporter, Florida Cases* is the official reporter for Florida in lieu of the *Florida Reporter*, which ceased publication in 1948.

The *Southern Reporter, Florida Cases* is a unit of the national reporter system developed by West Publishing Company, which includes the federal units described above and the following state and regional reporters:

Atlantic Reporter: contains cases for Connecticut, Delaware. Maine, Maryland, New Hampshire, New Jersey, Pennsylvania, Rhode Island, and Vermont.
North Eastern Reporter: contains cases for Illinois, Indiana, Massachusetts, New York (court of appeals only), and Ohio.
North Western Reporter: contains cases for Iowa, Michigan, Minnesota, Nebraska, North Dakota, South Dakota, and Wisconsin.
Pacific Reporter: contains cases for Arizona, California (supreme court only), Colorado, Idaho, Kansas, Montana, Nevada, New Mexico, Oklahoma, Oregon, Utah, Washington, Wyoming, Alaska, and Hawaii.
South Eastern Reporter: contains cases for Georgia, North Carolina, South Carolina, Virginia, and West Virginia.
South Western Reporter: contains cases for Arkansas, Kentucky, Missouri, Tennessee, and Texas.
Southern Reporter: contains cases for Alabama, Florida, Louisiana, and Mississippi.
New York Supplement: contains cases for New York only from 1887 to the present.
California Reporter: contains all California cases from the supreme court, the district courts of appeal, and the appellate division of the California Superior Courts since 1960.

Since the inception of the national reporter system in the late 1800s, the states (which had or have official reporters) had parallel reporters—one official and the other unofficial, the commercially published edition. Many decisions reported in the unofficial reporters were not reported in the official reporters; this, together with the headnoting system, makes research in the unofficial publications a bit more thorough and informative than that allowed in the official reporters. Unofficial reporters published by West will contain the same topic name and key numbers that are used in all West digest series, making it possible to research the same issue in several jurisdictions very quickly.

All reporters, whether official or unofficial, include similar elements in their publication format, such as:

1. The docket number assigned by the court and the date of the decision;
2. The full caption of the case;

3. A summary of the case;
4. Headnotes;
5. Identity of counsel for the parties, including any counsel submitting briefs as *amicus curiae* (friend of the court); and
6. The actual opinion.

The actual opinion of the court on the subjects at issue is the only "authority" in the reports. Unless otherwise indicated, the summary is prepared by the editor of the reporter to assist the researcher in deciding whether to read the entire opinion or not. While this is helpful, it is not authority and, conceivably, may be in error. The headnotes (short paragraphs with numbers) list the legal issues and points of law covered in the opinion but are not authority. The headnotes are prepared by the editor and are a great aid in quickly determining (1) whether the opinion deals with or relates in any way to the researcher's current specific problem and (2) where in the opinion the particular point of law covered by the headnote is discussed. They are also very important when updating research by Shepardizing (*see* Section 2.06). The actual language in the opinion must be checked to verify that what the summary and the headnotes indicate is truly supported by the opinion text.

The opinion usually starts with the name of the judge writing it, though opinions may be written as *per curiam* decisions—those written expressing the court's view (even if all the judges were not there), or as *en banc* views—those written with all members of the court present and agreeing on the decision. The opinion is followed by a statement of the fact situation of the case, analysis of the points of law argued by the various parties, and the court's opinion and decision on each point raised. The court then states its decision(s) on the case as a whole. Because judges sometimes disagree, a decision may also carry one or more dissenting or minority opinions. The footnotes can also be helpful in finding supporting cases. Many lawyers start by reading the decision at the end of the report as an aid in understanding the language of the opinion that resulted in that decision.

As mentioned in other sections, many state courts opinions are now available on the Internet, although most such state court sites do not contain cases any older than 1990.

2.06 Use of *Shepard's Citations* or "Shepardizing"

Query: "Can the cases and laws be brought up to date? Have any of the cases been reversed on appeal or overruled by subsequent cases? Have the laws been amended or repealed? In essence, is our authority really valid authority?"

Shepard's Citations are published for the cases in the U.S. Supreme Court reports, federal reports, National Labor Relations Board (NLRB) reports, some other federal departments reports, the national reporter system, and state reports. This material is accumulated through searches of the various court decisions, agencies' decisions, opinions of attorneys general, articles in legal periodicals, and annotated reports, and is available in electronic editions as well as print.

Shepard's publishes for statutory citations as well, including the *U.S. Constitution, U.S. Code, U.S. Statutes at Large*, treaties and other international agreements, United States court rules, state constitutions, codes, session laws, municipal charters, ordinances, and state court rules. These resources are also available in both print and electronic media, such as CD-ROM and via on-line services such as WESTLAW and LEXIS-NEXIS.

Every reported case is collected and examined at Shepard's, and the cases and statutes mentioned in each reported case are recorded and printed under their own citations in the Shepard's publications. By this process, the history of the cited cases and laws is developed. Editors read the cases and, where required, note the history and treatment of the case. A table of abbreviations for consultation is provided at the front of each volume. If the same case is affirmed on appeal, a lowercase *a* appears in front of the citation; *cc* represents a connected case that is a different case but arising out of the same subject matter; capital *D* stands for dismissed, *m* for modified, *r* for reversed, *s* for same case, and *v* for vacated. Capital *S* for superseded case, and parentheses indicate parallel citations. In the treatment of the case, *c* indicates criticized, *d* distinguished, *e* explained, *f* followed, *h* harmonized, *j* dissenting opinion, capital *L* limited, *o* overruled, *p* parallel, and *q* questioned. If any of these symbols appears at the front of a citation, for example, "s 167 FS 405," (*see* Exhibit 2-9 under Vol. 364, page 339), check the table of abbreviations at the front of the volume to confirm what the abbreviation means.

Frequently a case will cite another case for only one point of law in the cited case that may have had as many as twenty points of law analyzed in headnotes. In order to indicate to the researcher that the citing case discussed only one point of law, a smaller number, called a superior figure, appears before the page number a little elevated from the line of type to show which headnote relates to the discussion in the citing case: for example, "377 US[1] 555" (*see* Exhibit 2-9 under Vol. 364, page 339).

As stated before, the resources of the law library will control the scope of the research to a large extent. This chapter covers a variety of the Shepard's publications in the hope that the legal assistant has access to some of the titles or at least similar titles so that these techniques may be applied to the resources at hand.

2.061 Case Research

The scope of case research in *Shepard's* can be limited to the state jurisdiction, expanded to neighboring states, to federal cases, or to all reported cases in accordance with the titles selected.

2.062 State *Shepard's Citations*

Shepard's Citations cover every state with volumes listing every case in that state that has been subsequently discussed in any later case in that state or federal system. The state *Shepard's* edition also incorporates any state case that is not reported in the national reporter system (primarily those decided prior to 1887). *ALR* and legal periodical citations are included in the *Citator*. The first time a case is mentioned in *Shepard's Citations*, the parallel citation to the National Reporter System is given but not repeated in subsequent volumes.

Every unit of West's national reporter system has a companion *Shepard's Citator*. To use the contents, convert the state citation to the regional reporter citation. Under the reporter citation will be listed every case discussed in any later case in that regional reporter and all other reporters in the national reporter system as well as federal reporters. *ALR* and *American Bar Association Journal* citations are also included. The first time a case is mentioned in *Shepard's Citations*, the parallel citation to the state reports is given but not repeated in subsequent volumes.

2.063 Federal *Shepard's Citations*

Shepard's United States Citations and *Shepard's Federal Citations* list every case citing the federal cases in alphabetical order by state, given the state or national reporter citation.

EXHIBIT 2-9 Sample Page from *Shepard's*

UNITED STATES SUPREME COURT REPORTS				Vol. 364
Cir. 4	237FS¹566	456FS³673	j306F2d¹476	255So2d69
537FS393	CtCl	506FS³2	313F2d¹38	Md
	198CCL624	541FS¹872	314F2d¹228	226Md600
– 297 –	461F2d1379	76FRD³600	355F2d¹362	174A2d783
s278F2d446	Mo	82FRD⁴609	362F2d¹120	NY
Cir. D.C.	352SW681	94FRD³241	410F2d81	33Msc2d521
292F2d756	NY	Cir. 7	445F2d832	227S2d87
293F2d153	13Ap2d209	346F2d³251	191FS¹683	Ore
294F2d221	215S2d191	f525F2d¹764	d222FS¹986	229Or246
j294F2d228	Pa	408FS⁴1161	238FS¹757	230Or6
547F2d699	497Pa63	68FRD⁴385	242FS¹298	235Or66
Cir. 2	498Pa535	85FRD20	326FS530	366P2d886
380F2d777	439A2d103	98FRD721	Cir. 3	367P2d400
205FS836	448A2d1048	13BRW860	486F2d¹1105	383P2d1004
	Wis	18BRW⁴798	330FS¹496	Pa
– 298 –	53Wis2d400	Cir. 8	361FS21	222PaS372
s371US807	192NW897	476F2d⁴60	28FRD440	295A2d100
s371US907	47ABA458	Cir. 9	28FRD495	Wash
s371US944		316F2d⁴789	39FRD¹340	63W2d323
s374US203	**– 310 –**	337F2d¹750	Cir. 4	387P2d80
s177FS398	(5LE8)	f399F2d895	344F2d¹742	
s184FS381	(81SC13)	481F2d¹1190	351F2d¹422	**– 336 –**
s195FS518	s361US958	487F2d¹675	202FS¹664	**Case 1**
s201FS815	s364US938	708F2d⁴1492	218FS¹597	s76Nev157
Cir. 3	s270F2d290	38FRD²197	237FS¹65	Nev
j465F2d863	s301F2d133	Cir. 10	Cir. 5	s350P2d724
Cir. 9	379US¹158	446FS⁴908	286F2d¹752	
77FRD36	401US⁴335	76FRD346	290F2d¹398	**Case 2**
Cir. 10	406US¹17	Alk	290F2d¹431	s18Il2d506
689F2d914	j449US926	499P2d602	291F2d¹420	Ill
Md	52FC€1271	632P2d543	297F2d¹417	s165NE322
228Md247	Cir. D.C.	DC	319F2d¹366	
228Md259	424F2d⁴907	305A2d530	322F2d¹159	**– 337 –**
179A2d702	Cir. 2	468A2d1342	335F2d¹197	**Case 1**
179A2d709	392F2d384	Ind	346F2d¹874	s364US925
	522F2d158	263Ind195	405F2d⁴949	s170OS393
– 299 –	f541F2d¹952	325NE843	585F2d¹741	Ohio
s279F2d289	568F2d⁴906	Mich	249FS¹379	s165NE642
s290F2d858	668F2d108	99McA858	331FS1289	
Cir. 6	226FS²372	390Mch656	426FS¹375	**Case 2**
311F2d47	349FS705	213NW136	514FS¹1204	s359Mch430
	359FS914	298NW870	Cir. 6	Mich
– 300 –	440FS1092	Mo	340F2d¹730	s102NW552
s271Ala22	445FS⁴722	572SW867	662F2d¹434	
Ala	506FS⁴308	Ohio	305FS¹1185	**– 338 –**
s122So2d280	63FRD50	33€A228	Cir. 7	**Case 1**
	66FRD⁴228	293NE329	322FS519	Mo
– 301 –	82FRD4	Ore	Cir. 8	s335SW118
(5LE1)	23BRW283	271Or311	401FS17	
s185Kan274	Cir. 3	532P2d4	Cir. 9	**Case 2**
Kan	312F2d³372	Tenn	d343F2d¹221	s171OS192
s341P2d1002	407F2d673	637SW884	369F2d¹300	Ohio
Cir. D.C.	420F2d⁴1276	Wash	371F2d¹783	s168NE409
419F2d¹312	534F2d569	100W2d349	495F2d916	
Cir. 1	663F2d⁴425	670P2d243	d203FS¹725	**– 339 –**
f254FS¹255	346FS⁴994	MFP§6.16	213FS¹356	(5LE110)
369FS¹1114	382FS474		Cir. 11	(81SC125)
Cir. 2	484FS409	**– 325 –**	224FS¹249	s362US916
190FS¹625	519FS¹562	(5LE20)	Calif	s270F2d594
Cir. 3	561FS¹137	(81SC6)	228CA2d697	s167FS405
356F2d¹654	58FRD447	s362US909	44CA3d355	j366US¹573
347FS1254	81FRD³662	s271F2d194	39CaR763	369US¹229
Cir. 5	89FRD64	j375US212	118CaR518	369US¹244
333F2d¹640	96FRD⁴235	379US¹672	Conn	j369US¹284
523F2d1286	Cir. 4	51USLW	153Ct78	j369US¹335
319FS522	484FS312	[4103	171Ct276	d372US¹376
Cir. 6	37FRD⁴435	63MC935	214A2d366	j372US¹386
421F2d¹765	Cir. 5	66MC1561	368A2d230	376US56
489FS¹43	413F2d1281	67MC2155	Fla	376US¹58
Cir. 9	616F2d¹747	Cir. 1	139So2d403	j376US¹59
377FS¹152	639F2d⁴1284	434F2d¹122	Ill	j376US¹68
Cir. 10	661F2d¹52	608F2d18	79Il2A594	374FS¹377
513F2d137	Cir. 6	608F2d¹20	399NE175	376FS1352
620F2d779	429FS183	Cir. 2	La	411FS¹654
		297F2d¹11	260La46	568FS¹1460

379US¹143	j568FS1461
380US¹540	Cir. 1
383US¹311	376F2d¹541
j383US¹672	570F2d¹1075
385US¹130	295FS¹206
387US¹108	385FS¹882
d391US¹384	405FS¹1394
393US¹391	j451FS¹154
j393US589	70FRD¹655
j396US453	Cir. 2
j398US¹193	j294F2d¹44
400US¹126	j379F2d497
j400US¹283	482F2d¹265
400US¹389	c482F2d266
402US141	510F2d514
403US¹5	e510F2d¹522
d403US¹149	j510F2d530
j403US¹177	512F2d49
403US¹225	e191FS¹184
j403US¹264	196FS¹762
405US¹70	202FS¹744
j406US¹576	202FS¹754
407US¹194	202FS755
j407US¹483	d211FS¹466
j408US¹390	j211FS¹468
409US¹521	j211FS¹473
412US¹751	d214FS¹901
413US¹368	j229FS¹779
j418US¹778	d238FS¹926
j418US¹808	260FS¹208
422US378	d266FS¹325
425US¹142	j271FS¹16
j425US¹148	271FS¹499
426US¹254	290FS¹883
429US¹266	j311FS¹55
430US¹165	341FS¹148
430US¹170	d377FS¹1166
430US¹179	386FS7
j430US¹181	429FS¹212
j430US¹511	473FS¹495
433US¹414	476FS323
442US¹272	f535FS¹1017
j442US283	Cir. 3
445US¹62	j535F2d¹812
e446US¹85	563F2d¹582
j446US102	564F2d¹141
j446US127	d648F2d¹182
j446US214	233FS¹620
j458US652	262FS¹828
51USLW	j262FS¹857
[4858	419FS¹273
51USLW	468FS¹951
[4861	536FS¹584
j51USLW	567FS¹1515
[5116	Cir. 4
Cir. D.C.	397F2d¹41
395F2d587	442F2d¹572
452F2d¹1306	459F2d¹097
459F2d1247	j459F2d¹1100
465F2d¹638	j459F2d¹1109
j481F2d530	462F2d1068
j489F2d¹1174	j462F2d1078
520F2d¹70	463F2d56
j559F2d694	j473F2d¹1021
593F2d1111	573F2d¹190
661F2d1303	588F2d¹424
255FS¹299	664F2d919
j333FS¹590	710F2d¹135
349FS¹729	198FS¹503
d354FS¹1030	245FS¹245
374FS¹377	d267FS267
376FS1352	269FS848
411FS¹654	d276FS¹668
568FS¹1460	313FS386

– 336 –		
230US6	j369US¹284	

Additional circled entries: s167FS405, j366US¹573, 377US¹555, j377US¹613, j377US¹744, 378US¹287

Continued
297

To research a federal case in Florida, for instance, consult the proper federal *Shepard's* and find a Florida case or a *Southern Reporter* citation. Then take that citation to the *Florida Shepard's Citations* or the *Southern Reporter Citations* and research that case through the state or regional system.

2.064 Statutory Research

Knowing the wording of a law may be insufficient to resolve a controversy between litigants, and resorting to court interpretation of the law is required. *Shepard's Citations* exist for state and federal statutory research, giving the citations to cases interpreting the laws as well as editorial notations as to changes in the law by legislative bodies.

Armed with the proper citation to state or federal constitutions, codified law, or session laws, it is possible to determine what courts have mentioned the laws in their opinions as well as subsequent changes in the law. Cases holding a law unconstitutional will have *U* prior to the citation alerting the researcher to this important fact. Tables of abbreviations at the front of the volume explain the meaning of the symbols used in the text. Again, law review articles, attorney general opinions, and *ALR* annotations specifically identifying the law will be cited in *Shepard's*.

Laws frequently are known by popular names but cannot be identified in indexes that way. *Shepard's* incorporates a "Table of Acts by Popular Names or Short Titles" in its statutory division as well as in a separate publication, *Shepard's Acts and Cases by Popular Names*. This is frequently the best source to consult for the proper statutory citation.

Municipal or county ordinances are included in the state *Shepard's Citations* when they have been interpreted and construed by the courts. These are usually arranged in alphabetical order by geographical unit and then alphabetically within the unit by catchword identification of the ordinance. Usually an index accompanies these for easy identification.

2.065 Court Rules

State and federal court rules can be Shepardized either in the state *Shepard's Citations* or the *Shepard's Federal Citations*. The latest cases are cited under the number of the rule along with changes in the rules and periodical citations.

2.066 Administrative Decisions

Shepard's United States Administrative Citations include other decisions by administrative agencies, such as the tax court, Interior Department, Federal Communications Commission, Federal Trade Commission, Treasury decisions, opinions of the Attorney General of the United States, and many others. Again, these decisions will be included if they have been mentioned specifically by name in later decisions. Notes will accompany the citations of subsequent changes in the points of law considered.

2.067 *Shepard's Federal Labor Law Citations*

This very specialized system includes decisions and laws relating to labor. NLRB decisions and orders form the basis for the content. Extensive coverage of periodical literature is included. One of the distinct advantages of this title is the reporting of the parallel citations for the different commercial services publishing editions of labor materials. Patents and trademarks are also the subjects of specialized treatment in *Shepard's United States Citations*.

2.068 Law Review Articles

Shepard's Law Review Citations lists law review articles by citation and subsequent articles and court decisions that cite the original article. This permits one to locate a good article on a given subject and then trace it through later literature for other good articles on the same subject. New in 1974 was *Shepard's Federal Law Citations in Selected Law Reviews*. This compiles references from nineteen law reviews to federal court cases, federal rules decisions, and the *U.S. Constitution*, *U.S. Code*, and federal court rules. From these federal sources of primary authority, it is now possible to pinpoint law review articles that mention them specifically by name.

2.069 Supplements

Supplements to *Shepard's Citations* take the form of bound volumes and cumulative paper pamphlets in red or ivory color, with individual advance sheets in white. As information accumulates, the red pamphlet is revised and reissued with instructions to discard previous pamphlets. Be sure to check the notice on the front cover of the pamphlet as to the parts of the series that make up the whole unit of *Shepard's Citations*. The hard copy supplements to *Shepard's Citations* are published and delivered several weeks behind the available information. With on-line services such as WESTLAW or LEXIS, the time for *Shepard's Citations* updates moves to within 24–48 hours. Many judges (or their clerks) will check case law submitted via WESTLAW or LEXIS to confirm it is good law before a ruling. It is crucial that all memoranda are citing good law when submitted to the court to as close to the date of filing as possible.

Total reliance on *Shepard's Citations* without substantiation from other sources could be fatal. *Shepard's* gives the history and treatment of a case by judges in later decisions. It does not cite all cases on a point of law. It should not be used as a substitute for a researcher bringing the search up-to-date through the reporter or statute being searched. *Shepard's* is designed as a complementary aid to research. Cases can cite other cases, not for the point of law involved, but for the amount of damages or some other phase of the case; therefore, cases cited in *Shepard's* must be checked for their pertinence to the question at hand. On the other hand, a case can completely change the areas of the law by a grand, sweeping statement that "all former decisions not in accord with this opinion are overruled." If such statements include no reference to cases affected (either by name or citation), they never will appear in *Shepard's Citations*.

The use of *Shepard's Citations* may yield more cases on the subject of inquiry and shed some light on the direction the law is taking in the area. In addition, it should turn up related sources that were not uncovered in prior research. Finding a case in *Shepard's Citations* may at first glance seem to be confusing, but it is easily resolved by consulting the back side of the title page to each volume. This page indicates the volumes of citing materials included in the *Shepard's* volume. Start with the first volume of *Shepard's Citations* (of any series) and examine the contents indicated on the spine. If the case or statute is of early vintage, in all likelihood it will be in this volume. Examine every subsequent volume for newer cases, law review articles, and other sources that cite the given case or statute. However, if the case is a relatively recent one, it may not be in the first volume. Advance forward through the volumes until you find the first mention of the case citation of interest. This procedure should become apparent when the volume itself is used, not just read about.

2.07 Review of the Basic Research Process

1. If unfamiliar with the particular area of law, locate a reference that discusses it, such as a legal encyclopedia or other commentary.
2. Identify a number of different terms that pertain to the topic of research. A legal thesaurus or dictionary may be helpful in doing this task.
3. If the research question involves or is likely to involve a statute, go to the subject index of the appropriate code and use the terms previously identified to locate the appropriate reference to a statutory chapter (title) and section number.
4. After locating the statute, read the text and examine any relevant annotations that might follow. If the allocation of billable hours permits, check the legislative history (analysis) available either in the firm's legal research file system or other official sources.
5. If the issue is not statutory, or if there are no annotations, go to the digest. Again, use the identified terms with the descriptive word index (subject index) of the digest. These will help locate the topic and key number (section) for finding annotations or case summaries (also called headnotes) on the specific subject.
6. After reading the annotations, select those most applicable to the case at hand and locate the complete decision in the reporter system by using the citation given in the annotation. This citation will contain the case name, the reporter volume and page, and the year of the decision.
7. After reading the complete judicial opinions, note those that most closely resemble the research issue and general facts of the case at hand. Generally, those decisions that come from the same jurisdiction and most closely parallel the case being researched will be the most persuasive.
8. Prepare the correct citation for those authorities that are going to be used to respond to the research issue. Develop a handwritten outline, based on the priority of the cases, and the issues each represents. This is the beginning of your memoranda and, because these notes may be discarded after preliminary research, should be only a rough map so you won't get lost along the way. Then go to the *Shepard's Citations* volume for the reporter where the case or statute is published, and using the volume and page number, locate the *Shepard's Citations* volume for that particular case or statute. The volume and page will appear in boldface and any subsequent references will appear immediately below.
9. In all stages of research, be aware that most publications, whether commentary, statutes, digests, or *Shepard's*, contain supplements or pocket parts with the most up-to-date information. These must be consulted to determine the most current law on a particular subject.

2.071 Let's Research

As you prepare to do your research, get ready to be alert, dig out facts needed to prove the client's side of the case, alert the lawyer to strong cases adverse to the client's position, and find or distinguish cases in rebuttal. Above all, be prepared to accept constructive criticism. Such criticism is an invaluable learning aid, and a lawyer who takes time to give thoughtful advice and constructive criticism is one who is interested in helping the legal assistant advance and improve. One common criticism of a new legal assistant's work is that it does not express the lawyer's own personal style. In both legal research and legal writing, a legal assistant should try to style his or her work in a way that complements the attorney's. Don't be offended if the lawyer doesn't accept the offered writings in every instance or totally rewrites a proffered offering; try to think as the lawyer does and gear the style of the work product to his or her liking.

The research examples given here will be simple; they are illustrations of the sequence of researching and will pertain to one point of law only.

2.072 Facts—Example No. 1

In 1994, Sam Smith (plaintiff) sued General Hospital (defendant) and other medical practitioners at the hospital (codefendants) for malpractice. In 1985, that suit was settled and an order of dismissal, with prejudice, was entered by the court.

In 1997, General Hospital (plaintiff), represented by the legal assistant's firm, filed a collection suit against Sam Smith (now the defendant), in the amount of $1,800, representing the 1994 hospitalization expense. Smith filed an answer and counterclaim, alleging malicious prosecution among other things. In Smith's counterclaim, the amount sought for relief exceeded the jurisdictional dollar amount in Municipal Court and the action was transferred to Superior Court.

The legal assistant for the firm representing General Hospital is asked to determine whether (1) the counterclaim of Smith states a valid cause of action for malicious prosecution; and (2) can an action for malicious prosecution be raised by way of a counterclaim.

A review of defendant Smith's counterclaim by the legal assistant reveals that Smith alleged the amount of the bill ($1,800) was included in the settlement of his medical malpractice claim in 1994 and that General Hospital waived payment of the bill as part of the settlement at that time. General Hospital's position is that the settlement only included the cause of action for malpractice against the hospital, that the release signed by Smith released only General Hospital from such a claim, and the release neither contained a provision for waiving the amount of the bill nor was authority for waiving the bill given by the hospital in settlement of that case.

Beginning with a secondary source, such as *Corpus Juris Secundum* (*also see* 2.052, *Secondary Authority* and 2.061d, *Legal Encyclopedias, supra*) or in California perhaps, *Witkin, Summary of California Law, 8th edition,* the legal assistant determines that to establish a cause of action for "malicious prosecution of a civil proceeding" a plaintiff must plead and prove three points:

a. that the prior action was commenced by or at the direction of the defendant and was pursued to a legal termination in his (the Plaintiff's) favor;
b. that the prior action was brought without probable cause, and
c. was initiated with malice.

In reading the secondary sources the legal assistant noted the cases cited or referred to and now begins reading them. The legal assistant quickly learns that malicious prosecution is a cause of action not favored by law. Shepardizing (*see* Shepardizing, *supra*) develops cases the legal assistant reads and finds that malicious prosecution cannot be raised by way of cross-complaint. The legal assistant's memorandum to the lawyer might take the form shown in Section 2.074.

2.073 Facts—Example No. 2

John Law, a California highway patrolman, was injured while making an arrest and attempting to prevent Willy Henry from falling down. Law subsequently filed a civil suit against Henry and John Smith for personal injury. Law's employment records were subpoenaed, and the state of California claimed they were privileged. Determine whether the claimed privilege applies, and draft a letter in support of the contention that they are not privileged, if so indicated. The state claims privilege under California Government Code Section 6254 and California Evidence Code Section 1040. Begin the research by reading the code sections cited.

It appears clear they to not apply to a private citizen who files a civil suit for injury. Then read the California Code of Civil Procedure's applicable sections relating to discovery and confirm that the records are not privileged under those provisions.

2.074 Research Memorandum—Example No. 1

MEMO

To: Ace, Attorney at Law
From: Deuce, Legal Assistant
Re: *General Hospital v. Smith*
Date: 1/26/97

Issue 1: Does Smith's Counterclaim state a valid cause of action?
Issue 2: Can Malicious Prosecution be raised by way of a Counterclaim?

Issue 1: Elements of Proof
1. Prior action was commenced by or at the direction of the Defendant (General Hospital) and pursued to legal termination in favor of Plaintiff (Smith).
2. Prior action was brought without probable cause.
3. Prior action was initiated with malice.

Conclusion:

Smith's counterclaim fails to state a cause of action upon which relief can be granted, or facts sufficient to constitute proof of any of the above necessary elements. Smith's inability to plead favorable termination of the prior action will prove fatal through a motion to dismiss. *Bertero v. National General Corp.*, 13 Cal.3d 43, 50, 118 Cal.Rptr. 184, 529 P.2d 608 (1974); *Tool Research & Engineering Corp. v. Henigson*, 46 Cal.App.3d 675, 120 Cal.Rptr.29 (1975).

Issue 2: Discussion

The case of *Babb v. Superior Court*, 3 Cal.3d 841, 92 Cal.Rptr. 179, 479 P.2d 379 (1971), involved the question of whether a defendant in a civil action might file a cross-complaint seeking declaratory judgment; that in the event the action terminated favorably to him the action be adjudged to have been instituted and prosecuted maliciously and without probable cause. The trial court overruled a demurrer contending that favorable termination of the prior proceeding is a necessary precondition to the maintenance of a malicious prosecution action, on the ground the cross-complaint was not premature since it sought only declaratory relief. The Supreme Court reversed the ruling and ordered the lower court to vacate its order and sustain the demurrer without leave to amend. This decision was based on the "conclusion that precedent, principle, practicality and policy forbid such a cross-complaint, which entails the risk of discouraging legitimate claimants . . .". The Court stated, at page 846:

First, there is a certain metaphysical difficulty in permitting malicious prosecution since theoretically that cause of action does not yet exist.

The Court further stated, at pages 847 and 848:

Third, the rule of favorable termination is supported by strong policy considerations. (5) Since
malicious prosecution is a cause of action not favored by the law, it would be anomalous to
sanction a procedural change which not only would encourage more frequent resort to malicious
prosecution actions, but would facilitate their use as dilatory and harassing devices. Abolition of
the requirement that malicious prosecution suits be filed as separate actions after termination of

the main litigation would surely increase the incidence of such suits, since filing a cross-action requires less time, expense, and preparation than does initiation of a separate action. Furthermore, the introduction of evidence on the issues of malice and probable cause may prejudice the trier of fact against the plaintiff's underlying complaint, or enhance the possibility of a compromise verdict. Even if, as here requested, consideration of those issues is deferred until the principal action has been completed, an outcome of that trial adverse to the plaintiff may unduly enhance the defendant's chances in his malicious prosecution action. Finally, as was the case here, the plaintiff and his attorney may be joined as cross-defendants in the malicious prosecution suit. This not only places the attorney in a potentially adverse relation to his client, but may well necessitate the hiring of separate counsel to pursue the original claim. (*See* Note, *supra, 58 Yale Law Journal* 490, 493, and fn. 13.) *The additional risk and expense thus potentially entailed may deter poor plaintiffs from asserting bona fide claims.* (Emphasis added.)

It is hornbook law that the plaintiff in a malicious prosecution action must plead and prove that the prior judicial proceeding of which he complains terminated in his favor.

> ". . . Because of this requirement it is obvious that a defendant cannot cross-complain or counter claim for malicious prosecution in the first or main action, since a claim cannot state a cause of action at that stage of the proceedings. This appears to be the rule, not only in California, but generally." *Babb v. Superior Court*, 3 Cal.3d 841, 845-846, 92 Cal.Rptr. 179, 180-181, 479 P.2d 379, 380-381 (1971).

Conclusion:

Malicious prosecution should not be allowed by way of cross-complaint in the main action. Failure to plead prior favorable termination is fatal; cross-complainants cannot allege a favorable determination of the underlying action.

2.075 Memorandum and Draft Letter—Example No. 2

MEMO

To: Ace, Attorney at Law
From: Deuce, Legal Assistant
Date: 6/6/97
Re: Privileged Records—Draft of Letter to State

Gentlemen:

We are in receipt of your records, forwarded to Naida Love, C.S.R., with your letter of May 11, 1997. We are also in receipt of the declaration attached thereto for the records withheld and deemed privileged, signed by Jack W. Lewis, state services analyst. You cite as authority for claiming privilege Government Code section 6254(b) (c) (f) and Evidence Code section 1040. We submit that under the fact situation in this lawsuit, the privilege does not apply to "(3) Correspondence and reports pertaining to the December 10, 1984, injury which occurred on duty and from which Officer Law sustained a lower back injury. Injury Record card excluded." We are not concerned with the records listed in the balance of the declaration.

In support of our position, we call your attention to the following facts:

1. Enclosed is a copy of the amended complaint for personal injury filed by John Law. You will note that the charging allegations are that John Smith provided defendant Willy Henry with alcoholic beverage during the course and scope of his employment, that defendant Henry negligently and wrongfully assaulted, battered, and struck plaintiff about the face, head, back, body, and legs, causing severe bodily injuries, frightened plaintiff, and placed plaintiff in great fear for his life and physical well-being. In addition, the complaint alleges

that these acts were done with malice and ill will and with the intent and design of injuring and oppressing plaintiff. The claim for punitive damages in the complaint has been dropped by stipulation of counsel. These injuries allegedly were the result of acts required of plaintiff in the course and scope of his employment. Further, in verified answers to interrogatories, plaintiff contends that defendant violated "ordinances, codes and statutes relating to reckless driving, speeding, improper lane change, failure to yield to a red light, resisting arrest, failure to obey lawful order of police officer, drunk driving and public drunkenness, and assault and battery."

2. Mr. Law is claiming back pain at the conclusion of putting the defendant in the car and that he later developed left leg problems. Further, he had surgery that he relates to this accident and may need further surgery. Asked why the facts surrounding the arrest as described by him in deposition were not included in his arrest report, he pointed out it is the Garden City's California Highway Patrol office policy not to charge intoxicated persons with resisting arrest or assault and battery on a peace officer unless the officer has actual signs of injury, such as lacerations, broken bones, etc., and, therefore, he felt the facts stated by him in deposition were not relevant to the charge of driving under the influence. He further testified that he reported the incident at the jail to his superior, Sgt. Lager, and later that evening the sergeant completed an injury report.

3. Your cited subdivisions to Government Code section 6254 (b) (c) and (f) are not applicable in this instance. Subsection (b) relates to "pending litigation to which the public agency is a party or to claims made pursuant to Division 3.6 (commencing with section 810) of Title 1 of the Government Code. . . ." In this instance, the "public agency," or the California Highway Patrol, is not a party, nor is this suit filed against public entities or public employees (section 810). Rather, it is a private lawsuit by a California Highway Patrol officer for injuries resulting of an arrest made by him while on duty as an officer. Subsection (c) relates to personnel, medical or similar files, the disclosure of which would constitute an unwarranted invasion of personal privacy. Here, again, we submit that by filing a civil action for personal injuries as a private citizen, plaintiff Law has subjected himself to the normal discovery available to defendant to prepare a defense to the suit and, thus, correspondence and reports pertaining to the injury are a proper subject of discovery to substantiate the injuries and the circumstances surrounding same and that he has, in essence, waived the privilege regarding his reports and work records relating to the injury. This material is relevant and should be produced. Subsection (f) does not appear to state a privilege insofar as this lawsuit is concerned.

4. Your cited Evidence Code section 1040 refers to "official information," which is defined as "information acquired in confidence by a public employee in the course of his duty. . . ." We submit that the correspondence and reports pertain to the December 10, 1984, injury of plaintiff Law. We suggest that they are, in view of his personal civil lawsuit, business records and should be produced as such under the provisions of California Evidence Code section 1560. Further, provision (b)(2) provides for privilege if disclosure of the information is against public interest because there is a necessity for preserving the confidentiality of the information that outweighs the necessity for disclosure in the interest of justice. Our position is that the withholding of this information would be against public interest and prejudicial to the defendants in preparation of their defense.

Defendants cannot obtain this information through their own efforts, and under the facts, the necessity for disclosure in the interest of justice outweighs the necessity for preserving the confidentiality of the information.

We will appreciate your forwarding the material described under number (3) of your declaration relating to privileged and withheld records.

Sincerely,
Ace, Attorney at Law

2.08   Modern Technology and Legal Research

The reliance by courts and lawyers on precedent, the recorded accounts of the decisions in past litigation, as well as the gradual proliferation of statutes (whether amplifying old law or creating new), have made big business out of libraries and publishing houses. The increasing volume of decided cases and learned dissertations on facets of the law, the growth in regulatory agencies with their obligatory rules and regulations, increasing numbers of law schools and students, and the continuing legal education courses across the country all assure that the production of law source, reference, and citator books will greatly expand in the years ahead. It also ensures that an adequate law library is no mean investment to create or to maintain. Large firms, of course, find it necessary to equip their libraries with more than one volume of some law books, even of some sets of books. It is one of the observed, but untitled, laws that whenever a particular law book is desperately needed to check an authority, form, or reference for a last minute filing at court, that book will be checked out or misfiled within the library or another attorney is also engaged in a last minute research project in the same volume.

Other types of library problems are the need for a dedication of labor time in posting and updating the reference books with pocket parts, rearranging shelves to make space for new acquisitions and replacement volumes, restoring books to the proper shelf, and performing emergency searches for wanted but checked out volumes. The space needed to create a law library is another consideration. At current commercial property rates in metropolitan areas, the financial impact of space alone is substantial.

The modern technologies of photography and computers can be applied to solve some of these nagging problems.

Perhaps the greatest strides in legal research have been made in the area of computer access to resource materials. The developments in the last few years alone are phenomenal and can only be expected to continue. It is entirely conceivable, if not probable, that in the not too distant future, most bound-volume libraries will be replaced by computer terminals with access to the resources located in databases (collections of information that can be retrieved through a computer) on-site or across the country. Already these terminals are an integral part of most comprehensive libraries.

One of the major computer research systems is WESTLAW, created by West Publishing, which provides access to such sources as statutes, the West digest series, the national reporter system, *Shepard's Citations*, and *Black's Law Dictionary*. Another similar system is LEXIS, offered by Mead Data Central. There is also a system similar to *Shepard's Citations* known as *Auto-Cite*, offered by the Lawyers Cooperative Publishing Company. One of the more recent developments is West Publishing's CD-ROM Libraries, which allow research for a specific jurisdiction rather than a nation-wide scope, a much less expensive system. CD-ROM will be discussed in greater detail below. Additionally, certain governmental entities have similar computer research systems. In all of these systems, the user inputs a query into the system, and receives an information response relevant to the query. This is seemingly a simple process. However, as with all legal research, a particular skill must be developed in formulating the appropriate question in order to gain the most valuable information and the least amount of irrelevant information.

2.081 Computer-Based Systems

2.0811 On-line Sources. "On-line sources" generally refers to those resources available through use of a computer with a modem, although many use the term loosely to include any computer based reference material.

2.08111 Database Service Providers. The two major database service providers for legal research are WESTLAW and LEXIS-NEXIS. Both services require that accounts be established in advance, and charge for use on a per minute basis, although some "flat rate" plans are also available. Because charges for use are time-based, it is imperative that the attorney or legal assistant have a query formulated prior to "signing on." It is also a wise practice to narrow the issues as much as possible before using these resources.

The benefits to both of these services is that they are updated on a daily basis and contain thousands of state and federal legal documents such as published and unpublished opinions, constitutions, statutes, regulations, court rules, presidential papers, law reviews, legal periodicals, and special databases on select topics of wide interest. Some of the special topical databases include civil rights, workers compensation, family law, insurance, commercial litigation, asbestos litigation, and many others. Additionally, each has an on-line system for "Sheparizing" cases.

Search results from both these systems, including the full text of any document, are available by "downloading" the information to the computer's hard drive (allowing the ability to "cut-and-paste" quoted portions into legal memoranda and briefs), by fax transmission (useful when away from the office), and by printing to a printer attached to the computer. The ability to send the results via fax is especially helpful in situations where the attorney needing a printed copy of a case is elsewhere, such as in a judge's chambers or a courtroom.

2.08112 The Internet. One of the fastest growing "on-line" legal research sources is the World Wide Web, generally known as the Internet. The vast majority of the information available on the Internet is available at no additional charge, which is a great benefit. Additionally, most Internet Service Providers ("ISP") provide flat fee accounts at extremely low cost when compared to the "on-line" charges that can quickly accumulate with WESTLAW, LEXIS, or services.

The organizations who sponsor sites of interest for legal research purposes tend to be major universities and law schools, state and federal governmental agencies, state and federal court systems, the U.S. Congress, and national legal professional organizations. The legal sources available are not as extensive as those available through WESTLAW and LEXIS, although the collections are growing by the hour, with the largest limitation being the time period covered (many collections do not have materials prior to 1990). The other major drawback to Internet research is that the "search engines" available are often not as discriminating as those provided by WESTLAW and LEXIS, making it more difficult to narrow a search quickly. In general, this is because WESTLAW and LEXIS are a series of structured, related, and linked databases, while the Internet is a collection of unrelated and often unlinked databases with no consistent structure.

The most effective use of the Internet for legal research is to consider it a secondary source for locating information. For example, the U.S. Supreme Court maintains a website where its decisions are published instantly when announced. An Internet subscription service called *LLI Bulletin* prepares a synopsis of the opinions which it sends its subscribers within hours by e-mail.

The e-mail, in addition to containing the opinion synopsis, contains a "hypertext" link to the U.S. Supreme Court's official full text opinion as well as to a related site at Cornell University which maintains a collection of prior decisions. Another excellent resource in the area of constitutional law is provided by the House of Representatives in the form of a full text version of the U.S. Constitution, Amendments, and the Bill of Rights which is "annotated" by citation and "linked" to interpreting decisions of the U.S. Supreme Court.

2.08113 Court System Services. In addition to the Internet, the federal courts (and a growing number of state and local courts), are providing bulletin board systems ("BBS") which allow certain kinds of access to court files. In general, these services are more useful for pre-trial investigation purposes because they usually do not include access to case law or statutory law, although they do provide access to court rules (*see* Chapter 7, Section 7.0331, Court Records).

2.0812 CD-ROM Libraries. Another component of computer-assisted research is CD-ROM libraries. The development of this system has made computer research affordable for virtually any size firm or organization. The concept is quite simple. Compact discs containing research materials for a particular subject of law or jurisdiction are loaded into a compact disc player attached to a personal computer and the information on them retrieved by the computer. As with WESTLAW, one can retrieve headnotes, cases, statutes, and so on. However, because the user purchases only those discs his or her library needs, there is no cost for access through telephone lines to the WESTLAW database or for access to all published statutes and cases nationally. Because approximately three hundred thousand pages of information can be contained on a single disc, space requirements are extremely low, compared with a standard library. Additionally, updated discs allow the researcher to retrieve the most current information. CD-ROM also has word processing capabilities that enable the researcher to lift information from the disc and incorporate it into a brief or other document.

2.082 Computer-Assisted Research Methods

2.0821 Formulating a Query. The first step in computer-based research is to formulate a query. This is the discipline of writing down what it is you are really interested in finding. It is always a good practice to refine your search topic before you "log on" to an on-line service, because this saves significant time—and on-line services charge for the time you spend using them.

2.0822 Boolean Logic and Wildcards—Tool to Refine a Search. George Boole, a 19th century mathematician, developed a system to describe language in mathematical/logical terms. The Boolean Search System is traditionally used by most on-line services, as well as by many Internet search engines, to retrieve documents. Although "natural language" tools also exist, they are based on the Boolean system.

Boolean Logic uses words and connectors to create phrases and concepts based on certain set rules. When using the basic framework of Boolean Logic, the computer can search for documents containing specific words or combinations of words requested. Some common words such as "the", "and", or "when" cannot be searched because of the number of document "hits" this would generate. (A "hit" is a document that matches search criteria.) Some letters in a word can be replaced in the search by an asterisk (*) or exclamation point (!). To denote variations of a root word, or a different spelling (for example: wom*n will search for women and woman; child! will search for child, children, and childish in addition to any plural or possessive forms).

By placing quotation marks around words, the entire word grouping will be searched (example: "clean air act"—without the quotes, it would list every document that contained either "clean", "air", or "act", or any combination of those three words).

"Natural" or freestyle language is also used by on-line services to enable simple queries, such as "Does Massachusetts law contain a common law marriage provision?" The search is broader in this form, but will find documents or cases based on a computer-generated Boolean search.

2.0823 Example of a WESTLAW Search Query

Step 1: Understand how the system works. The user will have a computer with a monitor and a keyboard and a telephone. The computer is connected to a phone line that sends the information projected on the screen—the user's queries, for example—and receives information back from the WESTLAW databases. If the user wishes to receive a hard (paper) copy of the information obtained, a local printer, or a fax machine is also needed.

Though the query process will be discussed briefly here, the reader who anticipates using a computer research system is encouraged to obtain and study a tutorial or reference manual, such as the *WESTLAW Reference Manual*. An example of a computer tutorial is *Westrain*. There are similar tools for the other systems. *Westrain*, which can be used on any personal computer, is a step-by-step approach to effective computer research that can be employed at the user's own pace and convenience.

The process of legal research is quite similar for most systems. For the purposes of demonstration here, reference will be made to the WESTLAW system. As with any type of legal research, the first step is to identify the jurisdiction whose authority is being sought. For example, if research is being done for a case pending in Pennsylvania, the researcher would be primarily concerned with the legal standards issued by the courts and legislature of that state. In computer research, this step is known as identifying the "field." Once the correct field has been entered into the computer, all queries will be directed to the law of that field.

Step 2: Formulate the query. Because the cost of computer research is based on the time the system is in use and because research should be performed efficiently, it is important to adequately prepare before accessing the system. In all legal research, including that which is computer-assisted, it is necessary to determine the issue with as much specificity as possible. Once the issue has been defined, the researcher must select those terms relevant to the issue and identify any variations or synonyms of them.

To arrive at variations that might be used in place of the original term, the researcher needs only to identify the root of the term and follow it immediately with an exclamation point (!). This instructs the database to produce all authorities in the field that contain the root of the word and any variation. If the only relevant variations differ by only a few letters, an asterisk (*) can be used within the original term at any place where a different letter might appear in a variation. The system automatically searches for plurals, so these need not be identified as variations.

Step 3: After the terms and their variations are selected, it is important to connect the terms properly. This will aid in limiting the information retrieved to relevant authorities. The system interprets a space between letters as the word or; for example, the system would interpret a query of "malicious prosecution" to mean locate any authority containing the word malicious or the word prosecution, but not both. Thus, one should be especially aware of spaces in the query before inputting it into the system.

Connectors are symbols that tell the computer how closely terms in the query must appear to one another in order to be retrieved. For example, the symbol "/s" between two terms means that the terms must appear within the same sentence of an authority before the system will retrieve it. Similarly, the symbol "/p" means that the terms must appear within the same paragraph of an authority before the system will retrieve it. The "/s" symbol is so limiting that relevant cases or statutes may be missed, while the "/p" symbol may cause numerous irrelevant authorities to appear. Basically, a knowledge of the subject and the likelihood of authority will guide the researcher in determining which connectors or combination of connectors to use between terms. When an authority is retrieved, the terms of the query will be highlighted where they appear in the authorities. It is possible to retrieve only the citations of the authorities or to examine the specific text of each authority.

The researcher who has a specific citation of a relevant authority may call up that citation without going through the query process by using the "find" command or by doing a field search. To do this, the name of the statute or case, the volume, page, and report citation, or both, if available, are input. The computer will then retrieve all cases in the field by that name; if the volume and page are available, the specific case will be called up. Insta-cite can be used to provide the researcher with direct and indirect history in the particular case.

Step 4: Identify variations of the terms that might be used in authorities on this issue:
Elements—element
Malicious—maliciously, maliciousness, malice
Prosecution—prosecute

Step 5: Construct the query. Element requirement factor component and or /p malic! malevolent wanton and /p prosecut***

Step 6: Input the query, review the headnotes, and select the decisions that appear to address the issue most directly.

Step 7: If the results are not satisfactory, modify the query and input it.

Step 8: Call up the complete decisions of the selected headnotes and review.

Step 9: Shepardize those decisions that will be used as authority.

At virtually any point, the research process can be converted to standard book research. For example, if the printed materials are also available, it may be more cost effective to perform the research by computer through Step 7 and then read and Shepardize the decisions in the actual books. This compatibility with book research is an additional benefit of computer-assisted research.

2.083 Benefits of Computer-Based Media

As the power, efficiency, ease of use, and economics of computer research continues to improve, it is becoming more widespread and commonplace. Computer-based libraries have become more cost-effective than traditional bound volume collections because of the cost savings available in terms of both shelf space and updates of hardbound volumes. Additionally, the portability of CD-ROM volumes, along with the capability of using laptop computers with modems to access the growing number of on-line services, are benefits of computer-based media that simply cannot be matched by traditional bound volume libraries.

2.084 Photography, Microfilm, Microfiche, and Microform

Photography, Microfilm, Microfiche, and Microform are older technologies for storage of data which the researcher may encounter in public libraries, government institutions, and private industry, although the trend has been and continues to be a move towards electronic and digital media such as CD-ROM. Because these various media may still be encountered, this section will briefly describe them.

Photography can reduce printed pages to the size of a typewriter's letter m with resolution quality that allows a lighted viewing screen to restore the image to clear, readable size, even allowing the production of hard copy prints of the image. Whole volumes can be reduced onto one or several cards of Microfiche or Microform, or rolls of Microfilm.

Microfilm usually refers to the reduction of material into photographs on film rolls. Several thousand page-size images can be stored on one roll. The roll of film can be equipped with keyed film image counters that allow the indexing of its contents.

Microfiche began as transparent cards with sleeves into which microfilm strips were slipped, allowing the assembly to be handled as a four-by-six-inch card, easily filed and easily adapted to the assembly of one increment of information or topic. The reader equipment is less expensive than for microfilm, since no transport mechanism is needed and focusing problems are minimized. Copying requires slightly different equipment, however.

Microforms are microfiche further reduced to exceptionally small size, allowing hundreds or thousands of images on one card. One such form, "ultrafiche," has been used to provide units of the *National Reporter System* to subscribers. Each volume (approximately 1,450 pages) is on one ultrafiche card. The readers for the process have a nine-by-twelve-inch screen and can be mounted on a library table or office desk. Separate equipment is needed to make paper copies.

Such devices as these eliminated the space requirements where mass storage of hard copy volumes were involved, producing a major space and economic benefit. They also reduced the problem of the "borrowed but not returned volume."

2.09   Research Delegation Considerations

The most commonly delegated research assignments to legal assistants consist of Shepardizing cited cases, reviewing cases for proper citation, and locating cited cases for review by the attorney. As the attorney becomes more confident in the legal assistant's abilities, the types of research projects may be expanded to include finding relevant cases, statutes or relevant sections of constitutions underlying a point of law, review and summarize cases, and prepare internal memoranda of law.

At first the legal assistant's research projects will be basic and carefully detailed in scope, purpose, form, and time allowed for completion. Typically the problem may be one requiring little interpretation, such as "identifying each state code section or reference relating to riparian water rights. . . ." The project has easily defined parameters and can be checked easily by the attorney in order to verify the accuracy and thoroughness of the legal assistant's work. A second assignment might be "locate each riparian water rights case decided since 1850 and distinguish each to our present case issue of beneficial water use, briefing chronologically those cases which mention this issue."

Legal research requires skill, perception, hard work, and a candid and forthright recognition by the legal assistant of his or her own limitations. The lawyer has a wealth of knowledge obtained both at law school and in practice which allows him or her relatively quick recognition and appreciation of the sometimes complex and/or convoluted views expressed in some case opinions. The legal assistant cannot, without equivalent training and experience, expect to, or be expected to, perform with the same insight, legal writing skills, and appreciation of legal expressions as the employing attorney.

Both the attorney and the legal assistant must adopt a mutually confident and comfortable posture which recognizes these differences in training and performance.

2.10 Research Tasks

Before allowing a legal assistant to do legal research, the attorney must have confidence that the legal assistant is trained, well-informed, and capable. A working rapport and understanding must be established between the attorney and the legal assistant. The following checklist is actually one of capabilities. Most of the tasks can be performed either by the attorney or the legal assistant; however, some require more knowledge and insight than a legal assistant might have or more than his or her training will allow. Other tasks can and should be performed by a legal assistant as a great time saver to the attorney, some of which are:

Research Tasks	Attorney	Legal Assistant
Check cites and Shepardize a brief.	X	X
Prepare a table of authorities for a brief.	X	X
Given a West key number, a fact situation, and a point of law: Read summaries of cases listed under this number to find relevant cases.	X	X
Given a fact situation and a point of law: Go to appropriate sources to find relevant cases; update those cases to see if there have been any decision changes regarding that point of law.	X	X
Given a fact situation and a point of law: Find statutes or ordinances bearing on the issue and update statutes through supplements and session laws.	X	X
Given a particular question or point of consideration: Find relevant sections of constitution (federal and state).	X	X
Read cases and prepare a brief synopsis of each.	X	X
Organize research results into memo form.	X	X
Given a fact situation and a point of law: Determine whether there are constitutional considerations.	X	
Write a brief.	X	*

* Primarily an attorney's job; however, a legal assistant can assist in drafting and supplying technical information, such as legal descriptions, cites, and organizing exhibits.

2.11 Summary

The more experience and expertise the legal assistant demonstrates, the more complex the research possibilities will become. BE ABSOLUTELY CERTAIN to understand what is expected and avoid assignments totally beyond current skills and knowledge, as this will result in disaster both for the legal assistant and the supervising attorney.

One of the basic concepts of the role of the legal assistant is to enable the lawyer to provide legal services at less cost to the client. The competent research of legal assistants will enhance this aim, and the legal assistant will become an even more valuable member of the staff in the law office.

Bibliography

Cohen, Morris L., *Legal Research in a Nutshell*. 6th ed. St. Paul: West, 1996.

How to Find the Law. Edited by Morris L. Cohen and Robert C. Berring, St. Paul: West, 1989.

How to Use Shepard's Citations. Colorado Springs, CO: *Shepard's Citations,* n.d.

Jacobstein, J. Myron and Mersky, Roy M., *Fundamentals of Legal Research*. 3rd ed. Westbury, NY: Foundation Press, 1985.

Jacobstein, J. Myron and Mersky, Roy M., *Legal Research Illustrated: An Abridgement of Fundamentals of Legal Research*. Westbury, NY: Foundation Press, 1987.

Price, Miles O., et al., *Effective Legal Research*. 4th ed. Boston: Little, Brown & Co., 1979.

Rombauer, Marjorie Dick, *Legal Problem Solving: Analysis, Research, and Writing*. 5th ed. St Paul: West, 1991.

Statsky, William P., *Legal Research and Writing: Some Starting Points*. 3rd ed. St. Paul: West, 1985.

Statsky, William P., *Legislative Analysis and Drafting*. 2nd ed. St Paul: West, 1983.

Statsky, William P., *West's Legal Thesaurus-Dictionary*. St. Paul: West, 1986.

A Uniform System of Citation. 16th ed. Cambridge: Harvard Law Review Association, Gannett House, 1996.

West's Law Finder: A Legal Research Manual. St. Paul: West, 1990.

Walker, Janice. *"MLA Style Citations of Electronic Sources."*
     http://www.cas.usf.edu/english/walker/mla.html (October 13, 1996).

Harnack, Andrew and Kleppinger, Gene. *"Beyond the MLA Handbook: Documenting Electronic Sources on the Internet."* June 10, 1996.
     http://www.falcon.eku.edu/honors/beyond-mla (October 13, 1996).

3 Ethics

3.00 Introduction

Ethics are guideposts for measuring conduct and for conforming behavior to meet accepted standards for legal assistants in their role in the judicial system. Ethics, simply put, are proper professional conduct. Ethics are critical for legal assistants and should not be taken lightly. Legal assistants work under the supervision of attorneys in the delivery of legal services. The legal profession traditionally has pursued and maintained a goal of assuring high standards of professional competence and ethical conduct. As part of the attorney team in the rendering of legal services, a legal assistant should pursue and maintain this same level of high standards of professional competence and ethical conduct.

The past two decades have brought many changes and advances in the legal assistant profession and the recognition and increased utilization of legal assistants by attorneys. But this advancement and utilization have also raised questions about what activities a legal assistant may perform and still remain within accepted professional boundaries and ethical limitations. One must ascertain what standards and principles exist for a legal assistant to follow to assure that the conduct and activities performed do not cross the boundary into the realm of potential liability for the unauthorized practice of law. Questions on legal ethics, however, are not always easily answered. Conduct cannot always be simply categorized as right or wrong. A knowledge of ethical considerations will assist in this decision process. The NALA *Code of Ethics and Professional Responsibility*, the NALA *Model Standards and Guidelines for Utilization of Legal Assistants* (Annotated), provisions of the American Bar Association *Model Rules of Professional Conduct*, provisions of the American Bar Association *Model Guidelines for the Utilization of Legal Assistant Services*, and similar state codes of professional conduct for attorneys and legal assistants, and case law are necessary sources for the legal assistant to obtain this knowledge. The NALA *Code of Ethics and Professional Responsibility* with its *Model Guidelines* has provided legal assistants with meaningful guidelines to enable them to perform their duties and remain within all ethical boundaries relating to standards of competence and ethical requirements imposed on attorneys.

The American Bar Association has traditionally provided attorneys with meaningful guidelines for competent and proper representation of their clients and the public interest as a whole. The ABA's most recent formal attorney conduct guidelines are found in the *ABA Model Rules of Professional Conduct*, adopted in 1983. The predecessor to the *Model Rules* was the *ABA Model Code of Professional Responsibility*, which consisted of canons, ethical considerations, and disciplinary rules. Provisions of the former *Model Code* have been incorporated into the present *Model Rules*, and the provisions of each consider substantially similar subject matter or reflect similar concern. To the extent that the ethics and disciplinary rules of the *Model Code* offer further explanation or clarification, they can and should be relied on as a resource for professional standards and as a supplement to the current *Model Rules*. The *ABA Model Guidelines for the Utilization of Legal Assistant Services*, adopted August 1991, is another source of ethics guidelines. Guidelines 2 and 3 relate to the actual utilization of legal assistants, while Guidelines 1 and 4–10 are specific to the ethical requirements imposed on the lawyer who employs legal assistants. These ethical considerations, guidelines and disciplinary rules of the ABA have direct prescription only on attorneys who belong to the ABA or who practice in states which have specifically adopted them. But all states have at least some equivalent code of professional conduct or responsibility statute governing the conduct of attorneys within their jurisdiction. The legal assistant should be familiar with the provisions of the attorneys' code applicable in his or her jurisdiction because the employing attorney has a responsibility to see that the legal assistant abides by the standards for ethical conduct set out in the code. Rule 5.3 of the *ABA Model Rules* specifically requires that in employing a nonlawyer, the attorney "shall make reasonable efforts to ensure that the person's conduct is compatible with the professional obligations of the lawyer." This requirement is imposed on the attorney because the "assistants, whether employees or independent contractors, act for the lawyer in rendition of the lawyer's professional services" (Comment, Rule 5.3, *ABA Model Rules of Professional Conduct*).

Courts also continually render opinions interpreting the *ABA Model Code* and *Model Rules*, in addition to disciplinary code provisions for a particular jurisdiction. The American Bar Association maintains a Committee on Professional Ethics, which publishes formal and informal opinions relating to code provisions. State and local bar associations also may offer formal and informal opinions on questions relating to ethical conduct.

Self-regulatory efforts to pursue and maintain professional conduct and provide meaningful guidelines for ethical behavior are also a tradition in the legal assistant profession. In 1975, the National Association of Legal Assistants adopted its own *Code of Ethics and Professional Responsibility*. The NALA *Code* has been refined and amended over the years and is provided in its current form in Section 3.061 of this chapter. Each canon of the NALA *Code* considers the same types of subject matter and concerns which are addressed in the rules and codes governing attorney conduct, including attorney conduct involving the utilization of nonlawyers. NALA recognized that the legal assistant's conduct must be compatible with the obligations of the attorney since the ultimate interests served are the same. Accordingly, Canon 9 of the NALA *Code* mandates that a legal assistant is governed by bar associations' codes of professional responsibility and rules of professional conduct.

In 1984, NALA determined that the growing employment of legal assistants by attorneys made it necessary to develop an educational document relating to utilization standards and guidelines as guidance to the legal profession on acceptable conduct for legal assistants. The culmination of NALA's research and efforts in this area is the *Model Standards and Guidelines for Utilization of Legal Assistants* (Annotated), which is provided in Section 3.062 of this chapter. These guidelines were developed from existing case law, professional standards of conduct governing attorneys and their use of legal assistants, and other authorities. In short, the guidelines served to answer three basic questions about legal assistants: who are they, what are their qualifications, and what duties may they perform. Sections IV through IX of the *Model* provide an excellent outline of the ethical standards and principles for legal assistants and guidance for the attorney in utilizing a legal assistant.

3.01 Duties A Legal Assistant May Perform under the Supervision of an Attorney

As noted in the introduction to this book, the NALA definition of a legal assistant includes the caveat that the legal work being performed by the individual is done under the supervision of an attorney. The rationale for inclusion of this aspect will become obvious in the discussion of guidelines, codes, and case law that follows.

Kentucky was the first state to actually adopt a separate paralegal code within its supreme court rules; this code recognizes the use of paralegals and sets forth certain exclusions to the unauthorized practice of law. But the code also expressly mandates that the attorney must supervise the legal assistant and must remain responsible for the work.

> For purposes of this rule, the unauthorized practice of law shall not include any service rendered involving legal knowledge or advice, whether representation, counsel or advocacy, in or out of court, rendered in respect to the acts, duties, obligations, liabilities or business relations of the one requiring services where:
>
> a. The client understands that the paralegal is not a lawyer;
> b. The lawyer supervises the paralegal in the performance of his duties; and

c.   The lawyer remains fully responsible for such representation, including all actions taken or not taken in connection therewith by the paralegal to the same extent as if such representation had been furnished entirely by the lawyer and all such actions had been taken or not taken directly by the attorney.

Paralegal Code, Ky.S.Ct. R. 3.700, Sub-Rule 2.

Canon 2 of the *NALA Code of Ethics and Professional Responsibility* addresses this question as follows: "A legal assistant may perform any task which is properly delegated and supervised by an attorney so long as the attorney is ultimately responsible to the client, maintains a direct relationship with the client, and assumes professional responsibility for the work product." This language is not only compatible with the *Kentucky Code* but also with EC 3-6 of the *ABA Code of Professional Responsibility*, which provides:

A lawyer often delegates tasks to clerks, secretaries, and other lay persons. Such delegation is proper if the lawyer maintains a direct relationship with his clients, supervises the delegated work, and has complete professional responsibility for the work product.

Various states have included similar provisions in attorney professional responsibility codes. For example, EC 3-6 of the *Florida Code of Responsibility* provides:

A lawyer or law firm may employ nonlawyers such as secretaries, law clerks, investigators, researchers, legal assistants, accountants, draftsmen, office administrators, and other lay personnel to assist the lawyer in the delivery of legal services. A lawyer often delegates tasks to such persons. Such delegation is proper if a lawyer retains a direct relationship with his client, supervises the delegated work, and has complete professional responsibility for the work product.

The work which is delegated is such that it will assist the employing attorney in carrying the matter to a completed product either by the lawyer's personal examination and approval thereof or by additional effort on the lawyer's part. The delegated work must be such, however, as loses its separate identity and becomes either the product or else merged in the product of the attorney himself.

In addition to the general professional responsibility codes regulating the use of nonlawyers by attorneys, many states have adopted specific guidelines for the use of legal assistants.[1] These guidelines are generally not part of the attorney's professional responsibility code but have been developed to emphasize the requirement that attorneys must supervise the work that is delegated to the legal assistant and must accept complete responsibility for the final work product. Case law is also useful in determining what constitutes the unauthorized practice of law. The legal assistant should from time to time research recent decisions relating to the unauthorized practice of law. Thus, the legal assistant should be familiar with not only the professional code for attorneys in his or her state or practice jurisdiction but also with any additional guidelines or decisions regarding the use of legal assistants.

---

[1] *See*, for example, *Guidelines for the Utilization of Legal Assistants in Kansas*, adopted by the Kansas Bar Association and *Guidelines for Legal Assistants*, adopted by the Colorado Bar Association. Guidelines have been adopted by a majority of the state bar associations.

> ## PRACTICE TIP
>
> - Be familiar with the content and know where to find all rules, codes, and other regulations governing the attorneys in your firm and locale.
>
> - Confirm answers to any ethical questions you may have by consulting the regulations and following up with your supervising attorney.
>
> - Know that an attorney's livelihood demands that legal assistants strictly adhere to the ethical rules.

3.02   Ethical Considerations in the Work Environment

The ethical considerations for legal assistants do not end with proper delegation and supervision by the attorney. The legal assistant must be conscious of other ethical considerations when carrying out assigned tasks. The legal assistant must examine and be aware of the relationship between specific concepts and principles contained in the codes of professional responsibility and the conduct and activities performed by the legal assistant as part of the legal services team.

3.021   The Legal Assistant in the Client-Lawyer Relationship

3.0211 Accepting Clients and Setting Fees. Canon 3 of the NALA *Code* specifically prohibits a legal assistant from engaging in the practice of law by accepting cases and setting fees. (*Also see* NALA *Model Standards*, Section VI for a discussion of case law regarding such prohibited acts.)

The legal assistant may not establish the attorney-client relationship. While the legal assistant may be involved in obtaining initial information from a prospective client, the attorney must make the final decision to accept the case. The legal assistant must also be extremely cautious in quoting fees for legal services. Making general statements about approximate fees that might be charged for a particular service is a very unwise practice, even when the employer may have an established schedule listing fees for various services. There may always be exceptions to the set fees, and until the attorney has discussed the specific legal problem with the client, neither the services required nor the reasonable fee is certain.

> ## PRACTICE TIP
>
> - Make it clear to prospective clients or existing clients with new matters that only the attorney may agree to provide legal services.
>
> - Be aware that in some kinds of cases, e.g., class actions, legal assistants in some jurisdictions may accept as new clients, members of the class who meet specific criteria which has been defined by the attorney.
>
> - Tell individuals who are persistent in asking for an estimate of the fee that it is unethical for you to quote fees.

3.0212 Competence and Integrity. Canon 6 of the NALA *Code* stresses competence and integrity. Rules 1.1 and 8.4 are the counterpart rules in the *ABA Model Rules of Professional Conduct*. As with attorneys, legal assistants must not only maintain present skills and knowledge, they must also keep current and informed about changes in procedures and the law. Knowing how things used to be done and what the law was will not enable the legal assistant to perform competently. The legal assistant is a professional. To retain that status, a competent legal assistant must pursue a continuous program of self-education and reeducation. Attendance at workshops and seminars in substantive areas of the law and in the legal assistant's specialty is essential. Reading legal publications, case summaries, and professional association publications will keep the legal assistant on the cutting edge. Integrity means strict personal honesty and independence and is generally understood to preclude any dishonest or unethical conduct. The legal assistant must adhere to the highest standards of truth, honesty, and loyalty to assist the attorney in maintaining integrity, not only in the attorney-client relationship, but in all activities conducted in the professional capacity.

PRACTICE TIP

- Arrange to receive announcements of upcoming seminars given for attorneys or legal assistants.

- Submit a request to attend relevant seminars.

- Supplement your request with the seminar brochure and comment on how such attendance would benefit your employer.

- Read promptly periodicals from attorneys' professional organizations as well as those from legal assistant organizations.

3.0213 Diligence and Communication. Canon 8 of NALA's *Code of Ethics* requires a legal assistant to do ". . . all other things incidental, necessary, or expedient for the attainment of the ethics and responsibilities as defined by statute or rule of court." In a profession fraught with deadlines, diligence and an absence of procrastination cannot be emphasized too strongly.

A legal assistant is often responsible for docket control on matters involving time deadlines. The employer will depend on the legal assistant to meet the attorney's obligation to act with "reasonable diligence and promptness in representing clients," as required by Rules 1.3 and 1.4 of the *ABA Model Rules of Professional Conduct*. The legal assistant will also frequently keep clients updated on the status of cases or matters. Clients will often rely on the legal assistant to get information because they may prefer to talk to the legal assistant rather than the attorney. A legal assistant may explain procedural matters to clients, but making a legal judgment on a client's behalf as to what procedure is best would be improper. If the legal assistant is merely passing on information or a decision made by the attorney, the communication by the legal assistant is not improper. A legal assistant must be on guard in these situations to ensure that he or she does not give legal advice or perform any acts that involve professional legal judgment. Such activities are addressed in Canons 3, 4, and 5 of the NALA *Code* because the exercise of professional legal judgment is the practice of law.

> ## PRACTICE TIP
>
> - Discipline yourself to timely performance of duties and responsibilities.
> - Advise your supervisor if your workload is so excessive you are unable to perform tasks in a timely manner.
> - Learn to prioritize your work.
> - Other things being equal, tackle first the tasks you are unsure how to do.
> - Remember many tasks are not difficult once you start.
> - Be cautious in communications with clients and others to avoid giving legal advice.
> - Make certain that all with whom you communicate are aware that you are not an attorney.
> - Make certain that a system of docketing filing deadlines, statute of limitations and other important dates is used and that such information is regularly communicated to the attorneys.

3.0214 *Confidential Information and Privileged Communications.* A legal assistant is constantly exposed to confidential matters which concern the affairs of clients as well as information about client matters or cases in performing job functions. All of this information must be kept confidential and should not be revealed in casual or indiscreet conversations, particularly with individuals outside the workplace. Canon 7 of the NALA *Code* addresses this ethical responsibility for legal assistants, and the ABA counterpart for attorneys is Rule 1.6.

A communication made to an attorney in professional confidence within the realm of the attorney-client relationship is considered a privileged communication. Under the Federal Rules of Evidence, these communications are generally not permitted to be disclosed, or allowed to be discovered, by third parties except where there may exist an exception to the general rule. Other similar privileged relationships exist, such as those between physician and patient or husband and wife, which are established by statute, constitutional mandate, or common law. Any communication made by a client to the legal assistant in confidence while in the course and scope of professional employment is generally considered to be as if the communication were made to the attorney, and therefore will be considered to come under the attorney-client privilege. Disclosures to third persons of any such communications should never be made by the legal assistant unless directed to do so by the attorney, by court order, or expressly consented to by the client.

Work done by the attorney for a client as part of the attorney's work product is also subject to privilege considerations. When the work of the legal assistant is directed, supervised, authorized, and required by the attorney as part of the service provided the client, it is generally considered to fall under this same attorney work product privilege. The legal assistant must assume that each communication sent or received, each document generated, every note taken, and so on, falls under this privilege and must protect the privilege until the attorney, the client, or the court authorizes or orders disclosure. It is critical to remember at all times that these privileges can be lost through unintentional and inadvertent disclosure to third persons.

Confidentiality takes on a whole new meaning with the advent of computerized information and electronic data transfer. The use of cellular phones carries with it responsibility for safeguarding information which can be accessed by outside parties. The legal assistant should be aware that the confidentiality of sensitive information may be at risk when such information is transmitted by cellular phone. "Courts have repeatedly held in Fourth Amendment cases that there is no reasonable expectation of privacy in the content of cellular or cordless phone conversations." (*See* Association of the Bar of the City of New York Committee on Professional and Judicial Ethics, Formal Opinion 1994-11, October 21, 1994.) Fax transmittals should always be accompanied by a cover sheet containing a disclaimer that the information is confidential and for the use of the intended recipient only. Care should be taken to ensure that faxes are sent to the correct location. By the same token, Internet e-mail should be used with caution as it carries with it the same risk characteristics as fax transmittals and cellular or cordless phone transmission—all can be intercepted by or inadvertently disclosed to third persons.

Internet and digital technologies provide a broader level of communication, but that benefit is at the expense of privacy and confidentiality. Rule 34(a) of the Federal Rules of Civil Procedure allows a party to serve on any other party a request to permit the "inspection and copying of . . . data compilations . . . through detection devices." Courts have interpreted this language to include access to computer disks, hard drives, backup tapes, e-mail and other electronic data. Every user should be aware that e-mail messages, file transfers and Internet conduct are all potentially discoverable by a knowledgeable party. (*See "The New Age of Electronic Discovery,"* Legal Assistant Today, Wendi Webb, May/June 1996 and *"O What A Tangled Web We Weave,"* Facts & Findings, James A. Powers, May 1996.)

PRACTICE TIP

- When speaking with a client, close doors and make sure that no third party is listening to the conversation.

- Protect your computer screen from being read by other persons by turning it away from office doors and windows, or by obtaining a filter screen to place over the monitor.

- Do not talk about work-related matters when socializing with friends or in any public place.

3.0215 Conflict of Interest. The avoidance of any conflict of interest or the appearance of impropriety is important to consider because loyalty is an essential element of the attorney-client relationship. Canon 8 of the NALA *Code* expands the general requirement for protection of the confidences of a client to include the avoidance of conflicts of interest or any activities that might present the appearance of impropriety. Rule 1.7 of the ABA *Model Rules* addresses the attorney's responsibility to avoid conflicts of interest.

The growth in the utilization of legal assistants has increased the potential for conflicts of interest. Recognizing that conflicts may arise when a legal assistant moves from one employer to another, the ABA Committee on Ethics and Professional Responsibility issued an opinion on this topic:

> A law firm that hires a nonlawyer employee, such as a paralegal, away from an opposing law firm may save itself from disqualification by effectively screening the new employee from any participation in the case the two firms have in common.

ABA Opinion No. 88-1526 (6/22/88).

This screening (sometimes referred to as the "Chinese wall," the "firewall," the "cone of silence," or the "ethical wall") seeks to protect the confidences of a client and any information that pertains to the attorney-client relationship. Several courts have been faced with requests for disqualification on the basis of nonlawyers' conflicts of interests, primarily resulting from a job change from one firm to another.[2] Just how far disqualification may extend is an issue still under scrutiny by the courts. It certainly extends to the new employer who utilizes the legal assistant to perform work on cases it has in common with the old employer. While the New Jersey Supreme Court Advisory Committee on Professional Ethics issued Opinion 665 (1993) supporting its position for the "Chinese wall" theory, the Nebraska Supreme Court rejected the "Chinese wall" as a means of avoiding disqualification stating that it does little or nothing to ease the appearance of impropriety.[3]

EC4-2 and DR4-101(D) of the *ABA Code of Professional Responsibility* impose requirements on the attorney to exercise care in selecting and training employees to ensure that such client confidences are preserved. In addition, the new employer is prohibited from attempting to obtain information from a legal assistant that was acquired as a result of a prior employment. The California Court of Appeals addressed the issue of whether there were any additional precautions a new employer might take to prevent disqualification when it discovers that a legal assistant was previously employed by an adverse party in a common case. In its 1993 ruling on a case involving a change of employment by nonlawyer employees, the Court found that in addition to the cone of silence, a law firm has the option of obtaining a waiver from the former employer that it does not object to the switch in employment.[4] It is important that the legal assistant be alert to any situations that might present a conflict of interest or the appearance of impropriety as a result of information gained during a past employment and should immediately disclose any questionable situation to the employer.[5]

PRACTICE TIP

- Keep track of former employment and former clients to prevent any potential conflicts.
- Do not enter into business transactions with clients or ever use any information you receive from a client to your own advantage.
- Do not accept gifts from clients.

3.0216 Safekeeping of Property. A final area deserving of mention is the safekeeping of property. Rule 1.6 of the ABA *Rules* prohibits the commingling of funds. Law offices maintain separate trust accounts for holding monies related to client transactions, and strict accounting

---

[2] *Grant v. Thirteenth Court of Appeals,* (Texas Sup.Ct., No. 94-0581, 10/6/94, rev'g 877 S.W.2d, 10 Law.Man.Prof. Conduct 173); *Phoenix Founders Inc. v. Marshall,* 10 Law.Man.Prof. Conduct 316 (Texas Sup. Ct. 1994).

[3] *FirsTier Bank N.A. v. Buckely, State (Nebraska) ex rel.,* 503 N.W.2d 844, 9 Law. Man.Prof.Conduct 244 (Neb.Sup.Ct. 1993).

[4] *In re Complex Asbestos Litigation,* (1991) 232 Cal. App. 3rd 572, 283 Cal. Rptr. 732.

[5] For a thorough discussion of the considerations for a legal assistant in changing jobs, see Cohn, Steven, *"Beyond the 'Chinese Wall',"* Legal Assistant Today (November/December 1995); Emert, Laurence T., *"Preserving a Client's Confidences,"* XIX Facts & Findings 5 (February 1993), and Voisin, Vicki, *"Changing Jobs: Ethical Considerations for Legal Assistants,"* XV Facts & Findings 12 (March 1989).

procedures must be followed in these accounts. The legal assistant is often involved in setting up these accounts or in disbursements and should become familiar with, and strictly follow, all procedures required of the law firm in such transactions.

PRACTICE TIP

- If you are given responsibility for handling client trust fund accounts, maintain a separate ledger that shows the date and amount of funds received; the date and amount deposited; and the date, amount, and purpose of any disbursements.

- Keep bank deposit slips for client trust fund accounts separate from other law office deposit slips.

3.022 Transactions with Persons Other than Clients

The legal assistant's ethical obligations are not confined solely to activities within the employer's office or activities involving the clients represented by the employer.

3.0221 Truthfulness in Statements. Rule 4.1 of the ABA *Model Rules* mandates that false statements cannot be made and facts cannot be misrepresented. Such a responsibility extends to the legal assistant. The legal assistant's nonlawyer status must be clearly stated and conveyed in any communications, oral or written, to anyone with whom the legal assistant has contact during the course and scope of employment. This practice will ensure that there is no misrepresentation or misunderstanding about the legal assistant's nonlawyer status, and will avoid the problems that arise from the failure to disclose nonlawyer status.

3.0222 Improper Communications. Just as attorneys are prohibited from any direct communications with persons and adverse parties known to be represented by counsel (*see* Rule 4.2 of ABA *Model Rules*), legal assistants cannot make such a contact or be utilized in such a manner as to circumvent that prohibition.

PRACTICE TIP

- Do not commnicate with parties to a litigation or employees of such parties where opposing counsel is not present.

- Do not initiate communications with a judge and avoid communications with members of a jury.

3.023 The Legal Assistant and the Law Firm

3.0231 Attorney Responsibility regarding Nonlawyer Assistants. As noted in the introduction to this chapter, Rule 5.3 of the ABA *Model Rules* specifically discusses the responsibilities of an attorney regarding the use of nonlawyer assistants and the need to take measures to ensure the nonlawyer's conduct is compatible with the professional obligations of the lawyer.

Some states have enhanced Rule 5.3 to provide that a partner in the law firm, in addition to the supervising attorney, has these responsibilities (e.g., Montana, Idaho, and South Carolina).

EC 3-5 of the ABA *Model Code of Professional Responsibility* also relates to the attorney's use of nonlawyers.

3.0232 Sharing of Legal Fees and Partnership. Rule 5.4 of the ABA *Model Rules* states that legal fees may not be shared with nonlawyer personnel. This rule is not intended to deny legal assistants salary, bonuses, or benefits, even though they may be tied to the profitability of the law firm. Instead, the prohibition applies to any form of compensation that is based on the existence or amount of a particular fee. Bonuses paid to nonlawyers are to be distinguished from fee splitting. Fee splitting occurs when a payment to the nonlawyer is tied to a particular client; bonuses, however, are not tied to receipt of a particular fee for a particular case. Thus, a legal assistant's regular compensation may not include a percentage of the profits of a law firm, nor can the compensation be based on fees received in the general course of business, from any referrals of legal business, or from a particular client or case. However, subparagraph (a)(3) of Rule 5.4 provides an exception to the extent that the law firm may include nonlawyers in a compensation or retirement plan, even though that plan is based in whole or in part on a profit-sharing arrangement. This is permitted since participation in these plans does not encourage or aid nonlawyers in the unauthorized practice of law, and because such plans have been authorized by Congress (i.e., qualified plans under ERISA, 401K, etc.)

The same rule also prohibits the lawyer from establishing any business with a nonlawyer if any part of that relationship would involve the practice of law (DR 3-103). This rule is supplemented by DR 5-107(C) which forbids an attorney to practice law in any organization or professional corporation where a nonlawyer holds any interest or is a director of officer of such group.

PRACTICE TIP

- Do not participate in, or agree to, any compensation arrangement which involves, or appears to involve, the sharing of legal fees with an attorney.

- You may refer clients to an attorney, as long as you are asked to do so by the client and you do not accept a fee for such referral.

- Do not go into business with an attorney when such business involves, or appears to involve, the practice of law.

3.0233 Listing on Letterhead, Use of Business Cards, and Signing of Letters. Questions arise frequently as to whether a law firm may list legal assistants and other nonlawyers on the firm letterhead, whether such individuals may have business cards also containing the law firm name, and whether legal assistants can sign letters under the lawyer's letterhead.

ABA *Model Rules* 7.1 and 7.5 govern what information may be provided on lawyers' letterhead. While these rules do not specifically address the listing of nonlawyer personnel, the ABA has issued an informal opinion (89-1527, 2/22/89) stating that the listing of nonlawyer support personnel is not prohibited by the rule or any other rules, provided the listing is not false or misleading. To avoid being misleading, the title of the nonlawyer personnel should clearly appear on the letterhead so that the public is not misled into believing that the nonlawyer is an attorney. The same findings are made with regard to business cards for nonlawyers. The primary concern is to avoid confusion about the status of the nonlawyers which may arise from the use of any title or other designation. The use of letterhead and business cards by freelance or independent paralegals must also conform to these rules as well as the specific rulings of the jurisdiction in which the legal assistant operates.

Rules regarding nonlawyer use of business cards and listing on letterheads vary from state to state. A legal assistant should be familiar with and follow the appropriate rules of the jurisdiction involved. The form and language of any listing on letterhead or business cards should also be approved by a supervising attorney. Freelance or independent paralegals should seek the advice of an attorney and/or request an opinion from the appropriate state bar entity or supreme court commission prior to printing or disseminating letterhead or business cards.

It is generally accepted that a legal assistant may sign letters on law firm letterhead so long as the nonlawyer status of the legal assistant is clear. This is accomplished by stating an appropriate nonlawyer title immediately below the signature. The contents of a letter signed by a nonlawyer must also be considered. No direct legal advice or opinion should be contained in correspondence sent under the legal assistant's name. If any doubt exists, a supervising attorney should be consulted.

3.024 The Legal Assistant and Public Service/Pro Bono Activities

Attorneys have a basic responsibility to provide public-interest legal services without a fee or at a reduced fee (ABA Rule 6.1). To meet public concern about the availability of legal services to the indigent, many bar associations have established programs to provide such low-cost or free services to these individuals. Some legal assistant professional associations are even working with the organized bar associations in these programs. Legal assistants may assist attorneys in these public service activities in the same manner and under the same delegation and supervisory obligations previously discussed. As with the attorney, the legal assistant is bound by the same standards of professional conduct in offering pro bono services as with any other services.

3.03 The Legal Assistant and the Unauthorized Practice of Law

ABA *Model Rule* 5.5 specifically prohibits an attorney from assisting a nonlawyer in the performance of any activity that would constitute the unauthorized practice of law. Canon 3 of the NALA *Code of Ethics and Professional Responsibility* prohibits a legal assistant from engaging in any activity that would constitute the unauthorized practice of law. Canon 1 of the NALA *Code* prohibits a legal assistant from the performance of any duties that may only be performed by lawyers.

The proper starting point for any discussion of the unauthorized practice of law is to have a basic understanding of what constitutes the practice of law. The ABA has been reluctant to formulate a single specific definition of what constitutes the practice of law except to stress that it relates to the rendering of services to others which call for the exercise of professional legal judgment (*see Model Code* EC 3-5).

Various courts have addressed the definition of the practice of law. In *Davis v. Unauthorized Practice Commission*, 431 S.W.2d 590 (Tex. 1968), that Court stated:

> According to the generally understood definition of the practice of law, it embraces the preparation of pleadings and other papers incident to actions of special proceedings, and the management of such actions in proceedings on behalf of clients before judges in courts. However, the practice of law is not confined to cases conducted in court. In fact, the major portion of the

practice of any capable lawyer consists of work done outside of the courts. The practice of law involves not only appearances in court in connection with litigation, but also services rendered out of court, and includes the giving of legal advice or the rendering of any service requiring the use of legal skill or knowledge, such as preparing a will, effect of which under the facts and conclusions involved must be carefully determined.

A cursory reading of this definition might lead one to the inaccurate conclusion that anyone who prepares legal documents could be engaged in the practice of law. The important distinguishing fact, not present in the *Davis* case but later articulated by other courts in other opinions, is that a legal assistant performs these functions under the direct supervision of a licensed attorney. An example of the continuing development of this line of thought is represented by opinions from South Carolina:

"Paralegals are routinely employed by licensed attorneys to assist in the preparation of legal documents such as deeds and mortgages. The activities of a paralegal do not constitute the practice of law as long as they are limited to work of a preparatory nature, such as legal research, investigation, or the composition of legal documents, which enable the licensed attorney-employer to carry a given matter to a conclusion through his own examination, approval, or additional effort." *In re: Easler*, 275 S.C. 400, 272 S.E.2d 32 (1980).

"[T]he preparation and filing of legal documents involving the giving of advice, consultation, explanation, or recommendations on matters of law [is the practice of law]." *State v. Despain*, 460 S.E. 2d 576 (S.C. 1995) and *State v. Buyers Service Co.*, 357 S.E.2d 15 (S.C. 1987).

"[T]o legitimately provide services as a paralegal, one must work in conjunction with a licensed attorney." *State v. Robinson,* Opinion 24391, SC Supreme Court, March 1996.

In addition, as discussed above, attorney standards of professional conduct recognize the use of nonlawyer personnel in performing many tasks that the lawyer would otherwise do.

PRACTICE TIP

- When in doubt, do not proceed! Ask your supervising attorney for guidance.
- Join a local, state, and/or national legal assistant association which may provide guidance.
- Know your state's professional responsibility codes for attorneys and legal assistants.
- You may relay legal advice and opinion from the supervising attorney to the client, but may not independently give legal advice or opinion.

The importance of being familiar with your jurisdiction's definition of the unauthorized practice of law cannot be over emphasized. Most states have adopted their own definition of the unauthorized practice of law, which have been interpreted according to specific areas of law. California Attorney General Opinion 93-416 found that a nonlawyer, acting on the basis of a power of attorney, may not engage in the practice of law on behalf of the client. Idaho has opined that lawyers may not enter into an arrangement with a corporation of nonlawyers to review living trust documents. It was found that the preparation of such documents is the practice of law (*see* Op. 135). Representation of individuals at real estate closings has been found to be the unauthorized practice of law in Pennsylvania (Op. No. 96-102).

Another aspect of the practice of law is the appearance in proceedings on behalf of clients in courts. Canon 3 of the NALA *Code of Ethics* prohibits the appearance of a legal assistant in court in a representative capacity for a client, unless such appearances are authorized by court or agency rules. The basis for this guideline is the requirement that the legal assistant's work must be under the direct supervision of an attorney. Unless there has been a waiver, either through statute, or a court or agency rule, specifically permitting a nonlawyer to perform such services independently and without the supervision of an attorney, the legal assistant will be crossing the boundary and could be subject to charges of unauthorized practice of law. As an example, Kentucky is a state which has long held that an attorney may not send a nonlawyer to do anything in a courtroom with respect to the representation of a client, this would be the unauthorized practice of law. (Ethics Opinion E-266, Supreme Court of Kentucky, 93-C-159-KB, 4/20/83). Kentucky also extended this provision to include the taking of depositions by nonlawyers (*see* Op. 341, 11/90).

The appearance by nonlawyers in a representative capacity in administrative proceedings is authorized by a number of state and federal agencies. Before a legal assistant engages in such activities, appropriate steps should be taken to ensure that such appearances are sanctioned by the agency rules, the supervising attorney has authorized and endorsed the appearance, court approval for the legal assistant to appear has been obtained, and, if appropriate, the client has consented to the legal assistant appearing on his or her behalf.[6]

What constitutes a court appearance is somewhat vague, depending on the activities involved in the appearance, and at least one court has held that preparation of a court order and transmission of information to the court was not the unauthorized practice of law because of the ministerial nature of the act.[7] As noted in the NALA *Code* (Canon 3), exceptions allowing court appearances by legal assistants may exist, and local, state, and federal rules applicable for the jurisdiction where the legal assistant works should be consulted. (As noted in Section 3.01 of this chapter, the *Kentucky Paralegal Code* specifically allows for some court appearances by legal assistants but only if the client understands the legal assistant is not an attorney, the lawyer supervises the legal assistant in the performance of his or her duties, and the lawyer remains fully responsible for such representation, including all acts taken and not taken.)

In the early 1990s, a movement developed for nonlawyers to offer legal services directly to the public. These individuals are often referred to as legal technicians. In 1992, in response to the push to allow nonlawyers to serve the public, the ABA established a Commission on Nonlawyer Practice. The Commission consisted of lawyers and nonlawyers, and received written statements, along with hearing testimony at sites across the United States. The Commission published a 173-page report entitled *Nonlawyer Activity in Law-Related Associations*. One of the items noted in the report is that the role of traditional paralegals should be expanded, while still under the supervision of lawyers. In 1996 Pennsylvania addressed their concerns on this issue by revising their UPL statute to include a reference to legal assistants. It states:

---

[6] The California Bar has issued an advisory opinion regarding the use of a paralegal employed by a law firm for appearances before the Workers' Compensation Appeals Board (WCAB). While under certain labor code sections, nonlawyers are authorized in California to represent applicants before the WCAB, the California Bar's Standing Committee on Professional Responsibility and Conduct was dealing with the effect of the representation by the nonlawyer as an employee of a law firm and on behalf of the firm's client. The committee noted the need for adequate supervision by the employing attorney and the requirement that the clients be informed and consent to the use of the nonlawyer.

[7] *People v. Alexander*, 53 Ill.App.2d 299, 202 N.E. 2d 841 (1964).

(a) General rule—Except as provided in subsection (b), any person, including, but not limited to, a paralegal or legal assistant, who within this Commonwealth shall practice law, or who shall hold himself out to the public as being entitled to practice law, or use or advertise the title of lawyer, attorney at law, attorney and counselor at law, counselor, or the equivalent in any language, in such a manner as to convey the impression that he is a practitioner of the law of any jurisdiction, without being an attorney at law or a corporation complying with 15 Pa.C.S. Ch. 29 (relating to professional corporations), commits a misdemeanor of the third degree, upon a first violation. A second or subsequent violation of this subsection constitutes a misdemeanor of the first degree. Penn.Cons. Stats. Title 42 Sect. 2524(a)

States are also adopting definitions of legal assistants. In 1992 South Dakota adopted a definition for legal assistants and included a list of seven minimum qualifications for legal assistants. In Illinois, Senate Bill 995, effective January 1, 1996 states:

Sec. 1.35 Paralegal. "Paralegal" means a person who is qualified through education, training, or work experience and is employed by a lawyer, law office, governmental agency, or other entity to work under the direction of an attorney in a capacity that involves the performance of substantive legal work that usually requires a sufficient knowledge of legal concepts and would be performed by the attorney in the absence of the paralegal. A reference in an Act to attorney fees includes paralegal fees, recoverable at market rates.

Many bar associations are also adopting definitions in an effort to clarify proper utilization of legal assistants, all in an attempt to stay clear of the unauthorized practice of law.

3.04   Adequate Supervision by the Attorney

The requirement that a legal assistant work under the direct supervision of an attorney is embodied in ethical guidelines, case law involving the unauthorized practice of law, and rulings in disciplinary proceedings against attorneys. As a result of this clear ethical precept for the use of nonlawyers in the delivery of legal services, the National Association of Legal Assistants has incorporated this principle into its definition of a legal assistant, as discussed in the introduction of this book. The importance of adequate supervision by the employing attorney cannot be overemphasized. As is made clear in the guidelines and accepted standards of professional conduct for attorneys, the ultimate responsibility rests with the supervising attorney. The professional codes and case law establish that the attorney must be responsible for the assignment of the tasks to be performed, must supervise the manner in which the legal assistant performs the duties and tasks, and must merge the work products of the legal assistant into the attorney's final work product. The attorney must maintain a direct relationship with the client and a managerial role in the representation of the client.

The managerial role came into question in New Jersey with lawyers entering into contracts with independent or freelance legal assistants. Opinion No. 24 was entered in November 1990 stating this practice was an unauthorized practice of law. However, this ruling was appealed. The Supreme Court opinion issued May 14, 1992 found:

The evidence does not support a categorical ban on all independent paralegals practicing in New Jersey. Given the appropriate instructions and supervision, paralegals, whether as employees or independent contractors, are valuable and necessary members of an attorney's work force in the effective and efficient practice of law.

On March 1, 1997 the North Dakota Rules of Professional Conduct were amended to include:

Rule 5.3 Responsibilities Regarding Nonlawyer Assistants:

With respect to a nonlawyer employed or retained by or associated with a lawyer:

    a. The lawyer shall make reasonable offers to put into effect measures giving reasonable assurance that the nonlawyer's conduct is compatible with the professional obligations of the lawyer;

    b. The lawyer having direct supervisory authority over the nonlawyer shall have reasonable efforts to ensure that the nonlawyer's conduct is compatible with the professional obligations of the lawyer; and

    c. The lawyer shall be responsible for a violation of these rules by the nonlawyer if the lawyer knows of the violation at a time when its consequences can be avoided or mitigated but fails to take reasonable remedial action.

    d. In addition to paragraphs (a), (b) and (c), the following apply with respect to a legal assistant employed or retained by or associated with a lawyer;

        1. A lawyer may delegate to a legal assistant any task normally performed by the lawyer except those tasks proscribed to one not licensed as a lawyer by statute, court rule, administrative rule or regulation, controlling authority, or these rules.

        2. A lawyer may not delegate to a legal assistant:

            i.   responsibility for establishing an attorney-client relationship;

            ii. responsibility for establishing the amount of a fee to be charged for a legal service;

            iii. responsibility for a legal opinion rendered to a client; or

            iv. responsibility for the work product

        3. The lawyer shall make reasonable efforts to ensure that clients, courts, and other lawyers are aware that a legal assistant is not licensed to practice law.

Failure by an attorney to adequately supervise nonlawyer staff can result in harsh disciplinary consequences, including disbarment. Sections VI and VIII of the NALA *Model Standards and Guidelines for Utilization of Legal Assistants* provides detailed annotations to case law dealing with the duties of the attorney and instances where sanctions have been imposed for the attorney's failure to perform these duties.

PRACTICE TIP

- Do not sign attorney's name to any legal documents. The supervising attorney must review and sign any legal document you have drafted.

- Make sure the work you are doing has been delegated by your attorney.

- If you are unsure of any aspect of any delegated work, ask for guidance from the supervising attorney.

3.05 Summary

The placement of responsibility on the attorney does not relieve the legal assistant from an independent obligation to follow the same professional conduct obligations required of attorneys and certainly to refrain from illegal conduct. While the provisions of standards and disciplinary rules for attorneys are not binding on nonlawyers, the very nature of a legal assistant's employment imposes an obligation to not engage in conduct that would involve the supervising attorney in a violation of attorneys' codes. This obligation has been codified in Canon 9 of the NALA *Code*.

The legal assistant must take additional individual steps to ensure protection from potential liability for the unauthorized practice of law. While statutory provisions concerning the unauthorized practice of law often do not describe such conduct with exactitude, precautionary steps can be taken by the legal assistant to stay within proper and accepted boundaries. As an example, the Virginia Alliance of Legal Assistant Associations has adopted *Educational Standards and Professional Responsibility Guidelines* for legal assistants.

From the compendium of material discussed in this chapter, the legal assistant can analyze professional conduct by considering the presence or absence of the following factors:

1. Are the tasks the legal assistant performs being delegated by an attorney?
2. Are the tasks and activities of the legal assistant being performed under the supervision of an attorney?
3. Are the tasks being performed ministerial or information gathering for an attorney's use?
4. Are the tasks and activities performed being given final approval and/or personal examination by an attorney, and does the work performed by the legal assistant merge into the attorney's final work product?
5. Has the attorney maintained a direct relationship with the client, or is the legal assistant managing the attorney-client relationship?
6. Has the legal assistant disclosed his or her nonlawyer status at the outset of any professional relationship with a client, other attorneys, a court or administrative agency (and personnel), or members of the general public?
7. Has the legal assistant established attorney-client relationships by accepting cases?
8. Has the legal assistant set the fees for the services to be performed?
9. Has the legal assistant rendered professional legal opinions or advice?
10. Has the legal assistant represented a client before a court when such activity is not authorized by the court or agency rules and when appropriate approval is obtained?

3.06 Codes and Guidelines

3.061 National Association of Legal Assistants, Inc. *Code of Ethics and Professional Responsibility* (As amended through 1995)

Preamble

A legal assistant must adhere strictly to the accepted standards of legal ethics and to the general principles of proper conduct. The performance of the duties of the legal assistant shall be governed by specific canons as defined herein so that justice will be served and goals of the profession attained. (*See* NALA *Model Standards and Guidelines for Utilization of Legal Assistants, Section II.*)

The canons of ethics set forth hereafter are adopted by the National Association of Legal Assistants, Inc., as a general guide intended to aid legal assistants and attorneys. The enumeration of these rules does not mean there are not others of equal importance although not specifically mentioned. Court rules, agency rules and statutes must be taken into consideration when interpreting the canons.

Definition

Legal assistants, also known as paralegals, are a distinguishable group of persons who assist attorneys in the delivery of legal services. Through formal education, training, and experience, legal assistants have knowledge and expertise regarding the legal system and substantive and procedural law which qualify them to do work of a legal nature under the supervision of an attorney.

Canon 1—A legal assistant must not perform any of the duties that attorneys only may perform nor take any actions that attorneys may not take.

Canon 2—A legal assistant may perform any task which is properly delegated and supervised by an attorney, as long as the attorney is ultimately responsible to the client, maintains a direct relationship with the client, and assumes professional responsibility for the work product.

Canon 3—A legal assistant must not: (a) engage in, encourage, or contribute to any act which could constitute the unauthorized practice of law; and (b) establish attorney-client relationships, set fees, give legal opinions or advice or represent a client before a court or agency unless so authorized by that court or agency; and (c) engage in conduct or take any action which would assist or involve the attorney in a violation of professional ethics or give the appearance of professional impropriety.

Canon 4—A legal assistant must use discretion and professional judgment commensurate with knowledge and experience but must not render independent legal judgment in place of an attorneys. The services of an attorney are essential in the public interest whenever such legal judgment is required.

Canon 5—A legal assistant must disclose his or her status as a legal assistant at the outset of any professional relationship, with a client, attorney, a court or administrative agency or personnel thereof, or a member of the general public. A legal assistant must act prudently in determining the extent to which a client may be assisted without the presence of an attorney.

Canon 6—A legal assistant must strive to maintain integrity and a high degree of competency through education and training with respect to professional responsibility, local rules and practice, and through continuing education in substantive areas of law to better assist the legal profession in fulfilling its duty to provide legal service.

Canon 7—A legal assistant must protect the confidences of a client and must not violate any rule or statute now in effect or hereafter enacted controlling the doctrine of privileged communications between a client and an attorney.

Canon 8—A legal assistant must do all other things incidental, necessary, or expedient for the attainment of the ethics and responsibilities as defined by statute or rule of court.

Canon 9—A legal assistant's conduct is guided by bar associations' codes of professional responsibility and rules of professional conduct.

3.062 National Association of Legal Assistants, Inc. *Model Standards and Guidelines for Utilization of Legal Assistants* (Annotated)

Introduction

The purpose of this annotated version of the National Association of Legal Assistants, Inc. (NALA) *Model Standards and Guidelines for the Utilization of Legal Assistants* is to provide references to the existing case law and other authorities where the underlying issues have been considered. The authorities cited will serve as a basis upon which conduct of a legal assistant may be analyzed as proper or improper.

The *Guidelines* represent a statement of how the legal assistant may function in the law office. The *Guidelines* are not intended to be a comprehensive or exhaustive list of the proper duties of a legal assistant. Rather, they are designed as guides to what may or may not be proper conduct for the legal assistant. In formulating the *Guidelines*, the reasoning and rules of law in many reported decisions of disciplinary cases and unauthorized practice of law cases have been analyzed and considered. In addition, the provisions of the American Bar Association's *Model Code of Professional Responsibility* and the *Model Rules of Professional Conduct,* as well as the ethical promulgations of various state courts and bar associations have been considered in development of the *Guidelines*.

While the *Guidelines* may not have universal application, they do form a sound basis for the legal assistant and the supervising attorney to follow in the operation of a law office. The *Model* will serve as a definitive and well-reasoned guide to those considering voluntary standards and guidelines for legal assistants. If regulation is to be imposed in a given jurisdiction the *Model* may serve as a comprehensive resource document.

Preamble

Proper utilization of the services of legal assistants affects the efficient delivery of legal services. Legal assistants and the legal profession should be assured that some measures exist for identifying legal assistants and their role in assisting attorneys in the delivery of legal services. Therefore, the National Association of Legal Assistants, Inc., hereby adopts these *Model Standards and Guidelines* as an educational document for the benefit of legal assistants and the legal profession.

COMMENT

The three most frequently raised questions concerning legal assistants are: (1) how do you define a legal assistant?; (2) who is qualified to be identified as a legal assistant?; and (3) what duties may a legal assistant perform? The definition adopted answers the first questions insofar as legal assistants serving attorneys are concerned. The *Model* sets forth minimum education, training, and experience through standards which will assure that one denominated as a legal assistant has the qualifications to be held out to the public in that capacity. The *Guidelines* identify those acts which the reported cases hold to be proscribed and give examples of services which the legal assistant may perform under the supervision of an attorney.

The three fundamental issues in the preceding paragraph have been raised in various cases for the past fifty years. In *Ferris v. Snively,* 19 P.2d 942 (Wash. 1933), the Court stated work performed by a law clerk to be proper and not the unauthorized practice of law required supervision by the employing attorney. The Court stated:

We realize that law clerks have their place in a law office, and we recognize the fact that the nature of their work approaches in a degree that of their employers. The line of demarcation as to where their work begins and where it ends cannot always be drawn with absolute distinction or accuracy. Probably as nearly as it can be fixed, and it is sufficient to say that it is work of a preparatory nature, such as research investigation of details, the assemblage of data and other necessary information, and such other work as will assist the employing attorney in carrying the matter to a completed product, either by his personal examination and approval thereof, or by additional effort on his part. The work must be such, however, as loses its separate identity and becomes either the product, or else merged in the product, of the attorney himself. (19 P.2d at pp. 945–46.) (*See* Florida EC3-6, infra at, Section IV.)

The NALA *Guidelines* constitute a statement relating to services performed by non-lawyer employees as approved by court decisions and other sources of authority. The purpose of the *Guidelines* is not to place limitations or restrictions on the legal profession. Rather, the *Guidelines* are intended to outline for the legal profession an acceptable course of conduct. By voluntary recognition and utilization of the *Model Standards and Guidelines* the legal profession will avoid many problems.

Definition

Legal assistants, also known as paralegals, are a distinguishable group of persons who assist attorneys in the delivery of legal services. Through formal education, training, and experience, legal assistants have knowledge and expertise regarding the legal system and substantive and procedural law which qualify them to do work of a legal nature under the supervision of an attorney.

COMMENT

This definition has been used to foster a distinction between a legal assistant as one working under the direct supervision of an attorney and a broader class of paralegals who perform tasks of similar nature, but not necessarily under the supervision of an attorney. In applying the standards and guidelines it is important to remember that they in turn were developed to apply to the legal assistant as defined therein.

Standards

A legal assistant should meet certain minimum qualifications. The following standards may be used to determine an individual's qualifications as a legal assistant:

1. Successful completion of the Certified Legal Assistant ("CLA") examination of the National Association of Legal Assistants, Inc. (*see* attached Exhibit A, page 107);
2. Graduation from an ABA approved program of study for legal assistants;
3. Graduation from a course of study for legal assistants which is institutionally accredited but not ABA approved, and which requires not less than the equivalent of 60 semester hours of classroom study;
4. Graduation from a course of study for legal assistants, other than those set forth in (2) and (3) above, plus not less than six months of in-house training as a legal assistant;
5. A baccalaureate degree in any field, plus not less than six months in-house training as a legal assistant;

6. A minimum of three years of law-related experience under the supervision of an attorney, including at least six months of in-house training as a legal assistant; or

7. Two years of in-house training as a legal assistant.

For purposes of these standards, "in-house training as a legal assistant" means attorney education of the employee concerning legal assistant duties and these guidelines. In addition to review and analysis of assignments, the legal assistant should receive a reasonable amount of instruction directly related to the duties and obligations of the legal assistant.

COMMENT

The standards set forth suggested minimum qualifications for a legal assistant. These minimum qualifications as adopted recognize legal related work backgrounds and formal education backgrounds, both of which should provide the legal assistant with a broad base in exposure to, and knowledge of, the legal profession. This background is necessary to assure the public and the legal profession that the one being identified as a legal assistant is qualified.

The Certified Legal Assistant ("CLA") examination offered by NALA is the only voluntary nationwide certification program for legal assistants. The "CLA" designation is a statement to the legal profession and the public that the legal assistant has met the high levels of knowledge and professionalism required by NALA's certification program. Continuing education requirements, which all certified legal assistants must meet, assure that high standards are maintained. Certification through NALA is available to any legal assistant meeting the educational and experience requirements.

Guidelines

These guidelines relating to standards of performance and professional responsibility are intended to aid legal assistants and attorneys. The responsibility rests with an attorney who employs legal assistants to educate them with respect to the duties they are assigned and to supervise the manner in which such duties are accomplished.

COMMENT

In general, a legal assistant is allowed to perform any task which is properly delegated and supervised by an attorney, so long as the attorney is ultimately responsible to the client and assumes complete professional responsibility for the work product.

The *Code of Professional Responsibility* of the American Bar Association, EC3-6 states:

> A lawyer often delegates tasks to clerks, secretaries, and other lay persons. Such delegation is proper if the lawyer maintains a direct relationship with his clients, supervises the delegated work, and has complete professional responsibility for the work product.

ABA *Model Rules of Professional Conduct,* Rule 5.3 provides:

> With respect to a nonlawyer employed or retained by or associated with a lawyer:
>
> a. a partner in a law firm shall make reasonable efforts to ensure that the firm has in effect measures giving reasonable assurance that the person's conduct is compatible with the professional obligations of the lawyer;

  b. a lawyer having direct supervisory authority over the nonlawyer shall make reasonable efforts to ensure that the person's conduct is compatible with the professional obligations of the lawyer; and

  c. a lawyer shall be responsible for conduct of such a person that would be a violation of the rules of professional conduct if engaged in by a lawyer if:

    1. the lawyer orders or with the knowledge of the specific conduct ratifies the conduct involved; or

    2. the lawyer is a partner in the law firm in which the person is employed, or has direct supervisory authority over the person, and knows of the conduct at a time when its consequences can be avoided or mitigated but fails to take reasonable remedial action.

The Florida version of EC3-6 provides:

> A lawyer or law firm may employ nonlawyers such as secretaries, law clerks, investigators, accountants, draftsmen, office administrators, and other lay personnel to assist the lawyer in the delivery of legal services. A lawyer often delegates tasks to such persons. Such delegation is proper if a lawyer retains a direct relationship with his client, supervises the delegated work, and has complete professional responsibility for the work product.
>
> The work which is delegated is such that it will assist the employing attorney in carrying the matter to a completed product either by the lawyer's personal examination and approval thereof or by additional effort on the lawyer's part. The delegated work must be such, however, as loses its separate identity and becomes either the product or else merged in the product of the attorney himself.

The *Kentucky Paralegal Code* defines a legal assistant as:

> . . . a person under the supervision and direction of a licensed lawyer who may apply knowledge of law and legal procedures in rendering direct assistance to lawyers engaged in legal research; design, develop or plan modifications or new procedures, techniques, services, processes or applications; prepare or interpret legal documents and write detailed procedure for practicing in certain fields of law; select, compile, and use technical information from such references as digests, encyclopedias or practice manuals; and analyze and follow procedural problems that involve independent decisions.

Kentucky became the first state to adopt a *Paralegal Code,* which sets forth certain exclusions to the unauthorized practice of law:

> For purpose of this rule, the unauthorized practice of law shall not include any service rendered involving legal knowledge or advice, whether representation, counsel or advocacy, in or out of court rendered in respect to the acts, duties, obligations, liabilities, or business relations of the one requiring services where:
>
> a. The client understands that the paralegal is not a lawyer;
>
> b. The lawyer supervises the paralegal in the performance of his duties; and
>
> c. The lawyer remains fully responsible for such representation, including all actions taken or not taken in connection therewith by the paralegal to the same extent as if such representation had been furnished entirely by the lawyer and all such actions had been taken or not taken directly by the attorney.

Paralegal Code, Ky. S.Ct. R 3.700, Sub-Rule 2.

While the Kentucky rule is an exception, it does provide a basis for expanding services which may be performed by legal assistants.

There are many interesting and complex issues involving the use of legal assistants. One issue which is not addressed in the *Guidelines* is whether a legal assistant, as defined herein, may make appearances before administrative agencies. This issue is discussed in Remmer, *Representation of Clients Before Administrative Agencies; Authorized or Unauthorized Practice of Law?*, 15 Valparaiso Univ. L.Rev. 567 (1981). The State Bar of California Standing Committee on Professional Responsibility and Conduct, in Opinion 1988-103 (2/8/89) has stated a law firm can delegate authority to a legal assistant employee to file petitions, motions, and make other appearances before the Workers' Compensation Appeals Board provided adequate supervision is maintained by the attorney and the client is informed and has consented to the use of the legal assistant in such fashion.

In any discussion of the proper role of a legal assistant, attention must be directed to what constitutes the practice of law. The proper delegation of work and duties to legal assistants is further complicated and confused by the lack of adequate definition of the practice of law and the unauthorized practice of law.

In *Davis v. Unauthorized Practice Committee*, 431 S.W.2d 590 (Texas, 1968), the Court found that the defendant was properly enjoined from the authorized practice of law. The Court, in defining the "practice of law," stated:

> According to the generally understood definition of the practice of law, it embraces the preparation of pleadings and other papers incident to actions of special proceedings, and the management of such actions in proceedings on behalf of clients before judges in courts. However, the practice of law is not confined to cases conducted in court. In fact, the major portion of the practice of any capable lawyer consists of work done outside of the courts. The practice of law involves not only appearance in court in connection with litigation, but also services rendered out of court, and includes the giving of advice or the rendering of any service requiring the use of legal skill or knowledge, such as preparing a will, contract, or other instrument, the legal effect of which under the facts and conclusions involved must be carefully determined.

The important distinguishing fact between the defendant in *Davis* and a legal assistant is that the acts of the legal assistant are performed under the supervision of an attorney.

EC3-5 of the *Code of Professional Responsibility* states:

> It is neither necessary nor desirable to attempt the formulation of a single, specific definition of what constitutes the practice of law. Functionally, the practice of law relates to the rendition of services for others that call for the professional judgment of a lawyer. The essence of the professional judgment of the lawyer is his educated ability to relate the general body and philosophy of law to a specific legal problem of a client; and thus, the public interest will be better served if only lawyers are permitted to act in matters involving professional judgment. Where this professional judgment is not involved, nonlawyers, such as court clerks, police officers, abstracters, and many governmental employees, may engage in occupations that require a special knowledge of law in certain areas. But the services of a lawyer are essential in the public interest whenever the exercise of professional legal judgment is required.

There are many cases relating to the unauthorized practice of law, but the most troublesome ones in attempting to define what would or would not form the unauthorized practice of law for acts performed by a legal assistant are those such as *Crawford v. State Bar of California*, 355

P.2d 490 (Calif. 1960), which states that any act performed in a law office is the practice of law because the clients have sought the attorney to perform the work because of the training and judgment exercised by attorneys.

See also, Annot. *"Layman's Assistance to Parties in Divorce Proceedings as Unauthorized Practice of Law,"* 12 ALR4 656; Annot. *"Activities of Law Clerks as Illegal Practice of Law."* 13 ALR3 1137; Annot. *"Sale of Books or Forms Designed to Enable Layman to Achieve Legal Results Without Assistance of Attorney as Unauthorized Practice of Law,"* 71 ALR3 1000; Annot. *"Nature of Legal Services or Law-Related Services Which May Be Performed for Others By Disbarred of Suspended Attorney,"* 87 ALR3 272. See also, Karen B. Judd, CLA, *"Beyond the Bar: Legal Assistants and the Unauthorized Practice of Law."* VIII Facts & Findings 6, National Association of Legal Assistants, May-June, 1982.

Legal assistants should:

1. Disclose their status as legal assistants at the outset of any professional relationships with a client, other attorneys, a court or administrative agency or personnel thereof, or members of the general public;
2. Preserve the confidences and secrets of all clients; and
3. Understand the attorney's *Code of Professional Responsibility* and these guidelines in order to avoid any action which would involve the attorney in a violation of that *Code,* or give the appearance of professional impropriety.

COMMENT

Routine early disclosure of the legal assistant's status when dealing with persons outside the attorney's office is necessary to assure that there will be no misunderstanding as to the responsibilities and role of the legal assistant. Disclosure may be made in any way that avoids confusion. If the person dealing with the legal assistant already knows of his or her status, further disclosure is unnecessary. If at any time in written or in oral communication the legal assistant becomes aware that the other person may believe the legal assistant is an attorney, it should be made clear that the legal assistant is not an attorney.

The attorney should exercise care that the legal assistant preserves and refrains from using any confidence or secrets of a client, and should instruct the legal assistant not to disclose or use any such confidences or secrets.

DR 4-101 (D). ABA *Code of Professional Responsibility,* provides in part that:

> A lawyer shall exercise reasonable care to prevent his employees, associates, and others whose services are utilized by him from disclosing or using confidences or secrets of a client . . .

This obligation is emphasized in EC4-2:

> It is a matter of common knowledge that the normal operation of law office exposes confidential professional information to nonlawyer employees of the office, particularly secretaries and those having access to the files; and this obligates the lawyer to exercise care in selecting and training his employees to that the sanctity of all confidences and secrets of his clients may be preserved.

The ultimate responsibility for compliance with approved standards of professional conduct rests with the supervising attorney. *In the Matter of Martinez,* 107 N.M. 171, 754 P.2d 842 (N.M.

1988). However, the legal assistant should understand what he may or may not do. The burden rests upon the attorney who employs a legal assistant to educate the latter with respect to the duties which may be assigned and then to supervise the manner in which the legal assistant carries out such duties. However, this does not relieve the legal assistant from an independent obligation to refrain from illegal conduct. Additionally, and notwithstanding that the ABA *Code* is not binding upon nonlawyers; the very nature of a legal assistant's employment imposes an obligation not to engage in conduct which would involve the supervising attorney in a violation of the *Code*. NALA has adopted the ABA *Code* as a part of its *Code of Ethics*.

Legal assistants should not:

1. Establish attorney-client relationships; set legal fees; give legal opinions or advice; or represent a client before a court; nor
2. Engage in, encourage, or contribute to any act which could constitute the unauthorized practice of law.

COMMENT

Reported cases holding which acts can and cannot be performed by a legal assistant are few:

The legal assistant cannot create the attorney-client relationship. *DeVaux v. American Home Assur. Co.,* 444 N.E.2d 355 (Mass. 1983).

The legal assistant cannot make court appearances. The question of what constitute a court appearance is also somewhat vague. See, for example, *People v. Alexander,* 53 Ill, App.2d 299, 202 N.E.2d 841 (1964), where preparation of a court order and transmitting information to court was not the unauthorized practice of law, and *People v. Belfor,* 611 P.2d 979 (Colo. 1980), where the trial court found that the acts of a disbarred attorney did not constitute an appearance and the Supreme Court of Colorado held that only the Supreme Court could make the determination of what acts constituted an appearance and the unauthorized practice of law.

 The following cases have identified certain areas in which an attorney has a duty to act, but it is interesting to note that none of these cases state that it is improper for an attorney to have the initial work performed by a legal assistant. This again points out the importance of adequate supervision by the employing attorney.

Courts have found that attorneys have the duty to check bank statements, preserve a client's property, review and sign all pleadings, insure that all communications are opened and answered, and make inquiry when items of dictation are not received. *Attorney Grievance Commission of Maryland v. Goldberg,* 441 A.2d 338,292 Md. 650 (1982). See also *Vaughn v. State Bar of California,* 100 Cal. Reptr. 713, 494 P.2d 1257 (1972).

The legal assistant cannot exercise professional legal judgment or give legal advice. In *Louisiana State Bar v. Edwins,* 540 So.2d 294 (La. 1989) the court held a paralegal was engaged in activities constituting the unauthorized practice of law, which included evaluation of claims and giving advice on settlements. The attorney who delegated the exercise of these acts aided in the unauthorized practice of law. See also, *People of the State of Co. v. Gelker,* 770 P.2d 402 (Col. 1989).

Attorneys have the responsibility to supervise the work of associates and clerical staff. *Moore v. State Bar Association,* 41 Cal. Rptr. 161, 396 P.2d 577 (1964); *Attorney Grievance Committee of Maryland v. Goldberg, supra.*

An attorney must exercise sufficient supervision to insure that all monies received are properly deposited and disbursed. *Black v. State Bar of California,* 103 Cal. Rprt. 288, 499 P.2d 968 (1972); *Fitzpatrick v. State Bar of California,* 141 Cal. Rptr. 169.569 P.2d763 (1977).

The attorney must insure that his staff is competent and effective to perform the work delegated. In *Re Reinmiller,* 325 P.2d 773 (Oregon, 1958). See also, *State of Kansas v. Barrett,* 483 P.2d 1106 (Kansas, 1971); *Attorney Grievance Committee of Maryland v. Goldberg, supra.*

The attorney must make sufficient background investigation of the prior activities and character and integrity of his employees to insure that legal assistants have not previously been involved in unethical, illegal, or other nefarious schemes which demonstrate such person unfit to be associated with the practice of law. See *In the Matter of Shaw,* 88 N.J. 433, A.2d 678 (1982), wherein the Court announced that while it had no disciplinary jurisdiction over legal assistants, it directed that disciplinary hearings make specific findings of fact concerning paralegals' collaboration in nefarious schemes in order that the court might properly discipline any attorney establishing an office relationship with one who had been implicated previously in unscrupulous schemes.

Legal assistants may perform services for an attorney in the representation of a client, provided:

1. The services performed by the legal assistant do not require the exercise of independent professional legal judgment;
2. The attorney maintains a direct relationship with the client and maintains control of all client matters;
3. The attorney supervises the legal assistant;
4. The attorney remains professionally responsible for all work on behalf of the client, including any actions taken or not taken by the legal assistant in connection therewith; and
5. The services performed supplement, merge with, and become the attorney's work product.

COMMENT

EC3-6. ABA *Code of Professional Responsibility* recognizes the value of utilizing the services of legal assistants, but provides certain conditions to such employment:

A lawyer often delegates tasks to clerks, secretaries, and other lay persons. Such delegation is proper if the lawyer maintains a direct relationship with his client, supervises the delegated work, and has complete professional responsibility for the work product. This delegation enables a lawyer to render legal services more economically and efficiently.

In the supervision of a legal assistant, consideration should be given to:

1. Designating work assignments that correspond to the legal assistant's abilities, knowledge, training, and experience;

2. Educating and training the legal assistant with respect to professional responsibility, local rules and practices, and firm policies;

3. Monitoring the work and professional conduct of the legal assistant to ensure that the work is substantively correct and timely performed;

4. Providing continuing education for the legal assistant in substantive matters through courses, institutes, workshops, seminars, and in-house training; and

5. Encouraging and supporting membership and active participation in professional organizations.

COMMENT

Attorneys are responsible for the actions of their employees in both malpractice and disciplinary proceedings. The attorney cannot delegate work to a legal assistant which involves activities constituting the unauthorized practice of law. See *Louisiana State Bar v. Edwins,* 540 So.2d 294 (La. 1989), and *People of the State of Colorado v. Felker,* 770 P.2d 402 (Col. 1989). In the vast majority of the cases, the courts have not censured attorneys for the particular act delegated to the legal assistant, but rather, have been critical of an imposed sanctions against attorneys for failure to adequately supervise the legal assistants. See e.g., *Attorney Grievance Commission of Maryland v. Goldberg, supra.*

The attorney's responsibility for supervision of legal assistants must be more than a willingness to accept responsibility and liability for the legal assistant's work. The attorney must monitor the work product and conduct of the legal assistant to insure that the work performed is substantively correct and competently performed in a professional manner. This duty includes the responsibility to provide continuing legal education for the legal assistant.

Supervision of legal assistants must be offered in both the procedural and substantive legal areas in the law office.

In *Spindell v. State Bar of California,* 118 Cal. Rptr. 480,530 P.2d 168 (1975), the attorney was suspended from practice because of the improper legal advice given by a secretary. The case illustrates that it is important that both attorneys and legal assistants confirm all telephonic advice by letter.

In all instances where the legal assistant relays information to a client in response to an inquiry from the client, the advice relayed telephonically by the legal assistant should be confirmed in writing by the attorney. This will eliminate claims if the client acts contrary to the advice given. It will establish that the legal advice given is in fact that of the attorney, not the legal assistant, and obviate any confusion resulting from transmission of the advice through the legal assistant.

The *Spindell* case is an example of an attorney's failure to supervise and educate his staff. Not only was the secretary uneducated as to the substantive provisions of the law, but more importantly, she was uneducated as to her duty and authority as an employee of the attorney.

Except as otherwise provided by statute, court rule or decision, administrative rule or regulation, or the attorney's *Code of Professional Responsibility,* and within the preceding parameters and proscriptions, a legal assistant may perform any function delegated by an attorney, including, but not limited to the following:

1. Conduct client interviews and maintain general contact with the client after the establishment of the attorney-client relationship, so long as the client is aware of the status and function of the legal assistant, and the client contact is under the supervision of the attorney.

2. Locate and interview witnesses, so long as the witnesses are aware of the status and function of the legal assistant.
3. Conduct investigations and statistical and documentary research for review by the attorney.
4. Conduct legal research for review by the attorney.
5. Draft legal documents for review by the attorney.
6. Draft correspondence and pleadings for review by and signature of the attorney.
7. Summarize depositions, interrogatories, and testimony for review by the attorney.
8. Attend executions of wills, real estate closings, depositions, court or administrative hearings, and trials with the attorney.
9. Author and sign letters provided the legal assistant's status is clearly indicated and the correspondence does not contain independent legal opinions or legal advice.

COMMENT

The U.S. Supreme Court has recognized the variety of tasks being performed by legal assistants and has noted that use of legal assistants encourages cost effective delivery of legal services, *Missouri v. Jenkins*, 491 U.S. 274, 109 S.Ct. 2463, 2471, No. 10 (1989). In *Jenkins*, the court further held that legal assistant time should be included in compensation for attorney fee awards at the prevailing market rate if it is shown to be prevailing practice in the relevant community to bill legal assistant time.

Except for the specific proscription contained in Section 6, the reported cases such as Attorney Grievance Commission of *Maryland v. Goldberg, supra,* do not limit the duties which may be performed by a legal assistant under the supervision of the attorney.

The *Guidelines* were developed from generally accepted practices. Each supervision attorney must be aware of the specific rules, decisions, and statutes applicable to legal assistants within his jurisdiction.

Exhibit A

To become eligible to sit for the NALA certifying examination ("CLA"), candidates must meet one of the following requirements:

1. Graduation from a legal assistant program that is:
   a. Approved by the American Bar Association, or
   b. An associate degree program, or
   c. A post-baccalaureate certificate program in legal studies, or
   d. A bachelor's degree program in legal assistant studies, or
   e. A legal assistant program which consists of a minimum of 60 semester (or equivalent quarter)* hours of which at least 15 semester hours (or equivalent quarter hours)** are substantive legal courses.

---

 * 900 clock hours of a legal assistant program will be considered equivalent to 60 semester hours. 90 quarter hours of a legal assistant program will be considered equivalent to 60 semester hours.

 ** 225 clock hours of substantive legal courses will be considered equivalent to 15 semester hours. $22\frac{1}{4}$ quarter hours of legal courses will be considered equivalent to 15 semester hours.

2. A bachelor's degree in any field plus one year's experience as a legal assistant.*

---

 * Successful completion of at least 15 semester hours (or $22\frac{1}{4}$ quarter hours or 225 clock hours) of substantive legal courses will be considered equivalent to one year experience as a legal assistant.

3. A high school diploma or equivalent plus seven (7) years' experience as a legal assistant under the supervision of a member of the Bar plus evidence of a minimum of twenty (20) hours of continuing legal education credit to have been completed within a two-year period prior to the examination date.

Bibliography

American Bar Association, *Model Code of Professional Responsibility* (1969, as amended).

American Bar Association, *Model Rules of Professional Conduct* (1983, as amended).

National Association of Legal Assistants, *Code of Ethics and Professional Responsibility* (As amended through 1995).

National Association of Legal Assistants, *Model Standards and Guidelines for Utilization of Legal Assistants* (Annotated).

ABA Commission on Nonlawyer Practice, *Nonlawyer Activity in Law-Related Associations.* American Bar Association (1992).

National Association of Legal Assistants, *Summary of Definitions of Terms Legal Assistant and Paralegal,* XXIV Facts & Findings 1 (May 1997).

Cohn, Steven, *Beyond the "Chinese Wall,"* Legal Assistant Today (November/December 1995).

Emert, Laurence T., *Preserving a Client's Confidences,* XIX Facts & Findings 5 (February 1993).

Voisin, Vicki, *Changing Jobs: Ethical Consideration for Legal Assistants,* XV Facts & Findings 12 (March 1989).

Judd, Karen B., *Beyond the Bar: Legal Assistants and the Unauthorized Practice of Law,* VIII Facts & Findings 1 (NALA), (May–June 1982).

Webb, Wendi, *"The New Age of Electronic Discovery,"* Legal Assistant Today, (May/June 1996).

Powers, James A., *"O What A Tangled Web We Weave,"* XXIII Facts & Findings 1 (May 1996).

4 Judgment and Analytical Ability

4.00 Introduction

The scope and diversity of duties delegated to legal assistants depends primarily upon the trust and confidence the supervising attorney accords the legal assistant as an individual, not upon assumptions based solely on the title "legal assistant" or "certified legal assistant." This trust and confidence are earned recognitions of the personal attributes of the individual, including intelligence, a positive attitude, a willingness to assume responsibility, communication skills, ethical and moral standards, imagination, reliability, analytical ability, and good judgment.

The utility and value of a legal assistant to the lawyer depend more on the last two personal skills than all the others. Weakness in analytical abilities or judgment capabilities seriously limits the duties delegated to the legal assistant, for the entire legal process requires these two qualities. *Analyze* is defined as "to separate a thing, idea, etc. into its parts so as to find out their nature, proportion, function, interrelationship, and other properties." *Judgment* is defined as "the capacity to perceive, discern, or make reasonable decisions."

Legal assistants and attorneys work in an atmosphere of good and bad judgments. These two modifiers expand that passionless and risk-free definition of judgment into a qualitative evaluation of the action or inaction that flowed from the "formation of the opinion." That is the nature of legal work—participation and involvement, rather than uninvolved observation or comment.

Judgment is necessarily followed by a decision which sets in motion some act or causes some act not to be done. The result is then measured to determine whether a particular judgment in a particular situation was good or bad. For instance, one does not need to go to law school nor enroll in a course for legal assistants to understand that if an automobile driver deliberately runs a red light, a police officer may issue a citation calling for a fine or trial. Everyone is generally acquainted with good and bad judgments and the acts, consequences, and results that can flow from them. This chapter stresses more definitive aspects of judgment and analytical ability as they relate to legal assistants in large and small law offices, nontraditional legal assistant settings, and in simple and complex cases.

4.01   How to Develop Good Judgment

If good judgment in any given situation involved facts, statistics, or objects, each considered without self-will, opinions, biases, prejudices and preferences, tempers, egos, and feelings, then a computer could be used to sort all the factors and select the optimum decision. Reliable good judgment and productive analytical ability are developed by exercise and practice and, even more important, through mistakes. Good judgment requires the leavening of experience with analytical ability and other personal characteristics, such as compassion and flexibility, applied within a framework of the following basic guidelines:

a.   Understand the reporting system and delegation of responsibilities;
b.   Understand the scope, instructions, and authority delegated;
c.   Appreciate priorities;
d.   Honor time committments;
e.   Recognize exceptional situations;
f.   Accept guidance, directions, and comments constructively; and
g.   Enthusiastically observe moral and ethical standards.

4.011   Understand the Reporting System and Delegation of Responsibilities

Every law firm or legal department has a reporting system of personnel and specific reservations and/or delegations of responsibilities. Clearly, the librarian is responsible for the selection, purchase, and maintenance of the materials in the library. Sometimes, the office manager is the coordinator for "extra help," overtime, or other personnel adjustments and is responsible for equipment purchase, service contracting, petty cash expenditures, travel arrangements, and so on. The senior attorneys and their secretaries have certain stated, or unstated but well understood, prerogatives, and other attorneys, secretaries, and legal assistants have another set of prerogatives or guidelines. It is essential that areas of authority and responsibility of the office as a whole be generally understood by the legal assistant, including the avenues for inquiry, suggestions, and requests.

For example, in a firm that uses a well-established and rigidly controlled file system requiring every file to be returned to the file room daily (except with special permission), the legal assistant should learn the background of the current procedure from the files supervisor before attempting to introduce changes. It is bad judgment to attempt to resurrect an old system without knowing its history and without having substantial justification and a well-founded plan or recommendation for changing it. Personal opinions and convenience simply do not qualify as justifications, even though the legal assistant's suggested system may have worked beautifully and masterfully in other and even larger firms.[1]

As the legal assistant becomes more and more familiar with office organization and distribution of operational authority, his or her good judgment is demonstrated by posing appropriate questions to the properly responsible parties. Learning the reporting system or assumption of roles within the office ensures that few, if any, inadvertent cases of "going over the head" of a responsible person occurs. Understanding the office dynamics gives the legal assistant the proper perspective and prepares him or her to handle the other guidelines effectively.

4.012 Understand the Scope, Instructions, and Authority Delegated

Legal assistants are an ambitious group who will generally accept all responsibility delegated to them and additionally create, or even usurp, other areas of responsibility. They also devise new methods and procedures not previously tried and proven, which can be effective in certain situations. That frequently becomes true but never suddenly nor without a period of gradual demonstration of reliable judgment and analytical ability. An overly aggressive or presumptuous legal assistant will never achieve a high level of responsibility as a valued professional as quickly as one who proceeds with preparation, study, and deliberation.

Legal assistants entering a law office or legal department must become aware of and understand the office concept of the legal assistant, as well as the kinds of duties performed; who directs their work and whose work (if any) they direct; if they can spend funds, and if so, to what dollar limit; if they can contract for the firm, and if so, what kinds of contracts (travel, document copying, photography, model making, and so on). They must obtain information concerning how billable and nonbillable hours are recorded; who makes decisions about billable expenses; how the secretarial support system functions for the legal assistant; the mail system; the docket system; and any other system that may directly or indirectly affect them.

No matter how restrictive, inefficient, or ridiculous the system first seems, the legal assistant should make every effort to follow the stipulated procedures while establishing an independent level of respect in the office. Most of the poor or inefficient practices encountered in an office are the compromises of past internal struggles or "hand-me-downs" of long ago that remain through inertia. Legal assistants must be flexible enough to adapt to the internal situation until they have an opportunity to make proper, thoughtful, and constructive suggestions for change to the appropriate person at the proper time.

Once the office concept and general administration procedures are understood, the legal assistant seeks to understand the kinds of cases handled by the attorney as well as the preferred techniques for every procedure in which the attorney intends to involve the legal assistant. The next most important area of concern is the comfortable and effective integration of the lawyer, the legal assistant, and the secretary in all phases of the working relationship; this is a changing and vitally important team that requires consideration and participation from all three parties.

---

[1] This should not, however, deter a legal assistant from taking the initiative to promote efficiencies within the office setting.

Becoming familiar with the attorney's schedule allows the legal assistant's work efforts to be adapted to and compliment the lawyer's work habits. For example, some lawyers prefer the first hour to be undisturbed for handling mail and dictation, others the last hour. Some prefer to have the legal assistant meet with them once a week for a general review of all active files, while others prefer more frequent meetings for case-by-case discussions; still others are "hit it while I'm hot" advocates who are likely to say, "We'll do it right now, regardless of your previous assignments." Here again, flexibility and patience are important characteristics of a legal assistant.

Legal assistants specializing in real estate must be familiar with the real estate laws in their state, mortgage rates, property descriptions, title information, closing statements, zoning board regulations, local, state, and federal regulations or statutes concerning purchasing, leasing, landlord-tenant situations, and all other pertinent areas of real estate law.

Corporate legal assistants must be familiar with state and federal laws concerning corporations and procedures for incorporation, including: tax and other laws pertaining to different types of corporations, such as domestic, foreign, Chapter S, closed, nonprofit, charitable or eleemosynary corporations; stock splits and stock options, dividends; pension plans; minutes of meetings of shareholders, directors, and incorporators; mergers; acquisitions; blue sky laws; and certain requirements of the Securities and Exchange Commission.

Legal Assistants specializing in Bankruptcy Law must be familiar with the Bankruptcy Code (Title 11 U.S.C. and Title 28 U.S.C.), bankruptcy rules and procedures, including the applicable Federal Rules of Civil Procedure and Federal Rules of Evidence, with regard to debtors and creditors.

Legal assistants involved in estate planning must necessarily keep abreast of the everchanging tax laws affecting estate planning for particular clients and be familiar with proper auditing procedures; valuation of assets; preparation of federal and state tax returns; proper acquisition of bank accounts; insurance proceeds; Social Security regulations; and many other areas. The same is true in all other specialty areas—the legal assistants first are thoroughly familiar with the area or areas in which they work. Then they apply judgment and analytical ability in a particular area or areas.

While there are many specialty areas in which legal assistants operate, there is one area of specialization that will often encompass any one or all of the other specialty areas, and that is litigation. A litigation legal assistant, of necessity, becomes involved in real estate, probate, estate planning, bankruptcy, and family law; or possibly in real estate and corporate, criminal and corporate, criminal and tax, or other combinations, depending on the case. For that reason, we shall use the area of the litigation specialist to illustrate the concept of judgment and analytical ability. The same principles can be applied in any other specialty area but can be explored in more depth in the area of litigation. Therefore, as we explore the remaining five guidelines, the illustrations we use will deal primarily in litigation.

Litigation legal assistants must be familiar with the rules of federal and state courts, either criminal or civil, depending on the bulk of office practice. If the court rules state (for civil matters) that "all law and motion matters must be filed forty-eight hours prior to the hearing," a legal assistant must determine whether this means forty-eight actual hours or "no less than two full working court days before the hearing." Similarly, court rules or local interpretation give rise to such questions as: "Does the court accept pleadings on $8\frac{1}{2}$t · 14t paper, $8\frac{1}{2}$t · 13t paper, or only $8\frac{1}{2}$t · 11t paper?" "Will the court allow legal assistants at the counsel table during trial?" And if not, what accommodations will need to be made? Other similar questions may arise to a legal assistant. The failure to resolve such questions may confound the best efforts of the legal assistant, result in embarrassment to the attorney, and frustrate a tactical objective.

4.013 Appreciate Priorities

Priorities in legal assisting lie first in the court docket, including deadlines, orders, and applicable city, state, and federal rules and regulations, and then in personal preferences. Also of importance are less well-defined priorities, the most vexatious of these being the priority of work production accorded the various personalities within the firm. It is obvious that the managing partner with a job to be expedited will receive all the necessary resources to complete the assignment in a timely and diligent fashion. Less clear and compelling is the need of a junior attorney's legal assistant for extra help in completing a long-term project on schedule.[2] Yet the objective merit of the situations appears to be the same. The legal assistant needs to properly evaluate and predict the need for assistance before the situation becomes a panic as he or she is in the best position to make such predictions. The occasional panic situation could be avoided by the legal assistant's attention to prioritization and initiative. Such foresight is helpful not only to the lawyer but also to the office manager, who is responsible for coping with unanticipated peaks in workloads created by "Please expedite" or "panic" operations. Choosing between two necessary activities for first attention and effort is the most difficult priority judgment a legal assistant makes. Pulling together a list of the pending tasks, with an outline of "pros and cons" associated with your recommendation or prioritization, should be submitted to the person(s) who assigned the tasks. It is for them, then, to decide which task has priority. For example, develop the document control plan or assemble all the documents? Draft additional interrogatories or summarize the depositions? Thoughtful analysis can lead the way to making the decision. The work obviously cannot be predicated on the likes and dislikes of lawyers, legal assistants, or secretaries, since all aspects must be done sooner or later. Ignoring logical priorities results in creating additional problems, such as doing necessary but less challenging work under inordinate and unnecessary time pressures. The usual result of panic work is often poor quality and lost time which is the result of material being improperly prepared, proofed, and/or corrected. Unreliable and incomplete material is of little or no use to the employing attorney and seriously affects the trust and confidence placed in the legal assistant.

4.014 Honor Time Commitments

Time is the most important commodity of a lawyer. It determines work schedules, which may be planned many weeks in advance. In private practice, it is a primary basis for certain charges to the client. Court rulings, codes, and statutes all provide for certain periods of time to elapse in the normal course of pleadings, motions, discovery, trial, and appeal. A legal assistant who is consistently and conscientiously aware of the importance of time is highly valued. It is true that many time periods may be waived or extensions granted; however, the attorney should not be forced into seeking such favors from the adversary or the indulgence of the court because of the failure or inability of the legal assistant to perform. A legal assistant usually knows well before a deadline whether a project can meet a specified schedule with the resources currently in use. If the schedule cannot be met, the legal assistant should not hesitate to request or recommend additional help, overtime, a reshuffling or prioritization, or a combination.

Many legal assistants face having too much to do in too little time. A legal assistant's challenge, then, becomes acquiring time management techniques in order to optimize efficiency. Developing systems and starting form files are examples of how a legal assistant can manage time, whether done "manually" or by computer. Computers, document management systems, desktop avail-

---

2 Many firms and legal departments have established a less hierarchal approach and more of a team effort of prioritization.

ability of electronic research programs, and the Internet are a few of the technological advances that have given the legal assistant a set of tools to help manage the workload.

One system of time management involves establishing task lists with individual items placed in order of priority. Analyze the list for items that can be combined. For instance, when summarizing a deposition, concurrently create a list of the names of other potential witnesses on a separate document along with a listing and description of the exhibits introduced on yet a third document. This can be done very efficiently when using a computer and working from the disk version of the transcript provided by court reporters. Another time management technique is to anticipate future needs when accomplishing present tasks.

Think in terms of working "smarter not harder." For example, in a situation where a deposition must be scheduled which involves several parties, first review your attorney's calendar and select at least three dates and times which are convenient. Then, instead of telephoning each party (which can take an inordinate amount of time), send a letter by fax which asks each party to respond concerning availability on the suggested dates and to provide alternate dates if not available. Go ahead and have the draft deposition notice and subpoena prepared so that when the responses are received, all that need be added is the agreed upon date and time. The resulting time savings to the legal assistant can sometimes be counted in hours.

4.015   Recognize Exceptional Situations

Every legal assistant, after some time with a firm or legal department, may become a secondary target (in the absence of the case attorney) for requests, questions, and demands that involve routine matters clearly within the legal assistant's knowledge and functional ability to resolve. Other requests, questions, or demands may constitute serious questions involving the propriety of the legal assistant to respond either affirmatively or negatively. These instances usually involve such questions as, "If I do this, will it be all right?" or "What do you think I should do?" or "If I don't know how to act on this immediately, will the chance be gone?" These all pose ethical problems regarding the unauthorized practice of law by the legal assistant (*see generally,* Chapter 3, Ethics). Let us consider three basic problems in this area (commentary is provided in Section 4.04):

PROBLEM NO. 1

The client is involved in personal injury litigation resulting from injuries she received in an auto accident. She calls your office first asking for the attorney representing her on this case, but the attorney is out of the office for the day. The client states that an insurance adjuster is at her home and wants to take a written statement regarding the details of the auto accident.

Query: How should the legal assistant handle this situation?

PROBLEM NO. 2

Preparations are nearly complete for allowing an adversary to inspect documents under a "Request to Produce" that required "each and every copy" of a specified variety of records and files. Some 3,700 pages of material, already screened, are ready. Two hundred and fifty pages of privileged material have been removed, and the appropriate list prepared, when the client reveals that a wholly owned subsidiary has nearly an exact duplicate file, plus several individual personal files reasonably responsive to the request. Seventy-five work hours have already been expended, and the inspection is scheduled for the day after tomorrow.

Query: What does the legal assistant need to do to allow the lawyer to select a course of action? Can the legal assistant suppress this information until it is too late to act on it? Should the legal assistant simply throw up his or her hands and leave for the day?

PROBLEM NO. 3

A client is involved in a difficult contested divorce involving substantial assets in real estate, stocks, bonds, annuities, and other property. In the course of interviewing and assembling the property and asset descriptions, it becomes apparent that the client has been siphoning community property assets into a separate fund over the past two or three years. It has been skillfully done, and only the legal assistant's intimate involvement and careful analysis allowed the discovery.

Query: Does the legal assistant punish the client by advising the attorney, become a part of the client's fraud by remaining silent, or send an anonymous note to the adversary attorney ensure that the client gets his just desserts?

These are but a few of many exceptional situations that will arise in a law office from time to time. After many such experiences, a legal assistant's good judgment will become second nature, provided there is no compromise with loyalty to the lawyer and observance of good ethics.

4.016 Accept Guidance, Directions, and Comments Constructively

Legal assistants need help, suggestions, guidance, and—most important—constructive criticism to improve their skills and to serve as a reminder of the legal activity they have yet to learn and master. The same can be said of attorneys and other law office personnel. Judgment often is learned through painful postmortems—the examination, after the fact, of alternatives that had not been considered. In other words, the legal assistant did not appreciate all the legal issues involved, did not assemble, analyze, and evaluate all the facts or factual circumstances, or simply did not delve deeply enough into background or peripheral matters. The unsatisfactory result could be caused by a failure of the legal assistant's comprehensive analytical ability. Legal assistants should take initiative and responsibility for their own training and continuing legal education, whether or not their employer is supportive in those efforts.

PROBLEM NO. 4

A simple lawsuit involving the blowout of an oil well during drilling, under circumstances where an error by the drilling crew appears to be the cause, has been filed against the drilling contractor by the client oil company. The issues are simple negligence and contractual indemnity.[3] One of the officers of the drilling contractor has left that firm and lives and works out-of-state. He was not present at the blowout. His deposition is scheduled in Houston. An appropriate commission has been obtained, and one of the firm's junior attorneys is drafted into replacing the case lawyer at the deposition, for it seems to be a routine deposition. At the deposition, little

---

[3] *simple negligence*—Such consists of failure to exercise for protection of others that degree of care and caution that would, under prevailing circumstances, be exercised by an ordinary, prudent person.
contractual indemnity—A contact between two parities whereby one undertakes and agrees to indemnify the other against loss of damages arising from some contemplated act on the part of the indemnitor, or from some responsibility assumed by the indemnitee, or from the claim or demand of a third person, that is, to make good to him such pecuniary damage as he may suffer.

was learned that was not learned from the crew. The witness clearly was not experienced, did not volunteer anything, had no personal records, did not refresh his memory prior to deposition, and relied on what he was told by others. The deposition therefore proved to be simple, straightforward, and unproductive.

>   **Query:**   What if the witness were known before deposition to be an author of *"Blowouts and Blowout Prevention;"* taught seminars in safe drilling practices; served on the board of the American Petroleum Institute; and was sought as a technical consultant on special construction problems concerning blowout equipment?

4.017 Enthusiastically Observe Moral and Ethical Standards

Every profession that exists to serve people has recognized its obligation to provide this service within certain standards of proper conduct. Doctors follow the Hippocratic oath, lawyers the *Model Rules of Professional Conduct;* pharmacists, real estate salesmen, bankers, and other professionals all create (or have created by legislation or regulatory agency) guidelines for proper and proscribed conduct. The direct beneficiary is the patient, the client, the customer, or the "civilian" who uses the offered service.

This is as it should be, and these constraints on conduct are ones that legal assistants must enthusiastically endorse, accept, and observe, for the legal assistant profession serves two levels of users, lawyers and clients. The first endorsed, published, and adopted code of ethics in the legal assistant profession was written by the ethics committee of the National Association of Legal Assistants in 1975 and is discussed in Chapter 3, Ethics.

4.02 Analytical Ability

Analyzing is the process of separating a thing, idea, etc. into its parts so as to find out their nature, proportion, function, interrelationship, and other properties. It is from this process that relevant facts are identified as being applicable to a given situation. The ability to analyze is an essential skill for the legal assistant to develop. Creative thinking, imagination, and inspiration are excellent attributes; however, the routine, methodical assembly of every relevant fact or evidentiary fact is also essential. Analytical ability that cannot be demonstrated to the satisfaction of the employing attorney in direct relation to a particular case, or set of circumstances surrounding a particular case, has no merit or usefulness. However, when the legal assistant can supply the attorney with reliable control and retrievability of the analyses of facts, testimony, or source information, then the legal assistant's system and analytical ability become invaluable.

Before beginning the analysis and evaluation of facts and/or testimony in a case to determine the relevant facts, the legal assistant must be aware of the essential elements of the case. For instance, a case of misrepresentation is founded on proving at least the following seven points:

1. The representation was to a material fact.
2. The representation was false.
3. The falsity was known to the party making it.
4. The representation was made with the intent to induce the other party to act.
5. The representation was relied upon by the party to whom it was made.
6. The acting party was ignorant of the falsity of the representation and reasonably believed it to be true.
7. The acting party suffered damages as a result of the act.

There may be side issues of intentional or negligent misrepresentation and oral or written contract to be considered as well. The legal assistant therefore has factual categories established, each of which relates to the issues that must be proved or disproved (depending on the client's position). Otherwise, the pattern of facts assembled by the legal assistant is worthless to the lawyer.

Suppose this case involved the purchase of machinery designed for a specific agricultural harvesting function and the representation involved the cost of purchase and maintenance, the speed of operation, reliability, and the capability of operation by only two people. Is it relevant that the operation damaged 50 percent of the crop? Yes! Items of proof will be necessary for the issue. Is it relevant that the machine works so slowly that the prime picking period cannot be exploited without two of the machines? Yes! Again, proof may be documentary or testimonial. Is it relevant that its dimensions prevent it from being stored in existing equipment buildings? Probably not, unless some additional representation on ease of storage can be developed. Building an additional shed may not be a supportable item of damage.

Analysis of factual situations in simple cases is often more challenging than in complex cases, for the simplicity of the case issues places a premium on identifying each relevant evidentiary fact and assigning it a value that reflects its help or hindrance to the client's case.

Consider the following hypothetical case and proceed through an interview or fact-gathering session:

> Mr. Jones called an attorney and made arrangements to be represented in a personal injury suit arising from an automobile accident. He is uninsured and has been served with a complaint as the defendant in the suit. After the initial interview with the attorney, the legal assistant is the first person in the office with whom he will fully discuss the accident. He arrived by appointment and, after a few minutes of casual conversation, discussion of the case and the gathering of information begin.

The initial questions seek background information, such as name, address, telephone number, place of employment, and marital status. Since this is a case involving an automobile accident, it is essential to ask questions about his driving record, how long he has been driving, and what is the model, make, and condition of his car, where it was repaired, and whether it was in prior accidents. These background questions will give insight into the client's nature. For instance, if Mr. Jones has never had a traffic citation in his thirty years of driving, presumably he is a careful driver. If his driving record discloses a number of citations, then clearly there are times when Mr. Jones has disregarded the law. Also, what kind of a car does he drive and what color is it? Psychologists have determined that there is a link between the type and color of a car a person drives and the individual's personality; for example, a souped up red car indicates an aggressive person, while a conservative model and color suggests a conservative individual. Is the client a steady worker, or does he flit from job to job? Is he happily married, miserably married, or in the process of a divorce? The answers to these questions should be used to assist in evaluating the answers the client gives in response to questions related to the facts of the case.

> Mr. Jones admits to two speeding citations in the last eighteen months. He drives a bright yellow car with a large, modified engine with two four-barrel carburetors and is, according to him, "the fastest thing on the road." He is between jobs, and he does not approve of his wife's job. The interview proceeds into the discussion of the case.

L.A.: Now Mr. Jones, where did this accident occur?

Jones: In the driveway of Sam's Go-Go Bar.

L.A.:   What was the date, the day of the week, and the time of the accident?

Jones: It was April 24, 1997, a Saturday, and it was just before closing time, around 1:45 a.m.

(His testimony established that the accident occurred on private property, on a weekend and late at night. A few questions on weather, lighting, visibility, vehicle conditions, and so on should be asked.)

L.A.:   Mr. Jones, had you been in Sam's prior to the time of the accident?

Jones: Yes, I had been there. My wife works as a go-go girl for Sam, and I pick her up after work.

(Now the legal assistant knows why Mr. Jones was at Sam's, but the question arises, "If he picks his wife up after work, why was he leaving before closing time?")

L.A.:   According to the complaint, Mr. Smith says that you deliberately drove your car into the side of his as he was leaving the parking lot and that, after you hit his car, you left your car and attempted to pull him from his vehicle. Please tell me what really occurred in the sequence it happened.

Jones: Well, I didn't see his car in the driveway, and I only left my car to go over to him to see if he was injured.

There are now two entirely different and conflicting accounts of the same accident. The accident could have occurred as the client alleges, or it could be that he did not disclose that the plaintiff had been over-friendly with Mrs. Jones in Sam's Go-Go Bar, that Jones became enraged, left Sam's to follow the plaintiff, and in a fit of temper hit the plaintiff's car and assaulted him. With the background information about Mr. Jones along with his account of the accident, it is now time to proceed with more detailed investigation for corroboration, identification of other witnesses, and so forth. (*See* Chapter 6, Interviewing Techniques and Chapter 7, Investigations.)

Keep in mind that clients will usually tell their story in a manner that places them in the best light. They do not do this intentionally to deceive; it is a subconscious rationalization to avoid embarrassment or criticism for their actions. In the case of Mr. Jones, continue to question him to gather more facts and information to substantiate his presentation of the accident. This is done without expressing doubt and without being accusatory. If there is any doubt about the actual facts of the case, independently question the witnesses to the accident and/or to events that occurred prior to the accident. This information, along with the information given by Mr. Jones, will allow the legal assistant to analyze the facts and reach a conclusion that will be helpful to the lawyer in representing Mr. Jones, including providing a basis on which the attorney can further investigate other avenues of defense or settlement. The prime rule of legal assisting is "Never let the attorney be surprised by harmful information!" Find it and defuse it so the attorney can adapt to its impact.

In more complex cases, "Requests for Production of Documents" sometimes seek invoices, purchase orders, employee lists, time cards, expense accounts over a period of time, books, records, histories, and other comparative data surrounding the particular action. Responses to these requests may result in boxes and boxes of materials or may state that certain records will be available for counsel to inspect or reproduce at a particular time and place. Here, again, the ability of the legal assistant to index and analyze comparative data will be of invaluable assistance to an attorney. The attorney can instruct the legal assistant on the issues involved and the comparative data needed. The legal assistant may then spend days or weeks reviewing statistical data, documents, manuscripts, depositions, records, invoices, or purchase orders, making comparative analyses and chronologic sortings and gathering other information. For example, perhaps the adverse party's attorney has produced computer printouts in answer to a request for certain documents or information from those documents. The legal assistant must then become familiar with the computer printouts; how to read them, and how to trace the source documents from which the information on the printouts came. Then, the legal assistant begins comparing the printouts with the source documents to verify the accuracy of the information contained on the printouts. In performing this verification process, the legal assistant may discover discrepancies between the source documents and the computer printout. This use of good judgment and analytical ability is an example of what makes the work product and effort of the legal assistant invaluable to the attorney. Document cases are discussed in more detail in Chapter 9, The Legal Assistant and Document Discovery Cases.

4.021 Basic Rules

As a legal analyst, (whether an attorney or legal assistant) an established structure is required before approaching any form of analysis. Analytical ability is founded on a few basic rules which all legal assistants should be familiar.

First, you need to understand what is the objective of the analysis. Without a clear understanding of your objective, you will lack focus to your work and will not be able to develop a structure to achieve the objective. If you are unclear about the objective, seek more guidance from the attorney who assigned the project to you until you feel comfortable in knowing what you are to accomplish. Many times you can review an example of a similar project which was completed in another case; this will give you a guide to follow as you plan your strategy.

Next, you will need to comprehend the resources that are available for you to utilize in achieving the objective of your analysis. Not only will you need to assemble the data which is the subject of your analysis, but you will need a general understanding of how the data is presented and how to interpret the data. As part of your analysis, you will need to determine the function of the materials or documents to be analyzed. Knowing the purpose and function of the materials you will evaluate is paramount before performing any analysis of data. These concepts will be discussed in more detail in Sections 4.0212 and 4.0213.

Finally, after you have an understanding of the assignment and the data to be analyzed, you will need to establish the parameters of the project, to develop some structure to your approach. A key element in choosing the techniques, systems, and detail which you will utilize in establishing the structure is the time you will take to complete the assignment. All of these make up the factors that will provide the structure to your analysis. Some possible suggestions on this topic is covered in Sections 4.0214 and 4.0215.

4.0211 Understand the Final Objective of the Analysis.
It is important to understand the final purpose of the analytical effort. Are you determining the cause and effect between two events? Are you categorizing items to illustrate their relationship to each other? Are you evaluating events to create a time line of events? These are scenarios which you may be asked to accomplish and your understanding of the basic assignment is paramount to producing the desired result.

Initially, you need to know some basic facts before you can begin your analysis, such as who are the parties involved in the event, where did the event take place, what motivating factors, if any, played a role in triggering the event, and what duties existed, if any, on one party to another? If you cannot answer these basic questions, begin with an overview of the facts of the case by reading case memos, complaints, and other foundational pleadings. If the facts are not clearly in focus, look to other written material which discusses the factual issues, the legal issues and/or the question of law which brought the client to the attorney you are assisting.

A different situation exists when the final objective is to provide demonstrative exhibits for use in helping a jury to understand the lawyer's case. Little learning is involved, although a testing of different mediums might be needed, such as photography, sketches, graphs, charts, maps, videotape, and models.

If the need is simply to identify and retrieve exhibits easily and quickly that were introduced in single depositions, solve that problem alone in lieu of expanding it into a case-wide indexing system. Do not develop complex procedures when there is no need for them. If the utility of the deposition exhibits requires only identifying duplicates (many times several witnesses will identify the same object or document during their depositions resulting in that one exhibit having several exhibit numbers), a detailed history or summary of each exhibit may be unnecessary. A workable, understandable, cross-reference system of duplicate exhibits would suffice. Effective analysis should fit the needs of the case.

4.0212 Comprehend the Resources Available. Analysis can sometimes only be accomplished within the mind of one person. At other times, it requires the assembly of information, data, documents, records, photos, and other material to allow sorting, copying, indexing, and physical comparison. Large and complex tasks are sometimes better handled by breaking them into smaller, simpler tasks which can be divided among a team. For instance, one person is responsible for creating a chronologic history, while another person assembles and collates all witness statements for points of agreement or conflict, and yet another person copes with analysis and cross-referencing the data from interrogatories, requests for admission, and other discovery devices.

If only one legal assistant is assigned to a large and complex task, with no extra help or funds available, then extra document reproduction, document imaging, scale model construction, and other such items, may be unrealistic. Each necessary act or function must be scheduled to fit available equipment and personnel hours. A realistic approach to time estimates and dollar values is essential. The legal assistant who, without protest, accepts or acquires more projects than can realistically be completed hurts the employing attorney and commits cumulative professional suicide. Effectiveness is measured by successfully completed projects.

As an example of a situation, you may be asked to analyze how an accident occurred in a manufacturing plant. This might require a broad study of a complex manufacturing process in order to comprehend the relationships of people, plans, and documents—obviously a major learning effort—before undertaking any analysis of the evidentiary material. In order to accomplish this assignment, you need a clear understanding of the answers to the questions posed above regarding the players, event location, motivating factors, and responsibilities of each person or entity. You may need to seek educational material on the subject before you can proceed with your analysis. A trip to a public or university library may provide you with the resources you need, or you may utilize the Internet as a resource or even a retained expert to provide documentation on the process.

If you are assigned the task of coordinating an analysis of documents produced by an adverse party for use in an upcoming deposition, you will first need to make sure your work environment is conducive to doing an effective job. Select a place and time to review the documents where interruptions will be minimal and your full attention can be devoted to the task. You will need to understand the issues in the case so that you can flag documents which relate to each issue. All these steps require concentration and your greatest analytical ability. Plan your work schedule accordingly so that important details will not be overlooked.

Remember to schedule demanding projects for the time of day when you are the most mentally alert. For many people, this time will not be right after lunch. Most of us know when our peak productive time period occurs. This is the time to schedule the important task of analyzing documents produced by adverse parties. Early in the morning may be the best time for you, when you are rested and ready to tackle the day's assignments. For others who are slow morning starters, a late-morning block of time is best. Still others reach their most productive time in the afternoon, so adjust your time accordingly. Once you have the appropriate time designated for the assignment, and you have identified the resources you need to help you comprehend the documents, your next step is to make some initial analysis about the function of the materials or documents to be reviewed.

4.0213 Determine the Function of the Materials or Documents to be Handled. Legal assistants do not analyze abstract philosophies but testimony, recorded events, groups of documents, production systems, material objects, and/or locations. If the material involved is evidentiary in nature, it must be preserved, protected, and prepared for production at trial. If the analytic process requires use of that object, a surrogate must be developed, a duplicate obtained, or a model created. For instance, an original evidentiary document is stored in the safe, but a photocopy is adequate for the legal assistant's analytical purpose. It can be written upon, recopied (with a legend as described in the Pretrial Litigation Skills chapter), or annotated. The analysis may be to summarize and simplify the utility of a document, a few documents, or all the documents, and it is important to create the proper framework to meet the need established by the attorney.

Many trial advocacy seminars bring out the fact that a good advocate does not *tell* the jury what to believe, but instead *shows* them. In order to show the jury what they need to know to render a decision, an attorney needs to have the evidence organized in a logical manner as it relates to the issues. This job is usually delegated to the legal assistant to prepare before trial.

How do we ensure that our efforts contribute to a successful trial outcome? We cannot routinely prepare and answer discovery and document production requests, or summarize documents without some direction in mind. This would be like driving to an unfamiliar destination a thousand miles away without using a road map. Formulate a trial plan early in the case by identifying the issues; that way all efforts are directed toward proving those issues at trial. Armed with a clear view of the case issues, the legal assistant can begin the review of documents and materials and determine their function in the case by categorizing them to the issues. One method which may be helpful in accomplishing this task is to establish issue files. Separate files can be labeled with each case issue, then pertinent documents can be sorted into these files. This effort is the beginning of establishing the parameters of document analysis.

4.0214 Establish the Parameters of the Project. These parameters may be the rules of law in the case by which topical breakdowns can be established; the number of hours to be dedicated to specific projects; the date of origin of the action that is the earliest date documents can carry and still be relevant to the case; the related professions that have an impact on the standards of the industry involved in the case (a general contractor may be charged with safety orders on excavation, steel work, reinforced cement, electrical wiring, heating, cooling and environmental controls, worker's compensation, Occupational Safety and Health Act regulations, and so on); or possible expert witnesses who could be utilized, for example economists, statisticians, actuaries, psychiatrists, research analysts, and computer programmers.

If the need is to summarize depositions, then primary concentration should be placed on these summaries. Plans should not extend to cross-referencing Requests for Admission to the deposition testimony (even though it may become necessary at a later date). If the legal assistant feels such a cross-reference would be a possibility, then a note to this effect could be placed on a list of possible things to do.

If the legal assistant is to work on analyzing documents categorized into issue files, the first question which comes to mind may be how to identify the issues in the case. Usually, the attorney is the one to identify the issues in a case memo or in the complaint drafting. However, as a legal assistant gains experience identifying documents keyed to the case issue, the next logical step is to develop the skill to identify the issues, thus providing some high-level assistance to the attorney. Entry-level legal assistants may have difficulty identifying issues but, with practice, this valuable skill can be developed. By considering the factual outline of the case, the legal assistant can identify the issues by asking a couple of key questions:

1. What is the controversy in this case?
2. What questions of fact will the jury have to decide?

Wording the issues in a question form makes it easier to identify them. For example, in a construction defect case, an issue may be identified as follows:

Did the defendant perform the work in a negligent manner?
Did the defendant perform the work to industry standards?
Did the defendant use proper equipment for the job?
Did the defendant violate any statutory requirements on the job?
Did any of the subcontractors hired by the defendant perform in an incompetent manner?
Did the defendant follow the instructions give on the work assignment?

Another way to identify issues is to identify and review the jury instructions which are applicable to the facts of the case. Reviewing the areas of law on which the judge will instruct a jury makes it easier to formulate issue questions. This method will, in effect, work backwards in trial preparation. By starting with the law and then formulating a theory of what happened, a legal assistant can identify the important issues. From there, the legal assistant can find the documents relating to the issues, place them in the issue files, or use another method to group the documents by issue category. At first, it may seem unusual to start at the end and work backward to identify the issues, but many trial advocates favor this approach. By first establishing what issues are to be proved, all the effort is spent in gathering evidence to support the theory of the case. Experienced trial attorneys have reported that this method is effective in focusing on the important case issues.

4.0215 *Consider Time When Choosing Techniques, Systems, and Detail.* An extraordinary system that can be operated perfectly is worthless if it does not produce results on time. One of the frustrating elements of legal assisting is working within short time frames that require severely simple or incomplete solutions. It must be understood that attorneys are constantly faced with Hobson's Choice (taking what is offered or nothing at all for the lack of an alternative) in making the decision whether or not to dedicate time and money to projects that have a chance of ultimately being proven unnecessary. Sometimes, the attorney will make such a dedication based on an understanding that a certain method is "recommended by experts" in the field without attempting to adapt the method to the particular problem at hand. A prudent and efficient legal assistant will become familiar with methods and devices which are both cost effective and time efficient for the attorney, as well as the client, and will evaluate and identify necessary projects from unnecessary ones.

4.022 Analytical Techniques

4.0221 Data Comprehension. Understanding written material and data are paramount to being a successful legal assistant. A routine aspect of our job involves understanding instructions given both orally and in written form and in performing the task assignment. Some questions the legal assistant can go over mentally to make sure the assignment or the data is being understood include the following:

1. Do I know what I am supposed to do?
    a. Are the instructions clear? Do I understanding them?
    b. Am I sure of the objectives of the assignment?
    c. Are the planned actions defensible alternatives?
2. Can I do the task?
    a. Do I see its importance?
    b. How is it difficult for me?
    c. Have I made a plan?
    d. Have I made all the necessary preparations?
3. Do I know all the steps to complete the task?
    a. Have I checked my progress?
    b. Do I need more help?
    c. Am I so confused that I have set the project aside?
4. Have I achieved the established goal?
    a. Did I include everything that is relevant?
    b. Have I made the necessary revisions?
    c. Was any portion of the assignment hard for me? Which part and why?
    d. Did the procedure work?
    e. What aspect of my accomplishment was excellent?
    f. What aspect of my accomplishment was inferior?

By using the questions above as a checklist to evaluate performance, a legal assistant can ascertain where improvement in his or her performance is necessary. If the legal assistant is unfamiliar with the case, the attorney can give a brief outline of the facts or the assistant can read the pleadings and memos in the file before summarizing or beginning the analysis. If necessary, another meeting can occur between the attorney and the legal assistant to address areas of questions that are particularly important. Armed with a clear direction and focus, the next step is to begin the factual analysis.

4.0222 Factual Analysis. In law school, students are taught the structure of legal analysis early in their studies. Legal assistants can benefit from understanding the legal analysis formula and how it applies both in analyzing legal issues and applying the facts to reach legal conclusions. The structure of legal analysis takes on the following form:

Issue + Rule + Analysis = Conclusion

Referred to as the IRAC method of studying, it begins by stating the question of law or fact raised by the client's case, such as "Is the defendant liable for the alleged negligent construction on the plaintiff's property?" Once the issue, or question of law or fact is identified, the next step is to look at the applicable rule, statute, ordinance, or other regulation and analyze the facts to reach a conclusion which will answer the issue question posed. This type of exercise is an excellent way to develop analytical skills because it requires the use of deductive and analogous reasoning and distinguishing relevant versus irrelevant data, topics which are covered in Section 4.0223 and Section 4.0224. The legal assistant should feel challenged by this type of assignment, for it represents a substantive level of work which is more challenging than categorizing or indexing documents. The ability to review a document and extract factual information that is material to answering the issue being addressed is the resulting skill developed here and is one which every legal assistant should strive to fine tune. Opportunities to be challenged by taking on assignments of this nature should always be taken, even if it requires reorganizing the day's workload.

Let's look at an example of this type legal analysis:

FACTS: A city ordinance requires all businesses operating within city limits to have a business license. A client comes into your office to determine if a business license is necessary for a proposed nonprofit operation that involves the purchase of products at wholesale prices in bulk quantities and sale to its members. No formal business location is anticipated; the president of the nonprofit organization will warehouse the products in his garage, and no profit is expected.

ISSUE: The issue raised is whether the proposed nonprofit operation constitutes a business and is required to obtain a business license to operate.

ANALYSIS: Additional information that is relevant before analyzing the situation and reaching a conclusion includes the following questions which the legal analyst must discover:

1. Is a non-profit operation considered a "business" under the ordinance?

The legal analysis will have to review relating sections which define the term "business" as it applies to the ordinance.

2. Is the location of the president's garage where the products will be stored within the city limits?

If it is outside the city limits, then the ordinance would not be applicable since it states that a license is required of all businesses operating *within* city limits.

3. Are members of a nonprofit organization involved in this activity considered partners, customers, or some other status?

Further review of state business and nonprofit statutes will reveal the answers to the questions posed.

4. Does the nonprofit organization have its tax exempt clearance and will it be required to collect and report state sales tax on the items?

Again, further statutory review will provide the answer to these questions.

Once the answers to the questions are obtained, the legal analyst will be able to reach a conclusion to the issue question posed. The ability to use deductive and analogous reasoning will play a key role here.

4.0223 Deductive Reasoning and Analogous Reasoning. Being able to review facts to determine what conclusions can be reasoned or to determine whether the facts are analogous to those set forth in another source (case law or statutory language), is a challenging skill that is developed with experience. Once a legal assistant develops this skill, he or she can become a valuable member of the legal team, especially in litigation matters. One method of study which can help legal assistants learn to develop analytical skills is to look at the study of rhetoric and its application when preparing a legal memo that outlines the persuasive reasoning. Referring to the concept of rhetoric as taught at the University of West Los Angeles by veteran paralegal advocate, Janet Kaiser, we can see how this is helpful with legal reasoning:[4]

> Rhetoric is the art or the discipline that deals with the use of discourse, either spoken or written, to inform or persuade, or motivate an audience. Classical rhetoricians dealt with the problems of selecting and arranging material in order to effect their purposes. The Latin term *dispositio* and the Greek term *taxis* refer to the study of the various parts of discourse:
>
> 1. the *exordium* or introduction;
> 2. the *narratio* or statement of facts;
> 3. the *divisio* or outline of our points/steps;
> 4. the *confirmatio* or proof of our argument;
> 5. the *refutatio* or discrediting of opposing view; and
> 6. the *peroratio* or conclusion.
>
> Aristotle wrote about three types of artistic proofs, or appeals:
>
> 1. rational appeal (logos)
> 2. emotional appeal (pathos)
> 3. ethical appeal (ethos)

Quintilian, in his *Institutio Oratoria*, stated that writers needed to make judgment calls about issues such as these:

1. When should we make our statement of facts continuous, and when should we break it up and insert it *passim*?
2. When should we begin by dealing with the arguments advanced by our opponents and when should we begin by proposing our own arguments?
3. When is it advisable to present our strongest argument first and when is it best to begin with our weakest argument and build up to our strongest?
4. Which of our arguments will our audience readily accept and which of them must they be induced to accept?
5. Should we attempt to refute our opponents' arguments as a whole, or deal with them in detail?
6. Should we reserve our emotional appeals for the conclusion, or deal with them throughout the discourse?
7. What evidence or documents should we make use of, and where in the discourse will this be most effective?

---

[4] *Rhetorical Memory and Delivery*, edited by John Frederick Reynolds, Lawrence Erlbaum Associates, Publishers, Hillsdale, New Jersey, 1993; *Classical Rhetoric for the Modern Student*, by Edward P. J. Corbett, Oxford University Press, New York, 1990; and *Roots for a New Rhetoric*, by Daniel Fogarty, S.J., Columbia University, New York, 1959.

By thoughtfully reviewing these questions as we evaluate and perform deductive and analogous reasoning, one can see the evolution of legal analysis and the process that litigators go through, many without full realization of what they are actually doing as they prepare and conduct a case for trial.

As a legal memo is prepared covering the analysis, here are some thoughts to take into consideration to assist in the reasoning and writing effort:

GUIDE TO EVALUATING YOUR WRITTEN ANALYSIS[5]

1. Look at the questions presented. Are your questions written so that all necessary information is presented? For example, there is a world of difference between "What is the statute of limitations?" and "What is the statute of limitations for a negligence action in California?"
2. Look at your brief answers. Do your brief answers say the same thing as (i.e., draw the same conclusion as) your answers in the discussion section? If your brief answers are stated as "probably no" or "probably yes," do you give your reader the conditions under which the "yes" or "no" would apply?
3. Look at your statement of facts. Do you give all the facts necessary (i.e., all the facts needed to understand all the ideas presented in the discussion section)? Do you present your facts in a fair manner? Are your facts presented clearly, so that even someone unfamiliar with the matter could understand what had gone on?
4. Look at your discussion section. Check each paragraph carefully; see whether each paragraph (except, perhaps, those paragraphs that set the context of your various arguments) have the following: (1) legal principle; (2) facts; (3) analysis of how those facts relate to the legal principle; and (4) conclusion of analysis. Make sure that you never give a conclusion without having authority to back up that conclusion. Make sure that you always give proper citations for your case law; that means, for state cases, the official and unofficial citations plus the year of the decision, and, for federal cases, the citation(s) plus the court and the year of the decision. If you cite to statutory or regulatory law, be sure to give the name of the code or title along with the section or rule number. And remember never to cite first or only to secondary law.
5. Look at your conclusion. Is it succinct? Does it eloquently repeat the major conclusions reached in your memo? Does it give the "bottom line" (which bottom line is qualified or conditioned, if necessary)?
6. Make sure you have spelled all your words correctly. Make sure you have set forth only that which is relevant. Make sure that your legal memo has the appearance of professional done work product.

Some excellent points to remember when writing a memo regarding your analysis and conclusions include these four categories:[6]

1. Don't fail to explain your conclusions. You must show *how* your facts and your law relate, and you may not jump ahead to the conclusion without giving your analysis, even if you think your analysis is "obvious" to everyone.
2. Don't share irrelevant words from your quoted law. Quote only what you need. Paraphrase only if useful. Your memo won't look any better if you copy irrelevant words, no matter how eloquent those words may be.

---

[5] Janet Kaiser, Professor, University of West Los Angeles.

[6] Rombauer, *Legal Problem Solving*, West 1981, and Block, *Effective Legal Writing*, Foundation Press, 1992.

3. Don't think that string cites will impress. Some judges think that string cites are the mark of a poor argument. While the "weight" of authority can be helpful, string cites in and of themselves—without analysis—do nothing other than make many readers suspicious of your argument.

4. Don't fail to consider opposing view. Good lawyering does not mean hiding unhelpful law. Legal memos require a full airing of all the relevant law, good or bad. Yes, you may want to discuss counter-arguments to the bad law, or counter-arguments that the opposition may make to your good law.

If a legal assistant can keep these thoughts in mind while performing the legal analysis, the conclusions reached about what can be deduced from the facts and how it applies to the structure of legal analysis (Issue + Rule + Analysis = Conclusion) will likely be on point. Similarly, by developing one's ability to analyze facts, causal relationships, correlations, similarities, and contrasts between two or more situations, a legal assistant's analogous reasoning will be greatly enhanced. One last skill to develop is the concept of identifying relevant data from irrelevant data, which plays a key role in performing legal analysis.

4.0224 Relevant vs. Irrelevant Data. An excellent source of study in developing skill in identifying relevant versus irrelevant data is the sample tests for the law school admission test. These exercises are not only excellent for development of analytical ability, but are also an excellent tool to utilize in preparation for the Certified Legal Assistant examination administered by the National Association of Legal Assistants. Here is a sample along with some points on making the analysis:

<hr />

JUDGMENT AND ANALYTICAL ABILITY

Each of the sets in this section contains a statement of facts, a dispute, and two rules. The rules may be conflicting. Each rule should be applied independently and not as an exception to the other. The rules are followed by questions. Select from the answer choices below the one that most accurately classifies each question as it relates to the possible application of one or both of the rules to the dispute.

a. A relevant question whose answer requires a choice between the rules
b. A relevant question whose answer does not require a choice between the rules but requires additional facts or rules
c. A relevant question that is answerable from the facts or rules or both
d. An irrelevant question or one whose answer bears only remotely on the outcome of the dispute

FACTS: Andrew had been a member of the Citizens for Sobriety Society for ten years when he decided to run for the club presidency. His only serious competition was Timothy who, for several years, had been quietly campaigning for the position. When Andrew announced his candidacy, Timothy had him closely watched. Timothy hoped to find some grounds on which he could base his claim that Andrew was not a member in "good standing," as that phrase was defined in the society's rules. Just before the election, the members held a meeting during which they were to decide if each candidate was in "good standing." Timothy chose this opportunity to attempt to establish that Andrew, in fact, was not a member in "good standing."

DISPUTE: Timothy contends that Andrew is not a member in "good standing," as this phrase is defined in the rules; Andrew contends that he is a member in "good standing."

RULES:
   I.   Any member who pays his dues on time each year and who attends at least 50 percent of the meetings during the course of the year shall be considered a member in good standing.
   II. Any member who is convicted of a crime or who brings an alcoholic beverage into the club shall not be considered a member in good standing.

QUESTIONS:
D 1. If a vote is required, how many members will favor Andrew for the position of club president?
B 2. If Andrew paid his dues this year, did he pay them on time?
A 3. Assume that Andrew has attended 75 percent of the meetings each year for the past ten years and has always paid his dues on time. If Andrew was convicted of embezzlement six months ago, is he a member in good standing?
C 4. At the meeting, Timothy stated that Andrew has not attended any meetings for the past three years and that he brought beer to a private party that he hosted on the club premises. Would Andrew be a member in good standing if these allegations are true?

Correlate the terms, requirements, and responsibilities established by the rules with the person, institutions, and actions given in the facts.

■ Do both of the rules apply to the question? Are the outcomes of the rules conflicting? If so, then the response must be A.
■ Does only one of the rules apply to the question? Will the outcome resolve the dispute? If so, then the correct response will be C.
■ Do both of the rules apply to the question and produce identical outcomes? If so, then the correct response will also be C.
■ Can the question be answered from the facts alone? If so, then C is again the correct response.
■ Does one or do both rules apply to the question but not resolve it? Would additional information resolve it? If so, then the correct response will be B.
■ Does neither rule apply? Will the answer to the question serve to resolve the dispute? If not, then the correct response must be D.

(Answers to this and the following problem are provided in Section 4.04.)

Another sample of questions is the following set of facts, dispute, rules, and questions for your analysis:

FACTS: John was explaining the functions of state government to a social studies class when Albert hit Philip with his eraser. When a disruptive fistfight ensued between Albert and Philip, John attempted to separate the two. Albert, however, resisted and, in trying to pull away from John, dislocated his own right shoulder. After the fight had been stopped, John made both boys bend over in front of the class while he struck each one five times with a yardstick. John then took the boys to the office of the principal, but on the way John tripped, accidentally bumped into Albert, and caused Albert to fall and break his left arm.

DISPUTE: Albert's parents are suing John for battery on behalf of Albert; John contests the claim.

RULES:
  I.   A teacher in a public school is permitted to use corporal punishment on a student when such punishment is necessary to maintain order and discipline in the classroom.
  II. An intentional touching made by hand, or with an object, and without the consent of the person being touched is battery.

QUESTIONS:
1. Is John liable for battery for breaking Albert's arm?
2. Did John have the legal status of a teacher in the classroom?
3. Was Albert harmed when John struck him with the yardstick?
4. If John is a teacher in a public school and had to strike Albert with the yardstick in order to maintain discipline in the classroom, is John liable for battery for hitting Albert with the yardstick?
5. If corporal punishment may not be administered to a child less than eight years old, is John guilty of battery?
6. In the past, had John often struck students with a yardstick?

These samples are an excellent way to develop analytical skills and critical thinking, all of which will carry over into legal analysis in litigation, tort law, case law analysis, and legal research.

4.03 Summary

Following basic principles aids the legal assistant in analyzing factual situations. Analysis requires a good memory and the ability to link facts, testimony, or objects together in relationship to the issues of the case. Effective legal assistants persevere in reading and measuring each statement, reported act, or event against others, constantly thinking, "If this is so, how can that be true?" and then proceed to examine, study, and review to establish the answer. A good legal assistant who, after examining, studying, reviewing, and attempting to establish an answer, finds nothing conclusive will not hesitate to say so. Being able to say "I found nothing" is sometimes as important as saying "This is what I found."

Good judgment and analytical ability are developed attributes of successful legal assistants. It is the result of those attributes that is noticed. Judgment improves with experience, and both good and bad judgments, when analyzed and criticized retrospectively, contribute to the improvement. Interested legal assistants grasp every opportunity to make judgments in the course of their careers, no matter how small, to test the attitudes of the lawyer, their coworkers, and the firm. Such tests develop a feeling for the responsibility and authority the legal assistant is permitted to exercise, expose the legal assistant to others in the office, and provide the feedback that allows the legal assistant to identify sources of assistance or opposition in various activities.

Judgment and analytical ability go hand in hand with prudence—careful thought in acting and planning. What is excellent for one law office may be a disaster for another. Personnel valued by one law firm may not be appreciated by another. A particular method of filing and storage of files may work fine in one office but would not meet the needs of another.

The legal assistant works for people and with the problems of people. Prudence, discretion, respect, and consideration for others—coupled with a driving interest, professional pride, and the desire to perform satisfactorily—will compel the legal assistant to consider each assignment, analyze it, and use the best judgment possible.

4.04 Discussion Problems, Commentaries, and Answers to Sample Questions

Section 4.015   Problem No. 1—Commentary:

Since the client is represented by counsel, there should not be any direct discussions by the insurance company and the client. The fact that the client is represented by counsel should be conveyed to the adjuster immediately, and the interview /statement should not take place. The adjuster should then contact the responsible attorney as soon as the attorney's schedule allows.

Section 4.015   Problem No. 2—Commentary:

This is not an unusual occurrence in document production cases. The obvious alternatives include: (1) instituting a priority rush program to process the additional material (and later explaining how it first was missed); (2) seeking a postponement; (3) promising future production; or (4) ignoring the documents in hope that the adversary will not discover them. Each alternative should be presented with factual data (such as hours of work involved and cost) and the legal assistant's candid recommendation to the attorney. Ignoring the documents in the hope that the adversary will not discover them is not a viable alternative, as it would be ethically unacceptable and could subject the attorney and/or the client to court sanctions for discovery abuse.

Section 4.015   Problem No. 3—Commentary:

There are no decisions to be made here, no matter how many alternatives can be created intellectually. The legal assistant has a moral and ethical obligation to apprise the attorney of these unpleasant facts and to rely on the attorney's moral and ethical standards to guide any subsequent actions. This is not a totally unusual situation for legal assistants to encounter. It may not be diversion of assets (as in this example) but some other aspect of human weakness, avarice, greed, lack of virtues, or unscrupulous business practices. It should not affect the legal assistant's execution of duties for the employing lawyer.

Section 4.016   Problem No. 4—Commentary:

Part of the preparation of a potential witness, such as the one described in the above scenario, requires not only factual information relative to the situation that gives rise to the pending lawsuit, but there may be substantial information that this person could offer in a case like the one described. Advanced technology, such as the Internet, and electronic research services could have revealed this person's credentials and background, allowing for a more productive and successful deposition.

Section 4.0224   Problem No. 1—Answers:

1. The application of rule I depends upon whether Andrew paid his dues on time and attended at least 50 percent of the club's meetings during the year. Any application of Rule II depends upon whether Andrew was convicted of a crime or brought alcoholic beverages into the club. Therefore, a question that asks how many members favor Andrew for the position is irrelevant. The correct response is D.
2. This question is relevant solely to any application of Rule I since, under that rule, Andrew is entitled to be considered a member in good standing only if he has paid his dues on time. Additional information is necessary to answer this question. The correct response is, therefore, B.

3. Because Andrew has attended more than 50 percent of the club's meetings every year and has paid his dues on time, he is a member in good standing under Rule I. Since he has been convicted of a crime, Rule II states that he is not a member in good standing. In this situation, both rules apply, but there are no grounds for choosing between them. The question is relevant since it deals with the central issue, Andrew's status as a member in good standing. The correct response is, therefore, A.

4. If it were true that Andrew has not attended at least 50 percent of the club's meetings during the past three years, Rule I specifies that he is not a member in good standing. If it were also true that he brought an alcoholic beverage into the club, Rule II specifies that he is not a member in good standing. This question is relevant because it addresses the issue of Andrew's status as a member in good standing, and it may be answered by applying the rules to the facts. Therefore, the correct response is C.

Section 4.0224   Problem No. 2—Answers:

1. This clearly relevant question can be answered from the facts given and by using deductive reasoning; we can conclude that the breaking of Albert's arm was not "intentional." The correct answer is C.

2. A review of the facts reveals the lack of a clear answer as to whether John had the legal status of a teacher or some other positions. Therefore, since more information is needed, the correct response is B.

3. Whether Albert was harmed is not relevant to the outcome of the dispute since it has no bearing on the definition of the term "battery." The facts clearly reflect that John's striking of Albert with the yardstick was intentional, but the rules do not require any showing of harm to fulfill the definition of a battery. Therefore, since the answer is irrelevant, the proper answer is D.

4. This relevant question requires the choice between the two rules. The correct answer is A.

5. A review of the facts does not reveal the age of the two boys involved in the classroom scuffle. Since more information is needed, the correct response is B.

6. The history of John's striking of students with the yardstick is irrelevant and bears only remotely on the outcome of the dispute. The correct answer is D.

Bibliography

Black's Law Dictionary, 6th ed. St. Paul: West Publishing Company, 1990.

Rhetorical Memory and Delivery, edited by John Frederick Reynolds. Hillsdale, NJ: Lawrence Erlbaum Associates, 1993.

Corbett, Edward P. J., *Classical Rhetoric for the Modern Student*. NY: Oxford University Press, 1990.

Fogarty, Daniel, *Roots for a New Rhetoric*. Columbia University, NY, 1959.

Rombauer, M., *Legal Problem Solving*. West Publishing Company, 1981.

Block, G., *Effective Legal Writing*. Foundation Press, 1992.

Koerselman, Virginia, *CLA Review Manual*. West Publishing Company, 1993.

5 Communications

5.00   Communication Concept

"Communication," as defined by *Webster's Tenth New Collegiate Dictionary,* is "a process by which information is exchanged between individuals through a common system of symbols, signs, or behavior." Communicating is a skill each of us employs, some more successfully than others. To be a successful communicator, one must study the elements of communication and then develop the ability to use those elements that complement one's personality.

The scientific aspects of communication involve well-identified techniques that can inhibit communication or facilitate it, depending upon the circumstance.

5.01   Ultimate Skill

Communication is one of the most important skills the legal assistant must develop. Legal assistants are charged with the responsibility of assembling and conveying facts and factual situations accurately to attorneys from the data source. This test of communication skill relies not only on the identification of a known or believed "fact," but also the effect on it of any coloration of prejudice, self interest, credibility, and applicability to the problem. Every "fact" that comes to the legal assistant originates somewhere else, not in his or her own brain. Otherwise, the legal assistant would be the witness rather than the identifier of witnesses. As is discussed in other sections of this book, facts may be testimonial, physical, or material. Relaying needed information to the attorney, both clearly and fully, is the legal assistant's absolute duty; perhaps it is even more important than the duty to find and isolate the important facts from the unimportant or irrelevant ones.

It is true that a legal assistant can accomplish this simply by flooding the attorney with every fact, inference, and circumstance relevant to the case. Doing this without attempting to provide gradations of value to these facts essentially reduces the contribution of the legal assistant to little more than that of a clerk. It is important for the legal assistant to use the fewest words to convey the fullest message to the attorney or, conversely, from the attorney to such other person as the legal assistant is designated to contact. The legal assistant's function then is not to serve as an unfiltered conduit of word flow but rather to relay clear meanings and ideas. If there is one formula for communicating that legal assistants should adopt, it is the KISS formula—"Keep It Simple, Stupid." Simple words are easily understood and seldom misunderstood. Short sentences do not confuse readers or listeners, and short thoughts are more easily assimilated than long, involved sentences. Remember that one formula. It will be your salvation in all forms of communication—KISS—the minimum needed for full understanding.

5.02   Methods of Communication

There are increasing numbers of communication techniques, most of which are variations or amplifications of the three most common means of communication available to each of us:

a. *Nonverbal*, sometimes referred to as body language, or the associative image we project by the posture of our body, the clothes we wear or the way they are worn, as well as the expression on our faces or the manner in which we look (or avoid looking) at others;

b. *Verbal*, or the process of speaking, either directly to someone or through mechanical devices such as a telephone, dictating machine, tape recorder, television camera, or, in some cases, a computer; and,

c. *Written*, where we put our thoughts on paper in print and convey them to someone else.

Communication is also possible by use of any one of the five physical senses of sight, smell, taste, touch, or hearing. However, the message then is frequently shallow and incomplete. A combined use of these senses can afford us a fully textured communication experience with the aggregate impression triggering our "sixth sense," *instinctive reaction.*

Why people instinctively like or dislike others, trust or fear them, are attracted to or repelled by them, are questions too complex for us to study definitively. Legal assistants must be aware that the total communication effort is affected by the impressions they give others, whether in the form of body impressions they give others, whether in the form of body image (good or bad), facial expressions, body language (we'll discuss this later), voice tone, phrasing and vocabulary, or writing style and technique.

Each of these, singly or in combination, affects the legal assistant's professional productivity and effectiveness directly or through stimulation of the "sixth sense."

It is not the decision reached that is critical. What is vital is that the legal assistant consider, test, modify, alter, adapt, or reject concepts in establishing the technique that fits the individual's personality and contributes to strengths while minimizing the effect of weaknesses.

5.03 Basic Communication Skills

It is possible through study to improve the quality of one's communication skills. Numerous courses are available at junior colleges, community colleges, universities, private schools, or through seminars sponsored by professional associations that greatly enhance these abilities. Some of the courses that should be considered by persons entering the legal assistant field are public speaking, debate, appreciation and analysis of English literature, creative writing, and spelling. All will play a distinct part in raising the communication skills of the legal assistant to the highest possible level.

5.031 Public Speaking and Oral Presentations

Public speaking or acting classes, debate societies, and similar activities will assist legal assistants in learning to think on their feet, to select effective and persuasive words under the press of time, and to listen to an adversary or partner.

Public speaking classes teach the skill of organizing a presentation into four steps:

1. the introduction;
2. a bridge from the introduction to the topical matter;
3. the argument; and
4. the closing summation.

Following these four simple steps will assist the legal assistant in preparing presentations to attorneys, clients, or adversaries.

The introduction (step 1) in a speech should accomplish three things: introduce the speaker to the audience; bring the attention of the audience to the presentation in comfort or ease (thus the frequent use of a suitable joke to break the tension and build a little rapport); and provide a preliminary statement of the overall topic.

The bridge to the topic matter (step 2) is a departure from the introduction and a transition to the true body of the presentation. Usually this bridge points out to the audience the timeliness, importance, or value of the material the speaker will cover.

The argument (step 3) is the presentation of viewpoint or data. It is organized in logical, progressive steps that allow the audience to follow the reasoning from a basic fact analysis, with a definition of all issues, choices, procedures, or proposals, and any major alternatives.

The conclusion (step 4) is a statement of the speaker's decision, recommendation, or request. Frequently, this is presented as a recapitulation where the salient thoughts are briefly restated and a persuasive conclusion is offered.

5.032 Reading and Writing

Creative writing or literature appreciation classes increase the ability of the legal assistant to write, to read, and to understand what is written. How to select words to convey the precise image desired is learned through the reading of essays, speeches, fiction and nonfiction works, and periodicals and daily newspapers.

Reading and writing legal material is a specialized activity that the legal assistant must study and practice in the course of the day-to-day job. Seek critiques, discussions, and the opportunity to draft material for others to accept or reject, edit, or totally rewrite. Do not take offense: take the suggestions and criticism and modify the technique used to match the style and technique of the office. Legal writing courses may help develop these skills.

5.033　Special Problems

In communication, special problems must be overcome to accomplish a given purpose. Among those the legal assistant may anticipate are communicating with people with different levels of literacy or different lifestyles and backgrounds, with people who are more fluent in a language other than English, and with those who have some form of physical handicap, such as a hearing, vision, speaking, or endurance problem. In each of these situations, it is the duty of the legal assistant to find solutions to the problems. The ability to solve such problems is one measure of his or her value to attorneys.

With the aged and the young, where attention problems may be a difficulty, schedule a series of visits of short duration or handle only one small problem, fact, or issue at a given meeting. For a person of limited literacy, word selection and the pace of conversation must be adapted to the comprehension level of that individual. If foreign languages are a barrier to direct communication, the use of an interpreter is essential for efficiency and desirable for the interviewee's confidence. Similarly, the handicapped who cannot hear, see, or speak have substitute means of communication that should be explored and used whenever possible.

5.04　Nonverbal Communication

This term relates to the image we create around ourselves as a matter of choice. It includes body language and sometimes is called the "associative image." It is that aura in which people clothe themselves and by which they project their self-image to others. Body language can be extremely important because the clients who visit law firms frequently differ in age, social status, levels of wealth, and backgrounds.

Lawfirms operate successfully on the trust of their clients, and each person who is employed by a firm to provide services to clients can reasonably be expected to contribute to that comfortable image of trust. To damage that image with whimsical or bizarre clothing or personal grooming is inexcusable and unnecessary. Each law office generally has some form of standard of dress for both men and women. It should be sufficiently flexible and comfortable so that none of the employees feels unduly constricted, nor should the attorneys feel the firm is being adversely affected or exploited by their employees' manner of dress, grooming, or personal hygiene.

5.041　Facial Expressions

A legal assistant's demeanor is as important as his or her grooming. A pleasant, cheerful expression will generally elicit a responding smile from even the most unhappy or dissatisfied person.

We seldom fully appreciate the effect of the image we present to the world by the expression we wear on our faces. Actors, of course, make their living by conveying emotion, attitude, and meaning through their faces. Comedians have built their whole careers on wearing a particular expression. If the legal assistant watches the attorneys' conduct in court, he or she will see that they, too, make use of the same communication techniques with the jury in trying to convey emotion, attitude, or belief to supplement or add impact to the words they are using.

Similarly, each of us, as we pass through our offices, meet each other, clients, or witnesses, and convey something about our attitude simply by looking at them and exposing our faces to their inspection. A legal assistant's attitude signals to the interviewee and to everyone else whether the legal assistant is serious or jocular, cheerful or sullen, interested and attentive, or bored and tolerating. Belief and disbelief often can be conveyed simply by the movement of eyebrows, and acceptance or rejection of a story can be expressed by wrinkles, motions, or lack of motions in the face. Surprise, shock, and revulsion are betrayed by facial expressions. The legal assistant who does much interviewing should perform "mirror practice" so that appropriate expressions can be adopted as needed. Practice allows analysis of the effect the legal assistant may create in the mind of a viewer by a particular grimace, scowl, or smile. It helps to see what the other party sees.

Remember, the most effective tool a legal assistant has in a repertoire of facial expressions is that of interested, cheerful, attentive, professional concentration. It encourages interviewees to talk; it makes the employing attorney believe in the legal assistant's dedication; and it assists the office manager in determining if the legal assistant will properly carry out the functions delegated.

5.042 Hands and Gestures

Some gestures may be offensive to others. Be careful of such actions as pointing fingers, spearing someone in the chest or shoulder while making a point in a discussion, or touching others. Many people resent the unwanted physical contact and miss the point of the argument because they are preoccupied with the contact.

5.043 Eye Contact and Body Position

These are vitally important in communication. Books are filled with descriptive terms such as "shifty-eyed liar," the "darting glance of fear," the "stern gaze of righteousness," as well as "a stiff-backed rage," "trembling with terror," or "crouched in shame." These vivid descriptions engender images in our minds based on past experiences or remembered characterizations in plays, movies, and television. It is a fact that various emotional conditions produce physical changes of posture and conduct that others interpret. The legal assistant is concerned with the messages given with the body or received from others. Project supportive, professional competence and avoid reflecting uncertainty, fear, confusion, irritation, or anger, unless there is a tactical need for such display.

5.0431 Nervous System. The body's autonomic nervous system is a complex mechanism that aids it in preparing for, or responding to, stress. It is sometimes called the "fight or flight" condition. As stress increases, most people find their heart rate increases, their breathing rate and/or volume of each breath changes, more adrenaline is produced, and the body temperature may rise. Additional perspiration is generated, and muscle tension increases, sometimes causing trembling. The body is preparing itself for combat or escape, depending on the situation and its development.

Legal assistants should observe such symptoms and try to place them in the context appropriate to the situation—normal nervousness in anticipation of a novel experience, fear of the unknown, or fear of being detected in a lie.

Common nervousness can be dispelled by accommodation to the circumstance and the establishment of a comfortable situation. Other physical manifestations should be noted together with the stimuli that generated them. Legal assistants can adjust (or record) the condition, as needed, when it is reflected. The same messages sent by legal assistants may be irretrievable, however, and it is necessary to know, understand, and minimize the body language that adversely affects the legal assistants' function. Again, note the conduct appreciated or disliked in others and adopt that preferred conduct.

5.0432 Body Language. Among the most common types of body language with a high potential for adverse interpretation are:

a. No eye contact. Avoiding a person's eyes during conversation is very dangerous for a legal assistant. It has been said that the "eyes are the mirrors of the soul." Failure to look in the other person's eyes denies the legal assistant an excellent means of character evaluation and may create a doubt in the other party's mind as to the honesty, candor, or interest of the legal assistant. Practice looking at people when they talk. Hold their eyes and try to evaluate whether they shift their eyes because they are lying or embarrassed or just because they are nervous. Do they practice the "sincere look" when trying out a tall tale? Match the stress of the conversation with the appearance of their eyes. Stress causes the pupils to contract in some eyes; others become brighter and wetter, while others jerk back and forth. Joy, pleasure, and friendliness cause some eyes to sparkle. It is not the whole world of meanings that is most important to a legal assistant professionally but the changes that occur during the talks and the time in the talks when the changes occur.

b. Standing too close. Most people in Western cultures want some distance between themselves and those with whom they talk. It is an outgrowth of the "territory" theory that anyone who comes too close to you is "invading your territory." Big or tall people who stand very close to smaller or shorter people create both a physical intimidation and a difficult psychological problem of submission and/or anger. "Arm's length" negotiations imply an equality of bargaining position, physically and psychologically. Legal assistants who like being close to people must gain their trust first; then closeness is tolerable.

c. Slouching, stooping, and leaning. These postures suggest carelessness, lack of interest, and lack of intensity. They are acceptable with friends but should be avoided during first meetings. Erect posture may not prove the person is alert, but its lack makes the proof more necessary.

Body language and all its elements are important to a legal assistant in the employer-employee relationship as well as the interviewer-interviewee one.

5.044 The Office and the Image

Body control, personal grooming, manner of dress, and facial expressions must meet acceptable standards for the office. These standards must also extend to the order and arrangement of the desk or office. This is one place where the old adage "neatness counts" cannot be emphasized more. Neatness assists prompt location of a file when it is needed. It engenders confidence in the minds of visitors to the office, whether they are other legal assistants, lawyers, or witnesses. In many ways, the office and the desk are extensions of the legal assistant's self-image: organized or disorganized, neat or sloppy. Certainly for interviewees who visit the office on business, the neatness of the office and the fact that all materials relating to their case are immediately available, while the cases of everyone else are discreetly out of sight, engender confidence and the belief in their minds that they are important and that their affairs are important and confidential.

5.05 Verbal Communication—The Listening Portion

Verbal communication denotes dialogue, speaking, *and* listening. It requires the use of the voice and of the ear, the two essential tools in verbal communication. They function twelve to twenty hours of every day in some form or another, and of the two, the ear and its use may be the most important. It is the "inbound" half of a two-way street. Listening is not an easy skill, but it is one that should be practiced at every opportunity by every legal assistant. Most people like to talk, and in talking, they expose themselves to the listener. If the legal assistant will listen and keep his or her mouth shut, he or she has greater opportunity to hear what the speaker has to say, to comprehend the words the speaker uses, and to correlate these words with other things the speaker has said before. This allows the legal assistant to accommodate him or herself to the speaker's particular level of intelligence. The legal assistant is then better prepared to phrase productive questions at the appropriate time.

5.051 Fast Mind—Slow Mouth

The mind works much faster than the mouth. As a result, many people find their minds telling them to argue, analyze, interject, question, or comment rather than to continue listening for greater and greater detail. There is nothing wrong with the mind going faster than the words of another, provided the narration is not confused by the listener's interjecting comments, thereby making the speaker reflect and fully realize what he or she is saying. The trickiest part about listening is to listen accurately and absorb what is being said, rather than allowing the mind to be distracted with comparisons, analysis, and arguments about what is being said.

5.052 Listen and Note

The preferred technique is to listen and take notes while visually observing the person doing the talking. The change of facial expression, the onset of blushing, the movement of the eyes, the willingness to meet the listener's eyes or the avoidance of them, all are significant to the person who is listening. Whether it is an attorney giving instructions to a legal assistant for the first time or an interviewee telling a story for the fourth time, it is important to listen closely to what is said.

5.053 Words—The Key to Speaking

Everyone speaks thousands of words every day. Strangely enough, the number of *different* words used among those thousands of spoken words may be small; the rest are the same words used repeatedly. It is estimated that the average high school graduate uses only seven hundred different words in the course of normal conversations, and that figure does not increase appreciably with a college education. Twelve hundred is a fairly common number of different words in regular use by U.S. college graduates.

By contrast, a Japanese child entering school for the first time has a working knowledge of approximately six thousand different words. This is due in part to the structure of the Japanese language, in which verbs are combined to create conjugations reflecting tense and other grammatical elements. In English, however, we live through a memory course of strange rules and irrational pronunciations of certain combinations of letters. For legal assistants to communicate effectively, it is necessary to learn, appreciate, and correctly use these variations to the highest degree.

5.054 Jargon

Once a person has attained a position as legal assistant, some alchemy occurs in the personality requiring the adoption of Latin phrases and the jargon of the legal profession in that legal assistant's normal conversations with peers, clients, and others. This is a serious error because people outside of the legal community may not fully understand the meaning of these words; thus, their use tends to confuse rather than clarify the meaning intended by the speaker. A legal assistant needs a broad vocabulary, and toward that end, understanding legal terminology is necessary; however, legal terminology should be reserved for use in technical discussions with peers of the legal assistant where the exact meaning of the legal terms is important.

5.055   Meanings, Words, and Sounds

One of the unfortunate features of the English language is the number of words that sound the same phonetically and yet carry substantially different meanings. A different complication is words of similar sounds but different spellings. These words can pose very serious problems in the use of electronic dictating or recording equipment.

Despite the limited number of words used by the average American, *Webster's Unabridged Dictionary* modestly describes itself as containing twenty thousand different words. Add to that the amazing complexity of technical languages, such as those of the legal, engineering, and medical professions, as well as the jargons adopted in business and other fields. The volume increases dramatically and so does confusion.

Since legal assistants work in all of these areas, the demand for learning vocabulary is strong. However, great discipline should be exercised in the vocabulary that is used. Slang and jargon are often regional, having totally different meanings outside a given area. Learn everything but limit use to the right phrase at the right time. Do not simply exercise a specialized vocabulary to impress or awe listeners. Consider words as tools to convey appropriate meaning, not toys with which to satisfy the ego.

5.056   Ethnic Language and "Street Talk"

Complicating communication is the proliferation of slang and/or ethnic phraseology and "street talk" in modern language. Many community colleges and some universities are adopting literature classes particularly designed to satisfy the needs of ethnic language students. Whenever possible, legal assistants should be familiar with these vocabularies, particularly when interviewing or contacting these ethnic populations. "Street talk" is everchanging, as is slang, and staying abreast is difficult at best. A retentive memory, inquiring mind, and patient questioning when encountering street talk can clarify the needed meanings.

5.057   Understanding Is the Object

Remember, the essence of communication is understanding, by both the speaker and the listener. The legal assistant is at once a highly skilled listener, translator, and speaker. The use of profanity, slang, or ethnic stereotypes by legal assistants is inappropriate. However, the people the legal assistant will encounter may use them, and it may be necessary in the course of those conversations to be able to speak on a comfortable level with such people. The legal assistant must be aware of these language dissimilarities and be able to accept their use without shock, irritation, or condescension.

5.058   Voice Tone and Implication

Perhaps more important than the words they speak is the manner in which legal assistants use their voices: tone, modulation, inflection, and diction. A word correctly used but incorrectly pronounced loses the meaning ascribed to it. The legal assistant often discusses matters of great importance to people in stressful situations where the listener's critical examination of the legal assistant's verbal response is colored by anxiety. Many clients anticipate failure, and they expect their initial statements will be misunderstood. Support their hopes and dispel their fears as much as possible with a pleasant voice tone that is well modulated, with good diction, and with a relatively cheerful or at least neutral attitude.

5.059   Facial Expressions and Word Meaning

One delightful feature about person-to-person conversation is the ability to impute shades of meaning to another's words from the emotion displayed on the person's face and from characterizing the individual's voice tone, modulation, and diction as being helpful, supportive, confirming, or argumentative. Once the conversation is filtered through a mechanical phase, such as through the use of a telephone or of dictating or recording equipment, these supplemental clues to the meaning of the speaker are lost. Often it is not possible to ask for clarification if the communication is on electronic media. Therefore, careful use of words and language and of voice tone and modulation is critical when conducting a conversation or a verbal communication through mechanical or electronic means.

5.06   Telephone Techniques

The telephone, of course, is the most common electronic or mechanical device in verbal communication. We seldom consider it as an extension of our personality. However, the majority of a legal assistant's first contacts with people will be accomplished over the telephone and it is very important to seriously analyze the manner in which the legal assistant conducts him or herself on the telephone.

Telephone companies around the nation offer training courses in telephone techniques for people who work in offices and use the telephone as part of their daily business. One of the things they uniformly advocate, and rightly so, is to "put a smile in your voice." There is nothing more aggravating than to call an office seeking information and be switched from one phone to another seeking the one person who can provide the information. This is especially true if each of the people to whom the individual is transferred expresses by voice tone, inflection, or choice of words his or her lack of interest in the particular request or inability to assist the caller.

5.061   Telephone Etiquette

A quick way to alienate clients is to put a client on hold immediately after answering the phone, according to the Telephone Doctor, a St. Louis-based training company. An overwhelming 85 percent said telephone courtesy makes "a lot of difference" in their willingness to purchase goods or services.

Answering the call: Standards should be set throughout the company for proper phone etiquette. The content should be memorized by everyone as though it were a minicommercial. The phone should be answered in two to four rings with a standard greeting, such as:

"Good Afternoon, The Miller Law Firm, how may I direct your call?"

Transferring the call: Proper etiquette for transferring calls is essential. Tell the caller you are going to transfer him. ("Please hold" is unprofessional). Be sure you are transferring to the right person. If the call is not picked up, get back to the caller.

When you are asked to screen calls: Legal assistants, although they usually don't answer the phone initially, are often responsible for screening the calls for their attorneys. "I will see if Mr. Miller is available," and "Can you tell me what your call is in reference to?" are common and acceptable inquiries. Make sure you get the name correct! Ask for the proper spelling and the correct pronunciation, if in doubt. Pay attention to titles.

Managing difficult clients: Difficult callers fall into a few general categories, and there are certain helpful approaches to dealing with them:

1. Those who go on and on . . . ask questions.
2. Those who are angry . . . show empathy and respect.
   a. "What you are telling me is important."
   b. Listen to understand. "Tell me what happened."
   c. Uncover the expectations. "Will you tell me what you feel needs to be done."
   d. Repeat the specifics. "Let me be sure I understand."
   e. Outline the solutions. "You have several choices."
   f. Take action and *follow through*. "I will personally check and let you know."

3. Those who speak little or no English . . . listen carefully, speak slowly.
4. When you reach a boiling point, turn the call over to a coworker, whom you have briefed, and let the client know that "perhaps Ms. Jones can answer your questions. I'll transfer you to her."

Closing the conversation: Thank the client for calling. Provide assurances that any promises will be fulfilled. Most importantly, leave the customer with a positive feeling. Although they can't see you, the client can tell whether or not you're smiling by the tone of your voice, so SMILE! A courteous closing might include, "We're happy to help", "I have enjoyed talking to you", or "If you have additional questions, please call again." Let the client hang up first, as a courtesy.[1]

5.062 Identification and Notation

When placing or receiving a telephone call, the legal assistant must identify him or herself by name and title. Notes should be taken of all calls involving clients or other office matters, and a copy of such notes should be placed in the appropriate client file. Any agreements reached or information given or received should be noted. They should be complete and expository with date, time, and the parties identified even if it is for the file only. Anything involving a case, the attorney, or a client should be summarized with the same elements in a memorandum to the file, or to the attorney, a letter to the client, or both. A log of all telephone calls placed and received should be kept, not only by the receptionist but also by the legal assistant, particularly when he or she is accepting or placing calls on behalf of the employing attorney.

5.0621 The Telephone as an Aid.   *Voice Mail:* Communications through voice mail has greatly enhanced the productivity in the office. While busy on other telephone calls or being away from the office, voice mail picks up a messages while you are otherwise engaged. The caller leaves a detailed message so the person called can act on the message and then return the call with a response, without a loss of time. The importance of reviewing all voice mail messages and returning calls make it an effective and efficient way to handle communications.

---

[1] Benn, Martha, *Telephone Resources*, Albuquerque, New Mexico, 1997.

Answering machines: Answering machines are another tool used to record messages while the person called is away from the telephone. Taped machines or digitally recorded messages allow the communication to be delivered with the same clarity and efficiency as talking in person. Quality of equipment must be a prime consideration. Tapes that run out or digitally recorded messages that garble words are of no use in the efficient world of communications.

5.0622 *Proper Use of the Telephone.* The telephone should be held so that words are transmitted directly into the mouthpiece and words emanating from the earpiece may be clearly and easily heard. The use of *speakerphones* that allow for conference calls sometimes is beneficial if more than one person will participate on one instrument; however, the sound from such speakers can be eerie and distorted. The use of conference calls that interconnect several telephones so that each person can converse from his or her own office instrument may be used. In each of these cases, the participants must take turns talking.

5.063 Confirming Letters

When a telephone call involves matters of legal procedures, docketing, extensions of time to answer, arrangements for production of witnesses or documents, or other material relevant to a particular case, a confirming letter should be initiated immediately following the call. This letter should be a complete recapitulation of the discussed topics and arrangements to be included in the case file for the information and documentation of the attorney, with copies to the office docket control and each affected party in the case. Usual custom calls for the party requesting an accommodation to write the letter; however, legal assistants are best advised to initiate the confirming letter immediately for the protection of their own firms and attorneys. If two letters result, redundancy won't hurt and a difference of opinion in what the agreement was thought to be might be revealed.

5.064 Phonetics

Telephones and other mechanical or electronic equipment can alter voice tones in the normal speaking mode. As a result, the transmittal of information of any importance, particularly names, addresses, numbers, or initials, should always be double- and sometimes triple-checked to insure accuracy. Letters, particularly, are easily misheard over a telephone or on a tape recording; B, D, P, and V tend to be confusing and indistinct over the telephone. Compensate with phonetic spelling. When there is doubt, use a phonetic alphabet to clarify any ambiguities. The legal assistant who does not know the international alphabet must substitute his or her own, for instance "A as in apple," and "G as in George." Numbers, too, are difficult to hear clearly over the telephone. "Fifth" and "sixth" can be confused. Therefore, when discussing an address over the phone, first be sure that the other party understands the address and that the listener reads it back to the giver precisely the way it was heard. When there is doubt, use the phonetic alphabet to clarify any ambiguities or count the numbers as in "one, two, three, four, five— fi-yiv street!"

5.065 Recording Telephone Statements

Before using the telephone to record any statements or conversations, the legal assistant must first confirm with the supervising attorney that this is acceptable. If the attorney approves the use of telephone recording, the legal assistant must review and observe the federal laws on the use of tape recording equipment, particularly in connection with telephone company facilities. (*See* Chapter 6, Section 6.056, for a discussion on recording considerations.) Both participants must be aware the recording is being made, and both must agree to such recording. This acknowledgment should be stated at the outset of such a recorded conversation and repeated before its termination.

Do not forget to memorialize all important nonrecorded telephone conversations with clear, written notes as previously discussed in Section 5.062. Even recorded telephone conversations can more profitably be memorialized by a concise, written summary of the call, reserving any tape recording for future reference, if and when needed, rather than having the full dialogue transcribed and edited.

5.07   Dictating Equipment

The use of dictating equipment is well established as a timesaving operation in the conduct of work for attorneys and secretaries. This dictation process now extends to a large proportion of legal assistants who must convert their thoughts and notes into some less cryptic and more communicative form of preserved document. Legal assistants must learn the courtesies and practices of good dictation. One of the greatest helps, of course, is to understand fully the dictating equipment to be used, both in its use and its ability to reproduce the human voice. The user's manual supplied with each piece of equipment should be studied by each user before attempting to dictate.

Every dictated communication should carry some identifying data at the outset to insure that the material can be identified quickly and easily by the typist at the time of transcription, and, if necessary, later. Among the essential items are the date, the name of the dictator, the dictator's phone number or extension, the case or the topic of the dictation, whether or not there are copies intended for other parties, and whether this effort is for execution as a draft or final form.

The use of a dictation "log" is helpful to most secretaries, whether they are experienced legal secretaries or novices from typing pools (*see* Exhibit 5-1). The log usually has a tape reference number and identifies the dictator, the date, the type of case or topic, how many copies are needed, and the full names and addresses of all parties who are addressees or who will be mentioned in the course of the dictated material. This insures that the proper spelling of names and addresses is reflected in the final product. Including on the log any special, technical, or obscure words used in the dictation will save the dictator and the secretary/typist a great deal of time (the latter in research, the former in editing).

5.071   Voice Use

The next element encountered is how the voice is used in dictating material other people will type. The pace of dictation should approximate a normal conversational pace. However, it is necessary to use better diction and pronunciation. Slurring or the use of unnecessary words as "and," "oh," "or," and "er" are not helpful to the typist and, in a long tape, can be both irritating and distracting. Do not use a monotone, but use a modulated voice, as you would in conversation. If possible, place emphasis on the correct words and the usual voice inflections that reflect sentence closings, periods, or question marks.

EXHIBIT 5-1   Sample Dictation Log

Dictator:	Date:
Case:	Tape/Side:
	Attorney:
	Client Matter/File No.:
	Deadline:
Subject:	
To:	CC:
Special Notes: (Names, Addresses, Technical Terms, etc.)	

5.072 The Outline

An outline of the material to be dictated should be prepared either mentally or on paper before beginning dictation. The entire structure of the ultimate document must be conceived ahead of time, both in content and form. Its format should be thought out and described either on the dictation log or in the introductory portion of the dictated material. Any tabulated material to be included should be referred to, and if it is in a form that can be inserted as a separate sheet or some other variety of material, it should be attached to the dictation log.

The actual dictation should proceed smoothly and quickly, with little dead space on the tape where the dictator is thinking. The speaker must concentrate on enunciating correctly so the typist can correctly understand the words and translate them into written form. Be especially cautious of using words that have unusual or irregular spelling or are technical terms, trade jargon, or of foreign derivation. Note these on the log as well.

5.073 Verbalizing Punctuation

The speaking voice has a cadence and pace that must be represented in writing by punctuation marks. Since the conversion of dictation from spoken to written form involves two people, the dictator must see the punctuation that will structure the sentence for the reader, then speak that punctuation for the typist. For example: "paragraph, all in caps, now is the time, colon, your opportunity to buy in, quote, sunshine acres, close quote, is limited, exclamation point, write for details, period, end of dictation" will look like this: "NOW IS THE TIME: Your opportunity to buy in "Sunshine Acres" is limited! Write for details."

Often an experienced secretary, listening to a familiar voice, well-modulated and speaking conversationally, can impute commas, semicolons, and capitalization. Very few typists, experienced or not, can hear a new voice and correctly punctuate for it. Typing from voice dictation is a reflex process for many typists, and they can perform only as well as the dictator dictates. The combination of modulated voice and spoken punctuation promotes efficiency through clarity and by providing the maximum number of clues to the material possible.

5.074 Review, Edit, and Learn

It is not enough simply to dictate and pass the completed material over to someone to type. Legal assistants must periodically review the material dictated to detect failures in dictating technique and to improve delivery. No one can learn only from reviewing his or her own tapes. Consult the experts—the typists and secretaries whose work allows them to hear and appreciate the techniques of many dictators. A "partnership" feeling between secretaries and legal assistants can develop the dictating style of legal assistants into one of great efficiency that is pleasant and fulfilling for the secretaries and the legal assistants.

The legal assistant must be critical of his or her own work and accept the suggestions and criticisms of others with a positive and constructive attitude.

5.08   Using the Computer

As with every business around the globe, computers have become the backbone of organization and efficiency for a law practice. Every legal assistant must compile a working knowledge of computers. This requires a basic understanding of computer "hardware", which consists of the computer itself (with choices of processors, memory capability, disk drives, etc.), as well as an understanding of the various monitors, printers, modems, and other options that are available.

The type of software attorneys have incorporated into their computer systems require legal assistants to be trained and ready to perform with technical skills that cover a wide range of applications, including word processing programs such as WordPerfect® and/or Microsoft Word®; spreadsheet programs such as Lotus®, Excel®, and Quattro Pro®; timekeeping programs such as Timeslips® and TABS®; database programs such as Paradox®, MS Access®, dBASE®, and FoxPro®; and presentation programs such as Corel Presentations®, Astound®, and MS PowerPoint®.

Because computer technology is growing and changing so rapidly, and because of its rapid integration into the court system and courtroom, it is important for every legal assistant to stay abreast of advances, and retrain when needed.

5.081 Effective Use of Computers

Drafting documents at the computer is often more effective and time efficient than dictating. By looking at the document as it is being drafted, the drafter is able to revise on screen without the necessity of reading a print copy and making manual revisions which then must be retyped into the computer.

Saving documents in a computer file for easy retrieval is a great benefit to the legal assistant. Rather than reinventing the wheel each time you draft a letter or pleading, it is easy to retrieve a similar document from the computer and revise it. This saves time and guarantees consistency in the work product. Find out the forms that are used most often in your office. Investigate the use of "macros", which are computer commands that perform a task automatically. A macro can retrieve a file, give it a new name, and save it in another file format, for example.

Scanning incoming documents into the computer for later use, revision, and reference is one of the most recent technology advances to find its way into the law office. Scanning software and hardware prices are now less than the costs of many printers. Scanning is particularly useful when large documents from outside sources, which would otherwise have to be retyped, are being revised. Scanning is also a timesaver when preparing responses to discovery requests, since scanning eliminates the need to type in the propounded requests which must appear in discovery responses.

5.082 Effective Use of E-mail

With the advent of networking, or connecting computers so that they share resources, the use of electronic mail ("e-mail") in interoffice communications has become commonplace and, in some firms and companies, has taken the place of many other forms of written communication, such as phone memo slips, records of contact with clients and others, status memos, scheduling memos, and the transmittal of documents for internal review. It is important to realize that critical information which is transmitted within the office using e-mail should be saved and appropriately filed for future reference.

Electronic exchange of documents between offices, or between an office and the client, is also a common practice. This can be done via modem connections from computer to computer, or by e-mail through the Internet. This technology combines computers with telephone lines to relay messages almost instantly.

It is important to build safeguards into any e-mail system that you use so security is not a question. Without the use of encryption software, data that is transmitted via modem or by e-mail is easily accessible by unauthorized persons. As a legal assistant, you should take care that no confidential information is disseminated without taking appropriate action to ensure its confidentiality.

5.09 Written Communication

This section will not include legal briefs, pleadings, formal discovery documents, or other materials whose style and form or format can be established from form books or other research material available to the legal assistant and that are generally within the responsibility and editing purview of the attorney. We will discuss those elements of correspondence originated by the legal assistant to the members of the law firm and those documents of correspondence originated by the legal assistant, either individually or for the attorneys, from the firm to other people.

Simple, thoughtful writing is elegant. Even complex ideas can be expressed plainly. The heart of a good writing style is the ability to write short, simple sentences. However, do not make the mistake of talking down to your readers. Search for quality vocabulary and a style that best conveys your meaning. Mark Twain once said that there is as much difference between the almost right word and the right word as there is between the lightning bug and lightning. It's worth the effort to "hunt" for the word that most accurately expresses your thought. This is particularly true for legal writing, where the wrong word can result in a mistaken interpretation, or, in the extreme case, to malpractice.

Writing is easiest if you organize your thoughts before you start. Here is a successful approach to organizing legal writing, which applies to a broad spectrum of applications, from basic correspondence to intricate legal memorandum:[2]

1. Write down every idea you have on your subject, even fleeting thoughts, and in no particular order.
2. Write an introduction paragraph. You will probably rewrite it several times, even after you have completed the assignment. The purpose in writing the lead is to start you thinking about how you are going to organize what you have to say.

---

[2] Garner, Bryan A., "*Writing for Litigation,*" *Scribes Journal of Legal Writing*, The American Society of Writers on Legal Subjects, Dallas, TX, 1990, pp. 66–68.

3. With your list of ideas and your lead paragraph, write a simple outline, checking off points from your idea list as you write. When your outline is finished, you'll discover there are gaps in your list of ideas. These are the holes this method is designed to expose.

4. Now you are ready to write. You may think of new ideas to include, and because you have an outline, these additions need not crowd out the main points.

5. Let your organization show. Let your reader understand that you know where you are, where you are going, and what conclusions you have drawn.[3]

6. Rewrite. If you are typing directly into your computer, you have help. By using your spell check, thesaurus, or grammar check (when available) you can enhance your writing quickly and easily.

    An excellent reference book is *Elements of Style* by William Strunk Jr. and E. B. White.[4] A 43-page summation of the case for cleanliness, accuracy, and brevity in the use of English, this booklet combines academics and insight in a short text.

7. All written materials subject to approval by a supervising attorney should be double-spaced, marked "draft," and submitted to your supervisor for review. Maintain all drafts for your records.

8. Reread the final version with a fresh look to see if there is anything you missed. Make sure copies are sent to the designated recipients, and, without fail, file a copy of the final draft.

5.091 Internal Correspondence

The law firm's internal correspondence can take many forms, from slips of paper bearing cryptic notes, to e-mail, to full-scale studies and briefing materials. Regardless of the matter to be communicated, it is important that each item of correspondence be dated, signed, and when appropriate, directed to a specific addressee, even if that addressee is "memorandum to the file." Any correspondence originated in connection with a court action should refer to that case by suitable caption at the outset of the correspondence.

The correspondence may be generated in a form established by office policy. This may include multi-page materials, a typed master from which photocopies can be made, or interoffice e-mail. For correspondence within the office where an answer is requested, the use of multipage material is helpful. Many firms produce in-house memoranda forms using carbonless paper, with space provided for answering. This saves time and allows all parties to have the full text of the original communication and its answer. The electronic equivalent of this process is to use the automatic message quoting feature in e-mail which will then include the original message text when generating a reply or forwarding the message to others.

5.0911 "Tickler Systems." Different tickler systems can be used to direct certain actions from one person to another, saving time. Tickler/suspense, docket, and calendar systems are all useful in providing reminders of anticipated due dates and/or appearances. (*See* Exhibits 5-2 and 5-3.) A handwritten tickler or suspense file system can be very inexpensive, but very cost affective. A 3 · 5 index card is used detailing the information and placed in a file box set up for ninety days (three months) into the future. If a response is due thirty days from the date of a filing, a tickler card in inserted in that numbered date of the month thirty days hence. As the date arrives,

---

[3] Garner, Bryan A., "*Writing for Litigation*", *ibid.*

[4] Strunk Jr., William and White, E. B., *The Elements of Style*, 3rd ed. Macmillan Publishing Co., Inc., New York, NY, 1979.

EXHIBIT 5-2 Sample Tickler Card

To:	Due date:
File:	
Action taken:	
Clock starts on:	
Action needed, if no response:	

EXHIBIT 5-3 Sample Docket Card

Client:	Matter:	
File:	Timekeeper:	Manager:
Rule sets:		
Key code:		
Category:	Priority:	Location:
Due date:	Time:	
Reminders:		
Other:	Explanation:	

the anticipated reminder comes up and is handled. That numbered date is then placed at the back of the file, continuing the ninety days into new months.

Computer docketing systems are even more efficient than handwritten systems. A program is set up (or a preformatted program can be purchased) that requests the client name, matter/file number, court, due date, action required, and reminder dates for actions of paramount importance. A copy of the docket will print out what has been docketed for that specific file or case. A daily docket will list whatever is needed for a specific day or week concerning the case involved.

A thirty day calendar is also a very useful item in keeping track of actions and anticipated due dates. Recommended as a backup to any of the other systems, a large calendar (18 in. · 24 in.) can be used to write in due dates. Computerized calendars or schedulers are also very helpful.

Diligence is a must in keeping things scheduled. Any new item must be entered immediately so that any conflicts that may arise can be dealt with and arrangement made for alternative plans. Everything placed on a calendar or scheduler must be current. Any rescheduled items must update old dates to guarantee the efficiency of the system. If deadlines are missed, cases can be lost because of default, so a system is very important part of keeping track of filings in cases.

5.0912 *Memos and Full Documentation.* The preparation of a memorandum to file or to an individual is an important step and should be treated as such. Do not use cryptic notes that rely on mnemonics or association with other words in order to derive the exact meaning of the memorandum. Each document should be sufficiently detailed so that its meaning and purpose are easily discernable by anyone who reads it and it is as understandable next week or next year as it is on the day it is conceived. Each document should be an independent thought. The plan of any memorandum should always follow a logical path of having an introduction, a body, and a conclusion. The extent of these three elements for a given memorandum may vary; however, they should be considered at the outset and honored in the execution whenever possible.

    a. The introduction includes the reason for the memo—references to files, conversations, or correspondence that might be needed as background.

    b. The body is the discussion of matters to be recorded, paragraphed by major thought, or a review of the elements.

    c. The conclusion is the recommendation, decision, or statement of status. If any suspense date is involved, it is reflected here, and the means of observing the suspense is shown—the "writer will follow up" or "the docket clerk was notified."

5.0913 *Privilege.* In those written memoranda between the legal assistant and the attorney related to a given case, one of the desirable introductory sentences to be used is "In connection with the cited case, you directed me to _____, and the following is reported." Since the legal assistant addresses the memoranda to his or her employing attorney, and it is in relation to a particular case, that particular document may carry the attorney-client privilege or the attorney work-product privilege. Whether the attorney at some future date may waive that privilege is not a speculation to be made by the legal assistant at any time, and certainly not when conceiving the document. In each and every case, the legal assistant is working for and under the direction of an attorney, and every step should be taken to insure that the same privileges the attorney exerts on behalf of the client attaches to the work of the attorney's legal assistant.

    The policy and procedure of the office may or may not address this problem. If it does not, the question should be discussed with the attorney. An alternative technique may be preferred, such as the use of a stamp saying "Attorney Privilege" or "Confidential" on the top and bottom of every page of such material.

5.0914 *Brevity.* Correspondence within the office should be brief. It is reasonable to believe we all work toward the same ultimate goal, and the use of excess verbiage or stereotyped language does not contribute to the communication of facts and information between members of the same firm. Simple words, clear and unmistakable, should be used whenever possible within the firm. This does not mean that in-house correspondence should not be phrased logically and persuasively. Candor, truth, and directness have greater value within the firm than in correspondence going outside the firm, which must be phrased more diplomatically and be more generalized. The legal assistant can use technical phrases here or employ the jargon or acronyms so dear to the profession. The only caveat is, use them properly, spell them correctly, and if in doubt, look them up in *Black's Law Dictionary* or a set of legal *Words and Phrases* before trying to include them in an internal memorandum.

5.09154 *Project Memos or Reports.* Frequently, the legal assistant is directed to study, review, summarize, and make recommendations on a given problem, topic, or volume of data.

Such work requires extensive analysis, often supplemented by investigation or research, as well as the submission of a detailed report. Use an outline, such as the one shown in Exhibit 5-4, to organize your thoughts before beginning to write along with the approach detailed earlier in this section.

This format requires the legal assistant to assemble the basic data; identify the assumptions (time constraints, personnel costs, task-time allocations) that will affect the conclusions; and clarify the sources of information used (whether books, documents, reports, or interviews) and the resulting dissection and analysis of the material, information, and assumptions. In applicable circumstances, an analysis of each available alternative is made and the full project then reported in terms of a conclusion or recommendation.

In the course of the analysis, footnotes, marginal annotations, or parenthetical citations should be used to refer to factual statements supporting sources or inferences that are significant in the analysis or the conclusion.

Note that this format is an adaptation of the "introduction, body, and conclusion" form. Since the study may be lengthy, it may be efficacious to prepare a cover letter to the attorney setting out the problem presented and the recommendation or conclusion and indicating the detailed memo attached. This allows a quick perusal of the essence of the assignment on one page, while making the full report available for more thorough evaluation if needed.

EXHIBIT 5-4　Internal Memorandum Outline

TO:		
FROM:		
DATE:		
SUBJ:		
Date of Assignment:	Assigned by:	Deadline Date:
Statement of the Problem:		
Assumptions:		
Sources of Information:		
Analysis:		
Alternative Analysis:		

5.092　Correspondence—Out-of-Office

All correspondence from the firm to persons outside the firm, whether they are clients, the courts, adversaries, or sources of information, should follow the standard established by the office in the office manual. If no office manual exists, consult with the attorney to determine the form preferred, the conventions of salutation, case citation, signature blocks, and the policies and practices honored by the attorney that are to be followed by the legal assistant. Many attorneys prefer to have all correspondence go out over their signatures, while some attorneys will allow the legal assistant to write and sign correspondence connected with lawsuits as long as such correspondence does not contain legal opinions or give direct legal advice. Some attorneys mix it up. Follow the office procedures. Any questionable correspondence should be reviewed by the attorney for either his or her signature or your own. Letters signed by the legal assistant must clearly set forth his or her title, preferably as part of the signature block.

5.0921 *Style and Form.* Frequently, legal secretaries set the style and form of the correspondence. They have developed habitual forms of salutation, citation, paragraphing, signature blocks, attachment or enclosure reference, spacing, and so on, and are comfortable with the established procedure. The legal assistant adapts his or her writing to that style if at all possible, because his or her work and the secretary's are complementary. The choice of form, provided the alternatives are equal in clarity, should be made by the secretary or the attorney. If the form is clear, direct, and acceptable to the attorney and comfortable for the secretary, the legal assistant defers to their choice.

The organizational structure of letters leaving the office is extremely important, and each such letter must be composed with care. There is always the addressee identification. There may be a caption, for example, "Re: Smith vs Jones, Your file: XYZ 123, Our file: 77AB132." There may be a salutation (depending on office policy). There is always an introductory sentence or paragraph followed by the body of the correspondence, which should be limited to two or three major points (preferably one), and then a concluding paragraph in which the conclusion, decision, or request is stated and a deadline date established for any required action or response.

5.0922 *Review for Impact.* Following dictation and typing, read the letter in final form to evaluate its impact. Does it fulfill the intended purpose? Is it clear? Is it concise? Is it sufficiently courteous and expository? Does it sound like you? Does it sound the way it was intended to sound?

The review will expose any cliches or stereotyped phrases that may have slipped in. Composing often is done one sentence at a time, each of which may be great standing alone but poor when combined.

5.0923 *Purposes of Correspondence.* The purpose of legal correspondence, particularly that leaving an office, follows the same general principles as business correspondence. It should serve a combination of, or at least one of, the following four functions:

a. *To obtain action.* The letter should create action by the party to whom the letter is going. This is done by presenting a situation in which the recipient of the letter either must act or, by failure to act, accept the results of inaction. This is insured by establishing a date in the last paragraph of the letter by which an answer or response is expected and required to prevent an alternative action.

b. *To provide information.* The letter often is a response to an inquiry or a request by a client, adversary, court, or a source of information for information or further details. This type of letter tends to be a little longer and may be more discursive or more involved than other correspondence. Any letter whose major purpose is to provide information should contain a concluding sentence or paragraph requesting further contact if the information provided is insufficient or incomplete. It can be as simple as "Please call or write if further information or clarification is needed."

c. *To maintain goodwill.* Goodwill should obviously be maintained with the clients, with friendly witnesses, and with sources of information. Not quite so obvious is the necessity of maintaining goodwill with adversaries and with the court system employees. Many legal assistants tend to feel that adversaries are the enemy and, therefore, should be treated with disdain or without substantial courtesy. That attitude is wrong. Even though the adversary may act in a discourteous, abrupt, crude, or offensive manner, there is no excuse for the legal assistant's correspondence to reflect a similar attitude. Remember, the conduct of trials and pretrial discovery activity is often a complex series of maneuvers in which the advocate of the parties take on certain colorations and roles based on the factual situations with which they contend. It is foolish to allow an adversary to force the attorney or legal assistant into playing that kind of game. Correspondence reflecting discourtesy also reflects a lack of professionalism. Many times the present adversary in a difficult and contentious piece of litigation will be a codefendant in some future action. The effect on each other of courtesy, tact, and diplomacy—or the lack of them—carries over into the next case. Legal assistants are responsible for the relations between the attorney and any other person of the legal community. The correspondence should engender, not destroy, goodwill.

d. *To create a record.* The record to be created is one of courteous, disciplined, timely, professional, and appropriate conduct fully recognizing the rules of court. At the same time, the correspondence may create a record advantageous to the legal assistant's employing attorney and his or her client regarding the adversary's unwillingness to comply with those same rules of court. In the case of extensions of time where either side requested, or agreed to a request by the other, appropriately phrased correspondence will express an attitude either of cooperation or vexatious behavior. A letter following a telephone call involving delaying tactics can be used in lieu of formal legal motions to create a record forcing the adversary to respond appropriately or face the difficulty of explaining the letter at some future time. The letter can be courteous and effective. The more responsibility the legal assistant carries in any piece of legal service and the more contact he or she has with witnesses, the court, and the adversaries, the more important are his or her efforts to create a record in the files of the court and the parties to the case.

5.0924 Timeliness. Correspondence should never be postponed. As soon as the need presents itself, decide what is the most efficient way to respond. Will an e-mail message be quicker and more efficient than spending time dictating a letter? If so, e-mail to the person immediately, making a copy of the message to the file. That message will be taken care of in less time between the two parties involved than it would take for one person to dictate a letter and a secretary to transcribe it and prepare envelopes to mail. Always remember to save a copy of the communication for the file which will evidence action taken on your part and that the recipient is asked to respond.

If the action taken in e-mail is setting up a meeting, deposition, or other important case matter, use an internal docketing system, if available. The docketing will be performed in a few keystrokes, showing an anticipated event in a certain case, by particular individuals, at a designated location, and for an allotted period of time. The parties involved will be alerted to the anticipated action in their daily docketing report.

If time permits, draft the letter, have it checked by your supervisor for accuracy, approved or signed, and send it. All letters confirming appointments or arrangements made over the telephone with other law offices, courts, or sources of information should be sent out immediately. If a suspense date is set in the letter, it is imperative to signal that date in the files of the attorney and the legal assistant. If it effects the docket, be sure to notify, or send a copy to, whomever handles the docketing. Uniform understanding by everyone is the acme of communication.

If docket and calendar systems are used in conjunction, make sure all the dates are the same. If several people are calendaring (secretaries, legal assistants, and attorneys) make sure everyone is counting the same days. If holidays fall during the calculation of due dates, the consensus of *all* must be the date that should be noted on all calendars and dockets.

5.0925 *Stereotypes.*   There is a tendency among those who lack confidence in drafting letters to follow guideline books or electronic "forms" that provide examples of phrases, some of which can be adapted to the legal assistant's needs. This can be a crutch of faulty strength. The legal assistant does not have to create the thought, but often ends up substituting triteness for spontaneity. It also causes the legal assistant to rely on the book, or "forms," instead of learning the correct use of the English language and in place of creative analysis. Be certain that such "canned" letters or "boilerplate" phrases are appropriate to the situation and will fulfill the purpose of the letter before adopting their use.

5.0926 *Logical Presentation and Limited Topics.*   Of more importance than stereotyped methods of referral is a well-organized presentation of the facts in coherent and logical fashion following the three-step structure discussed previously—"the introduction, the body, and the conclusion." Holding each letter to a minimum number of different topics will allow for easy drafting and simplicity of construction. The letter will be comprehensible if not fashionable.

Often it is better to write three letters, conveying one or two ideas in each, rather than one long letter containing five or six points. Short letters will be read promptly, while longer ones may be scanned and put aside for later detailed review. If the purpose of the letter was to generate action, its very length may postpone that action.

5.093 Grammar, Vocabulary, and Spelling

Law office correspondence, internal and external, is often the first (and many times the only) impression others have of you as a legal assistant, and tends to make a lasting impression. Bad grammar, poor or inappropriate vocabulary, and misspelled words combine to create the image of an incompetant, uneducated, and inept individual who need not be taken seriously. It is therefore extremely important for the legal assistant to pay close attention to these basic elements of communication.

5.0931 *Grammar.*   The composition of legal correspondence follows certain basic rules, among which are the rules of English grammar. The lack of a solid foundation in grammar will inhibit the legal assistant's ability to communicate. Consequently, many legal assistants find writing an onerous burden because their grammar is inadequate for the task. Those legal assistants must undertake to improve their English grammar, their creative writing ability, their vocabulary, and their methods of expression if they expect to advance in the profession.

In the interim, however, work must go on, and the easiest rule to follow in writing letters is to write as you speak. The language used in daily life sometimes may be elliptical in nature, lacking a clearly defined subject, object, or predicate, but it is a form of expression that will usually be comprehensible to the reader. A legal assistant with severe problems in this area must seek and honor the advice of others and write, edit, and rewrite if necessary. In the interim, he or she should write with confidence in the same manner as he or she speaks. The legal assistant is hired, in part, because of his or her ability to communicate, and the only way to improve that ability is to expose the faults to the blue pencil of critics, take note of the weaknesses thus exposed, and attempt to eliminate them in future work. The most comforting thought a legal assistant can have in drafting legal correspondence is that grammar is important but generally follows the lead of everyday conversation (by a few years, unfortunately, but it does follow). If the usage in a letter is comfortable to the author, it is probably acceptable as communication and may even be correct grammatically. If it is not, critics may help and seem to enjoy doing so.

Some word processing programs contain grammar-checking programs. While these can be beneficial on some occasions, they are generally cumbersome to use and can result in work-product which is stiff and stilted.

5.0932 *Vocabulary and Spelling.*   The writing of letters necessarily involves vocabulary and spelling. No single skill is more important to the legal assistant than the ability to use and spell words correctly. Drafting letters by hand, to be typed later, pinpoints the ability to spell as essential to the finished product. In dictating and proofreading the drafted material, the ability to spell is essential to insure that the material does convey the idea intended by the use of given words. Misspelled words can alter meanings and content dramatically.

The use of spell-checkers in word processing programs are beneficial in locating and correcting misspelled words. However, a word of caution. Most spell-checkers do not find the misused words that may be spelled correctly. One of the dangers of reliance on spell-checking is the failure to find those misused words which change the content and intent of the communication.

5.09321 *Which Word Is It?*   We all are familiar with the simple word "to," or is it "too," or "two"? Each has a distinctly different meaning, is spelled differently, and yet sounds the same. In dictation, each can be confused, and in handwritten notes, the necessity of spelling each of those three words properly is apparent. A great number of other questions may arise over words of similar phonetic sound. As mentioned earlier, each of the words below is spelled correctly and would not be identified as misused by a word processing spell-checker:

council or counsel	advice or advise
summary or summery	access or excess
pistol or pistil	affect or effect
chorale or corral	conscience or conscious
tear or tare	farther or further
bow or bough	all ready or already
capital or capitol	any way or anyway
principle or principal	pen or pin
imminent or eminent	their or there or they're
compliment or complement	do or due or dew

Recognize these words and their meanings? If not, look them up and consider the difference of meaning implicit in using one for the other. These are but a few. Watch out for the others.

5.09322 *Typos and Word Meanings.*   There is also the problem with words that are not pronounced the same but have all of the same letters within them, or nearly the same letters within them. Minor misspelling or transposed letters change the meaning dramatically. With the word "casual," for example, a transposition of the "u" and "s" turns it into "causal." The word "did," if misspelled, can be "dead" or perhaps "deed." More dramatic would be the word "illusive," which could be misspelled as "elusive" or, even worse, "allusive," each of which has a distinctly different meaning. Will the letter then carry the intended communication? These are all additional examples of misused words which a computer word processing spell-checker would not bring to your attention or correct.

A legal assistant who cannot spell must work intensively and continuously to eliminate or minimize that basic weakness.

5.09323 *Vocabulary Improvement.*   Earlier we mentioned that the average range of words at the instant command of the average American is seven to twelve hundred words. The legal assistant's general vocabulary must be much greater, or it will be insufficient for the normal discharge of his or her duties. There are specialized areas in the legal field that will put demands upon the legal assistant's retentive and recollective abilities, such as the specialized terminology of medicine and all sorts of trade terms in marketing, construction, longshoring, maritime activities, business, engineering, and so on. The ability to learn new words accurately, understand their meanings, and incorporate them into our professional lives is important. Enrolling in English classes that emphasize spelling or creative writing is certainly beneficial and offers a working professional the opportunity to improve his or her command of vocabulary and of spelling under conditions where the effort is professionally judged and critiqued. Additionally, crossword puzzles and other word games are a fun way to enlarge the legal assistant's vocabulary. Each month, *Reader's Digest* contains a special vocabulary improvement section, and "Word-a-Day" calendars are a popular item at bookstores and card shops. Another method readily available to increase vocabulary is to make a habit of using the thesaurus offered by word processing programs. One's vocabulary also improves by reading good writing, such as Faulkner, Hemingway, Emerson, or Thoreau.

Bibliography

Benn, Martha, *Telephone Resources.* Albuquerque, NM, 1997.

Block, Gertrude, *Effective Legal Writing for Law Students, Lawyers, and Paralegals*, 3rd ed. Westbury, NY: Foundation Press, 1989.

Ebbitt, Wilma and Ebbitt, David, *Index to English*, 7th ed. Glenview, IL: Scott, Foresman & Co., 1982.

Fowler, H. Ramsey and Aaron, Jane E., *The Little, Brown Handbook.* 4th ed. Glenview, IL: Scott, Foresman & Co., 1989.

Garner, Bryan A., *"Writing for Litigation," Scribes Journal of Legal Writing*, The American Society of Writers on Legal Subjects, Dallas, TX, 1990, pp. 66–68.

Gordon, Karen E., *The Well-Tempered Sentence: A Punctuation Handbook for the Innocent, the Eager, and the Doomed.* NY: Ticknor & Fields, 1983.

Hodges, John C., et al., *Harbrace College Handbook*, 10th ed. San Diego: Harcourt Brace Jovanovich, 1986.

Kirkland, James W., et. al., *Writing and Revising: Modern College Workbook.* Lexington, MA: D. C. Heath, 1986.

Mager, Nathan and Mager, Sylvia, *Encyclopedic Dictionary of English Usage.* Englewood Cliffs, NJ: Prentice-Hall, 1975.

Mellinkoff, David, *Legal Writing: Sense and Nonsense.* St. Paul: West, 1981.

Rodale, J. I. and Urdang, Lawrence, *The Synonym Finder*. Emmaus, PA: Rodale Press, 1990.

Sisson, A. F., *Sisson's Word and Expression Locater*. Englewood Cliffs, NJ: Prentice-Hall, 1966.

Strunk, William Jr. and White, E. B., *The Elements of Style*, 3rd ed. NY: Macmillan, 1979.

Venolia, Jan, *Write Right!* rev. ed. Berkeley, CA: Ten Speed Press, 1988.

Webster's Tenth New Collegiate Dictionary. Springfield, MA: Merriam-Webster, 1993.

Wydick, Richard C., *Plain English for Lawyers,* 2nd ed. Durham, NC: Carolina Academic Press, 1985.

6

Interviewing Techniques

6.00 Introduction

Because each interview presents unique challenges, and each interviewer has his or her own strengths, no one can script a universally applicable interview. At best, one can relate prior experiences, explain techniques that have worked in the past, point out inherent hazards, and offer potential solutions.

The ideal interviewer has a photographic memory, a broad knowledge base, a commanding yet comfortable personality, a well-timed sense of humor, is a patient and careful listener, meticulous, trustworthy, and appropriately empathetic. The ideal interviewer glows with the aura of dignity.

Of course, few people meet this ideal, but we can all be effective. In the coming pages, we will learn how to adapt to certain situations, how to exploit our strengths while recognizing and improving weaknesses. By studying the work of others and applying reasonable effort, a personal interviewing style can be developed that produces desirable results and elevates self-confidence.

The concept of an interview is based on the supposition that the interviewer controls the direction and pace of the dialogue. Though not always simple or easy, this can be accomplished (and accomplished with gentleness), provided the legal assistant enters the interview with predefined goals and a workable strategy in mind.

Experience is the best teacher, especially for refining skills like interviewing. The legal assistant's abilities will develop by trial and error. This is a sometimes frustrating truth that requires us to remain flexible, to adjust our approach when necessary, and to maintain composure through it all.

6.01   The Interview: What It Is and What It Is Not

The interview is a special form of verbal exchange in which information is transferred between parties. It is not a conversation but a polite, unofficial form of interrogation. The interview seeks to separate matters of belief and/or conjecture from those which are evidentiary facts. It is also used to develop leads to other witnesses. The legal assistant must control the direction and set the pace of the interview in order to successfully accomplish the task of gathering data.

We are all involved in interviews on a daily basis. Employment interviews, tax counseling, and credit applications are examples of common interviews which require the directed exchange of information. The sheer volume of interviews conducted leads to the belief that many are "canned" and, in fact, many are. However, the legal assistant's task of assembling evidence admissible in courts of law is too specialized to conduct according to a standard format. Because of the unique circumstances and complexities of individual cases and witnesses, each interview the legal assistant conducts presents a unique set of challenges. Flexibility and imagination, combined with skilled questioning, will produce better results than any standard set of questions and forms.

Interviews are usually one-on-one conversations but exceptions do exist. Experience shows that the amount of useful information obtained from interviews is inversely proportioned to the number of people involved: the more people involved, the less information is obtained. For this reason, whenever possible, group activity surrounding the interview should be limited to the professional introduction of the legal assistant by the attorney.

People are often surprised to learn that interviewing does not require a licensed attorney. However, using legal assistants as interviewers is a common practice for identifying potential witnesses, recreating corporate organizational histories, establishing time lines, etc. A thorough interview performed by a legal assistant, including end report and evaluation, will provide the attorney with necessary information in a manner that is both cost effective and efficient, which clients appreciate.

Interviewing is a learned skill requiring carefully considered, often intense preparation, and responsive adaptation in pursuit of the necessary testimony which extends to a thorough evaluation of the interview and the witness. Because the findings of the interview are a critical source of information, the quality of work must be high, and the attorney is best aided by the legal assistant who treats every interview as worthy of preparation, skillful execution, thorough review, and corroboration and report.

6.011   Obtaining a Statement

Statements are used in preparation for, and during, trial. In preparation for trial, the written statement allows reference to all facts known by the witness. At trial, the statement, whether or not it is "sworn," can be used to *impeach* the testimony of a witness who states something different or contrary on the stand than what was stated during the interview. To impeach a witness's testimony is to damage that witness's credibility. Because juries frequently determine cases based on the perceived credibility of witnesses, the potential value of a well taken statement is immeasurable.

6.0111   Negative Statements. Negative statements are statements made by witnesses that, in and of themselves, provide no advantage to either party. The majority of legal interviews conducted only yield negative statements. With many occurrences, such as bar fights, neighborhood disputes, and automobile accidents, there are often people who have only witnessed a portion of the event. Few will have knowledge of evidentiary value for either side in the case, but all should be interviewed because it is probable that people in the vicinity of the accident can direct the investigator to other witnesses.

6.0112   Questionable Statements. Questionable statements are those which may or may not constitute admissible evidence because of some extenuating circumstance. For instance, the mental state of a witness could make what at first appears to be a valid statement inadmissable or uncredible. Traumatic shock, whether triggered by physical or mental injury; alcohol or drug use, including some legitimate medications; psychological instability and impaired mental development—these are all conditions that can adversely affect a person's ability to accurately perceive, recall, or articulate the course of an event. How close or how far away a witness is to the event, weather conditions, time of day, the presence or absence of distractions, and the level of attention are additional factors which effect the validity or credibility of testimony. One of the objectives of effective questioning is to explore whether or not any of those factors apply.

6.012   Written Statements

Written statements are desirable for several reasons, particularly if they are in the witness's own words and handwriting, and not simply a product of the legal assistant paraphrasing the witness's story. If the legal assistant does draft the statement, the witness should be required to correct and initial any errors, initial each page, and sign the last page of the statement. It is not unusual for the witness to request a copy of the statement, which should then be provided. It is already a requirement in many jurisdictions that a copy of the statement be provided to the witness. The purpose of this procedure is to ensure the validity of the statement, so that neither side can dispute it later.

It is essential that the statement contain the witness's full identity: name, age, home address, occupation, employer, employer's address, work and home phone numbers. The relationship of the witness to the case should be included and described in narrative form. For instance, describe the witness as a "witness to the event," an "accountant involved in the accumulation of records concerning project costs," or as a "party to the discussions which resulted in the agreement." A clause must be included which states that the witness has provided the statement freely and without coercion or promise of reward.

6.0121 When Not to Take a Statement.   One of the first things a legal assistant should ask in an interview is whether or not the individual is represented by counsel. If the answer is yes, especially if the interview is being recorded, the legal assistant must state for the record that the representation by counsel was previously unknown. The legal assistant must then ask the individual being interviewed to identify his or her counsel fully, the circumstances of the representation, and whether or not the representation is related to the matter at issue. If it is, the legal assistant must immediately terminate the interview and advise the employing attorney of the situation.

The legal assistant should also be careful about how information harmful to the client's case is documented. Formal discovery procedures usually require the production of all nonprivileged statements when requested by the adversary. Witness statements usually are not privileged. Client statements may or may not be privileged, depending on the form and manner in which they were taken. For this reason, even if the legal assistant knows, or believes, the witness is lying, documenting the adverse information in the statement is dangerous. If the legal assistant knows the witness is lying and can prove it, that ammunition should be saved for a later time, like when the opposition introduces the witness.

If the individual being interviewed shows evidence of incapacity, such as being under the influence of alcohol, drugs, or medications, the interview should not go forward.

6.013 Formal Statements

In addition to interviewing, there are several other more formal methods of obtaining statements from witnesses. The affidavit, the declaration, and the deposition are all examples of methods for taking testimony that is bound by oath. The legal assistant should always conult the supervising attorney about what method is to be used for a given witness. Depending on what the attorney hopes to do with the testimony, different types of statements may be desired.

6.0131 Depositions.   The most solidly admissible type of formal statement is the deposition. The deposition is a recorded interrogation of the witness by counsel. The deponent (witness) is subject to the penalties of perjury and the testimony is transcribed by a certified shorthand reporter and/or recorded on audio/video tape. The witness's counsel has the opportunity to cross-examine the witness. Witnesses who are subpoenaed to provide deposition testimony can often be compelled to travel to a different location to give that testimony, although this ability is limited by the statutes of the particular jurisdictions. Depositions, while powerful, can be expensive to take, given reporting costs, possible travel costs, and witness fees.

6.0132 Affidavits.   Affidavits take two forms. They are either oral statements made under oath and transcribed by a certified shorthand reporter, or written statements signed under oath in the presence of a notary public. Because there is no opportunity for the witness's counsel to examine the witness, the affidavit does not have the impact or admissibility of the deposition.

6.0133 Declarations.   The declaration is the simplest of the three types of formal statements to obtain. It is a written statement concerning the matter at hand, prepared and signed by its author, the declarant. It must include the explicit disclaimer that the statement was voluntarily made under the penalty of perjury.

6.02   The Participants

6.021   The Legal Assistant

This book is written for the legal assistant. In the legal interview, it is the legal assistant's job to obtain pertinent information from a witness who may or may not be agreeable. This task requires disciplined communication, sound judgment, adaptability, and confidence.

6.022   The Client

Because of the wide variety of entities that employ legal assistants today, the type of client encountered ranges from individuals seeking some form of government assistance to executive officers of multinational corporations. In most cases, the client is the best source of information on a matter, though this is not the rule. One interview rarely completes the legal assistant's contact with the client, and each interview should be treated as a separate, important step in a well-arranged process. Clients take their problems seriously and want their perception of events taken for truth, a highly stressful situation that can make a client nearly irrational. Often this results from a deeply held faith in Murphy's Law: whatever can go wrong, will go wrong. But most clients are fine people who revert to reasonable standards of behavior on learning that the attorney and legal assistant will help them succeed in their efforts so far as the facts, the law, professional ethics, and abilities allow.

6.023   Witnesses

6.0231   Friendly Witnesses. "Friendly" witnesses are usually related to the client by blood, viewpoint, common business interests, occupation, or social acquaintance. They usually require little pressure to speak freely and fully but usually present rather biased opinions. This bias must be considered when evaluating their information. They are helpful in corroborating the client's viewpoint and can offer a means of evaluating the testimony of adversary or hostile witnesses.

6.0232   Hostile Witnesses. The legal assistant can anticipate that some witnesses will be antagonistic to the purposes of the interview, such as witnesses directly aligned with the client's opposition. Hostile witnesses do not necessarily conduct themselves in a rude manner; rather, the term, is used to describe a witness who either does not wish to provide any information from the start, or who during the course of the interview becomes increasingly reluctant to provide information. The truly hostile witness does exist, though, and it is not always possible to know in advance which witnesses may become hostile.

If a witness becomes hostile, it is the legal assistant's challenge to identify the source of the witness's discomfort because that discomfort is the reason information is not being exchanged. It is good to remember that, for a variety of reasons, interviewing can be an unnerving experience for the person being interviewed. To minimize this effect, one should give the impression of relaxed efficiency, which necessitates preparedness, smiling, appearing interested, and being focused. A sincerely interested, non-judgmental attitude generates trust and encourages the witness to speak freely. When the hostility is not a result of the stress of being interviewed, it is important to identify other possibilities. It may relate to the case, the attorney, or the client, and therefore be significant. It may relate only to the legal assistant, and that is important also, though less important than the other reasons. If the legal assistant projects arrogance, superiority, or condescension, the witness may respond with hostility. It is citical for the legal assistant to recognize such mannerisms and work to change them. If the legal assistant cannot solve the hostility problem, or otherwise doubts the validity of the information obtained, he or she must seek help from the attorney. Perhaps another interviewer will be more successful.

6.0233 Official Witnesses. Official witnesses are crucial to many cases because of the positions they occupy. They can be municipal employees, state employees, federal employees, or officers of corporations. They can belong to associations, business groups, ad hoc citizen committees, or other organized, identifiable entities. Official witnesses are usually personally removed from the dispute, although this is not always the case. Like all witnesses, official witnesses can be friendly, neutral, or hostile. Ideally, official witnesses are impartial and objective. They neither enhance nor inhibit the development of information for either side of the dispute, but offer only those facts of which they have personal knowledge or which can be ascertained from their files, where those files are open to the public.

6.0234 Expert Witnesses.   Legal assistants encounter experts in many situations. Often there is a need for an expert consultant rather than a witness. Expert consultants usually are not hostile. They have no personal stake in the outcome of the case and provide only general information, often about the expert's field. The expert witness is a different sort, providing testimony to support the contentions of one side and refute those of the other. The expert witness can usually be identified as friendly or hostile by the name on his or her paycheck, though few experts become truly hostile and attack the interviewer personally.

Expert witnesses tend to possess a narrow spectrum of information with regard to any given case and typically should not be used to develop information outside their areas of expertise. When interviewing experts, close attention should be paid to their ability to communicate so that an assessment of their potential impact on a judge or jury can be made. The degree of preparation and poise under fire should also be analyzed and assessed. The best expert witnesses are identified by their ability to cope effectively and dispassionately with attacks on their credibility and the soundness of their conclusions.

6.03   General Considerations for Every Interview

6.031 Language
The language, vocabulary, and communication skills the legal assistant uses may not match the language, vocabulary, and communication skills of the witness. It is incumbent on the legal assistant to seek a comfortable level of dialogue that will allow a thorough and effective exchange of thoughts and information.

6.0311 Jargon and Slang.   The language used should be comfortable for the person being interviewed. Legal assistants should be careful about using legal jargon and technical terms, because it may be confusing to someone with no legal background.

Professional jargon or any slang used by the witness must be identified and explained. The meaning of such words and phrases must be explored with the witness to ensure there is a common understanding. Once a common understanding of the language being used is obtained, the legal assistant should explore whether that is really what the witness meant, and whether the terms have meaning within the context of the case.

6.0312 *Profanity and Abuse.* Occasionally the legal assistant will encounter an individual who cannot speak without being profane or abusive. It is imperative that the legal assistant exercise restraint, keep emotions in check, and not reply in kind. The legal assistant's purpose is to obtain information. The wintess should be encouraged to speak even when that speech is laced with expletives and vulgarity. The more the witness says, the more information will be revealed. The attorney may never use this particular witness at trial; however, the information obtained may be of use, leading to the discovery of a more presentable witness or source of evidence.

Offensive language, in and of itself, is not hostility. Some witnesses speak profanely, even obscenely, as a matter of habit. If such remarks are so offensive that the ability to function, control, and direct the interview is lost, then it may be an indication that the legal assistant is too sensitive to interview. However, if the remarks are directed at the legal assistant personally, action is required. Legal assistants do not have to endure personal abuse or vilification; when it occurs, a prompt, dignified termination of the interview is appropriate.

6.0313 *Body Language.* During an interview, the legal assistant should observe witnesses as much as possible. Body language can be very revealing and indicative of some major or minor internal conflict. For example, during a particular line of questioning, the witness may avoid eye contact. Later in the interview, the legal assistant should return to the issue which appeared to cause the witness discomfort. If the witness avoids eye contact again, the legal assistant may reasonably conclude that either the witness is being dishonest or is uncomfortable with the subject matter. This would be important to note, especially in the case of perceived dishonesty, because the attorney will want to know whether or not the witness appeared to be straightforward and credible.

Arm-crossing is another body language expression which may have various meanings. It may simply mean the witness is cold, or it could mean that the witness is feeling defensive in some way. The legal assistant should make a notation next to the line of questioning which appeared to cause this behavior and return to it later in the interview. If the behavior is repeated when the same topic is reviewed later in the interview, it may indeed indicate that the witness is responding to an unconscious feeling of needing self-protection. If this is true, then the arm-crossing may signify that the witness is withholding information.

Active listening includes the ability to observe the reactions of the witness as responses to questions are given while at the same time making note of any apparant inconsistencies between the spoken words and the body language responses. These inconsistencies can be explored at a later date in a follow-up interview.

6.032 Listening

The legal assistant must listen to the witness. One of the most common mistakes made is the failure to listen. This is often perceived as insulting or condescending to witnesses. From their point of view, the interview is a unique event which may be burdensome or unfair. The legal assistant who fails to listen with focused intent on what the witness is saying may be perceived as disinterested or uncaring, often resulting in the witness becoming hostile.

When a client is interviewed, the responsibility to listen attentively increases exponentially. The client is there because they are either seeking or have obtained representation. Clients are paying for legal services and they notice when the people handling their affairs appear unconcerned or disinterested about the task at hand.

Attentive and active listening is necessary to conduct a productive interview. It will allow facts and erroneous beliefs to be exposed, and will enable the legal assistant to recognize mistaken interpretations. Such interpretations and beliefs should be heard in context, without argument or correction, until the full account is told. Correction of even a minor but obvious error during the narration may unnecessarily create an argument. It may also unnerve the witness so badly that the interview must be terminated. Worst of all, it causes the legal assistant to talk while the witness listens, a reversal of roles.

6.0321 Empathy and Interest. The legal assistant must generate a feeling of empathy and understanding as well as sincere interest in the witness. Lack of empathy by the legal assistant, or harsh judgment of the witness, even if conveyed by body language alone, can cause an otherwise cooperative witness to become hostile.

6.0322 Personality Clash or Lack of Rapport. Incompatibility between the legal assistant and the witness should be promptly identified. If such a personality conflict arises, a courteous inquiry should determine if the witness would feel more comfortable with a different interviewer.

The incompatibility may develop during the interview as a result of the legal assistant's manner or style of interviewing. If possible, identify and modify the cause of the problem. If unsuccessful, the legal assistant should consult the attorney and if necessary, arrange for another interviewer to reschedule and conduct the interview.

6.033 Confabulation and Deception

Confabulation is a special word used in psychiatry to describe the unconscous process of replacing gaps in memory with detailed accounts of fictious events, giving the impression of a coherent story which is more believable. All witnesses want to be believed. Frequently, when witnesses only have a disjointed knowledge of an event, they infer the connections between known facts to make the story logical and less subject to challenge. The legal assistant who understands this process will carefully establish each known fact and allow the interpolated events to be established by later testimony or information from other sources.

6.0331 Correction of Erroneous Information. It is not unusual to find that the initial statement of a witness is incorrect or incomplete. A second interview may be needed during which the legal assistant can attempt to clarify inaccuricies, errors, or omissions in the account of events given by that witness.

The determination of the foundation for any error along with the motivation of the witness for correcting the erroneous information is also important to the accurate assembly of facts. This will necessitate a thorough dissection of the substance of the first interview with the witness to learn what was in error and what was correct.

6.0332 Handling the Deceptive Witness. Sooner or later, the legal assistant will encounter the situation where a story told by a witness cannot be reconciled with the known facts of the case. Even tactful questioning may fail to develop explanations that account for the discrepancies. Repetition and review may convince the legal assistant that the witness is deliberately telling lies, concealing the truth, or misrepresenting the sequence of events. When this happens, the interview should be concluded, and the legal assistant should consult with the supervising attorney. Referring the matter to the attorney may seem to be an expression of defeat, but it is not. The legal assistant's job is to assist the attorney. Knowing when to seek help is an example of using good judgment.

6.034   The Motivation to Speak

6.0341 Ego Satisfaction.   Many people derive a high level of ego satisfaction from public recognition of their knowledge and/or their willingness to testify. Sometimes this recognition is limited to that of the client, an employer, or a committee; sometimes it is even more expansive. It is the attention given by people of different professions; people who weigh the individual's words as though they are gold; people who will rely upon those words to resolve a dispute. This motive for cooperation is rarely admitted to openly, but will be recognized if looked for.

6.0342 The Desire to Be Liked.   Some witnesses agree to be interviewed or testify because they want to please others and be liked by them. This causes the witness to look for opportunities to do or say what they believe the interviewer wants, whether that individual is the client, the attorney, or the legal assistant. These witnesses do not intend to deceive or mislead, but their need to please and to be liked may interfere with, and take precedence over, their desire to be honest. A witness with this motivation will attempt to determine that the legal assistant wants by paying close attention to facial expressions and the way questions are phrased. Their responses are generally calculated to provide what they believe is expected and therefore to be liked for it.

If leading questions are used, this witness type will give the answers the questions suggest. For that reason it is important to carefully construct questions using the six basic interrogatories, "who, what, when, where, why, and how," to ensure that the witness responds with a narrative based on individual recollection and not on suggestion.

6.0343 Altruism.   Some witnesses are motivated to speak from an unselfish concern for the welfare of others and are willing to provide the facts in their possession if they think it will help someone. Others in this category are motivated by a belief that justice must be served. These witnesses are usually objective, seldom having any personal interest in the outcome or proceeding, and are often strangers to the parties involved in the case. They have the potential to be extremely credible witnesses. Official witnesses are often fall into this category.

6.0344 Novelty and Excitement.   Another common motivation for some witnesses is the perception that the opportunity to testify is novel and exciting. These witnesses may actively seek to participate and become involved. They often appear to ask as many questions as they answer and are persistent in attempts to probe the interviewer for details. However, despite their eagerness, these witnesses rarely possess information of evidentiary value. When they do, it is even rarer for them to present such information in a credible manner.

6.0345 Catharsis.   Some witnesses, including many clients, find that the interview is an opportunity to vent their frustrations, clear their conscience, and give voice to deeply held feelings of suspicion, mistrust, anger, and other emotions. It is a form of catharsis. These individuals relate everything they know, believe, or suspect about the matter in question. Sometimes they are so profuse that it is difficult to record all of the information they are attempting to provide. Subsequent questioning may expose the story as a fabrication woven of rumors and conjecture. The legal assistant should understand and accept this as part of basic human nature, even though it can be time-consuming and frustrating. By the same token, the legal assistant should not criticize a witness who suddenly recants an earlier story by confessing to exaggeration or embellishment. This effectively begins the interview process all over again, but with a new set of parameters by which to measure the credibility of the witness.

6.0346 Loyalty and Friendships. Personal friendship or loyalty with one of the parties involved in the case often provides a motivation to speak. Witnesses motivated in this fashion often feel an obligation to provide testimony that will benefit a friend, acquaintance, employer, or coworker. Others may be driven by the desire to be part of a winning side and attempt to join it. The testimony in either case, though voluntary, is colored by these motivating factors and becomes suspect.

When the legal assistant suspects that a witness may be shading the truth because of personal loyalty or friendship to a party, an explanation of the problems that can arise from reliance on questionable testimony will often cause the witness to reexamine their own testimony and offer more credible responses.

6.0347 Extrinsic Reward. The most difficult motive for cooperation to overcome is that caused by the desire for some extrinsic reward. Although expert witnesses receive fees, there is usually little personal stake in the outcome of the case. An expert receives payment which is based on special qualifications and knowledge for research, analysis, and testimony needed by the parties, the court, and jury in understanding a specific case issue in their field of expertise. This is very different from the witness who testifies for some perceived personal gain, such as a coveted job with an entity involved in the litigation, a portion of any money damages awarded, or a favorable recommendation by one of the parties to some other organization. A typical example would be a criminal case where one criminal testifies against another in exchange for immunity from prosecution, favorable recommendations to a parole board, or the promise of employment following release. Family disputes may also give rise to similar situations, especially if there are estates involved. The legal assistant should never suggest that a witness will receive any extrinsic reward for his or her testimony.

If a witness does offer information in exchange for money or other reward, the legal assistant should advise the witness that any decision concerning such an offer must be made by the supervising attorney. It is unethical to buy testimony or information. As a practical matter, the credibility of the witness suffers, the benefit to the case is questionable, and the effect on a judge and jury can be disastrous if the circumstances become known. Witnesses who sell information are perceived as amoral opportunists prepared to edit his or her story to fit with the best interests of the purchaser. Parties who pay such witnesses may be subject to criminal charges of suborning a witness.

6.035 Confirming Interviews by Letter

Every interview should be confirmed in advance in writing. This serves as a reminder to the client or witness and is an opportunity to provide written directions or maps showing the office location or interview site. Written confirmations are also an opportunity to remind the witness or client of items you would like them to bring to the interview, serving as an informal checklist. This is especially important when the items being requested from clients or witnesses are needed to meet pleading deadlines, discovery deadlines, or other deadlines established by court order.

6.04 Questioning Techniques

6.041 Question Construction

The legal assistant should use simple, commonly understood words and straightforward questions that do not address multiple issues. Each question should generate one answer and should not combine more than one unknown quantity. Use questions that require narrative answers rather than leading questions which suggest a desired response or those which require a yes or no answer.

6.0411 Narrative Questions. Consider this question to a witness: "Were you at the corner of 15th and A Streets, Seattle, Washington, on February 12, 1997, when an auto accident occurred in which John Doe was injured?" A question constructed in this manner will usually result in a yes or no response. A negative response to this question will require five or six additional questions to find out which part of the question caused the negative response. The witness may not have been at that particular location. Perhaps the witness honestly believes the accident they saw occured on a different date. It is also possible that the witness might remember seeing an accident at that location but did not believe that anyone was injured or that John Doe was involved. Better question construction uses the six interrogatories: who, what, where, when, why, and how. For instance, the question "Where were you on February 12, 1997?" allows the witness to answer in narrative form. It may require a series of follow-up questions to explore the sequence of acts over a span of time. Similarly, the question "While you were there, what did you see?" requires a narrative answer that can be explored and evaluated with further questions later in the interview. Questions are designed to elicit information. Well-designed questions allow witnesses to talk at their own pace, in their own language, and to create their own frames of reference concerning the time and location of an event.

6.0412 Supportive Questioning. During the course of the interview, supportive questioning helps witnesses provide all the information they know. Words or phrases that are argumentative or indicate a lack of belief in what the witness is saying will generate anger, self-consciousness, and lack of cooperation. It is easy to alienate people by asking overly blunt questions and/or confronting them with their own inconsistencies. The goal is to frame questions that encourage a response which is a voluntary explanation in narrative form.

Supportive questioning can begin during the initial storytelling phase of the interview with such phrases as "And then what happened?", "Who said that?", and "What did he say then?" Follow-up questions might include: "I'm a little confused now, on June first, did you write the agency or call them?" "Did this follow his letter or did his letter follow this?" "Now that we know this, how can we prove it to the other people?" Many times the explanations to supportive questioning will clarify otherwise conflicting points. Get the witnesses to help in resolving conflicts, instead of confronting them with accusations of errors or falsehoods.

6.0413 Leading Questions. Leading questions can make witnesses uncomfortable, turning otherwise friendly witnesses into hostile ones. Questions like "You saw the accident, didn't you?" when posed to a witness who is a friend or associate of the client, may generate a sense of obligation in the witness, and may cause the witness to answer the question based on a perception that the legal assistant (on behalf of the friend) expects a certain answer. Instead, ask questions that allow a witness to provide a narrative answer, such as "Where were you when the accident happened?", "How far were you from the point of impact?", or "Which way were you looking when you heard the sound of the squealing tires?" This technique will produce more reliable answers than leading questions without causing the witness to wonder what they might be expected to say.

6.042 Refining Judgment Statements

Special care must be used when a witness is asked to provide or offers judgment statements such as estimations of distance, elapsed time, or an individual's ability to carry out a certain act. For instance, consider the statement "He was 100 feet away." Explore the accuracy of that "100 feet" by having the witness estimate distances. Use easily estimated or checked distances. Have the witness estimate distances at the scene if possible, or have the witness mark the important reference points on a witness sketch, then measure the distance in reality. Do not let an important witness testify concerning a distance or length without first checking its reasonableness.

Understandably, time estimates can also be dangerous. "It just took a minute" must be explored to determine if "a minute" was sixty full seconds, a split second, or a figure of speech. Ask the witness to recreate the time by saying, "I'll time a full minute; you tell me if it is too long." Use a watch or clock with a sweep second hand, or a stop watch, and sit quietly through the full period estimated by the witness. Seldom will it feel correct. Have the witness reenact or "role play" the time period as originally experienced while discretely marking the actual time. Record the actual elapsed time period and discuss this with the witness.

Initial descriptions can be treacherous if they are accepted at face value. Have the witness provide a description, then check its salient points. Remember, people are identified by race, sex, age, height, weight, general physical build (slim, stocky, stout, fat, etc.), hair color, eye color, and outstanding physical characteristics or distinguishing marks. These latter two characteristics include scars, disfigurements, hairstyles, glasses, limping, the use of crutches or braces, tattoos, cosmetics, wigs, jewelry, and watches.

Physical objects often require a description. Vehicles and colors can often be troublesome elements. For example, red does not mean quite the same thing to everyone. It could be "tomato" red, "fire engine" red, or "beet" red. An artist's color chart is a good aid for defining colors. Vehicle makes, models, and production year are difficult for most witnesses to quickly identify. A good method for aiding vehicle identification is to visit new and used car lots with the witness to locate similar or identical cars.

Conduct is another judgment element which often needs additional description. If a witness says the plaintiff or defendant was "acting strangely," follow-up questions should be used to add specifics. What do you mean by strange? Glassy, unfocused eyes? Staggering? Unresponsive to direct questions? Grimacing from pain? Sorrow? Shock? It may be difficult for the witness to put into words, but it is easier to do so in an interview than in a deposition or on the witness stand during cross-examination by opposing counsel.

Occasionally, a witness will have a solid factual foundation on which to base a statement. A time estimate may be based on an event occuring at the same time a favorite television show was starting. A vehicle description might be based on the fact that a relative "owns one just like it." A time period might be correlated to a timed activity: "I had just put a dish in the microwave and started it on high for thirty seconds when I heard the sound and looked out the window. The time went off at the same time the police were driving up and I noticed a man running down the alley in the opposite direction." Ask questions designed to help the witness remember any details which will help frame or define a judgment statement.

6.043 Recapitulation

Another important questioning technique in an interview, called recapitulation, is to go back through the major details of testimony with the witness. This is done after the witness has provided narrative testimony and the legal assistant has asked follow-up questions. This is accomplished by restating each major element of the testimony. This process should be repeated until the witness is satisfied that the legal assistant understands what has been said.

6.05   Interview Preliminaries

6.051   Scheduling Considerations

When a person is known to have information that the legal assistant wants to document, a statement should be taken via interview. But first, the legal assistant must decide whether to contact the individual in advance to schedule an appointment or approach the individual unannounced. This first decision can be very important because each method of approach has its particular drawbacks and advantages.

Scheduling the interview in advance gives a witness time to prepare. The witness can gather and review documents, notes, memorabilia, and/or other materials for the coming interview which serve to refresh memory. While this process may help the interviewer's search for truth, it also has the disadvantage of giving the witness time to prepare mentally, to compose responses that provide minimal information, obscure important facts, or limit the information to only those facts the witness to reveal.

Although approaching the witness unannounced generally prevents the kind of mental preparation which inhibits spontaneous production of the desired information, surprising the witness can backfire. When confronted by unknown individuals about potentially volatile matters, people may experience fear. Fear often causes witnesses to employ delay tactics, and may trigger aggressively defensive behavior, both of which hinder the interview's progress. Try to get as much information about the intended witness and his or her relationship to the matter at hand in advance, it will help in planning the correct method of approach.

6.052   Review of Law and Facts

It is important to have a basic understanding of the general areas of law which are applicable to the client's case. If time allows, research and review those general areas of law expected to arise in the case, particularly those with which the legal assistant is unfamiliar or has not worked in some time. The legal assistant should never hesitate to seek the advice of the supervising attorney when approaching a new or unfamiliar area of activity, and must develop the confidence to face the attorney and say, "What do you recommend I read or study to prepare?", or "I'm not familiar with this type of case; can you brief me or point me toward reference material I can study?"

In addition to having a basic understanding of the law which may come into play, a thorough review of all available factual information is essential in preparing for an interview. This review should include all documents in the file, including internal notes and memorandum, which concern or relate to the matter to be discussed in the interview. This review may involve a multitude of facts in the form of documents, statements, and/or citations of code, statute, or case law. Because of this, the legal assistant needs to devlope a method of coordinating existing facts with supporting references. Each fact can be listed chronologically, with its corroboration, on the left side of a piece of paper, with questions needed to develop, corroborate, or attack the information listed to the right. For instance, if the dispute involves a contract and the client seeks specific performance, the contract may be the physical fact and a client statement may corroborate it. The questions on the right side might include "Novation?", "Rescission?", "Consideration made?", "Is the contract capable of performance?", or "Who drafted the document?"

6.053 Gathering Checklists and Forms

The law office should have checklists and forms concerning the type of legal services performed. The legal assistant's use of the appropriate forms during interviews will expedite parts of the interview but should not replace the legal assistant's good judgment. The legal assistant should take all forms that could apply to the given situation to the interview; it is better to have more forms and checklists on hand than will actually be needed, they can be returned to stock more easily than the interview can be interrupted to obtain them. Many jurisdictions have standard forms which have been approved by the courts or the legislature, such as living wills, powers of attorney, and probate declarations. Using these forms contributes to the smooth, efficient management of the case. For example, in a personal injury case, the names and addresses of doctors, hospitals, insurance companies, employers, and witnesses, among others, will be needed. Using a form for gathering the information increases efficiency and ensures that nothing is forgotten. Other type of standardized forms commonly used are those to be signed by the client which authorize the release of medical records or other privileged information from doctors, hospitals, therapists, accountants, and employers. Whenever possible, the legal assistant should develope forms for gathering the basic information used in specific kinds of cases to maximize efficiency. Think ahead, save time, and be professional.

6.054 Planning the Interview Site

Selection and arrangement of the interview site may be a problem unless adequate notice is given. Ideally, the interview should be in an uncluttered conference room of an appropriate size, comfortably furnished and arranged to avoid distraction or unease. During the interview, the legal assistant needs to keep the witness focused on the issues at hand. Eliminating unnecessary files and materials not related to the interview will help the legal assistant with this task. The room should also be equipped with all necessary miscellaneous supplies, such as scratch pads, pencils, a carafe of water, and glasses. Arrange the chairs and tables so that the legal assistant sits alongside the witness or at the corner of the table. (*See* Exhibit 6-1.) Placing the table directly between the interviewer and the witness creates a physical barrier and the classic posture of confrontation: eye-to-eye. Barriers and confrontation, whether actual or implied, physical or psychological, are not conducive to the feeling of rapport the legal assistant needs to cultivate in order to uncover the true facts.

If the interview cannot be conducted in an ideal setting, such as the conference room previously described, but occurs at the legal assistant's desk, clear the desk of all other materials. Put away correspondence, files, and reference materials. Create the impression that the interview is the most important thing occurring at that time and place. Arrange for the phone to be answered elsewhere. Not every interview can be conducted under ideal conditions, but they should always be controlled to the largest extent possible. Interviewing is difficult enough without allowing distracting influences to inhibit or interrupt the dialogue between the interviewer and the witness.

EXHIBIT 6-1   Arranging the Interview Room

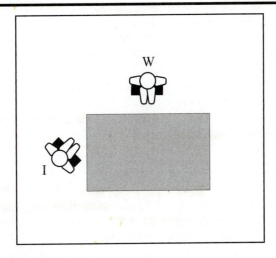

Sometimes the interview must be conducted in an uncontrolled environment. Special problems arise when this is the case. Frequently, time pressures exist because the interview is being fit into the witness's schedule. Distractions, like windows and telephones, throw the interview off course. Courtesy, sincerity, and a dogged willingness to adapt the interview to the situations encountered will serve the legal assistant well. Occasionally, the legal assistant can arrange to interview the individual at lunchtime or during a work break; sometimes immediately after work, sitting in a car. These conditions, of course, are not conducive to the contemplative, thorough, and deep-ranging discussions legal assistants prefer; but situations are not always perfect.

Regardless of the interview setting, the legal assistant must be alert and sensitive to any special needs the witness may have. For example, someone may be hard of hearing in one ear and may ask that the legal assistant sit on a particular side so the witness can hear better. Others may be uncomfortable if the legal assistant happens to be sitting too close. Be observant and do whatever needs to be done to put the witness at ease.

6.0541 *The Young and the Old.* Children should never be interviewed without the consent of their parents. They usually speak more easily if their parents are with them. However, the presence of a parent complicates the interviewing process because children often look to parents for guidance or approval when speaking. Preparing parents properly for involvement in such interviews, teaching them not to coach the child by word or gesture, presents an interesting challenge to the legal assistant. One possible remedy is to arrange the chairs so the legal assistant and the child are sitting side by side at the table or desk and the parent is to the rear of the child and out of sight. However, this does not prevent the parent from speaking to the child.

It may be necessary to conduct interviews of older persons under circumstances that are a little unusual for the legal assistant. Many times the interview will be conducted in the home of the witness. Interviewing an aged person in his or her own environment may be more advantageous than putting that person through the difficulty of traveling to an office for an interview. This possibility should be given serious consideration if a very aged or infirm person must be interviewed.

6.0542 Telephone Interviews. Telephone interviews can be a cost-effective method of identifying witnesses or obtaining basic facts from a client. They allow the legal assistant to make many contacts in short periods of time, to terminate the interview quickly if it appears unproductive, or to be expanded if the interview is going well. During a telephone interview, the legal assistant should work to establish rapport with the individual, with the goal of making a face-to-face interview easy to schedule if the witness has, or contends to have, information bearing on the facts of the case. As discussed in the section on body language, people exhibit certain tendencies during an in-person interview which are an aid in determining credibility. A disadvantage of using a telephone interview is the inability to make personal observations of the witness's behavior and body language.

6.0543 Other Special Cases. In addition to the problems associated with interviewing children and older people, other types of witnesses will make the arrangement of an interview site difficult. These include people who are hospitalized or under medication at the time of the interview, prisoners in correctional facilities or jails, and people who are willing to provide information but are unwilling to be identified as the souce of that information.

This last category of witnesses, also known as anonymous or confidential sources, may volunteer information that is actually available publicly but which would not be requested in the course of a normal investigation because of its relative obscurity. These individuals may offer contacts who, because they are aware of the legal assistant's particular interest, generate more information than would be obtained by a routine request. The identity of these contacts and confidential sources must be protected if the legal assistant agrees to accept their information. The major danger in using confidential sources is the inadvertent exposure of them to others involved in the case.

The legal assistant who develops confidential sources, whether they are neighbors who volunteer information of a private and personal nature regarding the adversary, or government officials who have provided special information from their own and other departmental files, must keep these sources strictly confidential. Their value in assisting the legal assistant and lawyer in other phases of formal discovery cannot be measured because it places the attorney in a superior position with regard to knowledge of facts.

6.055   Notetaking

The legal assistant conducting the interview should always make notes during its course, even when consent is obtained to record the interview electronically. These notes should not be transcriptions. They should be succinct, reflect relevant portions of the interview, and include physical observations and mental impressions about the witness. Take the notes in such a manner that the witness cannot read what is being written; this prevents the witness from being distracted or influenced by the notes and modifying behavior as a result. After the interview, use the notes to prepare a quick summary of events, saving both documents for permanent storage in the case file. Remember: notes are not transcripts, they are meant to aid the legal assistant's recollection of the interview. Keep them short.

6.056   Electronic Recording Decisions

The decision whether or not to use recording equipment to memorialize the interview depends on several things, including the opinion of the attorney, the attitude of the client or witness toward the recording device, and the circumstances or purposes of the interview. While electronic recording of interviews by legal assistants is not common in many jurisdictions, it is important to understand the concepts and procedures.

First, as we have seen, interviews are conducted for a wide variety of purposes, some of which do not necessitate recording. Second, because recording the interview can be costly, it is a good idea to limit the number of recorded interviews to include only those expected to generate critical information; for this reason, it may be advantageous to conduct a preliminary oral interview or document review to determine the extent of the witness's pertinent knowledge. Finally, even though the ultimate decision to record the interview must be cleared with the supervising attorney, unless the interview is a formal deposition, the witness may prevent the interview from being recorded by refusing to give permission.

The tapes serve a second purpose, beyond that of data storage; they are a wonderful teaching aid for the legal assistant trying to perfect the art of interviewing. There is no cure for backward mannerisms like watching yourself do them, or hearing yourself say them. If you are allowed to tape any interviews, review them with a critical eye and ear, noting areas that need improvement as well as those that don't.

6.0561 *Special Considerations for Audio and Video Tape Recording.* If audio, video, or other electronic devices are used to record an interview, there are some conventions that should be observed:

   a. The legal assistant (or investigator) introduces him or herself, gives the date, location and purpose of the interview, and provides the case reference or title; for example, "This is Robert Smith, a legal assistant employed by Jane E. Jones, attorney for Alice S. Brown, who is the Plaintiff in Brown vs. ABZ Corporation. The following will be a tape recorded interview with Ms. Brown conducted in the law offices of Jones, Jones, and Day at 1655 North Street, Jonesville, Ohio. Today is April 3, 1989; it is now 10:05 a.m."
   b. The witness to be interviewed should be introduced; for instance, "Ms. Brown, please state your full name and spell your last name." Allow the witness to answer. Then ask, "Ms. Brown, will you allow us to record the discussion we have planned to have today?" The next question may be "Our discussion will deal with the events that gave rise to this legal action. Will you freely and voluntarily relate your best knowledge and recollections of this matter?"
   c. Each person present in the room must also be introduced and asked to state their identity, relationship to the case, and willingness to have the session recorded.
   d. If a tape log or counter is used, the tape identification should be spoken onto the tape, both early (during the initial introduction preferably) and at the conclusion of the tape.
   e. All interruptions of the recording should have the time (hour and minutes) and the reason for stopping read onto the tape at the point when stopped. The date, time, and a brief restatement of the people present should be made when the recording is resumed.
   f. Some jurisdictions require that witnesses be supplied with copies of their statements when preserved in writing or by recording. Some witnesses will agree to make a statement only if they can have a copy of it.
   g. At the conclusion of an interview, the legal assistant should have the witness reaffirm that the statement was recorded knowingly and voluntarily and ask whether the witness wishes to add, delete, or clarify anything discussed during the interview.

If audio equipment is used and more than two people are present for the interview, it is important that microphones be positioned to pick up each voice equally. If various people speak intermittently during the interview, each person should state his or her name before injecting comments. This allows a more accurate transcription of the tape.

When video equipment is used, it is important that the camera(s), and any microphones if separate, be positioned so that all of the participants can be seen and heard. To facilitate this, the chairs should be arranged so that no one's back is to the recording device.

6.0562 Drawbacks and Benefits of Audio Tape Recording.

Audio taping an interview, while a way to guarantee total recollection of the dialogue, does have its drawbacks. The first is the general problem associated with any means of recording an interview; the taped record of the interview will almost certainly be subject to discovery by the adverse party. If favorable testimony is expected, recording may be helpful; but if it is anticipated that the testimony will not be helpful, or perhaps even harmful, the interview should not be tape recorded. Instead, a preliminary interview should first be done orally, with the interviewer's notes serving as the only record. Then, if the information is not harmful, a second interview can be conducted which may be recorded on tape, or a written statement may be prepared for signature by the witness. The attorney directs which method is preferred.

The second drawback to audio taped interviews is that it adds a significant number of procedural steps that must be followed during the course of the interview. For this reason, it is generally a good idea for legal assistants with relatively little interviewing experience to avoid taping their sessions. Additionally, taping itself is a distraction that may adversly affect both the interviewer and the witness.

Finally, many witnesses are intimidated by recording devises and may not speak as freely as they would during an unrecorded interview, or may refuse to speak at all.

6.0563 Drawbacks and Benefits of Video Tape Recording.

The drawbacks that applied to audio taped interviews apply equally to those recorded on video tape, although the procedural complications are lessened by the fact that on video tape there is no need for constant verbal identification of the speaker. However, the nature of video tape presents its own special circumstance: some individuals, while entirely honest, give the appearance on video as shifty or crooked, while some individuals who are completely crooked look like saints. Video tape allows the personality of a witness to affect the testimony, whether or not the witness is conscious of that fact. For this reason, video tape should not be used to record an interview until the subject has been contacted in person and an assessment made of that subject's dynamic effect.

It is worth noting that video tape's greatest potential drawback, its ability to either subdue or enhance certain aspects of the individual, is also its greatest potential strength. A client whose image to a judge and jury is positively enhanced by video tape will be very appreciative; that same client will also appreciate the tape that reveals the nervous nature of an adversary. Video tape, then, is a two-edged sword with no handle; do not pick it up until it has been thoroughly examined and all caution is employed.

6.06 The Interview Proper

6.061 Introductions

The introduction of the legal assistant to the involved parties is extremely important because it puts the relationship of the legal assistant to the attorneys, the client, and the witness in proper perspective. The introduction to the client should be performed by the attorney. The introduction should be professional and reflect the attorney's full confidence in the legal assistant's capabilities. Ideally, the attorney will discuss the legal assistant's role in the case with the client before this formal introduction occurs.

If the lawyer is not present when the legal assistant first meets the witness, it is the legal assistant's duty to clearly delineate the differences between lawyers and legal assistants and to explain the legal assistant's role in the coming interview. The witness must be made fully aware of the object and purpose of the interview, the parties involved, and the legal assistant's connection to the matter. It is not uncommon for a witness to refer to the interviewer as an attorney during the course of an interview, even when the status and role as legal assistant has been previously explained. When this occurs, the witness must be immediately reminded that the interviewer is a legal assistant conducting the interview at the request of an attorney for the benefit of the client.

6.0611 Walk-Ins. In many law offices, particularly those of solo practicioners and small firms, the legal assistant will be the first to encounter the walk-in person seeking aid or advice. In these instances, while there is little or no opportunity to prepare for the interview, the legal assistant must be well acquainted with the ethical considerations and requirements as well as the predefined limits of authority and responsibility (*see generally,* Chapter 3, Ethics). The legal assistant must also be knowledgable concerning the various types of inquiries which are likely to be received in this situation. Checklists, forms, and resource material covering the routine problems the legal assistant will generally encounter with walk-in clients must be kept at hand for immediate reference. When the legal assistant is asked for information not routinely handled, or outside the scope of authority, responsibility, or ethical restraints, it is best to make a clear explanation to the client that the information requested needs to be provided by the supervising attorney.

6.062 Establishing the Purpose of the Interview

The purpose of the interview should be one of the first things established. For instance, a common purpose for the initial interview of a client is to prepare for or respond to litigation. Such preparation may develop enough information to clarify the issues and lead to a settlement of the dispute that first brought the client to the office. To most clients, a quick resolution to their problem which avoids litigation is preferable to a lawsuit filed, fought, and won at some uncertain future date.

Legal services which do not involve litigation may also require the use of interviews to develop the necessary information for successful completion. These include such tasks as researching corporate organizational structures, estate planning, probate, difficult and complex commercial transactions, business mergers, applications to governmental agencies, drafting contracts, and employer-employee matters.

6.063 The Meeting and the Establishment of Rapport

From the moment the legal assistant meets the witness, a rapport should be cultivated. As the witness is being escorted to the interview site, the legal assistant should make every effort to put the witness at ease. It helps to engage in casual conversation, during which the legal assistant may gain insight into the personality of the witness. The exchange of pleasantries, comments on the weather, inquiries into the traffic situation, or how the ball team did are opportunities for the legal assistant to determine the presence of any hostility in the witness as well as the level of communication skills. It also allows the witness to evaluate the legal assistant and to some extent overcome any initial apprehension they move concerning the interview.

Coffee, tea, or a glass of water should be offered at this time. It allows witnesses to do something with their hands and helps to establish a connection with the legal assistant. Rapport is the establishment of a harmonious relationship based on mutual trust and respect between people. The legal assistant's appearance, sincerity, cheerful attitude, and demonstrated courtesy will aid in dispelling any fears and will help to generate rapport and the feeling of working together toward a common goal. If a decision to tape record the interview has been made, the legal assistant should take the opportunity at this time to learn how the witness feels about the use of recording equipment, whether the idea makes them nervous and uncomfortable, or is objectionable for other reasons. This inquiry should be done tactfully and discretely to avoid destroying the rapport which has been established to this point. If the witness is obviously uncomfortable with the idea of being recorded, the legal assistant should not go forward with recording plans at that time. It is possible that as more rapport is established, the witness will become more comfortable with the idea.

6.064 Beginning the Interview

Following the introduction and attempt to build rapport with the witness, the legal assistant begins taking down preliminary data. This process serves to calm emotions in most witnesses because these things are routine, well-known, not in dispute, yet essential to the identification of the people involved in the case, the dates at issue, and the establishment of the purpose of the interview. If permission has been obtained to record the interview, the requirements discussed in Section 6.056 are followed.

Once the preliminary information about the witness has been noted, the legal assistant should ask whether the witness has brought any documents, photographs, sketches, drawings, or other items to the interview. Each item brought by the witness should then be described and physically identified. The witness should be asked for permission by the legal assistant to take custody of the items. In the event the witness refuses to allow the legal assistant to keep any originals, permission should be obtained to have copies made of any documents or computer disks and photographs taken of any physical objects. It is also a good idea at this time to have copies made of any documents so that both the witness and the legal assistant can refer to them during the interview.

6.065 The Body of the Interview

Usually a witness has a preconceived idea or sequence of thoughts to present. The most effective way of gauging the value of a witness is to begin by encouraging a general narration of what the witness knows while the legal assistant takes notes of points that need corroboration or further detail, information which is in conflict with other known facts, or information which appears difficult for the witness to have obtained firsthand. During this stage, the legal assistant encourages the narration by using supportive questioning techniques and body language, such as nodding the head, empathetic facial expressions, and extensive eye contact. Many people, once they begin talking, like to talk. One of the difficulties the legal assistant may have during this portion of the interview is keeping the focus and direction of the witness away from peripheral issues or irrelevant matters.

Once the legal assistant has heard the story offered by the witness, the next phase of the interview begins. The points and facts raised by the witness are categorized through gentle but focused questioning as either arising from personal knowledge, inference, or supposition. Search for corroboration of every point of the story through skillful questioning which invites additional narrative, refines judgment statements, and recapitulates what the witness has said. Determine whether the witness knows of other potential related parties, remembers any photographs being taken, recalls the existence of maps, or can identify any other documents or objects from the case file.

Another final essential topic to be explored in the interview is whether the witness has previously provided any written or recorded statement to anyone about the case. The firm's policy will determine what advice or instructions should be given the witness about how to handle any approach by an adversary for an interview. The policy may be to cooperate or to decline to give another statement, referring the requesting party to the client's attorney. The goal is to avoid an inconsistent statement, which can cause an otherwise competent, honest witness to loose credibility.

6.066 Concluding the Interview

The interview should be brought to a close politely with an understanding that additional information may be needed in the future. Obtain an agreement about a completion date of any checklist, form, or other document or information that the individual has agreed to provide. The legal assistant should remember to calendar that date for follow-up at the appropriate time.

The legal assistant should escort the witness and any other participant back to the door of the office or, if an appointment has been scheduled with another individual in the firm, to the next person the witness is to see. Never abandon a witness, client, or other participant after completing this first interview. Keep in mind that rapport is to be nurtured throughout the case, not just during the first meeting.

6.07   Summarizing the Interview

As soon as possible after conclusion of the interview, the legal assistant should prepare a summary for the attorney which contains a succinct description of the interview and its basic facts. If the interview was recorded, it may be necessary at some future time to have a full transcription prepared. In addition to a recapitulation of the important facts both supporting and refuting the client's position, the summary should include an evaluation of the witness and the elements of proof provided in the testimony, a listing of potential additional witnesses, evidence or other documents, and descriptions of any documents or objects received from the witness.

6.071 Evaluation of the Witness

The opportunity to evaluate a witness, in terms of potential impact on a jury or the liklihood of changing testimony under the pressure of cross-examination, is one of the major benefits of the interview. The attorney will want the legal assistant's general impressions of the witness, such as the witness's overall appearance and image, whether they appear sincere or deceitful, whether they have mannerisms which would affect their ability to communicate with a jury, and so on.

These opinions should be based on any perceived inconsistencies in the story, knowledge the witness could not have but claims to know directly, and any physical mannerisms or other observations the legal assistant observed during the course of the interview. This evaluation and its foundation are important for supplementing the attorney's opinion about the witness and for alerting the attorney to areas requiring special consideration.

6.072 Elements of Proof

What evidentiary value does the story have on its own? What other evidentiary facts does it corroborate or refute? What conflicts in fact, opinion, or allegation does it create? Facts provided by a witness's testimony should be evaluated in terms of use as an element of proof. The evaluation should also differentiate testimonial proof from documentary, or demonstrative proof. Points of corroboration or points of refutation should be outlined for each statement that could have a bearing on the factual issues relevant to the case. Additionally, testimonial proof needs to be identified as "inferred," "deduced," "hearsay," or "firsthand, personal" knowledge. This information will also be used by the legal assistant to assist the attorney in preparing for trial by incorporating it into a master index of the facts and proofs for each issue of the case along with a listing of the witnesses who can offer testimony on those points.

6.073 Possible Remedies, Responses, and Additional Potential Defendants

Some matters discussed by the supervising attorney and the legal assistant, such as potential remedies, strategy or planned courses of action, are items which the legal assistant should not discuss with either a witness or a client.

During client interviews, the legal assistant always seeks to have the client articulate as many acceptable remedies, solutions, or recourses as possible. Identification of potential additional defendants or other interested parties is always important whether the client is a plaintiff, defendant, or other interested party. Equally important is the investigation, discussion, and possible mediation of disputes, which can often resolve the issues without the need to file suit. In some cases, the client's position can be advocated for him or her in a forum that has not already been considered.

The legal assistant should not suggest or comment on the probability of success or propriety of pursuing any potential resolutions to the client. Such comments or suggestions to a client may be interpreted as the practice of law because they have the appearance of being independant legal opinion or advice. The legal assistant should voice any such comments or suggestions to the attorney, as they are often an important element in the attorney's process of reaching a conclusion on those issues.

6.074 Leads to Additional Witnesses, Evidence, or Documentation

The interview summary should include a list of additional potential witnesses or interested parties as well as a list of documents or objects which need to be obtained. Time, location, the technical nature of the matter, or other impediments should be identified. The legal assistant should make a note to discuss with the supervising attorney the arrangements which will need to be made to meet with these additional witnesses and obtain the additional documents or objects.

Bibliography

"Investigation" presentation to Paralegal Association of Santa Clara County—Litigation Section, May 23, 1996 by Ken Edick, P.I., ACTION P.I., San Jose, CA.

General References for Further Study

California Legal Assistant Handbook. 1st ed. James Publishing, Inc., 1996.

Dwight, Jennifer, *The Nuts and Bolts of Civil Litigation Practice.* Clark, Boardman, Callahan with Estrin Publishing, 1994.

Weinstein, Mark, *Introduction to Civil Litigation.* 3rd ed. The Philadelphia Institute, West Publishing Company, 1993.

Koerselman, Virginia, *CLA Review Manual.* West Publishing Company, 1993.

7 Investigation

7.00   The Gatherer of Facts

The gatherer of facts in a situation where a client is seeking services or advice from an attorney may be any one of a broad range of people. The attorney clearly has the first responsibility of gathering sufficient facts on which to base his or her opinion as to the proper course of action to pursue. Additionally, since the attorney is not an expert in many other fields, he or she may employ the services of such gatherers of facts as accountants, engineers, doctors, real estate appraisers, or any of the whole gamut of professional people peculiarly suited to provide the special type of information required. In cases where litigation or some form of legal representation or advocacy may be required, the employment of an investigator may be indicated. Investigators may be called "private investigators," "insurance adjustors," "police officers," or "legal assistants." Clearly there may be other titles in other jurisdictions that denote the same function. However, these people are all alike in the purpose they serve. They do not dispense legal advice but take directions from an attorney to follow the legal theory that he or she has created and support or refute that theory through the careful and thorough assembling of all pertinent and relevant evidentiary facts within their ability to locate, identify, corroborate, and report.

A thorough investigation, prior to the filing of a lawsuit, can change not only the decision as to whether to file a case, but also the end results of the case. The rule-of-thumb is, if a case is filed today, be prepared to start trying the case tomorrow. That's how thorough the investigation prior to filing a suit should be. By out-preparing and out-working the opposing side, the attorney will be able to provide the client with the best representation.

Investigation basically is going where specific information is suspected to be, determining whether or not it exists, and collecting it if it does. This may involve searching official records, unofficial records, or quasi-official records of any form, type, or nature. It may involve obtaining the testimony of those people who have direct, peripheral, or hearsay information bearing on the matter at issue. It may involve creating evidence in the form of photographs, drawings, reproduction of documents, models of places, things, and conditions, or preserving physical objects for later use. This is done in an efficient manner, without intending to harass anyone, and solely to accomplish the basic purpose of supplying the attorney with reliable information of a factual nature on which to base his or her legal conclusions and advice to, or advocacy for, the client. The investigator should be thorough in this fact-finding process. If that is done, the attorney can then select and rely on the information he or she deems important. Investigations should also be conducted in a courteous and professional manner so that witnesses are willing to submit to follow-up interviews by either the investigator or the attorney.

7.001   Informal Discovery—Basic Elements

Investigation is "informal discovery" in the sense that it is a unilateral collection of facts ordered by one attorney, not the court, and without specific notice to the adversary. Whether the investigation consists of one or two letters and phone calls or a full team of field investigators, the basic principles are the same:

   a. Define the issues in dispute.
   b. Identify the essential elements of proof involved in the case.
   c. Identify the facts needed to prove each of the elements.
   d. Analyze the potential sources and locations of evidentiary factual data and/or witnesses that may contribute or impede the establishment of the facts.

e. Elect the method of investigation most likely to produce timely, reliable results commensurate with time, distance, economy, and the importance of the data to the case.

f. Find, preserve, and present both the evidentiary facts (with foundation) to the attorney and an explanation of nonavailability of those facts that could not be obtained or established.

g. Reevaluate, reinvestigate, and develop data needed and/or revealed right up to conclusion of the case.

7.002 Judgment and Ethics

In the course of this work, a substantial amount of judgment is required of the investigator. It is not enough simply to produce evidence; it must be done in an ethical and acceptable manner. The investigator should never stoop to burglary, robbery, embezzlement, extortion, corruption of any variety, or blatant misrepresentation in order to obtain facts, physical evidence, or cooperation from witnesses. There is a fine line between dissembling and misrepresentation, but the legal assistant must distinguish it. Particularly in litigation, it is important to be able to go to court with clean hands and an honest case. The legal assistant, even when acting as an investigator, must follow the attorney's policies and guidelines in contacting parties to obtain information, documents, and other items connected to the case. If any of the parties is represented by an attorney, the legal assistant must discontinue all communication except through that party's attorney. The investigator, and particularly a legal assistant who is acting as an investigator, works at the direction of and under the control of the attorney. Illegal or improper conduct reflects on the attorney and, in serious cases, may jeopardize his or her right to practice law. Private investigators and independent adjustors usually are regulated by state law, licensed by a state agency, insured, and bonded. Unethical or illegal conduct by them will jeopardize their own businesses, as well as their licenses.

7.01 The Investigation Plan

The investigation plan is a preliminary examination of the problem presented to the attorney and the considerations that are to be made in developing the form of work to be done by the investigator or the legal assistant in generating the information needed to provide the service to the client.

Among the major considerations to be discussed at the outset is whether or not the firm is acting in behalf of the plaintiff, the defendant, or an applicant. The needs are different in most cases, and the time element involved varies widely according to the circumstances under which the investigation is to be made. If the client is the plaintiff, the investigation can be made before the complaint is served and often before a claim is presented to the potential defendant. Most litigious matters begin with the plaintiff's attorney having a tremendous advantage since the only time compulsion is to insure that the claim or case is filed prior to the expiration of the applicable statute of limitations. This usually provides plenty of time in which to perform the investigative tasks necessary to establish firmly the factual foundation of the right of the client to the remedy selected. Another advantage is that the client usually has a substantial number of facts ready at hand. As the injured party, he or she has personal knowledge of the circumstances that caused the action to arise, the names of witnesses, the types of documents involved, and the potential issues that the attorney will define. This is a major head start for an investigator in assembling the evidentiary facts necessary to proving the case.

The defendant, on the other hand, has a different set of problems. Time frequently is a handicap if the action is one that began sometime in the past and a response is statutorily required within a short period of time. While the plaintiff's investigator could speak freely to each person in seeking witness statements, the defendant now is precluded from talking to the adverse party (or the party's employees) without the agreement of the plaintiff's counsel. Thus a substantial source of testimonial fact is denied the defendant through informal discovery.

Applicants for licenses or permits generally are not in a litigious mood but are assembling data required by statute or code in order to comply with the minimum requirements of a governmental entity. Time may be a problem, but it seldom is a crushing load on the investigator. Accuracy and thoroughness are just as important as in any other form of legal action. Intervention in administrative hearings by interests opposed to the applicant's objective is more and more common, particularly where the environmental regulations are involved; these interventions can require "crash" programs to develop information countering the unanticipated allegations of the intervenors.

The plan always considers the possible theories of action the attorney contemplates at the outset. From these, the essential elements of proof can be identified and serve as guidelines to the investigator in seeking out the testimony and factual support for the attorney's positions. The elements of proof are easily obtained in most jurisdictions by consulting the approved jury instructions, the appropriate code or statute to be litigated (or the standards to be met in applications), or the texts and commentary that define the common law actions. Identities, locations, and physical evidence are always critical for the investigator to consider, examine, obtain, and preserve.

7.011 The Plan Outline
The plan outline always covers the following:

1. What facts are believed known? How can they be proved? Supported?
2. What facts must be corroborated?
3. What evidentiary facts are needed to prove?
4. How do we locate and establish them?
5. Where may the needed evidentiary facts or information be found?
   - Federal, state, local governments, agencies, and commissions
   - Business, trade, and professional associations
   - Private firms' or businesses' records
   - Public domain sources (libraries, newspapers, TV stations)
   - Individuals' files, memories, and knowledge
6. How best can the inquiries be made?
   - By telephone
   - By letter
   - By physical contact, examination, or interview
   - Through employment of associated investigators who will perform informal discovery tasks
   - By formal discovery methods
7. When must it be available for the attorney?

7.012 Inhibitors of Investigation
The investigation may be inhibited by a variety of factors, such as cost, the geographic location where the investigation must take place, document volume, or the time available for the work.

7.0121 The Cost versus the Value. The method of investigation has a tremendous impact upon its economics. Obviously, if a legal assistant can conduct the investigation by letter or telephone from the office, the cost will be minimized. If it requires the employment of a special outside investigator on a retainer for a substantial period of time, the cost of proving the elements of the case may outweigh the value of the information. Formal discovery may be more economical and effective.

7.0122 Geography. Geography can be a barrier to investigation if time or cost is a major element in the choice of technique. Witnesses can be located in remote areas by physically going there and talking to people, examining records, directories, and so forth, but only occasionally can they be located by telephone or letter. Locating relevant documents from large volumes in diverse locations requires time and knowledgeable eyes and is best accomplished by an investigator fully versed in the case background and issues. Telephones and letters are weak substitutes for physical examination.

7.0123 Volume of Material. If the matter is one involving large volumes of documents for review and analysis, alternative means of accomplishing that task should be explored. Alternatives to it being done internally by the attorney's existing staff include the temporary employment of a special staff for this particular project or the use of the client's own personnel under the supervision of a legal assistant. (*See* Chapter 8, Pretrial Litigation Skills, and Chapter 9, The Legal Assistant and Document Discovery Cases.)

7.0124 Time Considerations. Investigation is vital to gaining an outcome that is most favorable to the client in a legal action and a thorough investigation prior to a suit being filed is essential to the case. Once an action has begun, time is no longer under the control of the attorney. The attorney must out-work and out-prepare the opposing side by knowing everything available about the case, the issues involved and the documents to be presented as evidence, than the opposing side in order to provide the best representation to his/her client. Therefore, prior investigation is necessary to insure that nothing is missed and that everything is checked and rechecked. As indicated previously, the rule-of-thumb is, when the complaint is filed, the attorney should be ready to try the case tomorrow.

In federal criminal litigation, where a plea of not guilty is entered, the trial commences within seventy days from the date of filing (F.R.Cr.P 3161(c)(1)). This does not allow much time to secure documents from the government, experts to review the documents, meet with witnesses, research the law, and prepare for trial. Therefore, when a client indicates that he or she has been contacted by the government, or that business acquaintances are getting subpoenaed regarding the client's business and/or activities, it is essential to begin gathering information and preparing for trial; do not wait for the indictment to come down. You can be sure the government has been conducting their investigation for months and you do not want to wait until the indictment is filed to begin preparation on the case. Also, by doing a thorough investigation prior to indictment, in some instances it is possible to avoid an indictment altogether.

7.013 Formal and Informal Discovery and Privilege

Investigation, as a term, reflects that work which is performed by an investigator or a legal assistant during the informal discovery phase of the case for the benefit of the client. This is distinguished from the formal discovery process made available through the code sections of the jurisdiction and the rules of the court in which the case is being handled. Formal discovery procedures are interrogatories, depositions, requests for admission, requests for production of documents, and all of the related law and motion matters associated with those functions (*see generally,* Chapters 8 and 9). Informal means are those conducted solely for the attorney by his or her employees and without consulting, or needing to consult, the adversary counsel in the process. Much of the information obtained in this manner is covered under the "work product" privilege, since it is obtained for and by direction of an attorney in contemplation of litigation. The legal assistant and the investigator must insure that they handle all of the material obtained, as well as any reports they may prepare, in a manner that will not breach, or waive, that privilege. The assertion of the "work product" privilege is exclusively the right of the attorney. Ruling on whether the privilege applies or has been waived is the duty of the court.

The physical evidence, photography, documents, and statements of witnesses (if written or recorded), will not usually be privileged and thus will be available to the adversary through formal discovery. This lack of privilege and the potential for discovery must constantly be considered by the investigator and legal assistant when locating information adverse to the attorney's client. In many cases, a memorandum or report of examination to the attorney may be the best method of alerting the attorney to the adverse data without creating a discoverable windfall for the adversary.

7.0131 *Investigator Notes and Reports.* In the investigation process, the legal assistant or investigator must take detailed notes to ensure the attorney receives an accurate and factual account of the information learned. Opinions differ on how such notes ought to be preserved and maintained.

One viewpoint is that such notes are a temporary account of details which need not be maintained or preserved once the details have been included in a confidential memorandum to the attorney. The rationale is that notes usually are abbreviated, sometimes cryptic, seldom narrative, and often undated and unsigned. Whether the notes themselves are privileged is questionable—particularly when they are used for memory refreshment in any manner. If the privilege protection is lost months or years after the notes were made, the investigator may find that explaining the cryptic, abbreviated entries can be personally embarrassing and/or damaging for the attorney's case. Therefore, the conversion of the notes into a privileged memorandum in full narrative detail shortly after the notes are made is safer and more beneficial to the attorney, provided the notes are then destroyed. It is important to remember that such memorandum, whether formal or informal, may be subject to disclosure by discovery requests. Therefore, the legal assistant or investigator should request direction from the attorney before preparing any such memorandum.

Seldom must an investigator or legal assistant testify at trial or deposition, but occasionally, he or she may be called upon to explain photos that were taken, sketches that were made, or a physical examination made of the scene or of document files. When this happens, the natural reflex is to review all the documents available to prepare for the proceeding. That reflex may be wrong. Talk to the attorney first. Remember, anything personally reviewed to refresh a memory may have to be made available to the "noticing" or cross-examining attorney. A better procedure is for the attorney to review the memoranda, then interview the legal assistant or investigator. The attorney can refresh the memory of the legal assistant or investigator with questions while preserving the privilege of a specific report or memoranda.

7.02   Public Relations in Investigation

Investigative activities create contacts with a wide variety of people in private and public roles. The legal assistant's conduct can reflect favorably or unfavorably upon the employing office and attorney. The legal assistant's manner of speech and dress, the arrangement and honoring of appointments, the efficiency displayed in the conduct of the business, particularly in public offices, are all contributing factors to the public image and impression made by the legal assistant and the attorney's office. The rule then, of course, is: "Be pleasant, be cooperative, be firm, but be reasonable." Doggedness does not necessarily require rudeness. Thoroughness does not require argumentative behavior. The importance of the matter is no excuse for arrogance by the legal assistant.

When the legal assistant presents a request to others that is clear and easily inderstood, half the problem is solved. Before asking others for assistance, the legal assistant must have a clear concept of the kind of help expected. For example, asking for real property assessment information from the city planning office will waste the time of the city employee as well as the legal assistant, since that kind of information is not maintained at that public office. Make plans and preparations ahead of time. Try to work efficiently, in concert with others. Above all, make every effort to ensure that requests are reasonable. Avoid "panic" searches, last minute certifications, and/or "rush" filings. Those activities tend to irritate everyone and reflect poorly on the office.

The people contacted by the legal assistant, particularly those in public offices, are people the legal assistant can expect to see again and again. Custodians of Record for public agencies and offices are the "official witnesses" who have custody and control of documents and files. It is essential to meet these people with a deep appreciation for the information they have, their expertise in locating and producing data, and their willingness to assist, even when those efforts may seem feeble, inefficient, or untimely. The successful investigator is one who hides irritation and accepts help cheerfully, graciously, and with sincere gratitude. The next trip to that office will result in smiles, friendly words, and the best assistance to which anyone is entitled. An arrogant, irritable, or abrasive attitude will insure that the information sought will only come after additional time and effort and virtually without assistance from others who might have made the search effortless. Cooperation is the essential element needed from those contacted. The way to obtain it is to give cooperation and consideration.

7.03   In-Office Investigations

7.031 Telephone

The legal assistant who must gather information without leaving the office is not precluded from conducting investigations. The telephone can be a versatile and powerful tool for information gathering. A drawback is that it is difficult to evaluate the credibility of the person on the other end of the line solely by voice tones and words.

Visit the county clerk's office and learn what kinds of records are kept there. Make at least one trip to the courthouse in the company of a more experienced person who can explain the offices in the building and detail the files that are kept there. Knowledge of how recording and retrieval are accomplished in the ordinary course of business, along with names and phone numbers of contact personnel, will be a valuable resource.

Similarly, assessors' offices, public defenders' offices, law libraries, secretary of state offices, the corporation filings offices, and others all have tremendous amounts of information and various files that can be accessed by phone in many cases if the legal assistant knows the questions to ask, the phone numbers to call, and the protocol needed to obtain assistance from each particular source. Many of these directories are also available at no cost on the Internet, or are incorporated in CD-ROM programs available for purchase. Most, if not all, state and federal agencies publish special directories of phone numbers (at nominal cost). General information numbers to assist in locating the correct source for particular kinds of data are usually available from the telephone company directory assistance or are published in the local phone books.

Often it is not necessary to call a particular governmental office, commission, or department. In addition to resources available on-line, many private firms perform research functions for clients within the governmental files of state and federal agencies. Using these resources allows the legal assistant to verify or obtain a variety of information from such things as drivers' licenses, car titles, official government or agency filing forms, to copies of proposed legislative bills, and other government documents or reports. Search inquiries must be clearly defined as to topic, scope, and acceptable costs before they are initiated, or the single document expected to cost five dollars may grow into several expensive boxes of material.

Another resource for information compiled by government agencies are subscriptions to periodic reports. For instance, monthly climatological data segregated by specific location is available from the National Oceanic and Atmospheric Administration, Environmental Data Service, National Climatic Center, in Asheville, North Carolina. A listing of all such available subscription services, as well as a listing of all government publications can be obtained from the U.S. Government Printing Office.

Establishing personal and direct contacts with the people who staff government agencies, whether local, state, or federal, and building a relationship of mutual trust and respect with those individuals, will eventually make it possible to call a person by phone and ask for a timely search, photocopying, mailing, and billing of specific information. Asking others to search records in this manner is acceptable, efficient, and reliable when the volume of material to be screened is small and the facts or issues are clearly defined and easily recognizable. If the issue or fact is affected by the context of the documents, personal examination is required, and the telephone inquiry should be avoided.

7.032 Correspondence

Correspondence is another investigative tool which can be effectively utilized to gather information without leaving the office. A singular advantage of using correspondence, as opposed to the telephone, is that there is a record created which makes follow-up easier to track. Most offices have form files which contain letters of inquiry for basic types of information relating to particular kinds of cases handled in the past. These letters may include requests for such things as medical records from doctors and other care providers, employment records from employers, accident reports and other reports of investigation from police or regulatory bodies, or studies from governmental agencies.

Potential witnesses can be contacted by a letter which includes "form" questions that serve to identify those with helpful information. Enclosing a self-addressed, stamped, envelope makes it as easy as possible for prospective witnesses to provide the basic information needed to determine whether or not they should be contacted personally for further details. This technique is relatively inexpensive but may not always result in a response from the prospective witnesses. It is *not* a good technique for important or complex cases where solid evidentiary representations by each potential witness are required.

7.033 Computer Resources

7.0331 Court Records. Electronic access makes court records available by using a computer, modem, and phone line. Almost all federal and state courts have established some form of electronic access to records using a variety of methods which allow the legal assistant to obtain desired information quickly and almost immediately. PACER, ABBS, VCIS, BBS, ACES, ELF, and the Internet are the names of the most widely used court information access methods.

PACER, Public Access to Court Electronic Records, is used by most U.S. District Courts. PACER is a dial-in service that allows access to court information including the status of the case, the participants, deadlines in force, scheduled hearings, and significant dates. You can access a case by searching a name or case number, you can obtain a list of cases before the specific court, track case updates, review recent docket entries, and retrieve case summary records. To use PACER, you must contact the PACER Billing Center in San Antonio, Texas at 800-676-6856 for registration information.

ABBS is the Appellate Bulletin Board System and is another dial-in service used by the Court of Appeals. It is an electronic bulletin board containing opinions and dockets that may be viewed or downloaded in either WordPerfect 5.1 or ASCII text version. ABBS provides slip opinions (published and unpublished), amending orders, oral argument calendars, docket entries by case number, local rules, internal operating procedures, plans and forms, and notices such as press releases and bulletins. ABBS numbers can be secured through PACER at 800-676-6856.

VCIS, Voice Case Information System, uses a computer-generated synthesized voice device to read case information from the court's computer. By dialing from a Touch-Tone phone, you can retrieve case numbers, names of the parties, case filing date, attorneys' names and telephone numbers, assigned judge's name, and the case status. VCIS numbers can be received from the clerk's office of the applicable court.

BBS stands for Bulletin Board System and is a setup of computers accessible to outside users for trading software and communicating through typed messages. Users can post or reply to messages within BBS services designed around particular interests.

ACES, Appeals Court Electronic Service, is provided to participating courts in conjunction with the Federal Judicial Center. Using ACES you can obtain full text of slip opinions and orders, oral argument calendars, local rules and procedures, a list of dispositions, press releases, and general notices. ACES is accessed through ABBS by typing BBS at your log in prompt and following the prompts.

ELF is a pilot project being tried in some districts to allow attorneys to electronically file court documents directly to their computers. To use this system, contact the Clerk of Court for details and registration.

7.0332 Other Information and Research. The Internet contains a vast smorgasbord of information that is almost instantaneous and almost always free. Independent companies, individuals, legal publishers, universities, and local, state, federal, and foreign governments are providing free access to all manner of information and data using the Internet. However, the information can and does change frequently and should not be the only source of information or legal research.

For those accustomed to using WESTLAW and LEXIS for legal research, the Internet does not seem as comprehensive nor as easy to use (*see* Chapter 2, Legal Research). However, as a tool for obtaining scientific, corporate, and other kinds of information, the Internet is invaluable. There are several methods of searching available on the Internet. Two of the most widely used "search engines" are Yahoo® (http://www.yahoo.com) and Excite!® (http://www.excite.com). To begin a search with either of these tools all you need do is type in a key word or phrase. Advanced search functions are also available which help you narrow the focus of the search by using special terms and connectors which are familiar to anyone who has used WESTLAW, LEXIS, or a database program such as dBase.

Some Useful Internet Addresses

Internet Address	Description
http://www.sec.gov/edgarhp.htm	Securities and Exchange Commission
http://thomas/loc/gov/	Links to the White House, Senate, Congress, and all Federal Agencies
http://www.angelfire.com/biz/processservers/index.html	Process Servers on The Net
http://www.city.net/	Maps and information about cities and surrounding areas worldwide
http://www.irs.ustreas.gov/prod/	Internal Revenue Service
http://lcweb.loc.gov/homepage/lchp.html	Library of Congress
http://www.dowjones.com/	Dow Jones News Home Page
http://www.dbisna.com/	Dun & Bradstreet
http://www.fedex.com/	Federal Express
http://www.ncdc.noaa.gov/ushcn/ushcn.html	United States Historical Climatology Network
http://ipl.sils.umich.edu/	The Internet Public Library
http://lcweb.loc.gov/copyright/forms.html	U.S. Copyright Office Forms
http://www.scsl.state.sc.us/	State Courts & Statutes
http://www.verbatimreporters.com	Court Reporters

Both Yahoo and Excite! provide fast links to newspapers and magazines that publish on-line editions, as well as links to specialized indexes such as nationwide phone books, people and business directories, digital maps of every city in the U.S., thesaurus, dictionary, and other reference services. *See* Chapter 2, Legal Research, for information on how to properly cite an information source from the Internet.

7.034 Physical Examination

Physical examination by the legal assistant is the best form of inquiry, whether it is reading documents or inspecting the damaged home or vehicle, grazing land, or the scene of an accident. Personal observation allows automatic and reliable comprehension of related testimony, perception of related exhibits, and quick recognition of error, confusion, and mistake.

7.04 Locating Witnesses

Chapter 6, Interviewing Techniques, of this manual discusses many of the problems associated with interviewing people who may be witnesses in a given case. We did not at that time discuss the difficulty of locating the witnesses. It is advantageous to identify witnesses, locate them, and interview them in the informal discovery process of investigation, since this offers the lawyer an opportunity to determine the extent of the person's knowledge and whether it is helpful or damaging to the client's own position. The formal discovery process of deposing a witness unfortunately requires notice to the adversary counsel of the existence of the person and the possibility that his or her testimony is important to the case. It is also expensive.

The first step in locating potential witnesses is to identify those persons who are essential to obtain facts, authenticate other forms of evidence, and who can provide leads to other testimony and evidence. Any time a person is mentioned in oral or written form the investigator should at least note the name and source(s) that identify the name. Not all persons named become witnesses, but every person named becomes a potential witness. Potential witnesses are identified in many ways. Some are directly revealed by their names on official records and reports, news and media accounts, or within private documents that comprise part of the evidence in the case. Often the client, friendly witnesses, or hostile witnesses will refer to other people who they believe have knowledge of the circumstances. Crime or accident scene photographs may identify business logos or license plate numbers that can be used to trace individuals. Business and governmental organization rosters and in-house telephone rosters are also helpful in directly identifying witnesses when a person's position is known and their name is unknown.

If none of these sources works out, then inquiry must be made of persons who can reasonably be expected to be acquainted with the person. This may include all of the other witnesses previously interviewed on matters relating to the case and during which discussion they did not mention the person's name. Questions as to the identity and location of the new potential witness may bring forth the fact that the name is misspelled or mispronounced, that it is a nickname, or that it is only a diminutive of the real name. When interviewing any witness, it is a good habit to ask near the end of the examination: "Do you know anyone else who has knowledge of the events that we have been discussing?" As an interview progresses, many persons develop recall of names, descriptions, or work addresses through the process of talking about the events. Show photographs or diagrams of scenes to enhance witness memories.

After identifying various persons associated with the case, we frequently do not know where or how to locate them. This stage of investigation requires the qualities of persistence, patience, assertiveness, and an occasional dose of luck. The search commences by concentrating on any clue that leads you to the person's residence and occupation. Traditional sources of addresses include: accident and crime scene reports, local telephone directories, voters' registration roles, the city directory found in many metropolitan areas, driving license records, vehicle registration files, and electric and water utility registers. Each of these sources contain addresses. As these resources are used, be sure to consider different spellings of names, especially those received from oral testimony. Also beware of nicknames, maiden names, and misspelled names on documents. Exhibit 7-1 contains a checklist of traditional sources of addresses and telephone numbers.

In today's Information Age, the legal assistant can personally access nontraditional methods of locating prospective witnesses. Computers with modem connections are common in law offices, public libraries, educational institutions, and homes. A computer with Internet access provides several easy-to-use address directories with nationwide access and it is possible to readily program your electronic address book to automatically dial these nationwide address directories. This manual is not the forum to provide a treatise on how to use the Internet, however, legal assistants should not pass up the opportunity to learn and acquire skills using this vital research technology. Some Internet addresses that permit the user to input a name and location and retrieve the corresponding street address and existing telephone number are: Switchboard® (http://www.switchboard.com) and Bigbook® (http://www.bigbook.com). These online directories are extraordinarily useful and are the equivalent of having a white page telephone directory for the entire nation. Some of the Internet directories even provide street maps to business addresses.

EXHIBIT 7-1   Traditional Sources of Addresses and Telephone Numbers

Local telephone directories.

Local city directories.

State driver's licenses records.

Voter registration rolls.

Electric and water utility records.

Vehicle registration records.

Licensing agencies for regulated professions such as: physicians, pharmacists, private investigators, taxi drivers, land surveyors, certified shorthand reporters, private guard services, lobbyists, real estate brokers, and mortgage brokers.

Labor unions and union hiring halls.

Professional associations, such as engineering societies, bar associations, legal assistant associations, or academic honor groups.

Avocational groups such as: American Bowling Congress, the Women's International Bowling Congress, the Federal Aviation Administration for pilots, state or national golfing associations.

College alumni groups or booster clubs.

In addition to the Internet, computer modems provide direct gateways to very sophisticated investigative programs. For example, WESTLAW continually updates its services and it currently offers an investigative research program via InfoAmerica®. InfoAmerica can also provide address searches using surnames and social security numbers. There are several investigative database providers on the market who will permit you to directly link into their computers for nominal fees. These companies are sometimes regional and the number of providers is growing quickly. To find an investigative database provider best suited for your needs, scan legal periodicals for advertisements pertaining to investigative research.

Armed with an initial address or telephone number, the investigator attempts to make contact with the witness. If the obtained address is not a current one, the possibility always exists of seeking the assistance of the post office for a forwarding address. The U.S. Postal Service provides forwarding address data when requested in writing. (*See* Exhibit 7-2.) However, the Postal Service is required only to forward mail to new addresses for one year only. Neighbors and co-workers may also be able to provide clues as to the location of witnesses that have moved or transferred out of the area. Once an accurate name and at least one address for the witness is obtained, the credit bureau of the community may provide a reliable source of identifying past and present addresses. Under current laws regarding fair credit reporting, the credit bureau may have to reveal the legal assistant's interest to the individual, but that is not a particular concern in most cases. Motor vehicle and vehicle operator license bureaus often can furnish reliable data directly or through private services at nominal cost. If the residence cannot be determined, the legal assistant must work through the potential witness's occupation, and the problem becomes much more complex. If the occupation can be linked to a particular company, it sometimes is possible to obtain the address from the personnel department of that company. However, this possibility is diminishing with the right-to-privacy laws inhibiting the release of information. A next to last resort is to contact others with the same last name listed in local telephone books. It is possible they are related to the witness being sought. And lastly, if the legal assistant does not have the time or ability to locate witnesses or if all direct investigation fails, there are private investigation firms that specialize in "skip-tracing." When a witness is critical to the case, the cost to hire an outside investigator is reasonable.

EXHIBIT 7-2   U.S. Postal Service Request for Forwarding Address Information

_____

(DATE)

Postmaster
(Local Post Office)

Dear Sir or Madam:

In accord with the Freedom of Information Act, please provide me with the last known change of address for the following person:

       Name:
       Street Address:
       City, State, Zip:

Enclosed is a check in the amount of $1.00 for payment of the requested change of address. Please send the requested address to:

              Max A. Million
              Binotz & Berry, P.A.
              111 Maple Ave.
              New South, FL 32222

                        Very truly,

                        Max A. Million, CLA
                        Legal Assistant to James Beny, Esq.

_____

7.041 Experts

Investigations of areas beyond the expertise or personal experience of the legal team may require consultation with an expert witness.

a. Identify the need for expert help. Some cases require help to identify the theory of liability, to distinguish evidentiary facts, to prove some of the evidence involved in the case, or to refute the testimony of expert witnesses on the opposing side. Medical malpractice, products liability, and vehicle accidents, are but a few of the types of cases requiring insight into the standards of medical care, design and manufacturing practices, the maintenance principles for vehicles, etc. Surgeons, engineers, physicists, industrial hygienists, economists, and vocational placement counselors are among the experts the legal assistant must consult to establish a framework from which the attorney may deduce the existence of a desirable and productive course of legal action. Later on, damages, compensation, or recourse, for example, may compel the use of other experts to provide insight into the fairness of proposed settlements or to prove those elements to a judge or jury.

b. Expert witness qualifications. Expert witnesses need to be authorities in their particular field, effective communicators, and credible. Although expert witness opinions often influence settlement of cases prior to trial, an expert in a particular discipline should be selected with the intention of using him or her in trial. Accordingly, the expert should speak clearly and comfortably in front of an audience, and be able to present an image of a confident manner without being overbearing or pedantic. Gauges of credibility include: prior testimony on the subject, publications of articles or textbooks, educational background, training, and length of time as a practitioner in the subject field of expertise.

c. Locating experts. Law firms often have a list of experts, some for consultation and some for both consultation and use as witnesses. Not all experts are suitable for both purposes, and not all expert witnesses are the most knowledgeable people in their field. When seeking an expert's information, the best expert available should be obtained since the expert will contribute to the attorney's and the legal assistant's understanding of the technical material around which the factual issues revolve. If the legal assistant must locate an expert without the benefit of an office expert file or recommendations from a knowledgeable source, consider the following:

1. The *Lawyers Desk Reference* lists expert firms and individuals by their specialty and basic services offered (analysis, examination, exhibit preparation, testimony, and so on), together with addresses and phone numbers.

2. Research publications or home offices of attorney associations and specialty groups, State Bar Associations, Defense Research Institute, American Trial Lawyers Association, and American Board of Trial Attorneys are but a very small sampling of organizations that may have expert witness information files or listings.

3. There are numerous for-profit organizations which serve as clearinghouses for experts. TASA (Technical Advisory Service for Attorneys) is an example of this type of service. The Internet has become an increasingly valuable source for locating authorities and witnesses. Generally, a keyword search of "expert witness" or Internet research in the many legal web sites will result in useful leads.

4. Experts frequently are authors and simply reviewing professional journal articles and textbooks in the area of expertise will yield an author's name and business address of pertinent experts. Public libraries have reference sections, sometimes available by appointment only, where trade or specialty publications can be perused.

5. Review jury verdict publications or online services to identify experts used in particular cases. For example, WESTLAW offers searchable jury verdicts in the "LRP" database. If the legal assistant were to conduct a WESTLAW search using the terms " 'automobile accident' & Maryland," the result would identify experts involved a sampling of Maryland state auto accident cases. LEXIS-NEXIS also offers an expert witness database.

6. Trade libraries are fertile sources for locating knowledgeable authors. Utility companies, oil companies, merchandisers, contractors, and others often have professional associations or societies that maintain libraries for their members and may allow nonmembers access to these resources.

7. Professional, academic, trade, and industry associations and societies maintain membership lists that may serve as a starting point in seeking comments on the reputation of their individual members, a beginning in establishing the qualifications of an expert. The legal assistant can start the inquiry by contacting the membership secretary or by seeking the "best known" member in that organization.

8. Search courthouse case files for similar cases and identify which expert witnesses may have been used in local actions. When reviewing the case files, you may even be able to find a deposition of the named experts.

9. Word of mouth can reveal not only the identity of an expert, but also the referring person may have developed an information file on the expert which includes a curriculum vitae and transcripts of prior testimony.

d. When the decision has been made to retain an expert and the initial verbal contact has been made, an engagement letter should be prepared. The letter should contain the following elements: confirm the expert's fee schedule, describe the nature of the case, define the effort required from the expert, state applicable deadlines, state whether a written report is required, and define the scope of the report. At some point in the working relationship, material and evidence may be provided to your expert. WARNING: Any document or evidence provided to expert witnesses may be discoverable by the opposing party. Before providing confidential, privileged, or sensitive documents or evidence, check with the attorney first. It is good practice to send all material to experts under cover letter, with a complete description of the material provided.

7.05　Obtaining and Preserving Evidence

Evidence is that testimony or material that proves, or tends to prove, a specific fact. It may be testimonial in the form of the personal recollections of a person with firsthand knowledge of the matter; it may be documentary in the form of letters, notes, memoranda, tape recordings, photographs, movie strips, videotape, microfilm, or other recorded and retrievable information.

Evidence may be physical, such as a broken mechanical part, skid marks on the ground, an appliance that did not work correctly or failed to work at all, or the tools or devices used to commit the offense that is the subject of the action.

Evidence also may be demonstrative. Demonstrative evidence includes sketches, diagrams, maps, models, reconstruction, tests, or pieces of equipment identical to the item involved in the case.

7.051　Identification

Identifying potential evidence is perhaps the most difficult duty of the investigator. An investigator at an accident scene works under certain time constraints before the cleanup activity begins, and there is always a substantial amount of confusion regarding the circumstances of the event as well as the number and variety of people interested in the matter. Police, fire department, and public safety personnel all have responsibilities in any accident involving major property damage or injury to life.

The first step most investigators follow at an accident scene is to preserve that scene as best they can through immediate photography and/or sketches. This frequently requires a quick orientation sketch on which a diagram of the camera angles and distances is plotted. One technique for creating good proportionate sketches is to carry a quad-ruled tracing paper pad. After a basic sketch with the major geographic features (whether of an intersection or a room) is made, it is torn off the pad and slipped beneath the next sheet. Retrace the major features and add the specific data desired for that sketch. One sketch may be the photo reference sketch; another might be the positions of the vehicles (if it is a traffic collision); and a third may be a clear, basic sketch with the data supplied by each percipient witness. That data might include the location of the witness, the first point at which the witness saw each vehicle, and the locations of other vehicles or witnesses. These witness sketches can be amplified by adding trees, shrubs, buildings, or parked vehicles and supplemented by the investigator standing where the witness was to determine whether the story of the witness is physically possible. A composite sketch can be used to locate each witness graphically.

The diagram may be used to record such things as skid marks, significant buildings, vegetation, safety control devices, and the relationships of the objects involved in the incident. At an explosion scene, for instance, where a gas heater is considered to be the origin of the explosion, a photograph including both the thermostat and heater in one picture is desirable, if possible. If not, a sketch must be used to carefully reconstruct that relationship, keying the multiple photographs together with the sketch.

At accident scenes involving automobiles, the locations of the roadways, traffic control devices, visual obstructions (trees, fences, bridges, parked cars), skid marks, point of impact, and positions at rest of the involved vehicles are essential. While photographs can do this to a certain extent, detailed sketches are also necessary. In extremely important cases, these details should be surveyed by a qualified surveyor to ensure the accuracy and later admissibility of the sketch at trial.

Unfortunately, the investigator is rarely able to get to the accident scene before the vehicles are removed. The investigating police department usually makes a diagram of the accident scene, which is attached to the police accident report. Such a report and diagram can be obtained from the police department and will assist the investigator in creating additional sketches. Police departments also sometimes prepare accident reconstruction reports and diagrams that can be excellent resources for scale drawings.

7.052 Physical Evidence

Every time an object is identified as potential evidence, the investigator faces the problems of how to: (1) acquire, preserve, and identify it for future reference and retrieval for introduction at trial; and (2) create the foundation for its admissibility. In many cases, the investigator does not have legal title to the evidence he or she wishes to take into custody. Frequently, the ownership of the item is in question, and the propriety of taking custody calls the investigator's judgment to the test. In most cases of doubt, take custody of the documents, objects, or things and leave a receipt indicating the investigator's name and identity and the means by which people can contact the investigator if they wish to exert their ownership rights in the matter. Often police, fire, or safety investigators will be on the scene, and notification can be left with them if they allow the investigator to take possession of the item.

7.053 Documents

Documents are one of the most valuable tools in an attorney's case. How the documents are acquired is just as important as their safeguarding, and both must be preserved by the investigator.

The investigator must be careful to insure that each step of locating and acquiring documents is carefully documented to create a foundation for the attorney's later use. The "best evidence rule" as set forth in the Federal Rules of Evidence ("FRE") requires the original of a given document to be offered in evidence (FRE 1002). Only when the original cannot be located may copies be substituted (FRE 1004). However, sometimes copies may be admissible under exceptions to the "hearsay rules" (FRE 803). Neither the legal assistant nor the investigator can make assumptions as to the document's admissibility, or expect the attorney to rely on documents collected without some foundation. Foundation can be established by the answers to such questions as: Where was the document located? Who was the custodian? Why was the document in the file? If a copy, is it a notarized or certified copy? Where is the original? Where is a duplicate original? Who might have one?

The lawyer will also need the legal assistant's opinion of what evidentiary fact the document establishes. Perhaps in a contract case, it represents a contemporaneous memorial of the requisite "meeting of the minds" or acknowledges the tender of the consideration, or perhaps it is persuasive that the defendant's defense of "mistake of material fact" was not a mistake at all but a well-understood gamble. In a matter in probate, the document might represent support for a contention that the decedent had made a true gift *inter vivos* that should allow an asset to be exempted from the estate.

Each document in a case can be more than informational if the legal assistant continually seeks to locate and preserve the documents that, with proper foundation, constitute evidentiary facts proving or disproving the essential elements of the case, corroborate or refute testimonial evidence, or support or refute the credibility of the witnesses. The foundation may be established easily at the time the document is found by any of several methods:

1. In public records, the easiest is to obtain certified copies.
2. Records of private firms may be obtained with a short statement of the custodian identifying the document, the file, the firm, and the custodian with a notarization of the statement and document by a notary public.
3. Records of the client should be fully identified by file, location, and the identity of the person who will testify as to how, why, and where the document was kept.
4. Where certification or notarization is impossible, obtain full details of the document—identity, custodian, file identity, and purpose—for formal discovery proceeding.

Documents pose a special identification and storage problem for the investigator. They are most valuable to the attorney in their unaltered state yet the investigator usually must describe the document, provide a foundation for it's use, and attach it to a report. The FBI system of marking original documents with alpha-numeric or "bates" stamped numbers, or initialing the document with the date received and file number, is not considered by courts as an "alternation" of the original document. As long as the substance of the original document is not altered, some form of identification is allowed.

When the document is a letter, written memorandum, or pamphlet, many investigators mark the document "EXHIBIT" or "ATTACHMENT" and staple it to the report. Convenient? Yes!, but very poor technique, since the attorney now has an altered document, although not substantively, and the convenient title "EXHIBIT" or "ATTACHMENT" may have to be explained in the future. A better technique is to place the document in a transparent envelope (or even an opaque paper one) and apply the "EXHIBIT" or "ATTACHMENT" label to the envelope, together with a thorough description of the document (date, document type, author, addressee, topic or title, number of pages, and any attachments), as well as a short statement of the source of the document, the custodian, and the relevance of the document to the case. Alternatively, a "face sheet" can carry this information. A photocopy of the document can be used as a "work copy" during preparation of the case. Underlining, marginal annotation, or writing on the document cannot be allowed to happen to the original document (whether the true original, a duplicate true copy, or a photocopy). Evidence should be preserved in the discovered state. If a copy is made, it should be marked as a copy, preferably with a marginal label "Copy of a document in the file X vs. X." This avoids the problem of creating yet another piece of evidence that could confuse the future admissibility of the original document at the trial. Other forms of documents, such as movie films, tape recordings, even photographs are not quite so susceptible to contamination as paper documents; however, safeguards should be considered for any item that may become evidence at trial.

7.054 Control and Retrieval

Investigators need to properly manage physical evidence to ensure its identification and legal status. Attorneys and the court will require assurance that an object is what it is purported to be. A broken bolt, for example, has no significance in the courtroom unless it can be positively linked to a cause of action.

When the investigator takes evidence into custody, its later identification can be recreated by recording the "five Ws": WHO, WHAT, WHY, WHEN, and WHERE. Establish the name(s) of WHO takes custody of the evidence. Describe WHAT the evidence represents. Note WHY the evidence is obtained. Register WHEN the evidence is taken into custody, and state WHERE the evidence will be stored or located for later retrieval.

Record these five essential information elements either in writing, with a handheld tape recorder, or by video camera. If handling very large amounts of physical evidence or timeliness is a factor in the gathering process, use the faster means of recording—audio or video. In addition to recording facts pertaining to the material, objects may require minor but unique marking to allow absolute and unequivocal identification of that particular object as being the one taken into custody on the date and at the time involved. A forensic investigator kit commonly includes copper wire and lead seals with a sealing tool. Wire is passed around an object, then through the seal. The sealing tool squeezes the seal tightly around the wire and can impress designs, a logo, or numbers on the soft lead that can be recorded for later identification. For larger objects, nylon cable-ties can be obtained in a range of sizes. Some objects are too large or unsuitable for such seals, and a unique marking can be engraved or written on the object; initials and the date are best. Small objects can be placed inside plastic bags or envelopes and sealed with tape on which the date and initials can be written using laundry marker pens.

Any system may be used, so long as it provides a means of distinguishing that one object from all others similar to it and it is a credible basis for testifying that the object is the one collected as evidence on a given date. From the time that object is identified as potential evidence, its custody must be substantiated by a document trail showing every transfer of custody from the point of the incident or event to the trial. That chain is based on the investigator or legal assistant creating that first step in a proper, ethical, and careful manner and recording each subsequent transfer in detail. When physical evidence has been gathered, it is good practice to create a computer database or written log for incorporation in the case file.

Finally, investigators should occasionally physically check on the status of physical evidence that has been placed in storage or entrusted to the custody of others. The week before trial is a poor time to discover that important evidence has been lost or deteriorated into useless form.

7.055 Storage

Once the document or object is in custody, it cannot simply be placed in a file cabinet in an uncontrolled environment where anyone can obtain access to it, remove it, alter it, or damage it. Therefore, the investigator or the attorney must provide a safe and controlled environment within which the object is stored. Each event, between the time of taking custody and its introduction to trial, where people wish to examine the object should be recorded in detail to include the date and time, the person authorizing the particular examination or movement, the person benefitting from such activity or movement, the duration, and the return of the object to the place of storage. Anyone taking possession of the object must sign for it with a statement that it will be safeguarded and returned or preserved in the exact same condition. Polaroid photos may be appropriate for memorializing the transfer. A suitable form for controlling evidence is shown in Exhibit 7-3.

EXHIBIT 7-3   Example of an Evidence Log

Case:		Event:	
Description of Evidence:	Date Acquired:	Acquired by:	How Acquired:
	Identifying Marks:	Marked by:	Date Marked:
Storage Location:	Custodian:		Date:
Released To:	Date/Purpose:		

7.056 Testing and Examination

Often, evidence connected with an event over which litigation is to transpire must be tested, examined, or disassembled to validate it as evidence. Sometimes the examination, disassembly, or test will damage or destroy the object. If this situation arises, the attorney will ensure that the adversary and all other parties to the action have an opportunity to have representatives present.

The investigator generally is charged with taking custody of the item, removing it to the place of examination, and documenting the steps of the examination. The purpose of the examination and the anticipated method should be planned, and the scenario described and noticed in timely fashion to all parties of the action to allow them or their experts to participate or observe the necessary examination. The whole process may be recorded through the use of still photographs, movies, or videotape. The investigator records the presence of all witnesses, including their full identification and their association with their respective parties in the matter. All experts should be fully identified as to name, address, specialty, and employer. Remember, any examination, testing, or disassembly of the item that destroys or changes the physical characteristics of the item and is not accomplished with the knowledge, consent, and participation of all of the parties may prevent the use of any developed information at trial.

7.06 Surveillance and Activity Checks

Occasionally, there will be a need to verify the activities of certain parties to a lawsuit. This type of investigation is usually done when plaintiffs or claimants are alleging disabilities that either preclude them from certain activities or limit abilities to perform particular tasks.

Surveillance should be conducted by trained inve equipment to properly perform this type of investigation. Sometimes the alleged disabled party can be caught working around the yard or involved in sporting activities with little or no sign of physical limitations. A serious limp that was quite obvious in the doctor's office sometimes can miraculously disappear outside. Videotaped proof of these activities can be later used in the courtroom to raise questions of truthfulness in regard to the alleged disabilities. However, this kind of investigation may be expensive and may yield no useful information. Therefore, it is vital that a reliable, knowledgeable, and qualified investigator be obtained. Qualifications you should look for are:

a. Licensed and bonded—however, not all states require investigator's to be licensed or bonded.
b. Ask for a C.V. *(Curriculum Vitae)* or resume.
c. References—ask for recent job contacts; anyone can look good on paper.
d. Ask if the investigator ever has testified in court and if the investigator ever has been qualified as an expert.
e. Appearance and demeanor—your investigator may have to appear in court on your behalf and you want the jury to like the investigator, believe the investigator, and feel that the investigator is honest and has integrity.
f. Association affiliation—many investigators belong to state affiliations; this can show a dedication to the career and a willingness to keep up-to-date on new developments.
g. Ask local law enforcement—investigators may have to register with local law enforcement and, in some states, the investigator has to have the endorsement of both the sheriff and prosecutor in their principal residence county with their initial application and with renewals. Local law enforcement may also know if there have been any complaints made by citizens on the investigator and the way they were handled or questioned.
h. Check with the governmental agency that issued the investigative license. Not only will you find out if the investigator is truly licensed, but since these agencies issue the license, they can pull the license as well. Also, this agency may have information regarding the investigator that could be obtained under the Freedom of Information Act.

Obtaining an investigator is not just a matter of looking under "P.I." in the yellow pages; you want a reputable investigator that will do the job professionally.

Divorce and child custody disputes may require "domestic" surveillance. In states where grounds for divorce are required, surveillance may be used to establish the needed evidence to determine certain grounds, such as adultery. Surveillance in child custody cases may yield helpful evidence regarding the fitness of the adverse parent.

Activity checks are usually conducted by talking with neighbors or other persons who make frequent observations of the plaintiff or claimant. Though these checks may provide helpful information, they will often alert the plaintiff or claimant that an investigation is being conducted. For this reason, activity checks should be done as the last, or later part, of the investigation.

7.07 Demonstrative Evidence

Demonstrative evidence in the form of sketches, drawings, or surveys created as a means of preserving transitory physical evidence in retrievable form will require a certain amount of documentation for use at future times. The presence of a scale and the date and the name of the person who rendered the drawing is essential. The means and method of making the measurement represented in the drawing will be subject to question and must be supported by the proper foundation. The date of the examination and measurements is essential, particularly if it is different from the date of the event in question. It is helpful to support these drawings with photographs of the same area.

Demonstrative evidence that is a model, a replica, a reconstruction, or an exact duplicate of the object involved in the case requires the same establishment of the dates, times, scale, methods of calculation, sizes, and measurements. The accuracy of the representation probably still will be subject to questioning. Many of these demonstrative evidence procedures are very expensive and obviously should be discussed with, and authorized by, the attorney before they are undertaken.

7.071 Sketches and Drawings

Certain injury litigation cases and regulatory agency actions can benefit from the use of renderings by artists. Medical illustrators are talented at clarifying what otherwise might be very difficult explanations of X-rays (even if produced as positives) by converting them into easily understood colored drawings at relatively little cost. If a general medical illustration is all that is desired, many programs are now available on CD-ROM which allow the user to print standard depictions of human anatomy and disease. Graphic illustrators can show a proposed development or project in simplified (even idealized) form to assist the presentation for permits, zoning actions, and so forth.

7.072 Photography

Photography is both a blessing and a curse in litigation. It is a truism that almost any photograph related to an event is potentially admissible at trial. The opposite side of the coin is that almost any photograph may be subject to argument over its admissibility. The judgment of the person taking the photograph and his or her expertise are always subject to question. The average investigator or legal assistant who chooses to take his or her own pictures rather than to employ professional photographers must be prepared to defend the representations in the photographs. For this reason, many investigators have resorted to snapshots taken with simple cameras that are nonadjustable, or instant cameras. If the investigator is an expert, he or she understands that the use of an adjustable lens camera that allows shooting wide-angle, normal-angle, and telephoto views of the same scene alters perspective as focal length changes. In order to ensure that the investigator defend the photographic representation, he or she should employ some form of photo log. For every photograph taken, the focal length, f-stop, film speed, film type, filters, and whether or not artificial lighting equipment was used should be recorded. If possible, each photograph should be related to a sketch indicating the location of the camera and the direction it was pointed to get the view in the photograph. (*See* Exhibit 7-4.)

EXHIBIT 7-4   Example of Photo Log

Case:			Photographer:			
Camera/Equipment Used:						
#	Date	Time	Place	Details of shot	Notes	3

The use of filters is arguable at best and difficult to explain to a jury. At worst, the photograph will be excluded. If filters are used, an unfiltered shot of the same view should be made. A great deal of judgment must be exercised by the investigator or legal assistant in deciding whether or not to shoot photographs.

Obviously, if the client is a plaintiff and the accident investigation involves an automobile collision with injury, photographs of the amount of blood spilled in the vehicles may be desirable. If the client is a defendant, gory photographs can be no help at all. It is not enough to take them and destroy them because then the photographs and the destruction must be explained. The skilled legal assistant considers the evidentiary value of each photograph he or she intends to take—both its benefits and its detriments—and then decides whether the benefits outweigh the detriments.

Counsel for plaintiffs often find photographs of bodily injuries very early in the incident are shockingly persuasive to the jury to demonstrate the obvious pain and suffering caused by the injury. It is important to consider the type of camera and film used in making these photographs. For instance, a black-and-white photograph of a person showing massive bruises of an extremely dark nature may be the result of the use of film specially sensitive to the color red and generating a higher contrast than otherwise may be present. Similarly, color photographic film can show red, blue, or green very strongly, depending on the representation desired by the person taking the photograph.

The use of lighting will often have an effect on the photograph. Daylight provides one form of reflected light accepted, while incandescent light tends to throw a warmer red-toned color on the same object. Fluorescent light tends to provide more yellow-green, and flashbulbs, depending on their size and nature, affect the color quality of the image produced. Infrared film can be highly informational in cases involving vegetation growth, decline, and death or in heat gain and loss disputes.

When the investigation begins some time after the incident, a wide variety of sources of photographs should be explored. The police often take photographs, as do fire departments, coroner's officers, newspapers, wire services, and freelance photographers. The more important, dramatic, and long-term incident produces a veritable flood of photographs to which the legal assistant can gain access. Occasionally, a neighborhood canvass can locate snapshots of the immediate area.

It is always possible, and often desirable, to employ a professional photographer to take selected photographs for specific purposes. They are relatively expensive, but professionals can usually qualify their photos for introduction as evidence. Be specific in the request for the number, sizes, type of film, and views desired. Every photograph should benefit the case or the understanding of the jury.

Do not ignore the possibilities of overhead views obtained through aerial photos from a wide variety of sources. The U.S. Coast and Geologic Survey has a tremendous collection of recent and historical aerial photos in different scales. The U.S. Department of Agriculture, too, uses aerials in its studies. Forestry departments, state and federal highway projects or departments, city and county public works, and planning departments turn more and more to aerial photographs for planning, zoning, and traffic study work. Many have aerial photographs of diverse locations. Any area subject to land management or reclamation probably has been photo-mapped by the U.S. Department of the Interior. These governmental sources generally provide fine, full-frame prints at nominal cost but with a bureaucratic time delay problem. Using private aerial photograph sources often permits enlargements of all of a negative or only a portion, at the lawyer's election. The cost is a little greater for the custom work but is well worth it. Individually, photographs from an upper-story window or rooftop can be helpful. A photograph from a chartered airplane may be desirable. It is difficult for these photographs to be used to scale, however, and that is one of the major benefits of professional aerial photographs—the exact determination of scale.

7.073 Video

The video camera is quickly becoming a very valuable investigative tool. It is useful in illustrating accident scenes, roadway views taken from a vehicle traveling on the roadway, statements of witnesses, depositions of expert witnesses not available to testify at trial, and "day-in-the-life" videos of disabled plaintiffs. Accident-scene videos should adhere to the same standards required of regular photographs. When illustrating roadway views, the camera operator should be prepared to testify about the position of the camera and the general speed of the vehicle while the recording was being done.

"Day-in-the-life" videos should be recorded in the natural environment where the disabled plaintiff can illustrate daily routines. The video should, in a discrete manner, show the plaintiff in general daily routines, such as getting out of bed in the morning, taking care of personal hygiene, preparing and eating meals, and doing other chores. These videotaping sessions should not be rehearsed. Opposing counsel should generally be given notice that such videotaping will be done. These "day-in-the-life" videos can be very instrumental in representing to a jury the plaintiff's life in terms of pain and suffering and his or her general loss of enjoyment of life. While the scenes may be unpleasant, so are the plaintiff's injuries.

Although a legal assistant investigator may be familiar with the operation and functions of camcorders and video cameras, indispensable photographic evidence is generally best preserved by professional videographers. Professionally trained videographers can, under the guidance and direction of legal assistants, determine the cinematic angles, lighting, and distance to most effectively depict the intended video impression. Additionally, videographers typically possess sophisticated equipment which stabilizes their camera and reduce jerking, vibrating scenes. A videographer also is skilled in the art of accurately capturing sounds and dialogue which enhances the video record. The cost of a videographer is well worth the investment for vital evidence.

7.08 Preserving Digital, Electronic, and Photographic Documents and Objects

As discussed throughout this chapter, investigative evidence comes in many forms. Audio evidence may be created in several cassette sizes, on tape reels, on CD-ROM, or on video cassettes. With the recent proliferation of software and audio computer files, it is even possible that an investigator will store audio evidence on computer floppy disks. A quick search of the Internet reveals numerous downloadable audio files and audio file "readers." Photographic evidence also comes in numerous formats: video tapes of various sizes, photographs, undeveloped film, pictures from news articles, and computer graphic files. Electronic and digital data may be obtained in computer disk or CD-ROM form.

The preservation of digital, electronic, and photographic evidence is a challenge requiring foresight and planning. Some forms of this type of evidence is sensitive to environmental factors. All of the aforementioned evidence is susceptible to physical hazards such as crushing, tearing, or damage from being carelessly placed into case files. Computer disks and audio tapes are prone to destruction from exposure to magnetic fields or fluid spills. Excessive heat may warp video tapes or CD-ROM disks.

A special storage facility for such recorded evidence should be maintained, along with a system to identify the evidence for later use. A log for digital, electronic, and photographic evidence typically would include: an evidence identification number, a description of the evidence, a cross-reference to the case file, and a suspense date to dispose of the evidence following resolution of the case. An evidence identification number might consist of the last two digits of the year, the initials of the investigator, and the number of the tape (an increasing sequential series) to be affixed to the tape. (*See* Exhibit 7-5.) If the evidence log is maintained on a computer database or word processing program, it would improve the retrieval capabilities or pertinent items.

EXHIBIT 7-5 Log for Digital, Electronic, and Photographic Evidence

ID No.	Destruct Date	Case Name	Description of Evidence
97001	01/05/99	Jones v Martin	Microcassette recording of interview with Bob Marley.
97001	01/05/99	Jones v Martin	Microcassette recording of interview with Sarah Beechnut.
97003	01/05/99	Jones v Martin	Photographic negatives of Marvin Jones's early childhood.
97004	09/25/02	Niles v Mitchie	3.5† diskette of Mitchie Inc. quality assurance inspections during 1995 for the Whupmobile production line.

7.09 Discovery through Investigation

The informal discovery (investigation) by the legal assistant or the investigator is primarily to assist the attorney in developing the lines of inquiry that should be followed in formal discovery, and in evaluating the responses of the adversary to the questions and motions posed in the formal discovery actions.

Remember, no item of evidentiary fact will stand alone at trial. Each fact needs corroboration, and one of the best ways of corroborating a fact is to ask questions of the adversary under oath. Whether this is done through interrogatories, requests for admission, or in depositions is the choice of the attorney. Each is effective. Investigation provides the basis for specific and explicit questions to be posed to the adversary. It changes interrogatories from broadbased, shotgun, or generalized questions to specific, detailed, and pointed inquiries of specific interest.

Further, the investigation serves as a fountain of knowledge to assist the attorney in creating the deposition plan for any potential deponent. Statements taken of adversary witnesses often can be used in preparing the attorney to generate sworn testimony and depositions that might otherwise be overlooked. They will reveal motivation, relationships, background, and post-incident activities of intense interest to the attorney. The rule is to know as much about the witness and what he or she is going to say, before the questions, as it is possible to know. The use of testimonial statements, physical evidence, and photographs are essential to proper preparation of the attorney for the confrontation in the deposition procedure.

Bibliography

Buchanan, John C. and Bos, Carole D., *How to Use Video in Litigation: A Guide to Technology, Strategies, and Techniques*. Englewood Cliffs, NJ: Prentice-Hall, 1986.

Dudnik, Robert M., *Anatomy of a Personal Injury Lawsuit*. 2nd ed. Washington, DC: Association of Trial Lawyers of America, Education Fund, 1981.

Kirk, Paul L. And Thornton, John I., *Crime Investigation*. NY: Wiley, 1985.

Magarick, Pat, *Casualty Investigation Checklists*. 3rd ed. NY: Clark Boardman Co. Ltd., 1985.

Philo, Harry M., *Lawyers Desk Reference*. 7th ed. Rochester, NY: Lawyers Cooperative Publishing Co., 1987.

Criminal Justice, 12 ABA Journal 1 (Spring 1997).

Federal Civil Judicial Procedure and Rules. St. Paul: West, 1996.

Federal Rules of Criminal Procedures. St. Paul: West, 1996.

"Legal Research in the Information Superhighway." Legal Assistant Today (March/April 1997).

Legal Secretary Federal Litigation. 4th ed. Costa Mesa, CA: James Publishing, 1996.

1997 Wiley Expert Witness Update: New Developments in Personal Injury Litigation. John Wiley & Sons, Inc., 1997.

8

Pretrial Litigation Skills

8.00 Introduction

Litigation is the focal point of our legal system. Regardless of area of practice, attorneys are either working to prepare a legal dispute for trial or to avoid a dispute that could lead to suit, malpractice, or otherwise. The legal assistant must have a basic working knowledge of the litigation process, whether specializing in litigation or not. This chapter explores legal assistant duties in suit preparation and discovery practice.

The duties a litigation legal assistant perform vary widely, such as interviewing clients and witnesses, performing investigation such as searching public records and locating potential documentary evidence, performing legal research, and drafting pleadings and discovery documents. These tasks require extensive training and practice, along with solid written and verbal communication skills. A legal assistant with expertise in these areas is invaluable. Attention to detail, critical analysis of statutes and court opinions, and superior written communication skills are essential. While many pleadings, such as notices, are fairly simple and routine, others require creativity, as well as considerable familiarity with substantive and procedural law.

A legal assistant in an active trial practice makes substantial contributions in the area of discovery. All discovery requires a manager to oversee its organization, to systematize it, and to monitor its implementation. The legal assistant may draft interrogatories and other discovery requests, assist clients in preparing responses to discovery requests from opposing parties, prepare summaries and digests of discovery documents as the case progresses, and perform other tasks as delegated by the supervising attorney. Some legal assistants routinely attend depositions, although they are generally prohibited from asking questions during a deposition. Nevertheless, the legal assistant plays a valuable role in developing outlines of questions to be used at the deposition, taking notes and keeping track of exhibits during the deposition, and generally being another set of eyes and ears for the attorney.

As the trial date approaches, the legal assistant attends to crucial details, such as keeping track of witnesses, having subpoenas issued, and organizing the trial notebook. At trial, the legal assistant keeps track of exhibits, take notes, and performs other tasks delegated by the attorney.

Generally speaking, legal assistants cannot represent clients at court. However, they may represent clients before an administrative agency if the rules governing that particular agency permit nonlawyer representation. Assuming that nonlawyer representation is permitted and that both the attorney-employer and the client consent, it is critical that the legal assistant in this situation master the necessary advocacy skills and have a strong working knowledge of the substantive and procedural law. Many attorneys are reluctant to allow any nonlawyer to represent their clients in any setting. This is not a reflection on the legal assistant's capabilities so much as it is a reflection of the attorney's commitment to provide personal representation to clients.

8.01   The Advocacy System and the Legal Assistant

Clients, as consumers of legal services, are driving the legal market to become more competitive, just as in the business world. Low and moderate income families cannot afford to pay high prices for legal services and often must resort to poorly funded public assistance programs. More attorneys now recognize their moral duty to serve all phases of society and seek to deliver those legal services more efficiently. As clients become more knowledgeable of the value of legal assistants, they are seeking out firms who utilize highly educated, trained, and credentialed legal assistants. Terms such as cost-effective and cost-benefit analyses appear frequently in corporate memoranda. Competition for clients, particularly corporate clients, is fierce. Law firms must streamline procedures and computerize operations if they are to compete in today's world.

Many tasks previously performed solely by attorneys are now delegated to legal assistants. Discovery is one of these areas that has become more encompassing. Attorneys are becoming more skillful in identifying possible sources of evidence and information. The skilled legal assistant who accumulates, analyzes, collates and cross-indexes factual information, and drafts discovery requests ranging from the simple to the complex increases firm productivity. Firms not using legal assistants are at a serious disadvantage. Without legal assistants the attorney is forced to devote a higher percentage of time to factual matters in the case, while the adversary, reinforced by legal assistants, can spend more time on the law, tactics, and strategy of trial.

As every new case is commenced, the legal assistant should consult with the attorney and review the substantive law and court procedures and practices. Of course, this review should be incorporated into the legal assistant's ongoing continuing education habits. This ensures the legal assistant's place as an effective litigation team member. It further allows the legal assistant to anticipate the needs of the case, specifically the time elements, forms requirements, and policies that will affect its outcome.

The beneficiaries of the legal assistant's work are simultaneously the client, the attorney, and the legal system as a whole. The legal assistant, by performing many tasks formerly performed by the lawyer, accelerates the pace of discovery, leading to the ultimate resolution of the case in a more timely manner. The legal assistant improves the attorney's perception of the factual information developed in discovery by organizing and digesting it into compact summaries that are cross-referenced to exhibits. The attorney then applies the result to produce cogent, concise, and persuasive presentations. It allows thoughtful consideration and evaluation of the facts, law, timing, and suitability of settlement, along with evaluation and selection of the settlement options.

8.02   Specific Litigation Skills

Clearly, the benefits an attorney gains from utilizing a legal assistant increase as the legal assistant acquires more skill, knowledge of legal procedures, exposure to different situations, and awareness of the techniques and tactics preferred by the supervising attorney. Those skills include drafting complaints, subsequent pleadings, motions and related documents, discovery requests and responses, performing legal research and investigation, analyzing discovery responses from adversary parties, conducting interviews, and managing the information accumulated in the case file. Each of these activities enhances the value of the legal assistant to the attorney and clients.

As a case progresses, facts may develop that clearly indicate the case should not be tried, either from a plaintiff's or a defendant's point of view. The legal assistant, by carefully monitoring the factual development through discovery efforts, is in a unique position to identify such a situation, to refer it to the attorney, and to assist in a quick resolution of the dispute.

8.03   Preliminary Considerations in Litigation

Long before the pleadings are prepared and filed, the attorney and the litigation team must make some basic decisions about the case that will have long-reaching effects. During, or very shortly after the client's first interview, the facts of the case must be analyzed to determine whether the client has a valid cause of action. The legal theories and remedies that may be available to resolve the client's claim must be explored, as well as potential defenses that may be raised by the opposing party. A preliminary calculation of the damages or other relief to which the client may be entitled must be examined.

The attorney must develop the legal theories that will provide the framework for all that follows, from drafting the complaint through the trial itself. Experienced trial attorneys use checklists of the requirements for each legal theory of recovery and for each defense that may be used to avoid overlooking important details. As each requirement is drafted into the complaint or presented at trial, it is checked off the list to be certain that nothing is forgotten. For each element on the checklist, supporting facts must be outlined, along with all sources that prove the fact (make it more likely than not in civil cases or cause a reasonable doubt in criminal cases). Supporting facts may be in the form of one or more witnesses and/or one or more exhibits.

The checklist will be expanded, contracted, summarized, and cross-referenced as the case progresses. At the preliminary stage, the checklist is crucial more *because it exists* than because of what it contains. It provides the foundation for constructing appropriate legal theories which will result in a purposeful and thorough litigation plan. *See* Exhibit 8-1, page 212, for examples of possible legal theories which might be used in preparing such a checklist.

8.04   Pleadings and Pretrial Motions

8.041   Rules of Procedure

In addition to the substantive legal theories and rules, the litigation team must be familiar with the procedural rules that govern a particular case. At the federal level, all courts are governed by the Federal Rules of Criminal Procedure for criminal cases and by the Federal Rules of Civil Procedure for civil cases. Federal trial courts (U.S. District Courts) are permitted to adopt local court rules to supplement the federal rules; however, they may not replace the federal rules or materially change the character of the federal rules.

As an example of this interaction, Rule 12(b) of the Federal Rules of Civil Procedure permits motions to be filed to test the sufficiency of the complaint. The rule goes on to list specific bases

EXHIBIT 8-1   Examples of Legal Theories for Checklists

A. Law Action Theories
    1. Contract
    2. Personal Injury Torts
       a. General Negligence
       b. Products Liability
       c. Premises Liability
       d. Professional Liability
       e. Governmental Liability
       f. Worker Compensation Claim
    3. Other Torts
       a. Intentional Torts
       b. Defamation (Libel/Slander)
       c. Fraud/Misrepresentation

B. Equity Action Theories
    1. Mandamus
    2. Injunction
    3. Rescission
    4. Reformation
    5. Specific Performance
    6. Equitable Trust

C. Damages Recoverable
    1. Compensatory Damages
    2. Restitution Damages
    3. Punitive Damages
    4. Liquidated Damages
    5. Lost Profits
    6. Diminished Earning Capacity
       (reduced to present value)
    7. Future Medical Expenses
       (reduced to present value)
    8. Interest
    9. Attorney Fees

D. Defenses/Limitations to Recovery
    1. Performance
    2. Satisfaction/Accord and Satisfaction
    3. Statute of Limitations
    4. Statute of Frauds
    5. Privity of Contract

    6. Prior Breach (of contract)
    7. Duress
    8. Impossibility of Performance
    9. Illegality of Purpose
  10. Laches
  11. Agency/Independent Contractor Status
  12. Contributory Negligence
  13. Comparative Negligence
  14. Assumption of Risk
  15. Indemnity/Contribution
  16. Economic Waste
  17. Statutory Limitation of Damages
  18. Governmental Immunity
  19. Third-Party Liability
  20. Exhaustion of Remedies (administrative)

A portion of the legal theory checklist is reproduced below to demonstrate how it might be expanded.

    3. Other Torts
       a. Intentional Torts
          (1) Act by Defendant
          (2) Intent
          (3) Causation
          (4) Damage
       b. Defamation (Libel/Slander)
          (1) Defamatory Statement
              (Written/Oral)
          (2) Plaintiff Identified or Identifiable
          (3) Publication to Third Party
          (4) Plaintiff's Reputation Damaged
          (5) Calculation of Loss to Plaintiff
       c. Fraud/Misrepresentation
          (1) False Statement/Misrepresentation
              of Fact
          (2) Knowledge of Falsity by Defendant
              (for fraud only)
          (3) Intent that Plaintiff Rely
          (4) Plaintiff's Reliance Justified
          (5) Damage to Plaintiff

that can be included in such a motion, such as lack of jurisdiction over the subject matter, lack of jurisdiction over the person, improper venue, failure to state a claim upon which relief can be granted, etc. Under Rule 83, a particular federal district court would be permitted to adopt a local court rule requiring all Rule 12 motions to be filed in triplicate. This type of local rule does not change the character of the federal rule, but it does add another requirement. However, Rule 83(a)(2) states "A local rule imposing a requirement of form shall not be enforced in a manner that causes a party to lose rights because of a nonwillful failure to comply with the requirement."

State court systems also have procedural rules, many of which closely resemble the Federal Rules of Civil Procedure. These state rules of civil procedure are adopted either by the highest court of the state or by the state legislature. As in the federal system, many local courts are also permitted to adopt local court rules so long as the local rules do not supplant state rules of procedure. The discussion that follows uses the Federal Rules of Civil Procedure as its general basis.

8.042 Pleadings

Rule 7 states what documents constitute pleadings in a case: complaint, the answer, the reply to a counterclaim, an answer to a cross-claim (if the answer contains a cross-claim), a third party complaint, and a third party answer, if applicable. The pleadings inform the court of the allegations or contentions of each of the parties by outlining the claims of the plaintiff(s) and the affirmative defense(s) of the defendants. Pleadings also assist the court in formulating the issues.

The general rules of pleadings is covered in Rule 8. With regard to claims for relief, the pleadings:

1. Establish the court's jurisdiction or authority to adjudicate the controversy,
2. Briefly state the facts, circumstances, or theories that provide the basis of the plaintiff's claim against the defendant,
3. Briefly state any affirmative defenses that the defendant claims against the plaintiff, and
4. Include a demand for relief, remedy, or judgment sought by both the plaintiff and the defendant.

General rules of pleadings and language should be followed consistently. One should avoid expressions that are trite or mean the same thing, such as: each and every, due and owing, null and void, etc. A proper pleading must be able to stand alone, it must state facts, and not simply allege evidentiary matters. Often the pleadings will refer to a statute or authority under which the plaintiff bases his claim for relief. In matters involving contracts and real property matters, documents are often attached to the pleadings as numbered exhibits. See the Appendix of Forms attached to the Federal Rules of Civil Procedure for sample summons and complaints.

The key to drafting effective pleadings is to include only those matters that are absolutely necessary and to state facts in a simple, concise way. One should never admit unnecessary facts that may later become embarrassing obstacles in the proper presentation of the client's case. One should save righteous indignation and legal arguments for the trial brief, as these have no place in pleadings.

8.0421 *Complaints, Answers, Motions.* In a complaint (sometimes called a petition in state courts) the plaintiff formally notifies the court and the defendant of the basis for the plaintiff's claim. It is filed with the clerk of the court and served upon the defendant, along with a summons notifying the defendant that an answer must be given within a specified period or a default judgment will be entered. Rule 79(a) governs the manner in which the clerk of court assigns the civil docket number to each case. Actions are assigned consecutive file numbers and each document filed subsequent to the initial summons and complaint is assigned a folio number within that initial file number. The clerk maintains a chronological listing of all documents in the case.

When the complaint is received, the defendant's attorney analyzes it for legal sufficiency, in an attempt to weed out claims and defenses that are without merit. The defendant may challenge the legal sufficiency of the complaint by filing a motion to dismiss (called a demurrer in some state courts, but abolished by Rule 7(c) of FRCP in federal courts) and by serving a copy of the motion on the plaintiff, by mailing it to the plaintiff's attorney. In a motion to dismiss, the defendant asserts that the case should not be tried because of a specific defect. The defect, as described above and in Rule 12(b) may be lack of subject matter jurisdiction of the court, lack of personal jurisdiction of the defendant, improper issuance of summons, improper service of summons upon the defendant, or a failure to state a claim upon which the relief can be granted. The motion to dismiss and all other pretrial motions are set for hearing by the judge assigned to the case.

Depending on the jurisdiction, other pretrial motions may be used to refine the allegations contained in the pleadings. Among these are a motion for a more definite statement, a motion to strike (referring to statements in a pleading that are redundant, immaterial, or scandalous), and a motion for judgment on the pleadings (also called a motion for summary judgment in many state courts).

If the complaint survives the preliminary motions designed to test its sufficiency, the defendant must then file a written answer. The answer strives to minimize the damage and potential exposure to the client, not only monetary, but also to the client's business and/or personal reputation. The attorney will usually follow an issue analysis approach, seeking to separate known facts from those that must be proven by the plaintiff. The answer may contain admissions, denials, affirmative defenses, and counterclaims. If the defendant admits a particular allegation, there is no need to prove that fact at trial. If the defendant denies a particular allegation, a factual issue is created, and the plaintiff must then prove the fact at trial, unless he or she is able to do so before then.

After the defendant's answer has been filed, the plaintiff must file a reply if the defendant asserted any counterclaims in its answer. Some state jurisdiction also allow a reply to any affirmative defenses listed in Rule 8(c). In the reply, the plaintiff responds to the causes of action asserted (or any affirmative defenses stated when allowed) by admitting them, denying them, or stating any affirmative defenses, if applicable.

8.0422 *Affirmative Defenses.* Allegations contained in the answer that may bar (prevent) the plaintiff's recovery are called affirmative defenses. They describe acts or circumstances which may have occurred before, after, or concurrently with those alleged by plaintiff in the complaint. Defendant's alleging affirmative defenses must prove the allegations, similar to the plaintiff's, being required to prove their allegations. Rule 8(c) lists affirmative defenses as the following, along with very brief explanations:

1. Accord and satisfaction: payment in full or completion of obligation
2. Arbitration and award: prior agreement to arbitrate matter
3. Assumption of risk: plaintiff assumed risk and should accept consequences
4. Contributory negligence: plaintiff failed to exercise due and ordinary care
5. Discharge in bankruptcy: debt discharged or matter adjudicated by bankruptcy court
6. Duress: defendant's action caused by plaintiff's threats or inducements
7. Estoppel: plaintiff's action or silence in failing to assert a right
8. Failure of consideration: consideration for a contract no longer exists (i.e., house destroyed by fire, etc.)
9. Fraud: false representation, failure to disclose, etc.
10. Illegality: unlawful act
11. Injury by fellow servant: negligence by another employee was cause of plaintiff's injury
12. Laches: neglect in asserting right or claim

13. License: permission granted by law
14. Payment: prior discharge of obligation and acceptance by plaintiff
15. Release: relinquishment of a right
16. *Res judicata:* matter previously decided by court
17. Statute of frauds: agreement must be in writing to be valid
18. Statute of limitations: if applicable, and if expired, action may not be pursued
19. Waiver: intentional or voluntary abandonment (differs from estoppel in that it is a "knowing" abandonment, rather than to estoppel where intent is immaterial); and
20. Any other matter constituting an avoidance or affirmative defense.

8.0423 Counterclaims, Cross-claims, Third Party Pleadings. In a counterclaim, the defendant states a cause of action against the plaintiff. If the defendant's cause of action arises from the same facts as plaintiff's cause of action, the defendant's counterclaim is compulsory, i.e., the defendant MUST file the claim against the plaintiff in the existing action, or the claim is barred. If the defendant's cause of action against the plaintiff is based upon a different occurrence or a different set of facts, the defendant has a permissive counterclaim which may be filed in the same case, but the defendant is not barred from bringing a separate action for the claim. A counterclaim is usually included as part of a defendant's answer.

A cross-claim is a claim of one defendant against another defendant, and is also often included with an answer. Cross-claims are governed by Rule 13 of the Federal Rules of Civil Procedure and to be proper, must arise out of the same transaction or occurrence stated in the complaint or a counterclaim, or must relate to any property which is the subject matter of the complaint.

In a third party complaint, a defendant alleges a claim against a party not previously included in the lawsuit. In general, permission from the court must be obtained before a defendant is allowed to become a third party plaintiff. The party against whom the third party complaint if filed becomes know as a third party defendant. Rule 14 governs the procedures allowing third party practice.

An additional kind of "third party" pleading occurs when an outside party seeks permission from the court to intervene in a lawsuit. The motion to the court applying for intervenor status must contain an assertion that the right to intervene is: (1) conferred by a statute, *or* (2) based on an interest in the transaction or property which is the subject of the lawsuit, *and* (3) the party will be unable to protect its rights unless allowed to become a party to the lawsuit. Rule 24 of the Federal Rules of Civil Procedure governs interventions.

8.043 Administrative Controls
Administrative controls include all calendars, lists, document logs, numbering systems, etc. that are created and maintained throughout the case up to the time of trial. At that time, these items are incorporated into the trial notebooks. Keeping ticker files, case calendars, and to-do lists should be a daily ritual for the legal assistant. Methods for maintaining such controls vary from firm to firm based on the firm's and client's resources and size of the case. Deadlines for responding to pleadings and discovery requests are an inherent part of each case. The court will accept no excuses for missed deadlines. Such failure to adhere to deadlines may result in staff dismissal and attorney disbarment. The legal assistant should carefully review not only the rules governing time allotted for response to pleadings and discovery requests, but should coordinate any potential scheduling conflicts with the attorney and his/her secretary.

Calendaring and docketing software is often employed, and often recommended by malpractice carriers, to assist in assuring that no deadlines are missed and any scheduling conflicts are resolved. Of course, as with any software application, the results of its use are only as good as the information input into the computer. The responsibility for overseeing such tasks often falls on the shoulders of the legal assistant.

8.0431 Pleadings and Documentary Files. In complex litigation, particularly multiple party actions, simply keeping track of pleadings, discovery motions and orders, trial testimony, transcripts, evidentiary material, and other documents may prove cumbersome. There is no escaping the paper demon. Case documents are usually stored in chronological order and the legal assistant should formulate a cross-indexing system to facilitate reference and retrieval. This is no small or insignificant task; however, it may be accomplished manually or by computer. Filing and indexing systems should also include categories for all pertinent documents in the case, including lists of parties and witnesses. Such systems should be standardized wherever possible, and as succinct as possible, utilizing color-coded labels or whatever devices may be effective for the firm and that case.

It is essential to have indexed copies of all the pleadings filed in court, including the date on which filed. This index supports a file containing copies of these pleadings, and nothing else, marked by a numbered tab on each pleading, corresponding with the number listed in the index of pleadings. The index includes a description of the pleading filed, the date it was filed, the pleading number assigned and tabbed on the pleading, and any other desirable information. (*See* Exhibit 8-2.) A cross-index arranged by topics should also be prepared.

In the case of a multiparty suit, it may be desirable to prepare separate files to contain the following, all properly tabbed and indexed: correspondence and notes, pleadings (with subsections for complaints, answers to complaints, counterclaims and cross-claims, if separately filed, court orders and notices, proofs of service, subpoenas, etc.), discovery (interrogatories, answers to interrogatories, plaintiff or defendant objections, requests for admissions, requests for production of documents, motions to compel responses, etc.), documents (arranged by sources/parties), witness files (including expert witnesses), exhibits for trials, notebooks, and other files as needed. The same indexing method could be applied to other supporting documents in the files, including documents on microfilm, if any, and other recording mediums. For the most effective retrieval, the index should be established in both chronological and topical format. Throughout this process, the goal is to retrieve any document on a moment's notice.

Computerized databases to manage such indexing tasks are available commercially, and should be explored long before commencing work on such a case. Chapter 9, The Legal Assistant and Document Discovery Cases, discusses use of the computer in the area of discovery and document production, and the legal assistant could apply much of this discussion to the case management file. Other sources to explore include the firm's computer systems analyst and/or firm administrator, specialty vendors, and serial publications for attorneys and paralegals. Some legal assistants, possessing strong computer skills, have designed their own databases utilizing commercially available software. Of course, the legal assistant should elicit support from supervising attorneys before commencing such tasks.

8.05 Discovery and Pretrial Preparation

While the issues are being joined through the process of written pleadings and pretrial motions, formal discovery may also be undertaken by the parties. Formal discovery includes interroga-

EXHIBIT 8-2   Sample Pleadings Index

Index to Pleadings
Filed in Case 70-823

Doc. #	Vol. #	Date Filed	Description
8	II	7/11/90	Plaintiff's Rule 34 Request for Document Prod.
9	II	7/16/90	Order on Preliminary Pretrial Conference
10	II	7/15/90	Withdrawal of Appearance of Danny J. Jones
11	II	7/16/90	Order Consolidating Cases and Adding Counsel
12	II	8/09/90	Answers of the Lean Co. To Pl.'s Interrogs. #1
13	II	8/09/90	Answers of Pipe Corp. To Pl.'s Interrogs. #1
14	III	8/09/90	Answers of Clamor Co. To Pl.'s Interrogs. #1
15	III	8/09/90	Answers and Objections of U.S. Co. To Pl.'s Interrogs. #1
16	III	8/09/90	Def's Response to Pl.'s Rule 34 Req. for Prod. of Docs.
17	III	8/09/90	Answers of ASGO to Pl.'s Interrogs. #1
18	III	8/09/90	Def's Objections to Pl.'s Interrogs. #2
19	III	8/09/90	Answers & Objections of Clamor to Pl.'s Interrogs. #2
20	III	8/09/90	Answers of OUTGO to Pl.'s Interrogs. #1
21	III	8/12/90	Arno's Ans. & Objections to Pl.'s R. 34 Req. for Doc. Prod.
22	III	8/12/90	Arno's Ans. & Objections to Pl.'s Interrogs. #1
23	III	8/12/90	Answers of Met. Gov't. Of Anywhere to Def's Joint Ints. of June 25, 1990
24	III	8/12/90	Joint Response of Plaintiffs to Def's Joint Int.
25	III	8/12/90	Answers of CA to Def's Joint Int. Of June 25, 1990
26	IV	9/17/90	Def's Memo R. 37 to Compel Ans. by Pl.'s to Def's Joint Int. and Other Relief
27	IV	9/18/90	Pl.'s Motion & Memo. in Support of Class Actions
28	IV	9/20/90	Memo of all Def's in Opposition to Cl. Action
29	IV	9/20/90	Arno's Reply to Pl.'s Rule 37 Motion
30	IV	9/23/90	Def's Memo in Opposition to Pl.'s Motion for Order Pursuant to Rule 37
31	IV	9/23/90	Pl.'s Response to Def's R. 37 Motion & Memorandum
32	IV	9/23/90	Agreement Ltr. Between Met. Gov't. of Anywhere & Messrs. Brown & Moulder dated 1/21/90

tories, depositions, requests for production of documents and other things, and requests for admission. However, the ability of the parties to go forward in federal court with formal discovery is controlled, and may be limited, by Rule 26(a) and (f).

In the federal courts, Rule 26(a) requires that certain disclosures be made to the opposing party, without awaiting a discovery request and within a specified time period. These required initial disclosures may be waived or altered by order or local rule of the district court. Therefore, the legal assistant must check local rules when a lawsuit is filed in federal court to determine whether the initial required disclosures have been adopted or waived by local court rule or court order. If the initial disclosures are required, they must include information concerning:

- Identity of persons/entities having discoverable information about the claims and defenses in the lawsuit
- Copies or descriptions (by category and location) of documents, data compilations, and tangible things in the possession of the party that are relevant to the claims and defenses in the lawsuit
- A computation of damages claimed by the disclosing party and copies of documents and materials, not privileged or protected from disclosure, on which the computation is based
- Any insurance agreements under which any insurer could be liable for all or part of a judgment entered in the case
- Identity of expert witnesses who will be called to testify at trial, as well as a report from any such expert containing the expert's opinions, the facts considered in formulating such opinions, exhibits to be used by the expert, the qualifications of the witness, including a list of all publications the witness authored for the previous ten years, the compensation to be paid for the expert's work and testimony, and a list of other cases in which the witness has testified as an expert at trial or by deposition within the previous four years.

A party must also provide the other party with a list of potential witnesses, designating which witnesses will testify live and which by deposition, and a list of documents the party will introduce as exhibits at trial. Each category of these disclosures has different time periods assigned within which the disclosures must be made.

Rule 26(d) provides that no party can institute written or other discovery from another party before the parties have met, prepared a discovery plan, and submitted it to the court. The Rule 26(f) meeting of the parties must be accomplished and the report generated as a result of the meeting must be filed before the first scheduling conference is held or a Rule 16(b) scheduling order is due to be issued. The rule outlines what matters must be discussed at the Rule 26(f) meeting, but the overall thrust of the meeting is to plan the discovery phase of the case in as much detail as is possible at that early stage in the case.

Rule 26(a)(5) provides that parties may pursue discovery by more traditional methods as well: oral depositions; depositions by written question; written interrogatories; requests for production of documents or things or permission to enter upon land or property; requests for physical and mental examinations; and requests for admissions. However, if the local court in which the case is filed has not opted out of the Rule 26(f) requirements of a meeting of the parties to prepare a discovery plan by local rule or court order, Rule 26(d) provides that these traditional discovery methods may not be engaged in by the parties until after the meeting of the parties.

Other than those facts withheld for impeachment purposes and those facts that are privileged, the underlying philosophy of the Federal Rules of Civil Procedure and their state court counterparts is that all relevant facts should be available to all parties prior to trial, provided that the party has properly requested this information. If each party honestly and adequately responds to discovery requests by the other parties in the case in sufficient time prior to trial, the presumption is that many cases will be settled. This presumption is probably correct, since only a very small percentage of cases result in a full trial on the merits. The formal discovery process lends itself especially well to the skills of the legal assistant member of the litigation team.

The scope of discovery described in Rule 26(b) reflects this underlying philosophy. It provides that parties may discover any matter, not privileged, that is relevant to the subject matter of the action. Discovery may even be had of any information that is not admissible at trial, as long as it appears reasonably calculated to lead to the discovery of admissible evidence.

The most common privileges asserted in objections to discovery are attorney-client privilege, opinion work product (also known as the mental impressions, theories, and opinions of the lawyer), and material prepared in anticipation of litigation. Generally, information protected by the attorney-client privilege and the opinion work product privilege may not be obtained under any circumstances. Only if a party waives one of these privileges is such information usually made discoverable. However, the third category of privilege is more of an immunity than an absolute privilege. Rule 26(b)(3) provides that such material is protected from discovery unless the party seeking discovery can show that he/she is unable, without undue hardship, to obtain the substantial equivalent of the materials by other means. If such a showing can be made, the court may order that the material is to be produced to the party seeking discovery, but must protect against disclosure of the mental impressions, conclusions, opinions, or legal theories of an attorney or other representative of a party about the litigation.

Any party to the lawsuit, and any person not a party to the lawsuit, may obtain copies of statements they have previously given concerning the subject matter of the litigation, without any necessity of showing "good cause," or indeed any cause at all, and may move for an order compelling production of such statements if the party holding the statements refuses to provide it to the requesting party.

8.06 Interrogatories

Interrogatories are a discovery device specifically authorized in the Federal Rules of Civil Procedure under Rules 33 and 37. Rule 33 provides for the availability of the discovery method and procedures connected with interrogatories. It essentially provides that any party may serve any other party in a lawsuit with written interrogatories that must be answered within a specific time limit. Rule 33(a) also limits the number of interrogatories allowed to be served to no more than twenty-five, including subparts. That may seem very restrictive, particularly in those jurisdictions where the district court has opted out of the required initial disclosures discussed in Section 8.05 previously. Remember that the number limitation is not absolute. If you can demonstrate to the court what information is required from additional interrogatories and that the information is necessary to properly and fully prepare the case for trial, the court may grant an order giving permission to serve additional interrogatories.

In addition to the federal or state rule of procedure, there may also be conditions or limitations imposed by the rules of the local court in which the action is filed. These generally pertain to the form of the interrogatory and the number of interrogatories that may be propounded to an opposing party. Generally, these number limitations (ranging from fifteen to fifty, depending on the jurisdiction) include subparts of each interrogatory as part of the total allowed. The legal assistant should always check the local rules to discover whether this is the case, so that the attorney will not inadvertently violate a more restrictive local rule.

Interrogatories are self-executing discovery devices; each question must either be answered by the party served or by an officer or agent of a corporation, partnership, association, or governmental agency. Interrogatories must be answered under oath, in writing, and signed by the party who provides the answers. However, if objections are lodged to some or all of the interrogatories, the answers must also be signed by the attorney for the party. Objections must be detailed and must be made within the time limit permitted for responding. The rule provides that interrogatories may be used at trial "to the extent permitted by the rules of evidence." This statement reflects the fact that interrogatories may extend to matters that will not be admissible in evidence at trial, as is true of all discovery under the federal rules, given the scope of discovery provided in Rule 26.

Interrogatories and the answers or objections to interrogatories may be contained in separate documents. Many jurisdictions, however, have court rules which require the *engrossment* of the question and the answer to interrogatories in the interest of clarity. Simply put, this means that when answering an interrogatory, the entire question must be restated as propounded prior to the answer. Sometimes the propounded interrogatory format provides sufficient space between questions to permit the insertion of appropriate answers. These practices allow the court and the parties to look at one document and find, in successive order, question and answer, question and answer, and so on. Few courts, however, have solved the problem of supplemental answers, and few require engrossment of supplemental answers with the original questions and answers.

In this day of scanners and accompanying software, it is possible to scan a set of interrogatories propounded to the client by another party into your computer's word processing program. This allows the answers and any objections to be inserted after each interrogatory without having to retype them. If a scanner is not available to you, modern photocopy and computer copy equipment allows the "cut-and-paste" method to be used, although it is a time-consuming process if there are many interrogatories and/or subparts to interrogatories. Even if court rules don't require engrossment, it is a better practice to do so.

Under the federal rules, a party may serve more than one set of interrogatories but may be required to number the interrogatories sequentially in order. In other words, "Set one" may include questions from one to fifteen, and "Set two," filed at a later date, begins with question sixteen and extends to the completion of that set. In many ways, this is a desirable practice, whether in federal or state courts. It allows quick and easy reference to questions from the beginning of discovery in the case to its conclusion, and is a desirable system since it allows easy collation of one answer to another on a related point. This procedure, if the attorney will allow it, assists the legal assistant, and ultimately benefits the attorney.

8.061 Interrogatories as Part of the Discovery Plan

Interrogatories are only one part of the overall discovery plan. Effective discovery is the result of thoughtful planning to determine whether development of factual data is appropriate to a particular form of discovery. In interrogatories, almost anything can be asked; relevance to the issues or the possibility of leading to relevant, admissible facts are the only tests, and these tests are liberally construed. The only other possible limitation is the privileged status of the information being sought, but sometimes even a privilege may be breached and the information obtained from the adversary.

The timing of written interrogatories in the discovery process must be coordinated with depositions, requests for production, requests for admission, and the other discovery devices to ensure the maximum return for the effort. Similarly, many items may be better developed by independent investigation (informal discovery) or by using a different discovery method.

The resulting benefit of informal discovery is the ability to conceal the attorney's specific interest from the adversary. Because of the number limitation placed on interrogatories by the federal rule or a local rule, it may be more advantageous to convert an interrogatory that asks *about* a certain document or set of documents or a tangible piece of evidence into a request *for* the document, set of documents, or tangible evidence.

Filing interrogatories without a plan smacks of creating "busywork" for the adversary while appearing to advance the client's case. This conduct is unprofessional and, if not completely unproductive, usually yields only minimal discovery of the information required by the attorney, because the effort is not pointed or planned; the questions are general and lack specific application to the issues of the case. When such a set is received, the legal assistant and lawyer can easily recognize that the adversary is far behind in case planning and analysis, which gives them a tactical advantage over the adversary.

8.0611 *Forcing the Adversary to Prepare the Case.*

The untimely submission of extensive interrogatories of a highly pointed nature, especially where the adversary's case has substantial merit, may force the adversary attorney to prepare that case much earlier than otherwise. The attorney, of course, makes the tactical decisions; however, drafting interrogatories is frequently delegated to the legal assistant. In the early development of the discovery plan, the merits of the case as they are appreciated by counsel must take into account the effect that extensive and detailed interrogatories may cause. It is a fact of life that many lawsuits are filed on "bare-bones" allegation and seldom with a full set of supporting facts. Often both sides have good points in their favor and weaknesses in their positions. Discretion in drafting and answering interrogatories is not only appropriate, but necessary.

8.0612 *The Paper War.*

The filing of extensive and unnecessary interrogatories may spur the adversary into a similar response and create a "paper war." This is harassing and nonproductive in that it requires the expenditure of extensive blocks of both legal assistant and attorney time with little benefit to the client.

Rule 26(g), FRCP, is the discovery parallel to Rule 11. It requires that discovery requests be signed by an attorney, and provides that such a signature certifies that the discovery is: (1) consistent with the federal rules and warranted by existing law or a good faith argument for a change in existing law; (2) not propounded for any improper purposes such as harassment, delay, or increasing the cost of litigation; and (3) not unreasonable or unduly burdensome or expensive, given the needs of the case, the discovery already taken in the case, the amount in controversy, and the importance of the issues at stake in the litigation. If discovery is propounded in violation of these principles, the court is required to impose an appropriate sanction, usually monetary in nature, upon the party and/or the attorney who violates them, or both. Thus, it is not politic to file extensive and unnecessary interrogatories. Aside from provoking a like response from the adversary, it could, under the wrong circumstances, lead to sanctions.

These potential problems can be minimized by asking only cogent and relevant questions with obvious and focused purposes and by avoiding the trap of using reams of pattern or canned interrogatories of a general nature (sometimes called "boilerplate filings").

8.062 Objectives and Purpose

The major objectives of interrogatories are the identification of people and entities who have information concerning the subject matter of the action; the identification and location of documents or tangible evidence; the discovery and establishment of facts relevant to claims or defenses raised by the parties; the identification of contentions of fact; and to narrow the issues for trial. Interrogatories are also used as tools for piercing the corporate veil, establishing *res ipsa loquitur*, overcoming language problems, and to provide a foundation for summary judgment. Each of these objectives will be explored in some detail.

8.0621 Identification of People or Entities. In order to prepare a comprehensive deposition plan, it is necessary to obtain personal and employment information about individuals (whether parties or nonparties), their relatives, experts, or principal officers and directors of corporate bodies. Identifying "people" also involves identifying legally fictitious or jurisdictional entities, such as partnerships; corporations; company, corporate, partnership, or association names; or entities recognized at law that are business, government, or eleemosynary organizations. Exhibit 8-3 lists interrogatory topics which seek to meet this objective.

EXHIBIT 8-3   Topics for Identification of People or Entities

Identities of Parties. Identity and physical description to include full name, date of birth, Social Security number, height and weight, and color of hair and eyes. Depending upon the circumstances of each case, interrogatories may ask about nicknames, maiden or adoptive names, aliases, professional names, pen names, and identifying characteristics such as scars, tattoos, and/or deformities or disabilities, citizenship status, naturalization dates, immediate family, immigration sponsor. In any event, the thrust of these "identification" interrogatories should be used to gather necessary personal information about persons who are opposing parties.

Identities of Witnesses. It is essential to seek the identity of any witnesses known to the other party.

Note: If the matter is in federal court, and the federal district court in which the lawsuit is filed has not opted out of the requirement for initial disclosures required by Rule 26(a), F.R.C.P., this interrogatory will not be necessary, because this information must be given to opposing parties under this rule. However, if the district court has opted out of the provisions of Rule 26(a), or the case is filed in a state court which does not require a similiar disclosure, use the same language found in 26(a)(1)(A) to structure the question.

Official Identity of Fictitious Persons. If the defendant, or sometimes the plaintiff, is a business, a fictitious person, or a person doing business under a title not linked with his or her own name, interrogatories can be used to inquire into the identity of the organization, structure, officers, or managerial personnel of the business entity. Similarly, the authority under which the organization operates, such as articles of incorporation, partnership agreements, or the filing of the fictitious name with the appropriate regulatory agency are all suitable areas of inquiry. Distribution of stock, identity of agencies that regulate or license the business, identity of reports that must be filed with regulatory agencies, the identity of the agency or association that writes, adopts, and promulgates industry standards, as well as the actual

standards that have been adopted by the industry are also proper areas of inquiry.

Identities of Experts. Ask opposing parties to identify experts who will be called to testify at trial, the expert's area of expertise, the facts upon which his/her opinions are based, what those expert opinions are, and ask for production of the expert's *curriculum vitae*. It may even be necessary to ask for a list of articles or publications authored by the expert and/or a list of cases in which the expert has given deposition and/or trial testimony. This latter information may be necessary to attack the expert's opinions and credibility. This can be done by checking the contents of the articles or publications authored by the expert to see whether they contradict his opinions in the current case, and to check the expert's testimony in previous cases to see whether, given the same or similar facts, his opinion was different enough in the previous case to erode or eliminate his usefulness to the opposing party.

Note: If the matter is in federal court, and the federal district court in which the lawsuit is filed has not opted out of the requirement for initial disclosures required by Rule 26(a), F.R.C.P., this interrogatory will not be necessary, because this information must be given to opposing parties under this rule. However, if the district court has opted out of the provisions of Rule 26(a), or the case is filed in a state court which does not require a similiar disclosure, use the same language found in 26(a)(2) to structure the question.

Addresses. Addresses, both residential and business, should be obtained through interrogatories. Normally, questions on current residence and business addresses present few problems; however, the same may not be true regarding prior residences and prior employment. Interrogatories require the responding party to consult records and give complete and thorough answers; at deposition, the party may not recall this information and decline to speculate or guess, thus yielding no information.

8.0622 Identification of Documents and Objects. In relatively simple cases, relevant documents may be very limited in nature and easily characterized by the responding party through date, author, addressee, type of document, subject matter of the document, and/or file number. In other cases, it may be necessary to identify the size and character of the file, describe the filing system and method of identification of files, and storage location for subsequent examination and/or production.

Interrogatories may also be used to request information about tangible things that may or will be used as evidence at trial. For example, in a products liability case, one or more parties may propound interrogatories asking for identification of the object by asking for a physical description of the object, as well as information about each and every person who has had custody of the object since the time of the incident at issue up to the present time. This will enable the requesting party to check the chain of custody of the object in order to determine who has had the opportunity to inspect and test the object subsequent to the incident. This, in turn, may lead to the addition of names to the deposition and/or overall discovery plan.

Remember, however, that if your interrogatories are growing too large for the number limitation placed on you by either the federal or local rules in the specific case, you should consider converting interrogatories that ask *about* documents or things to a request *for* the documents or things. If what you really want is to obtain the document or thing, or an opportunity to inspect the document or thing or to test the thing, perhaps a request for production is the proper discovery tool to use. Exhibit 8-4 lists interrogatory topics which seek to meet this objective.

EXHIBIT 8-4 Interrogatory Topics for Identification of Documents or Objects

Documents. When asking about the existence of documentary items, request each item be identified by date, author, addressee, type of document, subject matter of the document, and/or file number. Other identifying characteristics could include the size and character of the file, the filing system, method of identification of files, whether the documents exist in electronic format (computer disks, e-mail, databases, etc.) and storage location for subsequent examination and/or production. When document identification is requested, the identity of the current custodian of each category of documents also is necessary, and should include a request for the name, business position or title, business address, home address, and business and home telephone numbers. Identification of the document custodian at the time of the event at issue, if different from the current custodian, should similarly be requested and should include all of the above information.

Existence of Tangible Evidence, Photographs, Videotapes, Maps, Sketches, and Models. In certain circumstances, photographs, videotapes, maps, sketches, and/or models will be made specifically for use at the trial by one party or the other. Appropriate interrogatories will reveal whether such items exist, their current location, the types of such presentations, and the name, address, and qualifications of the person who prepared them. In addition, a description of the facts and/or assumptions upon which the maker of the item based his/her finished product is necessary in order to test whether the maker's understanding of the facts and/or the assumptions made were accurate or appropriate. If the maker of the item had a poor understanding of the facts of the incident or made erroneous or inaccurate assumptions in making the item, the discovery of that fact will assist your attorney in attacking the opposing party's ability to use of the item in discovery or at trial, and may even lead to the item's exclusion.

Existence of Physical Evidence. Similarly, physical evidence may play a part in the case, and appropriate questions should be propounded to determine whether such physical evidence is held by any party or by his or her counsel. The propounding party is entitled to inquire into the nature of each item of evidence, the time and place the evidence was obtained or acquired and the name, address, telephone number, and place of employment of the person who is custodian of the evidence at the current time. Follow-up requests for production for purposes of inspection and perhaps even destructive or non-destructive testing of the evidence may be essential in order to provide your own expert witness(es) with pertinent factual information upon which their opinions may be based.

8.0623 Establishing Facts or Leading to the Discovery of Facts. Many incident cases are tried on facts solely in the personal knowledge of witnesses. Some witnesses are parties; some are not. Because interrogatories can be served only on parties, they may be used to elicit all discoverable information within the parties' knowledge. Often the questions are designed to elicit identification of sources of facts beyond the personal knowledge of the parties. Those sources (usually witnesses, documents, and tangible things) can then be explored: witnesses can be interviewed regarding their knowledge either by informal discovery or by deposition; documents and tangible things, if in the hands of nonparties, may be obtained through informal discovery means or by deposition in which the nonparty's knowledge of the document or thing may be explored. If they are in the hands of a party, they can be requested by a subsequent request for production.

A major benefit to using interrogatories is the fact that the answer of the responding party must be verified under oath and may used at the trial if the testimony is later changed. This advantage minimizes the chance of loss of memory or a change in testimony by parties during the life of the lawsuit, and reveals at least the sources of facts within the opposing party's knowledge as early in the lawsuit as possible, if not the factual information itself, depending on whether it is protected by a privilege. Even if the factual information itself is protected by a privilege, however, the information *about* the sources used by the opposing party to gather the information will be available to the requesting party. Exhibit 8-5 lists interrogatory topics which seek to meet this objective.

8.0624 Identification of Contentions. Properly timed and phrased interrogatories require the adverse party to state the contentions on which he or she relies in advancing his or her claims, or defenses, damages, or refutation of damages. From these responses, the merits of the adverse party's position may be deduced or weaknesses identified. Contention interrogatories usually are followed by questions requesting identification of the specific facts upon which the party's contentions are based.

The contentions may deal with whether the issue is one of law or fact and, if fact, the evidentiary facts on which the party relies, the source of the evidentiary facts, whether corroborated by documentary or physical evidence, and so forth. If the contention is not based on evidentiary facts, the attorney may then prepare to contest the issue based perhaps on the absence of facts or on the law, or both, and may attempt to have the matter decided by motion, that is, to have the matter either established or dismissed prior to trial. This eliminates the necessity of the court's having to adjudicate the issue later on, either by motion or at trial on the merits.

The legal assistant who drafts responses to such interrogatories must know the contents of previously filed answers to the complaint and answers to prior written discovery, as well as prior deposition testimony. There are few more embarrassing moments for a legal assistant than to prepare draft answers to a contention interrogatory or an interrogatory bearing on an important issue, only to have the lawyer point out that the issue was substantially admitted in the previously filed answer to the complaint or in deposition testimony or prior answers to interrogatories.

8.0625 Narrow the Issues for Trial. Cogent, timely interrogatories will force the exposure of information from the adversary under oath and thereby identify all issues, some of which may be disposed of before trial and some of which will be disputed matters in court.

The purpose of discovery is to learn what the other party knows, what the party will argue in answer to your client's contentions or defenses, and the strength or weakness of those

EXHIBIT 8-5   Interrogatory Topics for the Establishment or Discovery of Facts

Educational Background. It may be relevant to inquire into the educational background of the witness. Issues that might not have been apparent can be discovered, depending upon the level and type of education of the party.

Marital and Parental Status. The party's marital and parental status may be significant, as well as the status of the marriage (common domicile, legal separation, pending interlocutory decree, reconciliation, and/or child custody). The number of children and the quality of the family's relationships should be explored.

Employment History. Information about current and past employment, including names and addresses of employers, dates of employment or self-employment, hours worked in a typical week, job titles and descriptions of work performed, rate of pay, and monthly and/or annual income received, and reasons for termination of employment should be requested.

Military History. If a party has a history of military service, a search can be made of the military record to discover whether any facts or circumstances in that history have a bearing on the litigation, even if only to attack the party's credibility.

History of Crimes or Citations. Any criminal history of opposing parties should be explored. Sometimes criminal convictions have a direct bearing and effect on the litigation. Perjury is highly significant in any case. Violations involving alcohol or drugs and driving records could be significant.

History in Civil Litigation. Ask about any past claims or lawsuits of any kind in which the party may have been involved.

Compliance with Regulatory Rules. Compliance with, or citations for violations of, administrative rules, building codes, standards of health and hygiene, or environmental rules and regulations may be a proper area of inquiry, depending on the case and the identity or status of the opposing party.

Ownership Interest in Real Property. Ownership interest, or leasehold interest in real or chattel property may be highly relevant and pertinent to the case.

Insurance Coverage. The types of insurance coverage for the matter, incident, or accident giving rise to the litigation; the identity of the carrier, and the limits that are applicable to the subject matter of the litigation are all basic areas of inquiry. Ask whether the insurer has raised any coverage defenses; whether the accident occurred in the course and scope of the

defendant's employment; and whether any subrogation rights are claimed by an insurer.

Consumption of Alcohol or Drugs. In accident cases, questions regarding the events prior to the accident are appropriate. Such questions should specify a particular time preceding the event and explore the frequency and quantity of consumption, the place and location where the alcohol or drugs (whether legal or illegal) were ingested, the identities of witnesses who were present during the consumption, the quantity, quality, dosage, and name or type of drug, medicine, or alcoholic beverage taken, whether any of these were by doctor's prescription, the physician who prescribed the drugs, and the pharmacy providing the medication.

The Accident Scene and Conditions. Interrogatories requesting a description of the accident scene should include the date, time, and exact location of the accident, weather conditions, visibility, physical makeup of sidewalks and street surfaces, presence or absence of curbs, presence or absence of shrubbery, fences, street lights, holes, posts, traffic signals, warning signs, crosswalks, guards, or custodians, floor condition, presence of foreign substance/object, and efforts to clean up foreign substances/objects.

How the Accident Occurred. Ask for a description of how the accident/incident occurred, including each element that contributed to the accident. Follow-up questions ask the responding party to identify any documents, reports, photographs, or other records of the accident, the conditions, and circumstances surrounding it.

Plaintiff's Damages and Lifestyle. Ask about the injuries allegedly sustained by the plaintiff and damages being claimed as a consequence. Ask for bills, estimates, expert appraisals, financial records, hospital records, doctors' reports, medical bills, bills for miscellaneous out-of-pocket-costs, and indirect but consequential costs.

Knowledge of the Statements and Conversations with Others. Ask whether opposing parties have *taken* a statement from, or talked with, any other party or non-party witnesses concerning the lawsuit. Ask whether they have *given* any statement to, or talked with, other persons about the lawsuit. Ask to identify the person, the date, time, and place of the conversation, and the substance of the conversation. Ask for the location of any written statement or other record of the dialogue, the identity of the custodian, and how it can be obtained.

arguments. It will also reveal those facts about which the parties have no argument. This, in turn, will eliminate the necessity for court adjudication of undisputed facts. Also, discovery will reveal the legal issues that the court can determine without a jury, since the jury considers and renders verdicts only on the facts of a case and the court (judge) decides issues of law and instructs the jury.

8.0626 *Piercing the Corporate Veil.* The plaintiff suing a corporation can, through interrogatories, gather information that can be used to "pierce the corporate veil" as well as to identify that particular person, file, or policy most important to the establishment of the essential facts of the client's case. The corporation must provide all the information and facts available to it (and to its counsel and any other entity over which it has control) in response to any given question. Thus, the interrogatory is a highly effective tool for the individual plaintiff against an economically superior adversary.

The careful, methodical creation of appropriate interrogatories, whether one set or many, and analysis of the responses can provide a factual foundation for productive depositions and requests for production of documents by establishing such information as organization, chain of command, policies, practices, standards of the industry, applicable regulations, file systems, and other information concerning the corporation(s) that are the object of the effort to "pierce the corporate veil."

8.0627 *Res Ipsa Loquitur.* If a diligent discovery effort has been conducted to identify the cause of an accident, but the discovery has not elicited satisfactory or sufficient explanation of the event from the parties or percipient witnesses, and if independent investigation and expert witnesses have developed theories rather than facts, yet the accident could not occur if everything and everyone operated reasonably and properly, the attorney may have the data to support a plea of *res ipsa loquitur*, a Latin phrase meaning "the thing speaks for itself." This legal doctrine holds that there is a rebuttable presumption or inference that defendant was negligent, which arises when proof is given that: (1) the instrumentality causing injury was in defendant's exclusive control, and (2) the accident was one which ordinarily does not happen in the absence of negligence. The legal assistant must therefore look for facts in interrogatory answers that contribute to proof of these two elements of the *res ipsa* doctrine. If proof of these two elements can be identified in interrogatory or answers or other discovery responses, there is no need for the plaintiff to provide further explanation of the accident and the circumstances surrounding it; the burden shifts to the defendant to disprove the elements of the *res ipsa* doctrine.

8.0628 *Overcoming Language Problems.* Written interrogatories are an excellent means of surmounting communication obstacles of the adverse party. It matters little whether the obstacle is illiteracy or lack of English facility (sometimes a deadly problem in depositions), blindness, deafness, senility, incapacity due to illness, injury, or the side effects of medication. The written interrogatory must be answered by the party through whatever assistance is necessary. The opposing counsel has the burden of obtaining responsive answers from the client, the client's agents, or from the file and must submit the answers in a timely fashion. The questions and answers are in English, verified and under oath or, if in a foreign language, accompanied by an English translation.

8.0629 *Foundation for Summary Judgment.* Cogent, pointed, and extensive interrogatories are a legitimate and effective means of exposing a party who files an exaggerated or specious lawsuit or asserts improper, unfounded, or frivolous defenses. Similarly, it is an ideal and economic way to force the arrogant but unresponsive tortfeasor into a posture of truthful disclosure on the issues. The objective here, of course, is to force quick and timely resolution of the matter without extensive legal proceedings and their attendant cost. The correct and timely use of interrogatories often will elicit sufficient information so that, because they are given under oath, they can be used by the lawyer in support of a motion for summary judgment when that action is appropriate.

8.063 Drafting Interrogatories

Drafting interrogatories is a duty frequently assigned to legal assistants by the supervising attorney. To be done effectively, the legal assistant should be familiar with the facts, the pleadings (complaint, answer, and reply), and the elements of the causes of action involved. The type of case will often dictate whether the legal assistant must draft all new interrogatories or whether "canned" or pattern interrogatories may be used to find questions that have worked well in the past. Incident or accident types lend themselves to certain patterns of questioning. Contract disputes generate another set of typical questions. Product liability and antitrust cases often require extensive questions with different thrusts in several sets of interrogatories.

Previous sets of interrogatories used within the law firm on similar cases may be a great asset in learning certain preferences, information categories, and phrasings from past cases (so long as both the legal assistant and the attorney have weeded out the nonproductive, argumentative, and ambiguous ones). Commercially published "form books" containing pattern interrogatories are very helpful to the legal assistant, particularly to the inexperienced one, and should not be ignored. But neither should these pattern or "canned" interrogatories serve as the sole source of information for the creation of questions. The use of these canned interrogatories may be helpful in saving time, but they must be edited to conform to the needs of the individual case. Usually some additional specific questions are also necessary to make the "canned" set fit the case facts.

Some inexperienced or lazy legal assistants and lawyers have been known to select "nearly suitable" sets from canned or pattern interrogatories, insert the proper captions and certificates of service, and mail them out to the adversary. The danger of this practice is that a number of the questions may be inappropriate, and the adversary may object to the entire set as inappropriate, unintelligible, irrelevant, and unjustly burdensome. An example might be a car-pedestrian accident where the questions sent to the plaintiff (pedestrian) seek data about "the other car" or "plaintiff's automobile's speed at the time of the collision," its "mechanical condition," or "its maintenance record." The legal assistant, by careful editing and alteration, increases the attorney's effectiveness in the case by foreclosing the adversary from justified major or minor complaints and/or objections.

Early in the case, it is important to identify people, locations, sources of information, documents, and things. By tapping into the adversary's bank of information in these areas, the propounding attorney will then have a more complete picture of the people, locations, sources of information, documents, and things, so as to be able to prepare a more complete discovery plan. It is not so important at this stage to seek the contentions of the adversary.

Conversely, interrogatories submitted to the adversary late in the case can concentrate on contentions and on the facts on which they are based. Questions regarding identities (late in the case) may be used to check on whatever informal discovery the adversary may have conducted since the case began, identify expert witnesses, or focus on the discovery of documents which have been revealed during discovery, and which appear to have significance.

8.0631 *The Introductory Paragraph.* Every set of interrogatories has an introductory paragraph in which the propounding party should state that the responding party is directed to answer the questions that follow. In multiple party cases, this introductory paragraph may be directed to each adversary party separately, or to the parties jointly, with instructions that each must answer separately, in writing, under oath, and within the time limitation provided by law. This paragraph may even contain reference to the specific rule of procedure or code which governs interrogatories in the jurisdiction.

8.0632 *Definition of Terms.* Following the introduction may be a definition of terms used in the interrogatories. The definitions will include the identities of individuals or corporations, fictitious names, and so forth, which may be abbreviated or reduced to a one-word representation or acronym.

For instance, if the suit happens to be against the U.S. Bureau of Reclamation of the Department of the Interior, a definition might state that the acronym "USBR," when used within those interrogatories, refers to the U.S. Bureau of Reclamation, Department of the Interior. Use of that same definition throughout the interrogatories eliminates ambiguity, reduces the length of the interrogatories, and eliminates unnecessary words. Similarly, if the defendant in the case is the (fictitious) firm, The National Textile Corporation of the North American Continent, a single-word identification such as "National" or an acronym such as "NTCNAC" may be used in the definition and then throughout the interrogatories to refer to that firm.

Words that will be used repetitively in the set of interrogatories may also be defined at this time for accuracy, clarity, and understanding. For example, the word "documents" may be defined as "all writings, records, letters, memoranda, notes (whether handwritten or typed), studies, reports, books or volumes (bound or unbound), photographs, tape recordings, belt recordings, disc recordings, computerized or other electronic recordings, or other forms of recording, however produced or reproduced, whether a draft or final version, whether signed or unsigned, whether approved, sent, received, redrafted, executed, erased, or otherwise defaced or mutilated, from wherever obtained, which are in your possession or custody, or control."

The term "identify" may be used to shorten and make interrogatories clearer by defining it as the following: " 'Identify' when requested in relation to a natural person in these interrogatories, requires the full name, age, home address, home telephone number, business or occupational title, place of employment, address of employer, business telephone number, date of birth, and Social Security number, as minimum elements when available. 'Identify' when referring to documents requires the following minimum information to be provided: date, type of document, author, addressee, major topic or title of the document, the number of pages comprising the document, and a description of any attachments or exhibits incorporated by reference therein."

Another example of providing a useful definition is establishing what is meant by *accident*. " 'Accident' when used herein refers to that incident which occurred on the 10th day of June, 1995, in which two vehicles collided at the intersection of "A" Street and "B" Avenue in the town of Clearview, Arkansas, and is the focus of this lawsuit, unless otherwise specified."

Definitions of this general type allow the subsequent questions to be phrased with a minimum of words and a maximum of meaning, specifically and definitely. Proper use of such definitions almost demands productive answers. However, in very complex or technical litigation, there is a tendency to expand the definition of terms to such an extent that they become unwieldy and difficult to remember by any of the parties. When this occurs, the definition of terms has lost its purpose and may create a situation where the answering party may respond with an objection on grounds that the definitions, and thus the interrogatories themselves, are burdensome, oppressive, and confusing, and thus cannot be properly and accurately responded to by the objecting party.

8.0633 *Numbering System.* At the outset of drafting the interrogatories, it is important to establish the numbering system to be used and then to follow it consistently. Whether each question will receive a separate arabic number, or whether a decimalized system (a parent question with pointed numbers for each subsection), or an arabic number with alphabetic subparagraphs is to be employed is immaterial, so long as the decision is made early in the process and strictly followed. In many federal courts, it is necessary to number all questions sequentially in order, even when moving from one set of interrogatories to another, for the convenience of the parties and the court. This is a technique that may also be required in some state courts and is a great convenience to the legal assistant. If it is not required but permitted, use of the sequential numbers through several sets of interrogatories is a great help later on in collating answers and evaluating them in light of issues of fact and allegations.

8.0634 *Question Construction.*

a. Format. While "interrogatories" seems synonymous with "questions," in practice it is not unusual to find those that begin with terms such as "Please state . . .". The better and more professional practice for the legal assistant is to construct interrogatories in question format to avoid the possibility of creating a statement that does not require a response. Here is an example:

> "If you will do so without a motion to produce, attach copies of the above documents to the set of interrogatories."

This statement requires no answer; it requires no attachment of interrogatories and is a useless, wasted statement. The better practice is to include this request as a subpart to a series of questions regarding documents, such as:

> "3(a). Describe all the documents prepared by George Jones in response to requests by his supervisors for a justification of the research and development expenditures on the XYZ Widget during the time period January 1, 1990 through January 1, 1997.
> 3(b). Will you attach copies of the documents identified in response to 3(a) above without the necessity of a request for production or motion to produce?
> 3(c). If your answer to 3(b) above is 'yes,' please attach such copies to your answers."

Using this technique, the answering party must either provide a listing identifying all the responsive documents, or attach copies of the documents to the interrogatories; in either case, the party must respond.

Under the Federal Rules of Civil Procedure, and in many state and local jurisdictions, Rule 33 allows the answering party to produce business records when the answer to an interrogatory may be derived or ascertained from those records. For that reason, it is usually not necessary or effective to add a section to the "Definitions" which provides an option to attach the document or to require the responding party to identify the document, the storage location, and the custodian with sufficient specificity to allow filing an appropriate request for production. In addition to being unnecessary and redundant, there is a risk that the "definition" will provide the adversary with room for "inadvertent omission" or an objection to "complex, confusing, and oppressive instructions" if it is not clear and specific, and within the bounds of that which is stated in the rules as allowable.

b. Relevant Time Span. The time span to be covered in each interrogatory must be relevant to the matter being litigated. No matter whether the case arises out of an accident, business transaction, or alleged antitrust activity, many of the records, conduct, and actions of the party prior to the event giving rise to the litigation are important. However, seeking information preceding the event that gave rise to the action must be, in some way, relevant.

It is important that the inquiry into past events, documents, and conduct be sufficiently comprehensive to discover anything that is relevant or is capable of producing leads to admissible evidence in the case; however, it is also important to balance that need with the practical reality that a shorter period of time will involve a smaller volume of material for reasonable search and will be less likely to give rise to objections based on the burdensome nature of the interrogatory, particularly the requested time period. A short, relevant period may encourage the adversary party to respond to the request rather than to stonewall it, object to it, or provide partial or incomplete answers. This type of decision can be made only by the attorney; however, a careful analysis of the probability of obtaining usable data should be made. The legal assistant should be prepared to make a well-founded recommendation on the period of time to cover the various kinds of material sought. Some records have a reasonable life of only one year, some three years; some financial data must be preserved for seven years, and some corporate data may be permanent and/or perpetual (life of the corporation plus a statutory period). The purpose is discovery of factual data, not exercises in law and motion filings, and only reasonable requests will produce useful and informative discovery responses.

(c) Tense in Questions. Lawsuits concern matters in the past, and the phrasing of interrogatories in the proper tense is extremely important. If the current practice of a party is sought, the question must ask, "What is the practice . . . ?" If past practice is important, then the question must ask, "What was the practice of the company . . . ?" Consider only the pertinent time. The use of wrong verb tenses can result in a truthful but useless answer and wastes time.

The service of the interrogatory requires a few days, whether by hand or through the mail; then the responding party has thirty days in which to answer. An extension may be requested and granted, and additional extensions of time may be provided for any long or complex series of questions or because of illness, conflicting assignments of the adversary party's counsel, and so on. A poorly prepared question conceivably could waste anywhere from forty-five days to several months of time in the preparation of the case. Sloppy questions are expensive in terms of time. Remember also that discovery closes before the trial, and all answers must be submitted within a specified time period before trial. If a sloppy question is asked and the answer is due shortly before the close of discovery, it may be impossible to serve the rephrased question, taking even informal steps, to obtain the necessary information.

d. Simplicity. Keeping the question simple, partly through using the definition of terms described above and by restricting the use of adjectives and adverbs, will result in answers to the questions without evasions or objections. For instance, if the case involved an excavation by the defendant in which a pipeline was struck and damaged, there may be a tendency to ask a question like the following:

> "Did an employee of the defendant during excavation on June 12, 1979, strike, damage, and sever a five-inch cast-iron water pipeline three and one-half feet below the surface of Jackson Street, Oklahoma City, Oklahoma?"

The question is capable of easily being answered by the defendant with a "No." It is possible the defendant did not know whether it was a "cast-iron pipe;" it is possible he did not know he had "struck, damaged, and severed" the pipeline; it is possible he did not know how deep it was. It is far better to request the information in several questions:

"1. Did an employee of the defendant strike a buried pipeline on June 12, 1979?
2. How deep was the pipe buried at the point of contact?
3. Where did the defendant's employee report the contact to have occurred? (Please provide street, location, distance laterally from the south side of the road, distance from the nearest intersecting street, or alternatively, provide photographs and sketches that may have been made regarding this event.)"

Trying to write one clear but complex question, rather than a related pattern of simple questions—each with a specific, clearly focused object—is dangerous, may be unproductive and a waste of time, and may require additional questions in order to clarify the exact extent of the defendant's knowledge.

e. Belief Questions. Such questions as "Why did he do . . . ?" or "Why did he say . . . ?" are particularly unproductive, especially in the early stages of the case. Almost every such question will produce answers like "He believed he had a right to . . .", and "He said it because he believed it to be true." Depositions are usually far more productive than interrogatories for this type of question, because of the spontaneity of the answers, and because the deponent must respond to the question without an opportunity to consider the "best" answer and the adversary counsel cannot edit, phrase, or clarify the answers.

After drafting a question, or a series of questions, test them by answering them as unresponsively as possible. If the propounding party can answer the question unresponsively, a responding party should have no difficulty in providing the same unresponsive answers, perhaps in full truth and perhaps by rationalization.

f. Spelling. Good spelling is essential in writing interrogatories. Misspelling the name of the party or of any witness, the street, town, or any other identifiable feature, document, or matter of inquiry will result in an answer that negates the value of the question. It is true that a stipulation may be entered into in order to correct the spelling; however, it is equally true that a professional should be able to draft and double-check documents so as to eliminate or reduce the necessity for seeking favors from the adversary. Effective lawyers prefer to grant courtesies to the adversary rather than seek them.

8.0635 Contention Interrogatories. Among the types of questions that may be asked in interrogatories, usually late in the case and shortly before trial, are contention interrogatories in which the attorney asks the adversary party for an explanation of his or her legal and factual contentions. These may be phrased in very simple terms, such as in Exhibit 8-6, page 232.

Other alternatives are to pose a pattern of interrogatories based on a specific factual allegation which require the adversary to agree with the truth of the statement, to specifically deny the truth and expansively detail the grounds for the denial, or to admit the denial is not based on factual or evidentiary grounds. The format might appear as shown in Exhibit 8-7, page 232.

With the pattern established, statements can be inserted to force the adversary into admitting their truth, or alternatively, pinpointing areas of disagreement and the factual foundation on which he or she relies. Examples of the type of statement that can be inserted into these pattern contention interrogatories are: "Defendant was driving his own automobile in the proper traffic lane, at a lawful rate of speed immediately preceding the collision with plaintiff's car" or "There are no independent witnesses who have expressed the belief that plaintiff violated defendant's right-of-way."

EXHIBIT 8-6　Sample Contention Interrogatory

9. Do you contend that Plaintiff did not violate the right-of-way of the Defendant in the accident that is the focus of this lawsuit?

   A.   If so, please state:

      1.   Each fact on which you base your contention.

      2.   The identity of each person who has supplied you with information or testimony on which you base your contention. Identification requires names, addresses, telephone numbers, and relationships to plaintiff, at a minimum.

      3.   The location and description of any documents, objects, or other evidentiary facts or materials that you believe support your contention.

      4.   The name, address, telephone number, and name of employer of the custodian of any documents, objects, or other evidentiary facts or materials identified in (3) above.

EXHIBIT 8-7　Sample Pattern Contention Interrogatories

13. Do you contend that the following statement, or any portion thereof, is not true?
(Here set out the statement.)

14. If your answer to No. __ is in the affirmative, state which portion thereof you contend is not true.

15. Is your contention, described in No. __ above, based upon or supported by any facts known to you that are contrary to or inconsistent with the claimed truth thereof?

16. If your answer to No. __ is affirmative, state:
   a.   The evidentiary facts that support or tend to support your contention;
   b.   The identity of each person who has supplied you with information or testimony on which you base your contention. Identification requires names, addresses, telephone numbers, and relationships to plaintiff, at a minimum.
   c.   The location and description of any documents, objects, or other evidentiary facts or materials that you believe support your contention.
   d.   The name, address, telephone number, and name of employer of the custodian of any documents, objects, or other evidentiary facts or materials identified in (3) above.

17. If your answer to No. __ is negative, state whether you have conducted any investigation or inquiry as to the truth or falsity of said statement.

18. If your answer to No. __ is negative, state with particularity all bases, reasons, and grounds for your non-factual contention contrary to, or inconsistent with, the claimed truth thereof.

Such statements, if handled correctly in contention interrogatories, can dispose of many issues that otherwise would be tried in court. If the statements are contested, the patterned subparts and subsequent questions elicit an identification of the areas of disagreement, factual bases for the opinion, witnesses, disclose whether an investigation was conducted, and generally determine the sources of the contentions. This in turn assists the attorney in making further discovery plans, if there is still time to accomplish discovery prior to trial. At the very least, the attorney is made aware of the sources of the information on which the contentions are based and is better able to prepare to controvert or disprove the contentions at trial.

The execution of a few critical statements in contention interrogatories, which must be answered under oath, may eliminate a substantial number of issues from the trial, particularly if the submission of the interrogatories and the answers are very close to the trial. They are far more beneficial than requests for admissions, since they provide the opportunity for follow-up questions which explain a denial of the base question.

If contention interrogatories are used early in the case, the attorney is attempting to determine a better foundation for vague or uncertain allegations and forcing the adversary counsel to state the issues with specificity. However, it is difficult to elicit much data supporting the opposing party's contentions until the discovery process has matured, however; often contention interrogatories used early in the history of the case elicit answers indicating that discovery and investigation are not complete, and thus the question cannot yet be answered by the responding party.

8.0636 *Exhibits to Interrogatories.* The attachment of exhibits to interrogatories can be a very useful and inexpensive way of discovering relevant information. It can turn into a nightmare, however, if a proper procedure is not set up for controlling and retrieving such documents. If there is poor planning for identifying, indexing, controlling, and retrieving the exhibits and for identifying them with the relevant questions and answers related to them, their contents will be of little or no value to the attorney in future discovery, in settlement negotiations, or at trial.

From the beginning of the discovery plan, at least a general estimate of the numbers of exhibits pertinent to the case should be made and a system for identifying, indexing, numbering and control the documents chosen. This system should be organized so as to be able to identify, index, number, and control documents received from the client as well as from opposing parties throughout the discovery phase of the case. Once the control procedure is in place, it should be strictly adhered to, and every document that is received during discovery, no matter what its source, should be entered into the system immediately upon its receipt. This should result in the ability to easily and quickly retrieve any document produced in the discovery phase of the case.

8.06361 Case Exhibit Control Log. One effective system for controlling exhibits introduced from the outset of the case is the use of a Case Exhibit Control Log. This type of log identifies every exhibit introduced by each party, in chronological order. It permits the attorney to track his/her own, and other parties', exhibits in numeric or alphabetical or sequential order, no matter whether they were attached to the complaint, answer, interrogatories, depositions, requests for production of documents, requests for admissions, or motions. (*See* Exhibit 8-8 for an example of a Case Exhibit Control Log.)

EXHIBIT 8-8   Sample Case Exhibit Control Log

CASE:	Howard Jones v. Holiday Inn
ATTORNEY:	Jack Bonin
CLIENT:	Howard Jones
DATE LAST POSTED:	7/19/89
LEGAL ASSISTANT:	Jan Harlow

Pltf	Deft	Other Party	How Submitted	Description of Exhibit
X			Complaint—Ex 1	Holiday Inn Annual Report—1986
	X		Interrog. Answer #5	Financial Audit—Holiday Inn—1986
		X 3dp Def Comfort Inn	Depo.—30(b)(6)— Comfort Inn	Comfort Inn Annual Report—1985

8.06362 Discovery Exhibit Log. An alternative to the larger Case Exhibit Control Log is to maintain an integrated exhibit log for all exhibits produced through the all various discovery devices. (*See* Exhibit 8-9.) The object is to organize what can become a chaotic mass of paper, which in turn prevents you from locating any document easily and quickly, which is a necessary goal in litigation. If this is to accomplish the necessary organization, however, some sort of sequential numbering system should be used. How much simpler it is to refer to twenty exhibits introduced from various sources if they are numbered sequentially with cross-references to the identity of the party who submitted it, in connection with what pleading or discovery event it was introduced, and a description of the document. The attorney will then be able, by referring to the log, to simply call for Document #2, rather than having to ask for Exhibit D2 in the deposition of John Albert Thomas, taken by defendant on June 22, 1983.

EXHIBIT 8-9   Discovery Exhibit Log

CASE: Benjamin Jackson   ATTORNEY: Ford Mason
CLIENT: Aimes Alabaster
DATE LAST POSTED: 3/27/95
LEGAL ASSISTANT: Marilyn Afeman

Doc #	Who Submitted	Discovery Event	Description of Document
1	Def.—Aimes Alabaster	Pl. B. Jackson Int.Ans.	10 Photos of accident site
2	Def.—Aimes Alabaster	Pl. B. Jackson Int.Ans.	13 Photos of automobile
3	Def.—Aimes Alabaster	Pl. B. Jackson Int.Ans.	1989–94 Income Tax Returns
4	Def.—Aimes Alabaster	Pl. B. Jackson Int.Ans.	Johns Hosp. record 2/9/88–3/17/88
5	Pl.—B. Jackson	Def.—Aimes Int.Ans.	Videotape of accident site
6	Pl.—B. Jackson	Def.—Aimes Depo.	Sketch w/measurements of skid marks
7	Pl.—B. Jackson	Def.—Aimes Depo.	Photos of 18-wheel truck & trailer

Using a sequential numbering system requires close cooperation and discipline by the members of the litigation team, and if the case has more than one attorney assigned to it, it becomes even more complicated. There is a need for clear understanding of the procedure from the beginning of the lawsuit, so that each person who is involved in the logging process understands the process and the necessity for uniformity in maintaining the log.

8.064 Adversary Answers to Interrogatories

It is important for the legal assistant to carefully analyze, immediately on receipt, the answers provided by the adversary to the client's interrogatories. Evasiveness in answering any interrogatory should be discovered immediately, because there is a very short period between the time when the answers are served and the date by which any motions to compel further answers can legitimately be made. Occasionally, interrogatory answers are incomplete or unresponsive, but without determining a pattern of obvious deception or intent to deny the information called for by the interrogatory, it is difficult to win a motion to compel.

8.0641 Incomplete or "To Be Supplied" Answers. It is best to compare exactly what is requested by the interrogatory with the information provided in the answer. Where the relationship between the question and answer is reasonable, sometimes the matter can be resolved by phoning the adversary counsel's office, informally asking if the incomplete answers were inadvertently provided, and offering to grant an extension of time in which to answer. Of course, such an inquiry and offer should only be made by the legal assistant with the approval and the authority of the supervising attorney. The extension should be confirmed in writing to the other party and contain a provision that the other party agrees to have the time limit for filing a motion to compel tolled until the receipt of the supplemental or corrective answers or notification that the party will let the original answers stand.

Incomplete or "to be supplied" answers are very dangerous for the responding party. The propounding party has a right to complete answers. Any indication by the responding party that the answer is incomplete or will be supplied at a later date creates a burden that the responding party must honor in the future. It also places an additional burden on the propounding party to follow up such a response to ensure the answer is actually supplied. The legal assistant for either party should calendar the matter properly and be prepared, before discovery comes to a close, to remind the attorney to resolve such incomplete answers in a timely fashion.

Consider the effect of a plaintiff trying to move the case along to trial who, during discovery, files a "to be supplied" answer to an interrogatory propounded by the defendant. Discovery reaches the closing stages (usually about thirty days prior to the trial) when the defendant discovers that the plaintiff has not completely responded to the defendant's discovery. In many jurisdictions, the case may be removed from the trial calendar until discovery is completed. This can result in the case not being rescheduled for trial for a period of up to a year or more, depending on the size of the court's docket. The plaintiff's attorney has provided the defense attorney with a perfect opportunity for delaying a trial, which can be an effective method of delaying the financial burden of a judgment. Provided the defendant's actions are not obviously the grounds for the postponement, this kind of delaying tactic is seldom subject to sanctions of the court or bar association.

The lawyer and legal assistant should be a team that effectively moves the case forward and denies the adversary these types of "sitting duck" grounds for postponements and delays.

8.0642 Unresponsive Answers. Unresponsive answers are fairly common. Though they may appear on the surface to be a proper response, closer inspection may reveal that they have not answered the question asked. The propounding party's responsibility is to review the answers and determine whether or not they are acceptable and fully responsive to the question asked. If they are not, there is usually a limited period of time in which to compel responsive answers, because of the deadlines set in the court's scheduling order. Because of the self-executing nature of interrogatories, an attorney who allows that period to pass without action waives the right to have the unresponsive answers corrected, which means they may not be used at trial, or that their use may be severely curtailed.

The legal assistant who reviews the answers as they arrive can be of great assistance to the lawyer on this point alone. Analysis of the question and its answer may reveal the question to be unclear, ambiguous, or capable of various meanings. The answer may be an obvious evasion, a misunderstanding, a typographical error, or an inadvertent misstatement. Such an analysis will suggest the corrective action needed: a motion to compel, a phone call to the adversary to informally request that the answer be supplemented, or the submission of more specific and clarifying interrogatories.

In cases where the answers are obviously nonresponsive or appear to be deliberately incomplete, the same procedure for informally contacting the adversary to request that the answer be supplemented as outlined in Section 8.0641 may be followed. In this situation, the offer of additional time is made in writing, to the responding party as follows:

> "This will confirm the telephone conversation between my legal assistant, Mr. Jones, and Ms. Smith of your office regarding your incomplete Answers to our Interrogatories, Set No. 2, in which we offered to extend the time for your answers for an additional fifteen days from date of this letter. It is assumed that the time for us to file a motion to compel further answers will be tolled until we are notified that your answers will stand as submitted or we receive the full, complete answers."

This action places the burden on the responding party to decide whether to stand on the answers or provide additional information. At the same time, it protects the right of the propounding party to initiate a motion to compel further answers, yet shows cooperation and courtesy. This method may elicit the requested information in the fifteen-day period, which would eliminate the need to spend time preparing a motion, filing and serving it, and having it set for hearing, as well as the other potential delays in obtaining the information itself.

8.065 Answering Interrogatories

The party responding to properly served interrogatories has a duty to answer each question in writing, separately, fully, responsively, and under oath; the only limitation is that the information requested must be relevant to the subject matter of the action, and reasonably calculated to lead to the discovery of admissible evidence. The exceptions, of course, are where the information is privileged because it is protected by the attorney/client privilege, or the work product of the attorney, or is material prepared in anticipation of litigation, or when answering would be an oppressive burden on the responding party. Failure to answer a properly phrased, relevant interrogatory within the time allowed may result in an order to compel answers. Worse than that, the failure to respond on time may waive the attorney's right to object to answering any interrogatory for which a proper objection could have been made if responses had been filed within the deadline for answering.

Providing the information necessary to answer interrogatories, particularly personal information, is usually the duty of the client, with the help of the legal assistant, whose primary task is to assemble the factual data and provide draft answers from which the final responses are created.

"Responding" to interrogatories is the responsibility of the client's attorney. "Responding to" and "answering" interrogatories are not necessarily the same. "Answering" interrogatories includes expository answers, fully complete as to all relevant, known data; such answers may also include "volunteered" information that is beyond the scope of the specific question asked, or may be public information equally available to both sides. Such an answer may include the attachment of documents responsive to the question in lieu of a detailed, written response. On the other hand, a "response" to an interrogatory may consist of a complete refusal to answer stated in the form of an objection, or consist of an answer to the nonobjectionable portion of an interrogatory combined with an objection. This imposes a special responsibility on the legal assistant to ensure that all sources of information readily available to the client or the attorney are carefully searched, and that properly inclusive responsive answers are drafted for the consideration and editing of the attorney. It requires a careful analysis and full understanding of the interrogatories received and the issues in the case.

For instance, a question may seek a listing of "any and all evidence in your possession." This is not a well-crafted request. The word "evidence" is one with a specific legal meaning. Whether or not something qualifies as evidence is usually determined by a judge unless the parties stipulate to that fact. Therefore, the responding attorney could completely object to answering that interrogatory on the grounds that only a court may rule whether items or exhibits qualify as "evidence," or could object in part and answer in part: "we object to that portion which calls for a conclusion that all items in the possession of the party qualify as evidence; notwithstanding that objection, the party does possess the following items which may be offered as evidence at the trial of this case." The latter response is better practice, for it is in keeping with the spirit of the federal rules on discovery.

The legal assistant is responsible for making certain the responses to interrogatories are prepared and served within the established deadline. Making certain that the due date of the interrogatory answers, with appropriate warning dates, is recorded in the firm's or attorney's calendaring system is the best way of ensuring that the interrogatories are answered on time.

8.0651 *Time to Answer.* Every jurisdiction, whether federal or state, provides a specific period of time within which answers and responses to the interrogatories must be served. Any response which asserts an objection must be made within the applicable time period for answering. Unstated or untimely grounds for objection may be considered waived.

If additional time is needed to answer interrogatories, an informal request to the propounding party for an extension may be made by telephone or by letter; in most cases, one will be granted. There is no particular rule on the period of time to be granted as an extension. This is negotiated between the lawyers or their representatives under the provisions of Rule 29. Precision in language is important when requesting extensions. An agreement which allows additional time to *answer* interrogatories, but does not include additional time to *respond* may have the effect of responding party waiving the right to object. The better practice is for the responding party to include language which "extends the time to answer and/or otherwise respond to the interrogatories."

When either a full or a limited extension of time to answer or respond is given, that agreement should be confirmed in writing with the other party the same day it is granted. It is not good practice to give or receive verbal extensions of time to answer or respond to interrogatories without written confirmation. Often the attorneys for both parties will send letters confirming the terms of the agreement. When the other attorney's letter arrives in the office, the legal assistant or the lawyer should check it to make certain the terms of the agreement are accurately recorded in the letter. This alleviates future confusion and misunderstandings.

If the opposing party will not grant an informal extension of time and the attorney believes he or she has sufficient grounds to do so, a formal motion for extension of time may be filed. Often this formal motion will not be contested by the requesting party, even though he or she would not grant an informal extension of time. But the responding party should be able to provide specific and valid reasons for the requested extension of time.

8.0652 *Initial Review.* The interrogatories should first be read immediately on receipt, not analytically or argumentatively but from beginning to end, as a novel would be read. This allows an appreciation of the flow and scope of the interrogatories and suggests the approach of the adversary party and the overall thrust of the set of questions: Does the opponent seek facts, or identities? Does it seek contentions of the responding party? Are the questions specific or generalized and broadly inclusive? Does the requesting party aim at clarifying proximate cause or the affirmative defenses being asserted by the defendant?

Following the initial reading, a careful question-by-question reading of the set should be performed by the legal assistant independent of the attorney. Some questions are of a straight factual nature, while other questions appear to be mixed questions of fact and law, particularly susceptible to interpretation by the attorney; others ask for pure legal interpretation. The legal assistant should make notes during the analysis to include the probable responding responsibility as "legal assistant," "attorney," or "client," or any combination thereof.

8.0653 *Attorney and Legal Assistant Conference.* The third reading occurs during a planning meeting which the legal assistant should schedule with the attorney to formalize the answering procedure. The attorney probably will have read the interrogatories (or may read them during the course of the meeting), and decisions then can be made about how to proceed in the case. The responding responsibilities noted by the legal assistant are confirmed or modified, and decisions on how to handle the "client" answers can be made, that is, whether to call the client to the office, mail a set of the questions with instructions to return the answers by mail, mail a set of questions and then record the client's answers in a telephone conference, or coordinate with the client other means of obtaining the information within the client's knowledge and control necessary to prepare proper responses.

When the potential answer depends partially on a legal interpretation by the attorney, the legal assistant should assemble, in draft form, the factual data called for by the question. The legal assistant should then schedule a meeting with the attorney to discuss how best to respond to the interrogatory.

8.0654 *Source of the Answer, Responsibility, and Control.* Following the attorney's and legal assistant's review of the interrogatories, the legal assistant must try to decide on the best source(s) of the information from which to obtain answers to the questions the attorney delegated to the legal assistant to answer. If the information is in the case file, the legal assistant can simply extract it, draft the answers, and submit them for approval, editing, or rejection by the attorney.

If the client is a corporation, the legal assistant can establish a contact person in the corporation to coordinate the distribution of the interrogatories (or portions) to appropriate personnel within the corporation and to establish deadlines well in advance of the answer date for the return of appropriate information. It is essential for the legal assistant to have a follow-up procedure for contacting the contact person prior to the established deadline, so that the information gathered by the client will be received on time. This is particularly important when the client decides that objections to certain interrogatories should be made instead of answering them. The attorney will not be in a position to agree or disagree with this conclusion until the client's information is received and reviewed.

When questions will be answered using information and material from a variety of sources, it sometimes is helpful to photocopy the entire set of interrogatories and supply each source with those questions he or she is being asked to answer. A long or complex series of pattern interrogatories (one basic question followed by related subsections based on alternative anticipated answers) can be effectively controlled by photocopying the full set, then cutting and pasting each question onto paper punched for three-ring binders. As the source's material is received, it can be filed behind the question until it is time to draft answers. This system is helpful for the process of engrossing answers, if the material is carefully prepared and organized.

PRACTICE TIP — Casual Handling

Inexperienced legal assistants, and occasionally attorneys, under heavy calendar pressure will accept interrogatories from the adversary and forward them to the client for answer. When the answers prepared by the client are returned to the law office, the answers may be typed and filed without careful review or analysis of the questions or answers supplied by the client. Since the answers are required to be under oath, the client is bound by the answers in future court proceedings, and it is difficult and embarrassing to attempt to correct even inadvertent errors in such a situation. Preparing and submitting answers from information and materials provided by the client, or gleaned by the legal assistant from the attorney's work file without consultation with the attorney, and the client, and other knowledgeable sources is extremely dangerous.

Clients often do not understand the legal or factual import of some interrogatories, or they may misunderstand or misconstrue a word or phrase in an interrogatory. Using their unedited answers to interrogatories can therefore be damaging to the clients case. Preparing answers using information from the attorneys work file may inadvertently waive a discovery privilege or immunity. It is imperative that the attorney and/or legal assistant carefully peruse the questions that are posed and decide the best source of an answer, if any answer is to be given. Further, the answers must be checked for consistency with answers to pleadings, prior statements, prior depositions, prior responses to written discovery, and so forth, before they are finalized and submitted to the requesting party.

Another alternative is to make an extra copy of the interrogatories and mount them on the left-hand side of a file folder, then collect and file the data and draft answers on the right. A third method is to place the interrogatories (without cutting and pasting) in a three-ring binder, and then collect and file behind separate, labeled divider tabs the information and draft answers corresponding to each question. These organizational methods assist everyone in keeping track of the collection of the information by providing one place where that material can be stored until it is time to begin preparing the draft, and ultimately the final, answers and responses.

8.0655 *Format and Form of Answers.* As mentioned in the section on Drafting Interrogatories, the Federal Rules of Civil Procedure require the question and the answer to be engrossed in the final version of the answers, which means that each interrogatory appears first, followed immediately by the answer to that interrogatory. This practice is very helpful to all parties and to the courts and jury in the conduct of a case, whether that is a court rule or not. Many state courts have adopted the same or similar rules.

With the advent of scanners into the legal world, this procedure has become easier to accomplish. Each set of interrogatories is scanned into a computer, converted into the appropriate word processing program, and answers can then be inserted after each interrogatory. When a scanner is not available, the alternatives are to have the questions retyped, or to cut-and-paste the interrogatories, one to a page, to provide sufficient space for the answers, or to simply use addendum pages onto which the "overflow" of the longer answers can be typed.

8.0656 *Content of an Answer.* The Federal Rules of Civil Procedure places the responsibility on the responding party to provide full answers to the extent the interrogatories are not objectionable. If one question is objectionable on the grounds that it is too burdensome, it does not relieve the responding party of answering a similar question on a related topic or issue that asks for smaller amounts of information. Also, the fact that the responding party may need additional time to respond to some questions (or portions of some questions) does not justify a delay in responding to those questions (or portions of questions) that can be answered within the applicable time period.

Once a party decides to answer an interrogatory, the answer should be clear, concise, and directly responsive to the question. It should be based on information that the responding party has at hand. It is not necessary to provide information that is unavailable to the client or over which neither the client nor the attorney has possession, custody, or control. When answering an interrogatory based on lack of knowledge, the attorney, the legal assistant, and the client must be sure there is no access or control question that can be raised by the requesting party in a motion to compel.

A corporate client is very susceptible to a strict interpretation of the duty to answer in this situation because all information available to any employee of the corporation is considered equally available to the corporate entity and its counsel. If a court finds that the search made by the corporation was insufficient and the corporation had control of, or access to, the information through a subsidiary, branch, or other related entity, it may uphold the motion to compel and apply sanctions which may not only be monetary, but may also result in answers being stricken or matters being deemed admitted. Therefore, clients must be warned that a thorough search of all potential sources known to, or in the control of, the corporation must be made in gathering information with which to answer interrogatories. Additionally, lengthy answers that evade the question should be avoided since they will also often result in the filing

---

PRACTICE TIP — Unverified Answers

Unverified answers, though not proper, often occur through failure (inadvertent or deliberate) of the responding party to execute the verification to which the propounding party is entitled. This failure on the part of the answering party can be caught, however, if the propounding party checks the answers to determine that they were submitted in verified form. Unverified answers are not under oath and do not have the same force as verified answers, and cannot be used in the same way as verified answers, as the applicable rule intends. Due to the self-executing nature of interrogatories, the failure to detect the unverified answers, and to move timely and appropriately to compel verification in timely fashion, may require resubmission of the interrogatories to the adversary in order to obtain the verification, or a motion to compel if the party refuses to submit the appropriate verification, and will, at the very least, require extra work on the part of the attorney and legal assistant to obtain the proper verification by or some other, more informal method.

The attorney who uses legal assistants will usually designate either the legal assistant or the legal secretary to check incoming answers for verifications; however, the professional legal assistant recognizes that errors can occur and should double-check each set regardless of office procedure or custom and immediately call the lack of proper verification to the attention of the attorney so that prompt steps may be taken to correct the lack.

of a motion to compel by the propounding party, and may also result in sanctions against the answering party if successful. These activities create mistrust between the parties, wastes time and money, and does nothing to favorably advance the client's position.

8.0657 *Grounds for Objection.* If the legal assistant finds the interrogatory extremely complicated, difficult to understand, or that it requires excessive amounts of effort, research, assembly, collation, and reporting of information to enable the attorney to properly and fully answer the interrogatories, objection to those particular interrogatories (or the entire set, if appropriate) should be considered. In this situation, the grounds for objection are essentially those of injustice. For instance, it is immaterial that the information requested may require hearsay, since interrogatories have a much broader range than admissible evidence at trial. The purpose of discovery in general and interrogatories in particular is to learn about evidence that is admissible at trial or that may lead to the discovery of admissible evidence, not necessarily to provide the evidence itself, although any answer given may be used against the respondent. If this type of objection is raised, it must be couched in phrases the court will honor, and those always must include a showing of some form of injustice to the responding party.

The grounds for objecting on the basis of privilege or protection should also be stated specifically. Federal Rule 26(b)(5) requires a responding party to notify all other parties if it is withholding materials that are otherwise discoverable when the grounds for objection relate to any type of privilege or protection, including attorney work product and materials prepared in anticipation of litigation. Withholding such materials without notice violates Rule 26(b)(5); such action could be the subject of a motion for sanctions under Rule 37(b)(2) and the privilege could be deemed waived.

This rule also requires the responding party to provide enough information about the withheld materials to enable the other parties to evaluate the validity of the privilege or protection that is claimed. The other parties may believe that the privilege or protection invoked by the responding party is not valid, and may challenge the claim by motion to compel, in which case it is the court's duty to decide whether the privilege or protection applies to those materials. The type of information that should be provided by the party invoking the privilege concerns such things as general subject matter of the materials, applicable time periods, identity of persons who prepared, read, or received it, etc. If the materials being withheld are voluminous, the better practice might be to describe the documents by category instead of the more specific information.

The attorney is the authority on objections and whether to file them. The legal assistant may find at the conclusion of the meeting in which the decision has been made to object that the attorney will say, "Give me the draft answers and objections by tomorrow at ten, please, so they can be typed and filed by four." Because legal assistants often work on such short deadlines, familiarity with some of the language of objections can save substantial time and reduce the necessity for rewriting.

a. Continuing Answers. For interrogatories that require "continuing answers," the objection may say: "Plaintiff objects to this entire set of interrogatories on the grounds that the request to treat these interrogatories as a continuing obligation is not required under FRCP 26(e) or 33, and would constitute an unjust, oppressive burden." While the Federal Rules of Civil Procedure provide for certain circumstances when discovery answers and responses must be supplemented, there is no requirement that discovery responses be treated as "continuing." A party that seeks to obtain "continuing interrogatories" must petition the court specifically to be given permission to place such a burden upon the responding party, and must show good cause why it should be allowed to do so.

b. Confusing Instructions. If the propounding party includes instructions that are confusing or which contain confusing subinstructions, this may constitute a basis for objection by the responding party that may be phrased this way: "Defendant objects to the form of the instructions controlling these interrogatories on the grounds that the instructions are so complex and contain so many subinstructions and are so detailed that they require the respondent to spend unnecessary, extra, and unjustified time and effort to ascertain the impact of these instructions on succeeding interrogatories, and the instructions are therefore unjustly burdensome and oppressive."

This should serve as a warning that if instructions are going to be included in interrogatories, whether simple or complex, they should be relatively few and clearly and reasonably phrased; otherwise, the answering party will have grounds for objection on the basis that it will have a difficult time in either obtaining an answer or expressing its position in a motion to compel.

c. Public Records. Public records and documents are often sought by the propounding party and resisted by the responding party. The mere fact that the documents are a public record, equally available to both sides, is not necessarily a legitimate objection. However, if the objection is phrased in the proper way, the objection is more likely to be upheld. Here is an example: "Plaintiff objects on the grounds that the requested information is a matter of public record contained in public documents which are not in plaintiff's possession or control, and that this information is equally available to Defendant, such that requiring Plaintiff to locate, copy, and furnish such information would be unreasonable, unjust, burdensome and oppressive."

d. Irrelevancy. Some interrogatories go far afield and may intrude on areas not relevant to the issues raised by the claims and defenses in the lawsuit. In such a case, an objection may stand on the ground of irrelevance, but the objection, however phrased, must be combined with a statement that the question ". . . is not reasonably calculated to lead to the discovery of admissible evidence." The burden then shifts to the propounding party to file a motion to compel and show the relevance of the requested information to the subject matter of the lawsuit, the rationale behind the question, and in what manner the information sought would lead to the discovery of admissible evidence.

e. Uncertainty and Ambiguity. If an interrogatory is written in a vague and ambiguous manner, to the extent that the attorney and legal assistant must impute meaning to the request, there is a basis for an objection on those grounds. This objection may be phrased in this fashion: "Interrogatory No. 2 and particularly the phrase 'riding lawn mowers like the one involved in the accident sued on' is so ambiguous, uncertain, and unintelligible that defendant cannot frame a meaningful reply and therefore objects to the form of the question." Usually, the propounding party will rephrase the question in a more intelligible fashion and serve it again. Alternatively, the responding party could object in part as stated above and answer in part by imputing to the interrogatory the meaning most favorable to the client's case, and then providing an answer consistent with that view. This places the propounding party on a double hook. It is difficult to argue in a motion to compel hearing that you are entitled to the information that is sought by a poorly worded, vague, or ambiguous question when a free and willing offer of some information has been given by the responding party.

f. Burdensome and Oppressive Questions. Sometimes interrogatories impose severe burdens on the responding party to obtain the information upon which to base answers or responses.

Lack of time, money, available employees, and the necessity of travel are some of the reasons why such interrogatories may be burdensome or oppressive. In such a situation, the attorney will consider objecting to the interrogatories on those grounds.

Usually, the legal assistant is the person with the best command of the facts of the case and the sources of information that interrogatories of this nature will require. If it is anticipated that the search for the information required by interrogatories will be—or may become—"burdensome and oppressive," the legal assistant must assemble factual data on the nature and extent of the burden to assist the attorney in deciding whether to object to the interrogatory or to assemble all or a portion of the information for the answers. The foundation for such an objection will require calculation of the amount of time and the overall expense, including any necessary travel, cost of use of employees, or of hiring additional employees to perform the research, copying costs, and other such expenses. The legal assistant should confer with the client to ensure that all expense and time-related factors are included in the calculations, and that the calculations are as accurate as possible.

8.0658 *Final Draft.* The final draft of the answers must be proofread for form as well as content. Each answer should be checked to make sure it properly answers or responds to the question asked. All typographical errors should be corrected and the overall answers checked for compliance with form requirements. In addition, the legal assistant should check to make certain that any documents to be attached to the answers are copied and properly labeled to correspond to the number of the interrogatory to which they respond. All the answers should then be checked for internal and external consistency one last time.

8.0659 *Additional, Supplemental, or Correcting Answers.* Frequently, not all the information necessary to properly and fully answer or respond to interrogatories is available within the applicable time limit. In such cases, it is appropriate to say in the response that "supplemental information will be provided" or "will be supplied," or "documents will be supplied in a timely manner that respond to this interrogatory," or to use similar phrasing indicating that the information is not being provided, that no objection to the interrogatory is raised, and that it will be given to the requesting party when it is available to the responding party. When such commitments are made, however, it is important to record the promise and to follow up on fulfilling it.

When it is learned that information previously supplied in an interrogatory answer is incorrect, an amended answer correcting that information should be provided in order to clarify the record. It is extremely difficult to correct such errors at trial without doing serious harm to the client's credibility or the overall case. The legal assistant should constantly keep track of facts developed in a case and, as factual conflicts are identified, bring them to the attention of the attorney. The legal assistant can prepare drafts of amended answers or stipulations to correct and clarify the information previously given.

8.066 Motions to Compel Discovery

Rule 37 provides a method to force a party who has failed to answer interrogatories to answer them fully, completely, and responsively. A motion to compel under Rule 37(a) may be accompanied by a request that the party who failed to answer be ordered to pay the costs of making such motion (sanctions), including attorney's fees. Corresponding state rules or code sections allow substantially the same motion.

In every case, the rules of court outline the requirements necessary for filing such a motion. In almost every case, the moving party must submit several documents. There may be a requirement for a notice of the hearing date on the motion, the motion itself, a memorandum of points and authorities supporting the motion, and a declaration by the attorney as to the legitimacy of the motion. Some courts have local rules that require either an allegation in the motion or a separate certificate by the attorney for the moving party that the parties have met and made an effort to solve the discovery dispute, but have been unsuccessful in doing so.

One of the most common errors made by parties filing discovery motions is the general nature of stating the allegations that the responses to the discovery were unacceptable. Most courts require the moving party to state specific reasons why each disputed response is unacceptable. Most courts have adopted rules that require the following contents in the motion:

a. State the full text of each interrogatory that is not fully answered, then
b. Immediately follow with the full text of the response given by the answering party and/or the objection thereto, in full; and then
c. Provide a short statement of the moving counsel's contention that the interrogatory is not fully answered and/or the reasons why the responding party's objection should be overruled. The attorney may cite any legal and factual points and authorities applicable to his or her position; and
d. The moving party must serve the documents, along with the notice of the motion (if required by local rule) and any other papers required by law or local rules, upon the party or parties against whom the motion is directed, within the time period prescribed.

The burden is upon the party receiving the answers to interpret them correctly as being responsive or unresponsive, to determine whether the objections have merit or not, and to initiate such appropriate action as he or she feels appropriate and legitimate. Allowing any applicable time period to pass without action will waive the right to file a motion to compel further answers on that set of interrogatories. The movant must show that the information is reasonably believed to be available to the responding party and that the information sought is relevant to the proceedings and/or calculated to lead to the discovery of admissible evidence. Further, there must be a statement denying that answering the interrogatory will be burdensome, a harassment, or oppressive, if the adversary used those terms in objecting to the interrogatory.

The courts will often instruct responding parties to respond to the questions correctly and fully on an individual basis so long as there is not an extraordinary burden and so long as the questions do not constitute oppression. Oppression can mean inordinate expense for the value of the information provided, or excessive work effort necessary to locate the information or determine the existence of information over long spans of time or through huge masses of paper with little or no probative value to the case. The court may deny the motion to compel on these grounds if it finds the oppression or burden is too great on the responding party.

If the responding party has created an unreasonable burden (that is, the necessity of filing the motion to compel) on the propounding party in order to obtain the requested information, sanctions (the costs of the motion and attorney's fees for appearing in court for the motion) may be sought and obtained against the responding party. As a general and practical rule, courts are hesitant to grant sanctions early in a case or for failure properly to respond only to one set of interrogatories. A pattern of obstructive behavior or unwillingness to participate fairly and cooperatively in the process, however, may result in the court assessing financial sanctions against the noncooperating party.

If an order is issued as a result of a motion to compel, commanding the responding party to answer the discovery, and the responding party violates the court's order by failing to respond or failing to fully respond, as required by the order, Rule 37(b) provides that, in addition to monetary sanctions similar to those provided in Rule 37(a), the court may issue an order striking claims or defenses or other matters from the pleadings, order designated facts to be taken as established for purposes of the case, or to hold the party and/or its attorney in contempt of court.

8.067   Analysis and Use of Interrogatories

The legal assistant is usually charged with tracking and analyzing all interrogatory responses given by or on behalf of the client. It is necessary to accumulate both the questions and the answers and to relate them in some collated form to the issues or the elements of proof in the case. The plaintiff's claims must be outlined, detailing the elements of each type of claim for both liability and damages. The defenses, affirmative or otherwise, of each defendant must also be outlined, and the elements of proof for each affirmative defense should be included in the outline. The legal assistant then reviews each interrogatory and answer to determine its bearing on the various claims and defenses.

Analysis of the other party's answers is extremely helpful to the attorney, particularly where the interrogatories included documents attached as exhibits and answers were obtained that specifically or impliedly affirmed the documents as true or correct copies of originals. If the originals cannot be found, a foundation has been laid to introduce the exhibits as "secondary evidence" at trial.

Any information given by the attorney or the client in answer to interrogatories may be used by any other party as an admission against the interests of the client. In other words, a party cannot use his or her own answers to another party's interrogatories as proof of the fact in issue, although an adversary may be able to use those answers (because they are given under oath) as proof of a fact against the responding party. This emphasizes the importance of knowing the foundation of each answer supplied and that the answers are as factually correct and consistent as possible.

8.07   Depositions

Depositions are the method by which a party or a witness is examined orally under oath by counsel for each party to the action. Depositions in federal cases are governed by Rules 30 and 31 of the Federal Rules of Civil Procedure. State courts generally have similar provisions within their codes or statutes. These methods of taking a deposition, the oral deposition (Rule 30) and the deposition by written question (Rule 31), are sworn, out-of-court statements by witnesses during which counsel for all parties have an opportunity to ask questions of the deponent. The person whose testimony is taken during a deposition is commonly referred to as the "deponent."

Rule 30 provides that the oral deposition of any party or witness may be taken without leave of court. The deponent's attendance may be compelled by subpoena pursuant to Rule 45. Leave of court must be obtained to take a deposition in certain circumstances: when the proposed deponent is in prison; when a proposed deposition would result in more than ten depositions being taken by any one party under Rule 30 or 31 (except as may be amended by local rule or when the parties agree by stipulation to a different limitation); when the proposed deponent has already been deposed in the case; and when a party seeks to take a deposition before the meeting of the parties required by Rule 26(f).

8.071 Coordinating Depositions

One of the first tasks delegated to legal assistants is the coordination of depositions. This involves contacting the counsel for other parties, the witness, and a court reporter to set the date, time, and place for the deposition to be taken. Once a date, time, and place is established, the legal assistant is responsible for ensuring the Notice of Deposition required in Rule 30 and 31 is served on counsel for all parties, the witness, and the counsel for the witness (if any). In many instances, it will also be necessary to have the witness served with a subpoena to ensure their attendance at the deposition. Finally, arrangements for the deposition location and the court reporter are finalized, confirmed, and placed on the appropriate calendars for the firm and the supervising attorney.

8.0711 Arranging Depositions. As a matter of professional courtesy, all counsel and the witness are contacted by the legal assistant to arrange a mutually convenient date, time, and place for the deposition. When this is not possible, the date, time, and place is selected which meets the notice and location requirements of the rules or statutes, and fits the schedule of the supervising attorney and the client. The legal assistant must take into consideration whether the witness lives in the local area, within 100 miles, within the state, or in another state or country. Also, when the deponent is an expert or a professional, such as a physician or nurse, it is almost always necessary to consult them as to their availability. When the witness lives outside the local area, the supervising attorney should be consulted about whether the witness is to be brought to the local area, whether the deposition should be held in the place where the witness lives, or whether to arrange to take the deposition by telephone or video conference. If the deposition is to be held someplace other than the supervising attorney's office, arrangements for a suitable location will need to be made as well. Once all these details have been settled, the Notice of Deposition required by the rules (*see* Exhibit 8-10) should be served on the witness along with a subpoena (if not a party). Counsel of record for all parties are also served with the deposition notice. If any party is not represented by counsel or is acting *pro se*, the notice should be served on that party at the last known address. The next step is to make sure the date, time, and place is entered into the attorney's or firm's calendar system. Finally, arrangements are made with a court reporter to attend and take the deposition, along with any necessary additional arrangements if the deposition will be videotaped or taken by telephone.

EXHIBIT 8-10   Sample Notice of Deposition

[*CAPTION OF LITIGATION*]

NOTICE OF DEPOSITION

To: All Parties of Record and Their Counsel

PLEASE TAKE NOTICE that [*name of noticing party*] will take an oral deposition of the person specified below, on [*date*] at [*time*] at [*place and address*] before a certified court reporter authorized to administer oaths, for all purposes permitted by federal rules and statutes.

[*Name and address of deponent*]

Dated: _____   _____

                Name of Attorney
                Attorney for [*name of noticing party*]

Deposition arrangements are often subject to change for many different reasons. One of the counsel for the parties, or your own attorney, could be called to trial in another matter, the witness could become ill, an expert witness might be subpoenaed to testify in court in another matter—all these things happen more often than not, and can make deposition scheduling a frustrating and time consuming task. When it becomes necessary to reschedule a deposition, it generally requires the whole scheduling process to be repeated. It also requires an Amended Notice of Deposition be served as before, and the nonparty witness to be served with an amended subpoena as well.

8.0712 Subpoenas and Service. Witnesses must be subpoenaed to attend a deposition unless they are a party to the action. In federal court, and most other jurisdictions, it is not necessary to subpoena a party to require their attendance at a deposition. This is because parties to an action are already under the jurisdiction of the court, and proper notice in accord with Rule 30 or 31 is sufficient. In fact, Rule 37(d) provides for appropriate sanctions should any party fail to appear for their own deposition.

There are limitations imposed by each jurisdiction for the service of the subpoena. Federal and state courts do not allow parties in a lawsuit to indiscriminately impose burdensome travel requirements on witnesses. Rule 45 of the Federal Rules of Civil Procedure imposes specific mileage limitations for categories of witnesses in certain types of proceedings. The state courts, similarly, impose limitations on the distances over which a subpoena is effective. Rule 45 requires that a deposition subpoena may be quashed if it requires a witness who is not a party to travel more than 100 miles from the place where that person resides, is employed, or does business to give his deposition. Occasionally, it is possible to arrange for a witness to travel farther than the court order subpoena can normally enforce.

The service of a subpoena carries with it the responsibility of insuring that it is properly executed. Proper execution requires that the subpoena set forth the purpose of the subpoena. For instance, to take a deposition on oral examination, the subpoena should indicate that the person is required to "appear to testify." If the deponent is in custody of certain documents that are of interest to the case, the subpoena must specify that the deponent is "to appear to testify and to produce documents." This type of subpoena is called a subpoena *duces tecum* and must also comply with the requirements of Rule 34 concerning requests for production of documents and things including a description of the general categories of documents that are requested. Some jurisdictions also require that a subpoena *duces tecum* include a declaration by the attorney that they are necessary to the deposition, relevant to the case, and either constitute potential evidence or may lead to the discovery of admissible evidence in the case. Where such a subpoena is issued, the witness must appear with all of the documents specified in the subpoena and be prepared to discuss them.

Additionally, a subpoenaed witness is entitled to a statutory witness fee and mileage from home to the place of deposition at a fixed rate. Where a witness cooperates by traveling greater distances than required, loses wages, or incurs special expenses for the convenience of the lawyers and parties, arrangements to reimburse out-of-pocket costs can be made without tainting the witness's credibility and testimony. Most jurisdictions require that a check payable to the witness for the statutory fee and mileage be given to the witness at the same time the subpoena is served.

Some state courts require that the fees be presented only if requested, and some require that the fees be paid to the clerk of court, who in turn disburses the fees to the witness. It is proper and prudent in most cases to ensure that the person serving the subpoena has in a check available made out for the proper amount of witness fee or carries sufficient cash to provide the witness with those funds upon request. Otherwise, the subpoena may be unenforceable. Federal court subpoenas not only contain sufficient information to notify the witness what must be done to comply with the subpoena, but also contain information on the back of the subpoena explaining what their rights are if they believe the subpoena was for some reason wrongfully issued and served.

Subpoenas in federal cases may be served by any person who is not a party to the lawsuit and is at least eighteen years old, although in some limited kinds of civil cases, and in all criminal cases, the U.S. Marshal's Office is charged with the responsibility of serving subpoenas and other process. The wording "person not a party" means that legal assistants may be asked to serve subpoenas in federal court, and often do so. However, in some jurisdictions this same wording has been extended to exclude attorneys for a party and their employees as well, which would preclude legal assistants from serving subpoenas. In state courts, the sheriff's offices in each county or parish are often charged with the responsibility of serving subpoenas and other process. Some states have rules allowing the appointment of a private process server if after a specified time period the sheriff or constable has been unable to accomplish service of process on a subpoena or other document. The legal assistant should always make certain that the person charged with serving the subpoena is qualified and authorized to do so in the particular jurisdiction in which the lawsuit has been filed.

In federal court, the clerk of court may issue subpoenas, signed but otherwise blank, to any party who requests it. Rule 45 also allows an attorney to issue and sign a subpoena on behalf of a district court in which the attorney is authorized to practice, or for another district court when the requested deposition or production pertains to an action pending in a court in which the attorney is authorized to practice. Thus, in federal court it is easy to issue and serve subpoenas. The entire procedure can be accomplished by, and is in the complete control of, the attorney who desires the subpoena to be issued and served. In state courts, the rules generally require that the clerk of court issue the subpoenas and the sheriff or constable serve them, although some states follow the same or similar procedures set forth in the federal rules.

8.072 Deposition Purpose and Strategy

An oral deposition is one of the best discovery methods for obtaining information within the personal knowledge of a witness or a party to the action. Witness testimony is often the primary basis on which the trier of fact (whether judge or jury) will base a verdict. Therefore, the evaluation of the appearance, articulation, and credibility of witnesses expected to testify at trial is extremely important. Oral depositions afford the lawyers for each of the parties an opportunity to meet the witnesses who will probably testify at trial, to examine and cross-examine them before entering the courtroom for trial, and evaluate their credibility, appearance, and communication skills. Although questions at depositions are not subject to the more restrictive rules applicable to questioning at trial, they must be relevant to the subject matter of the litigation or be reasonably calculated to lead to the discovery of admissible evidence. Unlike interrogatories, witnesses must respond spontaneously in their own words to the questions asked, and generally are not allowed to consult with attorney before answering a question.

Depositions should be a part of a carefully scheduled, timed, and executed discovery plan and should involve both the attorney and the legal assistant. Deposition planning should include determining the types of information to be obtained from each potential witness and deciding the best order for taking their depositions. A common strategy is to depose the opposing party first in order to create a sworn record of his knowledge of the facts of the case before the opinions and recollections of other witnesses are heard, which prevents or limits the opportunity for rationalization, correction of any misinterpretations, or refreshing recollections. By the same token, it is good practice for both parties' depositions to be taken on the same day. This practice ensures that each party's testimony is recorded with little or no delay in the history of the lawsuit, and also ensures that neither party has the advantage of studying the other party's deposition testimony prior to their own. While these strategies are good practice in cases which have one party plaintiff and one party defendant, they are not as practical in cases with more than two parties or in complex, multiparty litigation. In those situations, decisions on which deposition to take first, and the order of those to follow, require careful thought and analysis. Some attorneys will base the order of depositions on which adversary they wish to attempt to settle with first, either based on the perceived weaknesses of the adversary's position, or because they believe their own position is weakest in terms of success at a jury trial. Other attorneys base the deposition order on what evidence they believe they need to obtain to either support or defend a motion for summary judgment. Of course, the ultimate order in which depositions are taken is also subject to the competing demands of the opponent.

8.073 Deposition Preparation

Depositions are an opportunity for the legal assistant to make effective use of case knowledge, organizational skills, judgment and analytical ability, and creative thinking.

The legal assistant's contribution to deposition begins with the preparation of a draft outline of facts known about the deponent, facts about which the deponent is expected to testify, and facts the attorney would like to develop through the deponent's testimony. The format of the outline should provide space for the attorney to make notes during the deposition and should also serve as a checklist of information to be verified and topics to be covered. Suggestions for exhibits to be used at the deposition should also be included in the outline and attached for review by the attorney (*see* Exhibit 8-11, page 250).

After the attorney has had an opportunity to review the draft outline, the legal assistant should schedule a meeting to finalize plans for the deposition. At this meeting, the attorney and the legal assistant discuss the upcoming deposition in detail to make certain they are both sufficiently familiar with the factual data to be developed, exhibits to be used, the critical areas to be covered, and any other considerations such as specialized terminology or credibility tests. The legal assistant then prepares the final deposition outline which incorporates the decisions made at the meeting as well as any additional information supplied by the attorney.

Final deposition preparation consists of organizing the proposed exhibits, including any demonstrative aids such as models of body parts, sketches, diagrams, photographs, charts, or graphs. A rule of thumb concerning deposition exhibits is that four copies of each proposed exhibit will be needed at the deposition: one for the lawyer, one to give the court reporter, one for the opposing attorney, and one for the deponent to review and to refer to during the deposition. The copies and the original, if available, of each exhibit may be packaged in an envelope or file folder, arranged in the order of their anticipated use during the deposition, or may be placed in three-ring binders with each exhibit behind an appropriately numbered divider tab. Which method to use will depend on the preference of the supervising attorney, and may vary from deposition to deposition.

8.0731 *Witness Preparation.*

One of the major services that a legal assistant can provide a lawyer is participation in the preparation of witnesses who are to be deposed by the adversaries.

EXHIBIT 8-11   Sample Deposition Outline

CASE: Smith v. Jones
DEPONENT: Albert Smith, plaintiff
DEPO DATE: 6 January 1990
LOCATION: 1421 6th Ave., Sacramento
ATTYS: E. Gibson for Jones
         N. Mason for Smith

Items to Cover	Testimony	Exhibit Desc. & No.
ID: Name, Address, & Telephone	Albert Smith 2130 "I" Street Sacramento 777/333-2222	
SSN	238-45-9726	
Age, DOB	47, 9/14/50	
Education	Wilson HS, Sacramento, 1968 Stanford, BS Math, 1972 UCLA, MS Math, 1974	
Employment	Stanford, Asst. Prof, Math Dept; 1973–1974 State of CA Dept of Highways Statistician; 1974–present	

Docs reviewed prior to deposition	Accident report
	Statistics on accidents in location of
	  accident in this matter
	Report of raw data on which statistics are
	  based
		Acc. Report, Exh. 1
		Statistics, Exh. 2
		
		Raw data docs, Exh. 3

The attorney will often assign the legal assistant the task of reviewing any documents the witnesses have been directed to produce, and then scheduling a meeting with the witness to find out what the witness knows about the documents, to discuss issues and topics it is anticipated will be covered, and to prepare the witness for what to expect during the deposition. This meeting is usually scheduled for a day or two prior to the deposition.

When the legal assistant reviews the witness's documents, it is very important to identify those which might fall under a protective privilege. Certain types of records of a personal or professional nature, such as medical records not directly connected to the case at issue, some tax records, or certain types of professional or "trade secret" records are examples of documents which may be shielded from discovery by the adversary. Whenever these types of documents are identified, they must be brought to the attention of the supervising attorney for a decision on how they are to be handled. In some cases, the documents may be withdrawn and not provided to the adversary parties; however, their existence must be identified along with the reason for their being withheld, i.e., the nature of the objection or privilege must be set forth during the preliminary phases of the deposition to meet the withholding party's obligations under the discovery rules. This also provides the adverse parties with sufficient information to make a decision whether to file a motion to compel the production of the withheld documents, as well as whether to go forward with the deposition before the motion to compel is decided or adjourn the deposition until a ruling has been obtained as to whether or not the documents must be produced.

The review with the witness covers several concerns: discussion of what takes place in a deposition, what to expect from the opposing attorney in terms of behavior and demeanor, the questions expected to be asked along with a review of the basic rules for testifying, and a review of the case-specific factual matters that are expected to be addressed in the deposition. It is important during the meeting to attempt to dispel any feeling the witness may have of anxiety, the fear of the unknown, or of going on the record. Explaining the process of a deposition helps dispel the fear of the unknown. Conveying and explaining the basic rules to follow in giving testimony also helps the witness:

a. Give only honest, responsive answers in the fewest possible words to the adversary attorney's questions.
b. Be aware that the "friendly" attitude of an opposing attorney at a deposition is for a purpose. Never forget that the attorney represents the opposing party.
c. The attorney for the client on whose behalf the witness is giving testimony will have a limited role in the deposition.
d. All questions asked in a deposition must be answered responsively unless they are totally irrelevant or constitute abuse, harassment, or humiliation of the witness.
e. The only other protection against full disclosure in a deposition is when a protective order limiting the topics is obtained prior to the beginning of the deposition (such orders are granted rarely and only in special circumstances).
f. Always allow the questioning attorney to complete the question and provide a short space for the friendly attorney to interpose objections, if any, before answering.
g. Avoid generalities, speculation, guessing, acting as an expert, and volunteering information not specifically required by a question.
h. Avoid estimating such things as time, speed, colors, distances, heights, weights, and so forth. (Many attorneys attempt to push witnesses into making such estimates, and then attack their testimony later when other sources of information reveal that the estimate was inaccurate or just plain wrong.) If you do not know the answer, you are not required to estimate or guess.
i. Avoid personal characterizations—for instance, "That boy's always been a smart aleck!" or "Everybody knows he's a drunk!"

No one can change a witness's basic manner of expression, but a few helpful hints can sometimes be the difference between a credible or discredited witness (*see* Chapter 6, Section 6.042, Refining Judgment Statements, for a related discussion of the topics of estimating and personal characterizations). Some witnesses want to review additional documents, reports, drawings, photos, or other items which may be in the possession of the attorney before beginning the deposition. Whether or not such a review would be helpful, few lawyers want their witnesses to review these materials because it then opens these documents to discovery by the opposing attorney and subject to examination.

There are commercially produced videotapes available that can take the place of direct participation by the legal assistant or the lawyer in this segment of witness preparation. Most of them review the rules for testifying (as discussed above), and then show short scenes that clearly demonstrate to the witness the consequences of not following the rules for testifying. Generally, these tapes last about one-half hour. Using this type of videotape frees the legal assistant and the attorney to do other work while the witness views the videotape. Afterwards, the legal assistant or attorney can meet with the witness to review the case-specific information necessary to fully prepare the witness for the deposition. It is also not unusual for the legal assistant to be asked to meet separately with the witness to review the specific factual matters connected with the upcoming deposition, take the position of devil's advocate, and walk the witness through the type of questioning which is expected to occur. This provides an opportunity for role-playing and give the witness practice in how to answer deposition questions.

The wise litigator always provides witnesses with some guidance in how to handle themselves at deposition (*see* Chapter 10, Exhibit 10-8, Sample Witness Instructions, for a set of witness guidelines that apply to depositions as well as trials). Most witnesses are reassured to be told that they need only tell the truth as best they can recall it.

8.074 Mechanics of a Deposition

On the date and time specified in the Notice of Deposition, the attorneys for the interested parties, the court reporter, the deponent, and often the parties themselves, appear at the location specified in the Notice. Once everyone is ready to begin, the court reporter begins the record with a required statement, administers the oath to the witness, and identifies all persons present for the deposition. Court reporters are considered officers of the court and are usually notaries public or otherwise empowered to give oaths, qualified to provide a written transcript of all of the words said during the course of the examination, and to prepare a booklet containing the transcript, including any documentary exhibits introduced during the deposition.

The attorney who noticed the deposition begins the examination by first explaining the ground rules of depositions to the witness. This generally includes a caution that everything said by the witness is being recorded under oath and may be used at a later time in a court of law to challenge anything he or she may say at that time that is different from what is said during the course of the deposition. The attorney may also advise the witness that there is no intent to trap or to take unfair advantage but simply to obtain honest and forthright answers to the questions asked. The witness is reminded to respond verbally to all questions and advised that responses made solely by head movements are unacceptable. The reporter must record the answers, and that requires an audible response. Usually the attorney will also ask the witness not to answer any questions he or she does not understand, that the witness should ask to have the question rephrased until it is clearly understood, and informs the witness that if a question is answered, it is presumed that the witness did understand the question. At this point, the attorney generally asks whether the witness wishes to read and sign the deposition, or waive that right. Unless that right is waived, under the federal rules, the witness will have thirty days after submission of the transcript to read it, to submit corrections, additions, or clarifications of the transcript, and to sign it. If the transcript is not signed or corrected within the specified time period, it may be used at trial as though it had been signed.

When all the parties and counsel are satisfied that the above preliminaries have been observed, the true examination begins with questions asked by the counsel who noticed the deposition. This is called "direct" examination, and is conducted in the same manner as allowed at trial under Rules 103 and 615 of the Federal Rules of Evidence. Subsequent examination by the opposing party is called "cross-examination," after which there may be "re-direct" by the party taking the deposition, and "re-cross" by the adversary. Because the counsel taking the deposition is considered to be taking the testimony of a "hostile" witness, the adverse party, or a witness identified with the adverse party, leading questions are allowed on direct examination. In each case, the attorney asking the questions will be identified by the court reporter either on a identifying line such as "Examination by [attorney's name]," followed by the marginal abbreviation "Q," or with the attorney's name shown on the left margin indicating the questions asked.

Exhibits will be introduced during the deposition and should be described verbally by the attorney to ensure the same object or document can be identified with accuracy from reading the text of the transcript. It is important to ensure that there will be no question later about what was actually introduced as an exhibit.

The transcript of the questions and answers will be prepared in booklet form with each line numbered, usually from one to twenty-five. Each page is sequentially numbered. An index will be included that lists each exhibit introduced. The actual exhibits will be attached at the back of the deposition booklet, unless they are too large to be accommodated. One or two pages of lined, but unnumbered, paper may be included at the back of each booklet for attorney comments or for the witness to enter corrections. The court reporter usually retains custody of the original exhibits, until they are sealed with the original transcript after the expiration of the time prescribed for reading and signing of the deposition by the witness. At that point, in federal court and many other jurisdictions, custody of the sealed original transcript and exhibits is transferred to the counsel for the party who originally noticed the deposition. Other jurisdictions require that the sealed original transcript and exhibits be filed immediately with the court. Copies of the transcript may be ordered by each party or counsel.

Videotaping of a deposition is a common practice in many jurisdictions. It is not unusual for the depositions of parties and other witness depositions to be videotaped, particularly when the deponent lives or resides more than 100 miles from the location where the trial is expected to take place. This should be done according to state or federal rules of procedure. Most rules will demand that either the court reporter or operator of the video equipment make an opening statement, on camera, prior to the beginning of the deposition. Under the federal rules, this opening statement must include: (a) the court reporter's ("officer's") name and business address; (b) the date, time, and place of deposition; (c) the name of the deponent; (d) the administration of the oath or affirmation to the deponent; and (e) an identification of all persons present. Items (a) through (c) must be repeated at the beginning of each unit of recorded tape. Other jurisdictions may also require the caption of the case, the party on whose behalf the deposition is being taken, and the party who requested that the deposition be included as well. At the end of the deposition, the "officer" must record a closing statement on camera that the deposition is complete, and state for the record any stipulations made by counsel concerning the custody of the transcript or recording, the custody of the exhibits, or any other pertinent matters, such as the length of the deposition and that the videotape has not been altered nor edited in any manner. These same general procedures also apply when the deposition is recorded in any manner other than stenographically, such as audio recording, by braille, or any other means.

8.075 Attending Depositions

Whenever given the opportunity by the supervising attorney, the legal assistant should attend depositions. Legal assistants can perform many duties during a deposition, such as making copies of documents brought to the deposition by the prospective witnesses and taking notes on the flow of the questions and answers during the course of the deposition. In a deposition where extensive exhibits are introduced, whether in a complex case or a single complicated deposition, the legal assistant can keep an independent record of the exhibits by recording each exhibit's number and a description of each exhibit. When breaks are taken during the deposition, the attorney and the legal assistant can compare notes, make changes to the deposition plan, double-check whether points have been covered or not, and discuss any issues or topics which were a surprise. Also, it is helpful later, when deposition summaries are being prepared, for the legal assistant to have had the benefit of hearing the testimony firsthand.

8.0751 Deposition Exhibits. Deposition exhibits may include photographs, documents, or other objects which were either obtained prior to the deposition, or produced at deposition in response to a subpoena, as well as documents created during the deposition such as sketches, diagrams, or drawings. The purpose of introducing these exhibits at a deposition is: (1) to have their nature, origin, content, and identity established under oath, or (2) to attempt to provide clarification of matters which are difficult to describe verbally. Often the introduction of copies of such things as letters, contracts, bills of sale, and warranty statements can establish a foundation for later introduction of the exhibit as secondary evidence at trial when the original or a duplicate original cannot be located.

During the deposition, it is the responsibility of the court reporters to either mark for identification the exhibits as they are offered, or in the case of exhibits which have been "pre-marked" by the offering party, to note and record that identification in the transcript. In the absence of other directions by the parties, court reporters will mark exhibits in numerical sequence from the first exhibit introduced through the last one introduced during the deposition, often with a designation of whether the exhibit was offered by the plaintiff or the defendant. Others use numbers for plaintiff exhibits and letters for defendant exhibits. Because there are a variety of methods which are used to mark deposition exhibits, it is important that the legal assistant develop a method of keeping track of all the exhibits introduced during the various depositions which take place in the normal course of litigation.

a. Deposition Exhibit Register. A system of exhibit identification requires sequential numbering (or lettering) of all exhibits introduced within a lawsuit. Establishing and maintaining the integrity of the system throughout the lawsuit is a task usually delegated to the legal assistant. Whether the decision is made to mark and list exhibits separately for each deposition, sequentially through all depositions, or sequentially throughout the case as a whole, a deposition register form, as shown in Exhibit 8-12, can be used to record the exhibits introduced at a particular deposition. A copy can be given to the court reporter to ensure the transcript matches the lawyer's notes and exhibit register.

EXHIBIT 8-12   Sample Deposition Exhibit Register

CASE: Wilson v. Horneker
DATE: 12/19/92
LOCATION: Hilton Hotel, Hilton Head Island
DEPONENT: Jack Horneker
ATTORNEYS: Fred Albanese—Wilson
                George Troutman—Horneker

Exh. No.	Pltf	Deft	Description of Exhibit	Notes
1.	X		Copy of 6/19/91 newspaper article of allegedly defamatory or slanderous material	Copy made for depo; Pltf retained original article
2.	X		Hornecker's Employment Contract with newspaper	
3.	X		Copy of letter from Wilson to Horneker and newspaper asking for retraction and apology	Find out date mailed to Horneker
4.	X	X	Copy of Horneker's notes containing what his source told him about Wilson	Horneker would not reveal ID of source; motion to compel?

If the exhibits are numbered *sequentially* by deposition, the entries made by the legal assistant might look like those shown in Exhibit 8-13.

EXHIBIT 8-13   Sample Deposition Exhibit Register

CASE: Smith v. Jones   DEPONENT: A.E. Robinson
DATE: 6/14/92   LOCATION: Hilton Hotel, Hilton Head Island
ATTORNEYS: J. Brooks—Smith
            V. Gallo—Jones

Pltf	Deft	Description	Notes
3		Contract of sale dtd 5/10/91 by Smith & Jones, 13 pgs with 3 addenda: A, B & C	Robinson relied on Contract in perf. Duty as Jones' agent
4		Change Order #10531, dtd 6/23/91 signed by Jones and initialed by Robinson	
5		Daily log book of Robinson from 5/18/91 to 10/12/91	Copied at depo; original retained by deponent
	2	Hard copy of e-mail sent by Smith to Robinson making 2nd change, dtd 6/4/91	Pltf to prepare computer disk w/copy e-mail on it

Because the exhibit numbers in the previous example are by *case*, rather than by deposition, the numbers in the "Pltf" and "Deft" column will not necessarily start with "1." Instead, they will pick up with the next number in sequence where the last deposition or discovery device left off.

When a sequential system is used, a master log must be employed to ensure control of the numbers, the exhibit description, and the witness or deponent by which it was introduced. (*See* Exhibit 8-14.)

EXHIBIT 8-14   Sample Master Exhibit Log

CASE: Smith v. Jones   DATE LAST POSTED: 6/15/92
ATTORNEY: V. Gallo   LEGAL ASSISTANT: Bob Brown

Pltf	Deft	Source of Exhibit	Description of Exhibit
1		Ans #3 to Int; P to D	Photo of tractor/trailer rig sold by Jones to Smith via Robinson
2		Resp #2 to RFP; D to P	Notice by Jones to Smith that rig was defective
3		Robinson Depo	Contract of sale dtd 5/10/91 signed by Smith & Jones; 13 pgs w/3 addenda: A, B & C
4		Robinson Depo	Change Order #10531 dtd 6/23/91 signed by Jones & initialed by Robinson
5		Robinson Depo	Daily log book of Robinson from 5/18/91 to 10/21/91
	1	Exh 3 att'd to Jones' MSJ	Affidavit of George Bowen, truck/trailer expert
	2	Robinson Depo	Hard copy of e-mail sent by Smith to Robinson making 2nd change, dtd 6/4/91

While each side can control only the numbering of its own exhibits, records of this type which track chronologically and descriptively all exhibits in the case, simplify the process of retrieving them when they are needed later to prepare for trial. Reliable identification, control, and retrieval are the prime functions of legal assistants, whether the attorney will need retrieval of all documents which contain particular *facts*, all documents connected to particular *parties*, all documents linked to a specific *witness*, or a particular exhibit.

8.076 Summarizing Depositions

Depositions, by the very nature of their question-and-answer format, involve many, many pages of testimony which record information in the order it is obtained from the witness. They are often bulky and difficult to use in the courtroom. Because of this, deposition transcripts are usually summarized either by the attorney or the legal assistant for use in final trial preparation. Summaries make it easier to prepare a witness to testify at trial and to prepare the questions the attorney will need to ask witnesses at trial. There are several methods of summarizing depositions: the chronological summary, the index or digest method, the narrative summary, and the topical summary, also known as the summary by category. The method chosen will vary according to the wishes of the attorney, the scope of the deposition, the importance of the case, and the number of issues in the case. The legal assistant is often assigned this task as a means of providing cost-effective and efficient legal services to the client. The old saying "Make haste slowly" applies to the task of preparing good deposition summaries. Among the rules to establish as a personal discipline are:

1. Ensure familiarity with the issues in the case. Review the deposition outline (if one was used) and the attorney's deposition notes. Identify the topics which are the main focus of interest.
2. First, read the entire deposition as if it were a novel. Place a post-it note next to passages that grab attention, but do not stop to analyze in detail at this point. See if the attorney followed the deposition outline and gain a general feeling for the flow of information.
3. Plan for an undisturbed block of time to go back through the transcript in detail and complete the summary. Continuity and quality suffer from interruptions in concentration.

8.0761 Chronological Summary.   The most common form of deposition summary is chrono-logical (sequential, logical), which is simply a page-by-page paraphrasing of the information contained in the deposition, eliminating extraneous material, condensing the evidentiary facts in the testimony, providing page and line references as to where they appear, and annotating all exhibits or references to any other documents or tangible evidence. In essence, this is simply a reduction of volume, both in the number of pages and the amount of material, rhetorical verbiage, colloquy of counsel, and the "fencing" or "game playing" dialogue employed by some witnesses and attorneys. It is the fastest method of summarizing a deposition.

The drawback to this method is a lack of order or organization in the entries. Following the progression of a particular deposition does not necessarily result in all the data on any one issue being developed in one set of questions and answers. A deposition is an interrogation with all the problems of memory refreshment and afterthought that occur from the witness's detailed retelling of a story and/or the accidental revelation of a fact the attorney had not previously known or considered. Because of these factors, the subject matters that are covered in the deposition are mixed in the transcript. On the other hand, in a relatively small case with uncomplicated factual and legal issues, this may be the better or more efficient method. (*See* Exhibit 8-15.)

EXHIBIT 8-15   Sample Chronological Deposition Summary

<table>
<tr><td colspan="2" align="center">Deposition Summary
Testimony of Albert Jones</td></tr>
<tr><td align="center">Page/Line</td><td>Testimony</td></tr>
<tr><td align="center">3/5</td><td>Albert Jones, 9637 Fujimori Way, Tokyo, Japan, 36 years old, DOB 1/2/63</td></tr>
<tr><td align="center">3/9</td><td>Married 10 yrs. to Sarah Conway Jones; 3 children: Jan, 9; Joseph, 6; Sally, 3</td></tr>
<tr><td align="center">3/12</td><td>Now employed at Conway Furniture, Tokyo, Japan, as Vice-President & Comptroller</td></tr>
<tr><td align="center">3/16</td><td>Graduated from Peoria HS, Peoria, IL, June 1981
B.S. from Univ. of IL, May 1985—Accounting</td></tr>
<tr><td align="center">4/3</td><td>Employed by Conway Furniture since college graduation</td></tr>
</table>

8.0762 *Index/Digest Method.* The index or digest method of summarizing a deposition lists the main topics covered in the deposition with page and line references "indexed" under each topic heading. Just as the index of a book is the quickest means to find where information on a word or phrase appears, this provides a quick reference to where testimony on each major topic is located. It can be used alone or as an accompaniment to the chronological summary. The drawback to this method is that, by itself, it does not provide any detail about the testimony, such as whether it is negative, positive, or of no use at all. (*See* Exhibit 8-16.)

EXHIBIT 8-16   Sample of Index/Digest Summary Method

<table>
<tr><td colspan="2" align="center">Deposition Summary
Testimony of Albert Jones</td></tr>
<tr>
<td>
Date of accident
p. 7, l. 4

Place of accident
p. 7, l. 14
p. 43, ll. 6–12
</td>
<td>
Description of vehicles
p. 10, ll. 1–13
p. 11, ll. 17–18
p. 33, l. 9
p. 62, l. 25

How accident occurred
p. 17, ll. 3–24
p. 18, ll. 7–19
p. 61, l. 9–p. 62, l. 22
</td>
</tr>
</table>

8.0763 *Narrative Summary.* The narrative summary, which is usually prepared by the attorney immediately after (or very soon after) the conclusion of the deposition, reports on the general nature of the testimony given and relates specific testimony on important facts provided by the deponent. It is not useful in trial preparation, but is commonly used to prepare progress reports for clients. This type of summary may also be used for short depositions of secondary or ancillary witnesses in a case. (*See* Exhibit 8-17, page 258.)

EXHIBIT 8-17   Sample of Narrative Summary Method

Deposition Summary
Testimony of Roxanne deBergerac

The deposition of Roxanne deBergerac was taken on June 15, 1996. She is twenty-five years old and works as a computer consultant for 9th Generation Computer Co. On November 9, 1996, she was walking from her car to the front door of 9th Generation Computers, when she claims to have slipped into a large pothole in the parking lot, causing her to fall and fracture her right ankle. She was not found for approximately fifteen minutes, at which time a coworker, Abel Sawyer, saw her and ran for help. She was given first aid by a coworker, John Jones, and then taken by ambulance to General Hospital, where she was seen in the ER. X-rays were taken in the ER, and the fracture in her right ankle was identified. The fracture was realigned by an orthopedist, Dr. Achord, who was on duty at the time, and the ankle was placed in a hard cast. She was hospitalized overnight and released the next afternoon.

When she returned to work a week later, she asked whether an accident report had been prepared, and her supervisor, Jasper Bardwell, told her one had not been prepared, because she had the responsibility to report the accident within seventy-two hours and had not done so. He informed her she would not be eligible for worker's compensation benefits because of her failure to promptly report the accident.

8.0764 Summary by Topic or Category. The summary by topic or category is the most detailed and most time-consuming method of summarizing depositions. There are several ways to proceed with this type of summary:

a. Dictate a detailed chronological summary of the deposition, make a copy of the summary, and then cut-and-paste statements from the summary about particular subjects into a group with page and line references.

b. Create an index/digest summary and then, using the page references under each topic as references to all the testimony in the deposition about that one topic or category of information, dictate or type a summary of the testimony about each topic or category with page and line references.

c. Label separate sheets of paper with headings for each important topic and write summaries of the testimony, with page and line references, while reading through the deposition.

d. Photocopy the deposition transcript, and then cut the various statements pertaining to each topic from the copy and paste them together to make the summary. You may need to duplicate parts of the transcript more than once if testimony on the same page pertains to more than one category.

Many specialized computer software programs are available which perform much of the manual work described in this section. Generally, these programs allow a deposition transcript which is on a computer disk (which are generally provided free or at a nominal charge along with the written deposition transcript) to be "loaded" into the software program for processing. The function of such programs is to locate portions of the deposition that refer to discrete topics which have been identified by the legal assistant and the attorney, and provide page and line references to transcript testimony containing the topic word(s) or phrases no matter where it appears in the deposition. This type of software is used extensively in complex cases where numerous depositions are taken, and is a valuable time-saving tool for the legal assistant and the lawyer.

In addition to the specialized software programs discussed above, many legal assistants use word processing software to perform the methods listed in (a) through (d) to "cut," "paste," and "copy" electronically from deposition transcripts on computer disk provided by court reporters. Sophisticated word processing programs like WordPerfect and Word have many powerful features, making them easy to use for this purpose and less time-consuming than manual "cut, paste, and copy" operations, and have the added benefit of being electronically "searchable" for words and phrases. They are cost effective because they are available within the office.

8.08 Requests for Admission

As stated in Rule 36 of the Federal Rules of Civil Procedure, requests for admissions may be simply defined as "a written request to a party to admit or deny the truth of any relevant fact or genuineness of any document." The actual effect of requests for admissions is far from simple. Results may be devastating to parties who overlook or ignore the importance of this discovery tool. The primary role of the legal assistant is to identify such issues which may be resolved by requests for admissions, and to draft appropriate responses in a timely manner when served by such requests.

The purpose of requests for admissions is to limit the number of disputed issues and material facts to be argued and proven at trial, or the necessity to create a further foundation for the introduction of evidentiary materials and documents. Requests for admissions are founded on matters developed during previous discovery procedures, interrogatories, depositions, or requests for production of documents. Usually, when a foundation has been developed, the answering parties will admit the truth of the facts or the genuineness of the documents, but there is no compulsion to do so. They may put the propounding attorney "on strict proof." When such proof is forthcoming at trial, the propounding party may ask the court to award the costs of the proof, such as the transportation of a witness or the expert witness's fee. Among the discovery tools, requests for admissions are relatively inexpensive considering the amount of court time usually devoted to resolving such discoverable issues.

The legal assistant is reminded that state practices vary and some may restrict the number of requests for admissions that may be served upon parties. State rules should always be consulted as to limitations and provisions for exceeding such limitations (which is usually upon consent of the parties or motion to the court).

8.081 Timing

The 1993 Amendment to Rule 36 reflected the change made in Rule 26(d) which prevented a party from seeking formal discovery until AFTER the parties meet in a scheduling conference, as required by Rule 26(f). Rule 16(b) sets forth guidelines and requirements for pretrial conferences in which parties schedule time limits for completing discovery and various pretrial motions.

The legal assistant contributes to the effectiveness of this process by assembling from previous discovery efforts those facts and documents important to the case that have not been specifically acknowledged by the other parties. This may include documents introduced at the depositions of witnesses or the client. It may also include requests for admission propounded by the other parties to obtain reciprocal admissions to the fact, document, or thing since answers to requests for admission are binding only on the answering party.

Rule 36 provides for a thirty-day response time. For the party on which the request for admissions is served, the legal assistant's duties are clear, action must be taken immediately. The attorney must read the request and response time must be calendared. If no response is filed, the matters are considered admitted and conclusively established. The propounding party in such instance should serve notice by registered or certified mail that they are deeming the answers to be admitted based upon Rule 36. The propounding party may also move the court for an order compelling further responses, if it believes a response is incomplete or evasive, or an objection is without merit. Parties may also amend their responses upon motion to the court, which may grant such motions if timely made and if such amendments will not prejudice the propounding party.

Responses to requests for admissions are limited. Parties may admit, deny, refuse to admit or deny, or object. Admitting has the force of a judicial admission, and may be used as evidence in court. Denying can be costly if the matter is later proven true at trial. Refusing to admit or deny has the effect of admitting by default if the request is not also objected to. It is difficult for a party to prove an objection to a request as they must prove lack of personal knowledge as the basis.

8.082 Form

Requests for admissions are usually posed in positive statements to which the answering party answers with "admitted" or "denied", as shown in Exhibit 8-18 and Exhibit 8-19 respectively. Objections or other answers may be provided, such as "Defendant can neither admit nor deny the truth of the matter because . . . ." Requests for admissions may be filed as one set or several sets. Federal court rules usually require sequential numbering for clarity and control, a good idea for use in all courts and a great idea for legal assistants charged with control and retrieval of the admissions.

EXHIBIT 8-18   Sample Request for Admissions Under Rule 36

Plaintiff AB requests Defendant CD within _____ days after service of this request to make the following admissions for the purpose of this action only, and subject to all pertinent objections to admissibility which may be interposed at the trial:

1. That each of the following documents, exhibited with this request, is genuine:
   (Here list the documents and describe each document)
2. That each of the following statements is true:
   (Here list the statements)

EXHIBIT 8-19   Sample Response to Request for Admissions Under Rule 36

Defendant CD responds to Plaintiff AB's Request for Admissions as follows:

Response to Request No. ___: Defendant CD admits that . . . *(here repeat the information)*

Response to Request No. ___: Defendant CD denies . . .

Response to Request No. ___: Defendant CD has no information with which to admit or deny this request. Defendant CD has made reasonable inquiry and the information known or readily obtainable by the party is insufficient to enable the party to admit or deny and, therefore, on the basis of this lack of information, denies the request.

Response to Request No. ___: Defendant CD objects to this request on the grounds that it seeks information that is privileged under the attorney/client privilege *(or state the grounds for objections)*.

8.084 Collation of Denials and Cost of Proof

Because Rule 36 allows the party who serves a request for admission to collect any costs from the responding party who denies a request which is later proven as true, the legal assistant collates all *denials* of requests for admission and coordinates with the lawyer on the method of proof. Once the plan of proof is selected, the legal assistant establishes a record of the costs associated with the proof of each disputed fact or document to serve the lawyer as the foundation for seeking recovery of those costs, if appropriate.

8.09   Requests for Production of Documents

Documents are both loved and feared by attorneys. Cases begin with a person telling an attorney of the "injustice of it all" and seeking help in gaining redress, often presenting letters, contracts, and bills in support of the story.

As the case progresses, other documents surface, some by design, some by accident, many in connection with various forms of informal discovery and others through formal proceedings. Occasionally, a case is truly a "document" case where something more than casual revelation of memorialized material is handled, ideally in an organized, thoughtful, and effective manner.

It is easy to understand how the gradual accumulation of documents through interrogatories, depositions, requests for admission, and the subpoena *duces tecum* can lull an attorney or the legal assistant into the belief that the "document" case, from one thousand pages on up, can be handled by the same manual procedures, only scaled-up just a bit. It may be possible to do that, but is that the most effective way? What if it involves ten thousand pages? What if it develops twenty-five thousand pages from each of two codefendants and fifteen thousand from plaintiff? Document cases are, or can be, lost in the planning stages and require far more than a "let's wing it" attitude from the attorney and the legal assistant. Chapter 9, The Legal Assistant and Document Discovery Cases, covers this topic in depth. This section is a brief introduction and overview.

Federal Rule of Civil Procedure 34, entitled "Production of Documents and Things and Entry Upon Land for Inspection and Other Purposes," permits any party to serve on any other party, including a person not a party to the action (by *subpoena duces tecum* under Rule 45), a request to produce and permit inspection of designated documents or any other tangible items and to permit entry upon designated land in possession or control of the parties. Designated documents or any other tangible items are itemized in the Rule as: "writings, drawings, graphs, charts, photographs, phone records, and other data compilations from which information can be obtained." The Rule sets forth procedures for parties to follow to respond to such requests, and further states that documents are to be produced as they are kept in the usual course of business. As technological advances in records management in business are made, this phrase, the "usual course of business" is constantly evolving to mean every sort of print, film, computer disk, and audio and visual media. Business records once kept in dusty archives and cumbersome ledgers are now stored in the "usual course of business" on microfilm, microfiche, computer disks, tapes, CD-ROMs, etc. This is another area where the legal assistant's enhanced computer skills and awareness are invaluable.

It sounds trite to state that this is the "age of information." However, there is no doubt we are in the midst of that age. Each day brings technological advances only dreamed of a few short years ago. Not only must the legal assistant be aware of new technology, but also must know how to utilize it and/or where to find vendors and specialists who may assist in utilizing such technology. Discoverable evidence can be found in clients' computers (and opposing parties' computers) in the form of correspondence, memoranda, spreadsheets, reports, databases, calendars and other forms of schedules, accounting records and data, and e-mail—both saved and deleted. A trained technician or "computer detective" is capable of retrieving smoking guns from computer disks and computer tape backups. E-mail can be especially dangerous as it brings a false sense of privacy to the user, often revealing the user's unguarded thinking. Throughout the following discussion, the legal assistant should keep in mind that the procedures also apply to all electronic data.

8.091 Basic Considerations

Whether the volume of documents is relatively small and manageable, or large and cumbersome, there are certain basic considerations which apply. When reviewing documents to be produced by the client, consider the following:

a. The adversary is entitled to those documents that can be described with sufficient specificity to allow the client, the client's counsel, and the legal assistant to identify them, provided the *scope* of the request is not burdensome and oppressive, the material is not privileged, and the documents are actually in the possession, custody, or control of the client.

b. The attorney and the legal assistant must review each document page before allowing the adversary to see it in order to ensure that no privileged documents, trade secret material, or documents not responsive to the specific request are included.

c. Client documents should be received and reviewed as they are kept "in the ordinary course of business" as well as in chronological context to determine whether the documents and records are complete. A chronological review helps detect files or documents which have been lost, misfiled, retired, or destroyed. These events must be explained, of course.

d. It is important to establish and maintain the source of each document, or sets of documents, produced during litigation. Source origination is very important as part of the foundation for offering a document as an exhibit at trial.

When reviewing documents obtained from other parties or nonparties, these are the considerations to bear in mind:

a. Are the items produced responsive to the request?

b. If an objection was made, was it reasonable, or will it be necessary to prepare a motion to compel?

c. If documents are being withheld subject to a privilege, has a list been provided with enough information to determine whether the privilege should be challenged?

d. Is the pertinent time period covered?

e. Do the records deal with the person, company, or entity directly or only by reference?

f. Do the records deal with the issues in the case?

g. Do the records refer to other records neither attached nor already obtained?

h. Do the records require expert help in interpretation or understanding?

8.092 Form

Requests for production have the same general format as interrogatories. A "Definitions" section may be used to identify common terms, words, and phrases. Each request is set forth in a separate sequentially numbered paragraph. The request must state the specific date, time, place, and manner of inspection, copying or testing, which may not be any sooner than the time within which the adverse party may respond under Rule 34 or its jurisdictional equivalent. Each requested item or category of items should be identified specifically enough to allow the opposing party to be able to determine what to produce, yet the terms used should be general enough so that all potentially responsive documents are included. For instance, the type of documents sought might be a company's internal policy and procedures manual for employees. Because the company might have internal policy and procedures, yet may not have them assembled in a volume called "policy and procedures manual," a request to obtain the equivalent information might state: "Produce all documents which detail, discuss, or relate in any manner the policy and procedures the company follows in regard to employees or expects the employees of the company to follow, including but not limited to reports, manuals, memoranda, statements, e-mail, or any other document whether written or recorded, for the period 1990 to 1997." It is good practice to state a reasonable and relevant time period. Failing to do so could result in the production being so large that it is overwhelming as well as significantly more expensive for the client in terms of both costs and fees. Stating a relevant time period also eliminates a reason for objection by the opposing party. An example of a Request for Production of Documents is contained in Exhibit 8-20.

EXHIBIT 8-20   Sample Request for Production of Documents, etc. Under Rule 34

Plaintiff AB requests Defendant CD to respond within _____ days to the following requests:

1. That Defendant produce and permit Plaintiff to inspect and to copy each of the following documents: *(Here list the documents either individually or by category and describe each of them, and state the time, place, and manner of making the inspection and performance of any related acts).*

2. That Defendant produce and permit Plaintiff to inspect and to copy, test, or sample each of the following objects: *(Here list the objects either individually or by category and describe each of them, and state the time, place, and manner of making the inspection and performance of any related acts.)*

3. That Defendant permit Plaintiff to enter *(here describe property to be entered)* and to inspect and photograph, test, or sample the following: *(here describe the portion of the real property and the objects to be inspected, photographed, tested, or sampled and state the time, place, and manner of making the inspection and performance of any related acts.)*

8.0921 *Requesting Documents from Nonparties.* Federal Rule of Civil Procedure 34 provides that the method of obtaining documents from nonparties is by issuing a subpoena pursuant to Rule 45, on a form provided by the local clerk of court. As previously mentioned in the section on depositions, this is called a *subpoena duces tecum,* which is a Latin phrase meaning "under penalty you shall take it with you." These types of document requests are most often issued to the custodian of record for a business or other entity to appear together with the records and be prepared to discuss the manner of origin and filing of the documents. If all that is sought is the records production, and not a deposition, the records custodian may be given the option of providing copies of the records in lieu of actually appearing. As a practical matter, many of the documents requested from nonparties are routine business records generated by neutral parties, and no dispute over the admissibility of the records exists: for instance, medical records of a plaintiff in a bodily injury lawsuit or employment, education, or military service records. It is common practice (on mutual agreement) for such subpoenas to be issued to a firm specializing in attorney's legal services to serve the subpoena on the custodian, take custody of the records, copy and notarize the relevant documents, deliver the copies to the attorneys, and return the originals to the custodian. In those cases where a dispute over admissibility of the records may exist, the custodian of record will be required to appear and give testimony concerning the records produced. When this occurs, the procedures discussed in the section on depositions should be followed.

8.093 Control Systems

Original documents must be preserved with care to avoid changing their character from the "as found" condition. Marking the original documents with a unique identifying number is a generally accepted practice which is not considered to have the effect of changing their character, just as placing an exhibit identification number on a document does not change its character. Marking documents in such a manner simplifies the process of accounting for those documents as the case progresses and makes subsequent retrieval and use much easier. Of course, when marking documents for identification, care must be taken not to obscure or obliterate any writing or other marking which appears on the document's face. It is also suggested that such marking be consistently placed, for example, the number always appearing in the lower right-hand corner, or if that is not possible, then at least on the right side of the document.

When documents and other items are assembled to be produced, or when they are received or inspected in response to a request, the legal assistant should prepare an index containing basic identification data which includes: any identification number which has been assigned, type of document, date, author, addressee, number of pages, and attachments. If there are characteristic file numbers or subject titles, they may be included. Chapter 9 covers document production in more depth and detail, and although it refers to large document cases, the same general principals apply to the management of small and medium cases as well.

8.10 Damage Calculation, Verification, and Settlement Offers

As discussed in Chapter 1, an essential element of any lawsuit is that the plaintiff suffered some form of damage. The most common type of damage, and the object of recovery in a civil tort case, is compensatory damages. The plaintiff is obligated during trial to prove any actual or special damages sustained. These are often documented by actual bills, canceled checks, employment or payroll records, W-2 forms and other earnings information, city assessment billings, financial statements showing profit and loss, and sometimes will include the testimony of expert witnesses. The goal is to attempt to restore the plaintiff to the same position, and reasonable expectations, held prior to, and "but for," the circumstance or incident at issue.

Every case contains elements of damage both of an objective nature and those of a subjective, speculative, mental, or emotional nature. For example, in bodily injury cases, the first element consists of the actual cost of past medical treatment and therapy associated with recovery from the injury, prospective costs of such future medical treatment and therapy, lost wages, and loss of future earnings, as well as the loss of future earning capacity. This element, or category, of damages is called "special damages." The second category is called "general damages," and encompasses those injuries referred to as "pain and suffering" and "mental anguish." General damages include recovery for the physical agony of the trauma itself; past and future pain, temporary or permanent disability, and deterioration of physical condition directly attributable to the accident sued on; scarring caused by the accident and injury; the loss of hobbies or pleasurable interests; and the disruption and loss of a choice of lifestyle (for instance, a broken hip may forever bar a marathon runner from competition, or an injured back may deny an interior decorator the ability to rearrange furniture on impulse and without assistance). Business litigation cases can contain both elements as well. For instance, in a dispute over a commercial building construction contract, there may be costs relating to the actual, necessary building alteration or reconstruction and costs related to loss of "return on investment," lost earnings because a higher than usual vacancy rate was experienced attributable to the defendant, or lost income which resulted from lessees who broke their leases as a result of the alleged actions or inactions of the defendant.

When attorneys enter into negotiations in an attempt to settle a case, they must first make an assessment of the value of their client's case, based upon their understanding of the facts, liability, and damages. The attorney then discusses this assessment with the client to determine an acceptable bargaining range for settlement. For plaintiffs, this bargaining range is usually the least amount of money the client is willing to receive in lieu of trial versus the maximum amount the client might receive if successful at trial. For defendants, it is the most amount of money the client is willing to pay to avoid a trial versus the least amount of money the client might be required to pay if the plaintiff is successful at trial. If the parties are reasonable in their assessments, there is usually a common area, known as the bargaining range, where these sums may overlap. The object then becomes to maximize (for the plaintiff) or minimize (for the defendant) the amount of money within the bargaining range. The success of negotiations depends to a great extent on the relative strengths and weaknesses of each party's case and their willingness to compromise. (*See* Exhibit 8-21.)

EXHIBIT 8-21   Factors Considered in Assessing Settlement Values

1. The ease or difficulty plaintiff will have in proving all elements necessary to fix liability on the defendant;
2. The ease or difficulty plaintiff will have in proving the damages claimed;
3. The nature of the injury, i.e., whether the injury is a relatively common one or has a "horror factor," such as serious burns and resulting scarring or the loss of a limb, eyesight, or hearing;
4. The quality (i.e., the credibility) of the witnesses, and particularly the witnesses whose testimony is important in proving important elements of liability or damages, or both;
5. The amount of the defendant's insurance coverage or the ability of the defendant to otherwise pay the judgment;
6. The plaintiff's financial status—that is, will the plaintiff's financial status support him during the time the case is pending;
7. The past record of the trial forum for large or small verdicts, including the known propensities of the judge and of past juries in similar cases;
8. The experience and ability of the opposing lawyer(s).

8.101 Damage Calculations

The plaintiff is the primary source of the documents necessary to prove the damages portion of the case, although such documents may also be collected from their originating source. These documents may include medical bills, checks, receipts, vehicle repair estimates and bills, invoices, financial statements, general ledgers, and any other document which supports an amount for any type of damage being claimed. The legal assistant should ensure (whether working for the plaintiff or defendant) that only legitimate and relevant amounts are included in the calculation. The bills should be assembled first into categories and then in chronologic order.

Sometimes figuring out a plaintiff's damages involves more than adding up the amounts in invoices, receipts, and estimates. For example, in a complex litigation a plaintiff may claim that the actions of the defendant were the proximate cause of the plaintiff declaring bankruptcy, during which the plaintiff's business loses all its inventory to creditors, although a portion of the original business remains. In this situation, some creative thought must be given to the various things which the plaintiff has lost, as well as a method of placing a value on those items.

Is the value of the lost inventory the amount owed the creditors, the original purchase price, or the amount the plaintiff would have received if the inventory were sold in the ordinary course of business? Did the plaintiff lose accounts or customers because there was no inventory to sell? If so, how is the value of that loss to be determined? The legal assistant working on damages in a lawsuit, whether for the plaintiff or the defendant, must be aware of circumstances where routine measures of the value of damages make little contribution to the lawyer's efforts. Flexibility and imagination are necessary. Every case has a unique set of facts that bear on the damage elements of the case. The legal assistant and the attorney must analyze the basis of the damages sought, seek expert help in valuing the claimed losses, and explore alternative methods of settlement where appropriate.

8.1011 *Damage Analysis.*   In cases involving injuries, or other damages for which the services of medical professionals were utilized by the plaintiff, a detailed examination of the medical bills should be made to separate bills related to diagnosis from those of treatment—whether the case is medical or not. Only amounts in medical bills related to diagnosis and treatment of injuries, illnesses, or conditions which are the subject matter of the lawsuit should be included in damage calculations. This requires a careful reading of each medical bill to eliminate those charges that are for routine checkups or other nonlawsuit-related treatments. Careful comparison of the medical history notes against the doctor's office or hospital billing may reveal that the bills include charges for medical treatment totally unrelated to the incident at issue, and that should be deleted from the damage total. For instance, a man suffering a minor knee injury who is treated by his family doctor may also be treated for allergy problems on a repetitive basis before and during the knee injury episode. All office visits, treatment, lab work, and other procedures related to the allergy condition can be identified by comparing the doctor's office notes or the treatment notes in the hospital record to the bills from these health care providers. Once they have been identified as unrelated to the plaintiff's claims in the lawsuit, they can be deleted from the list of damages.

In cases that are not medical, the value of estimates by professionals may be included. For instance, the damage to a home can be supported by estimates and bills, but not all proposed or actual repairs may be necessarily related to the actions or inactions of the opposing party. In business claims for lost earnings or profits, the accounting documents which support each amount must be verified. Where calculations are based on time periods, the validity of the time period as supported by documentary or testimonial evidence must be checked. If an interest rate is used, it must be verified that the use of that rate has a basis. These types of documents must also be examined carefully to identify items that do not relate to the matter which is the subject of the litigation.

Along with reviewing the documents for accuracy, foundation, and relevancy, every effort must be made to ensure that an item or amount is only counted once. Few plaintiff's bills are all of the same type. In a bodily injury case, there will be bills (some paid and some still owed), some vouchers showing insurance payments, some receipts for cash payments, canceled checks, charge account or credit card purchase slips, cash register tapes with handwritten notes identifying a purchase, and so on. These documents will come from different sources, and some may be duplications of others. Sometimes the duplication occurs from using one item as an element in arriving at the total for more than one category of damage. Such duplications may be innocent and thoughtless, or they may be preconceived and deliberate. The plaintiff's legal assistant must carefully examine all these documents, and where they are being used to support a total or subtotal, to avoid placing the supervising attorney in an embarrassing situation. By the same token, the defendant's legal assistant can prevent inflated damage totals by identifying such duplications and calling them to the attention of the supervising attorney.

The legal assistant's services in checking and rechecking all types of documents that support damage claims, in order to make certain that only the damages caused by the alleged actions or inactions of the opposing party are included in calculations, and that there is no duplication or overlapping of claimed items or amounts, is invaluable. This type of work by the legal assistant ensures that only valid claims are made and paid for injuries or damages (whether bodily injury or property damage) that were caused by the incident or accident which forms the basis of the litigation.

8.1012 Death Cases. How can a death be valued? How can money restore the survivors to the position they were in prior to the death? Actuaries can tell us the expected life span of an individual, economists and other experts can postulate that certain statistical methods provide an accurate estimate of the earning capacity of people of "X" ethnic groups, according to sex, age, education, and fields of endeavor. The U.S. Census Bureau has compiled figures considered reliable in making such calculations. With this basic data in hand, the application of a norm to the case at hand can be undertaken.

For example, an economic expert may calculate that a twenty-five year old man who has a college education and a job in a progressive company can be expected to earn not less than $750,000 over his working life. This is calculated by creating a facsimile of the specific individual's career in the company, with normal advancement, from date-of-death to retirement. Then a separate calculation is made for income from retirement and Social Security benefits.

A housewife's damage includes her marital interest in the earnings of her deceased husband (including retirement benefits), her loss of consortium and companionship with her husband, her loss of her husband's support in rearing the children, and out-of-pocket costs connected with the injury and death, such as funeral and related expenses.

A decedent's child is entitled to the value of the support the child would have had if the deceased parent had lived, loss of parental companionship, and loss of the parent's services. The legal assistant must consult with the attorney to determine the factual information that is necessary to make these calculations, convey them to the economic expert, and assist the expert in obtaining whatever other information may be necessary to make proper calculations of this nature.

8.1013 Continuing Damages. Some cases involve a situation that cannot be remedied or has not been resolved by the time of trial, and the damages are continuing or cumulative in nature, such as the contamination of an underground water source, or the accidental industrial poisoning of a person, where the poison's damage is a function of time of exposure and the material is slow to be expelled from the body, or a plaintiff with a medical condition caused by the accident or injury sued on that will require continuing medical treatment into the undetermined future. These circumstances require the lawyer and legal assistant to explore every available recourse for means of proof or refuting such proof, and to gather expert or lay testimony upon which calculations that are required to estimate duration and effect may be based, and to identify measures to correct, mitigate, or minimize the situation or circumstance.

8.1014 Alternative Recoveries. Damages usually are seen as a one-time cash payment placing the injured party where he or she would have been, but for the injury. In many cases, however, the aggregate dollar amount is so great that the defendant is incapable of paying such a judgment even when it is fair and reasonable. Bankruptcy may be the result of this type of situation, and the plaintiff will not be compensated if the defendant declares bankruptcy. In other cases, a large cash settlement may be insufficient to cover the rapidly expanding cost of future necessary medical care. An alternative method of settlement is necessary to address the needs of all parties in these situations. In the death case cited previously, annuities or endowments to guarantee the children's education as a part of the settlement might be considered. The mother might consider an investment portfolio with a projected or guaranteed annual income as a part of the settlement. Discharge of a mortgage, prepaid medical care plans, or real estate investments—all are possible alternatives to be explored to avoid destroying the defendant while justly compensating the plaintiff.

8.1015 *Present Values of Future Amounts.* When considering lost wage or lost earnings damages in any kind of lawsuit, the parties always begin with a calculation of all the dollars lost, including future lost dollars. Future dollars are always adjusted, first upwards to reflect the impact of inflation and then downward to reflect the benefit if receiving all the money at one time, rather than in a piecemeal fashion over a number of years, as most of us do by earning our salary. Clearly, the death case previously mentioned points out that the $750,000 the decedent would earn over forty years would not have the same value as that amount invested now and returning ten percent per year to the survivors. In effect, the survivors would receive an amount greater than what they would have received had their loved one lived, a "windfall" to which they are not entitled. Here are the calculations using that example: ten percent of $750,000 times forty years equals $2,000,000. There are economists and investment experts who can and do provide reliable foundations for calculating such adjustments. There are also computer software packages available commercially that have all of the basic assumptions, such as the U.S. Department of Labor's life expectancy and work life expectancy tables built into the program. The legal assistant and lawyer need only feed into the program the variables, such as the principal amount recovered or to be recovered, the inflation rate, and the rate by which it must be reduced in order to allow for the party's having received all the money in one lump sum, the time period over which the money would have been earned (i.e., the work life expectancy or life expectancy), and any provable raises or increases in salary and/or benefits over the term of the person's life or work life. The program then makes all the necessary calculations and arrives at the present value of the total raw-dollar sum. These calculations, whether made by an economic expert or by a computer program used in the office, provide the basis for calculating future lost earnings that can be claimed in any kind of lawsuit where lost earnings is an element of the damages claimed. The legal assistant should become familiar with the principles behind such calculations and the factual information upon which such information must be based, so as to be able to locate that information and either provide it to the expert or use it him/herself in making these calculations.

8.1016 *Arithmetic.* Because every damage claim involves some calculation of the value of a party's loss, the legal assistant can assist the attorney by checking the arithmetic used in the calculation process, and more importantly, the actual numbers supporting each subtotal and total. The legal assistant can pull all documents that provide a basis for each amount claimed by the party, double-check that each amount has been properly entered in the list of damages, and assemble copies of the documents that support the recapitulation of each category of damages. Although this is often a tedious and time-consuming task, it is one which is critical. Errors in numbers and calculations can cause the credibility of the damages to be weakened, both during settlement negotiations and when presented at trial.

8.102 Settlement Offers and Negotiations

Settlement offers are usually tendered by the plaintiff to the defendant, although it is also true that defendants will invite such offers and sometimes make the first offer to settle. The subject of settlement status and negotiations is one of the topics specifically listed to be discussed at the Rule 16(c) Pretrial Conference required under the federal rules. Many courts schedule a pretrial meeting between the parties and their respective counsel to encourage settlement discussions, particularly when it has come to the attention of the court that parties have not voluntarily entered into settlement negotiations.

The most common method by which a plaintiff will make an offer or demand for settlement to a defendant is to prepare and submit a written document called a settlement letter. The legal assistant for the plaintiff's attorney is usually involved in preparing the settlement letter and in locating and organizing any supporting documentation or other materials. The settlement letter should outline, in as much detail as necessary, the facts developed by the plaintiff that support plaintiff's settlement offer. (*See* Exhibit 8-22.)

EXHIBIT 8-22   Sample Settlement Letter Outline

1. An introduction of the plaintiff and his/her family, including personal statistics;

2. Statement of the facts of the accident/incident giving rise to the litigation;

3. Summary of the law applicable to the case, with emphasis on how and why liability can and will be proven if the matter is tried;

4. Description of the nature and extent of the damages plaintiff suffered, and the prognosis for partial or complete recovery;

5. Review of the different damage elements the plaintiff is claiming, such as:

   a. A review of jurisprudence that has made awards for damages similar or identical to those of the plaintiff;

   b. A demand for reimbursement for all past medical expenses incurred, with reference to the supporting medical recapitulation and supporting medical bills (all of which should be attached as an exhibit);

   c. A demand for reimbursement for future medical expenses which plaintiff's treating physicians have testified are necessary (if any), in a specific sum, with reference to the basic list of necessary treatments, drugs, equipment, etc., and the economic expert's calculations of the present value of such treatment (both of these documents should be included as supporting materials);

   d. A demand for reimbursement of past and future lost earnings, with reference to the economic expert's report (which should be included as an exhibit);

   e. A review of any other damage claims the plaintiff may have;

6. An offer to settle in a specific amount, along with a statement of any conditions, such as time limitations, who is to pay court costs, etc., that are a part of the offer to settle;

7. Supporting documents or materials:
   Examples for a personal injury case: Accident or incident report; Documents generated through discovery that demonstrate the manner in which the defendant was at fault, and the relationship of that fault to resulting damages; Excerpts of deposition testimony supporting plaintiff's claims (as to liability or damages, or both); Photographs of the plaintiff, both before and after the accident; Excerpts from hospital records and/or doctor's reports detailing the nature and extent of plaintiff's injuries and the treatments plaintiff was given to cure them, as well as the prognosis for plaintiff's partial or complete recovery from the injuries; Excerpts from treating physicians' depositions describing the nature and duration of the treatment plaintiff required; Information detailing plaintiff's work history and the nature of the work plaintiff was performing at the time of the accident; A recapitulation of the medical and related expenses plaintiff incurred while undergoing medical treatment; If appropriate, a list of expenses plaintiff can be expected to incur for medical treatment (or other items) in the future; Information relating to plaintiff's earnings at the time of the accident; A report from an economics expert detailing plaintiff's past and future lost earnings (or income and profits).

In cases where the potential monetary return justifies the effort and expense, consideration should be given to preparing a short videotaped introduction and summary presentation to accompany the written settlement brochure. The attorney may want to introduce himself and the client (or the client's decedent), give a short personal history of the client (and/or the client's decedent), and then proceed to verbally capsulize the thrust of the settlement proposal. Photographs or videotapes of family gatherings or activities can be included in the videotape, and will demonstrate more clearly than any words the impact the evidence about the injury or death will have on the trier of fact at the trial. Short presentations by key expert witnesses can also be included in the videotape.

The legal assistant can be of great help to the attorney in preparing such a videotape. Reviewing the photographs or videotapes provided by the family to select the best photographs or scenes to be used in the videotaped settlement presentation, interviewing the client and family members or any experts whose presentations are to be included, and participating in the final editing process are all tasks the legal assistant is well-qualified to perform, given his/her knowledge of the facts and issues involved in the lawsuit.

A well-prepared settlement letter that outlines all the elements of proof necessary for the plaintiff to prevail at trial, supported by documents and other evidence that will be used to prove each element, carries great weight with a defense attorney, the defendant, and the defendant's insurer. Often, this type of settlement proposal opens the door to negotiations with a view toward settling the case.

8.1021 *Statutory Offers.* The codes of civil procedure (or the equivalent) of some states provide for offers of settlement to induce the parties to make reasoned, good faith settlement offers to the adversary. The inducement to act in good faith lies in allowing the proponent to recover the costs of trial from the adversary who refuses the settlement offer if the ultimate jury award equals or exceeds the offer. For instance, if the plaintiff makes a formal offer to settle as provided by statute for $14,000 and the defendant declines, and if the jury then awards $15,000 at the end of the trial, the plaintiff may seek recovery of trial costs from the defendant. These statutes or code sections usually have a time limit within which both the offer and acceptance must be conveyed. This procedure is particularly effective when a defendant is represented by an insurance carrier with undisputed coverage, the offer made by the plaintiff is within policy limits, and a prospective jury award may exceed the policy limits. The insurance company must weigh the merits of the case itself, along with its responsibility to the insured defendant to act in "good faith" in indemnifying the insured, while representing the insured's and its own interests.

8.1022 *Negotiations and Settlement.* As stated above, when the parties voluntarily enter into settlement negotiations, the process is often begun by plaintiff's counsel, who sends some form of settlement letter. The process then continues with a series of interactions between counsel for the respective parties, in person, by telephone, by letter, or a combination of all three methods, in which counteroffers are exchanged.

If the judge enters the picture by scheduling a settlement conference or engaging in settlement talks during the pretrial conference, the judge may offer an assessment of the plaintiff's chances of proving the case on liability and damages, and the value of the case in the light of that assessment, along with a corresponding assessment of the defendant's case. This type of assessment is usually made after hearing each party's counsel verbally present the strong and weak points of each client's case, although some judges come to such a meeting with an assessment already made. The judge's participation in the settlement process sometimes acts to "break the ice," leading to a settlement of the case.

Another method of entering into settlement negotiations is through voluntary mediation, which is viewed by many in the legal profession as a much more cost effective means of resolving legal disputes than trial (*see* related discussion in Chapter 1, Section 1.05). In the mediation process, the parties choose a mediator and agree on who will pay the mediator's fees. A mutually available date and site is then chosen for the mediation. Usually the mediator asks that the parties as well as the attorneys attend the mediation, so that they can be fully involved in the process and be immediately on hand to consult with their respective attorneys and make quick responses to offers and counteroffers. Corporations, partnership, insurance companies, and other business entities who are parties to the lawsuit generally send representatives who have authority to negotiate on behalf of their principals. The mediator meets with all parties and counsel at the beginning of the day and some ground rules about the mediation are agreed upon. The plaintiff's attorney generally makes the first presentation, followed by the defendant's attorney. These verbal presentations may be very short and simple or long and elaborate. In the latter case, they greatly resemble opening statements given at the beginning of trials. The opening presentations may involve the use of charts, photographs, diagrams, or other forms of demonstrable evidence, or not, depending upon how much of their respective cases the attorneys are willing to reveal to the opposing side. The parties are then placed in different rooms with the mediator shuttling between them, pointing out strengths and weaknesses in both cases, conveying offers and counteroffers to both sides, and making recommendations about whether to accept or reject the offer or counteroffer. If the parties have realistically assessed the strengths and weaknesses of their respective cases and are willing to compromise to some extent, the mediator can usually find that bargaining range and the case can be successfully settled.

8.1023 Court Approval.   Some settlements require the approval of the court and may also require the appointment of a guardian or trust administrator. Such a procedure is most common in cases involving minors or those who have been adjudged incompetent to handle their own business and personal affairs. The procedures and requirements differ from state to state but where encountered, the legal assistant should review the current requirements of the jurisdiction and make certain that all necessary documents are prepared and all requirements are met so that settlement can proceed smoothly and correctly.

Bibliography

Baer, Harold and Broder, Aaron J., *How to Prepare and Negotiate Cases for Settlement*. Rev. ed. NY: Law-Arts Publishers, 1973.

Black's Law Dictionary. 6th ed. St. Paul: West Publishing Company, 1990.

Clermont, Kevin M., *Civil Procedure*. 3d ed. Black Letter Series. St. Paul: West Publishing Co., 1993.

Federal Civil Judicial Procedure and Rules, as amended to January 6, 1997. St. Paul: West Group, 1997.

Federal Practice and Procedure, as amended through December 1, 1996. St. Paul: West Publishing Company, 1997.

Federal Civil Rules Handbook. 1997 ed. St. Paul: West Publishing Co., 1997.

Fisher, Kathleen, *The Essentials of Civil Litigation.* National Center for Paralegal Training, 1995.

Anatomy of a Personal Injury Lawsuit, edited by Francis H. Hare, Jr. and Edward M. Ricci. NY: Association of Trial Lawyers of America, 1981.

Koerselman, Virginia, *CLA Review Manual, a Practical Guide to CLA Exam Preparation.* St. Paul: West Publishing Company, 1993.

Larbalestrier, Deborah E., *Paralegal Practice and Procedure, a Practical Guide for the Legal Assistant.* 2nd ed. Englewood Cliffs, NJ: Prentice-Hall, Inc. 1986.

Magarich, Pat, *Casualty Investigation Checklists.* NY: Clark Boardman Co., Ltd., 1985.

Mauet, Thomas A. and Maerowitz, Marlene A. *Fundamentals of Litigation for Paralegals.* 2nd ed. Little, Brown & Company, 1996.

Murvin, Jimmie W., *Paralegal Guide to Automobile Accident Cases.* John Wiley & Sons, Inc., 1995.

Osborne, Cynthia Monteiro, *Paralegal Preparation of Pleadings.* Santa Ana, CA: James Publishing Group, 1991.

Randall, Lynn M., *Litigation Organization and Management for Paralegals.* NY: Wiley Law Publications, 1993.

Signey, Phillip J., *Litigation Paralegal.* 2nd ed. NY: Wiley Law Publications, 1994.

9

The Legal Assistant and Document Discovery Cases

9.00 Introduction

Document production is an important part of the discovery process. Generally, legal assistants are more involved than attorneys are in requesting, reviewing, and inspecting and/or producing papers and records relating to the subject of the controversy. Therefore, it is important to learn the rules and general procedures for production of documents and things and inspection of land.

As discussed in Chapter 8, the document inspection phase of formal discovery is governed by Rule 34 of the Federal Rules of Civil Procedure. Many states have adopted a similar or identical rule which outlines the procedures in the state court system, but one should not assume that to be the case. It is important to locate and compare the applicable state rules regarding document requests and production and to note the variances. It is also important to review existing local rules for any court in which your action is pending.

The request for production of documents, whether initiated by the client's lawyer or by the adversary's lawyer, whether large or small, is designed to make available all the relevant facts in the case that have been memorialized in documents. The larger the volume of documents to be produced, the more difficult, time-consuming, and costly the effort will be. The basic concepts of document production apply to all cases, whatever the size, and should be followed to obtain the most cost effective and efficient results.

The attorney and the legal assistant must consider and analyze the value, the need for, and the utility of the discovery plan. They must weigh the time and cost against the anticipated benefits. It does little good to expend time and money designing and implementing a system that does not substantially contribute to reaching the goal in the case.

Document discovery cases and the systems developed to handle them require intensive thought and consideration early in the cases to produce effective and reliable results. Once committed to a given course, it can be difficult and expensive to change directions. Because the majority of the work with documents is a physical task, time is a critical element. The best work is conducted with intensity but not panic in a consistent and reliable manner.

9.001 The Discovery Plan

The initiation of discovery requires the attorneys and the legal assistants to consider jointly the problems anticipated in implementing any discovery plan for documents. There are two sides to this consideration: the client's documents and how to handle them and the adversary's documents and how to handle those. Decisions on the system to employ and the staff required will vary according to a number of factors discussed below.

9.0011 Plaintiff or Defendant. Whether the client is the plaintiff or the defendant in the case will play a part in staffing choices. If the client is the plaintiff, usually there is adequate time before filing the complaint to locate all of the client's documents and to arrange them in a reasonably ordered fashion. In this case, it is possible to work with a much smaller staff than when the client is the defendant responding to an aggressive plaintiff and suffering from the constraints of time created by court orders.

9.0012 Time Problems. Time constraints may arise from many sources. The statute of limitations effective in the case may have a bearing on the organization of personnel and equipment. The service of a request for production of documents with a statutory period in which to respond may present timing problems. It is axiomatic that the shorter the period of time in which to accomplish the production, the larger the staff needed and, generally, the more limited the choices of the manner in which the production will be performed.

9.0013 Volume. Documents in business litigation, product liability, and antitrust cases may vary from 1,000 pages of material to 200,000 or more pages of material. Documents in mass tort, class actions, and multidistrict litigation may number in the millions. Document volume has a major effect on the difficulty of production and will make demands both on the attorneys and the legal assistants in terms of the system employed and the manner of handling the documents (which are discussed later). Generally, one to two-thousand pages can be handled easily using either lists of documents or cards created for each document as a control device. A small team of one or two people can be used and becomes very familiar with the individual documents. Control and retrieval of the documents are thereby simplified.

As the volume of documents increases, the ability of the team to recall the important documents with certainty diminishes, regardless of the size of the team. If time is a problem, the team may be larger, and consequently, the number of "duplicate documents" that exist in all files may not have the same impact on the discovery team as they would if only one or two people worked on them. Generally, with a file of from 2,000 to 20,000 pages, "document databases" (which are discussed later) become necessary to handle the files properly. The "rule" in document discovery is the smaller the crew, the better. A small team gives each person a high degree of familiarity with the file, but it also means the routine tasks of numbering, indexing, and review will take longer and there is a greater impact on the effort if the team loses a member.

9.0014 Special Document Considerations. Routine correspondence, contracts, drafts of contracts, letters and memoranda, and so on, can be handled by legal assistants with reasonable training, time, and familiarity with the subject of the lawsuit. When the documents contain extensive and technical engineering reports, or highly complex studies and mathematical calculations related to those studies, the use of an engineering-qualified legal assistant or an engineer on loan from the company department in which the lawsuit originated may be absolutely essential.

Other special document problems can arise involving economic data, tax matters, or accounting documents peculiar to a large firm in which computer printouts and/or prenumbered forms might be adapted directly into the system without "special" or additional identifying data.

9.0015 Locating Responsive Documents. Among potential discovery production problems is the location and production of all responsive documents as opposed to the production of a representative copy of a particular type of requested document. The attorney must be consulted in determining whether all copies should be produced or whether a single copy will suffice. An example might be a personnel manual; it is probable that only one manual need be produced unless there are more than one version, in which case all versions may need to be produced. When the client is the plaintiff, thought should be given to identifying all categories of documents which have any relation to the issues in the lawsuit, including the proof of damages, with the idea of anticipating the documents which the adversary is most likely to request. Once through the files is difficult, but twice through is very expensive and time-consuming. The search must be thorough to identify all the documents within the guidelines established. Additionally, it is important to maintain the files "as kept in the ordinary course of business" unless the attorney makes a strategic decision not to do so. In any event, production of complete files is essential. Files of a fragmentary nature are extremely difficult to explain in discovery proceedings and will create many difficulties for the discovery team later in tracking the normal handling of such documents.

9.0016 File Location. One of the most difficult problems to overcome in document production is that of physical location. Files are often spread out among offices of a large corporation or the departments of small companies based on their duties, functions, and responsibilities. Sometimes the relationship between a file and an office or department is so tenuous that it is difficult to anticipate all the locations where the documents might be; this poses a substantial problem in the identification and location of those documents. The legal assistant's imagination should range as widely as the ability of the photocopy machine to produce documents in considering the possible resting places of potentially responsive material. It may be in a central file room, in one or more offices of individuals, or in storage. Consider each possibility, and then during the physical search ask each person, "Who else might have copies of this?", "Who do you send material to?", and so on.

9.0017 *Work Space, Equipment, and Budget.* The space in which the work is performed, the equipment with which to conduct the effort, and the budget within which the discovery team attempts to operate, all effect the team's ability to produce results. It does little good to rage against problems beyond one's control, and the legal assistant's flexibility in adjusting to any limitations will assist the discovery effort and present a positive and effective attitude.

9.0018 *Documents—Evidence and Company Operation.* The need to produce documents in a suit requires the attorney to take custody of potential documentary evidence. However, the client's daily work must continue with as little handicap as possible. Photocopying is simple and fast; however, simply copying the original material creates new documents potentially responsive to the case. Consider placing a legend on the copies of responsive documents and giving these "legend copies" to the operating office for convenience. The legend may consist of a unique identifying number, or may be a phrase such as "Copy of an original in the lawsuit file XYZ vs. ABC." Many clients will prefer the discretion of a unique number.

9.0019 *To Number or Not to Number.* Once the potentially responsive and relevant documents are identified, the problems of future reference to each one must be addressed. The documents may be marked with a unique identifying number, alphabetic character, or an alpha-numeric combination before any photocopying, sorting, or other handling is undertaken. Tactical or strategic considerations, or the personal preference of the attorney may dictate otherwise.

Early numbering establishes control over the documents and minimizes the chances of a document becoming lost or misfiled. It also has the benefit of dealing with a laborious job in the beginning of the case, simplifies the recognition of individual documents and their subsequent copies, the comparison of apparent duplicates, and facilitates the use of file indexing, databases, or other techniques. It allows quick relation of the document to its point of origin through the minimum number of reference elements, such as type, date, author, addressee, and topic. Some attorneys prefer not to number the documents until after the adversary has reviewed and inspected them. This creates difficult control and identification problems for the legal assistants (and ultimately for the attorney). Its worst feature is that it delays the labor of numbering until after the inspection by the adversary. This often means that a huge volume of documents must be numbered under a time constraint, as opposed to the more comfortable system allowed by the technique of numbering them as they are found. An additional drawback is that when an unnumbered document is used by the adversary later in the case, it may not be possible to know whether or not it originated from the client's production. When the documents have been numbered in advance, there is no doubt of their source.

9.00110 Document Control Methods. Since the documents may range in volume from 1,000 to 200,000 pages or more, the choice of control methods must be one of the first decisions made. Failure to do this will result in duplication of work, additional labor, and added cost and may result in documents being lost, misplaced, or misfiled. In addition to numbering the documents, which is generally considered the best method, other methods available are:

a. Document indexes using reference items, such as date, author, and addressee (discussed in Section 9.0122);
b. The use of surrogate documents, such as the "Document Screening Form" (discussed in Section 9.0132);
c. "Individual and Entity" form (discussed in Section 9.032);
d. Other indexes which include the identification numbers for each document.

9.00111 Privileged Documents. It is important to identify and segregate documents early in the review and control process which may carry any "privilege," such as that of attorney-client, attorney work product, proprietary information or trade secrets. The legal assistant often assists in this important assignment and should be briefed by the attorney concerning what specifically should be looked for, along with the criteria to be used, in evaluating the existence or absence of privilege. It is the attorney's responsibility to provide this guidance at the beginning of the case and to provide adequate supervision throughout the process.

9.00112 Issue Recognition. When the client is the plaintiff, it may be necessary early in the discovery operation to code the documents according to the issues of the case. A substantial amount of early thought and analysis by the attorneys to identify the case issues, along with some familiarity with the types of documents involved in the case, is needed to accomplish this task. One of the important elements to successful issue-coding is to establish a reference list of the issues which incorporates an understandable "plain language" definition.

When the client is the defendant in a case, issue recognition is often accomplished at a later stage when there has been more opportunity to define all the issues important to the defense. Instead, sortings may be performed according to each numbered request by the adversary, with the issues imputed to some degree from an analysis of the nature of the documents requested.

9.00113 Personnel Choices. Deciding what personnel resources to use in gathering and indexing the required documents must be done early in the process. Depending on the number of documents, using the client's personnel may be a cost effective alternative to relying solely on legal assistants or hiring temporary workers. However, when nonlegal trained staff are utilized, it is very important for the attorney and the legal assistant to closely supervise the work effort to ensure that the results are reliable and thorough, with all the records produced and properly indexed.

9.00114 Legal Assistant Conceptual Contributions. The attorneys in each case must rely on assistance to obtain enough data to allow intelligent decisions to be made about choosing a discovery plan. The legal assistant is often tasked with performing an initial screening review of the files and to participate in discussions on the possible paths the litigation may take. When a tentative choice of the document discovery plan is made, the legal assistant may often be tasked with generating a step-by-step procedure for implementing the plan, including estimates of time, personnel, space, equipment, and cost for consideration by the attorney in making the final decision. The legal assistant should be knowledgeable concerning the mechanical processes and should be a forceful advocate when necessary for the system of choice; but in the end, it is the attorney's decision.

9.00115 Attorney Reviews and Audits.   The attorney must be satisfied that the directions given the legal assistant for performing document searches are effective, and that the work is being properly accomplished. The legal assistant should welcome and encourage spot checks or audits of the work being done; it minimizes wasted work and reveals any weaknesses in communications.

9.00116 Documenting the Plan.   Once selected, the plan should be outlined in detail (in writing) with the control devices and procedures well explained. These terms to be used, acronyms, logos, codes, abbreviations, and so on all must be analyzed and the initial selections memorialized. The plan document will serve as a guide for use and modification as the case progresses.

9.01   Client Documents

Whether plaintiff or defendant, document discovery plans always involve a minimum of five basic activities to be considered, whether the ultimate effort is small and simple or huge and complex. These essential elements, or common principles are locating the documents, establishing document control, identifying the documents, retrieving and producing the documents, and ultimately returning the documents.

9.011   Locate

If the client is on the receiving end of a request for production of documents, the legal assistant will be involved in determining what material, if any, is responsive to the various requests and where it is located. In some types of cases, especially actions involving business entities and manufacturing processes, it will take a good part of the thirty-day response time to accomplish those tasks.

When the client is the plaintiff, the legal assistant is involved in locating and gathering together all the client's documents which relate to the lawsuit prior to formal filing of the summons and complaint. This is especially critical when lawsuits are to be filed in federal court, since Rule 26 of the Federal Rules of Civil Procedure requires the plaintiff to make initial disclosures concerning witnesses and documents at the time the lawsuit is filed.

9.0111 Attorney and Legal Assistant Review and Analysis.   The first step in responding to a production request is to carefully review and analyze the formal request. Note any individual requests as to which an objection might be asserted, and discuss them with the supervising attorney.

Whether responding to a production request or gathering documents during the pretrial investigation phase, the attorney and the legal assistant should carefully discuss the case to ensure both have the same understanding of the issues (actual or probable) of the case along with the parameters for locating the client's files and the screening and selection process that will follow. In some cases, particularly in complex litigation, it may be necessary for the attorney to assist in the early review of documents to obtain a perspective on the types of documents involved in the case in order to make the subsequent decisions. The types of documents, as well as the volume, often determine the control system used in the case.

9.0112 Locating Document Sources.   The next step in responding to a production request is to send a copy of the request to the client and then follow up with the client to determine the likely location of all responsive material. If the client is a business entity, the legal assistant will need to know all departments or individuals who have played a part in the contracting or manufacturing or other procedure which is involved in the subject of the litigation. If possible, it is best for the legal assistant or the attorney to talk with key employees. Ask them to provide a "walk-through" of the contracting or manufacturing process, identifying all other players or departments. Be on the alert for names, as well as types of documentation, which pass between or among employees. Typically, several copies of interoffice memoranda and correspondence are circulated to department heads or managers. If that is the case, the legal assistant should locate and produce as many copies of each document as were circulated throughout the company. In a case with a small number of issues, only one, two, or three departments may be involved which makes it easier to gather the documents. In large document cases, it is essential to prepare a full listing of all sources of records to be screened for discussion with the supervising attorney since this initial step may determine the completeness of the response to the adversary's document request.

After the types of potentially responsive records and the approximate volume have been tentatively identified, a strategy session may need to be held so that the attorney and client can decide whether responsive documents will be produced as they are kept in the normal course of business (generally in files or file cabinets at the client's place or places of business), or whether they will be organized and labeled to correspond with the categories in the request.

9.0113 Gathering the Documents and Taking Custody.   In small document cases, this process may be as simple as receiving a few file folders or a banker's box of documents from the client. In larger document cases, the process will involve arranging for all the documents to be collected in one place for transport to the law firm, or some other work area within the client's organization where they will be processed and segregated. In very large cases, this process can also involve arranging transport to a "joint document depository" which has been established by agreement among all the parties to a lawsuit, or by court order.

As each collection of documents, whether in file folders, boxes, or file cabinets, is identified as having a possible connection to the lawsuit, it is added to an inventory list that characterizes the location from which it was taken, the custodian (individual) who provided it, along with a general description of the contents. For instance, if the file has a number and a title, that identification should be used for clarity; if a box contains accounting records, that description along with the time period covered may be used for identification. When taking possession of a large number of documents or files, an estimate of the space involved should be made as well, such as a "one-half-inch linear measure" or "one full banker's box." This is important because at some later date if a decision to number is made, a reference to the inclusive numbers contained within the individual files or document collections should be added to the inventory list. (*See* Exhibit 9-1.) Receipts for the documents are prepared by the legal assistant team and left with the client or individual who provided them. The legal assistant team then takes the documents in whatever form provided into custody for transport to a work area.

EXHIBIT 9-1   Sample Inventory List

Page No. ___ of ___

Initial Client Document Inventory

Case: _____   Date: _____

Source / Location	General Description	Container / Size	ID / End	Produced	Date
		☐ Box ☐ Folder ☐ Loose ☐ _____ Size:_____			
		☐ Box ☐ Folder ☐ Loose ☐ _____ Size:_____			
		☐ Box ☐ Folder ☐ Loose ☐ _____ Size:_____			
		☐ Box ☐ Folder ☐ Loose ☐ _____ Size:_____			

PRACTICE TIP

When gathering files from a business client for your review, it is important to ascertain whether those particular records are active files. If so, every effort should be made to give those records priority for review purposes so that they can be returned to the department using them. If any active file contains material which is responsive to the request, you must devise a system to note the location of the active file and the custodian of that file so you can retrieve it for the inspection.

The material which was contained in the active file when you reviewed it should be marked, listed, or clipped in some manner so that employees will not disturb the portions you have already reviewed and it will be obvious if anything has been added to the file after your review; then you only have to review any new material before you produce that file for inspection. During the inspection, it is acceptable procedure to request that opposing counsel review active files first so that business interruption can be kept at a minimum.

9.0114 The "Evidence Room" Work Area. If the actual production for inspection will be held at the client's facility, a conference room or other working space should be selected. In most instances, that place will serve as your "office" for purposes of reviewing files and other records. Generally, inactive files which contain material responsive to the request should be segregated and kept in a designated area awaiting the production after you have reviewed them.

The work area for the legal assistant team should be removed from normal activity of the departments and of the functional personalities in a case. The room should be considered an "evidence room" with restricted entry and a firm control over the entry and removal of documents within it.

9.012 Control

Once the documents have been located and gathered together, some method of control for ensuring the integrity of the document collection while it is in custody must be established. The surest method is to number the selected documents as soon as the "responsive" identity is confirmed. Once each document is numbered with a unique identifying number, alphabetic character, or alphanumeric combination, the ability to maintain the documents in the same order and condition produced is certain. Additionally, unique identification numbers allow accurate records to be maintained of exactly what documents are produced to an adversary, ensure that the source of the particular document will be easily identified in the future, allow for the creation of easily searchable information databases, allow for cross-referencing use as exhibits, and simplifies accurate reference to the document during depositions.

PRACTICE TIP

There are several methods available to number the documents. An automatic numbering machine or "Bates Stamp" may be used. Electronic, or powered numbering machines are available to stamp the documents. Computer label programs are also widely available which print a series of numbers on "peel-and-stick" labels which are then affixed to the document pages. Finally, there are vendor services which will produce printed labels similar to those which may de done in-house as well as those who will also perform the actual task of document numbering. All of these methods allow for the use of a prefix or suffix with the number, which is useful for additional source identification.

Whichever method of numbering is used, the placement of the identifying number on the document should be consistent and regular. The number must not cover or obscure any writing or data on the original document. Nothing is more frustrating than having to hunt for the document number on a page, or not being able to read a word or phrase because it has been defaced by the number. It is suggested the whenever possible, the number be placed in the vicinity of the lower right-hand corner of a page, because most of us are already accustomed to looking in that area for a page number.

Although in small document cases it is not uncommon for a method other than numbering to be used, it is still the best control method. In large document cases, numbering is the only practical and reliable method. If numbering is not used, a more complex system must be created, which often consists of maintaining a duplicate "original" set and a series of duplicate copy sortings which represent what was produced or otherwise utilized. Working with a nonnumbered set of documents requires additional effort and extreme care to ensure that a document separated from the file is returned to the exact spot it was removed from. The relationship of a document to the file from which it was taken cannot be lost, and preserving the documents in the same condition in which they were discovered is extremely important. The legal assistant cannot

PRACTICE TIP — The Decision to Number

Numbering of documents prior to production (in the case of plaintiffs) or at the beginning of production (in the case of defendants) to the adversary, has great advantages for the legal assistant team, and by extension, the attorneys for whom they work. It improves control and simplifies referral, retrieval, and sorting. When the original documents are numbered, it makes it easy to provide a copy back to the client in the situation where the document is actually used by the client in its normal and continuing course of business. Numbered documents provide an easy reference between the client, the lawyer, witnesses, and other users from that point forward. When the decision to number is postponed to some future time, photocopies of the responsive documents should be limited to reduce to a minimum the duplicates, or near duplicates, that later will have to be located, purged, and/or substituted with the numbered copies.

A numbering system is sometimes perceived as imposing additional difficulties. Irrelevant or privileged documents may be numbered that later would not be produced to the adversary but might have to be explained. Gaps may occur where there are numbering errors, where irrelevant documents were initially included and later removed, and where privileged documents have been removed. The adversary will want to know why these gaps exist. However, under the Federal Rules of Civil Procedure (and state rules which are similar) the adversary is entitled to a listing of all documents withheld from production. The use of a numbering system under these provisions enhances the ability of the producing party to comply with those rules. It should be remembered that determinations of relevancy, responsiveness, and privilege may all be challenged by an adversary and ultimately ruled upon by a judge, therefore numbering the documents is a tool which ultimately aids in this process.

A numbering system is often more cost effective and efficient than a "no numbering" system. In order to maintain control and to minimize problems which arise from adversary challenges to the completeness of the production, such as claims of never receiving a document, or establishing the source of a document reviewed by expert witnesses, consultants and others, each document photocopied for production should have a legend on the side, at the top, or bottom of the page in a distinctive location that reads essentially "Copy of an original from the file of X produced on [date]." For extra security, it also requires that an exact duplicate of the material produced to the adversary be maintained. These duplicate copies are costly to the client and the attorney in both time, money, and storage space. Because a numbering system would allow the creation of an index of the documents produced, it eliminates the need for many duplicate copies.

change the character of the documents by assembling or disassembling stapled or bound material without the concurrence and direction of the attorney.

From this point forward, it is essential that whatever system of control is adopted, the legal assistant ensures its integrity. By doing so, the legal assistant ensures that the attorney will be able to establish that the method of production complies fully with discovery requirements and is not arbitrary, whimsical, or unreliable.

9.0121 Purposes. The purpose of the document control program is to ensure the following points:

1. That no document is made available to the adversaries without having been reviewed by the legal assistants and by the attorneys.
2. That no privileged document is ever accidentally exposed to the adversary in the course of the proceeding.
3. That every document responsive to the case is produced as required but that every appropriate defense to production of any document is exercised by the attorneys before its surrender.
4. That every highly significant document, whether helpful or harmful to the client, is referred to the supervising attorneys for evaluation before the adversary sees it.
5. That every document obtained from the adversary is correctly handled and cross-referenced in relation to the issues and to the "friendly" documents in the case.
6. That documents are maintained in an order allowing retrieval of any document as needed by the attorneys in timely fashion.

9.0122 Indexes. Indexing is an essential control element in all document cases. Good indexes are cost-effective because they make the process of analyzing, sorting, and retrieving documents less labor intensive and time-consuming. Indexes are really "mini" databases. By creating a master index on the computer in either "table" format or in "merge data file" format (if using word processing software such as WordPerfect or Word), the master index can be sorted in various ways to create additional indexes, such as by ID number, by date, by author, by issue, or any other combination. When the volume of documents to be indexed exceeds one thousand, it is more efficient to use a database program (such as Access, Paradox, or dBASE) to create the master index. The essential elements of the master index include the identification number, the original source, the date, document type, author, addressee, any "cc" recipients, and the subject or title of the document. Normally, the information for the index is collected on forms by the legal assistant or document production team as the documents are screened and numbered for entry into the computer at a later time. Sometimes, the information is entered directly into the computer while it is being gathered, if the legal assistant or team has a laptop computer available. The form used to gather the information is in the same format and order as the electronic version.

Indexing may be done at the same time the documents are screened and identified, or may be done separately as the first element of establishing control. The factors that effect that decision are usually the volume of the documents, the staff available to accomplish the task, and the time constraints. During the control phase, the only file that exists is the original document file collection. (*See* Exhibit 9-2, Sample Master Index.)

9.0123 Document Room Control. Control of documents in the document room or work area is critical for maintaining the integrity of the document collection. When an original document leaves the document room for any purpose, whether it is to be sent to an attorney for review, a technical expert for review or consideration, supplied for studies, or supplied for review by adversaries under a court order, it is essential that a record be created which gives the date, the name of the requester, the name of the person who physically removed the document, where the document is being sent, and the name of who will be responsible for the document (if different from the person who requested). This record should be in the form of an "out card"

EXHIBIT 9-2   Sample Master Index

Master Document Index

Case: _____   Date: _____

ID No.	Source	Date	Type	Author	Addressee	Other "cc"	Subj / Title / "re"
AB 10001 AB 10002	ABC Accounting Dept	97-01-11	Letter	John Doe	James Joyce	Annie Long	Payment of Invoice No. 77923
AB 10003 AB 10003	ABC Accounting Dept	97-01-12	Memo	Jane Roe	John Doe		Adjustment to Joyce Bill

or other surrogate document which is inserted in the file in place of the document, and should also be noted in a memorandum or on a Check Out Form. (*See* Exhibit 9-3, page 286.) This sounds burdensome, but it provides an essential check to ensure that the document is not lost or mislaid, and depending on the reason the original was taken, establishes a record which be useful in certain circumstances, such as when an adversary complains that the document was never provided or never seen, or to establish what an expert has or has not reviewed.

When a copy of a document is made for any purpose, it is also important to create a record which gives the date, the purpose of the copy, who requested it, and who it was provided to. This information should be noted on the master index and in a memorandum for the same reasons noted above concerning original documents.

9.013 Identify and Screen

The third phase of the document program is concerned with screening and identifying the document collection. No matter the volume of the documents involved, there is no shortcut for examining each document page-by-page. The identification process is not complete until all potentially relevant or responsive documents are distinguished and separated from documents that may be privileged and from those which are irrelevant documents.

For plaintiffs, the process of initial screening and examining each document page-by-page often occurs during the prelitigation phase of the case, and is conducted to identify all documents which may be potentially relevant to the anticipated lawsuit, as well as those supporting of, and troublesome to, the client's position. When done effectively, this process will also provide the necessary information needed to respond to production requests after the lawsuit has been filed.

For defendants, the initial screening and document examination is usually conducted to identify specific documents that fit the requirements of the production request, whether in hand or anticipated, as well as to identify documents which support or contradict the defenses asserted in the answer to the complaint.

9.0131 Legal Assistant Preparation and Training. It is extremely important for the attorney and the legal assistant to discuss the scope of the screening. This should be based on the issues of the legal pleadings and the discovery received or anticipated. The scope, issues,

EXHIBIT 9-3   Sample Check Out Form and Document Review "Out Card"

Document Check Out Sheet

CASE: Alpha Beta Corp vs Luke Skywalker   LOCATION: File Room "A" — Sixth Floor

Doc. ID Nos.	Date Taken / Name	Purpose	Destination	Date Return / Name	Notes
AB 115000 AB 125005	2/6/97 J. Greene	Issue Coding of Docs	J. Greene's Office	2/10/97 J. Greene	
AB2 007000 ABS 008500	2/9/97 Annie Long	Review for Damages Info	Jack Esquire's Office		

Sample Document "Out Card"

**DOCUMENT(S) PULLED FOR
REVIEW/PROCESSING
(SEE CHECK OUT SHEET)**

ID No. Start	ID No. End
~~AB 116000~~	~~AB126006~~
AB2 007000	AB2 008500

and other items deemed important to note during the review should be documented in a memo which is then available as a ready reference as the task is being performed. Additional items to include in the memo are standard designations for document types, issues, privilege designations, references to individuals and entities, and document sources. This ensures that references will be consistent, which is very important later, when searches are accomplished and indexes or databases are created. A Document Screening Form should be created which helps those performing the task maintain consistency. (*See* Exhibit 9-4, Sample Document Screening Form.)

EXHIBIT 9-4   Sample Document Screening Form

CASE: XYZ Construction vs Developments, Inc., et al   Screened by: Jack Palance   Date: 1/1/97

| Doc_ID Start: C 100001 | Doc_ID End: C 100010 | Date: 10/2/94 | Source: XYZ JOB FILE |

Type: ☐ Letter ☐ Memo ☐ Report ☐ Financial Notes ☐ Contract ☐ Invoice ☐ Medical ☐ Receipt
☑ Proposal ☐ Time Card ☐ Daily Job Report ☐ Meeting Minutes ☐ Other _____

| From: XYZ CONSTRUCTION | To: OWNER | "cc": ARCHITECT |

| Duplicate of Doc_ID: | ☑ Attached to Doc_ID: C 099999 |

| ☐ Subj: ☐ Re: ☑ Title:
Change Order Proposal 14 | ☐ Marginalia |

Privilege: ☐ AC ☐ WP   Protection: ☐ Trade Secret ☐ Research ☐ Development ☐ Commercial
☐ Other

☑ Relevant ☐ Not Relevant ☐ Helpful ☐ Problem ☑ Damage Info ☐ Liability ☐ KEY

Issues: ☐ Fraud ☐ Negligence ☑ Breach of Contract ☐ Bad Faith ☐ Notice ☐ Intent ☐ Reliance

Key Words: ☐ Bituthene ☑ Change Order ☑ Delay ☐ Acceleration ☐ Weather ☐ Generator ☐ Piles

Names Mentioned:

Doc. Mentioned: Contract dated 8/1/94

Notes/Summary: Subcontractor's itemized proposal to add waterproof membrane sub-roofing. Total cost $150,679. Attached to Cover Letter dated 10/3/94.

When there will be a team of personnel performing the review and screening tasks, one legal assistant should be designated as being the "lead." This legal assistant, with the assistance of the attorneys and any professional people recruited as consultants in the case, conducts training programs to ensure that the legal assistants, or other personnel, performing the screening operation have a working knowledge of the language and functions expressed in the documents to be read, and are familiar with the screening memo and the screening form. The training process may be a day or more, depending on the volume of the documents, the complexity of technical terms, the number of legal issues, and the experience of the discovery team.

9.0132 Reviewing and Screening the Material. The legal assistant, or discovery team, is now prepared to review and screen all of the enclosed documents within each folder according to the criteria established in the document screening memo. Every page must be read and analyzed. The legal assistant, or discovery team, reads and screens for "potential relevance" or "potential responsiveness" in this initial sorting process. If there is any question in the mind of the reviewer, the document should be included as relevant or responsive with a notation that it is questionable. The final decision on whether the document is included or not is made by an attorney.

PRACTICE TIP

In document cases where a decision has been made to produce the file material responsive to each discovery request, rather than producing all material "as kept in the ordinary course of business," initial physical sortings of material which is potentially responsive to a production request can often be made during the screening process.

All documents are organized in boxes for the legal assistant, or the discovery team, to review and screen. Place marker cards are used to ensure the legal assistant, or discovery team, is reviewing the documents progressively in order and covering all of the documents in a file. This card should be identified with the name of the reviewer, sufficiently tall so it can project vertically above a file, and distinctive in color to allow instant recognition as a "reviewing place card." The selection of responsive documents is initially indicated in the raw files by standing them vertically on their edges in the boxes. This makes it easy to pull the documents for production copying.

The documents should not be changed from their original condition during this initial screening process. No stapled or otherwise bound document should be taken apart to characterize some portion of it as responsive and another portion as irrelevant. Where files must be transported from the screening location to another place for advice or the consideration of another party, an "out card" fully identifying the document, dated, signed by the screener, and reflecting the person to whom the document was directed must be inserted in place of the document. The integrity of the individual files must be maintained.

9.0133 *Identifying and Segregating Privileged Material.* Identifying potentially privileged material is one of the critical purposes of reviewing and screening the document collection.

Privileged documents should be removed from the files as they are identified. A colored or special form sheet can be made for insertion in the file, indicating that a document has been removed due to claimed privilege. This "production document" (*see* Section 9.0143) should contain the document identification number, number of pages, date, author, addressee, any other recipients of the document, the document title or subject line (if any), and the type of privilege claimed. This is the same information which will be taken from the document screening form to create the "privilege document index," which will be used to create the "privilege log." The Federal Rules of Civil Procedure and many state discovery rules require that the producing party compile and produce to the adversary a "log" of material which is being withheld on the claim of privilege. Because the privilege log is given to the adversary, additional care is taken in the wording used to describe the type, subject matter or title of privileged document, and the persons involved so that the confidential or privileged information and content is not inadvertently disclosed. (*See* Exhibit 9-5, Sample Privilege Log.)

Again, legal assistants should include all documents which are "potentially" privileged. The final decision on whether a document is privileged or not is made by an attorney. What initially appeared to be a privileged document may not be. When this occurs, its "privileged" designation is removed from the index, log, and screening form, and the document is returned to its original place in the responsive file with the "Privileged Document" production form pulled and destroyed. The legal assistant must check to ensure that any copies of the document are properly redistributed. Any other indexes on which the document was listed as "privileged" must be corrected, and indexes listing material produced, or to be produced, must be changed as well.

EXHIBIT 9-5   Sample Privilege Log

PRIVILEGE LOG: XYZ Construction vs Developments, Inc., et al

Priv.	Doc. No.	No. Pages	Date	From	To	cc	Nature of Communication
AC	XYZ 1010012	2	08/26/87	Joe Client	H. Lawyer	none	Litigation Status
WP	XYZ 1079999	5	08/05/88	H. Lawyer	Joe Client	none	Analysis of Damages

9.0134 Types of Files Created. The two files that are created during the initial screening and review process consist of:

a. The Original Document File. It is best to maintain this file in the same manner and condition as the documents were first found. The only exception is that privileged documents are removed with cross-reference sheets, or "production documents," substituted in their place. Ideally, the original documents will have been numbered, allowing the file to be maintained in numeric order. A master index of the documents is created from the information contained on the Document Screening Forms. This index forms the basis for preparing working files and additional indexes later during the retrieval and production phase of the discovery process.

b. Privileged Document File. This file consists of all the original documents which have been determined to be potentially privileged (including those which are duplicates of another). This file must be separated physically from the original file and stored in a secure manner to prevent inadvertant disclosure to third parties. Depending on the volume of the privileged material, this can be accomplished by placing the documents in a sealed envelope or box and/or a locked file cabinet. A copy of the privilege index and/or the privilege log should be attached to the outside of the envelope, box, or file cabinet. Cross-reference "Privileged Document(s)" production forms (*see* Section 9.0143) are inserted in the original file in place of the documents. Care is taken to ensure that any photocopies made of the privileged documents for review by the attorneys are destroyed or stored in the same place as the originals.

9.014 Retrieve and Produce

Documents are discovered during the course of a case to determine those that contribute to establishing facts or the reasoning that led to events, practices, procedures, or representations at issue in the case. The assembly of documents without the ability to use them effectively later in supporting the client's case, or refuting the adversary's case, is virtually worthless.

The ability to retrieve any given document or set of documents reliably and timely from the assembled mass of produced material or reference material included within a document discovery file is vital. Additionally, where documents become exhibits in a case, the authors, addressees, and persons who have seen or acted upon the content of the document are potential witnesses and may need to see and examine those documents to refresh their memories. The ability to retrieve documents can be the difference between supporting or destroying a witness or winning or losing a case.

Documents often are assembled in a fashion that is solely a convenience for the department file clerk or an individual who has created his or her own personal reference file. The assembly

---

PRACTICE TIP — Screening Documents for Privilege and Protection

ATTORNEY/CLIENT PRIVILEGE

Privilege May Be Asserted

1. The document is written to the attorney from the client, or from the client to the attorney.
2. Third parties (other than the attorney's staff, partners, or associates) not listed as copy recipients.
3. The subject matter concerns this litigation or another litigation matter.

Privilege May Be Waived

1. Voluntary Disclosure to *anyone else* acts as waiver either during discovery or elsewhere.

Other Considerations

1. If the document, or portion of the document, is to be used at trial, it must be produced during discovery.
2. Parts of documents that are not subject to assertion of the privilege must be disclosed.

WORK PRODUCT/TRIAL PREPARATION MATERIALS

Privilege May Be Asserted

1. Document is prepared by, or on behalf of, an attorney.
2. Document prepared in anticipation of litigation.
3. Document prepared by a party or agent of the party.
4. Statement within a document contains mental impressions and legal evaluations of the attorney, investigator, or claims agent.

Privilege May Be Waived

1. Disclosure to *another party* is basis for waiver.

CONFIDENTIAL INFORMATION, NOT ABSOLUTELY PRIVILEGED

1. Trade secrets
2. Confidential research, development, or commercial information

---

of a large number of these accumulations can result in a hodgepodge of nonchronologic material in no particular order. Since the document discovery file generally must serve the purpose of relating one document to another and documents seldom are generated simultaneously, a chronologic sorting of copies of all of the responsive documents is always necessary. The peripheral benefits of chronologic sorting will be the identification of duplicate or near-duplicate documents resulting from the juxtaposition of all duplicate or near-duplicate documents. It allows comparison of drafts, marginal annotations, or distribution comments that individually may mean little but together reflect policy, decision, responsibility, and so on.

Retrieving and producing documents involves working with the original document file to either prepare working copies of specific documents or categories of documents, or to produce copies of documents responsive to an adversary's discovery request.

9.0141 *Working File and Index Categories.* The working file and index categories described below contribute significantly to the conduct of the case. Sorting and identifying the document collection to obtain these files is done very efficiently by using the master index created from the Document Screening Form during the identify and screening phase of the discovery process to create indexes. Using these indexes make the process of selecting the documents for inclusion much easier and less labor intensive, which results in cost savings to the client and the attorney in terms of both time and money.

a. Chronologic File and Index. A chronologic index and file is always necessary on document cases. The chronological index is created by using the computer to sort the master index by date. The file is then created by photocopying the original documents in the same order as the chronological index. This file should exclude privileged documents, irrelevant documents, and duplicate documents. "Production document" forms which included a detailed summary may be substituted on occasion for very large or bulky documents, depending on the preference of the case attorney. (*See* Section 9.0143.)

b. Issue File and Index. This index and file is organized by each case issue identified by the attorneys. This sorting is accomplished by using the master index mentioned above to sort by both issue topic and date. When the Document Screening Form has been used to identify issues during the review and screening phase, *and* that information has been included in the master index, this task is reasonably fast and simple because it can be done using the computer. If the issue identification is done separately from the initial review and screening, manually going back through the chronologic document file to identify all issue relationships can be time and labor intensive. The original documents are then photocopied in the same order as they appear on the index and placed in notebooks for review by the attorneys and technical personnel as needed. It is not unusual that subsequent reviews will reveal that a document pertains to additional issues, and should be included in other issue files, or that a document no longer has relevance to an issue. When this occurs, the master index is corrected to include the additional information, so that the corrected issue index can be generated.

c. Witness Document File and Index. In preparation for the deposition of a witness, copies are made of each document which refers or relates to that witness in any manner. Every document which mentions the witness as author, addressee, or other recipient, or mentions the witness in the text, is located and compiled in a notebook along with any documents which were connected to the witness through the testimony of another individual. This is generally a multistep process which includes sorting the master index to produce a listing of documents which contain the name of the witness, reviewing the documents *not* included on that list to ensure accuracy, and reviewing deposition testimony or statements of other witnesses for references to documents mentioned in connection with the witness. The master index is corrected to include any additional links to documents for that witness, and a new witness index is generated. Usually, the documents are set up in chronological order, but sometimes they are also further segregated by issue. These files are used either to prepare the friendly witness for deposition or to prepare for questioning an adversary witness at deposition.

d. Exhibit Files and Index. Every document introduced for the client or by the adversary as an exhibit, either to pleadings, at deposition, or at trial, must be identified and indexed. The index should include a historical background on the document, and cross-references to other related documents or to witnesses. This can be prepared using the master index, which is first amended to include a reference to the use of the document as an exhibit, then sorted to produce the exhibit index. It is recommended that the marked exhibits be maintained with the pleading or deposition in which they were used.

e. Documents Produced. This index, or file, tracks what documents have been produced to the adversary, and includes information such as the date produced, the receiving party, and what discovery request the production request is responsive to. When a small number of documents is involved, it is usually cost effective to maintain an exact duplicate of the documents produced along with a copy of the formal discovery response which makes them available to the adversary. When the volume of documents is large, it is more cost effective to prepare an index which lists the documents produced in numerical order, or lists them in order of the request they are responsive to. In either case, the master index is amended to note that the documents were produced to the adversary party.

f. Individual and Entity Database. In its simplest form, this is a listing of every name that appears in the case, whether discovered in documents or testimony. In its most complex form, it includes addresses, personal information and history, and a listing of each document which has been connected to that individual or entity. It is created by compiling information from a review of the master index, the adversary documents, and depositions. (*See* Section 9.032.)

9.0142 *Responding to Document Requests.* Most requests generate a mixture of types of formal written responses which include, but are not limited to, the following: (1) A statement that the material sought will be produced at a time and place to be agreed upon by counsel; (2) A statement that the documents sought will be produced on an agreed date to the extent that any responsive documents or records exist; (3) A statement that the responding party has no documents or records responsive to the request; and/or (4) An objection to the request.

If your client has records or documents which will be produced, it is not necessary that you identify the material with any specificity in the written response. It is sufficient to state that the party does have responsive documents which will be produced. The attorney and client can determine between the date of the written response and the date on which the material will be produced for inspection whether it will be produced as kept in the normal course of business, or whether it will be organized and labeled to correspond with the categories in the request; that is a choice afforded to the producing party.

In some cases, where responsive documents are small in number, the required written response and the document production can be taken care of simultaneously by attaching copies of responsive documents to the written response. When this occurs, it is a good idea to assign a different exhibit number or letter to each document or group of documents being produced in response to each request. When the actual production is done in this manner, it must be remembered that if any documents or records are being withheld under a claim of privilege, a "privilege log" is also required to be provided.

When the decision is made to allow the adverse party to inspect the documents and mark those for which copies are desired, the legal assistant will need to determine ahead of time how, when, and where the copies will be made of the documents the opposing counsel designates for copying. This can range from using copy facilities at the legal assistant's office, the client's offices, or the use of a commercial copying service. It is important to discuss this with the client and to make sure that the client feels comfortable with the copy method selected.

The first thing to be done when the production commences is to inform the opposing party's representatives as to the preferred procedure for marking records they want copied. If this procedure includes tabbing papers with "post-it notes," don't presume that they will bring their own. Have some handy where the inspection will take place. Be sure to tell the representatives what the copy cost will be. If you anticipate using a commercial copy center, discuss the possibility of direct billing to opposing counsel by the copy service.

Most attorneys and clients do not want the client's records produced without having a representative of the law firm present. This task is usually delegated to the legal assistant. If there is a large quantity of material being produced, the legal assistant may be kept busy rotating files in and out of the room where the inspection is taking place. Otherwise, it is a good practice to bring other work assignments along to help pass the time.

After the inspection is concluded, follow through with the arrangements made for having the documents copies. Prior to having the documents copied, annotate the master index for each document being copied as well as each document which was available during the inspection. As previously mentioned in this chapter, it may be advisable to maintain one complete set of the documents copied so that there is no question about what was copied by opposing counsel; this is particularly critical when the client's documents have not been numbered. If the client's documents have not been previously numbered, it is recommended that the documents to be copied be numbered at that time so that if they are utilized for any purpose in the future, there will be no question as to where they came from. Whatever numbering system is selected, care should be taken that the numbers are consecutive with no gaps, and that the duplicate set retained has the same numbers. Some copy services have photocopy machines which "stamp" a consecutive number on copies made from an original. In many cases, using a service such as this proves more cost effective in terms of both time and money, than numbering and producing the copies "in-house."

9.0143 Using "Production Documents." "Production documents" are divider sheets or inserts that function to preserve the original groupings or placement of materials within a document collection. When documents are obtained from clients, whether individuals or entities, they may be in folders, three-ring binders, stapled, bound, or in various forms of semipermanent binding. When these original documents or materials are selected to be photocopied, scanned, or otherwise reproduced, it becomes necessary to provide "Production Document" inserts which serve as placeholders for documents too large to be copied or processed, and which preserve the placement and grouping characteristics of the original document collection. Because they are placeholders, they should not receive a unique document identification number, but may contain the identification of the document whose place they are substituted for. Examples of Production Document forms commonly used are as follows:

"Begin Bound Document." This is a sheet placed ahead of photocopies made of a bound document, such as a hardbound book, a government pamphlet, or any other document that normally is an assembly of permanently bound pages. This sheet is followed by a sheet "End of Bound Document." (*See* Exhibit 9-6, page 294.)

"Begin Stapled Document." This is placed ahead of a series of pages stapled together before the copying process. As the staple is pulled, the integrity of the stapled document might be lost without this particular sheet. The one that follows the last page of this document would be the "End Stapled Document." These documents look essentially the same as those depicted in Exhibit 9-6.

EXHIBIT 9-6 "Production Document" for Bound Documents

Case _____	Case _____
Document ID No.: _____	Document ID No.: _____
BEGIN BOUND DOCUMENT	**END BOUND DOCUMENT**

These sheets should be on standard letter-size paper, and may be color-coded.

"Begin Loose-leaf Notebook." This is placed ahead of a document found contained in a three-ring binder or other loose-leaf notebook and may be supplemented, if there are divider tabs within the binder, by production sheets saying "Divider Tab" and carrying the title of the divider tab. The whole assembly at the end of the binder would be followed by "End Loose-leaf Notebook." These documents look essentially the same as those depicted in Exhibit 9-6.

"Reduced-Scale Document." This sheet would be inserted just ahead of a large document that has been photocopied in reduced size and scale to a more manageable document. It is only used where the document can be reduced to one page (either legal or book size). This will alert everyone that a document in the original file is larger than the copy produced. For handling large computer printouts, economic tabulation sheets, engineering drawings, and so on, this type of sheet is convenient and important. (*See* Exhibit 9-7.)

"Document Too Large to Copy." In some cases, a drawing or other document is too large to be copied, even with reduction, on a single sheet of paper. When this happens, the legal assistant must paste several copies of portions of the document together to achieve one larger one. It is important for persons using the file to know that what they are seeing is not an accurate representation of the original document. (*See* Exhibit 9-7.)

"Begin Stapled Series of Stapled Documents." Many times, stapled documents are assembled by purpose or by chance either in central files or in personal information files of individuals

EXHIBIT 9-7   "Production Document" for Reduced-Scale and "Too Large to Copy" Documents

Case: _____
Document ID No.: _____

**REDUCED-SCALE
DOCUMENT**

Original size: _____
Brief Description: _____
_____
_____

Case: _____
Document ID No.: _____

**DOCUMENT
TOO LARGE TO COPY**

Original size: _____
Description: _____
_____
_____

Where located: _____

These sheets should be on standard letter-size paper, and may be color-coded.

under circumstances incomprehensible to the legal assistant reviewing the document. It is inappropriate for the legal assistant to disassemble these documents. Thus, the condition of this assembly of documents is shown by the introduction of this sheet. It would immediately be followed by "Begin Stapled Document" and then "End Stapled Document," "Begin Stapled Document," and so on, through the total assembly of the stapled series. The last production document would be "End Stapled Series of Stapled Documents." These documents look essentially the same as those depicted previously in Exhibit 9-6.

Archiving. In large document cases, and increasingly in smaller ones, the document collection may be archived for ease of use and reference. In this instance, there may be a need for a production document entitled "Document not Processed." This would be used for bound documents, documents too large to be copied, roll charts, or other materials which may be unable to be processed. These documents look essentially the same as those depicted previously for "Document Too Large to Copy" in Exhibit 9-7. In the past, large volume files were microfilmed to create an archive. There is still a need for archiving in large document cases although microfilming is no longer being used. Instead, archives are now being created in CD-ROM format, and are processed by scanning equipment or digital photography.

Privilege. Privileged documents have been discussed in Section 9.0133. This production document is inserted in place of the "privileged" document it represents in the original file and in any file copies subsequently produced. (*See* Exhibit 9-8.) The information contained on this sheet is identical to that listed on the "privilege log" that is produced to any adversary party.

Other. Other production document forms may be generated as needed.

EXHIBIT 9-8   Privileged Document "Production Document"

Case: _____

PRIVILEGE DOCUMENT

Doc. ID No.:	No. Pages:	Date:
Author:		
Addressess:		
Other Recipients:		
Privilege Asserted:		
Description:		
Attachments (ID No.):		

This sheet may be color-coded.

9.015 Return and Destroy

When a lawsuit is ended or settled, original documents considered unnecessary for retention in the firm's permanent litigation file are returned to the client or source custodians from whom they were taken. Since lawsuits require extended periods of time and, in the course of such lawsuits, any given document may become the "best evidence," it is prudent to retain custody of the original documents until the last moment of the case.

9.0151 Use of the Screening Log. If the inventory and master index were used at the beginning of the case, returning each document and file to the original source will be much simpler. Documents should be returned in the same fashion (stapled, bound, in binders, and so on) as they were surrendered. At the time of return, any original documents which have been entered as evidence in the court file can be so noted on a copy of the document substituted in the client's or custodian's file. Each return should be logged and receipted.

9.0152 Retention of Indexes. Every document index and receipt created in the case should be preserved and stored in the case file to serve as a guide for future cases, or to answer questions regarding documents the client might have at a later time.

9.0153 Destruction of Photocopies. Once the case is concluded and all originals have been returned to the custodians, the photocopied document files should be destroyed. Destruction is exactly that: torn up, shredded, or burned, not simply placed in the trash for casual disposal. Any documents or their copies covered by protective orders should be obtained from the adversary and from the court file, the originals returned to the client or custodian, and the photocopies destroyed.

9.02 Adversary and Other Documents

Adversary documents and documents from other parties are received as a result of discovery requests or subpoenas. They are handled in much the same manner as client documents: the legal assistant must develop a plan to control and organize the documents as they are received; the documents must be reviewed and analyzed; a system must be established to work with the documents; and a plan developed to return or destroy the documents at the end of the case. Many of the same general principals discussed in handling client documents apply and will not be repeated.

9.021 Control and Organization

When discovery documents are received, the legal assistants task is easier when the adversary party has already numbered the documents. When the documents have not been numbered, decisions must be made on whether to do so, or whether to implement some other control method. It is always prudent to maintain a copy of the documents exactly as they were produced. Additionally, it is important to immediately prepare an index of the documents received, using a form similar to the one used to index client documents. This makes the later tasks of analyzing the produced documents in terms of responsiveness to the production request or subpoena and creating various working files and indexes much easier to accomplish.

9.022 Review and Analyzing

In general, the legal assistant and the lawyer should meet and review the purpose of the discovery request or subpoena to identify the items and issues which are considered important to the case. In many cases, these will be the same topics previously identified in preparation for screening the client's documents. With discovery documents there are two variables: (1) whether the documents to be reviewed are attached to the discovery request or subpoena response; and (2) whether the documents and items will be inspected in another location with the legal assistant or discovery team making decisions on what items should be copied, and whether the items produced for inspection were responsive to the discovery request.

9.0221 *Documents Received with Discovery Responses.* The documents should first be indexed and then reviewed to determine if they are responsive to the discovery requests. If the discovery response to which the documents are attached indicates that documents are being withheld because of a privilege, it should be noted whether or not a privilege log has been produced as well. The Federal Rules for Civil Procedure and many state rules have a time limitation during which the requesting party must move to compel further production from the responding party. If the appropriate motion is not filed within that time frame, the ability to require the other side to comply with the original request may be lost.

9.0222 *Documents Produced for Inspection and Copying.* Preparation for the actual document inspection should include becoming familiar with the request as well as the other party's written responses. As previously discussed, it is very important to know what to look for and understand the issues and theories which are being asserted on behalf of the client. It is helpful to prepare a summary of the material sought, noting the response.

The first step in the actual inspection should be to make a preliminary assessment of the material which is being produced for inspection. Compare the written responses with the categories or types of records produced. If any categories or types of promised documents appear to be missing, make inquiry as to their location or ask when they will be produced. Be sure to dictate or write a list of any material that is not produced. Also, ask if the records are being produced as they are kept in the normal course of business or whether they have been organized and labeled to correspond with the categories in your request.

Begin by taking an inventory of the files and records produced for your inspection. This may be done by using a Document Inventory Form similar to that used to inventory client documents, or it may be dictated. It is always good practice to either note on your inventory the files and/or documents designated for copying, or dictate such a list. Make sure to always ask whether any documents have been withheld on the basis of claimed privilege. If so, ask for the required list or ascertain when it will be given to you.

PRACTICE TIP

Certain basic supplies are recommended for performing an on-site document inspection, including gummed notepads (post-it notes), paper clips, legal pads, and inventory or screening forms. Portable dictating machines are also very useful. If the facts in your case include important dates and key players, lists of those things will prove helpful in locating key documents and records.

It is important to determine in advance what the page price will be for designated copies of records and/or photographs. Failure to do so can obligate the lawfirm and the client to pay exorbitant charges and/or incur additional attorneys fees and expenses to object to such charges. It is much easier to negotiate a fair price and/or explore alternative arrangements for having the material copied before the inspection begins than after the fact.

Take time to read or skim all material that is produced. This is important because another opportunity to inspect the requested records may not be offered. You owe it to your client to be thorough. When finished with the review, be sure that the method used to mark documents for copying is clear and that it can be understood by a copy clerk. Generally, a good method for designating such material is by tagging it with "post-it notes." Paper clips can be used to identify a group of documents so that time need not be wasted "tagging" every individual page. By the same token, if an entire folder contains documents to be copied, the folder may be tagged. Whatever method chosen, it should be uniform if more than one person is conducting the inspection for the client. It is also a good practice to leave a handwritten list of instructions for copying, particularly if you have any special requests (like "Copy file tabs," "Insert blank page between files," etc.). Leave a business card when the inspection is complete so the people responsible for making the copies can call if they have any questions.

When copies of the designated documents are received, the first task is to check the inventory made during the inspection against the records delivered. The next task is to determine what control method will be used. As previously mentioned, it is recommended that a master "original" set of all documents received be maintained from which copies can be made as necessary for attorney and other use.

9.0223 *Analyzing the Documents.* Once the documents have been indexed and reviewed for responsiveness to the discovery request, the next task is to analyze the documents in terms of their relationship to the legal issues in the case, how they fit in with chronologies and issue indexes developed from the client documents, whether new information is contained in any document, whether additional documents should be added to witness preparation files, whether documents which appear to be duplicates contain any additional notations or other writings, whether the documents contain any additional information on known individuals and entities, and whether the documents expose the identities of previously unknown individuals and entities. A Document Screening Form similar to the one used to screen client documents may be used to make the process more efficient. (*See* Exhibit 9-4.)

9.023 Working with the Documents

Just as with client documents, all the work of reviewing and analysis will be fruitless if the legal assistant is unable to develop a system for retrieving and working with the documents and the information they contain. Data from the discovery documents should be used to supplement the information gathered to create the Issues Files and Index, the Witness Documents Files and Index, the Chronologic Files and Index, and the Individual and Entity Files and Index. In addition, review of these discovery documents will provide information to create another useful file and index system to track additional potential discovery items that are mentioned in received documents, but whose existence has not otherwise been disclosed or produced by the adversary.

9.0231 *Documents Cited but Not Produced.* There will be cases where the adversary has produced documents that refer to other documents which were not produced, or show attachments which were not attached; a special indexing and file of these documents may be appropriate at some time, together with the cross-reference information needed to support a motion to compel or other motion to produce. In some cases, very significant documents within the files will refer to documents requested from the adversary which have not been provided. These should also be identified and included in that type of file and index. The indexes should be very specific as to the dates of the request, dates of the response, and the supporting but conflicting references. This may go so far as to use colored highlighting on the documents for quick and easy reference by the attorneys. During screening or review, this information may be noted on the Document Screening Form previously discussed, or on a special form "Production Discrepancy." (*See* Exhibit 9-9.)

EXHIBIT 9-9   Sample Production Discrepancy Form

Production Discrepancy List: XYZ Construction vs. Developments, Inc., et al

Document Mentioned	Source Document	Responsive to Discovery Request	Notes
Memo dated 7/15/95 from J. Astor	D1 200757 Letter to Alf Landon from Jay Lender	Pltf Set 1, RFP #7 dated 1/15/97	Source Document Produced 2/16/97; Cited Doc not listed on Privilege Log

9.024 Return and Destroy

When the litigation is concluded, whether through trial or settlement, the discovery documents received form other parties should be returned if they consist of originals or material which was provided subject to a protection or confidentiality order or agreement. Other discovery documents and copies may be destroyed in the same manner described in Section 9.0153.

9.03 Customizing Database Forms

A database is a collection of information arranged for retrieval, although usually discussed within the context of computerized information. However, legal assistants have been managing this task with and without computer aid for decades through the use of forms. The ready ease and availability of adapting these forms to computer systems in the law office has been a welcome tool to add to the arsenal of document control, sorting, indexing, and analysis.

9.031 Document Databases

Document Databases are forms which contain the information extracted from documents obtained during the course of a litigation. They serve as substitutes for the documents, and if done appropriately and correctly, much of the sorting and indexing can be accomplished by working with these "surrogate" documents rather than the original document collection. They may be prepared and "filled out" directly on a computer, or they may be sheets of paper or index cards which are filled out by hand and later entered into a computer. An example would be 5-by-8-inch card on which is recorded sufficient data to allow sorting of cards in chronological order, determining all documents authored by a given party, or identifying all of the letters that went from the client company to someone else on a particular topic. The same information contained on those cards can be sorted much faster, more efficiently, and in more ways when the information is digitized, either by keying it in or scanning it in to a computer. The Master

Index Form and the Document Screening Form are examples of database information which may be captured first on paper, and later input for sorting and indexing by a computer. (*See* Exhibit 9-4.) The most important element in creating or customizing a database is to think and plan in advance the kinds of information that are necessary to track, along with the kinds of sortings, indexes, and reports which may be needed. The organization of the record form should flow from the order of importance of the data and how the data is organized within the document. An example of a sample Document Database Form is shown in Exhibit 9-10. A listing of some

EXHIBIT 9-10   Sample Document Database Form

Document Database Form			
Case: _____ Coded by: _____ Date: _____			

Doc_ID Start:	Doc_ID End:	Date:	Source:

Type: ☐ Letter ☐ Memo ☐ Report ☐ Financial Notes ☐ Contract ☐ Invoice ☐ Medical ☐ Receipt ☐ Proposal ☐ Time Card ☐ Daily Job Report ☐ Meeting Minutes ☐ Graphic ☐ Photo ☐ Clipping ☐ Other _____

Author:	**Addressee:**	**"cc":**

☐ **Duplicate of Doc_ID:**	☐ **Attached to Doc_ID:**

Doc. Quality: ☐ Original ☐ Photocopy ☐ Carbon Copy ☐ Torn ☐ Thermal Fax ☐ Faded ☐ Illegible

☐ **Subj:** ☐ **Re:** ☐ **Title:**	☐ **Marginalia** ☐ **Other Markings**

Privilege: ☐ AC ☐ WP ☐ Other	**Protection:** ☐ Trade Secret ☐ Research ☐ Development ☐ Commercial

Sensitivity: ☐ Relevant ☐ Not Relevant ☐ Helpful ☐ Problem ☐ Damages ☐ Liability ☐ KEY

Issues: ☐ Fraud ☐ Negligence ☐ Breach of Contract ☐ Bad Faith ☐ Notice ☐ Intent ☐ Reliance

Key Words: ☐ Bituthene ☐ Change Order ☐ Delay ☐ Acceleration ☐ Weather ☐ Generator ☐ Piles

Individuals & Entities:

Doc. Mentioned (Not Attached):

Notes/Summary:

☐ **Deposition Exhibit**	Witness:	Ex. No.:	Date:
☐ **Pleading Exhibit** ☐ **Motion Exhibit**	Title:	Ex. No.:	Date:
☐ **Produced to Adverse**	Party:	Req. No.:	Date:
☐ **Trial Exhibit**	Witness:	Ex. No.:	Date:

common database fields or elements (in addition to those previously discussed) is shown in Exhibit 9-11.

Thought and consideration must be given as to which documents should be included in a database. Current case law trends view index listings and inventory listings which include every document in a collection, as items which may be discoverable by opposing counsel if they demonstrate to the court's satisfaction a substantial need along with inability to obtain the substantial equivalent without undue hardship by other means. Some courts have held that indexes and inventories which list only objective data, such as document number, date, author, addressee, and copy recipient cannot by their nature contain any mental impressions, conclusions, opinions, or legal theories of the party who created them, or in other words, protected

EXHIBIT 9-11   Some Common Elements to Include in a Document Database

• **The Date.** All documents must be identified by date. Where the date is shown on the document, an estimate may be used based on the document's location in the original file or other logical basis. When the date is estimated, a notation to that effect must be made. Dates should be written using six places in a year-month-day format for ease of sorting (i.e., 97-09-05).

• **Total Pages.** A space should be provided on the database form to show the total number of pages in the document.

• **Document Type.** It is very important that the legal assistant define the types of documents and provide a reference glossary for any individual who will be entering data in this field to ensure consistent information. This is done by analyzing the kinds of documents likely to be encountered and assigning certain arbitrary identification to them; for instance, correspondence between the client firm and outside parties might be called "letters," while all correspondence within the client firm or between employees are designated "memoranda." Among those to be considered are: letters, memoranda, studies, reports, contracts, graphics (such as drawings, sketches, plans, and surveys), clippings (newspapers and magazines), photos, minutes of meetings, and notes.

• **Document Quality.** This will assist in pointing out torn documents, partially illegible documents, or faded documents which are the best copy.

• **Document Sensitivity.** In some cases, content in document text or added notations are so significant in the context of the case that a document may be classified as harmful, "significant," and/or "privileged." These are simple gradations to make, and subtle shading should not be attempted in this area. Frequently, the legal assistants are limited to "privileged" entries under "document sensitivity."

• **Individuals and Entities.** This category is to include information concerning any person or entity mentioned within the document not included within the objective fields of author, addressee, or other recipient. Reference should include the context such as mentioned, attended, or conversation with. These references may be shown by a standardized abbreviation, such as: Mnt for mentioned; Attnd for attended, and phcon for phone conversation; or con for conversation. It is also very useful to develop a standardized method of abbreviating name references for companies and other entities, such as DOJ for Department of Justice; GM for General Motors; AMEX for American Express. These kinds of standardizations should be collected in a reference list to ensure accuracy and consistency—very important when the time comes to search for this information.

• **Related Documents.** It is important to note whether a document is attached to other documents or refers to other documents. This information may become important or relevant as the case develops, or it may point to additional documents to request. This is done by noting the Document ID number of an attached document (i.e., Doc# ABC–199999 attch), or the literal reference when a document is referred to but not attached (i.e., Ref: "Yesterday's Memo from Harry").

• **Issues.** If coding for issues or sorting the documents by issue, include a provision on the card to indicate issues by number or by topic. Similarly, if sorting the documents by document discovery order, a provision to indicate that appropriate paragraph on the surrogate document is very helpful.

• **Use of the Document.** An important function is to track the use of a document during the course of the case: whether it was produced to adversaries; whether it was copied by adversaries; whether it was used as an exhibit; whether it was produced to you or by you. All of these can, with proper planning, be reflected on the form.

Note: The above elements are in addition to those listed for the Document Screening Form. (*See* Exhibit 9-4.)

"work product." The analogy is that these indexes and inventories represent the same kinds of information which are discoverable in the initial disclosures required under Rule 26(a) of the Federal Rules of Civil Procedure or the similar "standard" interrogatories allowed by many state rules. A few courts have required the disclosure of more extensive "databases" which contain summary information on the content of the documents. One of the rationales for allowing these disclosures is that the party had included every document in the collection, making it indiscreet. On the other hand, counsel who have been able to argue that their databases or discrete indexes contained only selected documents, have been able to successfully demonstrate to the courts that revealing the identity of the documents selected would disclose to the opposing attorney their thought process, mental impressions, conclusions, and opinions, and have successfully prevented the disclosure of such databases. These kinds of discovery skirmishes usually take place in large document cases, but may occur in smaller cases as well. The net effect of these discovery battles has been recommendations that only selected "key" documents be input into substantive databases. To the extent that surrogate documents, such as the Document Screening Forms, contain mental impressions, opinions, and conclusions, (such as whether a document relates to a certain issue, whether it may be privileged, etc.) they will remain protected work product. To the extent that inventory lists or master indexes do not contain opinion information, they are open to discovery attacks.

9.032 Individual and Entity Database

Since documents are the products of people, the creation of data records for each of the names mentioned in the course of each case is essential. At the time the Document Screening Form or Document Database Form is being created, a form for every different name appearing on the document should also be created.

Provision on the form should include last name, first initial, first/middle name, and middle initial. All are included because a party may be referred to by initials on one document and by name on another, and it may take three or four documents before anyone is certain of the exact or preferred name of a given person. The business position of the individuals and their company affiliations, addresses, and phone numbers all should be accumulated as encountered and posted to show the month and year of the information. The form should also indicate each document where the name of the individual appears as author, addressee, copy recipient, or is mentioned. (*See* Exhibit 9-12, page 304.)

9.04 Advanced Document Management with Computers

The legal assistant's knowledge of the attorney's manner and style of conducting litigation, the information commonly needed during the course of a particular type of case, an understanding of database concepts, a familiarity with computers and various computer programs, combined with active participation in creating the design of the document database and establishing the necessary guidelines for managing the project, will make the legal assistant an even more valuable member of the litigation team.

9.041 Introduction

Large and very large document cases which involve thousands of documents and hundreds of thousands of pages are candidates for advanced document management with computers. This chapter takes a brief look at some of the considerations which must be addressed when the

EXHIBIT 9-12   Sample Individual and Entity Database Form

Case: _____ Date: _____ Updated: _____	

☐ Individual
☐ Entity   ☐ Last Name   ☐ Entity Name

First Name: | Middle Name:
Initials: | Alias:

Employment: | Title:

Bus. Street Address:	City:	State / Zip:
P.O. Address:	City:	State / Zip:
Phone 1:	Phone 2:	Phone 3:
Fax:	Mobil Phone:	Other:

Related Entities: ☐ Parent ☐ Subsidiary ☐ Affiliate

☐ Parent ☐ Subsidiary ☐ Affiliate

☐ Parent ☐ Subsidiary ☐ Affiliate

☐ Parent ☐ Subsidiary ☐ Affiliate

Related Individuals: | Relationship:

Notes/Comments:

Doc. No.	Context	Doc. No.	Context	Doc. No.	Context

decision is made to manage documents extensively using computer technology. Advances in technology have been tremendous in the last decade, and will continue to develop for the foreseeable future. New and innovative uses for existing technology are often taking place at the legal assistant's desk. Specialized service companies for projects such as document numbering, scanning, and indexing have become widely available and are often cost-effective alternatives to handling those tasks "in-house." However, the human factors involved in the process of converting the physical documents to useable electronic information are still considerations which must be fully understood.

  a. The initial work effort involved in numbering, screening, and analyzing the documents is unchanged.
  b. Added to the initial work effort is the task of entering the data into the computer at an early stage.
  c. The cost of file handling may increase during the initial work effort, but may decline during later stages of the case.
  d. Attorneys are forced to focus early on the scope and issues of the case, the nature of the discovery documents, and the standardized terms which will be utilized in designing a database system.
  e. Attorneys must devote time to understanding and approving the computer system and database design and implementation, unless it has been used in the past.
  f. Staff time must be devoted to training and operation of the chosen system, unless it has been used in the past.
  g. Staff time must be devoted on a continuing basis to quality control and review of information being entered into the computer system.
  h. Unless personnel resources are available "in-house," additional personnel must be hired and trained.
  i. The greatest benefits are the ability to retrieve data in various combinations nearly instantaneously, coupled with the ability to transport the data to remote locations for use in depositions, hearings, and trials.

9.042 Initial Work Effort Considerations

In a document production effort (as described earlier in this chapter), every document must be found, identified, controlled, evaluated, and preserved for retrieval. Computerization does not change that but adds other layers of special effort to it, which include the requirement for stringent quality control, early data entry, and additional planning considerations (such as creating a database design that is easy to understand for both the person(s) entering the information into the database and the person(s) retrieving the needed documents).

9.043 File Handling Costs

The initial increase which may occur in file handling costs are attributable to whether or not additional personnel must be hired to design, test, implement, and maintain a database program. This becomes largely irrelevant when the resources for these tasks already exist within a lawfirm or organization. Another area which might increase the initial file handling costs is whether a decision is made to scan the discovery documents into an electronic format. During the life of a case, this initial cost may actually result in overall savings, because it may decrease the need for a significant number of photocopies and the physical storage space required to maintain them. The ability to access the electronic documents on media such as computer diskettes, portable hard drives, and CD-ROM is a benefit that may far outweigh the initial costs incurred. Imagine the ease of producing the client's documents "as maintained in the ordinary course of business" on one CD-ROM—there could be no dispute as to exactly what was produced.

Most lawfirms and business entities have computers available, including networked systems which allow shared resources, and the ability for many people to work on one project simultaneously. Database programs, such as Paradox® and Access® are commonly included in the major "Office Suites" programs used widely in the legal field and the business world at large. However, lawfirms and businesses who do not have internal resources which include information technology personnel, scanners, CD-ROM recorders, current computer hardware and software, must consider additional costs which include: program design, program testing, creating loading forms, loading data, retrieval reports, the salaries of personnel to maintain the program and/or the computer system, the type of computer program, the type of computer equipment, and whether the project can be done in-house by the lawfirm or the client, or by out-sourcing with a vendor or consultant. Weighed against these costs must be the benefits which will be realized on future cases and improvements to the firms general computer operations.

9.044 Increased Attorney Involvement

Once the decision is made to use extensive computer support, the responsible attorney must be prepared to devote substantial concentrated time to flesh-out case issues, objectives, topics and discovery document types rather than having the luxury of spreading that effort over a longer period of time. Additionally, the attorneys involved must contribute to, evaluate, clarify, reject, and accept the proposals, conceptual approaches, and parameters of computer input and output designed by a computer professional and/or the legal assistants. It is important that the database be designed at the beginning of the case with enough flexibility to refine the form of the discovery file as the case develops. This design is dependant on the type of case that is being handled. A long-term benefit of a well designed database is that it can be used in the future for other similar cases, and to the extent that the law firm has experience in past cases, the human cost factor is reduced.

9.045 Additional Staff Time

A manual file index system can be established in broad topical outlines with additions and subdivisions added as the need appears. Nomenclature and filing terms are conventional and few, with little need for strict consistency in the method of recording the data. Usually, a mix of hand-printing, cursive writing, and printed material can be found in manual document discovery file index systems. That changes with computerization. Everyone involved must learn and adhere to standardized formats. Everyone must understand and use the same terms, abbreviations, words, and phrases consistently and in the same manner and context or the ability to provide accurate searches and reports from the program will be seriously compromised. In addition to finding, identifying, and coding the documents that are normal to any case, entering the data into the computer system must be done in a standard and systematic manner which is constantly reviewed to ensure that the correct information is in the computer database.

The extraordinary need for consistency among all persons involved in converting documents into electronic data creates a continuing need for training, and for quality control audits of the screening forms and the information entered from those forms.

9.046 Benefits

The benefits of computerization for complex litigation involving huge volumes of documents and multiple parties, issues, or witnesses are sometimes difficult to appreciate unless, and until, they have been experienced. Once a majority of the significant data has been entered into the computer and verified as accurately done, the flow of succinct collations, in loose sheet or bound form, is awe-inspiring. When a report of several pages, which may have taken days under a manual system, identifies a major adversary witness and all the documents that witness prepared, received, considered, testified about, identified as genuine, acknowledged as relevant, argued about, or took issue with, in a matter of minutes, the benefits become obvious. When a phone call from an attorney at a deposition is received asking for a report detailing each time a particular document has been produced, used as an exhibit, or referred to in other documents, and the legal assistant is able to fax the results within minutes, a true appreciation begins to form. When the attorney has a copy of the database and the documents with him at the deposition and is able to search and retrieve information and documents instantly as the need arises, the advantages are apparent. When another level of sophistication allows posting a summary of deposition, cross-referencing conflicts between testimony and documents or conflicts between the testimony of two witnesses, another benefit is obtained. When a report shows all the answers received from various parties to each individual interrogatory or production request, or collates all the interrogatories and production requests received from multiple parties, along with the client's answers, another advantage is realized.

Once a well-designed and accurate database is established, the benefits are limited only by the ability of the legal assistant and attorney to think of new applications of the information.

9.047 Evaluation Factors in Implementing Advanced Document Management

There are six main factors which should be considered prior to implementing an advanced document management system as illustrated by Exhibit 9-13.

EXHIBIT 9-13   Factors to Consider in Implementing Advanced Document Management Systems

1. Data Input Methods
   a. Full Text
   b. Coded Entry System
   c. Document Imaging
2. Hardware and Software
   a. In-house Resources
   b. Client Resources
   c. Third Party Resources
3. Database Design Considerations
4. Evaluating Time and Cost Estimates
5. Personnel Considerations
6. Security

9.0471 Data Input Methods.   The selection of the database program involves basically a choice of two information retrieval methods, full text search or keyword search, which use one or more of the three data input methods discussed below.

a. Full Text.   The first is a method in which the full text of each document is entered into the computer. Information is retrieved by searching the database much in the same manner as when searching WESTLAW, LEXIS, or the Internet.

The benefit of this system is the relative ease of loading the data, since the need for personnel training is limited to the selection of responsive or significant documents. In its simplest form, very little coding is required other than fields for the document number and the date. No subjective coding, evaluations, or colorations are required.

The problems of relying on this system alone are numerous, but the most important are:

1. Original documents must printed or typed material to be processed into text, or already be in electronic format (such as data stored on magnetic tapes, discs, or other storage medium). An original document that is handwritten, or contains handwritten notes, must be typed before it can be entered into the system.

2. Photographs, charts, forms, graphs, and drawings must be entered by using a summary description in their place.

3. Other information not available using this system with no coding is the inability of scanning recognition software to "recognize" document characteristics, such as marginal annotations, distribution block characterization or routings, doodles and underlining, interlineation of corrections or suggested phrasings on drafts, all of which may, in some instances, be highly significant to the interpretation of the meaning of the document or a response to a document.

4. The most dangerous weakness of the full text system is the perception that search results will be accurate, reliable, and comprehensive. For instance, consider a product liability case of an allegedly dangerous toy. The toy was originally titled "Project 1780-64" during development and placed in production under "Charge No. NY 10-472." Its name was originally the "Wonderful Widget" but was changed after the first year to the "Wacky Widget." Ordering from retailers was by "Item 6320, Wacky Widget, Model 2." Internally, the "Widget" was fondly referred to as "WW", "WW2," and 'The Wack." This results in at least nine methods of referring to the principal object in the litigation; a search request would not develop any document that referred to the product as "that thing," "John's brainstorm," or "blasted catastrophe" unless one or more of the specified nine equivalents occurred within the same document.

b. Coded Entry System. The coded entry method substitutes a surrogate document for the original and is dependant on usage of standardized references to characteristics, terms, words and phrases, names, and issues identification to be effective. The information is collected on forms to assemble data in an organized format for entry into the computer. These often are called "coding forms," and in reality are the same as the Document Screening Forms and other forms discussed earlier in this chapter. A lawyer, legal assistant, or other person reviews the document and fills out the form with information which will usually be entered by someone else directly into the database program on the computer. The "on-screen" form usually closely resembles the paper form.

The benefits of this system include the ability to control the search parameters closely and to code a synthesis of the significant documents according to their substantive content, regardless of their form, whether letters, memos, photos, studies, sketches, or preprinted forms. Further, it is simple to enter additional sorting data as the need arises, such as their use as exhibits in depositions, to the complaint, to the answer, to interrogatories, or the introduction of a new case issue or topic. It allows combining all documents into one database for subsequent sortings and printouts and precludes anyone (lawyer or legal assistant) from relying solely on computer information rather than the evidentiary documents.

The drawbacks to this system, when used alone, may include:

1. The attorney may have trouble accepting the need to give early planning and analysis of the case to set the coding and search parameters a higher priority over a workload of more mature cases. It is understandably difficult for an attorney to devote concentrated time at such an early point in a case, given the uncertainties of issues, facts, and legal theories characteristic of suits with relatively vague and inconclusive pleadings.

2. The long lead time between the decision to begin the project and the entry of sufficient data before useful output is obtained can be frustrating.

3. The demands imposed in selection and training of any additional personnel required to code the data and/or enter the data into the program, along with the stringent quality control, consistency audits, error correction, and program modifications such systems may require, are time-consuming and may be costly.

4. The dedication of time, thought, imagination, and practicality essential to database design and the "coding form" design is hard to anticipate. Usually, the fewest possible elements produce the maximum effectiveness in speed and accuracy of entry.

c. Document Imaging. The ability to scan the image of a document into the computer for viewing "on-line" has added an important tool to the electronic arsenal. The combination of document images with coding creates a system far superior to either full text or coding alone. When a search is done "on-line," each responsive record, or "hit," is linked to a picture of the original document or object, which makes it possible to determine whether a particular document or object is relevant or useful without the need to obtain a separate paper copy of the document. The potential savings in time are tremendous, as are the increases in accurate, reliable search results.

9.0472 Hardware and Software

a. In-house Resources. Nearly all lawfirms have an in-house computer system. This probably is ideal if the equipment capacity and availability match the needs of the case. In addition to a computer system, consideration should be given to the availability of scanning equipment and software as well as recordable CD-ROM hardware and CD-ROM players. These hardware items have become very affordable in the last several years, often costing less than good quality laser printers. In-house capacity must also include an understanding of systems analysis, some programming skills, report creation capability, and the employment of computer-knowledgeable litigation support personnel, whether legal assistants, programmers and consultants, or data entry personnel.

Software selection will depend on the available in-house talent, programs already available, and information from any outside consultants which may be retained. As previously discussed, many excellent database programs are already widely available as components of popular office suites, such as MS Office® (which includes Access) and Corel WordPerfect® (which includes Paradox). These programs have many built-in capabilities, which include the ability to link images to databases, generate reports, search and sort.

b. Client Resources. Many clients have available computer systems of varying complexity and sophistication. Some systems may be purchased or leased and located on the client's premises. In other cases, the client will have contracted services through a vendor who provides time-sharing on a remotely located computer. The client may have the staff to operate the system or may add temporary employees to do the work. Such a system has obvious problems of priority of work effort, training, and control of the people operating the system but may be more economical for the client. Unless control, management, software selection and design, and security of the program is vested in the lawyer and the legal assistant in charge, the loss of intensity can affect both the dollar cost and the ultimate success of the computerization effort, as well as the cost of litigation.

c. Third Party Resources.   A third resource available is that of vendors, contractors, and consulting firms. A number of independent firms supply litigation support programs, from document discovery plans through hardware, software, personnel selection and training, and the supervision of the entire coding and data entry process. Many firms specialize in numbering the documents and scanning them into electronic format, as well as providing text recognition capabilities for full text searching. Generally, these businesses will provide all, or any portion of, the services desired. As with any contract for services, the scope of the services to be provided need to be clearly defined, along with representations as to quality, accuracy, and reliability.

Every price, every time standard, and every volume standard considered by a vendor in submitting a proposal is a qualified estimate which is usually based on a brief study of the proposed project. The client, the lawyer, and the contractor are all making estimates at the beginning of a case, and it should be remembered that the estimates of dollars, time, and volumes may not reflect the ultimate cost and the ability of the vendor to deliver the contracted service on schedule.

It is essential to meet the contractor's employees who will be performing the work, whether it be analysis, system design, personnel training, document imaging, text recognition, data entry, document coding, or any other task. It is very important that the contractor's personnel who will be working on the project exhibit characteristics of perception, attitude, interest, and flexibility. Ask for references from other lawfirms and litigators who have used their services. The difference between performing a job for a general business or industry and a lawfirm can often be summed up in the phrase "Can you say 'Court Order'?"

9.0473 Database Design Considerations.   Not all cases consist either of document types or volumes suitable for inclusion in a sophisticated database. For instance, in a price-fixing case where there are hundreds of thousands of numbered invoices, bills of lading, receipts, purchase orders, and other similar material, but which contains only a limited number of material requiring "subjective" analysis, it might be better to set up the major volumes of different document types in numeric or chronologic order and image scan the material to create an archive and working file with the originals stored as evidence. A separate system for the subjective documents in a simple database may be perfectly adequate for the attorney's needs. This kind of analysis and decision making must occur when the location and gathering of the client files (discussed earlier) is being conducted.

Another consideration is the types of information upon which sorting capabilities will depend. If the attorneys wish to attempt sorting by complex legal theories, they must be capable of providing simple, discreet guidelines for objective determination as to which documents will fit the mold. Complex theories such as "horizontal integration," "denial of market access," or "ultrahazardous endeavor" are nearly impossible standards with which to categorize documents during the initial design of the database and coding of the documents. Attorneys must be reminded that such characterizations will need to be added at a later date as the development of those theories ripen.

A good objective coding system will allow orderly production of documents with provision for entering additional characterizations as the case progresses and the documents begin to acquire characterizations such as significant, insignificant, damaging, or innocuous.

9.0474 Evaluating Time and Costs Estimates. The project proposal, whether an offer or formal proposal, by a vendor or an estimate by the client's or lawyer's in-house personnel, must be analyzed for the dollar and time bases giving rise to the ultimate commitment. Basic to every proposal are the salaries paid the personnel who will be coding the documents and entering the data into the system along with the estimate of the "minutes per page" necessary to process the documents, create the computer coding form, and enter the data into the system. The salary structure must be examined to ensure it is competitive for the area and adequate to attract quality people.

The industry standard for the ratio of pages per document is an average of three pages. It is further estimated that a legal assistant can perform "full" coding at a rate of ten documents per hour. This quantity would increase for "objective only" coding, and decrease when the documents involved are complex or highly technical. Using these estimates, a collection of 120,000 documents (360,000 pages) would take one legal assistant 12,000 hours to process. This is the equivalent of 1,500 "eight-hour" days, 300 "forty-hour" weeks. If ten legal assistants are used, the processing time is shortened to thirty weeks. Each document collection is different. To obtain a more accurate estimate, the legal assistant and the attorney responsible for making the system work should take a sample of at least one hundred documents and actually process them according to the intended program. If the material results in a figure of five pages per document and an "objective element only" coding rate of twelve documents per hour, then a collection of 120,000 documents will require 10,000 hours. Using this information, the same hypothetical team of ten legal assistants would require twenty-five weeks to accomplish the task. Realistic adjustments must be planned for personnel attrition, illnesses, errors, and error corrections. Provision must be made for production quality control, quality consistency audits, and program adjustments and changes. Interference with document processing by the ongoing discovery operations of the case should also be taken into consideration.

No estimate or proposal is capable of considering all the potential unknowns in a case. For instance, what happens to a half-processed file if the plaintiffs seek and obtain permission to amend the complaint by adding two more causes of action based on revelations during discovery? The processed documents may have to be reevaluated if subjective coding by issues was part of the coding plan. Such unforeseen developments may result in unanticipated costs, which emphasizes the necessity for a realistic, skeptical examination and testing of each estimate and/or proposal at the beginning of a project.

9.0475 Personnel Considerations. Recruitment can be handled in-house or through temporary help agencies. In either event, a "work sample" test is helpful in selecting people. The work sample may be a selected group of twenty to one hundred documents of varying types bundled into a file either bound or in an envelope. Copies of the same documents should be used for each applicant. A set of instructions should be provided that might, for example, direct that:

a. All names be circled.
b. All dates be underlined.
c. All references to money, dollar costs, expenditures, budgets, and so on be indicated on the left margin with an asterisk.
d. That the number of different names shown in the document be written in the top right corner of the top page of the document.
e. Other elements be identified as desired.

The work sample must be carefully checked before being presented to the applicant and a master file carrying all the correct entries for each page created. This is compared against the applicant's test file to measure error rates and the time used by the applicant. The test will weed out inaccurate or inordinately slow applicants. Standards must be high and must be maintained. It is better at the outset to quickly identify those who can follow instructions, whether fully understood or not, reliably and productively, from those who cannot. Inconsistency, error, and exceeding slowness are deadly to the document discovery effort. A separate test for reading comprehension, vocabulary, handwriting, and printing is desirable.

Training of selected applicants must involve more than "do this and then do that." The team members must feel like a team. An orientation on the factual history of the case, the legal issues, and the anticipated defenses, as well as an opportunity to meet each of the attorneys, is indispensable to the project. Training usually is staged by succeeding degree of complexity. It includes training on all the machinery to be used, such as computers, photocopiers, numbering methods, scanning equipment, the filing systems to be screened, company organization, and the team's filing and handling systems, as well as basic instructions of how to select, code, and process the various documents.

Refresher sessions will be needed to update procedures, correct detected errors, and give the attorneys a chance to talk directly to the discovery team and ensure they are in it together.

Every team must have a quality control auditor assigned to monitor, spot-check and even "work behind" each team member to ensure consistency in use of the selected coding parameters and other procedures. The audit is a check to assist each team member, not simply to criticize. It helps detect weaknesses in the training presentation and in the coding manual supplied each team member. It identifies ambiguities that creep into the program through documents that may fit more than one category. The audit will reveal the quality of each person and can serve as a foundation for dismissal of the lazy or careless worker, an unpleasant but essential task.

9.0476 Security. The use of computers for maintenance and storage of documents and information adds to the control problems of a document discovery effort and increases the need for security against natural disaster, negligent damage, and negligent compromise of the computer file. It represents a substantial dollar investment in time, labor, and other costs.

Natural disasters include fire, flood, and power supply aberrations that can damage or destroy the computer and essential hardware and software components. Computer data may be archived or "backed up" on tapes or other storage media, such as optical disks and CD-ROM, at little cost and stored in a separate location as a security archive against accidental disasters. Similarly, other archive copies of the database and the document image files can be separately maintained.

Negligent compromise of a computerized system can be minimized by controlling the numbers of coding manuals created and distributed and by limiting the report generation responsibility to certain members of the team. Every computer system can be programmed to grant access only through the use of passwords, special access codes, and "log in" identities. The production of reports must also be closely monitored to create as few as possible and to ensure that each report generated is shredded when superseded by another—not thrown away, but physically destroyed.

Little can be done to prevent intentional theft, espionage, or sabotage of the computerized file outside of the normal security steps. A determined crook can and will penetrate the usual business office protections of a client's business, vendors' facilities, or lawfirm's offices. The only extra security step possible is to detect that such an entry has occurred. Lock all the doors, filing cabinets, vaults, and desks that contain essential data and/or evidentiary documents. Being burglarized is bad, but being burglarized unknowingly can be fatal to the case.

9.05   Technology for Document Storage and Transportability

Document discovery often involves mountains of documents that may be necessary in a case being tried miles or thousands of miles from the file repository. Having documents image-scanned and placed on portable electronic media, such as CD-ROM, portable hard drives, or other computer media, solves a multitude of problems by reducing document volume from several boxes to one or two easy to carry disks. Be sure to mark each disk with "targets" that will identify the contents of the disc and will protect any privilege or confidentiality agreement. Producing copies from documents in electronic format is much less time consuming than the old method of microfilming and also has another advantage in that the copies generated from computer disks are much cleaner and legible, in addition to having your documents much more easily accessible.

Bibliography

Black's Law Dictionary. 6th ed. West Publishing Company, 1990.

Federal Rules of Evidence for U.S. District Courts and Magistrates with Amendments Effective Dec. 1, 1996. West Publishing Company, 1997.

Manual for Complex Litigation, 3rd ed. Federal Judicial Center Staff, 1995.

Federal Civil Judicial Procedure and Rules, as amended to January 6, 1997. St. Paul: West Group, 1997.

Federal Practice and Procedure, as amended through December 1, 1996. St. Paul: West Publishing Company, 1997.

Federal Rules of Civil Procedure. West Publishing Company (as amended through December 1, 1996).

Hutson, Beverly K., *Paralegal Trial Handbook.* 2nd ed. John Wiley & Sons, Inc., 1995.

Towne, V. Sheri, *"Organizing Your Client's Documents,"* Institute for Paralegal Education, May 1996 Seminar, Charleston, SC, *"Document Production and Organization in South Carolina: Management Strategies for the Litigation Paralegal."*

10 Assisting at Trial

10.00 Introduction

Trials are as varied as people and have just as diverse a selection of personalities. One trial may simply contest the damages involved with the liability issue already admitted. Other cases may be solely a trial of the legal issues or only of the factual issues, the damages or remedy having been established beyond dispute or by stipulation. Criminal trials may involve only one defendant and one violation of code or statute or may be complicated by multiple issues and defendants. Business litigation, product liability, and antitrust cases may involve complex and interdependent issues of law and fact, extensive discovery that generates hundreds or thousands of pages of potential exhibits, scores of witnesses, multiple defendants and, perhaps, hundreds of plaintiffs, cross-defendants, and cross-plaintiffs. There may even be interested parties who seek standing as a friend of the court *(amicus curiae)* and file legal briefs for the court's consideration. (*See* e.g. Appendix, Appellate Brief of the National Association of Legal Assistants.)

The duties delegated to a legal assistant in preparing a case for trial depend first and foremost on the unique nature of the individual case. Two additional determining factors are always: (1) how much help the lawyer feels is necessary, and (2) whether the legal assistant is the proper person to supply the needed assistance.

10.01   Trial Preparation

Knowing who is on the prospective juror list, having the trial materials ready, getting all the witnesses lined up and set to go, organizing all the exhibits: these are the elements that must be combined at the right time, in the correct order, and in the courtroom, for trial preparation to have been judged successful.

10.011   Investigation of the Jury Panel

A listing of every jury panel is available from the jury commissioner or clerk of court prior to the scheduling of a trial date for any particular case. Many firms now obtain these jury lists and supplement them by adding limited background information on each prospective juror. More detailed juror reports can often be purchased from firms who specialize in this service. If a firm handles a high volume of trials in one city, the use of such services can be a wise investment. In any event, obtaining jury listings and background information is often a task that is delegated to the legal assistant. Investigating jury lists is not particularly difficult, but it can be expensive and time-consuming.

Obvious sources are voter registration records, tax records, credit bureaus, and, depending on access, credit records maintained by the client. Be sure to check whether any person listed as a potential juror is known by the client (and in the case of a corporation, the client's employees), and if so, whether that information is negative or adverse. Another area of investigation is whether the prospective juror has been a plaintiff or defendant in any civil or criminal matter within the past several years. This can be checked by reviewing the records of the state trial courts, both civil and criminal. City directories give names and occupations for other household members which can also be important in the areas of prejudice or bias. Voter registration records generally provide information on age, residence, occupation, and political affiliation. Tax records provide information on ownership of real and personal property, such as homes, cars, and boats. Depending on the case, any or all of these facts could be important. Knowing that a particular juror is or is not a homeowner, is or is not a good paying customer, has initiated litigation, or has been a defendant in a criminal matter, aids the attorney during *voir dire* in the process of determining whether a juror is being truthful as well as whether the juror has any prejudices. Juror notebooks can be set up with an individual page for each potential juror. The attorney will find it works very systematically flipping pages from one juror to the next in voir dire.

10.02   Trial Notebooks

Trial notebooks are a particularly personal and individual creation of each attorney and legal assistant. Some use three-ring loose-leaf notebooks with dividers, others use multi-part file folders, and still others use special ledger-type hardboard covers within which legal- or accounting-size sheets can be added. Whatever the form, the trial notebook contains the attorney's trial plan and functions as a reference manual for all matters of law and fact related to the trial. Depending on the size and complexity of the case, a trial notebook may involve one or more volumes. Many law firms also utilize electronic versions which are contained on laptop computers brought into the courtroom. Regardless of the physical form, a trial lawyers' notebook will usually include the following sections: (1) Planning/"To Do" List; (2) Trial Notes;

(3) Key Pleadings; (4) Pretrial Motions; (5) *Voir Dire*; (6) Opening Statement; (7) Witnesses; (8) Exhibits; (9) Closing Argument; and (10) Jury Instructions. Preprinted index divider tabs can be purchased from several legal publishing companies covering almost every imaginable notebook section. Exhibit 10-1 is an example of a detailed trial notebook index which might be found in a complex case. A more detailed explanation of certain notebook sections is provided in the following sections.

EXHIBIT 10-1   Possible Trial Notebook Sections

1. Trial Notes	12. Witness Index
2. Things to Do	13. Direct Examination
3. Trial Preparation Agenda	14. Cross Examination
4. Trial Briefs	15. Expert Witnesses
5. Pretrial Motions	16. Exhibit Index
6. *Voir Dire*	17. Closing Arguments
7. Opening Statement	18. Jury Instructions
8. Outlines of Proof	19. Pleadings
9. Outlines of Damages	20. Discovery Index
10. Law and Evidence Briefs	21. Deposition Index and Summaries
11. Case Law and Summaries	

10.021   Trial Plan/"To Do" List

Each attorney expects to prove certain facts or introduce certain evidence at specific times or through specific witnesses. To do this, a trial plan must be devised to organize the questioning of each witness and the introduction of evidence in a coherent, persuasive manner, easy for the judge or jury to both understand and relate to the case issues.

Many attorneys begin the trial plan process by first preparing a brief of the case by cause of action to identify the essential elements of alleged conduct and the legal foundation for each cause of action. Then the answers and affirmative defenses are briefed; the admissions on both sides are posted (obtained from the answer to the complaint and from any responses to requests for admission or answers to interrogatories from the parties), and the remaining disputed elements isolated.

A trial plan is then created which incorporates the information from the trial brief and, in addition, outlines not only the attorney's own perception of the posture of the case but countermeasures for the discerned positions of the adversary. Once established, the trial plan falls easily into order by collating the available sources of testimony against the factual and legal demands of the trial brief. The plan then reflects the order of presentation along with the points to be covered, which are in turn cross-indexed to witnesses, exhibits, or other sources of information.

10.022   Key Pleadings

This generally contains an index with appropriate tabbed dividers for such legal documents as trial briefs, memoranda of points and authorities, case law, citations, and authorities on anticipated points of dispute, the most recent complaint and responsive pleadings, and key pretrial orders. These represent the pleadings and documents the attorney will need to refer to most often during the course of the trial.

10.023 Witness Section

This section should be indexed and tabbed with a separate section for each witness, including experts, listed by the parties to be called at trial. The first sheet in each section will usually be the attorney's outline of direct or cross-examination for that witness, followed by a fact sheet which lists the identifying personal data for the witness, the dates of each statement and/or deposition, answers to interrogatories attributed to the witness, a "conflicts" index if any conflicting points or story have been detected, and identification of each exhibit that the witness may be used to introduce. A summary of each statement and/or deposition is also included in chronologic order, perhaps highlighted with tabs or color markings of significant passages and cross-indexed to the separate file of statement and deposition transcripts.

10.024 Exhibit Section

This contains a listing of every exhibit, for both sides. All federal courts, and state courts whose rules follow the form of the Federal Rules of Civil Procedure, require each side to disclose and identify the documents or other exhibits it intends to use at trial prior to the trial. A copy of each party's exhibit disclosure pleading should always be maintained in this section, in addition to any other listing formats which may be used. (*See* Exhibit 10-2.) Many jurisdictions also require that each side mark intended exhibits with identification numbers prior to trial. Even if not required, this is a good organizational practice, which will make the presentation of the case go much smoother.

EXHIBIT 10-2   Sample Exhibit Disclosure Pleading

In the United States District Court
District of _____
Civil Action No.: _____

Plaintiff   )
)
   vs.   )   **PLAINTIFF'S TRIAL**
)   **EXHIBIT LIST**
Defendant   )
_____)

Plaintiff, by and through its attorneys, hereby submits its listing of exhibits to be offered at trial in accord with Local Rule 83.V.2 DSC as follows:

1. May 7, 1996 letter from John Doe to Jane Roe (Exhibit 1 to Deposition of Roe).
2. May 25, 1996 Contract of Sale for residence at 999 Governor's Road (Exhibit 5 to Deposition of Doe).
3. June 25, 1996 HUD Settlement Statement for sale of residence at 999 Governor's Road (Exhibit 7 to Deposition of Doe).

Respectfully submitted,

Because proposed exhibits may or may not actually be utilized, a common practice is to maintain an exhibit listing in the form of a log or chart. Exhibit 10-3, page 318, is an example of an Exhibit Log for use at trial. At a minimum, the log contains the identification for each exhibit (sequentially in order of introduction as well as the adverse party's assigned number for the exhibit if it appears on their exhibits list and preassigned numbers have not been given prior to trial); a description of the exhibit; the expected introduction witness; and columns to

EXHIBIT 10-3 Sample Trial Exhibit Log

Pltf Ex. No.	Deft Ex. No.	Obj.	Grounds	Witness	Description	Identified	Marked	Offered	Entered

record the exhibit's offer, its acceptance, or its rejection by the court as evidence. Some attorneys also like the log to include the needed foundation for admissibility as evidence (possibly the evidence citation); whether the attorney intends to object to an adversary's exhibit (cross-indexed to the foundation for objection, the evidence rule, and so on); or whether the attorney expects an objection from an adversary (cross-indexed to the foundation, case law, or evidence rule which supports admission).

10.025 Jury Panel

The jury commissioner or clerk of court usually publishes a roster of potential jury members with sufficient identification to allow some background inquiry as described earlier in Section 10.011. The legal assistant takes the information obtained on each juror and combines that data with information obtained during *voir dire* to prepare a twelve-block chart which correctly identifies each empaneled juror.

The twelve-block chart is organized just as the chairs in the jury box and, upon completion of the jury selection process, contains the name, age, address, occupation of each juror, and the attorney's notes regarding each. Alternate jurors, if used, are identified in separate blocks and annotated in the same fashion. (*See* Exhibit 10-4, Sample Jury Roster Form.) Some attorneys prefer to have a new roster prepared each day which also contains a description how the juror is dressed. In some jurisdictions, depending on how jury selection is accomplished, this form may also be used during the actual selection process to aid in determining which potential jurors are, or should be, stricken for cause.

EXHIBIT 10-4 Sample Jury Roster

Jury Panel — Case:				Date:		Alternates	
7	8	9	10	11	12	3	4
1	2	3	4	5	6	1	2

10.026 The Legal Assistant and the Trial Notebook

The trial notebook varies from lawyer to lawyer, partly as a function of the manner in which they learned their trial practice, and partly through their own ideas of emphasizing their trial effectiveness. The legal assistant's contribution to the trial notebook includes preparation of various indexes, entry and cross-referencing of factual material, and organization for instant retrieval back-up material for the various notebook sections, such as:

a. Testimony transcripts, tape recordings, signed statements, declarations, and affidavits listed in the Witness section.

b. The most recent amended complaint and answers, requests for admissions, interrogatories, production requests, pretrial motions and supporting briefs, pretrial orders for the Key Pleadings section.

c. The exhibits, organized, maintained, and easily available, including cross-references to summaries of depositions, requests for production, one-line summaries of interrogatories.

d. The case books, statutes, law review articles, the benchbook, regulations, or textbooks on which the attorney relies, available either as the entire volume or copied portions for the law section. Additionally, some matters in the law section may be delegated to the legal assistant for drafting, such as jury instructions—particularly in jurisdictions where a detailed book of approved jury instructions is available and citation of the exact language from approved instructions is persuasive. Similarly, the cross-citing of the attorney's anticipated authorities to the judge's preferred reference book may be drafted for the attorney's consideration.

Where such matters are delegated, they must be completed in timely fashion to allow time to review, edit, and verify those entries on which the case relies.

10.0261 Identities.   Another important contribution by the legal assistant is the compiling of a section which contains information on all individuals and entities associated with the case. This will be several sheets on which the name of every individual or entity in the case is recorded together with addresses, phone numbers, and the exact relationship to the case. Always included in detail are the names of the parties and their counsel, including investigators

TRIAL NOTEBOOK CHECKLIST

☐ Checked Pleadings for Amendments and Amended as Necessary	☐ Exhibits Exchanged
☐ Courtroom Evaluated for Special Needs	☐ Pretrial Report to Client Drafted and Sent
☐ Court's Special (Local) Rules Reviewed	☐ Motion in Limine Prepared
☐ Final Witness List Prepared	☐ Anticipated Legal Issues Identified and Researched
☐ Client Availability at Trial Confirmed	☐ Original Depositions Available
☐ Lay Witnesses Notified and Subpoenaed	☐ Depositions Digested
☐ Expert Witnesses Scheduled and Subpoenaed	☐ Offer of Settlement Filed
☐ Final Exhibit List Prepared	☐ Jury Pool Information Obtained and Reviewed by Client and Others
☐ Exhibits Numbered	☐ Jury Instructions Prepared

Source: *"It's Enough to Boggle Your Mind: the true meaning of trial preparation."* Jay J. Purcell, CLA, XXIII Facts & Findings 1 (May 1996).

and/or legal assistants if known, and every identified or probable witness, with an indication of the witness type, such as plaintiff, defendant, neutral, or expert witness. Include addresses and telephone numbers, business name and office personnel to contact in case additional information is needed from the expert's office, in addition to local addresses and phone numbers when witnesses are brought into town for the trial.

Also included in this section are references to persons, firms, or agencies that may be called upon to provide services to the trial team, such as a company for audio-video equipment, copy services, subpoena service, or convenient hotels where accommodation arrangements can be made for experts, witnesses, as well as the trial team and clients when the trial setting takes place out of town.

10.03 The Legal Assistant at the Trial

If the trial is expected to be of some duration, thought should be given to the economics of requesting daily transcripts. If this is done, and it usually is advisable and economical in multi-party cases, a legal assistant could see that an alphabetical index to witnesses is prepared on a daily basis. The index would include names of the witnesses, the date they appeared on the stand, names of interrogating attorneys, volume and page numbers of testimony of all witnesses, whether on direct examination and by whom, whether on redirect examination and by whom, and whether on cross or recross-examination and by whom. (*See* Exhibit 10-5.)

EXHIBIT 10-5 Sample Index of Trial Witnesses from a Daily Transcript

Witness	For	Date	Direct	Cross	Redirect	Recross
Doe, Jane L. (A), (1)	Defense	7/26	Vol. III., pp3102-3300; JONES			
		7/27	Vol. IV., pp3304-3400; JONES	Vol. IV., pp3401-3475; DOW	Vol. IV., pp3475-3500; JONES	NONE
Roe, John D.	Defense	7/27	Vol. IV., pp3502-3700; ABLE	Vol. IV., pp3701-3927; DOW	NONE	NONE
Buck, James X. (d) (I) (A)	Defense	7/28	Vol. V., pp4003-4150; DOW	Vol. V., pp4153-4200; CAIN	Vol. V., pp4200-4225; DOW	Vol. V., pp4225-4229; CAIN

(A) Abstract in File   (I) Topical Index in File   (d) Testimony Presented by Deposition

In addition to the index of trial witnesses, an index of the entire trial transcript may also be beneficial. (*See* Exhibit 10-6.)

Many courtrooms and court reporters are equipped with the capability of providing daily transcripts of the proceedings which include an index. These may be obtained on diskette for

EXHIBIT 10-6 Sample Index to Trial Transcript

Volume I — July 23, 1997 — Pages 1–975

Description	Page
Opening Statement by James S. DOW (Plaintiff)	175
Opening Statement by Ivan M. ABLE (Defendant Roe)	350
Opening Statement by Richard K. Jones (Defendant Doe)	500
Jason D. Shooter, sworn — DIRECT by DOW	800
Plaintiff's Exhibit 1: Letter from Roe to Shooter dated 1/15/95	803
Plaintiff's Exhibit 2: Contract between Roe and Shooter dated 2/1/95	815
Proceedings outside presence of jury — Objections to Plaintiff's Exhibit 3	845
Plaintiff's Exhibit 3: Letter from Roe to Doe dated 1/18/95	875

Volume II — July 24, 1997 — Pages 976–1500

Description	Page
Proceedings outside presence of jury — Objection to Plaintiff's Exhibit 4	976
Jason D. Shooter — Continued DIRECT by DOW	1050
Plaintiff's Exhibit 4: 1/28/95 tape recorded conversation between Shooter, Doe, and Roe	1060
CROSS of Shooter by ABLE	1149
Defendant's Exhibit 1: Letter from Shooter to Adams dated 1/26/95	1155
Defendant's Exhibit 2: Draft of 2/1/95 Contract between Roe and Shooter	1165
Proceedings outside presence of jury — Objection to Defendant's Exhibit 3	1199
Defendant's Exhibit 3: 2/12/95 Video tape of Shooter's delivery vehicle	1295
CROSS of Shooter by JONES	1400

use on a computer, and can form the basis for the index described above. Many courtrooms and court reporters are also equipped to provide a service known as "real time" reporting. This allows testimony to either be downloaded immediately to diskette for viewing on a computer, or allows a connection by which testimony can be viewed at the same time it is being taken on a computer at counsel table. Not only does the availability of these "real time" transcripts enhance the trial team's ability to prepare for the next day's courtroom activity, they are also a good tool for use in cross-examining a witness still on the stand.

In some instances, testimony at trial may be presented via depositions. This should be noted in the index, along with whether the file contains a deposition, abstract, or topical index of the deposition of certain witnesses. Here again is another avenue of comparison and analysis.

In instances where there are a large number be made prior to trial with the trial judge and/or the clerk of court to review all exhibits presented during that day's proceeding to determine the accuracy of your records and, when necessary, to obtain on a daily basis copies of the exhibits entered. The legal assistant can then supervise the reproduction, tabbing, and indexing of all exhibits, furnish copies to the attorney, and return any original exhibits obtained from the clerk to the court prior to trial the next day.

An index of these trial exhibits should reveal to the attorney the dates, volumes, and page numbers in the transcript on which the particular exhibit was identified, marked, received into evidence, and mentioned; the interrogating attorney and witness on the stand at the time; a brief description of the exhibit; the plaintiff or defendant exhibit number as actually entered in court; and the legal assistant's tabbed document number. (*See* Exhibit 10-7.) Not all exhibits are entered in sequence of plaintiff and defendant numbers in court; therefore, an independent chronological numbering system is preferred which also allows cross-referencing to the exhibit number entered by the court. (*See* previous discussion in Section 10.024.) As mentioned earlier, the use of "real time" or daily transcripts from the court reporter will assist in this task. Make sure you ask the court reporter to provide you with an index to each day's proceedings.

EXHIBIT 10-7   Sample Index of Exhibits Introduced at Trial

Court Ex. No.	Party Id. No.	Date	Vol. / Page	Exami- nation	Description	Identified	Marked	Offered	Entered	Mentioned
(P) 12	(P) 15	7/15	IV / 1753	ROE by ABLE	6/15/95 Visa Charge Slip Totaling $150.00	4	4			
		7/15	IV / 1754					4	4	
		7/15	IV / 1755		Explanation					4
		7/15	IV / 1890	ROE by CAIN	Cross					4
(P) 13	(P) 16	7/16	IV / 1987	ROE by ABLE	6/15/95 Report of Investigating Officer	4	4			
		7/16	IV / 1988		Direct					4
		7/17	V / 2350	ROE by CAIN	Cross					4
		7/18	VI / 3675	Bull by	Direct			4	4	
		7/18	VI / 3690	ABLE						4
		7/18	VI / 3895	Bull by CAIN	Cross					4

(P) = Plaintiff   (D1) = Joe's Bar & Grill   (D2) = Roe

This kind of trial support may require round-the-clock assistance with the legal assistant supervising a crew that might be required to work in shifts. Not all trials require this kind of massive assistance, indexing, and cross-referencing. The signs pointing to such a need are evident early in the case from the number of parties and witnesses, the complexity of issues, the factual material to be presented to the judge or jury for decision, and where it becomes obvious that, whatever the outcome, the matter will be appealed by one of the parties. Detailed transcripts and indexes are invaluable to the attorney in pinpointing the points of contention to be appealed and the testimony, factual data, and exhibits supporting those contentions.

10.031 Witnesses, Control, and Liaison

It is normal for witnesses to be nervous and apprehensive before a trial. They have had to disrupt their daily lives to attend. Such disruption is particularly difficult in trials that will take only one, two, or a few days but are delayed for administrative reasons by the court. The legal assistant should make periodic contacts with each witness, informing them of the progress of the case on the trial docket, but not on substantive matters. This allows the witness the utmost personal freedom possible without discussing the case itself. Some witnesses might have to travel to the place of trial, and the legal assistant often coordinates transportation, lodging, and/or meals for them. Having the witness available at the right time is important.

The legal assistant may also be called upon to help prepare the witness to testify. The degree of witness preparation depends on the type and complexity of the case. Many attorneys prepare detailed outlines of their witness examinations which are in part based on previously prepared summaries of statements or depositions. These are often reviewed with the witness prior to trial. In such instances, the legal assistant follows the planned testimony of each witness against the topical summaries previously prepared from statements or depositions to check off anticipated testimony story changes or conflicts. Another area of preparing witnesses often delegated to the legal assistant involves educating them about the purpose and procedures associated with court testimony. Many law firms maintain a brief set of instructions which are provided to the witness for review ahead of time. (*See* Exhibit 10-8.)

EXHIBIT 10-8   Sample Witness Instructions

- Above all else, always tell the truth.

- Be sure you understand the question before you answer.

  - Your attorney is not allowed to ask leading questions that suggest an answer. You will need to tell all the details you remember with as little prompting from your attorney as possible.

  - If you do not understand what is being asked, say so—politely ask the attorney to rephrase the question so that it is clear.

- Answer only the question asked as briefly as possible.

  - If possible, answer the questions of the opposing attorney with a yes or no response; if it makes you uncomfortable, then ask to explain or clarify your yes or no answer. Stop and wait for the next question.

  - Do not volunteer any additional information unless asked to do so.

  - Do not expand on the question.

  - Do not be evasive or give "smart" or sarcastic answers.

- Admit lack of knowledge. Do not guess or speculate. "I don't know" or "I don't remember" can be a perfectly acceptable answer.

- Avoid exaggeration.

- Make an effort to speak clearly and slowly.

  - Address your answer to the jury; they are the people who must decide whether to believe what you are saying.

- Dress conventionally and act with restraint.

- Maintain a respectful and pleasant demeanor.

- Avoid nervous gestures.

- Do not qualify favorable facts.

Source: *"The Whole Truth On How to Prepare a Witness."* Michael K. Gaige, CLA, XXIII Facts & Findings 2 (August 1996).

10.032 Fees, Costs, and Expenses

The legal assistant frequently monitors all the fees, costs, and expenses associated with the trial. These may include witness fees, transportation and lodging expenses, meal expenses for the trial team, witnesses, and the client, parking fees, subpoena service fees, photocopying charges, audio/video equipment costs, court reporter fees, and any hotel/motel charges. Usually, the method of handling such matters are determined by established office policy and procedure. The attorney or the office manager should be consulted to determine the manner of handling any unusual situations or expenses on each case.

10.033 Exhibit/Evidence Log

The legal assistant should maintain an independent log of every exhibit introduced by the plaintiff or the defendant and record its marking for identification, the foundation and offering as evidence, any objections, and the court's ruling. (*See* Exhibit 10-9.) During courtroom breaks and recesses, the legal assistant should confer with the attorney to ensure that desired exhibits have not only been identified and marked, but have also been formally offered and entered. It is normal for the trial team to meet after court has been adjourned for the day to review the day's events. During the course of the daily meeting, discussed in more detail below, the attorney and the legal assistant reconcile their logs to ensure they are consistent.

EXHIBIT 10-9   Sample Trial Exhibit Log

Exhibit List—Case:

P/D No.	Date	Witness	Description	Status
P 13	7/16	ROE	6/15/95 Invoice for Roof Repairs	OBJ; RR
P 14	7/16	ROE	6/15/95 $150.00 Canceled Check	O; A
P 13	7/17	BUCK	6/15/95 Invoice for Roof Repairs	OBJ;OR; A
P 15	7/17	BUCK	6/15/95 Invoice for Asphalt Shingles	O; A

O = Offered   OBJ = Objection   RR = Ruling Reserved   OR = Overruled   S = Sustained   A = Admitted

The legal assistant is usually in charge of the exhibits and must be ready to provide a desired exhibit as the attorney is ready to introduce it. This is particularly important where special arrangements are needed, such as the provision of videotape machines, televisions, computers, scale models, large sketches, drawings, or photographs.

10.034 Daily Trial Review and Planning Meeting

Every day following adjournment of the court and after the witnesses have been released, the legal assistant participates in the daily trial review and planning meeting. Testimony and courtroom observations are discussed. Trial notes and exhibit logs are compared, and final arrangements and plans for the next day's activity are outlined, including decisions on any changes to the order of appearance of witnesses, and identification of exhibits expected to be used with each witness. It is not unusual for these meetings to result in the need to set up morning or evening meetings with witnesses, clients, or other attorneys, the creation of additional exhibit enlargements, or new demonstrative exhibits. As a result of these meetings, it may also be necessary to assist with additional research and supervise the preparation of briefs on issues the trial team has decided to bring up in court. The next day's witnesses must be notified or subpoenaed when appropriate, and arrangements for transportation and other logistics are completed. Finally, the various indexes, logs, and summaries discussed earlier in Section 10.03 are revised and updated.

10.035 Trial Notes

One of the most helpful and important jobs performed by the legal assistant at trial is that of taking detailed notes of the proceedings. Of particular importance are notes and observations of testimony, particularly during cross-examination of the adversary's witnesses. Cross-examination is one period where the lawyer cannot witnesses response. Even when daily or "real time" transcripts are available, careful and detailed notes which include courtroom observations of the testimony will aid the lawyer during breaks and recesses, as well as at the daily trial review and planning meeting. Notes may be taken in a variety of methods which may include the utilization of computers in the courtroom, as well as the more traditional pen and paper.

One effective method is to use a lined, legal pad, notebook paper, or spiral-bound $8\frac{1}{2}$-by-11-inch pad, fifty to eighty pages thick (or more than one, if for a complex case). If time permits, the top margin of each page should be marked in advance with the case name and a place to fill in the date, time, and consecutive page number. This information will be entered as the case progresses, creating a chronology of the case presentation. A vertical line one-quarter or one-third of the way from the right edge of every page will create a margin for noting exhibit introduction, important admissions, important conflicts, and other courtroom observations. When trial begins, the legal assistant fills in the date and time, along with the court and the judge. It is also useful to note the names of the court clerk, the court reporter, the bailiff, the adversary attorneys, experts, and the presence or absence of parties. For example:

Case: Smith vs. Jones
Date: 6/14/90   Time: 9:30 am   Lincoln Co. Sup. Crt., Courtroom 3. Judge I. M. Wright

Note taking begins in earnest as the opening statements are made by each attorney. When the first witness is called, the entry may look like "9:35 am—Thompson sworn. Darrow Direct." The testimony is then noted as given, with additional notations in the margin concerning exhibits, objections, rulings by the judge, and jury observations. As exhibits are offered, that information is also recorded on the evidence/exhibit log for identification. Although objections and rulings are recorded in the trial notes, they are not noted on the evidence/exhibit log. When an exhibit is admitted, a notation to that effect is made in both places. The current time should also be entered on the top of each new page. That chronology, along with the times recorded for breaks and recesses (logged both at the time granted and the time trial resumes), is useful in estimating when to notify witnesses to come to the courthouse, when looking back through notes during the daily trial review and planning meetings, and when requesting certain portions of the daily trial transcripts. When the trial is over, the notebook, together with the copies of the trial exhibits and the lawyer's trial book, is stored for use in appellate procedures.

10.036 Polling the Jury

When a verdict is rendered that surprises the lawyer, interviewing the jurors to identify the reasoning behind the verdict is important. What fact, exhibit, or testimony caused the result? Which witnesses did they believe, and which did they find not credible? Why did they not believe the client or the client's witness? Asking the members of the jury these kinds of questions after a verdict has been rendered and the jurors excused is often informally referred to as polling the jury. The formal use of that term refers to a demand by a party that the jury be polled to verify that the verdict is unanimous prior to the verdict being entered and the jury discharged.

Usually, there is a reasonable and understandable basis for the decision. Sometimes it is simply common sense or a spirit of equity. For instance, in a condemnation case, the landowner wanted two million dollars, and the public agency offered only two thousand dollars. Both sides had experts supporting their respective but opposing valuation theories. The jury awarded the landowner two hundred thousand dollars in a decision which recognized the difference in the two valuations, one so unreasonably high and the other so unreasonably low, and honored the spirit of compromise, if not the facts submitted by the adversaries.

In other cases, the severity and continuing nature of an injury to an individual may arouse the sympathies of the jury, leading them to decide in favor of the injured party on a compassionate basis even though there is only the slightest thread of causal connection to the defendant's conduct.

On occasion, decisions are rendered against a party because of tactics or actions that upset, anger, or offend the jury. The offending tactic or trial strategy used by the attorney may be perfectly ethical, correct, and even necessary or required, such as a tough impeachment cross-examination. The action that angered might have been an obvious lie by a critical witness, or a pattern of behavior by the party that the jury acknowledged as legal but unworthy of being rewarded by it in the verdict.

Jury polling is best done immediately after the jury is discharged but can be pursued later. Each juror is interviewed and the notes are all collated for what value such a postmortem may provide. Some jurisdictions have placed constraints on this kind of post-verdict investigation, and a legal assistant should never initiate this kind of action without the attorney's express authorization, and without being familiar with any such restrictions.

Comment

There is nothing quite like the experience of seeing a case through to a jury verdict. The preparation in the weeks and days preceding a trial can be demanding, exhausting, and stressful. Every jury trial is a miniature stage drama, with the characters, props, and carefully choreographed moves. The legal assistant often functions as stage master, copywriter, propmaster, and set designer, as well as bookkeeper, concierge, limo service manager, and drama critic. This chapter is but a brief look at the way in which the legal assistant aids in trial preparation and provides assistance as an integral part of the trial team during presentation of the case to a jury. (*See* Exhibit 10-10.) Trial lawyers with a great deal of experience always say that a case should be prepared from the very beginning as if there is no chance of settlement and going to trial is definite. It pays to be prepared. If you are, the attorneys cannot afford to try a case without you.

EXHIBIT 10-10   The Legal Assistant at Trial

Courtroom Check
1. Arrange and set up counsel table.
   a. Have adequate chairs for attorney(s), legal assistant, and parties.
   b. Arrange files and documents (know where everything is).
2. Check on any requested easel, video player, etc.

Jury Selection
1. Assist attorney in gathering data on jury panel.
2. Use forms for jury selection.
3. Instruct parties to take notes during voir dire and to communicate thoughts regarding potential jurors to you or to the attorney.
4. Take complete notes during jury selection.
5. Be prepared to give opinion regarding potential jurors to the attorney and make sure he or she sees any notes from the parties.
6. After selection, make list of sworn jurors and fill out Jury Selection Roster form.

Witnesses
1. Coordinate attendance using information provided on a Witness Control Sheet (keep in contact prior to the time needed; make any hotel arrangements if necessary).
2. Know your witness and client.
   a. Make sure witnesses can find the courthouse, nearby parking facilities, and the assigned courtroom.
   b. Make sure witness is ready to testify.
   c. Check what the witness plans to carry on to the witness stand.
   d. Help calm down or psych up the witness.
   e. Have props, magic markers, etc. ready; tell witness where they are or how he or she will get them.
   f. Have Kleenex, aspirin, mints, cough drops, and water handy.
   g. Caution witness not to talk about testimony or the case in halls or restroom.
   h. After witness is excused, check with attorney to see if he or she will be needed again. Remind witness of no obligation to discuss case or testimony with anyone. Beware of press.
3. Track outline, unanswered questions, leads, inconsistencies not caught, etc.

Handling Documents
1. Anticipate need; have ready for witness and extra copies for court and opposing counsel.

2. Stay alert and pull pleading/documents referred to by other attorneys or witnesses; hand to attorney.
3. Keep documents organized at all times.
4. Remind attorney to offer exhibit into evidence as each witness testifies.
5. Keep careful records of exhibits offered and received (by all parties) on an Exhibit Control Sheet and compare your records with those of the court clerk at the close of each day's session.

Notetaking
1. One of the most important duties you can have.
2. Use computer for notetaking, if allowed.
3. Take as extensive notes as possible. Good notes by you can alleviate the need and expense for daily transcripts. One good method is to listen to the question and the answer and try to summarize the two into a statement.
4. Make notes as to objections and court rulings.
5. Print out and make notes available to attorney at the end of each day. Make sure the attorney has a complete set of notes of all testimony for use in preparing closing argument.

Telephone Contact with Office
1. Arrange procedure with Court Clerk's office for incoming messages.
2. Call office at prearranged times. (Check with attorney for instructions prior to placing calls.)
3. Keep attorney contact with office to a minimum (you act as the go-between).

Overnight Recesses
1. Go over office crisis list with attorney—get instructions or answers to telephone back to the office.
2. Ask attorney what you can do to help prepare for next day.
3. Review trial notes—make list of inconsistencies of points that need elaboration or clarification.
4. Assist with preparation of jury instructions, if requested.
5. Do not make any personal plans—be available.

Closing Arguments
1. Assist attorney in preparing for closing argument.
   a. Outline pertinent testimony from trial notes.
   b. Check with clerk to make sure exhibits are in proper numerical order.
2. Monitor outline as argument is being presented.
3. Monitor time of argument for attorney.
4. Take notes of opposing counsel's closing argument.

Source: *"Trial Conduct for the Legal Assistant."* Karen B. Judd, CLA, XXI Facts & Findings 3 (November 1994).

Bibliography

Federal Practice and Procedure, as amended through December 1, 1996. St. Paul: West Publishing Company, 1997.

Hutson, Beverly K., *Paralegal Trial Handbook.* 2nd ed. John Wiley & Sons, Inc., 1995.

Purcell, Jay. J., *"It's Enough to Boggle Your Mind: the True Meaning of Trial Preparation."* XXIII Facts & Findings 1 (May, 1996).

Robtoy, Pam, *"Seating a Jury."* XXIII Facts & Findings 2 (August, 1996).

Gaige, Michael K., *"The Whole Truth On How to Prepare a Witness."* XXIII Facts & Findings 2 (August, 1996).

Judd, Karen B., *"Trial Conduct for the Legal Assistant."* XXI Facts & Findings 3 (November, 1994).

Glossary: Legal Terminology

[*Copyrighted source material: The entire section on Latin words and phrases and all other definitions followed by an asterisk have been taken from* Black's Law Dictionary *(revised sixth edition, West Publishing Company)*.]

Introduction

This chapter is not a dictionary of all legal terms but rather a selection of frequently used terms. These words have been sorted into categories, though words found under "Business and Corporate Terms" are also used by professionals who specialize in real estate. This glossary is arranged to give legal assistants easily scanned word lists with barebones definitions that serve as memory aids or refreshers.

The definitions provided are accurate but do not constitute every possible definition or contextual meaning. They are the basic, generally accepted, meanings; there is insufficient detail to provide the legal assistant with a means of outlining the elements of proof for a cause of action. For instance, assault in the "General Legal Terms and Phrases" section is defined as "an unlawful offer or attempt with force to do corporeal hurt to another." The elements for a civil action require a showing that there was no consent by the plaintiff. The legal assistant must consult the codes, annotated cases, texts, and other references when outlining the elements of cases and their defenses.

Those seeking in-depth meanings must consult more authoritative and detailed definitions than this book can accommodate. *Black's Law Dictionary* and the multivolume sets of *Legal Words and Phrases* are recommended.

Latin Words and Phrases

A fortiori With stronger reason; much more.

A posteriori From the effect to the cause; from what comes after.

A priori From the cause to the effect; from what goes before.

A vinculo matrimonii From the bond of matrimony.

Ab actis An officer having charge of acta, public records, registers, journals, or minutes; an officer who entered on record the acta or proceedings of a court; a clerk of court; a notary or actuary.

Ab initio From the very beginning.

Ad damnum clause A clause in pleadings praying for claimed money loss or damages or other relief.

Ad hoc For this; for this special purpose; one time only.

Ad infinitum Without limit; to an infinite extent; indefinitely.

Ad litem For the suit; for the purposes of the suit; pending the suit. A guardian ad litem is a guardian appointed to prosecute or defend a suit on behalf of a party incapacitated by infancy or otherwise.

Ad respondendum For answering; to make answer.

Ad satisfaciendum To satisfy.

Ad valorem According to the value. A tax imposed on the value of a property.

Adieu Without delay. A common term in the yearbooks, implying final dismissal from court.

Aggregatio mentium The meeting of minds. The moment when a contract is complete.

Alias dictus Otherwise called. A fictitious name assumed by a person is colloquially termed an alias.

Alibi In criminal law, elsewhere; in another place.

Aliquot A proportional part; fractional.

Alius Other. Something else; another thing.

Alter ego Second self; the same entity under a different name or title.

Amicus curiae A friend of the court. A person who has a strong interest in, but who has no right to appear in, a suit but is allowed to introduce argument, authority, or evidence to protect his or her interest.

Animus Mind; intention; disposition; design; will.

Anno domini In the year of the Lord. Commonly abbreviated A.D. The computation of time, according to the Christian era, dates from the birth of Christ.

Ante Formerly; heretofore; synonymous with supra.

Arguendo In arguing; in the course of the argument.

Assumpsit He undertook; he promised.

Bona fide In or with good faith; honestly, openly, and sincerely; without deceit or fraud.

Causa A cause, reason, occasion, motive, or inducement.

Causa mortis In contemplation of approaching death.

Caveat Let him beware; warning.

Caveat actor Let the doer or actor beware.

Caveat emptor Let the buyer beware.

Certiorari To be informed of, to be made certain in regard to. The name of a writ of review or inquiry. The writ of a superior court directing an inferior court to send up a pending pleading, as the U.S. Supreme Court honoring a petition for writ of certiorari.

Civiliter Civilly. In a person's civil character or position or by civil (not criminal) process or procedure.

Civiliter mortuus Civilly dead; dead in the view of the law.

Consortium Conjugal fellowship of husband and wife and the right of each to the company, cooperation, affection, and aid of the other in every conjugal relation.

Contra Against, confronting, opposite to; on the other hand; on the contrary.

Contra bonos mores Against good morals.

Contra pacem Against the peace.

Coram Before; in the presence of. Applied to persons only.

Corpus Body; an aggregate or mass; physical substance, as distinguished from intellectual conception; main part as opposed to appendages.

Corpus delicti The body of crime. The body (material substance) upon which a crime has been committed; for example, the corpse of a murdered man, the remains of a house burned down. Fact or evidence that proves the crime.

Corpus juris A body of law. A term used to signify a book comprehending several collections of law.

Corpus juris civilis The body of the civil law.

Cum testamento annexo With the will annexed. A term applied to administration granted where a testator makes an incomplete will, without naming any executors, where he or she names incapable persons, or where the executors named refuse to act.

Curia A court.

Damnum Damage; loss.

Damnum absque injuria Loss, hurt, or harm without injury in the legal sense.

Datum A first principle; a thing given; a date.

De bonis non An abbreviation of *de bonis non administratis*. Of the goods not administered. When an administrator is appointed to succeed another who has left the estate partially unsettled, he or she is said to be granted "administration de bonis;" that is, of the goods not already administered.

De facto In fact, in deed, actually; legitimate or correct in fact.

De jure Of right; legitimate; lawful; by right and just title.

De minimus Short for *de minimus non curat lex*. The law does not care for, or take notice of, very small or trifling matters.

De novo Anew; afresh; a second time.

Dicta Opinions of a judge that do not embody the resolution or determination of the court. The plural of *dictum*.

Dictum A statement, remark, or observation.

Donatio A gift. A transfer of the title to property to one who receives it without paying for it.

Duces tecum Bring with you. The name of certain species of writs of which the *subpoena duces tecum* is the most usual, requiring a party who is summoned to appear in court to bring with him or her some document, piece of evidence, or other thing to be used to inspected by the court.

Durante During.

Durante minore aetate During minority.

Durante viduitate During widowhood.

E converso Converse hand; on the contrary.

Ergo Therefore; hence; because.

Erratum Error.

Et al. An abbreviation for *et alii*. And others.

Et alius And another.

Et cetera And others; and other things; and others of a like character; and others of the like kind.

Et seq Abbreviation of *et sequentes*. And the following; sometimes shown as *et. seq*.

Et ux An abbreviation of *et uxor*. And wife.

Ex contractu From and out of a contract.

Ex delicto From a delict, tort, fault, crime, or malfeasance.

Ex necessitate legis From or by necessity of law.

Ex officio From office; by virtue of the office.

Ex parte On one side only; by or for one party; done for, in behalf of, or on the application of, one party only. Hearing with only one party present or represented.

Ex post facto After the act; by an act or fact occurring after some previous act or fact, and relating thereto; by subsequent matter. The opposite of *ab initio*.

Ex rel From the relation of; a form of pleading by the state on a matter arising from another case. Used in citations to indicate that a case is brought on behalf of another person or entity.

Exempli gratia (e.g.) For example.

Facto In fact; by an act; by the act or fact.

Felonice Feloniously.

Feme covert A married woman.

Feme sole A single woman, including a woman who has been married but whose marriage has been dissolved by death or divorce.

Fiat Let it be done. An authority issuing from some competent source for the doing of some legal act. A command.

Filius A son; a child.

Filius familias In the civil law, the son of a family; an unemancipated son.

Filius nullius An illegitimate child; son of nobody.

Filius populi A son of the people.

Flagrante delicto In the very act of committing the crime.

Forum A court of justice or judicial tribunal; a place of jurisdiction; a place where remedy is pursued.

Guardian ad litem Appointed by the court to prosecute or defend the interests of another person (usually a minor or an incompetent) in litigation.

Habeas corpus You have the body. The name given writs having for their object to bring a party before a court or judge.

Ibid. Abbreviation of *ibidem*. In the same place; in the same book; on the same page.

Ignorantia Ignorance; want of knowledge.

Ignorantia legis neminem excusat Ignorance of the law excuses no one.

Illicit Not permitted or allowed.

Illicitum collegium An illegal corporation.

Illud That.

Impotentia excusat legem The impossibility of doing what is required by the law excuses from the performance.

In bonis Among the foods or property; in actual possession.

In camera In chambers; in private.

In esse In being; actually existing.

In extremis In extremity; in the last extremity; in the last illness.

In forma pauperis In the character or manner of a pauper. A poor person may proceed without incurring costs or fees of court.

In fraudem legis In fraud of the law with the intent or view of evading the law.

In futuro In future; at a future time.

In hoc In this; in respect to this.

In loco parentis In the place of a parent; instead of a parent.

In omnibus In all things; on all points.

In pari delicto In equal fault or guilt.

In personam Against the person. Type of jurisdiction or power that a court may acquire over a defendant's person in contrast to jurisdiction over his or her property.

In praesenti At the present time.

In re In the affair; in the matter of; concerning; in reference to; regarding.

In rem Proceedings or actions instituted against the thing, as opposed to actions against persons.

In specie Specific; specifically. In kind; in the same or like form.

In toto In the whole; wholly; completely.

Indebitatus assumpsit Being indebted, be promised, or undertook.

Infra Below, under, beneath, underneath.

Innuendo Meaning. In a pleading in libel action, a statement by plaintiff of construction that he puts upon words that are alleged to be libelous.

Inter Among; between.

Inter vivos Between the living; from one living person to another.

Interim In the meantime; meanwhile; between.

Intra In; near; within.

Ipse He himself; the same; the very person.

Ipse dixit He himself said it; a bare assertion resting on the authority of an individual.

Ipso facto By the fact itself; by the mere fact; by the mere effect of an act or a fact.

Ita est So it is; so it stands.

Jura Rights, laws.

Jura personarum Rights of persons; rights that concern and are annexed to persons.

Jura rerum Rights of things; rights that a person may acquire over external objects or things, unconnected with his or her person.

Jure divino By divine right.

Jure uxoris In right of the wife.

Juris publici Of common right; of common or public use.

Jus (pl. jura) Right; justice; law; the whole body of law.

Jus accrescendi The right of survivorship.

Jus ad rem A right to a thing.

Jus civile Civil law. The system of law peculiar to one state or people.

Lis pendens A pending suit. Jurisdiction, power, or control that courts acquire over property in suit pending action and until final judgment.

Locus A place; the place where a thing is done.

Locus delicti The place of the offense; the place where an offense was committed.

Mala Bad; evil; wrongful.

Mala fide Bad faith. The opposite of *bona fide*.

Mala in se Wrongs in themselves; acts morally wrong; offenses against conscience.

Mala praxis Malpractice; unskillful management or treatment.

Malo animo With an evil mind; with a bad purpose or wrongful intention; with malice.

Malum Wrong; evil; wicked; reprehensible.

Malum in se A wrong in itself; an act or case involving illegality from the very nature of the transaction, upon principles of natural, moral, and public law.

Mandamus We command. A writ issued from a court of superior jurisdiction and directed to an inferior court, a private or municipal corporation, or an executive, administrative, or judicial officer commanding performance of a particular act therein stated.

Mens Mind; intention; meaning; understanding; will.

Mens rea A guilty mind; a guilty or wrongful purpose; criminal intent.

Modus Manner; means; way.

Nil Nothing.

Nisi Unless.

Nisi pruis Trial courts where issues of fact are tried before a jury and one presiding judge.

Nolle prosequi A formal entry on the record by the prosecuting officer in criminal action declaring that the prosecutor decides not to pursue the case.

Nolo contendere I will not contest it; a plea in a criminal case that has a similar legal effect as a plea of guilty.

Non compos mentis Not of sound mind; insane.

Non obstante Notwithstanding.

Non obstante veredicto Notwithstanding the verdict.

Nudum pactum A voluntary promise, without any consideration other than mere goodwill or natural affection.

Nul No; none.

Nul tort In pleading, a plea of the general issue to a real action, by which the defendant denies that he or she committed any wrong.

Nunc pro tunc Now for then. A phrase applied to acts allowed to be done after the time when they should be done, with a retroactive effect.

Omnibus For all; containing two or more independent matters.

Pactum An agreement without consideration that might produce a civil obligation.

Pari delicto In equal fault; in a similar offense or crime; equal in guilt or in legal fault.

Particeps criminis A participant in crime; an accomplice.

Pendente lite Pending the suit; during the actual progress of a suit; during litigation.

Per annum By the year; annually; yearly.

Per capita By the heads or polls. According to the number of individuals; share and share alike.

Per curiam By the court. A phrase used to distinguish an opinion of the whole court from an opinion written by any one judge.

Per se By himself or itself; in itself; taken alone; inherently; in isolation; unconnected to other matters.

Per stirpes By roots or stocks; by representation. This term, derived from the civil law, is much used in the law of descents and distribution and denotes a method of dividing an intestate estate.

Post mortem After death; pertaining to matters of death.

Persequi To follow after; to pursue or claim in form of law.

Praecipe An original writ, drawn up in the alternative, commanding the defendant to do the thing required or show the reason why he or she had not done it.

Prima facie At first sight; on the first appearance; on the face of it; so far as can be judged from the first disclosure; presumably; a fact presumed to be true unless disproved by some evidence to the contrary.

Prima facie case Such as will prevail until contradicted and overcome by other evidence.

Prima facie evidence Evidence good and sufficient on its face; such evidence as, in the judgment of the law, is sufficient to establish a given fact or group or chain of facts, constituting the party's claim or defense and that, if not rebutted or contradicted, will remain sufficient.

Pro For; in respect of; on account of; in behalf of.

Pro bono For the good; used to describe work or services done or performed free of charge.

Pro bono publico For the public good.

Pro confesso For confessed; as confessed.

Pro forma As a matter of form or for the sake of form.

Pro rata Proportionately; according to a certain rate, percentage, or proportion.

Pro se For himself; in his own behalf; in person.

Pro tanto For so much; for as much as may be; for as far as it goes.

Pro tempore For the time being; temporarily; provisionally.

Quantum meruit As much as he deserves; the extent of liability on a contract implied by law.

Quantum valebant As much as they were worth.

Quare Wherefore; for what reason; on what account.

Quasi As if, almost as it were; analogous to.

Quid pro quo What for what; something for something. Used in law for the giving of one valuable thing for another.

Quoad hoc As to this; with respect to this; so far as this in particular is concerned.

Quo animo With what intention or motive.

Quo warranto An extraordinary proceeding, prerogative in nature, addressed to preventing a continued exercise of authority unlawfully asserted.

Ratio decidenti The ground or reason of decision. The point in a case that determines the judgment.

Remittitur Power of a trial court to diminish the award of damages by a jury.

Res A thing; an object, subject matter, or status is considered as the defendant in an action or as the object against which, directly, proceedings are taken; subject matter of a trust or will.

Res gestae Things done; the whole of the transaction under investigation and every part of it.

Res ipsa loquitur The thing speaks for itself. The foundation of a legal pleading in common law in negligence, which, if accepted by the court, allows the burden of proof to be imposed on the defendant instead of the plaintiff.

Res judicata A matter adjudicated; a thing judicially acted upon or decided; a thing or matter settled by judgment.

Respondeat superior Let the master answer. Maxim meaning that a master is liable in certain cases for the wrongful acts of his or her servant and a principal for those of his agent.

Scienter Knowingly. Frequently used to signify the defendant's guilty knowledge.

Scilicet (SS. or ss.) To wit; that is to say. A word used in pleadings and other instruments as introductory to a more particular statement of matters previously mentioned in general terms.

Scintilla A spark; a remaining particle; a trifle; the least particle.

Se defenendo In defending oneself; in self-defense.

Semper Always.

Semper paratus Always ready. The name of a plea by which the defendant alleges that he or she has always been ready to perform what is demanded of him or her.

Seriatim Severally; separately; individually; one by one.

Sigillum A seal; originally and properly a seal impressed upon wax.

Simplex Simple, single; pure; unqualified.

Simplex obligato A single obligation; a bond without a condition.

Sine Without.

Sine die Without day; without assigning a day for a future meeting or hearing.

Sine qua non Without which not; that without which the thing cannot be; an indispensable requisite or condition.

Situs Situation; location.

Stare decisis To abide by or adhere to decided cases. A decision that establishes precedent in law.

Status quo The existing state of things at any given date.

Sub Under; upon.

Sub nomine Under the name of; in the name of; under the title of.

Sub silentio Under silence; without any notice being taken.

Sui generis Of its own kind or class; peculiar.

Sui juris Of his own right; possessing full social and civil rights; not under any legal disability, the power of another, or guardianship.

Supersedeas The name of a writ containing a command to stay the proceedings at law.

Supra Above; before.

Terminus Boundary; a limit, either of space or time.

Tort A private or civil wrong or injury. A wrong independent of contract.

Ultra Beyond; outside of; in excess of.

Ultra vires Acts beyond the scope of the powers of a corporation, as defined by its charter or the laws of the state of incorporation.

Versus Against. In the title of a cause, the name of the plaintiff is put first, followed by the word *versus*, then the defendant's name. The word is commonly abbreviated *vs.* or *v.*

Vi et armis With force and arms.

Via Way; road. In civil law, a right of way.

Vice In the place or stead; substitution for.*

Vice versa Conversely; in inverted order; in reverse manner.

Voir dire To speak the truth. Denotes the preliminary examination that the court may make of one presented as a witness or juror, where his or her competency, interest, or other quality is objected to.

General Legal Terms and Phrases

Abrogation The destruction or annulment of a former law by an act of the legislative power, by constitutional authority, or by usage.*

Acceptance Agreeing to an offer, thereby creating a contract.

Accommodation An arrangement or engagement made as a favor to another not upon a consideration received.

Acknowledgment An admittance, affirmation, declaration, testimony, avowal, confession, or owning as genuine.

Adhesion contract Standardized contract form in which one party, normally the weaker, has little or no bargaining power or choice as to its terms.

Administrative law A body of law in the form of rules and regulations promulgated by an administrative body created by state legislature or Congress to carry out a specific statute.

Affiant One who swears to or affirms the statement in an affidavit.

Affidavit A voluntary statement in writing sworn or affirmed to before an official, usually a notary public, who has the authority to administer an oath or affirmation.

Agent A person authorized by another to act for him, one entrusted to another's business.*

Allegation The assertion claim, declaration, or statement of a party to an action, made in a pleading, setting out what he or she expects to prove.*

Amnesty A sovereign act of oblivion for past acts; often conditioned on acceptance within a trial period. Amnesty is the abolition and forgetfulness of the offense; a pardon is forgiveness.

Anticipatory breach Before the legally required performance of a contract duty, an announcement by one party to another party to the contract that he or she will not or cannot perform his or her contract duty.

Antitrust laws Federal and state laws designed to protect trade and commerce and to prevent restraint of trade, price-fixing, price discrimination, monopoly, and unfair practices in interstate commerce; for example, Sherman Act, Clayton Act, Federal Trade Commission Act.

Appraisal A valuation or an estimation of value of property by disinterested persons of suitable qualification.*

Assault A willing unlawful threat or attempt to do corporeal hurt to another by force so that the intended victim has reason to fear or expect immediate harm.

Assets All the items of value owned by an individual, association, estate, business, or corporation.

Assignment A transfer or making over to another of the whole of any property, real or personal in possession or action, or of any estate or right therein.*

Attestation The act of witnessing the signing or execution of a document by signature.

Attorney-in-fact One who is appointed by another to act for him or her in specific actions described in a power of attorney or letter of attorney.

Bailment A delivery of goods or personal property by one person to another for some particular purpose, upon a contract, express or implied, that the property will be returned to the person delivering it after the accomplishment of the purpose for which it was delivered.

Bankruptcy A state of insolvency under the Federal Bankruptcy Law in which the property of a debtor is taken over by a receiver or trustee in bankruptcy for the benefit of the creditors. A voluntary bankruptcy is brought about by the filing of a petition in bankruptcy by the debtor. An involuntary bankruptcy is brought about by the filing of a petition by the creditors against an insolvent debtor.

Battery An unlawful application of force to another's person, or other wrongful physical violence or constraint, inflicted on a human being without his or her consent.

Breach of contract Failure, without legal excuse, to perform any promise which forms the whole or part of a contract.*

Capacity Legal qualification (such as legal age), competency, power, or fitness.

Censure An official reprimand or condemnation.

CLA Abbreviation for Certified Legal Assistant; a term earned through and awarded by the National Association of Legal Assistants to legal assistants who successfully complete an extensive written test of their general skills and specific knowledge of four areas of substantive law practice and procedure.

CLAS Abbreviation for Certified Legal Assistant Specialist; a term earned through and awarded by the National Association of Legal Assistants to Certified Legal Assistants who successfully complete an extensive written test of knowledge and skills in specific areas of substantive law and procedure.

Civil law Laws adopted by local, state, and federal governments and known as codes or statutes and that concern civil or private rights and remedies, as contrasted with criminal laws.

Codes A systematic collection, compendium, or revision of laws, rules, or regulations enacted by legislation; statutes. *See also* Ordinance.

Code Civil The code embodying the civil law of France, framed by a commission of jurists, passed by the tribunate and legislature, and promulgated in 1804 as the *Code Civil des Francais*. When Napoleon became emperor, the code was changed to *Code Napoleon* for many years. The law of the state of Louisiana is based historically on the Napoleonic Code.

Common law All statutory and case law background of England and the American colonies; laws of legal rules that are developed as a result of decisions by judges based upon accepted customs and traditions and that do not rest upon any express and positive declaration of the will of the legislative body.

Community property Property owned in common by husband and wife, each having an undivided one-half interest by reason of their marital status.*

Conciliation The adjustment and settlement of a dispute in a friendly, unantagonistic manner. Used in courts before trial with a view toward avoiding trial and in labor disputes before arbitration.*

Consideration The price, motive, cause, impelling influence, or matter of inducement of a contract, which must be lawful in itself.

Contract An agreement between competent parties upon a legal consideration to do or to abstain from doing some lawful act.

Copyright A right of literary property as recognized and sanctioned by positive law.*

Creditor A person to whom a debt is owing by another person, who is the debtor.*

Criminal law That law that for purposes of preventing harm to society declares what conduct is criminal and prescribes the punishment to be imposed for such conduct.

Debtor One who owes an obligation.

Decree The judgment of a court of equity or chancery, answering for most purposes to the judgment of a court of law; a sentence or order of the court, pronounced on hearing and understanding all the points in issue and determining the rights of all the parties to the suit, according to equity and good conscience.*

Discharge To release; liberate; annul; unburden; disencumber; dismiss.

Duress Unlawful constraint exercised upon a person whereby he or she is forced to do some act that he or she otherwise would not have done.

Equity Justice administered according to fairness, as contrasted with the strictly formulated rules of common law.*

Evidentiary Having the quality of evidence; constituting evidence; evidencing.*

Exemptions Freedom from a general duty or service; immunity from a general burden, tax, or charge.* In bankruptcy proceedings, amounts of property allowed to be kept by the debtor.

Felony A crime of a graver or more serious nature than those designated as misdemeanors. Any offense punishable by death or imprisonment for a term exceeding one year.

Fraud Any kind of artifice employed by one person to deceive another.*

Guardian A person lawfully invested with the power and charged with the duty of taking care of the person and managing the property and rights of another person who, for defect of age, understanding, or self-control, is considered incapable of administering his or her own affairs.*

Hypothetical question A combination of assumed or proved facts and circumstances, stated in such form as to constitute a coherent and specific situation or statement of facts, upon which the opinion of an expert is asked, by way of evidence on a trial.*

Indorsement The act of a payee, drawee, accommodation indorser, or holder of a bill, note, check, or other negotiable instrument, in writing his or her name upon the back of the same, with or without further or qualifying words, whereby the property in the same is assigned and transferred to another.*

Interstate commerce Traffic, intercourse, commercial trading, or the transportation of persons or property between or among the several states from or between points in one state and points in another state; commerce between two states or between places lying in different states.*

Judgment The official and authentic decision of a court of justice upon the respective rights and claims of the parties to an action or suit therein litigated and submitted to its determination.*

Legal assistant A distinguishable group of persons who assist attorneys in delivering legal services. Within this occupational category, some individuals are known as paralegals. Through formal education, training, and experience, legal assistants have knowledge and expertise regarding the legal system and substantive and procedural law that qualify them to do work of a legal nature under the supervision of an attorney.

Legal ethics Usages and customs among the members of the legal profession involving their moral and professional duties toward one another, toward clients, and toward the courts.*

Lien A charge, security, or encumbrance upon property.*

Liquidation Payment, satisfaction, or collection; realization on assets and discharge of liabilities.*

Litigation Contest in a court of law for the purpose of enforcing a right or seeking a remedy.*

Long-Arm Statute A state law extending personal jurisdiction over out-of-state persons or entities who own real property in the forum state, conduct business in the forum state, or commit certain actions in the forum state, such as entering into a contract or committing an alleged tort or crime.

Misdemeanor Offenses lower than felonies and generally punishable by fine or imprisonment other than in the penitentiary.* Defined by local, state, and federal code and statute.

Mitigation of damages Duty of parties to minimize damages after an injury has been inflicted or a breach has occurred.

Napoleonic Code *See* Code Civil.

Notary Public An official authorized by law to administer oaths and to attest to and certify by his or her hand and official seal the identity of persons executing documents.

Novation Substitution of a new contract, debt, or obligation for an existing one between the same or different parties.*

Oath An affirmation of truth of a statement that renders one willfully asserting untrue statements punishable for perjury.*

Offer A promise; a commitment to do or refrain from doing some specific thing in the future.

Offeree The person to whom an offer is made.

Offeror The party who makes the offer.

Ordinance A law, statute, or regulation passed by a local governmental body below the state level. *See* Codes.

Parol A word; speech, hence, oral or verbal.*

Parole A conditional release of a prisoner, generally under the supervision of a parole officer, who has served part of the term for which he or she was sentenced to prison.

Patent A grant made by the government to an inventor, conveying and securing to him or her the exclusive right to make, use, and sell his or her invention for a term of years.*

Pecuniary Monetary; relating to money; financial; consisting of money or that which can be valued in money.*

Power of attorney An instrument authorizing another to act as one's agent or attorney. Power may be made general or specific.

Privilege An immunity which exists under law, and which may constitute a defense to a tort (such as self-defense as a counter to a charge of battery); protected relationships existing under law or statute, such as attorney-client, husband-wife, or doctor-patient. The assertion of a privilege under the work product rule to protect or prevent disclosure of confidential information, such as notes, working papers, memoranda, or similar materials, prepared by an attorney [or a legal assistant acting under the direction of an attorney] in anticipation of litigation or for trial. The work product rule has been interpreted to include private memoranda, written statements of witnesses, and mental impressions of personal recollections prepared or formed by an attorney in anticipation of litigation or for trial.

Privileged communication Those statements made by certain persons within a protected relationship, such as husband-wife, attorney-client, priest-penitent, and the like.*

Probation A sentence releasing the defendant into the community under the supervision of a probation officer.*

Promissory estoppel Legal theory that prevents one party to a contract from denying that consideration was given in that contract.

Rescission An action of an equitable nature in which a party seeks to be relieved of an obligation under a contract on the grounds of mutual mistake, fraud, impossibility, and so forth.*

Restitution The measure of damages according to the defendant's gains rather than the plaintiff's losses.

Revocation Taking back some power, authority, or thing granted; to make void a contract.

Specific performance The carrying out or performance of a contract according to its exact terms. Matters of specific performance are enforced by a court of equity.

Statute An act of the legislature declaring, commanding, or prohibiting something; a particular law enacted and established by the will of the legislative branch of government.*

Substantive law That part of the law that creates, defines, and regulates rights and duties. Substantive law is the opposite of adjective or procedural law, which provides for the method of administering and protecting the rights, duties, and obligations created by substantive law. All states of a general nature are substantive law; those regulating administrative and court proceedings are adjective law.

Tort A private or civil wrong or injury. Three elements of every tort action are: (1) existence of legal duty from defendant to plaintiff, (2) breach of duty, and (3) damage as a proximate result.*

Trademark A distinctive mark, motto, device, or emblem that a manufacturer stamps, prints, or otherwise affixes to the goods it produces, so they may be identified in the market and their origin vouched for.*

Undue Influence Illegal threats or pressure that take away the other party's free will.

Uniform laws A considerable number of laws have been approved by the National Conference of Commissioners on Uniform State Laws, and many of them have been adopted in one or more jurisdictions in the United States and its possessions.* Some of the more important uniform laws are the Uniform Negotiable Instruments Act, the Uniform Partnership Act, the Uniform Stock Transfer Act, and the Uniform Warehouse Receipt Act.

Void; voidable That which is void is of no legal force or effect; that which is voidable may be avoided or declared void.

Business and Corporate Terms

Antitrust acts Federal and state protecting commerce and trade from unlawful restraints, price discriminations, price fixing, and monopolies.

Articles of incorporation Basic instrument filed with the appropriate governmental agency on the incorporation or formation of a business and organized under general corporation laws.*

Assumed business name The name under which an individual, partnership, or corporation conducts business.

Blue Sky law A popular name for statutes providing for the regulation and supervision of investment companies and securities, offerings, and sales.

Bond A written obligation; a certificate or evidence of a debt.

Bylaws Regulations, ordinances, rules, or laws adopted by a corporation or association for the regulation of its own actions and the rights and duties of its members among themselves

Calendar year The period from January 1 to December 31, inclusive.*

Capital The principal invested in a business.

Capitalization The total amount of various securities issued by a corporation.

Clayton Act An act to supplement the Sherman Antitrust Act against unlawful monopolies and restraints.

Cooperative An organization for the primary purpose of providing economic services for its members for their benefit or gain rather than that of the organization.

Copyright A right granted by statute to the author or originator of certain literary or artistic productions, whereby he or she is invested, for a limited period, with the sole and exclusive privilege of multiplying copies of the same and publishing and selling them. A patent relates to the invention of an article; for example, a typewriter.

Corporation An artificial person or legal entity created by, or under the authority of, the laws of a state or nation composed, in some rare instances, of a single person and his or her successors, being the incumbents of a particular office, but ordinarily consisting of an association of numerous individuals who subsist as a body politic under a special denomination, which is regarded in law as having a personality and existence distinct from that of its several members and which is, by the same authority, vested with the capacity of continuous succession, irrespective of changes in its membership, either in perpetuity or for a limited term of years, and of acting as a unit or single individual in matters relating to the common purpose of the association, within the scope of the powers and authorities conferred upon such bodies by law.*

Domestic A corporation created by or organized under the laws of the state in which it does business;

Foreign A corporation created by or under the laws of another state, government, or country.

CUSIP Committee on Uniform Securities Identification Procedures.

Debenture A promissory note or bond issued by a corporation as evidence of an obligation to pay money.

Depreciation An allowance for the exhaustion or wear and tear of tangible property and certain intangible assets that have a limited useful life.

Director An individual appointed or elected to manage and direct the affairs of a corporation.

Dissolution The termination of a corporation as a body politic. Dissolution may occur voluntarily or involuntarily.

Dividend The share allotted to each of several persons entitled to share a division of profits or property. Dividends may denote a fund set apart by a corporation out of its profits to be apportioned among the shareholders or the proportional amount falling to each.*

EIR Environmental impact report.

Excise tax A tax imposed by legislature on the performance of an act, the engaging of an occupation, or the enjoying of a privilege.

FELA, Federal Employers Liability Act Protects employees engaged in interstate and foreign commerce. Payments are made for death or disability sustained in the performance of the duties of employment.

Fiscal year The year between one annual time of settlement or balancing of accounts and another. A period of twelve consecutive months (not necessarily concurrent with the calendar year) with references to which appropriations are made and expenditures authorized and at the end of which accounts are made up and books balanced.

Franchise A special privilege conferred by government or individual or corporation and that does not belong to citizens or country generally of common right.* A privilege granted or sold so as to use a trade name or to sell products or services of a company. Usually conferred for a consideration.

Goodwill The favor that the management wins from the public. The fixed and favorable consideration of customers arising from established and well-conducted business.

Incorporators Individuals who join together for the purpose of forming a corporation.

Insolvency Inability to pay debts as they become due in the usual course of business.

Interstate commerce Traffic, intercourse, commercial trading, or the transportation of persons or property between or among the several states or from or between points in one state and points in another state; commerce between two states or between places lying in different states.*

Interstate Commerce Act The act of Congress of February 4, 1887, designed to regulate commerce between the states and particularly the transportation of persons and property by carriers between interstate points; prescribing that charges for such transportation shall be reasonable and just; prohibiting unjust discrimination, rebates, drawbacks, preferences, pooling of freights, and so on; requiring schedules of rates to be published; establishing a commission to carry out the measures enacted; and prescribing the powers and duties of such commission and the procedure before it.*

Interstate Commerce Commission Federal regulatory agency; no longer in existence, discontinued by Congress in 1996.

Inventory A detailed list of articles of property; an itemized list or schedule of property with appraised or actual values.

Keogh Plans An enactment by Congress that allows self-employed persons to establish and participate in tax-favored retirement plans similar to qualified pension and profit sharing plans.

Liquidation Payment, satisfaction, or collection; realization on assets and discharge of liabilities.

Majority The number greater than half of any total.

Merger The fusion or absorption of one thing or right into another.* In regard to corporations, the union of two or more corporations by the transfer of property of all to one of them, which continues in existence, the others being swallowed up or merged therein.*

Monopoly A privilege or peculiar advantage vested in one or more persons or companies, consisting in the exclusive right (or power) to carry on a particular business or trade, manufacture a particular article, or control the sale of the whole supply of a particular commodity.*

National Labor Relations Act (Taft-Hartley Act of 1947) A federal law regulating the relationship between employers and employees or their union representatives.

Nonprofit corporation A corporation or organization of which no part of its income is distributable to its members, directors, or officers.

Officer A person holding office of trust, command, or authority in a corporation with the power and duty of exercising certain functions. An officer of a corporation carries out the directives of the board of directors.

Organizational meeting A meeting of the original board of directors named in the articles of incorporation at which the adoption of bylaws, election of officers, and transaction of any other necessary business usually takes place.

OSHA, Office of Safety and Health Administration A federal agency.

Partner A member of a partnership or a firm; one who has united with others to form a partnership in business.

Partnership (general) An association of two or more persons by voluntary contract, to carry on, as co-owners, a business for profit.

Partnership (limited) A partnership formed by two or more persons that includes, along with one or more general partners, one or more limited partners, who, as such, are not bound by the obligations of the partnership.

Patent A grant made by the government to an inventor, conveying and securing to him or her the exclusive right to make, use, and sell his or her invention for a term of years.*

Pension plan A plan that requires the employer to make a certain rate of contribution into a retirement fund each year per employee.

Profit sharing plan A plan that provides the employer make contributions into a retirement fund based solely on the profits of the corporation.

Proprietorship (sole) Business completely and directly owned by a single person.

Proxy A person who is substituted by another to represent him or her and act for him or her, particularly at some meeting.* An agent representing and acting for a principal.*

Quorum The number necessary to be present in order to conduct business.

Recapitalization An arrangement whereby stock, bonds, or other securities of a corporation are adjusted as to amount, income, or priority.*

Redemption A repurchase; a buying back.*

Registered agent of a corporation An individual resident (or corporation authorized to do business in the state), located at the listed registered office, upon which service or notice can be made on the particular corporation.

Reorganization The act or process of organizing again or anew. As to corporations, the carrying out, by proper agreements and legal proceedings, of a business plan for winding up the affairs of or foreclosing a mortgage or mortgages upon the property of insolvent corporations.

Resolution A formal expression of the opinion or will of an official body of a public assembly, adopted by vote.*

Royalty A payment reserved by the grantor of a patent, lease of a mine, or similar right and payable proportionately to the use mode of the right by the grantee.*

Securities Evidences of obligations to pay money or of rights to participate in earnings and distribution of corporate, trust, and other property.

Securities and Exchange Acts to provide for the regulation of securities, exchanges, and over-the-counter markets operating in interstate and foreign commerce and through the mails and to prevent unfair practices covering same. The Securities Exchange Commission (SEC) is the federal agency that administers these acts.

Shares A part or indefinite portion of a thing owned by a number of persons in common that contemplates something owned in common by two or more persons and has reference to that part of the undivided interest that belongs to some one of them. A definite portion of the capital of a company.*

Shareholder *See* Stockholder.

Sherman Act or Sherman Antitrust Act An act to protect trade and commerce against unlawful restraints or monopolies.

Stock (corporate) Stock is distinguished from bonds and ordinarily from debentures in that it gives right of ownership in a part of the assets of a corporation and the right to interest in any surplus after payment of debts.* Stock is the capital of a corporation, usually divided into equal shares.

Stockholder A person who owns shares of stock in a corporation.*

Taxable year Annual accounting period of a taxpayer.*

Trademark A distinctive mark, motto, device, or emblem that a manufacturer stamps, prints or otherwise affixes to the goods it produces, so that they may be identified in the market and their origin be vouched for.*

Truth in Lending Act A federal act that ensures that every person needing consumer credit is provided full disclosure of finance charges, including disclosure in the advertisement of credit transactions; amended in 1970 to regulate issuance, holder's liability, and the fraudulent use of credit cards.

Usury An illegal contract for a loan or forbearance of money, goods, or things in action, by which illegal interest is reserved, agreed to be reserved, or taken.*

Worker's compensation The name commonly used to designate the method and means created by statutes for giving greater protection and security to workers and their dependents against injury and death occurring in the course of employment.

Litigation Terms

Abatement A reduction, decrease, or diminution; the suspension or cessation, in whole or in part, of a continuing charge, such as rent.

Abstract of record A complete history in short, abbreviated form of the case as found in the record, complete enough to show that the questions presented for review have been properly reserved.

Accident report (auto) A report filed with the designated authorities by the operators of motor vehicles involved in an accident that sets forth the names of the parties and the circumstances surrounding the accident.

Affidavit A statement in writing sworn or affirmed to before an official, usually a notary public, who has the authority to administer an oath or affirmation.

Affirmative defense A new matter constituting a defense to the complaint, which is not merely a denial of facts asserted by the plaintiff. The defendant generally has the burden of proving any affirmative defenses.

Alienation of affection The robbing of husband or wife of the conjugal affection, society, fellowship, and comfort that inheres in the normal marriage relation. The deprivation of one spouse of the right to the aid, comfort, assistance, and the deprivation of consortium or society of the other spouse in family relationships.*

Allegation The assertion, claim, declaration, or statement of a party to an action, made in a pleading, setting out what he or she expects to prove.*

Allocution In criminal proceeding, the process during which the court allows the defendant to say a few words before sentencing.

Answer A pleading setting forth matters or facts as defense(s) to allegations made in a complaint.

Appeal The petition to a superior court of an injustice done or error committed by an inferior court, whose judgment or decision the superior court is called upon to correct or reverse. The removal of a cause from an inferior court to one of superior jurisdiction, for the purpose of obtaining a review of a decision in the lower court.*

Appellant A party who petitions a higher court for review of a decision made by a lower court.

Appellee The party against whom the appeal is taken.

Arbitrary Nonrational; not done or acting according to reason or judgment. Without fair, solid, and substantial cause; that is, without cause based upon the law.*

Arbitration The referring of a dispute to an impartial third person chosen by the parties to the dispute to adjudicate the dispute. An alternative method of dispute resolution as opposed to litigation.

ATLA American Trial Lawyers Association.

Attorney-client privilege *See* Privilege.

Attorney work-product privilege *See* Privilege.

Bail To procure the release of a person from legal custody, by undertaking that he or she shall appear at the time and place designated and submit him- or herself to the jurisdiction and judgment of the court.

Bifurcation Separation of issues at trial.

Burden of proof The necessity or duty of affirmatively proving a fact or facts in dispute on an issue raised between the parties in a cause. The degree of proof necessary for a judge or jury to render a verdict in a criminal prosecution or civil lawsuit. In criminal matters, the burden of proof standard is "beyond a reasonable doubt." In civil cases, the standard is usually "a preponderance of the evidence," although in some cases the civil standard may be raised to a higher level of proof, which is "to a reasonable degree of certainty." Both civil standards are less stringent than that required for a criminal conviction.

Cause of action The grounds, or legal theory, on which a lawsuit may be brought.

Certified shorthand reporter A shorthand reporter tested and approved as to speed and accuracy by the court and empowered to administer oaths and record sworn testimony.

Circumstantial evidence Evidence of facts or circumstances from which the existence or nonexistence of a fact in issue may be inferred. The proof of various facts or circumstances that usually attend the main fact in dispute and therefore tend to prove its existence or to sustain, by their consistency, the hypotheses claimed.*

Civil action Action brought to enforce, redress, or protect private rights.

Class action An action brought on behalf of other persons similarly situated.* This refers to persons in the same situation; for example, all persons given false information about a particular product by the manufacturer.

Codes A collection of laws; a system of law promulgated by legislative authority.

Competent Duly qualified; answering all requirements; having sufficient ability or authority. Legally fit.*

Complaint The first pleading in a lawsuit, also known as a "declaration," "petition," or "bill of complaint" in some jurisdictions. Its purpose is to notify the court and the defendant of all material facts, as well as the legal basis (cause of action), on which a plaintiff relies to support a demand for remedy or relief.*

Conciliation The formality of bringing the parties of a case before a judge who attempts to reconcile the parties. Common in domestic relations matters.

Condemnation The process by which property of a private owner is taken for public use through the power of eminent domain.

Contempt (of court) Any act that is calculated to embarrass, hinder, or obstruct the court in its administration of justice or that is calculated to lessen its authority or its dignity.

Contingent fee An arrangement between attorney and client whereby the attorney agrees to represent the client with compensation to be a percentage of the recovered amount.

Conviction In a general sense, the result of a criminal trial that ends in a judgment or verdict that the accused is guilty as charged.*

Cost Expenses awarded by a court to the prevailing party.

Court reporter *See* Certified shorthand reporter.

Counterclaim The defendant's claim against the plaintiff usually set forth in the defendant's answer to the complaint.

Crime A positive or negative act in violation of penal law; an offense against the state or the United States.*

Cross-claim The claim by a party to a lawsuit against a co-party that arises out of the transaction that is the subject of the lawsuit or of a counterclaim to the original action (such as one defendant's claim against another).

Cross-examination The examination of a witness during a trial, hearing, or the taking of a deposition by the party opposed to the one who produced the witness concerning the evidence (or testimony) given by the witness during the case in chief, to test its truth, to further develop it, or for other purposes.*

Damages A pecuniary compensation or indemnity, which may be recovered in the courts by any person who has suffered loss, detriment, or injury, whether to his or her person, property, or rights, through the unlawful act or omission or negligence of another.* The most common damages requested are: (1) general, which are to compensate the injured party for the injury sustained; (2) punitive or exemplary, which are to "punish" the liable party by awarding to the injured party additional sums, over and above the general damage amount, where the wrongful tort was aggravated by circumstances of violence, malice, fraud, and so forth; and (3) special, such as wage loss and medical expenses.

Declaratory judgment One that simply declares the rights of the parties or expresses the opinion of the court on a question of law, without ordering anything to be done.

Decree A sentence or order of the court, pronounced on hearing and understanding all the points in issue and determining the rights of all the parties to the suit, according to equity and good conscience.*

Defamation Holding up of a person to ridicule, scorn, or contempt in a respectable and considerable part of the community; may be criminal as well as civil; includes both libel and slander.

Default judgment A judgment for the plaintiff where the defendant has failed to appear or file an answer in a timely manner.

Deposition A written record of the oral testimony of a witness under oath, in the form of questions and answers made before a public officer for use in a lawsuit.

Directed verdict Procedure whereby a judge directs that a jury reach a certain determination in cases where the evidence is such that a reasonable person could not disagree.

Discovery The ascertainment of that which was previously unknown; the disclosure or coming to light of what was previously hidden. The phase in a lawsuit when parties may use formal methods provided by court rule or statute to obtain information from other parties to a lawsuit or from nonparties.

Dismiss without prejudice Dismissal of a case allowing a party to refile the same cause of action.

Domicile That place where a person has his or her true, fixed, and permanent home and principal establishment and to which whenever he or she is absent, he or she has the intention of returning.* Domicile is not synonymous with residence, the difference being one of intention. A person may have more than one residence, but not more than one domicile.

Due process The fundamental procedural rights which must be followed by court, agency or other entity prior to depriving an individual of life, liberty, or property. It is a protection granted by the Fifth and Fourteenth Amendments to the U.S. Constitution.

Enlargement Applies to the extension of time in legal proceedings.

Estoppel A bar or impediment at law that prevents one from alleging or denying a fact.

Evidence Relevant information presented in accord with applicable evidence rules for the purpose of aiding the "trier of fact" in making a determination of the truth of facts at issue. Includes testimony of witnesses, documents, objects, and admissions of parties.

Exhibit A paper, object, or document produced and exhibited to a court during a trial or hearing, to a commissioner taking depositions, or to auditors, arbitrators, or others as a voucher, or in proof of facts, or as otherwise connected with the subject matter which, on being accepted, is marked for identification and annexed to the deposition, report, or other principal document, filed of record, or otherwise made a part of the case.*

Felony A crime of a graver or more atrocious nature than those designated as misdemeanors.* Generally, an offense punishable by death or imprisonment for a term of greater than one year.

Filiation Judicial determination of paternity. The relation of the child to the father.

Filiation proceeding A special statutory proceeding, criminal in form but in the nature of a civil action, to enforce a civil obligation or duty specifically for the purpose of establishing parentage and the putative father's duty to support his illegitimate child.*

Fraud A false representation of a matter of fact, whether by words or by conduct, by false or misleading allegations, or by concealment of that which should have been disclosed, which deceives and is intended to deceive another so that he or she shall act upon it to his or her legal injury.*

Garnishment A statutory proceeding whereby a person's property, money, or credits in the possession or under the control of or owing by another are applied to payment of the former's debt to a third person by proper statutory process against the debtor and garnishee.*

Guardian A person lawfully invested with the power and charged with the duty of taking care of the person and managing the property and rights of another person who, for defect of age, understanding, or self-control, is considered incapable of administering his or her own affairs.*

Guardian ad litem A guardian appointed by the court to represent an individual during the pendency of a lawsuit.

Hearsay Evidence not proceeding from the personal knowledge of the witness but from the mere repetition of what he or she has heard others say.* Secondhand evidence, as distinguished from original evidence.

Hypothetical question A combination of assumed or proved facts and circumstances stated in such form as to constitute a coherent and specific situation or set of facts upon which the opinion of an expert is asked, by way of evidence on a trial.*

Impeachment The adducing of proof that a witness is unworthy of belief.*

Impleader A procedure by which a new party is brought into an action on the ground that the new party is or may be liable to the party who brings him or her in for all or part of the subject matter of the claim.

Indictment An accusation in writing found and presented by a grand jury, legally invoked and sworn, to the court in which it is impaneled, charging that a person therein named has done some act or been guilty of some omission that by law is a public offense, punishable on indictment.*

Inference A truth or proposition drawn from another that is supposed or admitted to be true. A process of reasoning by which a fact or proposition sought to be established is deduced as a logical consequence from other facts or a state of facts already proved or admitted.*

Information An accusation exhibited against a person for some criminal offense, without an indictment. A written accusation made by a public prosecutor, without intervention of a grand jury.*

Injunction A prohibitive writ issued by a court of equity forbidding the defendant to do some act or to permit his or her servants or agents to do some act that he is threatening or attempting to commit.

Intent Generally the same as *mens rea*. The state of mind of an individual at the time of the alleged offense.

Interpleader A procedure by which persons having claims against another person may be joined as parties to a suit and required to set up claims, if their claims are such that the person initiating such procedure is or may be exposed to multiple liability.

Interrogatories A set or series of written questions used in the judicial examination of a party or a witness.

Intervention The procedure by which a third person, not originally a party to the suit but claiming an interest in the subject matter, comes into the case in order to protect his or her right or interpose his or her claim.*

Joinder Uniting with another person or party in some legal step or procedure.

Judgment The official and authentic decision of a court of justice upon the respective rights and claims of the parties to an action or suit therein litigated and submitted to its determination.*

Jurisdiction The authority or power of a court to decide or deal with the subject matter of an issue.

Jury A certain number of citizens selected according to law and sworn to inquire of certain matters of fact and declare the truth upon evidence to be presented before them.

    Grand Jury Considers whether the evidence presented by the state against a person accused of a crime warrants his or her indictment.

    Petit jury The ordinary jury for the trial of a civil or criminal action. So called to distinguish it from the grand jury.

Jury panel The assembly of citizens called to court where a group will be selected for a given jury. More than one jury can be filled from one panel.

Laches An omission to assert a right for an unreasonable and unexplained length of time under circumstances prejudicial to the adverse party.

Leading question One that instructs a witness how to answer or puts into his or her mouth words to be echoed back. Questions are leading that suggest to the witness the answer desired.

Libel Almost any written language, picture, or sign that upon its face has a natural tendency to injure a person's reputation, either generally or with respect to his or occupation, and is published to a third party and is not privileged or permitted and is not true.

Litigation Contest in court of law for the purposes of enforcing a right.*

Malice The intentional doing of a wrongful act without just cause or excuse with an intent to inflict an injury or under circumstances that the law will imply an evil attempt.*

Malpractice Any professional misconduct, unreasonable lack of skill or fidelity in professional or fiduciary duties, evil practice, or illegal or immoral conduct.*

Mediation An informal, nonbinding process wherein an impartial third party assists the parties to a dispute in a direct negotiation to resolve the dispute. An alternative form of dispute resolution as opposed to litigation in the court system.

Misdemeanor Offenses lower than felonies and generally punishable by fine or imprisonment otherwise than in the penitentiary.* Defined by local, state, and federal code and statute.

Mistrial An erroneous, invalid, or nugatory trial; a trial of an action that cannot stand in law because of want of jurisdiction, a wrong drawing of jurors, or disregard of some other fundamental requisite before or during trial.*

Mitigation Alleviation, reduction, abatement, or diminution of a penalty or punishment imposed by law.* Actions taken by an injured party to reduce the amount of damage being suffered.

Motion An application for a rule or order made to a court or a judge for the purpose of obtaining some act to be done in favor of the applicant or moving party.

Motive Cause or reason that moves the will and induces action. An inducement or that which leads or tempts the mind to indulge in a criminal act.*

Negligence The omission to do something that a reasonable person, guided by those ordinary considerations that ordinarily regulate human affairs, would do or the doing of something that a reasonable and prudent person would not do.*

Oath An affirmation of truth of a statement, which renders one willfully asserting untrue statements punishable for perjury.*

Opinion The statement by a judge or court of the decision reached in regard to a cause tried or argued before them, expounding the law as applied to the case and detailing the reasons upon which the judgment is based.*

Order Direction of a court or judge made or entered in writing and not included in a judgment. An application for an order is a motion.*

Paralegal *See* Legal assistant.

Parol evidence Oral or verbal evidence; that which is given by word of mouth; the ordinary kind of evidence, given by witnesses in court.*

Parole A conditional release; the condition being that, if the prisoner observes the conditions provided in the parole order, he or she will receive an absolute discharge from the balance of sentence, but if he or she does not, he or she will be returned to serve the unexpired term.

Paternity The state or condition of a father; the relationship of a father.*

Paternity proceeding *See* Filiation proceeding.

Peremptory challenge The right to challenge a juror without assigning a reason for the challenge.*

Perjury The willful assertion as to a matter of fact, opinion, belief, or knowledge made by a witness in a judicial proceeding as part of his or her evidence, either upon oath or in any form evidence given in open court, in an affidavit, or otherwise, such assertion being material to the issue or point of inquiry and known to such witness to be false.*

Personal injury A hurt or wrong to the physical body or reputation of a person or both.

Personal property (personalty) Rights or interests a person has in things movable; for example, an automobile or furniture.

Plea A pleading; more particularly, the first pleading on the part of the defendant.*

Pleadings The formal allegations by the parties of their respective claims and defenses.*

Preponderance of evidence Greater weight of evidence or evidence that is more credible and convincing to the mind. That which best accords with reason and probability.

Pretrial conference or hearing A meeting of the judge and counsel for the parties preliminary to the trial of a lawsuit.

Presumption An assumption that the law expressly directs to be made from particular facts.

Probable cause A reasonable ground for belief in the existence of facts warranting the proceedings complained of.

Privilege An immunity which exists under law, and which may constitute a defense to a tort (such as self-defense as a counter to a charge of battery); protected relationships existing under law or statute, such as attorney-client, husband-wife, or doctor-patient. The assertion of a privilege under the work product rule to protect or prevent disclosure of confidential information, such as notes, working papers, memoranda, or similar materials, prepared by an attorney [or a legal assistant acting under the direction of an attorney] in anticipation of litigation or for trial. The work product rule has been interpreted to include private memoranda, written statements of witnesses, and mental impressions of personal recollections prepared or formed by an attorney in anticipation of litigation or for trial.

Probation Allowing a person convicted of some lesser offense to avoid imprisonment under a suspension of sentence, during good behavior, and generally under the supervision of a probation officer.*

Recidivist A habitual criminal.

Recission of contract Annulling or abrogation or unmaking of a contract and the placing of the parties to it in *status quo.*

Record A written account of some acts, court proceedings, transaction, or instrument drawn up, under authority of law, by a proper officer and designed to remain as a memorial or permanent evidence of the matters to which it relates.*

Relevancy The tendency of the evidence to establish a proposition that the evidence is offered to prove.

Replevin Redelivery to the owner of the pledge or thing taken in distress. A local action to be brought where property is taken or where property is detained, unless statute regulates the matter.

Rules of court Rules established by a court for the regulating of conduct of business of the court; for example, rules of civil procedure, criminal procedure, and appellate procedure.

Sequester To separate or isolate; for example, to sequester a jury by requiring it to stay apart from society until a trial is concluded and a verdict returned.

Settlement An agreement by which parties having disputed matters between them reach or ascertain what is coming from one to the other.*

Slander The speaking of base and defamatory words tending to prejudice another in his or her reputation, office, trade, business, or means of livelihood.*

Statutes *See* Codes.

Statute of limitations A statute prescribing limitations to the right of action on certain described causes of action or criminal prosecutions; that is, declaring that no suit shall be maintained on such causes of action nor any criminal charge made unless brought within a specified period after the right accrued.*

Stipulation The name given to any agreement made by the attorneys engaged on opposite sides of a cause (especially if in writing) regulating any matter incidental to the proceedings or trial, which falls within their jurisdiction*; for example, agreements to extend the time for pleading or to take depositions.

Subpoena A command to appear at a certain time and place to give testimony upon a certain matter.

Subpoena *duces tecum* In addition to being a subpoena to appear, it requires a person to produce books, papers, documents, and other materials.

Subrogation The substitution of one person in the place of another with reference to a lawful claim, demand, or right, so that the one who is substituted succeeds to the rights of the other in relation to the debt or claim and its rights, remedies, or securities.*

Summons A writ or process directed to the sheriff or other proper officer, requiring him or her to notify the person named that an action has been commenced against that person and that he or she is required to appear, on the day named, and answer the complaint in such action.*

Transcript of record The printed record as made up in each case for appeal to a superior court.

Venue The neighborhood, place, or county in which a particular lawsuit should be tried.

Verification A sworn statement confirming that the allegations in the pleadings are authentic, correct, or true.

Witness fees Fees for mileage and appearance in court or at a deposition that are paid to a witness and often prescribed by law.

Workers' compensation A procedure created by statutes that provides for fixed awards to employees or their dependents in case of employment-related accidents and diseases, dispensing with the proof negligence and legal actions.*

Work-product privilege *See* Privilege.

Real Estate Terms

Abatement The suspension or cessation of a continuing charge; for example, rent.

Abstract of title A condensed history or summary of public records relating to the title to a particular parcel of land.

Access A right vested in the owner of land to enter and leave a tract of land from a road or other highway without obstruction; the right to enter and leave over lands of another.

Acceleration clause (in a mortgage) Specifies conditions under which the lender may advance the time when the entire debt that is secured by the mortgage becomes due.

Accretion A gradual and imperceptible accumulation of land by natural causes, as out of the sea or a river.

Acre A tract of land containing 43,560 square feet of land; that is, 208.71 feet square.

Adverse possession Physical possession of land inconsistent with the right of the owner. In most states, a party in adverse possession, after satisfying fully the requirements of the relevant statutes, thereby acquires the title to the land. Usually requires: actual possession, adverse, under claim of right, notorious, open, exclusive, hostile, continuous, and uninterrupted.

Air rights The right to use all or a portion of the space above a designated tract of land.

ALTA American Land Title Association, a national association of title insurance companies and title abstract organizations. This term is used most frequently as part of the identification of standard policy forms adopted by that association.

Amortize To reduce debt by means of regular periodic payments, including amounts applicable both to principal and interest.

Appurtenances Things deemed to be incidental to the land when they are by right used with the land for its benefit.

Assessed valuation The valuation placed upon land for purposes of taxation; however, valuation does not necessarily represent the market value of the property.

Assessment A special tax levied upon property for the purpose of paying for improvements (sewer lines, sidewalks, street paving, and so on) benefitting the land.

Assessor A public official who evaluates property for the purpose of taxation.

Assignment A transfer or making over to another of the whole of any property, real or personal.* Used often in transferring interests of a mortgagee or of a lessee.

Assignee One to whom an assignment or transfer of interest is made; for example, the assignee of a mortgage or contract.

Assignor One who makes an assignment; for example, the assignor of a mortgage or contract.

Assumption of mortgage An obligation undertaken by the purchaser of land to be personally liable for payment of an existing note secured by a mortgage. As between the lender and the original borrower, the original borrower remains liable on the mortgage note.

Attachment Legal seizure of property to force payment of a debt.

Attorney in fact One who holds a power of attorney from another allowing him or her to act in the other's place and stead and to execute legal documents such as deeds and mortgages.

Base title or basic title Title to an area or tract out of which parts are subsequently conveyed or from which a subdivision or development is made. Thus, the title to farm acreage that has been subdivided would be the base title to the entire subdivision.

Beneficiary (of a trust) A person designated to receive some benefit from the trust estate.

Binder or commitment An enforceable agreement that, upon satisfaction of the requirements stated in the binder, the insurer will issue the specified title insurance policy subject only to the requirements being met prior to closing and exceptions stated in the binder. A binder sets forth status of title as of a particular date.

Bond (1) An insurance agreement under which one party becomes surety to pay, within stated limits, financial loss caused to another by specified acts or defaults of a third party. (2) An interest bearing security evidencing a long-term debt, issued by a government or corporation and sometimes secured by a lien on property.

Building (restriction) line or setback A line fixed at a certain distance from the front and/or sides of a lot or at a certain distance from a road or street that marks the boundary of the area within which no part of any building may project. This line may be established by a filed plat of subdivision, by restrictive covenants in deeds or leases, by building codes, or by zoning ordinances.

Bureau of Land Management A branch of the U.S. Department of the Interior charged with the surveying and management of natural resource lands and their resources.

Chain and links Units of length in the measurement of land. A chain is a land measurement being 66 feet in length; a link is a land measurement being 1/100th of a chain or 66/100th of a foot. *Caveat:* Modern surveyors use a steel tape 100 feet long in manual measurement, and it commonly is called a chain.

Chain of title A term applied to the past series of transactions and documents affecting the title to a particular parcel of land.

Clear title One which is not encumbered or burdened with defects.

Closing (1) A process by which all the parties to a real estate transaction conclude the details of a sale or mortgage. The process includes the signing and transfer of documents and the distribution of funds. (2) A condition in the description of real property by courses and distances at the boundary lines where the lines meet to include all the tract of land.

Closing costs Miscellaneous expenses involved in closing a real estate transaction, over and above the price of the land; for example, pro rate of taxes, insurance, or recording fees.

Cloud on title An outstanding claim or encumbrance that adversely affects the marketability of title.

Collateral Marketable real or personal property that a borrower pledges as security for a loan. In mortgage transactions, specific land is the collateral.

Commitment *See* Binder.

Community property A category of property existing in some states in which all property (except property specifically acquired by husband or wife as separate property) acquired by a husband and wife or either during marriage is owned in common by the husband and wife.

Condemnation The process by which property of a private owner is taken for a public use, without his or her consent but upon the award and payment of just compensation, being in the nature of a forced sale and condemner stands toward owner as buyer toward seller.

Condition precedent A specified event that must occur before all or part of a contract or document takes effect.

Conditions and restrictions A common term used to designate the uses to which land may not be put and providing penalties for failure to comply. Commonly used by land subdividers on newly subdivided areas.

Condominium A system of individual fee ownership of units in a multi-unit project, combined with joint ownership of common areas of the structure and land.

Construction loan A loan made to finance the actual construction or improvement on land; disbursements may be made in increments as the construction progresses.

Contract of sale An agreement to sell and purchase under which title is withheld from the purchaser until such time as the required payments to the seller have been completed.

Conventional loan A contract between a lender and a borrower without government loan guaranty or regulation.

Convey An act of deeding or transferring title to another.

Conveyance A document that transfers an interest in real property from one person to another; for example, a deed.

Cooperative A residential multi-unit building owned by a corporation and in which tenancy in a unit is obtained by purchase of the pertinent number of shares of the stock of the corporation and where the owner of such shares is entitled to occupy a specific unit in the building.

Cotenancy Ownership of the same interest in a particular parcel of land by more than one person.

Covenant An agreement between the parties in a deed whereby one party promises either (1) the performance or nonperformance of certain acts with respect to the land, or (2) that a given state of thing with respect to the land is so; for example, a covenant that the land will be used only for residential purposes.

Cul de sac A blind alley; a street open at one end only.* Usually laid out by modern engineers to provide a circular turnaround for vehicles.

Curtesy A husband's life estate in the property of his deceased wife. By statute in most states, it is a life estate in one-third of the land she owned during their marriage. Curtesy has been abolished by statute in some states.

Deed A written document by which the ownership of land is transferred from one person to another.

Deed of trust A conveyance of a land title by a maker of a note (the debtor) to a third party, a trustee, as collateral security for the payment of the note, with the condition that the trustee shall reconvey the title to the debtor upon payment of the note, and with power in the trustee to sell the land and pay the note in the event of a default on the part of the debtor. Also called a trust deed.

Default Failure to perform a contractual obligation in a timely manner.

Deficiency judgment A judgment against a person liable for the debt secured by a mortgage in an amount by which the funds derived from a foreclosure or trustee's sale are less than the amount due on the debt.

Delivery The final and absolute transfer of a deed from seller to buyer in such a manner that it cannot be recalled by the seller.

Demised premises Property or a portion thereof that is leased to a tenant.

Devise A gift of land by will or to give land by will.

Devisee The person to whom property is given by a will.

Dower A wife's life estate in the property of her deceased husband. The reverse of curtesy.

Draw Disbursement of a portion of the mortgage loan. Usually applies to construction loans when partial advances are made as improvements to the property progress.

Earnest money Advance payment of part of the purchase price to bind a contract for property.

Easement A right of use over the property of another.

Egress The right to leave a tract of land. Many times used interchangeable with access. *See* Access.

Eminent domain The right of a government to appropriate private property for a public use by making reasonable payment to the owner of such property.

Encroachment An improvement, such as a house, driveway, wall, or fence, that illegally intrudes upon another's property.

Encumbrance Any right or interest in land held by persons other than the fee owner which right or interest lessens the value of the fee title; for example, judgment liens, easements, mortgages, and restrictions.

Endorsement Form issued by the insurer at the request of the insured that changes terms or items in an issued policy or commitment.

Equity (1) The interest or value that an owner has in real estate over and above the debts against. (2) A type of court of record.

Erosion Wearing away of real property by the action of water, wind, or other elements.

Escheat A reversion of property to the state in those cases where an individual dies without heirs and without a will.

Escrow Money, securities, documents, or other property deposited with a third disinterested party who completes the transaction in accordance with the instructions of the parties.

Estate (1) The degree, quantity, nature, and extent of interest that a person has in real and personal property. (2) The property comprising the assets of a decedent.

Exceptions (1) Those matters affecting title to the particular parcel of realty which matters are excluded from coverage of the particular title insurance policy. (2) In legal descriptions, that portion of lands to be deleted or excluded.

Exclusion Those general matters affecting title to real property excluded from coverage of a title insurance policy.

FNMA, Federal National Mortgage Association (Fannie Mae) A federally sponsored private corporation that provides a secondary market for housing mortgages.

Fee simple An estate in which the owner is entitled to the entire property, with unconditional power of disposition during his or her life, descending to his or her heirs upon death, intestate.

FHA, Federal Housing Administration An agency of the federal government, that insures private loans for new and existing housing and for home repairs under government-approved programs.

FHLMC, Federal Home Loan Mortgage Corporation (Freddie Mac) An affiliate of the Federal Home Loan Bank, which creates a secondary market in conventional residential loans and in FHA and VA loans by purchasing mortgages from members of the Federal Reserve System and the Federal Home Loan Bank System.

Financing statement Under the Uniform Commercial Code, used to create a public record that there is a security interest or claim to secure a dept on personal property; filed with the secretary of state or the county recorder.

Fixtures Any item of personal property so attached to real property that it becomes a part of the real property.

Foreclosure Legal process by which a mortgagor of real property is deprived of his or her interest in that property due to failure to comply with terms and conditions of the mortgage.

General warranty deed *See* Warranty deed.

GI or VA loan A loan for purchase of land in which the Veteran's Administration guarantees the lender payment of a home mortgage granted a qualified veteran.

GNMA, Government National Mortgage Association (Ginnie Mae) A government corporation that provides a secondary market for housing mortgages and special assistance to mortgagee financing housing under special FHA mortgage insurance programs.

Grantee A person who acquires an interest in land by deed, grant, or other written instrument.

Grantor A person who, by a written instrument, transfers to another an interest in land.

Guaranty policy A title insurance policy that insures only against defects of title appearing in the public records. Other policies insure against defects whether or not they appear in public records.

Habendum The "to have and to hold" section of a deed.

Heir The person who, at the death of the owner of land, is entitled to the land if the owner died intestate.

Heirs and assigns Terminology used in deeds and wills to provide that the recipient receives a "fee simple estate" in lands rather than a lesser interest.

Homestead, declaration of A recorded document whose primary importance to the homeowner is protection against the forced sale of property in satisfaction of certain debts.

Improvements Additions to raw lands tending to increase value, such as buildings, streets, and sewers.

Inchoate interest An interest in real estate that is not a present interest but may ripen into a vested estate, if not barred, extinguished, or divested.*

Indemnity agreement An agreement by the maker of the document to repay the addressee of the agreement up to the limit stated for any loss due to the contingency stated on the agreement.

Ingress The right to enter a tract of land. Many times used interchangeably with access. *See* Access.

Insurable title A land title that a title insurance company is willing to insure.

Joint protection policy A title insurance policy in a form suitable to insure the owner and/or lender.

Joint tenancy Where two or more persons hold real estate jointly for life, the survivors to take the interest of the one who dies.

Judgment A court's final determination of the rights of the parties in an action.

Judgment lien A statutory lien created by recording an abstract or certified copy of a money judgment.

Junior mortgage A mortgage, the lien of which is subordinate to that of another mortgage; for example, a second mortgage.

Lease A grant of the use of land for a term of years in consideration of the payment of a monthly or annual rental.

Leasehold An estate in realty held under a lease; an estate for a fixed term of years.*

Lessee One who takes lands upon a lease.

Lessor One who grants lands under a lease.

Lien A claim or charge on property of another for payment of some debt, obligation, or duty; for example, mortgage liens, judgment liens, and mechanics' liens.

Lien waiver or waiver of liens A document signed by the general contractor, each subcontractor, and each materialman of a construction project whereby the signators waive their right to mechanics' liens on the land involved in that particular project.

Life estate A grant or reservation of the right of use, occupancy, and ownership for the life of an individual.

Links *See* Chains and links.

Lis pendens A legal notice that there is litigation pending relating to the land, the outcome of which could affect the title to specified real property.

Loan policy, mortgage policy, or mortgagee's policy A title insurance policy in which the insurer insures the mortgagee against loss it may suffer because the title is not vested as stated in the policy and insures the validity and priority of the mortgage lien over any other lien not excepted to in the policy.

Lot A measured parcel of land having fixed boundaries.

Marketable title Such title as is free from reasonable doubt in law and fact.

Mechanic's lien and materialmen's lien The lien that by statute, a laborer or materialman may have against the land by reason of furnishing labor or material for the improvement of the property. The priority of such lien varies among the states; in some states mechanic's and materialmen's liens take priority over prerecorded mortgages.

Metes and bounds A description of a parcel of land by boundary lines in length and direction from point to point, circumscribing the parcel.

Mineral right An interest in minerals in land. A right to take minerals or a right to receive a royalty.*

Mortgage An instrument granting an interest in real property as security for payment of a note or performance of some other obligation.

Mortgage policy *See* Loan policy.

Mortgagor The person who borrows the money from the mortgagee and signs the mortgage as security.

Notary public An official authorized by law to administer oaths; to attest by his or her hand and official seal; and to identity persons executing documents.

Note A written promise to pay a certain amount of money at a certain time or in a certain number of installments. It usually provides for payment of interest, and its payment is at times secured by a mortgage.

Open-end mortgage A mortgage or deed of trust providing for future advances on the given mortgage and increases the amount of the existing mortgage.

Option The right, acquired for a consideration, to buy, sell, or lease property at a fixed price within a specified time.

Ownership The right to possess and use property to the exclusion of others.

Owner's policy A title insurance policy insuring the owner against loss due to any defect of title not excepted to, or excluded from, the policy.

Personal property Any property that is not real property.

Plat (of survey) A map of land made by a surveyor showing boundary lines, buildings, and other improvements on the land.

Points Charge imposed by a lender in consideration for making a loan secured by real property. A point equals one percent of the loan.

Power of attorney An instrument in writing by which one person, the principal, authorizes another, the attorney-in-fact, to act in his or her stead regarding the specific actions described in the instrument.

Prepayment penalty Penalty to the mortgagor for payment of the mortgage debt before it becomes due.

Prescription The doctrine by which a particular easement is acquired by long, continuous, and exclusive use and possession of property. *See* Adverse possession.

Public records Records that under the recording laws impart constructive notice of matters relating to land.

Quiet title The removal of a cloud on title by proper action in a court.

Quitclaim A deed that transfers whatever interest the maker may have in a particular parcel of land, containing no warranties as to title.

Reconveyance A document evidencing the extinguishment of the lien of the deed of trust; may be full or partial.

Redemption The right of the owner in some states to reclaim title to his or her property if he or she pays the debt to the mortgagee within a stipulated time after foreclosure.

Regress To return, go back, or reenter.

Release A deed from a mortgagee or trustee of a deed of trust that releases specific property from the lien of the mortgage or deed of trust.

Remainder An interest or estate in land in a person other than the grantor in which the right of possession and enjoyment of the land is postponed until the termination of some other interest or estate in that land.

Reserve Account The portion of funds included in a mortgage payment which are set aside for some specific purpose; e.g., insurance, taxes, etc.

Restriction or restrictive covenant Limitation imposed on a deed or lease respecting the use to which the property may be put; for example, building setback lines and limitations to residential uses.

Reversion Provision in conveyance by which, upon the happening of an event or contingency, title to the land will return to the grantor or his or her successor in interest in the land.

Riparian Pertaining to the banks of a watercourse. The owner of land adjacent to a watercourse is called a riparian owner, and the rights of the riparian owner related to that watercourse are called riparian rights.

Sale and leaseback A financial device that an owner of land may employ to raise money and still have the use of the land by selling the land to his or financier and immediately leasing it back for the period he or she wishes to use it.

Section or section of land A parcel of land comprising one square mile, or 640 acres.

Settlement *See* Closing (1).

Special warranty deed A deed containing a covenant whereby the seller agrees to protect the buyer against being dispossessed because of any diverse claims to the land by the seller or anyone claiming through him or her.

Standard coverage policy A form of title insurance that contains certain standard printed exceptions not included in the ALTA policies. This form of policy is used primarily in some of the western states.

Straw party Nominee; one who acts as an agent for another for the purpose of taking title to real property.

Subdivision A tract of land surveyed and divided into lots for purposes of sale.

Subordinate Placed in a lower order, class, or rank; occupying a lower position in a regular descending series;* the act of a creditor acknowledging in writing that the lien of debt due him or her from a debtor shall be inferior to the lien of the debt due another creditor from the same debtor.

Sub surface right Ownership of a right beneath the physical surface of the property.

Survey The process by which a parcel of land is measured and its contents ascertained; also a statement of the result of such survey, with the courses and distances and the quantity of the land.*

Take out loan A permanent mortgage loan that a lender agrees to make to a borrower upon completion of improvements on the borrower's land. The proceeds of the loan are used principally to pay off the construction loan.

Tax deed The deed given to a purchaser at a public sale of land for nonpayment of taxes. It conveys to the purchaser only such title as the defaulting taxpayer had and does not convey good title to that extent unless statutory procedures for the sale were strictly followed.

Tenancy by the entirety Created by a conveyance to husband and wife, whereupon each becomes seized and possessed of the entire estate and, after the death of one, the survivor takes the whole.

Tenant One who has right of possession of land by any kind of title. The word tenant used alone in modern times is used almost exclusively in the limited meaning of a tenant of a leasehold estate.

Tenancy in common An estate or interest in land held by two or more persons each having equal rights of possession and enjoyment but without any right of survivorship between the owners.

Title Evidence of a person's right or the extent of his or her interest in property.

Title defect Any legal right held by others to claim property or to make demands upon the owner.

Title insurance Insurance against loss or damage resulting from defects or failure of title to a particular parcel of real property; insures against past loss.

Title search An examination of public records, laws, and court decisions to determine the current ownership of and encumbrances on a parcel of land.

Torrens system A system of registering titles to lands that presumes an adjudication of title each time a deed or claim is filed.

VA loan *See* GI loan.

Vendee Purchaser of real or personal property.

Vendor The seller of real or personal property.

Vest To become owned by.

Waiver of liens *See* Lien waiver.

Warranty An agreement and assurance, binding upon the grantor of real property for the grantor and his or her heirs to the effect that he or she is the owner and will defend the title given.

Warranty deed Deed by which the seller implicitly or specifically agrees to protect the buyer against certain matters of title, usually including one or more of the following: lawful ownership of the property; rights of conveyance and quiet possession; freedom from all encumbrances; and warranty and defense of premises against all lawful claims.

Probate Terms

Abate To throw down, to beat down, destroy, quash.* To reduce a devise due to the insufficiency of property in the estate to pay all claims, expenses, and devises in full.

Ademption The act by which a testator in his or her lifetime pays his or her legatees a general legacy that, by will, he or she had proposed to give them at his or her death.

Administration of an estate The process of assembling a decedent's assets, paying debts, claims, and taxes and making distribution according to the will or the laws of succession.

Administrator An individual appointed by a court to settle the financial and legal affairs of a person who has died without a will. If the individual appointed is a woman, she is called an administratrix. In some states, this person is known under the general term of "personal representative."

Administrator *de bonis non* (Administrator d.b.n.) When the office of administrator becomes vacant for any reason, the court will appoint another person to complete the estate's administration. The new administrator is called the administrator *de bonis non,* which is an abbreviation of *de bonis non administratis,* meaning "of the goods not administered."

Administrator *cum testamento annexo* (CTA) An administrator of a decedent's estate appointed after the executor named in the will refused to act.* Since this person must distribute the estate under the terms of the will, rather than under the intestacy laws, he or she is called the administrator *cum testamento annexo,* meaning "with will annexed," to distinguish him or her from an administrator of an intestate estate.

Administratrix *See* Administrator.

Advancement That portion of an heir's inheritance given to him or her by the decedent during the decedent's lifetime.

Ancillary administration The administration of assets in the local state when the principal administration is in another state.

Annuitant A person who receives an annuity.

Annuity A yearly payment of money for life or years. A fixed sum, granted or bequeathed, payable periodically but not necessarily annually*.

Assets Property of all kinds, real and personal, owned by the decedent.

Attestation The act of witnessing the execution of a will or other document by signature.

Attesting witness A person witnessing to the genuineness of a will or other document.

Beneficiary One for whose benefit a trust is created; called a *cestui que trust* in Latin. A person having the enjoyment of property over which a trustee, executor, or other has the legal possession. The person to whom a policy of insurance is payable.*

Bequeath The act of making a bequest.

Bequest A gift by will of personal property; a legacy.* Distinguished from a devise that is a transfer of real property by will.

Codicil A supplement or an addition to a will; it may explain, modify, add to, subtract from, qualify, alter, restrain, or revoke provisions of a will.*

Death taxes Estate taxes and inheritance taxes.

Decedent A deceased person, especially one who has lately died.*

Devise A testamentary disposition of land or realty; a gift of real property by the last will and testament of the donor.* Distinguished from a bequest, which is a transfer of personal property by will.

Devisee The person to whom lands or other real property are devised or given by will.*

Distributee An heir; a person entitled to share in the distribution of an estate.

Domicile That place where a person has his or her true, fixed, and permanent home and principal establishment and to which whenever he or she is absent, he or she has the intention of returning.* Domicile is not synonymous with residence, the difference being one of intention. A person may have more than one residence but not more than one domicile.

Donee One to whom a gift is made or a bequest given or to whom a power of appointment is given.

Donor The party conferring a power. One who makes a gift.*

Duress Coercion that overcomes a person's free will.

Election Generally, the act of an heir choosing to take a statutory share of an estate in lieu of the share provided in a will.

Escheat A reversion of property to the state in those cases where an individual dies without heirs and without a will.

Estate (1) The property comprising the assets of a decedent. (2) The degree, quantity, nature, and extent of interest which a person has in land.

Estate plan An arrangement for the management and disposition of a person's property during his or her lifetime and at his or her death. Can be accomplished by a will, one or more trusts, gifts made during life, or a combination of these.

Estate tax An excise tax upon privilege of transferring or transmitting property by reason of death and is not a tax on property itself.*

Executor A person appointed by a testator to carry out the directions and requests in his or her will and to dispose of the property according to his or her testamentary provisions after his or her decease.* In some states, this person is known under the general term of "personal representative."

Expenses of administration All filing fees, costs of publication, compensation of personal representative and of his or her attorneys, and all other costs necessary to carry out the administration of a decedent's estate.

Fiduciary Any person who handles property or transacts business for the benefit of another person in a relationship of special trust.

Gift A voluntary transfer of personal property without consideration. Essential requisites of a gift are capacity of donor, intention of donor to make gift, completed delivery to or for donee, and acceptance of gift by donee.*

Gift *inter vivos* A gift between living parties and not in contemplation of death by the giver.

Gift tax The tax on a gift from one to another. A graduated tax levied by the federal government and some states on gifts made during life.

Grantor The person by whom a grant is made.*

Gross estate The total value, for federal estate tax purposes, of all a person's property before deducting debts, administrations expenses, marital deduction, charitable deductions, and so on.

Guardian A person lawfully invested with the power and charged with the duty of taking care of the person and managing the property and rights of another person, who for some peculiarity of status, or defect of age, understanding, or self-control, is considered incapable of administering his or her own affairs.*

Heir One who inherits property, whether real or personal.*

Income The return in money from one's business, labor, or capital invested; gains, profits, or private revenue.*

Income tax A tax levied by the federal and some state and local governments on a person's income, wages, and profits.

Incompetent A person legally declared to be incapable of managing his or her affairs.

Inheritance An estate or property that a person has by descent, as heir to another or that he or she may transmit to another, as his or her heir.*

Inheritance tax A tax on the transfer of passing of estates or property by legacy, devise, or intestate succession.*

Intangible property Such property as has no intrinsic and marketable value; that is, stocks, bonds, goodwill, trademarks, and so forth.

***Inter vivos* trust** Between the living; from one living person to another.* A trust created during the grantor's lifetime.

Interested persons Heirs, devises, children, spouses, creditors, and any others having a property right or claim against the estate of a decedent that may be affected by the proceeding, including fiduciaries representing interested persons.

Intestate One who dies without leaving a valid will, or the circumstance of dying without leaving a valid will effectively disposing of an estate. Partial intestacy occurs when the will does not dispose of all the estate.

Intestate succession Succeeding to or receiving property from a decedent as an heir, by virtue of statute rather than by will.

Irrevocable trust A trust that cannot be revoked or terminated by the grantor.

Issue Descendants. All persons who have descended from a common ancestor.*

Legacy A disposition of personal property by will. Legacy and bequest are equivalent terms.*

Legatee The person to whom a legacy is given. However, the term may be used to denote those who take under a will without any distinction between realty and personalty.

Letters of administration A certificate issued by the court identifying the administrator of the estate of a person who died intestate.

Letters testamentary A certificate issued by the court identifying the executor of a decedent's estate, as named in the will.

Life insurance trust A trust created by agreement by a person during his or her lifetime whereby the trustee receives proceeds of insurance on the life of the creator of the trust, to be held and used as stated in the trust agreement.

Marital deduction A deduction for federal estate tax purposes measured generally by the value of property passing to the decedent's surviving spouse; under federal tax laws, the deduction is unlimited.

Minor An infant or person who is under the age of legal competence.* This age varies from 18 to 21, depending upon the state, and may even vary within a state, depending on the purpose.

Net estate The real and personal property of a decedent, except property used for the support of his or her surviving spouse and children and for the payment of expenses of administration, funeral expenses, claims, and taxes.

Net intestate estate Any part of the net estate of a decedent not effectively disposed of by his or her will.

Partial distribution A distribution of a part of the decedent's estate before administration of the estate is complete.

Per stirpes By roots or stocks; by representation. This term derived from the civil law and denotes a method of dividing an intestate estate where a class or group of distributees take the share that their deceased ancestor would have been entitled to, taking thus by their right of representing such ancestor and not as so many individuals.*

Personal representative A term used in some states to take the place of executor, administrator, administrator with will annexed, or administrator *de bonis non.*

Posthumous child One born after the father's death.

Pretermitted child A child of the testator born or adopted after the execution of the will who is neither provided for in the will nor in any way mentioned in the will and who survives the testator.

Probate The act or process of proving a will. A judicial act or determination of a court having competent jurisdiction establishing the validity of a will.*

Remainder An interest or estate in land in a person other than the grantor in which the right of possession and enjoyment of the land is postponed until the termination of some other interest or estate in that land.

Remainderman The person who is entitled to an estate after the previous estate has terminated.

Residuary estate (1) That which remains after debts and expenses and devises have been satisfied; or (2) all that has been legally disposed of by will by the residuary clause.

Reversion Provision in conveyance by which, upon the happening of an event or contingency, title to the land will return to the grantor or his or her successor in interest in the land. Reversion differs from remainder in that remainder does not come back to the grantor but goes to someone else.

Revoke To cancel or make ineffective a will or codicil.

Settlor One who creates a trust; also, one who furnishes the consideration for the creation of a trust, though in form, a trust is created by another.*

Special administrator A temporary representative appointed in an emergency situation to avoid loss, injury, or deterioration of decedent's property or to provide for disposition of decedent's remains.

Specific devise A devise of a specific thing or specified part of the estate of a testator that is so described as to be capable of identification; a gift of a part of the estate identified and differentiated from all other parts.

Surety A person or corporation executing the bond of a personal representative, thereby agreeing to make good any loss suffered by one interested in a decedent's estate by reason of the failure of the personal representative to carry out his or her duty.

Tangible property Property that has physical characteristics. It includes movable items such as jewelry, animals, furniture, and cash.

Testamentary disposition The act of disposing of property by will.

Testamentary trust A trust created by a will.

Testate Leaving a valid will at death.

Testator One who makes or has made a testament or will; one who dies leaving a will.*

Testatrix A woman who makes a will; a female testator.*

Trust A right of property, real or personal, held by one party for the benefit of another.

Trustee The person appointed, or required by law, to execute a trust; one in whom an estate, interest, or power is vested, under an express or implied agreement to administer or exercise it for the benefit or to the use of another.*

Trustor One who creates a trust. Also called settlor.*

Undue influence Improper influence to control the disposition of another's property.

Will A document that directs the disposition of the testator's property, executed in accordance with statutory requirements. The term includes codicils and a document that merely appoints a personal representative or merely revokes or revives a will.

Will contest A proceeding in probate court questioning the validity of a will or codicil.

Appendix

Appellate Brief of the National Association of Legal Assistants Submitted to the Court

Statement

The National Association of Legal Assistants, Inc. submits this brief *amicus curiae,* pursuant to Rule 36 of the Rules of the Supreme Court of the United States, in support of respondents.[1] This brief is submitted upon the written consent of petitioners and respondents.[2]

Interest of the Amicus Curiae

Legal assistants[3] are a distinguishable group of persons who assist attorneys in the delivery of legal services. Through formal education, training and experience, legal assistants have knowledge and expertise regarding the legal system and substantive and procedural law which qualify them to do work of a legal nature under the supervision of an attorney.

National Association of Legal Assistants, Inc., Model Standards and Guidelines of Utilization of Legal Assistants (1984).

The National Association of Legal Assistants, Inc. (NALA) was incorporated in 1975 as a nonprofit organization, in recognition of and in response to the burgeoning use of legal assistants in the delivery of legal services throughout the United States. Representing some 8,000 legal assistants through individual membership or affiliated associations, NALA seeks to promote professional development and continuing education for legal assistants, and to provide a strong national voice to represent this growing and significant profession.[4]

Consistent with these goals, NALA, in 1975, adopted a Code of Ethics and Professional Responsibility for legal assistants to serve as a guideline for the proper conduct by legal assistants in the performance of their duties (reprinted in full in the Appendix to this brief). In 1976, NALA administered the first national legal assistant certification examination, testing skills basic to the profession as well as substantive knowledge of law and procedure. Currently, the voluntary two-day examination program is administered three times yearly. As of July, 1988, 2,327 participants have earned the title CLA (Certified Legal Assistant).

In 1984, NALA adopted its Model Standards and Guidelines for Utilization of Legal Assistants to serve as a guide for legal assistants and supervising attorneys, by describing the role of a legal assistant in the delivery of legal services. Finally, NALA works hand-in-hand with local,

---

[1] The National Association of Legal Assistants, Inc., submitted this brief, in substantially the same form, as *amicus curiae* in support of petitioner, in the case *Blanchard v. Bergeron,* 831 F.2d 563 (5th Cir. 1987), *cert. granted,* 108 S.Ct. 2869 (June 27, 1988) (No. 87-1485), currently pending before the Court.

[2] The original of petitioners' written consent by Bruce Farmer, Esquire, counsel for petitioners, and the original of respondents' written consent by Jay Topkis, Esquire, counsel for respondents, are being filed with the Clerk of the Court under separate cover.

[3] The term "legal assistant" is preferred, as it represents those persons doing work of a legal nature under the direct supervision of an attorney, as opposed to a broader category of persons termed "paralegal," who perform work of a similar nature but not necessarily under the supervision of an attorney.

[4] Projections by the U.S. Department of Labor indicate an increase in the number of legal assistants from an estimated 53,000 in 1984 to 104,000 in 1995. U.S. Department of Labor, Bureau of Labor Statistics, *Occupational Outlook Quarterly* (Spring 1986).

state, and national bar associations to set standards for legal assistants, and provides continuing education for legal assistants through seminars, workshops, publications and videotapes.

The legal assistant is a recognized and desirable addition to the modern law office. The delegation of work, which would otherwise be performed by an attorney, to a skilled legal assistant reduces the cost of legal services to the client and increases attorney efficiency and productivity. The benefits of this cost-reducing, cost-effective delivery of legal services to the public through the attorney-supervised use of legal assistants will be promoted and encouraged if the work of legal assistants is recognized and compensated at the market rate as part of court-awarded attorney's fees.

Were the Court to reverse the ruling below by holding that the time spent by legal assistants in the successful prosecution of a civil rights case should not be compensated at the market rate, under 42 U.S.C. § 1988, the detrimental effect upon those seeking legal representation to redress civil rights violations, as well as in other types of cases in which Congress has provided for the recovery of attorney's fees, would be substantial. Such a result would either discourage attorneys from representing victims of civil rights violations, because they could not receive full compensation for their effort, or force attorneys to perform all tasks of a legal nature, thereby decreasing the utilization of legal assistants and increasing the cost of litigation.

Summary of Argument

The widespread use of legal assistants by attorneys to perform work of a legal nature which would otherwise have to be performed by an attorney at a much higher rate has significantly reduced the cost of legal services to the public and enhanced the quality of legal representation by promoting efficient utilization of attorney time. Compensation for the attorney-supervised work of legal assistants at an hourly rate less than that charged by attorneys, but high enough to cover the cost of overhead associated with the work of a legal assistant, is customarily included in attorney's fees charged private fee-paying clients.

A reasonable attorney's fee awarded pursuant to the Civil Rights Attorney's Fee Awards Act of 1976, 42 U.S.C. § 1988, should include market rate compensation for productive work of a legal nature performed by a skilled legal assistant, under the supervision of an attorney, in order to effectuate the purpose of Section 1988. Section 1988 was adopted by Congress to make available legal representation to victims of civil rights violations by fully compensating counsel for prevailing parties at a rate competitive with that charged in the private marketplace. An attorney's fee award which includes market rate compensation for the work of legal assistants is competitive with fees charged to traditional fee-paying clients, makes civil rights representation financially feasible for competent attorneys, promotes the cost-effective practice of utilizing legal assistants in the delivery of legal services, and is in accord with the goal of making available efficient and reasonably priced legal services, not only to victims of civil rights violations but also to the public at large.

Argument: The Work of Legal Assistants is Compensable at the Market Rate as Part of a Reasonable Attorney's Fee Award Pursuant to 42 U.S.C. § 1988.

> a. Compensating prevailing parties for the work performed by legal assistants on an hourly basis at the market rate comports with accepted practice in the private marketplace and is thus consistent with the purpose of 42 U.S.C. § 1988.

The Civil Rights Attorney's Fee Awards Act of 1976, 42 U.S.C. § 1988, provides that in federal civil rights actions, "the court, in its discretion, may allow the prevailing party, other than the

United States, a reasonable attorney's fee as part of the costs." On several occasions, the Court has visited the legislative history of Section 1988, finding that the purpose of the Fees Act was to provide a remedy necessary to obtain compliance with civil rights laws, and to promote respect for civil rights through effective citizen enforcement thereof. *Pennsylvania v. Delaware Valley Citizen's Counsel for Clean Air*, 478 U.S. 546, 561, 106 S.Ct. 3088, 3096 (1986) (*"Pennsylvania I"*); *Evans v. Jeff D.*, 475 U.S. 717, 731, 106 S.Ct. 1531, 1539 (1986). Unless the attorney's fee reimbursement pursuant to Section 1988 is " *full and complete'*, the statutory rights [created by civil rights legislation] would be meaningless because they would remain largely unenforced." *Pennsylvania v. Delaware Valley Citizens' Counsel for Clean Air*, 483 U.S. 711, 737, 107 S.Ct. 3078, 3093 (1987) (Blackmun, J., dissenting) (emphasis added), (*"Pennsylvania II"*).

Because most victims of civil rights violations are unable to afford legal representation, Congress found that the market itself would not provide adequate and effective access to the judicial process for vindication of rights violated. *Pennsylvania II*, 483 U.S. at 736–37, 107 S.Ct. at 3092 (Blackmun, J., dissenting); *City of Riverside v. Rivera*, 477 U.S. 561, 576, 106 S.Ct. 2686, 2695 (1986). Thus, to ensure that experienced competent attorneys would be willing to represent persons with legitimate civil rights grievances, Congress determined that it would be necessary to compensate lawyers for all time reasonably expended on a case, at a rate mirroring the prevailing market rate in the relevant community. *Pennsylvania II*, 483 U.S. at 742–44, 107 S.Ct. at 3095–96; *City of Riverside*, 477 U.S. at 578, 106 S.Ct. at 2696; *Evans*, 475 U.S. at 731, 106 S.Ct. at 1539; *Blum v. Stenson*, 465 U.S. 886, 895 (1984). Reasonable Section 1988 attorney's fees must be competitive with the private market for lawyers' services, *Pennsylvania II*, 483 U.S. at 736, 107 S.Ct. at 3092, 3093, 3095 (Blackmun J., dissenting), and "similar to what 'is traditional with attorneys compensated by a fee-paying client.' " *Id.* at 3093 (citation omitted). *See also City of Riverside*, 477 U.S. at 575, 106 S.Ct. at 2695.

Attorneys in the private marketplace traditionally charge fee-paying clients for supervised work of a legal nature performed by legal assistants at a lesser hourly rate than that charged by attorneys. Separate billing for the services of such nonlegal personnel as legal assistants and law students is an "increasingly widespread custom." *Ramos v. Lamm*, 713 F.2d 546, 558 (10th Cir. 1983).

> In the not so distant past the court would have frowned upon the practice of billing paraprofessional time separate from attorney time just as it might if a firm separately recorded and billed the hours spent by a secretary on a specific client . . . , but the standing of paraprofessionals has improved significantly as special training has enabled them to undertake a wide variety of more sophisticated tasks previously assigned exclusively to higher priced lawyers. The advent and widespread use of the paraprofessional has meant that the cost of effective legal counsel has been reduced and its availability enhanced without impairing the quality or delivery of legal services.

In re Chicken Antitrust Litigation, 560 F.Supp. 963, 977–78 (N.D.Ga. 1980) (citation omitted). *See also Parise v. Riccelli Haulers, Inc.*, 672 F.Supp. 72 (N.D.N.Y. 1987). That attorney's fees include compensation for time spent by legal assistants reflects "the realities of the marketplace and of modern, progressive law office management." *United Nuclear Corp. v. Cannon*, 564 F.Supp. 581, 589 (D.R.I. 1983).

This court implicitly recognized and encouraged the traditional marketplace use of nonlawyer personnel in the delivery of legal services by approving an award of attorney's fees, pursuant to Section 1988, which included compensation for time spent by a law clerk. *City of Riverside*, 477 U.S. at 566, 106 S.Ct. at 2690. Every federal circuit has likewise acknowledged the validity of delegating work of a legal nature to nonlawyer personnel under the supervision of an attorney by compensating for the work of legal assistants or law clerks pursuant to Section 1988,[5] or to an analogous fee-shifting statute or rule.[6]

   b. Compensating for the work of legal assistant time on an hourly basis at the market rate promotes the cost-effective delivery of legal services and enhances the quality of legal services.

Compensating for the work of legal assistant time as attorney's fees under Section 1988 "encourages cost-effective delivery of legal services and, by reducing the spiraling cost of civil rights litigation, furthers the policies underlying civil rights statutes." *Cameo Convalescent Center, Inc. v. Senn*, 738 F.2d 836, 846 (7th Cir. 1984), *cert. denied,* 469 U.S. 1106 (1985). Skilled legal assistants are capable of performing some work of a legal nature which would otherwise have to be done by an attorney. To the extent that such work is done by supervised legal assistants at substantially less cost per hour than would have been the case had the work been done by attorneys, the overall cost of legal services to the public is reduced. A rule prohibiting recovery for legal assistant time at the market rate would discourage the cost-effective delivery of legal services.[7]

---

[5] First Circuit: *Jacobs v. Mancuso*, 825 F.2d 559, 563 (1st Cir. 1987); *Furtado v. Bishop*, 635 F.2d 915, 920 (1st Cir. 1980); Third Circuit: *Daggett v. Kimmelman*, 811 F.2d 793, 799 (3d Cir. 1987) (fee reductions would be approved for work which should have been performed by paralegals; Fourth Circuit: *Vaughns v. Board of Educ. of Prince George's County*, 770 F.2d 1244, 1245–46 (4th Cir. 1985); Fifth Circuit: *Heath v. Brown*, 807 F.2d 1229, 1232 (5th Cir. 1987); Sixth Circuit: *Stewart v. Rhodes*, 656 F.2d 1216, 1217 (6th Cir. 1981), *cert. denied,* 455 U.S. 991 (1982); *Northcross v. Board of Educ. of Memphis City Schools*, 611 F.2d 624, 639 (6th Cir. 1979), *cert. denied,* 447 U.S. 911 (1980); Seventh Circuit: *Ustrak v. Fairman*, 851 F.2d 983 (7th Cir. 1988); *Cameo Convalescent Center, Inc. v. Senn*, 738 F.2d 836, 846 (7th Cir. 1984), *cert. denied,* 469 U.S. 1106 (1985); Eighth Circuit: *Jenkins v. Missouri*, 838 F.2d 260, 266 (8th Cir.), *cert. granted in part,* 109 S.Ct. 218 (Oct. 11, 1988) (No. 88-64), and *cert. denied,* 109 S.Ct. 218 (1988); Ninth Circuit: *Keith v. Volpe*, 833 F.2d 850, 859 (9th Cir. 1987); *Toussaint v. McCarthy*, 826 F.2d 901, 904 (9th Cir. 1987); Tenth Circuit: *Lucero v. City of Trinidad*, 815 F.2d 1384, 1385 (10th Cir. 1987); *Ramos v. Lamm*, 713 F.2d 546, 558 (10th Cir. 1983); Eleventh Circuit: *Walters v. City of Atlanta*, 803 F.2d 1135, 1151 (11th Cir. 1986).

[6] Second Circuit: *In re "Agent Orange" Prod. Liab. Litig.*, 818 F.2d 226, 238 (2d Cir.), *cert. denied,* 108 S.Ct. 289 (1987) (class action); *City of Detroit v. Grinnell Corp.*, 495 F.2d 448, 473 (2d Cir. 1974) (anti-trust class action); Third Circuit: *Brinker v. Guiffrida*, 798 F.2d 661, 668 (3d Cir. 1986) (recovery for law clerk under Equal Access to Justice Act); *Citizen's Council of Del. County v. Brinegar*, 741 F.2d 584, 596 (3d Cir. 1984) (Equal Access to Justice Act); Fourth Circuit: *Yohay v. City of Alexandria Employees Credit Union*, 827 F.2d 967, 974 (4th Cir. 1987) (law clerk under Fair Credit Reporting Act, 15 U.S.C. § 1681); *Lily v. Harris-Teeter Supermarket*, 720 F.2d 326, 339–40 n.28 (4th Cir. 1983), *cert. denied,* 466 U.S. 951 (1984) (employment discrimination); Fifth Circuit: *Concorde Limousines, Inc. v. Moloney Coachbuilders, Inc.*, 835 F.2d 541, 546 (5th Cir. 1987); *Alter Fin. Corp. v. Citizens & Southern Int'l Bank of New Orleans*, 817 F.2d 349, 350 (5th Cir. 1987) (sanctions, 28 U.S.C. § 1927); *Richardson v. Byrd*, 709 F.2d 1016, 1023 (5th Cir.), *cert. denied,* 464 U.S. 1009 (1983) (Title VII sex discrimination class action); Sixth Circuit: *Chandler v. Secretary of Dept. of Health & Human Services*, 792 F.2d 70, 73 (6th Cir. 1986) (Social Security Act, 42 U.S.C. § 406); Seventh Circuit: *In re Burlington Northern, Inc. Employment Practices Litig.*, 810 F.2d 601, 609 (7th Cir. 1986), *cert. denied,* 108 S.Ct. 82 (1987) (employment discrimination action, 42 U.S.C. § 2000e); *Spray-Rite Serv. Corp. v. Monsanto Co.*, 684 F.2d 1226, 1249–50 (7th Cir. 1982), *aff'd,* 465 U.S. 752 (1984) (anti-trust, 15 U.S.C. § 1 *et seq.*); Eighth Circuit: *Hawkins v. Anheuser-Busch, Inc.*, 697 F.2d 810, 817 (8th Cir. 1983) (employment discrimination, 42 U.S.C. § 2000e); Ninth Circuit: *Thornberry v. Delta Air Lines, Inc.*, 676 F.2d 1240, 1244 (9th Cir. 1982) (employment discrimination, 42 U.S.C. § 2000e); *Todd Shipyards Corp. v. Director, Office of Workers' Compensation*, 545 F.2d 1176, 1182 (9th Cir. 1976) (Longshoremen's and Harbor Workers' Compensation Act, 33 U.S.C. § 928); *Pacific Coast Agricultural Export Ass'n v. Sunkist Growers, Inc.*, 526 F.2d 1196, 1210 n.19 (9th Cir. 1975), *cert. denied,* 425 U.S. 959 (1976) (anti-trust, 15 U.S.C. § 1 *et seq.*); Tenth Circuit: *Kopunec v. Nelson*, 801 F.2d 1226, 1229 (10th Cir. 1986) (Equal Access to Justice Act); Eleventh Circuit: *Allen v. United States Steel Corp.*, 665 F.2d 689, 697 (5th Cir. Unit B 1982) (employment discrimination, 42 U.S.C. § 2000e); D.C. Circuit: *Wilkett v. Interstate Commerce Comm'n*, 844 F.2d 867, 877 (D.C.Cir. 1988) (law clerk; Equal Access to Justice Act); *Save Our Cumberland Mountains, Inc. v. Hodel*, 826 F.2d 43, 54 n.7 (D.C. Cir. 1987) *(en banc)* (Surface Mining Control and Reclamation Act of 1977, 30 U.S.C. § 1201).

[7] *See, e.g., Jacobs*, 825 F.2d at 563 *Spray-Rite Serv. Corp.*, 684 F.2d at 1250; *Todd Shipyards Corp.*, 545 F.2d at 1182; *Shorter v. Valley Bank & Trust Co.*, 678 F.Supp. 714, 724 (N.D.Ill. 1988); *Royal Crown Cola Co. v. Coca-Cola Co.*, 678 F.Supp. 875, 880 (M.D.Ga. 1987); *Chapman v. Pacific Tel. & Tel. Co.*, 456 F.Supp. 77, 83 (N.D.Cal. 1978).

In addition to reducing the cost of litigation, the use of legal assistants enhances the quality of legal representation. Legal assistants enable the attorney to spend his or her more costly time for greater productivity in more important areas where judgment and decision-making are required. The availability of legal assistants also promotes more thorough trial preparation by permitting a more efficient and economical utilization of staff time. *Chapman v. Pacific Tel. & Tel. Co.*, 456 F.Supp. 77, 83 (N.D.Cal. 1978). *See also Todd Shipyards Corp. v. Director, Office of Workers' Compensation Programs*, 545 F.2d 117. 1976); *Beamon v. City of Ridgeland, Miss.*, 666 F.Supp. 937, 946 (S.D.Miss. 1987).

Lawfirms in the private marketplace routinely include an hourly rate charge for legal assistants as part of the attorney's fee charged fee-paying clients. Indeed, seventy-seven percent of 1,800 legal assistants responding to a recent survey indicated that their law firm received compensation for their work from clients on an hourly billing rate basis. National Association of Legal Assistants, Inc., 1988 National Utilization and Compensation Survey Report (1989). "Lawfirms, like other businesses that sell time, must set their hourly rates at an amount greater than that needed to pay their attorneys' or paralegals' salaries; they must figure into those rates all their costs of doing business." *In re Burlington Northern Inc. Employment Practices Litig.*, 810 F.2d 601, 609 (7th Cir. 1986), *cert. denied*, 108 S.Ct. 82 (1987). The hourly rate of legal assistants must reflect not only base salary, but also fringe benefits and a proportionate share of firm overhead.[8] Additionally, the routine practice of law firms seeking reimbursement for the work of legal assistants at a rate sufficient to cover both the "actual cost" and overhead costs associated with that legally related work is a fairer billing procedure.

> Unlike the work of secretaries and other supporting personnel, . . . the work of paralegals and law clerks is ordinarily charged directly to particular litigation and is therefore a clearly identifiable cost. Were it to be treated as an overhead expense, payable out of the general receipts of the attorney, the across-the-board cost of services to the attorney's clients generally would be burdened by paralegal costs incurred in connection with particular matters of no interest or benefit to other clients.

Chapman, 456 F.Supp. at 82.

Consistent with the private billing procedure, a majority of federal trial and appellate courts approve compensation for legal assistant work hours, as well as the legally related work of other nonattorneys such as law clerks, based upon a reasonable hourly rate set lower than the hourly rate of attorneys but higher than the "actual cost" and sufficient to defray the cost of overhead. *See Jacobs v. Mancuso*, 825 F.2d 559, 563 n.6 (1st Cir. 1987) (legal assistant expenses are most frequently reimbursed based on an hourly fee).[9] This Court, in *City of Riverside, supra,* approved an attorney's fee award which included compensation for time spent by a student law clerk, at the rate of twenty-five dollars an hour, clearly more than the actual wages paid to the individual,

---

[8] *See Schwartz v. Novo Industri A/S*, 119 F.R.D. 359, 365 (S.D.N.Y. 1988) (citation omitted). *See also Williams v. Bowen*, 684 F.Supp. 1305, 1308 (E.D.Pa. 1988); *Garmong v. Montgomery County*, 668 F.Supp. 1000, 1011 (S.D.Tex. 1987); *Brewer v. Southern Union Co.*, 607 F.Supp. 1511, 1528 (D.Colo. 1984).

[9] *See also, e.g., Ustrak*, 851 F.2d 983; *Wilkett*, 844 F.2d at 877; *Save Our Cumberland Mountains, Inc.*, 826 F.2d at 54 n.7; *Tousaint*, 826 F.2d at 904; *Jacobs*, 825 F.2d at 563 & n.6; *In re "Agent Orange" Prod. Liab. Litig.*, 818 F.2d at 230, 238; *Lucero*, 815 F.2d at 1386; *In re Burlington Northern, Inc. Employment Practices Litig.*, 810 F.2d at 609; *Heath*, 807 F.2d at 1232; *Kopunec*, 801 F.2d at 1229; *Citizen's Council of Del. County*, 741 F.2d at 596; *Richardson*, 709 F.2d at 1023; *Louisville Black Police Officers Org., Inc. v. City of Louisville*, 700 F.2d 268, 273 (6th Cir. 1983); *Strama v. Peterson*, 689 F.2d 661, 663 (7th Cir. 1982); *Stewart v. Rhodes*, 656 F.2d at 1216–17; *Todd Shipyards Corp.*, 545 F.2d at 1182.

and obviously high enough to cover the overhead costs associated with the nonlawyer employee. *See* 477 U.S. at 566, 106 S.Ct. at 2690 & n.2.[10]

    c. The inclusion of compensation for legal assistants in an attorney's fee award does not offend ethical and legal tenets prohibiting the unauthorized practice of law.

Any objection to including compensation for the supervised legally-related work of legal assistants in a reasonable attorney's fee award because legal assistants are not attorneys is but a "technical" one. The work performed by legal assistants is work of the type necessary to the prosecution of the litigation which would otherwise be performed by attorneys. Indeed, this Court has recognized the validity of nonlawyer personnel performing services of a legal nature. In *Procunier v. Martinez*, 416 U.S. 396 (1974), the Court affirmed the striking of a prison administrative rule banning attorney-client interviews conducted by law students or legal paraprofessionals as constituting an unjustified restriction on the right of access to the courts. The Court agreed with the trial court's finding that prohibiting the use of law students or other paraprofessionals from conducting attorney-client interviews with prisoners would inhibit adequate professional representation of indigent inmates, or alternately, increase the cost of legal representation for prisoners. *Id.* at 419-20. Likewise, in *Johnson v. Avery*, 393 U.S. 483 (1969), the Court struck down a prison regulation prohibiting any inmate from advising or assisting another in the preparation of legal documents. The Court noted that "the type of activity involved here—preparation of petitions for post-conviction relief—though historically and traditionally one which may benefit from the services of a trained and dedicated lawyer, is a function often, perhaps generally, performed by a layman." *Id.* at 490 n.11. *See also City of Riverside*, 477 U.S. at 566, 106 S.Ct. at 2690 (affirming attorney's fee award which included compensation for work performed by a law clerk).

    Compensation for lawyer-supervised legally-related work performed by legal assistants conforms with the ethical canons and disciplinary codes governing lawyers and legal assistants. Lawyers are obligated to keep fees in check and take steps to provide efficient, cost-effective legal services. *See* ABA Model Code of Professional Responsibility EC 2-18 and DR 2-106(A)(B) (1976); ABA Model Rules of Professional Conduct, Rule 1.5(a) (1984). The delegation of tasks to lay persons is proper "if the lawyer maintains a direct relationship with his client, supervises the delegated work, and has complete professional responsibility for the work product. This delegation enables a lawyer to render legal services more economically and efficiently." Model Code EC 3-6. *See also* Model Rules, Rule 5.3.[11] Because the lawyer, or lawfirm, is the recipient

---

[10] To highlight the need for this Court's guidance, several courts have allowed the recovery of compensation for the work of legal assistants or law clerks based on an hourly-rate while at the same time calling it compensation for "expenses," rather than attorney's fees. *See In re "Agent Orange" Product Liab. Litig.*, 818 F.2d at 238; *Yaris v. Special School Dist. of St. Louis County*, 661 F.Supp. 996, 1002, 1003 n.9 (E.D.Mo. 1987); *PPG Industries, Inc. v. Celanese Polymer Specialties Co.*, 658 F.Supp. 555, 560, 565 (W.D.Ky. 1987), *rev'd on other grounds*, 840 F.2d 1565 (Fed.Cir. 1988). Some courts have held that law firms may only recover their paralegal "out of pocket" expenses, *see Thornberry*, 676 F.2d at 1244 (citing *Northcross*, 611 F.2d at 639), while others have permitted reimbursement for salary actually paid to a legal assistant, with no additional compensation for fringe benefits or overhead. *See, e.g., City of Detroit*, 495 F.2d at 473; *Illinois Migrant Council v. Pilliod*, 672 F.Supp. 1072, 1084 (N.D.Ill. 1987); *Campaign for a Progressive Bronx v. Black*, 631 F.Supp. 975, 983 (S.D.N.Y. 1986). Still others refuse to provide separate compensation for the work of legal assistants, taking the position that legal assistants represent overhead, such as clerical and office expenses, all covered by the attorney's hourly rate. *See Abrams v. Baylor College of Medicine*, 805 F.2d 528, 535 (5th Cir. 1986); *Roe v. City of Chicago*, 586 F.Supp. 513, 516 & n.6 (N.D.Ill. 1984).

[11] The American Bar Association emphasizes that the work of a legal assistant "involves the performance, under the ultimate direction and supervision of an attorney, of specifically-delegated substantive legal work, which work, for the most part, requires a sufficient knowledge of legal concepts that, absent such assistance, the attorney would

of an attorney's fee for legal services and not the salaried legal assistant, the inclusion of compensation for the supervised work of a legal assistant as part of a reasonable attorney's fee does not offend ethical rules prohibiting attorneys from sharing legal fees with laymen. *See* Model Code EC 3-8 and DR 3-102.

Legal assistants recognize the ethical ramifications of their performance of legally-related work, and emphasize, in self-policing ethics codes and guidelines, that legal assistants shall not undertake tasks which are required to be performed by an attorney, such as setting fees, giving legal advice, or appearing in any way to a court, the client, or the public to be practicing law.[12] Additionally, the rules stress that all work of a legal nature performed by a legal assistant must be delegated and supervised by an attorney, who retains ultimate responsibility to the client and assumes full professional responsibility for the work product. National Association of Legal Assistants, Inc., Code of Ethics and Professional Responsibility (1975, as amended through 1988); National Association of Legal Assistants Model Standards and Guidelines for Utilization of Legal Assistants (1984) (both reprinted in full in the Appendix to this brief). It is the close supervision by an attorney which keeps the legally-related work of a legal assistant from treading upon the prohibited and unacceptable unauthorized practice of law, and makes the work of a legal assistant no more than an extension of the work of an attorney at a less costly rate.[13]

> d. Courts scrutinize attorney's fee applications to assure the hourly rates of legal assistants and the time spent and nature of the work performed by legal assistants are all reasonable.

Courts compensating for the work performed by a legal assistant in connection with the award of a reasonable attorney's fee scrutinize the reported hours, the suggested rate, and the nature of the work performed in the same manner they scrutinize lawyer time and rates. *See Pennsylvania I*, 478 U.S. at 565, 106 S.Ct. at 3098; *Hensley v. Eckerhart*, 461 U.S. 424, 434 (1983);

---

perform the task." ABA Standing Committee on Legal Assistants, Position Paper on the Question of Licensure or Certification (1986).

[12] Though the American Bar Association has shied away from defining what constitutes the practice of law, ABA Code of Professional Responsibility, it notes that "[f]unctionally, the practice of law relates to the rendition of services for others that call for the professional judgment of a lawyer." ABA Model Code of Professional Responsibility ED 3-5 (1976). Courts faced with the question have attempted to craft a definition. For example, the Florida Supreme Court has stated that the giving of advice and the performance of services which affect important rights of a person under the law, and require legal skill and knowledge of the law greater than that possessed by the average citizen, constitutes the practice of law. *The Florida Bar v. Brumbaugh*, 355 So.2d 1186, 1191 (Fla. 1978).

[13] Courts awarding attorney's fees for the supervised work of legal assistants have delineated examples of legal services which would otherwise be performed by an attorney, and thus which are compensable if performed by a legal assistant. They include: investigation of the facts relating to the action, *In re Gas Meters Antitrust Litig.*, 500 F.Supp. 956, 969 (E.D.Pa.1980); assisting with discovery, including such tasks as statistical and financial analysis, inspection and production of documents, review of answers to interrogatories, and the compilation of statistical and financial data, *Bagel Inn, Inc. v. All Star Dairies*, 539 F.Supp. 107, 111 (D.N.J.1982); *In re Gas Meters Antitrust Litig.*, 500 F.Supp. at 967; *see also, e.g., Richardson*, 709 F.2d at 1023; *Spray-Rite Service Corp.*, 684 F.2d at 1250; doing legal research, *Morgan v. Nevada Board of State Prison Comm'rs*, 615 F.Supp. 882, 885 (D.Nev.1985); locating and interviewing witnesses, *Richardson*, 709 F.2d at 1023; *Garmong*, 668 F.Supp. at 1011; organizing and communicating with class members, *Richardson, supra*; *Edmonds v. United States*, 658 F.Supp. 1126, 1136 (D.S.C.1987); *In re Gas Meters Antitrust Litig.*, 500 F.Supp. at 970; assisting with preparation for depositions and trial, and organizing exhibits, *Easter House v. State of Illinois, Dept. of Children and Family Services*, 663 F.Supp. 456, 460 (N.D.Ill. 1987); *In re Gas Meters Antitrust Litig.*, 500 F.Supp. at 972; assisting with preparation of settlement and settlement administration, *In re Chicken Antitrust Litig.*, 560 F.Supp. 963, 978 (N.D.Ga.1980); *In re Gas Meters Antitrust Litig.*, 500 F.Supp. at 967, 972; compiling statistical and financial data, *Bagel Inn, Inc.*, 539 F.Supp. at 111; drafting pleadings, *Parise v. Riccilli Haulers, Inc.*, 672 F.Supp. 72, 75 (N.D.N.Y.1987); *In re Gas Meters Antitrust Litig.*, 500 F.Supp. at 969; and checking legal citations, *Beamon v. City of Ridgeland, Miss.*, 66 F.Supp. 937, 943 (S.D.Miss.1987).

Ramos, 713 F.2d at 559. Trial courts determine what portion of the work is of a clerical nature and is thus absorbed as part of the office overhead reflected in the attorney's billing rate and what portion of the work performed by the legal assistant constitutes legal services traditionally done by an attorney and which be performed by an attorney at a costlier rate. *Ramos*, 713 F.2d at 558; *Richardson v. Byrd*, 709 F.2d 1016, 1023 (5th Cir.), *cert. denied*, 464 U.S. 1009 (1983). "Such expenses are separately recoverable only as part of a prevailing party's award for attorney's fees and expenses, and even then only to the extent that the paralegal performs work traditionally done by an attorney. Otherwise, paralegal expenses are separately unrecoverable overhead expenses." *Allen v. United States Steel Corp.*, 665 F.2d 689, 697 (5th Cir. Unit·B 1982).

Indeed, when considering a reasonable attorney's fee award, courts have chastised attorneys for doing work which more properly could have been delegated to a legal assistant under the attorney's supervision, and have penalized the attorney by lowering the hourly rate charged.

> It is appropriate to distinguish between legal work, in the strict sense, and investigation, clerical work, compilation of facts and statistics, and other work which can often be accomplished by nonlawyers but which a lawyer may do because he has no other help available. Such nonlegal work may command a lesser rate. Its dollar value is not enhanced just because a lawyer does it.

Johnson v. Georgia Highway Express, Inc., 488 F.2d 714, 717 (5th Cir.1974). Wasteful utilization of expensive legal talent for work that may be delegated to nonlawyers is not condoned. "Routine tasks, if performed by senior partners in large firms, should not be billed at their usual rates. A Michelangelo should not charge Sistine Chapel rates for painting a farmer's barn." *Ursic v. Bethlehem Mines*, 719 F.2d 670, 677 (3d. Cir.1983). Accordingly, courts regularly reduce an attorney's hourly rate to that traditionally charged for a legal assistant, to reflect the nature of the legal work performed.[14]

   e. Permitting recovery for work of legal assistants promotes the availability of legal representation to victims of civil rights violations.

If the lawyer attempts to absorb the cost of the legal assistant into his or her regular hourly rate as an overhead expense, as is done for clerical work and office supplies, or to absorb the overhead costs associated with the work of a legal assistant, then all persons employing that attorney, including victims of civil rights violations, would suffer a higher hourly rate, regardless of whether their case necessitated the assistance of a legal assistant. More likely, the work currently performed by legal assistants would be done by attorney associates and billed at the higher attorney associate rate, clearly decreasing the utilization of legal assistants and increasing the cost of litigation. The attorney performing legal tasks which could be delegated to a legal assistant, however, faces the risk that his or her fee will be reduced by a court as being

---

[14] *See, e.g., Pennsylvania v. Delaware Valley Citizen's Council for Clean Air*, 478 U.S. 546, 553, 567, 106 S.Ct. 3088, 3092 (1986) (*"Pennsylvania I"*) (approving a lodestar which set different hourly rates for legal work requiring varying degrees of legal ability); *Dagget v. Kimmelman*, 811 F.2d at 799 (attorney hours devoted to tasks which should have been performed by associates or paralegals would warrant an hourly fee reduction); *Northcross*, 611 F.2d at 637, (necessary services performed by attorneys which could have reasonably been performed by less expensive personnel may be compensated at a lower rate than attorney's normal billing rate); *Drez v. E. R. Squibb & Sons, Inc.*, 674 F.Supp. 1432 (D.Kan.1987) (dropping attorney billing rate to law clerk rate where three attorneys sat through trial); *Beamon*, 666 F.Supp. at 941-42 (attorney fees for purely clerical work which is easily delegable granted at reduced hourly rate); *Skelton v. General Motors Corp.*, 661 F.Supp.1368, 1385 (N.D.Ill.1987) (court reduces time of attorney spent on administrative tasks); *Metro Data Systems, Inc. v. Durango Systems, Inc.*, 597 F.Supp.244, 246 (D.Ariz.1984) (gathering information and drafting answers to interrogatories not recoverable by attorney as work which could have been performed by paralegal).

unreasonably high for the quality of work performed. The only remaining alternative would be for the attorney to perform the work at a reduced rate, below and not competitive with the market rate. Such a result would make the representation of victims of civil rights violations cost prohibitive and unattractive, and discourage competent, experienced attorneys from undertaking such representation because they could not receive full compensation for their efforts.

The widespread practice of assigning less technical yet legal work to legal assistants to be performed under the supervision of an attorney promotes economy and efficiency in the administration of justice. Permitting reasonable compensation for such services at the market rate as part of a reasonable attorney's fee encourages this desirable practice, and makes legal representation more readily available to victims of civil rights violations, in accord with Congress' intent when adopting the Civil Rights Attorney's Fee Awards Act of 1976, 43 U.S.C. § 1988.

Conclusion

For the reasons set forth above, the National Association of Legal Assistants, Inc., as *amicus curiae*, respectfully urges the Court to affirm the decision of the Court of Appeals for the Eighth Circuit and permit recovery legal assistants at the market rate as part of a reasonable attorney's fee award made pursuant to 42 U.S.C. § 1988.

Respectfully submitted,

JOHN A. DEVAULT, III
Counsel of Record
JANE A. LESTER
Counsel
BEDELL, DITTMAR, DEVAULT & PILLANS, P.A.
The Bedell Building
101 East Adams Street
Jacksonville, FL 32202
(904) 353-0211

For *Amicus Curiae*
National Association of Legal Assistants, Inc.

The Court's Opinion: *Missouri v. Jenkins*, 109 S.Ct. 2463 (1989)

MISSOURI, et al., Petitioners

v.

Kalima JENKINS, by her friend,
Kamau AGYEI, et al.

No. 88–64.

Argued Feb. 21, 1989.

Decided June 19, 1989.

Prevailing plaintiffs in school desegregation case sought recovery of attorney fees. The United States District Court for the Western District of Missouri, Russell G. Clark, J., awarded attorney fees, and appeal was taken. The Court of Appeals for the Eighth Circuit, 838 F.2d 260, affirmed. On grant of certiorari, the Supreme Court, Justice Brennan, held that: (1) Eleventh Amendment did not prohibit enhancement of fee award under Civil Rights Attorney's Fees Awards Act against state to compensate for delay in payment, and (2) separate compensation award under Civil Rights Attorney's Fees Awards Act for paralegals, law clerks, and recent law school graduates at prevailing rates was fully in accord with Act.

Affirmed.

Justice O'Connor concurred in part and dissented in part and filed opinion in which Justice Scalia joined and Chief Justice Rehnquist joined in part.

Justice Rehnquist filed dissenting opinion.

Justice Marshall did not participate.

1. Federal Courts ⬡⟲265

Award of attorney fees ancillary to prospective relief in civil rights action is not subject to strictures of Eleventh Amendment. U.S.C.A. Const.Amend. 11; 42 U.S.C.A. § 1988.

2. Federal Courts ⬡⟲265

Not only is award of attorney fees in civil rights action beyond reach of Eleventh Amendment, so also is question of how

reasonable attorney fee is to be calculated. U.S.C.A. Const.Amend. 11; 42 U.S.C.A. § 1988.

3. Federal Courts ⬡⟲265

Eleventh Amendment does not prohibit enhancement of fee award under Civil Rights Attorney's Fees Awards Act against state to compensate for delay in payment. 42 U.S.C.A. § 1988; U.S.C.A. Const.Amend. 11.

4. Civil Rights ⬡⟲13.17(20)

Attorney fees under Civil Rights Attorney's Fees Awards Act are to be based on market rates for services rendered. 42 U.S.C.A. § 1988.

5. Civil Rights ⬡⟲13.17(19)

Appropriate adjustment for delay in payment—whether by application of current rather than historic hourly rates or otherwise—is within contemplation of Civil Rights Attorney's Fees Awards Act. 42 U.S.C.A. § 1988.

6. Civil Rights ⬡⟲13.17(19)
   Federal Courts ⬡⟲265

Eleventh Amendment has no application to award of attorney fees, ancillary to grant of prospective relief, against state; thus, it follows that same is true for calculation of amount of fee, and adjustment for delay in payment is appropriate factor in determination of what is reasonable attorney fee under Civil Rights Attorney's Fees Awards Act. 42 U.S.C.A. § 1988; U.S.C.A. Const.Amend. 11.

7. Civil Rights ⬡⟲13.17(18)

Phrase "reasonable attorney's fee" in civil rights attorney fees statute does not refer only to work performed personally by members of bar; rather, term refers to reasonable fee for work product of attorney, and thus, to work of paralegals as well as that of attorneys. 42 U.S.C.A. § 1988.

See publication Words and Phrases for other judicial constructions and definitions.

8. Civil Rights ⚖13.17(20)

Reasonable attorney fee under Civil Rights Attorney's Fees Awards Act is one calculated on basis of rates and practices prevailing in relevant market, and one that grants successful civil rights plaintiff fully compensatory fee, comparable to what is traditional with attorneys compensated by fee-paying client. 42 U.S.C.A. § 1988.

9. Civil Rights ⚖13.17(20)

Separate compensation award under Civil Rights Attorney's Fees Awards Act for paralegals, law clerks, and recent law school graduates at prevailing rates was fully in accord with Act, where prevailing practice in area was to bill paralegal work at market rates. 42 U.S.C.A. § 1988.

Syllabus *

In this major school desegregation litigation in Kansas City, Missouri, in which various desegregation remedies were granted against the State of Missouri and other defendants, the plaintiff class was represented by a Kansas City lawyer (Benson) and by the NAACP Legal Defense and Educational Fund, Inc. (LDF). Benson and the LDF requested attorney's fees under the Civil Rights Attorney's Fees Awards Act of 1976 (42 U.S.C. § 1988), which provides with respect to such litigation that the court, in its discretion, may allow the prevailing party, other than the United States, "a reasonable attorney's fee as part of the costs." In calculating the hourly rates for Benson's, his associates', and the LDF attorneys' fees, the District Court took account of delay in payment by using current market rates rather than those applicable at the time the services were rendered. Both Benson and the LDF employed numerous paralegals, law clerks, and recent law graduates, and the court awarded fees for their work based on market rates, again using current rather than historic rates in order to compensate for the delay in payment.

* The syllabus constitutes no part of the opinion of the Court but has been prepared by the Reporter of Decisions for the convenience of the

Held:

1. The Eleventh Amendment does not prohibit enhancement of a fee award under § 1988 against a State to compensate for delay in payment. That Amendment has no application to an award of attorney's fees, ancillary to a grant of prospective relief, against a State, *Hutto v. Finney*, 437 U.S. 678, 98 S.Ct. 2565, 57 L.Ed.2d 522, and it follows that the same is true for the calculation of the *amount* of the fee. An adjustment for delay in payment is an appropriate factor in determining what constitutes a reasonable attorney's fee under § 1988. Pp. 2466–2469.

2. The District Court correctly compensated the work of paralegals, law clerks, and recent law graduates at the market rates for their services, rather than at their cost to the attorneys. Clearly, "a reasonable attorney's fee" as used in § 1988 cannot have been meant to compensate only work performed personally by members of the Bar. Rather, that term must refer to a reasonable fee for an attorney's work product, and thus must take into account the work not only of attorneys, but also the work of paralegals and the like. A reasonable attorney's fee under § 1988 is one calculated on the basis of rates and practices prevailing in the relevant market and one that grants the successful civil rights plaintiff a "fully compensatory fee," comparable to what "is traditional with attorneys compensated by a fee-paying client." In this case, where the practice in the relevant market is to bill the work of paralegals separately, the District Court's decision to award separate compensation for paralegals, law clerks, and recent law graduates at prevailing market rates was fully in accord with § 1988. Pp. 2469–2472.

838 F.2d 260 (CA8 1988), affirmed.

BRENNAN, J., delivered the opinion of the Court, in which WHITE, BLACK-

reader. See *United States v. Detroit Lumber Co.*, 200 U.S. 321, 337, 26 S.Ct. 282, 237, 50 L.Ed. 499.

MUN, STEVENS, and KENNEDY, JJ., joined, and in Parts I and III of which O'CONNOR and SCALIA, JJ., joined. O'CONNOR, J., filed an opinion concurring in part and dissenting in part, in which SCALIA, J., joined and REHNQUIST, C.J., joined in part. REHNQUIST, C.J., filed a dissenting opinion. MARSHALL, J., took no part in the consideration or decision of the case.

Bruce Farmer, Jefferson City, Mo., for petitioners.

Jay Topkis, New York City, Russell E. Lovell, II, Des Moines, Iowa, for respondents.

Justice BRENNAN delivered the opinion of the Court.

This is the attorney's-fee aftermath of major school desegregation litigation in Kansas City, Missouri. We granted certiorari, 488 U.S. ——, 109 S.Ct. 218, 102 L.Ed. 2d 209 (1988), to resolve two questions relating to fees litigation under 42 U.S.C. § 1988. First, does the Eleventh Amendment prohibit enhancement of a fee award against a State to compensate for delay in payment? Second, should the fee award compensate the work of paralegals and law clerks by applying the market rate for their work?

I

This litigation began in 1977 as a suit by the Kansas City Missouri School District (KCMSD), the School Board, and the children of two School Board members, against the State of Missouri and other defendants. The plaintiffs alleged that the State, surrounding school districts, and various federal agencies had caused and perpetuated a system of racial segregation in the schools of the Kansas City metropolitan area. They sought various desegregation reme-

dies. KCMSD was subsequently realigned as a nominal defendant, and a class of present and future KCMSD students was certified as plaintiffs. After lengthy proceedings, including a trial that lasted 7½ months during 1983 and 1984, the District Court found the State of Missouri and KCMSD liable, while dismissing the suburban school districts and the federal defendants. It ordered various intradistrict remedies, to be paid for by the State and KCMSD, including $260 million in capital improvements and a magnet-school plan costing over $200 million. See *Jenkins v. Missouri*, 807 F.2d 657 (CA8 1986) (en banc), cert. denied, 484 U.S. 816 (1987); *Jenkins v. Missouri*, 855 F.2d 1295 (CA8 1988), cert. granted, 490 U.S. ——, 109 S.Ct. 1930, —— L.Ed.2d —— (1989).

The plaintiff class has been represented, since 1979, by Kansas City lawyer Arthur Benson and, since 1982, by the NAACP Legal Defense and Educational Fund, Inc. (LDF). Benson and the LDF requested attorney's fees under the Civil Rights Attorney's Fees Awards Act of 1976, 42 U.S. C. § 1988.[1] Benson and his associates had devoted 10,875 attorney hours to the litigation, as well as 8,108 hours of paralegal and law clerk time. For the LDF the corresponding figures were 10,854 hours for attorneys and 15,517 hours for paralegals and law clerks. Their fee applications deleted from these totals 3,628 attorney hours and 7,046 paralegal hours allocable to unsuccessful claims against the suburban school districts. With additions for post-judgment monitoring and for preparation of the fee application, the District Court awarded Benson a total of approximately $1.7 million and the LDF $2.3 million. App. to Pet. for Cert. A22–A43.

In calculating the hourly rate for Benson's fees the court noted that the market rate in Kansas City for attorneys of Ben-

---

1. Section 1988 provides in relevant part: "In any action or proceeding to enforce a provision of sections 1981, 1982, 1983, 1985, and 1986 of this title, title IX of Public Law 92–318 [20 U.S.C. 1681 et seq.], or title VI of the Civil

Rights Act of 1964 [42 U.S.C. 2000d et seq.], the court, in its discretion, may allow the prevailing party, other than the United States, a reasonable attorney's fee as part of the costs."

son's qualifications was in the range of $125 to $175 per hour, and found that "Mr. Benson's rate would fall at the higher end of this range based upon his expertise in the area of civil rights." *Id.,* at A26. It calculated his fees on the basis of an even higher hourly rate of $200, however, because of three additional factors: the preclusion of other employment, the undesirability of the case, and the delay in payment for Benson's services. *Id.,* at A26–A27. The court also took account of the delay in payment in setting the rates for several of Benson's associates by using current market rates rather than those applicable at the time the services were rendered. *Id.,* at A28–A30. For the same reason, it calculated the fees for the LDF attorneys at current market rates. *Id.,* at A33.

Both Benson and the LDF employed numerous paralegals, law clerks (generally law students working part-time), and recent law graduates in this litigation. The court awarded fees for their work based on Kansas City market rates for those categories. As in the case of the attorneys, it used current rather than historic market rates in order to compensate for the delay in payment. It therefore awarded fees based on hourly rates of $35 for law clerks, $40 for paralegals, and $50 for recent law graduates. *Id.,* at A29–A31, A34. The Court of Appeals affirmed in all respects. 838 F.2d 260 (CA8 1988).

II

Our grant of certiorari extends to two issues raised by the State of Missouri. Missouri first contends that a State cannot, consistent with the principle of sovereign immunity this Court has found embodied in the Eleventh Amendment, be compelled to pay an attorney's fee enhanced to compensate for delay in payment. This question requires us to examine the intersection of two of our precedents, *Hutto v. Finney,*

437 U.S. 678, 98 S.Ct. 2565, 57 L.Ed.2d 522 (1978), and *Library of Congress v. Shaw,* 478 U.S. 310, 106 S.Ct. 2957, 92 L.Ed.2d 250 (1986).[2]

In *Hutto v. Finney* the lower courts had awarded attorney's fees against the State of Arkansas, in part pursuant to § 1988, in connection with litigation over the conditions of confinement in that State's prisons. The State contended that any such award was subject to the Eleventh Amendment's constraints on actions for damages payable from a State's treasury. We relied, in rejecting that contention, on the distinction drawn in our earlier cases between "retroactive monetary relief" and "prospective injunctive relief." See *Edelman v. Jordan,* 415 U.S. 651, 94 S.Ct. 1347, 39 L.Ed.2d 662 (1974); *Ex parte Young,* 209 U.S. 123, 28 S.Ct. 441, 52 L.Ed. 714 (1908). Attorney's fees, we held, belonged to the latter category, because they constituted reimbursement of "expenses incurred in litigation seeking only prospective relief," rather than "retroactive liability for prelitigation conduct." *Hutto,* 437 U.S., at 695, 98 S.Ct., at 2576; see also *id.,* at 690, 98 S.Ct., at 2573. We explained: "Unlike ordinary 'retroactive' relief such as damages or restitution, an award of costs does not compensate the plaintiff for the injury that first brought him into court. Instead, the award reimburses him for a portion of the expenses he incurred in seeking prospective relief." *Id.,* at 695, n. 24, 98 S.Ct., at 2576, n. 24. Section 1988, we noted, fit easily into the longstanding practice of awarding "costs" against States, for the statute imposed the award of attorney's fees "as part of the costs." *Id.,* at 695–696, 98 S.Ct., at 2576, citing *Fairmont Creamery Co. v. Minnesota,* 275 U.S. 70, 48 S.Ct. 97, 72 L.Ed. 168 (1927).

[1, 2] After *Hutto,* therefore, it must be accepted as settled that an award of attorney's fees ancillary to prospective relief is

---

2. The holding of the Court of Appeals on this point, 838 F.2d, at 265–266, is in conflict with the resolution of the same question in *Rogers v. Okin,* 821 F.2d 22, 26–28 (CA1 1987), cert. denied *sub nom. Commissioner, Massachusetts Dept. of Mental Health v. Rogers,* 484 U.S. 1010, 108 S.Ct. 709, 98 L.Ed.2d 660 (1988).

not subject to the strictures of the Eleventh Amendment. And if the principle of making such an award is beyond the reach of the Eleventh Amendment, the same must also be true for the question of how a "reasonable attorney's fee" is to be calculated. See *Hutto, supra,* 437 U.S., at 696–697, 98 S.Ct., at 2576–2577.

Missouri contends, however, that the principle enunciated in *Hutto* has been undermined by subsequent decisions of this Court that require Congress to "express its intention to abrogate the Eleventh Amendment in unmistakable language in the statute itself." *Atascadero State Hospital v. Scanlon,* 473 U.S. 234, 243, 105 S.Ct. 3142, 3148, 87 L.Ed.2d 171 (1985); *Welch v. Texas Dept. of Highways and Public Transportation,* 483 U.S. 468, 107 S.Ct. 2941, 97 L.Ed.2d 389 (1987). See also *Dellmuth v. Muth,* 491 U.S. ——, —— S.Ct. ——, —— L.Ed.2d —— (1989); *Pennsylvania v. Union Gas Co.,* 491 U.S. ——, —— S.Ct. ——, —— L.Ed.2d —— (1989). The flaw in this argument lies in its misreading of the holding of *Hutto.* It is true that in *Hutto* we noted that Congress could, in the exercise of its enforcement power under § 5 of the Fourteenth Amendment, set aside the States' immunity from retroactive damages, 437 U.S., at 693, 98 S.Ct., at 2574–75, citing *Fitzpatrick v. Bitzer,* 427 U.S. 445, 96 S.Ct. 2666, 49 L.Ed.2d 614 (1976), and that Congress intended to do so in enacting § 1988. 437 U.S., at 693–694, 98 S.Ct., at 2574–2575. But we also made clear that the application of § 1988 to the States did not depend on congressional abrogation of the States' immunity. We did so in rejecting precisely the "clear statement" argument that Missouri now suggests has undermined *Hutto.* Arkansas had argued that § 1988 did not plainly abrogate the States' immunity; citing *Employees v. Missouri Dept. of Public Health and Welfare,* 411 U.S. 279, 93 S.Ct. 1614, 36 L.Ed.2d 251 (1973), and *Edelman v. Jordan, supra,* the State contended that "retroactive liability" could not be imposed on the States "in the absence of an extraordinarily explicit statutory mandate." *Hutto,* 437 U.S., at 695, 98 S.Ct., at 2576. We responded as follows: "[T]hese cases [*Employees* and *Edelman*] concern retroactive liability for prelitigation conduct rather than expenses incurred in litigation seeking only prospective relief. The Act imposes attorney's fees 'as part of the costs.' Costs have traditionally been awarded without regard for the States' Eleventh Amendment immunity." *Ibid.*

The holding of *Hutto,* therefore, was not just that Congress had spoken sufficiently clearly to overcome Eleventh Amendment immunity in enacting § 1988, but rather that the Eleventh Amendment did not apply to an award of attorney's fees ancillary to a grant of prospective relief. See *Maine v. Thiboutot,* 448 U.S. 1, 9, n. 7, 100 S.Ct. 2502, 2507, n. 7, 65 L.Ed.2d 555 (1980). That holding is unaffected by our subsequent jurisprudence concerning the degree of clarity with which Congress must speak in order to override Eleventh Amendment immunity, and we reaffirm it today.

[3] Missouri's other line of argument is based on our decision in *Library of Congress v. Shaw, supra. Shaw* involved an application of the longstanding "no-interest rule," under which interest cannot be awarded against the United States unless it has expressly waived its sovereign immunity. We held that while Congress, in making the Federal Government a potential defendant under Title VII of the Civil Rights Act of 1964, had waived the United States' immunity from suit and from costs including reasonable attorney's fees, it had not waived the Federal Government's traditional immunity from any award of interest. We thus held impermissible a 30 percent increase in the "lodestar" fee to compensate for delay in payment. Because we refused to find in the language of § 1988 a waiver of the United States' immunity from interest, Missouri argues, we should likewise conclude that § 1988 is not sufficiently explicit to constitute an abrogation of the States' immunity under the Eleventh Amendment in regard to any award of interest.

The answer to this contention is already clear from what we have said about *Hutto v. Finney*. Since, as we held in *Hutto*, the Eleventh Amendment does not bar an award of attorney's fees ancillary to a grant of prospective relief, our holding in *Shaw* has no application, even by analogy.[3] There is no need in this case to determine whether Congress has spoken sufficiently clearly to meet a "clear statement" requirement, and it is therefore irrelevant whether the Eleventh Amendment standard should be, as Missouri contends, as stringent as the one we applied for purposes of the no-interest rule in *Shaw*. Rather, the issue here—whether the "reasonable attorney's fee" provided for in § 1988 should be calculated in such a manner as to include an enhancement, where appropriate, for delay in payment—is a straightforward matter of statutory interpretation. For this question, it is of no relevance whether the party against which fees are awarded is a State. The question is what Congress intended—not whether it manifested "the clear affirmative intent ... to waive the sovereign's immunity." *Shaw*, 478 U.S., at 321, 106 S.Ct. at 2965.[4]

This question is not a difficult one. We have previously explained, albeit in dicta, why an enhancement for delay in payment

is, where appropriate, part of a "reasonable attorney's fee." In *Pennsylvania v. Delaware Valley Citizens' Council*, 483 U.S. 711, 107 S.Ct. 3078, 97 L.Ed.2d 585 (1987), we rejected an argument that a prevailing party was entitled to a fee augmentation to compensate for the risk of nonpayment. But we took care to distinguish that risk from the factor of delay:

"First is the matter of delay. When plaintiffs' entitlement to attorney's fees depends on success, their lawyers are not paid until a favorable decision finally eventuates, which may be years later.... Meanwhile, their expenses of doing business continue and must be met. In setting fees for prevailing counsel, the courts have regularly recognized the delay factor, either by basing the award on current rates or by adjusting the fee based on historical rates to reflect its present value. See, *e.g., Sierra Club v. EPA*, 248 U.S.App.D.C. 107, 120–121, 769 F.2d 796, 809–810 (1985); *Louisville Black Police Officers Organization, Inc. v. Louisville*, 700 F.2d 268, 276, 281 (CA6 1983). Although delay and the risk of nonpayment are often mentioned in the same breath, adjusting for the former is a distinct issue.... We do not suggest ... that adjustments

---

3. Our opinion in *Shaw* does, to be sure, contain some language that, if read in isolation, might suggest a different result in this case. Most significantly, we equated compensation for delay with prejudgment interest, and observed that "[p]rejudgment interest ... is considered as damages, not a component of 'costs.' ... Indeed, the term 'costs' has never been understood to include any interest component." *Library of Congress v. Shaw*, 478 U.S. 310, 321, 106 S.Ct. 2957, 2965, 92 L.Ed.2d 250 (1986). These observations, however, cannot be divorced from the context of the special "no-interest rule" that was at issue in *Shaw*. That rule, which is applicable to the immunity of the United States and is therefore not at issue here, provides an "added gloss of strictness," *id.*, at 318, 106 S.Ct., at 2963, only where the United States' liability for interest is at issue. Our inclusion of compensation for delay within the definition of prejudgment interest in *Shaw* must be understood in light of this broad proscription of interest awards against the United States. *Shaw* thus does not represent a general-purpose definition of com-

pensation for delay that governs here. Outside the context of the "no-interest rule" of federal immunity, we see no reason why compensation for delay cannot be included within § 1988 attorney's fee awards, which *Hutto* held to be "costs" not subject to Eleventh Amendment strictures.

We cannot share JUSTICE O'CONNOR's view that the two cases she cites, *post*, at 2474, demonstrate the existence of an equivalent rule relating to State immunity that embodies the same ultra-strict rule of construction for interest awards that has grown up around the federal no-interest rule. Compare *Shaw, supra*, at 314–317, 106 S.Ct., at 2961–2963 (discussing historical development of the federal no-interest rule).

4. In *Shaw*, which dealt with the sovereign immunity of the Federal Government, there was of course no prospective-retrospective distinction as there is when, as in *Hutto* and the present case, it is the Eleventh Amendment immunity of a State that is at issue.

MISSOURI v. JENKINS BY AGYEI   2469
Cite as 109 S.Ct. 2463 (1989)

for delay are inconsistent with the typical fee-shifting statute." *Id.*, at 716, 107 S.Ct., at 3082.

[4, 5] The same conclusion is appropriate under § 1988.[5] Our cases have repeatedly stressed that attorney's fees awarded under this statute are to be based on market rates for the services rendered. See, *e.g., Blanchard v. Bergeron,* 489 U.S. ——, 109 S.Ct. 939, 103 L.Ed.2d 67 (1989); *Riverside v. Rivera,* 477 U.S. 561, 106 S.Ct. 2686, 91 L.Ed.2d 466 (1986); *Blum v. Stenson,* 465 U.S. 886, 104 S.Ct. 1541, 79 L.Ed.2d 891 (1984). Clearly, compensation received several years after the services were rendered—as it frequently is in complex civil rights litigation—is not equivalent to the same dollar amount received reasonably promptly as the legal services are performed, as would normally be the case with private billings.[6] We agree, therefore, that an appropriate adjustment for delay in payment—whether by the application of current rather than historic hourly rates or otherwise—is within the contemplation of the statute.

[6] To summarize: We reaffirm our holding in *Hutto v. Finney* that the Eleventh Amendment has no application to an award of attorney's fees, ancillary to a grant of prospective relief, against a State. It follows that the same is true for the calculation of the *amount* of the fee. An adjustment for delay in payment is, we hold, an appropriate factor in the determination of what constitutes a reasonable attorney's fee under § 1988. An award against a State of a fee that includes such an enhancement for delay is not, therefore, barred by the Eleventh Amendment.

III

Missouri's second contention is that the District Court erred in compensating the work of law clerks and paralegals (hereinafter collectively "paralegals") at the market rates for their services, rather than at their cost to the attorney. While Missouri agrees that compensation for the cost of these personnel should be included in the fee award, it suggests that an hourly rate of $15—which it argued below corresponded to their salaries, benefits, and overhead—would be appropriate, rather than the market rates of $35 to $50. According to Missouri, § 1988 does not authorize billing paralegals' hours at market rates, and doing so produces a "windfall" for the attorney.[7]

---

5. *Delaware Valley* was decided under § 304(d) of the Clean Air Act, 42 U.S.C. § 7604(d). We looked for guidance, however, to § 1988 and our cases construing it. *Pennsylvania v. Delaware Valley Citizens' Council,* 483 U.S. 711, 713, n. 1, 107 S.Ct. 3078, 3080, n. 1, 97 L.Ed.2d 585 (1987).

6. This delay, coupled with the fact that, as we recognized in *Delaware Valley,* the attorney's *expenses* are not deferred pending completion of the litigation, can cause considerable hardship. The present case provides an illustration. During a period of nearly three years, the demands of this case precluded attorney Benson from accepting other employment. In order to pay his staff and meet other operating expenses, he was obliged to borrow $633,000. As of January 1987, he had paid over $113,000 in interest on this debt, and was continuing to borrow to meet interest payments. Record 2336–2339; Tr. 130–131. The LDF, for its part, incurred deficits of $700,000 in 1983 and over $1 million in 1984, largely because of this case. Tr. 46. If no compensation were provided for the delay in

payment, the prospect of such hardship could well deter otherwise willing attorneys from accepting complex civil rights cases that might offer great benefit to society at large; this result would work to defeat Congress' purpose in enacting § 1988 of "encourag[ing] the enforcement of federal law through lawsuits filed by private persons." *Delaware Valley, supra,* at 737, 107 S.Ct., at 3093 (BLACKMUN, J., dissenting).

We note also that we have recognized the availability of interim fee awards under § 1988 when a litigant becomes a prevailing party on one issue in the course of the litigation. *Texas State Teachers Assn. v. Garland Independent School Dist.,* 489 U.S. ——, ——, 109 S.Ct. 1486, ——, 103 L.Ed.2d 866 (1989). In economic terms, such an interim award does not differ from an enhancement for delay in payment.

7. The Courts of Appeals have taken a variety of positions on this issue. Most permit separate billing of paralegal time. See, *e.g., Save Our Cumberland Mountains, Inc. v. Hodel,* 263 U.S. App.D.C. 409, 420, n. 7, 826 F.2d 43, 54, n. 7

[7] We begin with the statutory language, which provides simply for "a reasonable attorney's fee as part of the costs." 42 U.S.C. § 1988. Clearly, a "reasonable attorney's fee" cannot have been meant to compensate only work performed personally by members of the bar. Rather, the term must refer to a reasonable fee for the work product of an attorney. Thus, the fee must take into account the work not only of attorneys, but also of secretaries, messengers, librarians, janitors, and others whose labor contributes to the work product for which an attorney bills her client; and it must also take account of other expenses and profit. The parties have suggested no reason why the work of paralegals should not be similarly compensated, nor can we think of any. We thus take as our starting point the self-evident proposition that the "reasonable attorney's fee" provided for by statute should compensate the work of paralegals, as well as that of attorneys. The more difficult question is how the work of paralegals is to be valuated in calculating the overall attorney's fee.

[8] The statute specifies a "reasonable" fee for the attorney's work product. In determining how other elements of the attorney's fee are to be calculated, we have consistently looked to the marketplace as our guide to what is "reasonable." In *Blum v. Stenson*, 465 U.S. 886, 104 S.Ct. 1541, 79 L.Ed.2d 891 (1984), for example, we rejected an argument that attorney's fees for nonprofit legal service organizations should be based on cost. We said: "The statute and legislative history establish that 'reasonable fees' under § 1988 are

to be calculated according to the prevailing market rates in the relevant community...." *Id.*, at 895, 104 S.Ct., at 1547. See also, *e.g.*, *Delaware Valley*, 483 U.S., at 732, 107 S.Ct., at 3090 (O'CONNOR, J., concurring) (controlling question concerning contingency enhancements is "how the market in a community compensates for contingency"); *Rivera*, 477 U.S., at 591, 106 S.Ct. at 2703 (REHNQUIST, J., dissenting) (reasonableness of fee must be determined "in light of both the traditional billing practices in the profession, and the fundamental principle that the award of a 'reasonable' attorney's fee under § 1988 means a fee that would have been deemed reasonable if billed to affluent plaintiffs by their own attorneys"). A reasonable attorney's fee under § 1988 is one calculated on the basis of rates and practices prevailing in the relevant market, *i.e.*, "in line with those [rates] prevailing in the community for similar services by lawyers of reasonably comparable skill, experience, and reputation," *Blum, supra*, 465 U.S., at 896, n. 11, 104 S.Ct., at 1547, n. 11, and one that grants the successful civil rights plaintiff a "fully compensatory fee," *Hensley v. Eckerhart*, 461 U.S. 424, 435, 103 S.Ct. 1933, 1940, 76 L.Ed.2d 40 (1983), comparable to what "is traditional with attorneys compensated by a fee-paying client." S.Rep. No. 94–1011, p. 6 (1976), U.S.Code Cong. & Admin.News 1976, pp. 5908, 5913.

If an attorney's fee awarded under § 1988 is to yield the same level of compensation that would be available from the market, the "increasingly widespread cus-

(1987), vacated in part on other grounds, 273 U.S.App.D.C. 78, 857 F.2d 1516 (1988) (en banc); *Jacobs v. Mancuso*, 825 F.2d 559, 563, and n. 6 (CA1 1987) (collecting cases); *Spanish Action Committee of Chicago v. Chicago*, 811 F.2d 1129, 1138 (CA7 1987); *Ramos v. Lamm*, 713 F.2d 546, 558–559 (CA10 1983); *Richardson v. Byrd*, 709 F.2d 1016, 1023 (CA5), cert. denied *sub nom. Dallas County Commissioners Court v. Richardson*, 464 U.S. 1009, 104 S.Ct. 527, 78 L.Ed.2d 710 (1983). See also *Riverside v. Rivera*, 477 U.S. 561, 566, n. 2, 106 S.Ct. 2686, 2690, n. 2, 91 L.Ed.2d 466 (1986) (noting lower-court approval of hourly rate for law clerks). Some

courts, on the other hand, have considered paralegal work "out-of-pocket expense," recoverable only at cost to the attorney. See, *e.g.*, *Northcross v. Board of Education of Memphis City Schools*, 611 F.2d 624, 639 (CA6 1979), cert. denied, 447 U.S. 911, 100 S.Ct. 3000, 64 L.Ed.2d 862 (1980); *Thornberry v. Delta Air Lines, Inc.*, 676 F.2d 1240, 1244 (CA9 1982), vacated, 461 U.S. 952, 103 S.Ct. 2421, 77 L.Ed.2d 1311 (1983). At least one Court of Appeals has refused to permit any recovery of paralegal expense apart from the attorney's hourly fee. *Abrams v. Baylor College of Medicine*, 805 F.2d 528, 535 (CA5 1986).

tom of separately billing for the services of paralegals and law students who serve as clerks," *Ramos v. Lamm,* 713 F.2d 546, 558 (CA10 1983), must be taken into account. All else being equal, the hourly fee charged by an attorney whose rates include paralegal work in her hourly fee, or who bills separately for the work of paralegals at cost, will be higher than the hourly fee charged by an attorney competing in the same market who bills separately for the work of paralegals at "market rates." In other words, the prevailing "market rate" for attorney time is not independent of the manner in which paralegal time is accounted for.[8] Thus, if the prevailing practice in a given community were to bill paralegal time separately at market rates, fees awarded the attorney at market rates for attorney time would not be fully compensatory if the court refused to compensate hours billed by paralegals or did so only at "cost." Similarly, the fee awarded would be too high if the court accepted separate billing for paralegal hours in a market where that was not the custom.

We reject the argument that compensation for paralegals at rates above "cost" would yield a "windfall" for the prevailing attorney. Neither petitioners nor anyone else, to our knowledge, have ever suggested that the hourly rate applied to the work of an associate attorney in a law firm creates a windfall for the firm's partners or is otherwise improper under § 1988, merely because it exceeds the cost of the attorney's services. If the fees are consistent with market rates and practices, the "wind-

fall" argument has no more force with regard to paralegals than it does for associates. And it would hardly accord with Congress' intent to provide a "fully compensatory fee" if the prevailing plaintiff's attorney in a civil rights lawsuit were not permitted to bill separately for paralegals, while the defense attorney in the same litigation was able to take advantage of the prevailing practice and obtain market rates for such work. Yet that is precisely the result sought in this case by the State of Missouri, which appears to have paid its own outside counsel for the work of paralegals at the hourly rate of $35. Record 2696, 2699.[9]

[9] Nothing in § 1988 requires that the work of paralegals invariably be billed separately. If it is the practice in the relevant market not to do so, or to bill the work of paralegals only at cost, that is all that § 1988 requires. Where, however, the prevailing practice is to bill paralegal work at market rates, treating civil rights lawyers' fee requests in the same way is not only permitted by § 1988, but also makes economic sense. By encouraging the use of lower-cost paralegals rather than attorneys wherever possible, permitting market-rate billing of paralegal hours "encourages cost-effective delivery of legal services and, by reducing the spiraling cost of civil rights litigation, furthers the policies underlying civil rights statutes." *Cameo Convalescent Center, Inc. v. Senn,* 738 F.2d 836, 846 (CA7 1984), cert. denied, 469 U.S. 1106, 105 S.Ct. 780, 83 L.Ed.2d 775 (1985).[10]

---

8. The attorney who bills separately for paralegal time is merely distributing her costs and profit margin among the hourly fees of other members of her staff, rather than concentrating them in the fee she sets for her own time.

9. A variant of Missouri's "windfall" argument is the following: "If paralegal expense is reimbursed at a rate many times the actual cost, will attorneys next try to bill separately—and at a profit—for such items as secretarial time, paper clips, electricity, and other expenses?" Reply Brief for Petitioners 15–16. The answer to this question is, of course, that attorneys seeking fees under § 1988 would have no basis for re-

questing separate compensation of such expenses unless this were the prevailing practice in the local community. The safeguard against the billing at a profit of secretarial services and paper clips is the discipline of the market.

10. It has frequently been recognized in the lower courts that paralegals are capable of carrying out many tasks, under the supervision of an attorney, that might otherwise be performed by a lawyer and billed at a higher rate. Such work might include, for example, factual investigation, including locating and interviewing witnesses; assistance with depositions, interrogatories, and document production; compilation of

Such separate billing appears to be the practice in most communities today.[11] In the present case, Missouri concedes that "the local market typically bills separately for paralegal services," Tr. of Oral Arg. 14, and the District Court found that the requested hourly rates of $35 for law clerks, $40 for paralegals, and $50 for recent law graduates were the prevailing rates for such services in the Kansas City area. App. to Pet. for Cert. A29, A31, A34. Under these circumstances, the court's decision to award separate compensation at these rates was fully in accord with § 1988.

IV

The courts below correctly granted a fee enhancement to compensate for delay in payment and approved compensation of paralegals and law clerks at market rates. The judgment of the Court of Appeals is therefore

Affirmed.

Justice MARSHALL took no part in the consideration or decision of this case.

Justice O'CONNOR, with whom Justice SCALIA joins, and with whom the Chief Justice joins in part, concurring in part and dissenting in part.

I agree with the Court that 42 U.S.C. § 1988 allows compensation for the work of paralegals and law clerks at market rates, and therefore join Parts I and III of its opinion. I do not join Part II, however, for in my view the Eleventh Amendment does not permit enhancement of attorney's fees assessed against a State as compensation for delay in payment.

The Eleventh Amendment does not, of course, provide a State with across-the-board immunity from all monetary relief. Relief that "serves directly to bring an end to a violation of federal law is not barred by the Eleventh Amendment even though accompanied by a substantial ancillary effect" on a State's treasury. *Papasan v. Allain*, 478 U.S. 265, 278, 106 S.Ct. 2932, 2940–41, 92 L.Ed.2d 209 (1986). Thus, in *Milliken v. Bradley*, 433 U.S. 267, 289–290, 97 S.Ct. 2749, 2761–2762, 53 L.Ed.2d 745 (1977), the Court unanimously upheld a decision ordering a State to pay over $5 million to eliminate the effects of *de jure* segregation in certain school systems. On the other hand, "[r]elief that in essence serves to compensate a party injured in the past," such as relief "expressly denominated as damages," or "relief [that] is tantamount to an award of damages for a past violation of federal law, even though styled as something else," is prohibited by the Eleventh Amendment. *Papasan*, 478 U.S., at 278, 106 S.Ct., at 2940–41. The crucial question in this case is whether that portion of respondents' attorney's fees based on current hourly rates is properly characterized as retroactive monetary relief.

statistical and financial data; checking legal citations; and drafting correspondence. Much such work lies in a gray area of tasks that might appropriately be performed either by an attorney or a paralegal. To the extent that fee applicants under § 1988 are not permitted to bill for the work of paralegals at market rates, it would not be surprising to see a greater amount of such work performed by attorneys themselves, thus increasing the overall cost of litigation.

Of course, purely clerical or secretarial tasks should not be billed at a paralegal rate, regardless of who performs them. What the court in *Johnson v. Georgia Highway Express, Inc.*, 488 F.2d 714, 717 (CA5 1974), said in regard to the work of attorneys is applicable by analogy to paralegals: "It is appropriate to distinguish between legal work, in the strict sense, and investigation, clerical work, compilation of facts and statistics and other work which can often be accomplished by non-lawyers but which a lawyer may do because he has no other help available. Such non-legal work may command a lesser rate. Its dollar value is not enhanced just because a lawyer does it."

11. *Amicus* National Association of Legal Assistants reports that 77 percent of 1,800 legal assistants responding to a survey of the association's membership stated that their law firms charged clients for paralegal work on an hourly billing basis. Brief for National Association of Legal Assistants as *Amicus Curiae* 11.

MISSOURI v. JENKINS BY AGYEI
Cite as 109 S.Ct. 2463 (1989)
2473

In *Library of Congress v. Shaw*, 478 U.S. 310, 106 S.Ct. 2957, 92 L.Ed.2d 250 (1986), the Court addressed whether the attorney's fees provision of Title VII, 42 U.S.C. § 2000e–5(k), permits an award of attorney's fees against the United States to be enhanced in order to compensate for delay in payment. In relevant part, § 2000e–5(k) provides:

"In any action or proceeding under this subchapter the court, in its discretion, may allow the prevailing party, other than the [EEOC] or the United States, a reasonable attorney's fees as part of the costs, and the [EEOC] and the United States shall be liable for costs the same as a private person."

The Court began its analysis in *Shaw* by holding that "interest is an element of damages separate from damages on the substantive claim." 478 U.S., at 314, 106 S.Ct., at 2961 (citing C. McCormick, Law of Damages § 50, p. 205 (1935)). Given the "no-interest" rule of federal sovereign immunity, under which the United States is not liable for interest absent an express statutory waiver to the contrary, the Court was unwilling to conclude that, by equating the United States' liability to that of private persons in § 2000e–5(k), Congress had waived the United States' immunity from interest. 478 U.S., at 314–319, 106 S.Ct., at 2961–2964. The fact that § 2000e–5(k) used the word "reasonable" to modify "attorney's fees" did not alter this result, for the Court explained that it had "consistently ... refused to impute an intent to waive immunity from interest into the ambiguous use of a particular word or phrase in a statute." *Id.*, at 320, 106 S.Ct., at 2964. The description of attorney's fees as costs in § 2000e–5(k) also did not mandate a contrary conclusion because "[p]rejudgment interest ... is considered as damages, not a component of 'costs,'" and the "term 'costs' has *never* been understood to include any interest component." *Id.*, at 321, 106 S.Ct. at 2965 (emphasis added) (citing 10 C. Wright, A. Miller, & M. Kane, Federal Practice and Procedure §§ 2664, 2666,

2670 (2d ed. 1983); 2 A. Sedgwick & G. Van Nest, Sedgwick on Damages 157–158 (7th ed. 1880)). Finally, the Court rejected the argument that the enhancement was proper because the "no-interest" rule did not prohibit compensation for delay in payment: "Interest and a delay factor share an identical function. They are designed to compensate for the belated receipt of money." 478 U.S., at 322, 106 S.Ct., at 2965.

As the Court notes, *ante*, at 2468, n. 3, the "no-interest" rule of federal sovereign immunity at issue in *Shaw* provided an "added gloss of strictness," 478 U.S., at 318, 106 S.Ct., at 2963, and may have explained the *result* reached by the Court in that case, *i.e.*, that § 2000e–5(k) did not waive the United States' immunity against awards of interest. But there is not so much as a hint anywhere in *Shaw* that the Court's discussions and definitions of interest and compensation for delay were dictated by, or limited to, the federal "no-interest" rule. As the quotations above illustrate, the Court's opinion in *Shaw* is filled with broad, unqualified language. The dissenters in *Shaw* did not disagree with the Court's sweeping characterization of interest and compensation for delay as damages. Rather, they argued only that § 2000e–5(k) had waived the immunity of the United States with respect to awards of interest. See *id.*, at 323–327, 106 S.Ct., at 2966–2968 (BRENNAN, J., dissenting). I therefore emphatically disagree with the Court's statement that "*Shaw* ... does not represent a general-purpose definition of compensation for delay that governs here." *Ante*, at 2468, n. 3.

Two general propositions that are relevant here emerge from *Shaw*. First, interest is considered damages, and not costs. Second, compensation for delay, which serves the same function as interest, is also the equivalent of damages. These two propositions make clear that enhancement for delay constitutes retroactive monetary relief barred by the Eleventh Amendment. Given my reading of *Shaw*, I do not think the Court's reliance on the cost rationale of

§ 1988 set forth in *Hutto v. Finney,* 437 U.S. 678, 98 S.Ct. 2565, 57 L.Ed.2d 522 (1978), is persuasive. Because *Shaw* teaches that compensation for delay constitutes damages and cannot be considered costs, see 478 U.S., at 321–322, 106 S.Ct., at 2965–2966, *Hutto* is not controlling. See *Hutto,* 437 U.S., 697, n. 27, 98 S.Ct., at 2577, n. 27 ("we do not suggest that our analysis would be the same if Congress were to expand the concept of costs beyond the traditional category of litigation expenses"). Furthermore, *Hutto* does not mean that inclusion of attorney's fees as costs in a statute forecloses a challenge to the enhancement of fees as compensation for delay in payment. If it did, then *Shaw* would have been resolved differently, for § 2000e–5(k) lists attorney's fees as costs.

Even if I accepted the narrow interpretation of *Shaw* proffered by the Court, I would disagree with the result reached by the Court in Part II of its opinion. On its own terms, the Court's analysis fails. The Court suggests that the definitions of interest and compensation for delay set forth in *Shaw* would be triggered only by a rule of sovereign immunity barring awards of interest against the States: "Outside the context of the 'no-interest rule' of federal immunity, we see no reason why compensation for delay cannot be included within § 1988 attorney's fee awards[.]" *Ante,* at 2468, n. 3. But the Court does not inquire whether such a rule exists. In fact, there is a federal rule barring awards of interest against States. See *Virginia v. West Virginia,* 238 U.S. 202, 234, 35 S.Ct. 795, 808, 59 L.Ed. 1272 (1915) ("Nor can it be deemed in derogation of the sovereignty of the State that she should be charged with interest *if* her agreement properly construed so provides.") (emphasis added); *United States v. North Carolina,* 136 U.S. 211, 221, 10 S.Ct. 920, 924, 34 L.Ed. 336 (1890) ("general principle" is that "an obligation of the State to pay interest, whether as interest or as damages, on any debt overdue, cannot arise *except* by the consent and contract of the State, manifested by

statute, or in a form authorized by statute") (emphasis added). The Court has recently held that the rule of immunity set forth in *Virginia* and *North Carolina* is inapplicable in situations where the State does not retain any immunity, see *West Virginia v. United States,* 479 U.S. 305, 310–312, 107 S.Ct. 702, 706–707, 93 L.Ed.2d 639 (1987) (State can be held liable for interest to the United States, against whom it has no sovereign immunity), but the rule has not otherwise been limited, and there is no reason why it should not be relevant in the Eleventh Amendment context presented in this case.

As *Virginia* and *North Carolina* indicate, a State can waive its immunity against awards of interest. See also *Clark v. Barnard,* 108 U.S. 436, 447, 2 S.Ct. 878, 882–83, 27 L.Ed. 780 (1883). The Missouri courts have interpreted Mo.Rev.Stat. § 408.020 (1979 and Supp.1989), providing for prejudgment interest on money that becomes due and payable, and § 408.040, providing for prejudgment interest on court judgments and orders, as making the State liable for interest. See *Denton Construction Co. v. Missouri State Highway Comm'n,* 454 S.W.2d 44, 59–60 (Mo.1970) (§ 408.020); *Steppelman v. State Highway Comm'n of Missouri,* 650 S.W.2d 343, 345 (Mo.App.1983) (§ 408.040). There can be no argument, however, that these Missouri statutes and cases allow interest to be awarded against the State here. A "State's waiver of sovereign immunity in its own courts is not a waiver of the Eleventh Amendment immunity in the federal courts." *Pennhurst State School and Hospital v. Halderman,* 465 U.S. 89, 99, n. 9, 104 S.Ct. 900, 907, n. 9, 79 L.Ed.2d 67 (1984).

The fact that a State has immunity from awards of interest is not the end of the matter. In a case such as this one involving school desegregation, interest or compensation for delay (in the guise of current hourly rates) can theoretically be awarded against a State despite the Eleventh Amendment's bar against retroactive monetary liability. The Court has held that Congress can set aside the States' Eleventh Amendment immunity in order to enforce the provisions of the Fourteenth Amendment. See *City of Rome v. United States,* 446 U.S. 156, 179, 100 S.Ct. 1548, 1562–63, 64 L.Ed.2d 119 (1980); *Fitzpatrick v. Bitzer,* 427 U.S. 445, 456, 96 S.Ct. 2666, 2671, 49 L.Ed.2d 614 (1976). Congress must, however, be unequivocal in expressing its intent to abrogate that immunity. See generally *Atascadero State Hospital v. Scanlon,* 473 U.S. 234, 243, 105 S.Ct. 3142, 3148, 87 L.Ed.2d 171 (1985) ("Congress must express its intention to abrogate the Eleventh Amendment in unmistakable language in the statute itself.").

In *Hutto* the Court was able to avoid deciding whether § 1988 met the "clear statement" rule only because attorney's fees (without any enhancement) are not considered retroactive in nature. See 437 U.S., at 695–697, 98 S.Ct., at 2575–2577. The Court cannot do the same here, where the attorney's fees were enhanced to compensate for delay in payment. Cf. *Osterneck v. Ernst & Whinney,* — U.S. —, —, 109 S.Ct. 987, 991, 103 L.Ed.2d 146 (1989) ("unlike attorney's fees, which at common law were regarded as an element of costs, ... prejudgment interest traditionally has been considered part of the compensation due [the] plaintiff").

In relevant part, § 1988 provides:

"In any action or proceeding to enforce a provision of sections 1981, 1982, 1983, 1985, and 1986 of this title, title IX of Public Law 92–318, or title VI of the Civil Rights Act of 1964, the court, in its discretion, may allow the prevailing party, other than the United States, a reasonable attorney's fees as part of the costs."

In my view, § 1988 does not meet the "clear statement" rule set forth in *Atascadero.* It does not mention damages, interest, compensation for delay, or current hourly rates. As one federal court has correctly noted, "Congress has not yet made any statement suggesting that a § 1988 attorney's fee award should include

prejudgment interest." *Rogers v. Okin,* 821 F.2d 22, 27 (CA1 1987). A comparison of the statute at issue in *Shaw* also indicates that § 1988, as currently written, is insufficient to allow attorney's fees assessed against a State to be enhanced to compensate for delay in payment. The language of § 1988 is undoubtedly less expansive than that of § 2000e–5(k), for § 1988 does not equate the liability of States with that of private persons. Since § 2000e–5(k) does not allow enhancement of an award of attorney's fees to compensate for delay, it is logical to conclude that § 1988, a more narrowly worded statute, likewise does not allow interest (through the use of current hourly rates) to be tacked on to an award of attorney's fees against a State.

Compensation for delay in payment was *one* of the reasons the District Court used current hourly rates in calculating respondents' attorney's fees. See App. to Pet. for Cert. A26–A27; 838 F.2d 260, 263, 265 (CA8 1988). I would reverse the award of attorney's fees to respondents and remand so that the fees can be calculated without taking compensation for delay into account.

Chief Justice REHNQUIST, dissenting.

I agree with Justice O'CONNOR that the Eleventh Amendment does not permit an award of attorney's fees against a State which includes compensation for delay in payment. Unlike Justice O'CONNOR, however, I do not agree with the Court's approval of the award of law clerk and paralegal fees made here.

Section 1988 gives the district courts discretion to allow the prevailing party in an action under § 1983 "a reasonable attorney's fee as part of the costs." 42 U.S.C. § 1988. The Court reads this language as authorizing recovery of "a 'reasonable' fee for the attorney's work product," *ante,* at 2470, which, the Court concludes, may include separate compensation for the services of law clerks and paralegals. But the statute itself simply uses the very familiar term "a reasonable attorney's fee," which to those untutored in the Court's linguistic juggling means a fee charged for services rendered by an individual who has been licensed to practice law. Because law clerks and paralegals have not been licensed to practice law in Missouri, it is difficult to see how charges for their services may be separately billed as part of "attorney's fees." And since a prudent attorney customarily includes compensation for the cost of law clerk and paralegal services, like any other sort of office overhead—from secretarial staff, janitors, and librarians, to telephone service, stationery, and paper clips—in his own hourly billing rate, allowing the prevailing party to recover separate compensation for law clerk and paralegal services may result in "double recovery."

The Court finds justification for its ruling in the fact that the prevailing practice among attorneys in Kansas City is to bill clients separately for the services of law clerks and paralegals. But I do not think Congress intended the meaning of the statutory term "attorney's fee" to expand and contract with each and every vagary of local billing practice. Under the Court's logic, prevailing parties could recover at market rates for the cost of secretaries, private investigators, and other types of lay personnel who assist the attorney in preparing his case, so long as they could show that the prevailing practice in the local market was to bill separately for these services. Such a result would be a sufficiently drastic departure from the traditional concept of "attorney's fees" that I believe new statutory authorization should be required for it. That permitting separate billing of law clerk and paralegal hours at market rates might " 'reduc[e] the spiraling cost of civil rights litigation' " by encouraging attorneys to delegate to these individuals tasks which they would otherwise perform themselves at higher cost, *ante,* at 2471, and n. 10, may be a persuasive reason for Congress to enact such additional legislation. It is not, however, a persuasive reason for us to rewrite the legislation which Congress has in fact enacted. See *Badaracco v. Commissioner,* 464 U.S. 386, 398, 104 S.Ct. 756, 764, 78

L.Ed.2d 549 (1984) ("[c]ourts are not authorized to rewrite a statute because they might deem its effects susceptible of improvement").

I also disagree with the State's suggestion that law clerk and paralegal expenses incurred by a prevailing party, if not recoverable at market rates as "attorney's fees" under § 1988, are nonetheless recoverable at actual cost under that statute. The language of § 1988 expands the traditional definition of "costs" to include "a reasonable attorney's fee," but it cannot fairly be read to authorize the recovery of all other out-of-pocket expenses actually incurred by the prevailing party in the course of litigation. Absent specific statutory authorization for the recovery of such expenses, the prevailing party remains subject to the limitations on cost recovery imposed by Federal Rule of Civil Procedure 54(d) and 28 U.S.C. § 1920, which govern the taxation of costs in federal litigation where a cost-shifting statute is not applicable. Section 1920 gives the district court discretion to tax certain types of costs against the losing party in any federal litigation. The statute specifically enumerates six categories of expenses which may be taxed as costs: fees of the court clerk and marshal; fees of the court reporter; printing fees and witness fees; copying fees; certain docket fees; and fees of court-appointed experts and interpreters. We have held that this list is exclusive. *Crawford Fitting Co. v. J.T. Gibbons, Inc.,* 482 U.S. 437, 107 S.Ct. 2494, 96 L.Ed.2d 385 (1987). Since none of these categories can possibly be construed to include the fees of law clerks and paralegals, I would also hold that reimbursement for these expenses may not be separately awarded at actual cost.

I would therefore reverse the award of reimbursement for law clerk and paralegal expenses.

Summary of Definitions of Terms: Legal Assistant & Paralegal

from the NALA Professional Development Committee
Published May 1997, XXIV Facts & Findings 1

Introduction

The National Association of Legal Assistants, Inc., is a professional association composed of individual members and ninety state and local affiliated association, representing over 17,000 legal assistants, Established in 1975. NALA goals and programs were developed by 800 charter members to:

- Increase the professional standing of legal assistants throughout the nation
- Provide uniformity in the identification of legal assistants
- Establish national standards of professional competence for legal assistants
- Provide uniformity among the states in the utilization of legal assistants

One of the services of this association is tracking legislative, court, and bar association activities related the paralegal profession. The following is a summary of the various definitions of the terms "paralegal" and "legal assistant" as of January 23, 1997, from twenty-six states, the U.S. Supreme Court, the American Bar Association, and the National Association of Legal Assistants.

Definition of Legal Assistant/Paralegal

National associations, bar associations, legislatures, and supreme courts have addressed the definition of legal assistants and paralegals. Through discussions within each group, similarities in the identification and duties of legal assistants are emerging with routine consistency. The common threads in these definitions and discussions are:

Legal Assistants
1. Have received specialized training through formal education or many years of experience;
2. Work under the supervision and direction of an attorney; and
3. Perform non-clerical, substantive legal work in assisting an attorney. This paper summarizes these definitions.

National Organizations

The definition of "legal assistant" adopted in 1984 by the National Association of Legal Assistants is as follows:

> *Legal assistants (also known as paralegals) are a distinguishable group of persons who assist attorneys in the delivery of legal services, Through formal education, training, and experience, legal assistants have knowledge and expertise regarding the legal system and substantive and procedural law which qualify them to do work of a legal nature under the supervision of an attorney.*

In 1986 the American Bar Association adopted the following definition:

> *A legal assistant is a person, qualified through education, training, or work experience, who is employed or retained by a lawyer, law office, governmental agency, or other entity, in a capacity or function which involves the performance, under the ultimate direction and supervision of an attorney, of specifically delegated substantive legal work, which work, for the most part, requires*

a sufficient knowledge of legal concepts that, absent such assistant, the attorney would perform the task.

In 1997, the ABA House of Delegates approved a streamlined definition of a legal assistant:

> A legal assistant or paralegal is a person, qualified by education, training, or work experience who is employed or retained by a lawyer, law office, corporation, governmental agency, or other entity, who performs specifically delegated substantive legal work for which a lawyer is responsible.

This definition maintains the similarities of those discussed previously by keeping the requirement that legal assistants work under the supervision of a lawyer, that delegated work be substantive in nature, and that legal assistants are qualified through education, training, or work experience.

Both definitions recognize the terms "legal assistant" and "paralegal" as identical terms.

State Legislatures

Legislatures among the United States have also addressed this question. The State of Florida Statute 57.104, effective 10/1/87, specifically states that legal assistants work under the direction of the supervision of an attorney.

Similar legislation was introduced in 1993 in the states of Indiana and Oklahoma. These bills call for the recoverability of legal assistant time in attorney fee awards. The Indiana bills (House Bill 1583; Senate Bill 424), passed April 27, 1993 are now Public Law 93-6. They define paralegals as persons (1) qualified through education, training, or work experience, and (2) employed by a lawyer, law office, governmental agency, or other entity to work under the direction of an attorney in a capacity that involves the performance of substantive legal work that usually requires a sufficient knowledge of legal concepts, and would be performed by the attorney in the absence of the paralegal. This definition is, essentially, the same as the definition adopted by the American Bar Association.

Oklahoma House Bill 1628 defined legal assistants in the same manner, using the ABA definition as a basis. This bill passed the Oklahoma House of Representatives on February 15, 1993. It did not reach the Senate floor during the session.

The definition of the term "paralegal" was addressed by the California legislature in Senate Bill 1455, which became Public Law 92-572 on August 30, 1992. This bill amended sections of the California probate code so that Section 2640 (a)(3)(c) provides:

> *Legal services for which the attorney may be compensated include those services rendered by any paralegal performing the legal services under the direction and supervision of an attorney.*

The statute also states that the attorney may "apply to the court for compensation" for services of a "paralegal."

Illinois Senate Bill 995, passed and signed by the governor on July 7, 1995, sets forth a definition of a paralegal. Effective January 1, 1996, the bill amended the Statute on Statutes by adding Section 1.35 as follows:

> *Sec. 1.35. Paralegal. "Paralegal" means a person who is qualified through education, training, or work experience and is employed by a lawyer, law office, governmental agency, or other entity to work under the direction of an attorney in a capacity that involves the performance of substantive legal work that usually requires a sufficient knowledge of legal concepts and would be performed by the attorney in the absence of the paralegal. A reference in an Act to attorney fees includes paralegal fees, recoverable at market rates.*

The Pennsylvania legislature has addressed paralegals in its unauthorized practice of law statutes. Effective July 11, 1996, Section 2524(a) of Title 42 of the Pennsylvania Consolidated Statutes now reads:

> *(a) General rule.—Except as provided in subsection (b), any person, including, but not limited to, a paralegal or legal assistant, who within this Commonwealth shall practice law, or who shall hold himself out to the public as being entitled to practice law, or use or advertise the title of lawyer, attorney at law, attorney and counselor at law, counselor, or the equivalent in any language, in such as a manner to convey the impression that he is a practitioner of the law of any jurisdiction, without being an attorney at law or a corporation complying with 15 Pa.C.S. Ch. 29 (relating to professional corporations), commits a misdemeanor of the third degree[,] upon a first violation. A second or subsequent violation of this subsection constitutes a misdemeanor of the first degree.*

This statute is in response to widespread concern that some individuals using the terms "paralegal" or "legal assistant" as their occupational title and in advertisements were doing so in a way that lead potential customers to believe they are authorized to deliver legal services. This legislation prohibits use of the terms "paralegal" and "legal assistant" in this fashion. Rather than serving as a definition of what paralegals may do, the statute informs the public that paralegals and legal assistants do not deliver legal services without attorney supervision and cannot hold themselves out as individuals entitled to practice law.

Supreme Court Recognition

The U.S. Supreme Court encourages and recognizes the use of legal assistants working under the supervision of an attorney.

> *It has frequently been recognized in the lower courts that paralegals are capable of carrying out many tasks, under the supervision of an attorney, that might otherwise be performed by a lawyer and billed at a higher rate* (*Missouri v. Jenkins*, 491 U.S. 274, 109 S.Ct. at 2471-72 (1989)).

State supreme courts have also addressed the definition of "legal assistant" or "paralegal" in their rules and in their opinions. Many of the state supreme court findings are included in this section. Further, the definitions of legal assistants or paralegals adopted by bar associations that are regulated by supreme courts are included in this section.

Kentucky.   Among the earliest to address the utilization of paralegals in its rules is the Kentucky Supreme Court in adoption of Rule 3.700 on September 4, 1979. The rule, revised through 1989, lists the following definition:

> *For the purposes of this Rule, a paralegal is a person under the supervision and direction of a licensed lawyer: who may apply knowledge of law and legal procedures in rendering direct assistance to lawyers engaged in legal research; design, develop, or plan modifications or new procedures, techniques, services, processes or applications; prepare or interpret legal documents and write detailed procedures for practicing in certain fields of law; select, compile and use technical information from such references as digests, encyclopedias, or practice manuals; and analyze and follow procedural problems that involve independent decisions.*

Rhode Island.   In Rhode Island Supreme Court Provisional Order No. 18, effective February 1, 1983, and revised through October 31, 1990, "legal assistant" is defined as follows:

A legal assistant is one who under the supervision of a lawyer, shall apply knowledge of law and legal procedures in rendering direct assistance to lawyers, clients and courts; design, develop, and modify procedures, techniques, services, and processes; prepare and interpret legal documents; detail procedures for practicing in certain fields of law; research, select, access, and compile information from the law library and other references; and analyze and handle procedural problems that involve independent decisions.

The guidelines accompanying this definition emphasize that legal assistants shall work under the direction and supervision of a lawyer who shall be ultimately responsible for their work product.

New Mexico.   The New Mexico Supreme Court Judicial Pamphlet 16, 1986, states that:

A 'legal assistant' means a person, not admitted to the practice of law, who provides assistance to a licensed lawyer and for whose work that licensed lawyer is ultimately responsible. The assistance may include, but is not limited to, record and statistical research; investigation; analysis of records, documents, and facts; problem analysis; preparation of legal memoranda; assistance in drafting legal documents, interrogatories, and correspondence; completion of forms which have been prepared by or under the supervision of the supervising attorney; location of reported decisions, cite checking, and shepardizing; and interviews of clients and witnesses. These and other types of assistance must be provided under the supervision and direction of a licensed attorney. . . .

The commentary to this definition includes references to the fact that the definition of "legal assistant" is intended to cover those persons usually designated as "legal assistants," "paralegals," and "lawyer's assistants."

In 1995 the Supreme Court amended SCRA 1986, 24-101 of the Rules Governing the New Mexico Bar to establish a division of the bar for legal assistants, affirming the definition and listing qualifications for division membership.

New Hampshire.   Supreme Court Administrative Rule 35, Guidelines for the Utilization by Lawyers of the Services of Legal Assistants Under the New Hampshire Rules of Professional Conduct, amended through 1987, define a legal assistant as:

. . . a person not admitted to the practice of law in New Hampshire who is an employee of or an assistant to an active member of the New Hampshire Bar; a partnership comprised of active members of the New Hampshire Bar or a Professional Association within the meaning of RSA Chapter 294-A, and who, under the control and supervision of an active member of the New Hampshire Bar, renders services related to but not constituting the practice of law.

South Dakota.   In Rule 92-5, March 6. 1992, the Supreme Court of South Dakota adopted the following definition of legal assistants:

Legal assistants (also known as paralegals) are a distinguishable group of persons who assist attorneys in the delivery of legal services. Through formal education, training, and experience, legal assistants have knowledge and expertise regarding the legal system and substantive and procedural law which qualify them to do work of a legal nature under the direct supervision of a licensed lawyer.

The rule further states that "any person having been convicted of a felony shall not serve as a legal assistant in the State of South Dakota, unless upon application to the Supreme Court of South Dakota, establishing good moral character and restoration of full civil rights, and its approval thereof."

The South Dakota rule goes on to list seven minimum qualifications as follows:

1. Successful completion of the Certified Legal Assistant (CLA) examination of the National Association of Legal Assistants, Inc.; or
2. Graduation from an ABA-approved program of study for legal assistants; or
3. Graduation from a course of study for legal assistants which is institutionally accredited but not ABA-approved and which requires not less than the equivalent of sixty semester hours of classroom study; or
4. Graduation from a course of study for legal assistants, other than those set forth in (2) and (3) above, plus not less than six months of in-house training as a legal assistant; or
5. A baccalaureate degree in any field. plus not less than six months in-house training as a legal assistant; or
6. A minimum of three years of law-related experience under the supervision of a lawyer, including at least six months of in house training as a legal assistant; or
7. Two years of in-house training as a legal assistant.

North Dakota. Amendments to the North Dakota Rules of Professional Conduct adopted December 11, 1996 by the North Dakota Supreme Court, with an effective date of March 1, 1997, include rules which govern legal assistants/paralegals in North Dakota. Rules 1.5 (Fees), 5.3 Responsibilities Regarding Nonlawyer Assistants, 7.2 Firm Names and Letterheads, and the Terms section of the NDRPC include a definition of "legal assistant," suggested minimum standards, and comments related to supervision of legal assistants, the unauthorized practice of law, and billing for work performed by a legal assistant.

The rules state the following definition:

"Legal Assistant" (or paralegal) means a person who assists lawyers in the delivery of legal services, and who through formal education, training, or experience, has knowledge and expertise regarding the legal system and substantive and procedural law which qualifies the person to do work of a legal nature under the direct supervision of a licensed lawyer.

Virginia. On March 8, 1996, the Virginia State Bar Standing Committee on the Unauthorized Practice of Law adopted a resolution stating that a legal assistant working under direction of a member of the Virginia State Bar in conformance with the Standards and Guidelines would not be engaged in the unauthorized practice of law and that the employment or supervision by a Virginia State Bar member of legal assistants who conform to the Standards and Guidelines would be in the best interest of the public.

The resolution recommends that members of the Virginia State Bar make all reasonable efforts to encourage all legal assistants to subscribe and conform to the Standards and Guidelines, This resolution adopts the following definition of a legal assistant (paralegal):

. . . as one who is a specially trained individual who performs substantive legal work that requires a knowledge of legal concepts and who either works under the supervision of an attorney, who assumes professional responsibility for the final work product, or works in areas where lay individuals are explicitly authorized by statute or regulation to assume certain law-related responsibilities.

Cases

Arizona. In *Continental Townhouses E. Unit One Ass'n v. Brockbank*, 152 Ariz, 537, 733 P.2d 1120, 73 A.L.R.4th 921 (1986), the Arizona Court of Appeals considered whether the time of a nonlawyer employee may be included in attorney fee awards. In its opinion, the Court relied upon the definition of "legal assistant" formulated by the American Bar Association. The court also used the terms "legal assistant" and "paralegal" interchangeably.

New Jersey. In 1990, the New Jersey Committee on Unauthorized Practice of Law issued Opinion No. 24 which held that legal assistants or paralegals who contract their services to attorneys are engaged in the unauthorized practice of law. The New Jersey Committee on the Unauthorized Practice of Law is appointed by the Supreme Court, thus its findings and opinions become Supreme Court Rule. This opinion was appealed to the New Jersey Supreme Court. The Supreme Court issued its Opinion on May 14, 1992, and held:

> The evidence does not support a categorical ban on all independent paralegals practicing in New Jersey. Given the appropriate instructions and supervision, paralegals, whether as employees or independent contractors, are valuable and necessary members of an attorney's work force in the effective and efficient practice of law.

The court further stated that charges for nonlawyers' time that properly fall within the definition of "attorney fees" are those that are clearly shown to have been made (1) for the delegated performance of substantive legal work, that (2) would otherwise have to be performed by a lawyer, and (3) at a rate higher than that charged for nonlawyers' time.

Oklahoma. In *Taylor v. Chubb*, 874 P.2d 806 (Okla. 1994), the Oklahoma Supreme Court held that charges for legal assistants could and should be included by courts in attorney fee award decisions. In its decision, the court refers to the definition of a legal assistant as promulgated by the American Bar Association, and specifically enumerated a list of duties that may be properly performed by legal assistants as follows:

1. *Interview clients;*
2. *Draft pleadings and other documents;*
3. *Carry on legal research, both conventional and computer-aided;*
4. *Research public records;*
5. *Prepare discovery requests and responses;*
6. *Schedule depositions;*
7. *Summarize depositions and other discovery responses;*
8. *Coordinate and manage document production;*
9. *Locate and interview witnesses;*
10. *Organize pleadings, trial exhibits, and other documents;*
11. *Prepare witness and exhibit lists;*
12. *Prepare trial notebooks;*
13. *Prepare for the attendance of witnesses at trial;*
14. *Assist lawyers at trials.*

South Carolina. In the *State of South Carolina v. Robinsan*, Opinion No 24391, filed March 18, 1996, the court stated the function of a paralegal was addressed *In re: Easler*, 275, S.C. 400, 272 S.E.2d 32 (1980):

Paralegals are routinely employed by licensed attorneys to assist in the preparation of legal documents such as deeds and mortgages. The activities of a paralegal do not constitute the practice of law as long as they are limited to work of a preparatory nature, such as legal research, investigation, or the composition of legal documents, which enable the licensed attorney-*employer to carry a given matter to a conclusion through his own examination, approval or additional effort.*

Id, at 400, 272 S.E.2d at 32-33. The opinions stated that while there are no regulations dealing specifically with paralegals, requiring a paralegal to work under the supervision of a licensed attorney ensures control over his or her activities by making the supervising attorney responsible. *See* Rule 5.3 of the Rules of Professional Conduct, Rule 407 SCACR (supervising attorney is responsible for work of nonlawyer employees). Accordingly, "to legitimately provide services as a paralegal, one must work in conjunction with a licensed attorney."

Washington. Adopted 12/3/94, the Washington State Bar Association Board of Governors has established guidelines for the utilization of legal assistant services. The guidelines are based on the ABA Model Guidelines for Utilization of Legal Assistants and adopt the definition of legal assistant/paralegal promulgated by the American Bar Association.

In *Absher Construction Company v. Kent School District*, 29 Wn. App. 841, (1995), the Washington Court of Appeals considered the question of the award of nonlawyer time in attorney fee awards if the nonlawyer is a legal assistant. The Court defined a legal assistant as one who is "qualified through education, training, or work experience, is employed or retained by a lawyer, law office, governmental agency or other entity in a capacity or function which involves a performance, under the ultimate direction and supervision of an attorney, of specifically delegated legal work, which work, for the most part requires a sufficient knowledge of legal concepts that, absent such assistant, the attorney would perform the task." The Court set forth the following criteria relevant in determining whether such services should be compensated:

1. The services performed by the nonlawyer personnel must be legal in nature;
2. The performance of these services must be supervised by an attorney;
3. The qualifications of the person performing the services must be specified in the request for fees in sufficient detail to demonstrate that the person is qualified by virtue of education, training, or work experience to perform substantive legal work;
4. The nature of the services performed must be specified in the request for fees in order to allow the reviewing court to determine that the services performed were legal rather than clerical;
5. As with attorney time, the amount of time expended must be set forth and must be reasonable; and
6. The amount charged must reflect reasonable community standards for charges by that category of personnel.

Bar Association Activity

Bar associations in the following states have defined legal assistants as qualified and educated individuals working under the supervision of attorneys:

Alaska, Arizona, California (Santa Barbara Bar), Colorado, Connecticut, Florida, Illinois, Iowa, Kansas, Kentucky, Massachusetts, Michigan, Minnesota, Missouri, New Mexico, New Hampshire, North Carolina, North Dakota, Ohio, Oregon, Rhode Island, South Carolina, South Dakota, Tennessee, Texas, Virginia, Wisconsin

The following are examples of bar resolutions or guidelines adopted by the associations to assist attorneys in the utilization of paralegal services.

Bar Sections and Divisions

Michigan. The Bylaws of the State Bar of Michigan, Article 1, Sec. 6, defines "legal assistant" for the purposes of membership in the State Bar Legal Assistant Section, as follows:

> *Any person currently employed or retained by a lawyer, law office, governmental agency, or other entity engaged in the practice of law, in a capacity or function which involves the performance under the direction and supervision of an attorney of specifically delegated substantive legal work, which work, for the most part, requires a sufficient knowledge of legal concepts such that, absent that legal assistant, the attorney would perform the tasks and which is not primarily clerical or secretarial in nature.*

On April 23, 1993, the Michigan State Board of Commissioners announced approval of Michigan Guidelines for the Utilization of Legal Assistants. In recognition of the professional status of legal assistants, the Guidelines cite *Missouri v. Jenkins* in allowing that a fee arrangement with a client may include a reasonable charge for work performed by legal assistants at market rates.

Nevada. As part of the creation of a Division of Legal Assistants, the State Bar of Nevada has adopted the following definition of a legal assistant (12/94):

> *A legal assistant (also known as a paralegal) is a person, qualified through education, training, or work experience, who is employed or retained by a lawyer, law office, governmental agency, or other entity in a capacity or function which involves the performance, under the ultimate direction and supervision of an attorney, of specifically delegated substantive legal work, which work, for the most part, requires sufficient knowledge of legal concepts that, absent such an assistant, the attorney would perform the task.*

This definition is identical to that adopted by the American Bar Association in 1986.

Texas. As early as 1981, the Board of Directors, State Bar of Texas, adopted General Guidelines for the Utilization of the Services of Legal Assistants by Attorneys. These guidelines require that a legal assistant work under the supervision of an attorney and shall not give legal advice or otherwise engage in the unauthorized practice of law. An attorney may allow a legal assistant under his or her supervision and direction to perform delegated services in the representation of that attorney's clients provided: (1) the client understands the legal assistant is not an attorney; (2) the attorney maintains a direct relationship with the client; (3) the attorney directs and supervises the legal assistant; and (4) the attorney remains professionally responsible for the client and the client's legal matters. The State Bar of Texas was the first state to establish a membership division for legal assistants within its bar association.

Bar Association Guidelines

Colorado. One of the first states to establish guidelines for paralegals in July 1986, the Colorado Bar has adopted the following definition of a paralegal:

> *Legal assistants (also known as paralegals) are a distinguishable group of persons who assist attorneys in the delivery of legal services. Through formal education, training, and experience, legal assistants have knowledge and expertise regarding the legal system and substantive and*

procedural law which will qualify them to do work of a legal nature under the direct supervision of a licensed attorney.

Connecticut. From a December 11, 1985 Report of Connecticut Bar Association Special Inter-Committee Group to Study the Role of Paralegals, the committee sets forth recommendations as to what the professional obligations of lawyers should be in relation to paralegals. The report uses "paralegal" and "legal assistant" as having identical meanings and define the terms as follows:

> *. . . persons employed by law offices who are not admitted to practice law but a major part of whose work is performing tasks commonly performed by lawyers and who are under the general supervision and control of lawyers. Paralegals may be salaried employees or independent contractors, such as freelance paralegals, utilized on occasion by lawyers for special assignments.*

Connecticut has recently announced the offering of associate membership to paralegals.

Georgia. Georgia Advisory Opinion No. 21, revised May 20, 1983, sets forth the following definition of legal assistant:

> *For the purposes of this opinion, the terms 'legal assistant,' 'paraprofessional,' and 'paralegal' are defined as any lay person not admitted to the practice of law in this state who is an employee of or an assistant to, an active member of the State Bar of Georgia or of a partnership or professional corporation comprised of active members of the State Bar of Georgia and who renders services relating to the law to such member, partnership, or professional corporation under the direct control, supervision, and compensation of a member of the State Bar of Georgia.*

Idaho. In State Bar Resolution 94-7, adopted November, 1994, the Idaho State Bar urged the Supreme Court to adopt the ABA Model Standards and Guidelines for Utilization of Legal Assistant Services, which includes the definition of a legal assistant/paralegal promulgated by the American Bar Association.

New York. The New York State Bar Association Committee on Law Office Economics and Management Subcommittee on Legal Assistants published a pamphlet entitled *"The Expanding Role of the Legal Assistant in New York State."* This references guidelines for the utilization of legal assistants, published in 1976, and adopts the definition of a legal assistant as promulgated by the American Bar Association.

Oregon. The Oregon State Bar Association has published a pamphlet entitled *"The Lawyer and the Legal Assistant"* (undated). This states the terms "legal assistant" and "paralegal" are synonymous terms, and that legal assistants must work under the direct supervision of a licensed attorney.

Utah. As published in January 1994, the Office of Attorney Discipline of the Utah State Bar has set forth standards related to the ethical use of paralegals in the practice of law. The office has reviewed the National Association of Legal Assistants Guidelines for Utilizing Paralegals as well as the ABA Model guidelines for Utilization of Legal Assistant Services and "in an attempt to provide a safe harbor for those lawyers utilizing paralegals until the Supreme Court Advisory Committee on Discipline formally considers amending Rule 5.3 and 5.5(b) of the Rules of

Professional Conduct, promulgates standards and guidelines." The guidelines require attorney supervision of legal assistants, and list general duties and responsibilities of a legal assistant.

Wisconsin. The following definition of a paralegal has been approved by the Wisconsin State Bar Paralegal Task Force, November 1996:

> A 'paralegal' is an individual qualified through education and training, who is supervised by a lawyer licensed to practice law in this State, to perform substantive legal work requiring a sufficient knowledge of legal concepts that, absent the paralegal, the attorney would perform the work.

Conclusion

All definitions describe a professional group working under the direct supervision of an attorney, and acknowledge that the terms "paralegal" and "legal assistant" are used synonymously. They intentionally exclude persons who do not work under attorney supervision even though they may perform law-related work. This direct supervision is required whether the legal assistant is utilized in the course of full time employment or is being utilized on a contractual basis by an attorney or firm. In both instances, the work-product of the legal assistant becomes merged into the final product of the supervising attorney.

Bar association definitions may be found in guidelines and informational materials developed by the bar associations to assist their members in understanding more about the utilization of legal assistants and how this may assist their practice. In addition, bar associations that offer associate membership to legal assistants include a definition of "legal assistants" or "paralegals" within the membership requirements.

Index